ARISTOTLE

XXI

POLITICS

264

ARISTOTLE

IN TWENTY-THREE VOLUMES

XXI

POLITICS

WITH AN ENGLISH TRANSLATION BY

H. RACKHAM, M.A.

FELLOW OF CHRIST'S COLLEGE AND LATE
UNIVERSITY LECTURER, CAMBRIDGE

CAMBRIDGE, MASSACHUSETTS
HARVARD UNIVERSITY PRESS
LONDON
WILLIAM HEINEMANN LTD
MCMLXXVII

American
ISBN 0-674-99291-1

British
ISBN 0 434 99264 X

First printed 1932
Reprinted with some corrections 1944
Reprinted 1950, 1959, 1967, 1972, 1977

CONTENTS

CONTENTS

" It is an amazing book.   It seems to me to show a Shake-spearian understanding of human beings and their ways, together with a sublime good sense."—Henry Jackson, *Letters.*

THE TRADITIONAL ORDER of the works of
Aristotle as they appear since the edition of
Immanuel Bekker (Berlin, 1831), and their
division into volumes in this edition

THE TRADITIONAL ORDER

THE TRADITIONAL ORDER

THE TRADITIONAL ORDER

INTRODUCTION

1. Practical Prolegomena

In this edition of *Politics* the Books are in the MS. order ; the division into chapters and sections is that of Schneider (1809) ; also, to facilitate reference, there are indicated in the margin the pages, columns and lines of Bekker's Berlin text (1831), which with its volumes of scholia (1836) and Bonitz's index (1870) has rendered invaluable service to students (its lines are numbered, and its two columns denoted by later editors by *a* and *b*, so that it affords a reference to every line of the extant works of Aristotle except *The Athenian Constitution*, only rediscovered in 1890).

Some modern editors have rearranged the Books, placing the 7th and 8th as 4th and 5th, and the 4th, 5th and 6th either as 6th, 7th and 8th, or as 6th, 8th and 7th. Also some number them by the Greek alphabet, but others by the Greek numerals, using ς, ζ, η instead of Z, H, Θ to denote 6, 7, 8. Moreover, two modes of dividing the Books into chapters are in vogue, and with one of these two different divisions of the chapters into sections have been used. The result is that such a reference as ' *Politics*, Z, v. 6 ' might denote twelve different passages in twelve different editions.

The arguments for the two different rearrangements of the order of the Books are based on their contents, and editors have made conjectural alterations of the cross-references in the text to suit these rearrangements ; but the reasons, based on these cross-references and on the general contents, in favour of retaining the traditional order seem to me almost or quite as strong, while the reasons of convenience (vigorously stated by Immisch in his edition, pp. vi f.) are overwhelming.

It also seems desirable to explain that this translation is designed primarily to serve as an assistance to readers of the Greek, not as a substitute for it ; it aims at being explanatory, so far as is possible without expanding into mere paraphrase. A version intended to be read instead of the Greek might well be on different lines. It might be quite literal and non-committal, keeping as close as possible to the form of the Greek and reproducing even its gaps of expression and what are or seem to our ignorance to be its ambiguities, and leaving the student to go for explanation to the commentators ; or, on the other hand, it might render the meaning but ignore the form, and substitute terse and finished English for Aristotle's great variety of styles—for he ranges from mere jottings and notes to passages of ample discourse, not devoid of eloquence, though hardly models of Attic distinction and grace.

A rendering on the latter lines was provided for English readers once and for all by Jowett, whose translation with notes and essays (1885) is an English classic. This version, revised by Ross (1921), is of the greatest service to the student who wants to know the things that Aristotle said, but not the way he had of saying them.

2. Mss. and Text of *Politics*

The mss. are not very old nor very good. The

oldest evidence for the text is a translation in bar-
barous Latin by a Dominican monk of the thirteenth
century, William of Moerbeke in Flanders. It is
occasionally quoted here as Guil., and when the
readings of its lost Greek original can be inferred
from it, they are given as L.[a] The five best extant
Greek copies are of the fifteenth century : one at
Berlin, Hamiltonianus (H), one at Milan (M), and
three at Paris (P^1, P^2, P^3). Of these H represents
an older text than any other ; M and P^1 form a
family with L ; P^2 and P^3 group with various inferior
mss., and are usually considered less reliable than
the other family.[b] The text of *Politics* is thus very
uncertain in detail, although uncertainties affecting the meaning are fortunately not very numerous.
Some inaccuracies of expression attested by all the
mss. are precisely similar to inaccuracies in other
places attested by some mss. and avoided by others ;
but as to how far the former inaccuracies are to be
accredited to the author and how far to his trans-
mitters, no two scholars will agree.

3. EDITIONS

The commentaries of Newman (1887–1902) and Susemihl and Hicks on five books are valuable. Besides
the Teubner edition (Susemihl revised Immisch, ed.
2, 1929) we now have the Oxford text, W. D. Ross,
1957, and in the Budé series bks. 1, 2 (1960) and 3,
4 (1971) by J. Aubonnet. Among translations E. Barker's (Oxford, 1948) has notes.

[a] Also the version of Aretinus (Leonardo Bruno of Arezzo),
1438, is once or twice cited as Ar.
[b] *Codd. cet.* in the critical notes of this edition.

INTRODUCTION

4. LIFE OF ARISTOTLE

Diogenes Laertius's *Lives of the Philosophers*, supplemented from other sources, gives us a fairly detailed knowledge of Aristotle's life. His father was an hereditary member of the medical profession, and physician to the king of Macedon, Amyntas II. Aristotle was born in 384 B.C. at the little colonial city of Stagirus, on the Gulf of the Strymon, of which he remained a citizen all his life, although he passed half of it at Athens. Perhaps it is possible to find some trace of his northern origin in his writings ; if in some details of his thought he is more Athenian than the Athenians, his style has little Attic neatness, fluency or grace, even though his vocabulary has no definitely non-Attic features. He came to Athens at the age of seventeen to pursue his education, and became a pupil of Plato, remaining a member of the Academy for twenty years, till Plato's death. Speusippus then became head of the school, and Aristotle left Athens for Atarneus in Asia Minor, where his former fellow-pupil Hermeias was now ' tyrant.' He entertained Aristotle for three years, and gave him his niece as wife ; but then he fell into the hands of the Persians. Aristotle fled to the neighbouring island of Lesbos, and in 342 was invited by King Philip to return to Macedon and become the tutor of Alexander, now thirteen years old. At sixteen the prince became regent, Philip being engaged in war with Byzantium. His tutor retired to Stagirus, which had been destroyed by Philip in the Olynthian war, but which Aristotle had been allowed to restore. But he returned to Athens when Alexander succeeded to his father's throne in 336 B.C., and set up as a professor of philosophy, breaking away from the Academy and establishing a kind of college in the Lyceum. This was a precinct of Apollo and the Muses just outside the city, and its περίπατος or walks, in which Aristotle taught, gave the new school its name of Peripatetic; he equipped it with a large library and a natural history museum.

Aristotle's professorship lasted till 322 B.C., when on Alexander's death Athens led a Greek revolt against Macedon. Aristotle, an alien, a protégé of the court and friend of the viceroy Antipater, and a critic of democracy, fell a victim to anti-Macedonian feeling; like Socrates before him, he was prosecuted for impiety. Saying that he would not let Athens 'sin twice against philosophy,' he withdrew to his estate at Chalcis in Euboea, and died in the same year.

His body was taken to Stagirus for burial, and his memory was honoured there by a yearly festival. He left his library and the originals of his own writings to his pupil Theophrastus, who succeeded him as head of the Lyceum.

5. ARISTOTLE'S WRITINGS

Aristotle's writings were partly more or less popular works on philosophical subjects, and partly scientific treatises. The former were published (ἐκδεδομένοι λόγοι), and are doubtless included among the 'exoteric discourses' referred to in his extant works (e.g. Pol. 1323 a 32), though that term seems to cover the writings of other philosophers also. They are all lost, unless The Athenian Constitution

INTRODUCTION

is held to belong to this group. No doubt they had the charm and flow of style which Cicero and Quintilian praise in Aristotle. To the latter group belong the extant works, and these are for the most part singularly devoid of those qualities of style. They are called 'lectures' (ἀκροατικοὶ λόγοι), and in fact each consists of a collection of separate discourses on different parts of a subject, loosely put together to form a treatise on the whole, with transitional passages of summary and preface, and cross-references, often untraceable. Some passages are mere outlines of the argument, others set it out fully but baldly, and others are copious and even eloquent, as if written to be read by the professor to his class. Doubtless they are actual drafts for courses of lectures, put together by Aristotle or his pupils to form treatises, and kept in the library of the school as an encyclopaedia for the use of students. It is to them that Cicero refers when in another passage he speaks of Aristotle's writings as ' notes ' (*commentarii*).

6. POLITICS AND ETHICS

For Aristotle Political Science is the second half of a subject of which Ethics is the first half; indeed in the opening chapters of *The Nicomachean Ethics* the term *Politiké* is applied to the whole subject. It is the science of human affairs, of man's happiness or good. This consists in a certain mode of life, and man's life is shaped for him by his social environment, the laws, customs and institutions of the community to which he belongs. Aristotle describes man in biological terms as ' by nature a political animal '; he only develops his capacities in society, rightly organ-

INTRODUCTION

ized for his welfare. The aim of *Politiké* is to discover first in what mode of life man's happiness consists, then by what form of government and what social institutions that mode of life can be secured. The former question requires the study of man's *ēthos* or character, which occupies *The Nicomachean Ethics* ; the latter is the subject of the constitution of the state, which is treated in *Politics*. *Politics* is a sequel to *Ethics*, the second half of a single treatise, although it bears the title that in the preface has been given to the whole subject ; this subject is covered by Plato in the single dialogue of *The Republic*.

In Aristotle's whole scheme of science, *Politiké* belongs to the group of Practical Sciences, which seek knowledge as a means to action, whereas the Theoretic Sciences (such as theology, metaphysics, pure mathematics and astronomy) seek knowledge for its own sake. The Practical Sciences fall into two groups again ; the ' Poietic ' or Productive Sciences, which tell us how to make things, and the Practical Sciences in the narrower sense of the term, which tell us how to do things : the former aim at some product or result, of the latter the actual practice of the art is itself the end. The former include the professions and the handicrafts, the latter the fine arts, like dancing and music, which are pursued for their own sake (though in Greek the term τέχνη, ' art ' or craft, is sometimes confined to the former group—compare the English word ' technology ').

The supreme Practical Science is *Politiké* ; it is the science of man's welfare or happiness as a whole. It is practical in the wider sense of the term, because it studies not only what happiness is (the topic of

Ethics), but also how it is to be secured (that of *Politics*) ; and it is also practical in the narrower sense, because happiness is found (in *Ethics*) not to be a product of action but itself to consist in action of a certain sort.

7. OTHER ARISTOTELIAN WORKS ON POLITICS

The short essay *Oeconomicus* included among the works of Aristotle is certainly by one or more Peripatetics of a later date. Other political works of Aristotle recorded are Πολιτικός (a dialogue), Περὶ Ῥήτορος ἢ Πολιτικοῦ, Περὶ Βασιλείας, Ἀλέξανδρος ἢ Ὑπὲρ Ἀποικιῶν (a dialogue on colonization), Δικαιώματα Πόλεων (formal pleadings on points of difference submitted by the Greek states to the arbitration of Philip), Νόμιμα or Νόμιμα Βαρβαρικά (an account of the institutions of non-Hellenic peoples, including the Etruscans), and most important of all, Πολιτεῖαι (a series of accounts of the constitutions of a large number of Greek states, enlivened with legends, local proverbs, and even anecdotes). This last work, until the discovery of *The Athenian Constitution* in 1890, was only known to us from a number of quotations and references in later writers. It was a collection of materials upon which *Politics* was based, and is referred to as such at the conclusion of *The Nicomachean Ethics*.

8. DATE OF COMPOSITION OF *POLITICS*

The latest event mentioned in *Politics* (V. viii. 10, 1311 b 2) is the death of Philip of Macedon, 336 B.C. The work is not finished, and Aristotle died in 322 B.C.

INTRODUCTION

9. STRUCTURE OF THE WORK

Most of Aristotle's extant works look like compilations of several *logoi* or discourses dealing with different parts of the subject, and somewhat loosely put together to form a treatise on the whole. This applies to *Politics* more than to any other ; it seems to consist of three sets of lectures, not completely finished, not systematically connected, and partly overlapping : viz. (1) Books I.-III., Prolegomena—the theory of the state in general and a classification of the varieties of constitution ; (2) Books IV., V., VI., Practical Politics—the nature of existing constitutions, and principles for their good government ; (3) Books VII., VIII., Ideal Politics— the structure of the best state (unfinished).

A probable view [a] is that the work was begun on one plan and later finished on another. Book I., a prefatory treatise on domestic economy, was probably written for the first plan ; it is unfinished, and clumsily fitted on to its present sequel. Book II. also looks like part of the first plan, kept to form part of the second one ; the same applies to Book III., perhaps the oldest part of all, which shows signs of incomplete revision to fit the new plan. Books IV., V., VI. are the newer work, and contemporary with the conclusion of *The Nicomachean Ethics*. Books VII., VIII., the Best State, are the earlier work, put aside unfinished when the plan was changed, and their substitute was never written.

[a] Stocks in *Classical Quarterly*, xxi., partly following von Arnim and Jaeger. Barker in *Classical Review*, xlv. p. 162, discusses the point in relation to Aristotle's life and political experiences.

10. Outline of Contents

(1) *Prolegomena*, Books I., II., III.

Book I. *The Family.*—The state (c. i.) is not merely
a large family (a retort to Plato's communism), but
different in kind, yet it is a natural outgrowth from
an aggregation of villages, as the village is from
an aggregation of families. The family (c. ii.) is a
partnership of master and slave, husband and wife,
father and children ; it involves the business of provision. Mastership (c. ii. continued) : the slave is a
live tool, and slavery is natural—the division into ruler
and ruled permeates nature (soul and body, reason
and appetites, man and animals, male and female),
and some men have only bodily capacities. Criticism
really hits ' legal slavery ' ; ' natural slavery ' is
recognized by common sense, and there is community
of interest and friendship between master and slave.
But the acquisition of slaves and the direction of
their tasks are not part of mastership proper. The
business of provision (c. iii.)—is it part of family
economy, or subsidiary ? Nature supplies food for
animals, and animals for the food and service of man ;
so one kind of acquisition—the supply of the limited
wealth needed for the good life—does belong to family
economy. But another kind uses goods for exchange,
aided by the invention of money, which led to commerce ; hence the mistaken beliefs that money is the
sole wealth and that the good life is bodily enjoyment.
The natural and necessary art of provision is subsidiary to family economy ; the other kind is justly
disliked, especially usury—money breeding money.
The branches of natural and unnatural provision are

outlined (c. iv.), with a third intermediate kind, the appropriation of the uncultivated gifts of the soil ; and reference is made to former treatises, dealing in particular with monopoly. The relation of the head of the family (c. v.) to the wife resembles republican government, and that to the children royalty. All three classes of household subjects have their virtues, the slaves' imparted by the master's admonition, the women's and children's by education directed in the interest of the state.

Book II., *The best Constitutions known*, theoretical and actual (c. i.).—Plato's *Republic* aims at unity by communism ; but complete unity of the state is not desirable, his system (c. ii.) will not produce it, his account is incomplete, and there are other minor objections. The communism of *Laws* (c. iii.) is less thorough-going. The equalitarian constitution of Phaleas and that of Hippodamus (cc. iv., v.) are criticized, with a short essay on the dangers of political innovation ; then the constitution of Sparta (c. vi.), that of Crete, said to have been its model (c. vii.), and that of Carthage (c. viii.). There follow notes on Solon and a few other law-givers (c. ix.).

Book III., *The Nature of the State.*—Political Science (cc. i.-iii.) asks 'What is a citizen ?' and ' Is the goodness of a citizen the same as the goodness of a man ? ' (in other words, What share in government constitutes citizenship and what classes should possess it ? and in order to perform its duties, must one possess all the moral virtues or only special political abilities ?). Citizenship means at least membership of the judiciary and the assembly, and therefore requires some property and leisure ; and manual work and trade are incompatible with the necessary mental qualities. On this basis the forms of government are classified (cc. iv., v.). They vary according as the sovereign is one man or a few or the many, and according as these govern for the common good or for their own ; this gives three Correct Constitutions —Royalty, Aristocracy, Constitutional Government ; and three Deviations—Tyranny, Oligarchy, Democracy (*i.e.*, essentially, the rule of the poor and unleisured, not the rule of the many). The distribution of power (c. vi.) : the state is a partnership for the good life, and in principle those who contribute most to this have most right to power. In practice, perhaps, the laws should be sovereign ; but they may be bad. The rule of the many is a simple solution— they have at least collective wisdom and wealth ; but they should not share the highest offices, only elect to and control them. The subject is treated afresh (cc. vii., viii.) : education and virtue are the best claims to power—wealth, birth and numbers have relative but not absolute claims. Supereminence puts a man or group of men above the law : hence the value of ostracism, for even in the ideal state supereminence would be dangerous—except supereminence in virtue, which should make a man monarch. Royalty (c. ix.)—Spartan, oriental, elective (the aesymnete), that of heroic times, and (c. x.) absolute monarchy. It calls for supreme virtue in an individual ; but royalty passed into aristocracy as virtue spread, and aristocracy degenerated into oligarchy ; this was overthrown by tyrants, and these put down by democracy. Truly (c. xi.) the law should rule, *i.e.* reason ; and the monarch must have helpers, which points to aristocracy. But surpassing individual excellence does occur, and then absolute monarchy is justified. Recapitulation on Royalty (c. xii.).

(Of the other five constitutions, four are treated, though not on a symmetrical plan, in Books IV., V., VI. Aristocracy was touched on as a variant to Royalty in III. x., xi., and actual cases of it are alluded to in IV. vii., but it is replaced by the Best Constitution, the unfinished essay on which forms Books VII. and VIII. The substitution of ἀρίστη πολιτεία as an equivalent for ἀριστοκρατία and βασιλεία is justified in IV. iii. 1 (1289 a 31 ff.) : is this an interpolation ?)

(2) *Practical Politics*, Books IV., V., VI.

Book IV. *Existing Constitutions.*—Science (c. **i.**) must study not only the ideally best form of state but the best under given conditions. Monarchy and Aristocracy (c. ii.) have been dealt with ; there remain Constitutional Government, and the Deviations (in descending order of merit), Democracy, Oligarchy, Tyranny—their varieties and their suitability to various peoples, their establishment and their preservation against revolution (the contents of Books IV., V., VI). Constitutions (c. iii.) vary in the distribution of power according to rank and wealth. Democracy and Oligarchy are usually thought the chief forms ; they really differ (c. iv.) not merely as the rule of the free and of the wealthy, but as that of the free majority and the wealthy minority. The necessary classes are farmers, artisans, shopkeepers, labourers, soldiers, councillors and judges, rich men, magistrates (Plato wrongly omitted the last three). Some may overlap, but rich and poor are distinct, so that Oligarchy and

INTRODUCTION

Democracy are the normal forms of government. Democracy (c. iv.) has four varieties, according as the qualifications of property and citizen-birth, and the supremacy of law over decrees of the assembly, are in force or are not. Oligarchy (c. v.) also has four varieties, according as power goes by a moderate or a high property-qualification, or by heredity, or is the arbitrary rule of powerful families called a Dynasty. The normal historical succession of the four varieties of Democracy and of Oligarchy are traced. Aristocracy, in a secondary sense, is a blend of these two, based on merit and numbers, or on merit, numbers and wealth. Constitutional Government (cc. vi., vii.) is also a blend of Oligarchy and Democracy (approximating more to the latter), being based on numbers and wealth; it is brought about by the institution of pay for service in the courts, and of either a moderate property-qualification for the assembly or else election without property-qualification of magistrates; it brings contentment, and so is stable. Tyranny (c. viii.) is monarchy based on force, irresponsible and selfish. Constitutional Government (c. ix.), based on the virtues of the middle class, is best on the average. But (c. x.) the best constitution for a given state depends on the relative numbers of the free, the middle class and the wealthy. Citizenship should be limited to those who bear arms, with a property-qualification admitting a majority. Classification of constitutions (cc. xi., xii.) is based on the distribution of deliberative, judicial and executive functions, the tenure and numbers of the executive, and their mode of election (fourteen modes are enumerated). The functions of the judiciary

INTRODUCTION

(c. xiii.), eight in number, are stated, and various modes of its appointment.

Book V. *Revolutions—their causes and their prevention.*—Revolution (c. i.) springs from a desire of the many or the rich for more power (though democracy is less liable to it than oligarchy). The various motives and circumstances that lead to it are set out (c. ii.), with historical instances of its arising from quite petty events (c. iii.) ; and special causes that operate in democracies, oligarchies and aristocracies (cc. iv., v., vi.). It is prevented (c. vii.) by the opposite causes and measures, which are discussed in general, and for oligarchy and democracy in particular, as well as (c. viii.) for monarchies, royalty and tyranny being contrasted : a variety of personal motives cause attacks on tyrants, but the monarchy of old days was only endangered by discord in the reigning house or by excessively harsh rule. Royalty is preserved (c. ix.) by moderation ; tyranny by two opposite methods, harsh repression or conciliatory public spirit (historical examples). Criticism (c. x.) of Plato's treatment of revolution in *The Republic*, with his theory of a regular cycle of constitutional changes.

Book VI. *(a) Democracy and Oligarchy.*—Democracy (c. i.) varies in form with the prevalent industries of the people, its basis being liberty and equality (not ' proportional equality,' balancing wealth against numbers). Agricultural democracy (c. ii.) is the best, pastoral next ; traders and labourers are too fond of politics and a field for demagogy. Devices to safeguard democracy (c. iii.), especially colonization. Oligarchy (c. iv.)—the more tyrannical its form the more protection it needs, an elaborate

military system and placation of the people by public
benefactions. (*b*) The various *Offices of Government*
are enumerated and discussed (c. v.).

(3) *Ideal Politics*, Books VII., VIII.

Book VII. *The Best Constitution : external conditions, population.*—The writer begins (cc. i.-iii.) with
a résumé of *Ethics* : the best life for the state
as for the man is the life of virtue with enough
external goods for virtuous action ; the highest form
of this for a man is the inner life of thought, and
similarly for the state external dominion is inferior
to the internal activity of politics. The necessary
conditions of the ideal but practicable state (iv., v.)
are a population not too small nor too large for the
best common life, a country large enough for the
temperate maintenance of this population and easily
defensible, a suitable city site (the advantages and
disadvantages of a sea-port are set out). The
citizens (c. vi.) should be of a race like the Greek,
at once spirited and intelligent. Of the necessary
classes (c. vii.), the artisans and farmers (c. viii.)
are unfit for citizenship, which must carry military,
political, judicial and priestly functions ; they should
be slaves or alien serfs. The history of the caste-
system (c. ix.) is discussed. The land must be
partly public, to support religion and the public
meals, partly private ; each citizen is to have one
farm near the city and another near the frontier.
The site and plan of the city (cc. x., xi.), water-
supply, fortifications, temples, state agora, market
agora, and guard-posts and shrines in the country.
The discipline and education of the citizens

(c. xii.) ; to natural gifts must be added training of habit and reason (c. xiii.), the psychology and objects of which are discussed ; and the life of leisure is the ultimate aim. To produce the finest human material (c. xiv.) the state must regulate marriage, and the training of infancy and childhood. Education proper (c. xv.) falls into two parts, for the ages 7 to 14 and 14 to 21.

Book VIII. *The Best Constitution* continued.— *Education* must be systematic, universal and public (c. i.). Studies (c. ii.) should be edifying, and useful studies should be pursued with a liberal tone. Gymnastics (c. iii.) are to train spirit ; for children (cc. iv., v.) they should be gentle, then three years of study should follow, then a period of rigorous bodily training. Music is not merely a harmless amusement or a rational pastime ; it is morally educative—it exercises and refines the emotions. Moderate skill in performance on the lyre (c. vi.) should be acquired, but the flute and cithara are too professional, and the flute too emotional ; and so (c. vii.) is the Phrygian mode—the ethical Dorian mode is more suited for education.

(The treatise here breaks off.)

ARISTOTLE'S POLITICS

ΑΡΙΣΤΟΤΕΛΟΥΣ
ΠΟΛΙΤΙΚΩΝ Α

I. Ἐπειδὴ πᾶσαν πόλιν ὁρῶμεν κοινωνίαν τινὰ 1
οὖσαν, καὶ πᾶσαν κοινωνίαν ἀγαθοῦ τινος ἕνεκεν
συνεστηκυῖαν (τοῦ γὰρ εἶναι δοκοῦντος ἀγαθοῦ
χάριν πάντα πράττουσι πάντες), δῆλον ὡς πᾶσαι
5 μὲν ἀγαθοῦ τινος στοχάζονται, μάλιστα δὲ καὶ
τοῦ κυριωτάτου πάντων ἡ πασῶν κυριωτάτη καὶ
πάσας περιέχουσα τὰς ἄλλας· αὕτη δ' ἐστὶν ἡ
καλουμένη πόλις καὶ ἡ κοινωνία ἡ πολιτική. ὅσοι 2
μὲν οὖν οἴονται πολιτικὸν καὶ βασιλικὸν καὶ
οἰκονομικὸν καὶ δεσποτικὸν εἶναι τὸν αὐτόν, οὐ
καλῶς λέγουσιν· πλήθει γὰρ καὶ ὀλιγότητι νομί-
10 ζουσι διαφέρειν ἀλλ' οὐκ εἴδει τούτων ἕκαστον,
οἷον ἂν μὲν ὀλίγων, δεσπότην, ἂν δὲ πλειόνων,
οἰκονόμον, ἂν δ' ἔτι πλειόνων, πολιτικὸν ἢ βασιλικόν, ὡς οὐδὲν διαφέρουσαν μεγάλην οἰκίαν ἢ
μικρὰν πόλιν· καὶ πολιτικὸν δὲ καὶ βασιλικόν,
15 ὅταν μὲν αὐτὸς ἐφεστήκῃ, βασιλικόν, ὅταν δὲ

ᵃ The Greek word had not acquired a specially political
connotation as the English word ' community ' has.
ᵇ Socrates and Plato.

2

ARISTOTLE'S POLITICS

BOOK I

1 I. Every state is as we see a sort of partnership,[a]
and every partnership is formed with a view to some good (since all the actions of all mankind are done with a view to what they think to be good). It is therefore
evident that, while all partnerships aim at some good, the partnership that is the most supreme of all and includes all the others does so most of all, and aims at the most supreme of all goods ; and this is the partnership entitled the state, the political associa-

2 tion. Those [b] then who think that the natures of the statesman, the royal ruler, the head of an estate [c] and the master of a family are the same, are mistaken ; they imagine that the difference between these various forms of authority is one of greater and smaller numbers, not a difference in kind—that is, that the ruler over a few people is a master, over more the head of an estate, over more still a statesman or royal ruler, as if there were no difference between a large household and a small city ; and also as to the statesman and the royal ruler, they think that one who governs as sole head is royal, and one who,

[c] οἰκονόμος denoting a higher grade than δεσπότης is unusual. For their ordinary use see c. ii. § 1 *fin.*

1252 a

κατὰ λόγους τῆς ἐπιστήμης τῆς τοιαύτης κατὰ
μέρος ἄρχων καὶ ἀρχόμενος, πολιτικόν· ταῦτα δ'
οὐκ ἔστιν ἀληθῆ. δῆλον δ' ἔσται τὸ λεγόμενον 3
ἐπισκοποῦσι κατὰ τὴν ὑφηγημένην μέθοδον· ὥσπερ
γὰρ ἐν τοῖς ἄλλοις τὸ σύνθετον μέχρι τῶν ἀσυν-
20 θέτων ἀνάγκη διαιρεῖν (ταῦτα γὰρ ἐλάχιστα μόρια
τοῦ παντός), οὕτω καὶ πόλιν ἐξ ὧν σύγκειται
σκοποῦντες ὀψόμεθα καὶ περὶ τούτων μᾶλλον τί
τε διαφέρουσιν ἀλλήλων καὶ εἴ τι τεχνικὸν ἐνδέχεται λαβεῖν περὶ ἕκαστον τῶν ῥηθέντων.

Εἰ δή τις ἐξ ἀρχῆς[1] τὰ πράγματα φυόμενα βλέ-
25 ψειεν, ὥσπερ ἐν τοῖς ἄλλοις καὶ ἐν τούτοις κάλλιστ'
ἂν οὕτω θεωρήσειεν. ἀνάγκη δὴ πρῶτον συν- 4
δυάζεσθαι τοὺς ἄνευ ἀλλήλων μὴ δυναμένους
εἶναι, οἷον θῆλυ μὲν καὶ ἄρρεν τῆς γενέσεως[2]
ἕνεκεν (καὶ τοῦτο οὐκ ἐκ προαιρέσεως, ἀλλ' ὥσπερ
καὶ ἐν τοῖς ἄλλοις ζῴοις καὶ φυτοῖς φυσικὸν τὸ
30 ἐφίεσθαι οἷον αὐτὸ τοιοῦτον καταλιπεῖν ἕτερον),
ἄρχον δὲ καὶ ἀρχόμενον φύσει,[3] διὰ τὴν σωτηρίαν
(τὸ μὲν γὰρ δυνάμενον τῇ διανοίᾳ προορᾶν ἄρχον
φύσει καὶ δεσπόζον φύσει, τὸ δὲ δυνάμενον τῷ
σώματι ταῦτα ποιεῖν[4] ἀρχόμενον καὶ φύσει δοῦλον·
διὸ δεσπότῃ καὶ δούλῳ ταὐτὸ συμφέρει). φύσει 5
1252 b μὲν οὖν διώρισται τὸ θῆλυ καὶ τὸ δοῦλον (οὐθὲν
γὰρ ἡ φύσις ποιεῖ τοιοῦτον οἷον χαλκοτύποι τὴν
Δελφικὴν μάχαιραν πενιχρῶς, ἀλλ' ἓν πρὸς ἕν·

---

[1] ἀρχῆς ⟨εἰς⟩ Richards.   [2] γεννήσεως Stobaeus.
[3] φύσει ante καὶ codd. cet. et Ald.
[4] ταῦτα ποιεῖν (ταῦτα ante τῷ σώματι MP¹): διαπονεῖν
Gomperz.

---

[a] A probable emendation gives 'that can carry out labour.'
[b] A dagger and carving-knife or knife and spoon in one?

4

while the government follows the principles of the science of royalty, takes turns to govern and be governed is a statesman ; but these views are not
3 true. And a proof of what we assert will appear if we examine the question in accordance with our regular method of investigation. In every other matter it is necessary to analyse the composite whole down to its uncompounded elements (for these are the smallest parts of the whole) ; so too with the state, by examining the elements of which it is composed we shall better discern in relation to these different kinds of rulers what is the difference between them, and whether it is possible to obtain any scientific precision in regard to the various statements made above.

In this subject as in others the best method of investigation is to study things in the process of
4 development from the beginning. The first coupling together of persons then to which necessity gives rise is that between those who are unable to exist without one another, namely the union of female and male for the continuance of the species (and this not of deliberate purpose, but with man as with the other animals and with plants there is a natural instinct to desire to leave behind one another being of the same sort as oneself), and the union of natural ruler and natural subject for the sake of security (for one that can foresee with his mind is naturally ruler and naturally master, and one that can do these things [a] with his body is subject and naturally a slave ; so
5 that master and slave have the same interest). Thus the female and the slave are by nature distinct (for nature makes nothing as the cutlers make the Delphic knife,[b] in a niggardly way, but one thing for one

The Family the primary association, for the necessaries of life.

5

1252 b

οὕτω γὰρ ἂν ἀποτελοῖτο κάλλιστα τῶν ὀργάνων
5 ἕκαστον, μὴ πολλοῖς ἔργοις ἀλλ' ἑνὶ δουλεῦον). ἐν
δὲ τοῖς βαρβάροις τὸ θῆλυ καὶ τὸ¹ δοῦλον τὴν αὐτὴν
ἔχει τάξιν· αἴτιον δ' ὅτι τὸ φύσει ἄρχον οὐκ ἔχουσιν, ἀλλὰ γίνεται ἡ κοινωνία αὐτῶν δούλης καὶ
δούλου. διό φασιν οἱ ποιηταὶ

βαρβάρων δ' Ἕλληνας ἄρχειν εἰκός,

ὡς ταὐτὸ φύσει βάρβαρον καὶ δοῦλον ὄν. ἐκ μὲν 6
10 οὖν τούτων τῶν δύο κοινωνιῶν οἰκία πρώτη, καὶ
ὀρθῶς Ἡσίοδος εἶπε ποιήσας

οἶκον μὲν πρώτιστα γυναῖκά τε βοῦν τ' ἀροτῆρα·

ὁ γὰρ βοῦς ἀντ' οἰκέτου τοῖς πένησίν ἐστιν. ἡ
μὲν οὖν εἰς πᾶσαν ἡμέραν συνεστηκυῖα κοινωνία
κατὰ φύσιν οἶκός ἐστιν, οὓς Χαρώνδας μὲν καλεῖ
15 ὁμοσιπύους, Ἐπιμενίδης δὲ ὁ Κρὴς ὁμοκάπους.²
    Ἡ δ' ἐκ πλειόνων οἰκιῶν κοινωνία πρώτη 7
χρήσεως ἕνεκεν μὴ ἐφημέρου κώμη. μάλιστα δὲ
κατὰ φύσιν ἔοικεν ἡ κώμη ἀποικία³ οἰκίας εἶναι,
οὓς καλοῦσί τινες ὁμογάλακτας [παῖδάς τε καὶ
παίδων παῖδας].⁴ διὸ καὶ τὸ πρῶτον ἐβασιλεύοντο
20 αἱ πόλεις καὶ νῦν ἔτι τὰ ἔθνη· ἐκ βασιλευομένων

---

¹ τὸ add. edd.   ² ὁμοκάπους ΓΜΡ¹.
³ ἀποικίαι ? ed.   ⁴ [παῖδάς τε—παῖδας] Susemihl.

ᵃ Euripides, *I.A.* 1400.   ᵇ *Works and Days* 405.
ᶜ A lawgiver of Catana in Sicily, 6th century B.C. or earlier.
ᵈ A poet and prophet invited to Athens 596 B.C. to purify
it of plague.
ᵉ Or Doric, 'with a joint holding.' The variant ὁμοκάπνους,
'smoke-sharers,' seems to mean 'hearth-fellows.'
ᶠ Perhaps the Greek should be altered to give 'consists of
colonies from.'

6

purpose ; for so each tool will be turned out in the finest perfection, if it serves not many uses but one). Yet among barbarians the female and the slave have the same rank ; and the cause of this is that barbarians have no class of natural rulers, but with them the conjugal partnership is a partnership of female slave and male slave. Hence the saying of the poets—

'Tis meet that Greeks should rule barbarians,[a]—

implying that barbarian and slave are the same in 6 nature. From these two partnerships then is first composed the household, and Hesiod [b] was right when he wrote :

First and foremost a house and a wife and an ox for the ploughing—

for the ox serves instead of a servant for the poor. The partnership therefore that comes about in the course of nature for everyday purposes is the ' house,' the persons whom Charondas [c] speaks of as ' meal-tub-fellows ' and the Cretan Epimenides [d] as ' manger-fellows.' [e]

7   On the other hand the primary partnership made up of several households for the satisfaction of not mere daily needs is the village. The village according to the most natural account seems to be a colony from [f] a household, formed of those whom some people speak of as ' fellow-nurslings,' sons and sons' sons.[g] It is owing to this that our cities were at first under royal sway and that foreign races are so still, because they were made up of parts that were

Related families formed a Village.

[g] The words ' sons and sons' sons ' are probably an interpolated note.

1252 b

γὰρ συνῆλθον, πᾶσα γὰρ οἰκία βασιλεύεται ὑπὸ
τοῦ πρεσβυτάτου, ὥστε καὶ αἱ ἀποικίαι διὰ τὴν
συγγένειαν. καὶ τοῦτ' ἐστὶν ὃ λέγει Ὅμηρος,

> θεμιστεύει δὲ ἕκαστος
> παίδων ἠδ' ἀλόχων·

σποράδες γάρ· καὶ οὕτω τὸ ἀρχαῖον ᾤκουν. καὶ
25 τοὺς θεοὺς δὲ διὰ τοῦτο πάντες φασὶ βασιλεύεσθαι,
ὅτι καὶ αὐτοὶ οἱ μὲν ἔτι καὶ νῦν οἱ δὲ τὸ ἀρχαῖον
ἐβασιλεύοντο· ὥσπερ δὲ καὶ τὰ εἴδη ἑαυτοῖς ἀφ-
ομοιοῦσιν οἱ ἄνθρωποι, οὕτω καὶ τοὺς βίους τῶν
θεῶν.

Ἡ δ' ἐκ πλειόνων κωμῶν κοινωνία τέλειος 8
πόλις, ἤδη πάσης ἔχουσα πέρας τῆς αὐταρκείας
30 ὡς ἔπος εἰπεῖν, γινομένη[1] μὲν οὖν τοῦ ζῆν ἕνεκεν,
οὖσα δὲ τοῦ εὖ ζῆν. διὸ πᾶσα πόλις φύσει ἐστίν,
εἴπερ καὶ αἱ πρῶται κοινωνίαι· τέλος γὰρ αὕτη
ἐκείνων, ἡ δὲ φύσις τέλος ἐστίν, οἷον γὰρ ἕκαστόν
ἐστι τῆς γενέσεως τελεσθείσης, ταύτην φαμὲν
τὴν φύσιν εἶναι ἑκάστου, ὥσπερ ἀνθρώπου, ἵππου,
1253 a οἰκίας. ἔτι τὸ οὗ ἕνεκα καὶ τὸ τέλος βέλτιστον·
ἡ δ' αὐτάρκεια τέλος καὶ βέλτιστον. ἐκ τούτων 9
οὖν φανερὸν ὅτι τῶν φύσει ἡ πόλις ἐστί, καὶ ὅτι ὁ
ἄνθρωπος φύσει πολιτικὸν ζῷον, καὶ ὁ ἄπολις διὰ
φύσιν καὶ οὐ διὰ τύχην ἤτοι φαῦλός ἐστιν ἢ
5 κρείττων ἢ ἄνθρωπος (ὥσπερ καὶ ὁ ὑφ' Ὁμήρου
λοιδορηθεὶς

> ἀφρήτωρ, ἀθέμιστος, ἀνέστιος,

---

[1] γενομένη ? ed.

---

a *Odyssey*, ix, 114 f. of the Cyclopes: the passage goes on:
ἐστὶν ἐκεῖνος | ὃς πολέμου ἔραται.

b A reminiscence of Xenophanes fr. 14.   *c* *Iliad* ix. 63.

under royal rule; for every household is under the
royal rule of its eldest member, so that the colonies
from the household were so too, because of the kin-
ship of their members. And this is what Homer [a]
means:

> And each one giveth law
> To sons and eke to spouses—

for his Cyclopes live in scattered families; and that
is the way in which people used to live in early times.
Also this explains why all races speak of the gods
as ruled by a king, because they themselves too are
some of them actually now so ruled and in other cases
used to be of old; and as men imagine the gods in
human form, so also they suppose their manner of
life to be like their own. [b]

8 The partnership finally composed of several villages
is the city-state; it has at last attained the limit of
virtually complete self-sufficiency, and thus, while it
comes into existence for the sake of life, it exists for
the good life. Hence every city-state exists by nature,
inasmuch as the first partnerships so exist; for the
city-state is the end of the other partnerships, and
nature is an end, since that which each thing is when
its growth is completed we speak of as being the
nature of each thing, for instance of a man, a horse,
a household. Again, the object for which a thing
exists, its end, is its chief good; and self-sufficiency
9 is an end, and a chief good. From these things
therefore it is clear that the city-state is a natural
growth, and that man is by nature a political animal,
and a man that is by nature and not merely by
fortune citiless is either low in the scale of humanity
or above it (like the 'clanless, lawless, hearthless'
man reviled by Homer,[c] for he is by nature citiless

*Neighbour-
ing villages
formed a
City-state,
for the
good life.*

9

1253 a

ἅμα γὰρ φύσει τοιοῦτος καὶ πολέμου ἐπιθυμη-
τής) ἅτε ὢν ὥσπερ ἄζυξ[1] ἐν πεττοῖς. διότι δὲ 10
πολιτικὸν ὁ ἄνθρωπος ζῷον[2] πάσης μελίττης καὶ
παντὸς ἀγελαίου ζῴου μᾶλλον, δῆλον. οὐθὲν γάρ,
ὡς φαμέν, μάτην ἡ φύσις ποιεῖ· λόγον δὲ μόνον
ἄνθρωπος ἔχει τῶν ζῴων. ἡ μὲν οὖν φωνὴ τοῦ
λυπηροῦ καὶ ἡδέος ἐστὶ σημεῖον, διὸ καὶ τοῖς
ἄλλοις ὑπάρχει ζῴοις (μέχρι γὰρ τούτου ἡ φύσις
αὐτῶν ἐλήλυθεν, τοῦ ἔχειν αἴσθησιν λυπηροῦ καὶ
ἡδέος καὶ ταῦτα σημαίνειν ἀλλήλοις), ὁ δὲ λόγος
ἐπὶ τῷ δηλοῦν ἐστι τὸ συμφέρον καὶ τὸ βλαβερόν,
ὥστε καὶ τὸ δίκαιον καὶ τὸ ἄδικον· τοῦτο γὰρ 11
πρὸς τἆλλα ζῷα τοῖς ἀνθρώποις ἴδιον, τὸ μόνον[3]
ἀγαθοῦ καὶ κακοῦ καὶ δικαίου καὶ ἀδίκου καὶ τῶν
ἄλλων αἴσθησιν ἔχειν, ἡ δὲ τούτων κοινωνία ποιεῖ
οἰκίαν καὶ πόλιν.

Καὶ πρότερον δὴ τῇ φύσει πόλις ἢ οἰκία καὶ
ἕκαστος ἡμῶν ἐστίν. τὸ γὰρ ὅλον πρότερον
ἀναγκαῖον εἶναι τοῦ μέρους· ἀναιρουμένου γὰρ τοῦ
ὅλου οὐκ ἔσται πούς οὐδὲ χείρ εἰ μὴ ὁμωνύμως,
ὥσπερ εἴ τις λέγει τὴν λιθίνην· διαφθαρεῖσα γὰρ[4]
ἔσται τοιαύτη, πάντα δὲ τῷ ἔργῳ ὥρισται καὶ
τῇ δυνάμει, ὥστε μηκέτι τοιαῦτα ὄντα οὐ λεκτέον
τὰ αὐτὰ εἶναι ἀλλ' ὁμώνυμα. ὅτι μὲν οὖν ἡ πόλις 12
καὶ φύσει[5] πρότερον ἢ ἕκαστος, δῆλον· εἰ γὰρ
μὴ αὐτάρκης ἕκαστος χωρισθείς, ὁμοίως τοῖς
ἄλλοις μέρεσιν ἕξει πρὸς τὸ ὅλον, ὁ δὲ μὴ δυνά-

---

[1] sic ? Richards : ἅτε περ ἄζυξ ὢν ὥσπερ.
[2] [ζῷον] ? ed.   [3] [μόνον] ? edd.
[4] γὰρ οὐκ Schöll.   [5] καὶ φύσει καὶ codd. plurimi.

---

[a] Or ' a hand thus spoiled will not be a hand at all.'

10

and also a lover of war) inasmuch as he resembles
10 an isolated piece at draughts. And why man is a
political animal in a greater measure than any bee
or any gregarious animal is clear. For nature, as
we declare, does nothing without purpose; and man
alone of the animals possesses speech. The mere
voice, it is true, can indicate pain and pleasure, and
therefore is possessed by the other animals as well
(for their nature has been developed so far as to have
sensations of what is painful and pleasant and to
signify those sensations to one another), but speech
is designed to indicate the advantageous and the
harmful, and therefore also the right and the wrong;
11 for it is the special property of man in distinction
from the other animals that he alone has perception
of good and bad and right and wrong and the other
moral qualities, and it is partnership in these things
that makes a household and a city-state.

Thus also the city-state is prior in nature to the The State
household and to each of us individually. For the prior in
whole must necessarily be prior to the part; since nature,
when the whole body is destroyed, foot or hand will
not exist except in an equivocal sense, like the sense
in which one speaks of a hand sculptured in stone as
a hand; because a hand in those circumstances will
be a hand spoiled,[a] and all things are defined by their
function and capacity, so that when they are no
longer such as to perform their function they must
not be said to be the same things, but to bear their
12 names in an equivocal sense. It is clear therefore
that the state is also prior by nature to the individual;
for if each individual when separate is not self-
sufficient, he must be related to the whole state as
other parts are to their whole, while a man who is

11

1253 a

μενος κοινωνεῖν ἢ μηθὲν δεόμενος δι᾽ αὐτάρκειαν
οὐθὲν μέρος πόλεως, ὥστε ἢ θηρίον ἢ θεός.

30 Φύσει μὲν οὖν ἡ ὁρμὴ ἐν πᾶσιν ἐπὶ τὴν τοιαύτην κοινωνίαν· ὁ δὲ πρῶτος συστήσας μεγίστων
ἀγαθῶν αἴτιος· ὥσπερ γὰρ καὶ τελεωθὲν[1] βέλτιστον
τῶν ζῴων ὁ[2] ἄνθρωπός ἐστιν, οὕτω καὶ χωρισθὲν
νόμου καὶ δίκης[3] χείριστον πάντων. χαλεπωτάτη
γὰρ ἀδικία ἔχουσα ὅπλα, ὁ δ᾽ ἄνθρωπος ὅπλα
35 ἔχων φύεται φρονήσει καὶ ἀρετῇ[4] οἷς ἐπὶ τἀναντία
ἔστι χρῆσθαι μάλιστα. διὸ ἀνοσιώτατον καὶ ἀγριώ-
τατον ἄνευ ἀρετῆς καὶ πρὸς ἀφροδίσια καὶ ἐδωδὴν
χείριστον. ἡ δὲ δικαιοσύνη πολιτικόν· ἡ γὰρ
δίκη[5] πολιτικῆς κοινωνίας τάξις ἐστίν, ἡ δὲ δίκη
τοῦ δικαίου κρίσις.

1253 b

II. Ἐπεὶ δὲ φανερὸν ἐξ ὧν μορίων ἡ πόλις συν- 1
έστηκεν, ἀναγκαῖον πρῶτον περὶ οἰκονομίας εἰ-
πεῖν· πᾶσα γὰρ σύγκειται πόλις ἐξ οἰκιῶν. οἰκονομίας δὲ μέρη ἐξ ὧν πάλιν οἰκία συνέστηκεν· οἰκία
5 δὲ τέλειος ἐκ δούλων καὶ ἐλευθέρων. ἐπεὶ δ᾽ ἐν
τοῖς ἐλαχίστοις πρῶτον ἕκαστον ζητητέον, πρῶτα
δὲ καὶ ἐλάχιστα μέρη οἰκίας δεσπότης καὶ δοῦλος,
καὶ πόσις καὶ ἄλοχος, καὶ πατὴρ καὶ τέκνα, περὶ
τριῶν ἂν τούτων σκεπτέον εἴη τί ἕκαστον καὶ ποῖον
δεῖ εἶναι, ταῦτα δ᾽ ἐστὶ δεσποτικὴ καὶ γαμική[a] 2

---

[1] τελεωθὲν secl. Jackson.
[2] ὁ om. codd. cet. et Ald.
[3] χωρισθὲν—δίκης secl. Jackson.
[4] ἀρετῇ ⟨ἐπιτήδεια⟩ ? Pearson.
[5] τὸ γὰρ δίκαιον Richards.

---

[a] The Greek word properly denotes the marriage cere-
mony, not the married state.

12

incapable of entering into partnership, or who is so self-sufficing that he has no need to do so, is no part of a state, so that he must be either a lower animal or a god.

Therefore the impulse to form a partnership of this kind is present in all men by nature; but the man who first united people in such a partnership was the greatest of benefactors. For as man is the best of the animals when perfected, so he is the worst of all when sundered from law and justice. For unrighteousness is most pernicious when possessed of weapons, and man is born possessing weapons for the use of wisdom and virtue, which it is possible to employ entirely for the opposite ends. Hence when devoid of virtue man is the most unscrupulous and savage of animals, and the worst in regard to sexual indulgence and gluttony. Justice on the other hand is an element of the state; for judicial procedure, which means the decision of what is just, is the regulation of the political partnership. *and the source of man's chief good.*

1 II. And now that it is clear what are the component parts of the state, we have first of all to discuss household management; for every state is composed of households. Household management falls into departments corresponding to the parts of which the household in its turn is composed; and the household in its perfect form consists of slaves and freemen. The investigation of everything should begin with its smallest parts, and the primary and smallest parts of the household are master and slave, husband and wife, father and children; we ought therefore to examine the proper constitution and character 2 of each of these three relationships, I mean that of mastership, that of marriage ᵃ (there is no exact *The head of the Family as master, husband, and father.*

13

1253 b

10 (ἀνώνυμον γὰρ ἡ γυναικὸς καὶ ἀνδρὸς σύζευξις)
καὶ τρίτον τεκνοποιητική[1] (καὶ γὰρ αὕτη οὐκ
ὠνόμασται ἰδίῳ ὀνόματι)· ἔστωσαν δὴ[2] αὗται τρεῖς
ἃς εἴπομεν. ἔστι δέ τι[3] μέρος ὃ δοκεῖ τοῖς μὲν
εἶναι οἰκονομία τοῖς δὲ μέγιστον μέρος αὐτῆς,
ὅπως δ' ἔχει, θεωρητέον· λέγω δὲ περὶ τῆς καλουμένης χρηματιστικῆς.

15 Πρῶτον δὲ περὶ δεσπότου καὶ δούλου εἴπωμεν,
ἵνα τά τε πρὸς τὴν ἀναγκαίαν χρείαν ἴδωμεν, κἂν
εἴ τι πρὸς τὸ εἰδέναι περὶ αὐτῶν δυναίμεθα λαβεῖν
βέλτιον τῶν νῦν ὑπολαμβανομένων. τοῖς μὲν γὰρ 3
δοκεῖ ἐπιστήμη τέ τις εἶναι ἡ δεσποτεία, καὶ ἡ
αὐτὴ οἰκονομία καὶ δεσποτεία καὶ πολιτικὴ καὶ
20 βασιλική, καθάπερ εἴπομεν ἀρχόμενοι· τοῖς δὲ
παρὰ φύσιν τὸ δεσπόζειν, νόμῳ γὰρ τὸν μὲν
δοῦλον εἶναι τὸν δ' ἐλεύθερον, φύσει δ' οὐθὲν διαφέρειν, διόπερ οὐδὲ δίκαιον, βίαιον γάρ.

Ἐπεὶ οὖν ἡ κτῆσις μέρος τῆς οἰκίας ἐστὶ καὶ ἡ
κτητικὴ μέρος τῆς οἰκονομίας[4] (ἄνευ γὰρ τῶν
25 ἀναγκαίων ἀδύνατον καὶ ζῆν καὶ εὖ ζῆν[5]), ὥσπερ 4
δὲ[6] ταῖς ὡρισμέναις τέχναις ἀναγκαῖον ἂν εἴη
ὑπάρχειν τὰ οἰκεῖα ὄργανα εἰ μέλλει ἀποτελε-
σθήσεσθαι τὸ ἔργον, οὕτω καὶ τῷ οἰκονομικῷ,
τῶν δ' ὀργάνων τὰ μὲν ἄψυχα τὰ δ' ἔμψυχα (οἷον

---

[1] τεκνοποιητική : πατρική Ar.
[2] δὴ Susemihl : δ' codd.
[3] ἔστι δ' ἔτι τέταρτόν τι (i.e. δ̄ τι) Schmidt.
[4] καὶ—οἰκονομίας secl. Susemihl.
[5] [καὶ εὖ ζῆν] ? ed. ; om. ΓΜΡ[1].
[6] δὴ Susemihl.

---

[a] No English word covers all the associations of the
Greek, which means ' dealing in χρήματα,' ' things,'—goods,
property, money—and so ' business.'

14

term denoting the relation uniting wife and husband), and thirdly the progenitive relationship (this too has not been designated by a special name). Let us then accept these three relationships that we have mentioned. There is also a department which some people consider the same as household management and others the most important part of it, and the true position of which we shall have to consider: I mean what is called the art of getting wealth.[a] *and as man of business.*

Let us begin by discussing the relation of master and slave, in order to observe the facts that have a bearing on practical utility, and also in the hope that we may be able to obtain something better than the notions at present entertained, with a view to a theo-3 retic knowledge of the subject. For some thinkers hold the function of the master to be a definite science, and moreover think that household management, mastership, statesmanship and monarchy are the same thing, as we said at the beginning of the treatise ; others however maintain that for one man to be another man's master is contrary to nature, because it is only convention that makes the one a slave and the other a freeman and there is no difference between them by nature, and that there-fore it is unjust, for it is based on force. *Mastership and Slavery. Various theories.*

Since therefore property is a part of a household and the art of acquiring property a part of household management (for without the necessaries even life, 4 as well as the good life,[b] is impossible), and, since, just as for the definite arts it would be necessary for the proper tools to be forthcoming if their work is to be accomplished, so also the manager of a household must have his tools, and of tools some are lifeless and *The slave a live tool for service (not for pro-duction),*

[b] ' As well as the good life ' is probably an interpolation.

15

1253 b

τῷ κυβερνήτῃ ὁ μὲν οἴαξ ἄψυχον ὁ δὲ πρωρεὺς
30 ἔμψυχον, ὁ γὰρ ὑπηρέτης ἐν ὀργάνου εἴδει ταῖς
τέχναις ἐστίν), οὕτω καὶ τὸ κτῆμα ὄργανον πρὸς
ζωήν ἐστι, καὶ ἡ κτῆσις πλῆθος ὀργάνων ἐστί,
καὶ ὁ δοῦλος κτῆμά τι ἔμψυχον. καὶ ὥσπερ
ὄργανον πρὸ ὀργάνων πᾶς ὑπηρέτης· εἰ γὰρ 5
ἠδύνατο ἕκαστον τῶν ὀργάνων κελευσθὲν ἢ προ-
35 αισθανόμενον ἀποτελεῖν τὸ αὑτοῦ ἔργον, ὥσπερ τὰ
Δαιδάλου φασὶν ἢ τοὺς τοῦ Ἡφαίστου τρίποδας,
οὕς φησιν ὁ ποιητὴς αὐτομάτους θεῖον δύεσθαι
ἀγῶνα, οὕτως αἱ κερκίδες ἐκέρκιζον αὐταὶ καὶ τὰ
πλῆκτρα ἐκιθάριζεν, οὐδὲν ἂν ἔδει οὔτε τοῖς
1254 a ἀρχιτέκτοσιν ὑπηρετῶν οὔτε τοῖς δεσπόταις δούλων.
τὰ μὲν οὖν λεγόμενα ὄργανα ποιητικὰ ὄργανά ἐστι,
τὸ δὲ κτῆμα πρακτικόν· ἀπὸ μὲν γὰρ τῆς κερκίδος
ἕτερόν τι γίνεται παρὰ τὴν χρῆσιν αὐτῆς, ἀπὸ δὲ
5 τῆς ἐσθῆτος καὶ τῆς κλίνης ἡ χρῆσις μόνον. ἔτι **6**
δ᾽ ἐπεὶ διαφέρει ἡ ποίησις εἴδει καὶ ἡ πρᾶξις,
δέονται δ᾽ ἀμφότεραι ὀργάνων, ἀνάγκη καὶ ταῦτα
τὴν αὐτὴν ἔχειν διαφοράν. ὁ δὲ βίος πρᾶξις, οὐ
ποίησίς ἐστιν· διὸ καὶ ὁ δοῦλος ὑπηρέτης[1] τῶν
πρὸς τὴν πρᾶξιν.

Τὸ δὲ κτῆμα λέγεται ὥσπερ καὶ τὸ μόριον· τὸ[2]
10 γὰρ μόριον οὐ μόνον ἄλλου ἐστὶ μόριον, ἀλλὰ
καὶ ἁπλῶς[3] ἄλλου, ὁμοίως δὲ καὶ τὸ κτῆμα. διὸ
ὁ μὲν δεσπότης τοῦ δούλου δεσπότης μόνον,

---

[1] [ὑπηρέτης] ? gloss ed.; cf. 1253 b 30.
[2] τὸ ed.: τό τε codd.   [3] ἁπλῶς Γ, ἁπλῶς ὅλως M¹, ὅλως cet.

ᵃ This legendary sculptor first represented the eyes as
open and the limbs as in motion, so his statues had to be

16

others living (for example, for a helmsman the rudder
is a lifeless tool and the look-out man a live tool—for
an assistant in the arts belongs to the class of tools),
so also an article of property is a tool for the purpose
of life, and property generally is a collection of tools,
5 and a slave is a live article of property. And every
assistant is as it were a tool that serves for several
tools ; for if every tool could perform its own work
when ordered, or by seeing what to do in advance,
like the statues of Daedalus in the story,[a] or the
tripods of Hephaestus which the poet says ' enter
self-moved the company divine,' [b]—if thus shuttles
wove and quills played harps of themselves, master-
craftsmen would have no need of assistants and
masters no need of slaves. Now the tools mentioned
are instruments of production, whereas an article of
property is an instrument of action[c]; for from a
shuttle we get something else beside the mere use
of the shuttle, but from a garment or a bed we get
6 only their use. And also inasmuch as there is a
difference in kind between production and action,
and both need tools, it follows that those tools also
must possess the same difference. But life is doing
things, not making things ; hence the slave is an
assistant in the class of instruments of action.

And the term ' article of property ' is used in the belonging
same way as the term ' part ' : a thing that is a part $\frac{\text{wholly to}}{\text{the master.}}$
is not only a part of another thing but absolutely
belongs to another thing, and so also does an article
of property. Hence whereas the master is merely
the slave's master and does not belong to the slave,

chained to prevent them from running away (Plato, *Meno*
97 D).   [b] *Iliad*, xviii. 369.

   [c] *i.e.* with it we do not *make* something but *do* something
(*e.g.* wear a dress, lie in a bed).

1254 a
ἐκείνου δ' οὐκ ἔστιν· ὁ δὲ δοῦλος οὐ μόνον δεσπότου
δοῦλός ἐστιν, ἀλλὰ καὶ ὅλως ἐκείνου.

Τίς μὲν οὖν ἡ φύσις τοῦ δούλου καὶ τίς ἡ δύναμις, 7
15 ἐκ τούτων δῆλον· ὁ γὰρ μὴ αὑτοῦ φύσει ἀλλ' ἄλλου
ἄνθρωπος ὤν, οὗτος φύσει δοῦλός ἐστιν, ἄλλου δ'
ἐστὶν ἄνθρωπος ὃς ἂν κτῆμα ᾖ ἄνθρωπος ὤν, κτῆμα
δὲ ὄργανον πρακτικὸν καὶ χωριστόν. πότερον δ'
ἐστί τις φύσει τοιοῦτος ἢ οὔ, καὶ πότερον βέλτιον
καὶ δίκαιόν τινι δουλεύειν ἢ οὔ, ἀλλὰ πᾶσα δουλεία
20 παρὰ φύσιν ἐστί, μετὰ ταῦτα σκεπτέον. οὐ 8
χαλεπὸν δὲ καὶ τῷ λόγῳ θεωρῆσαι καὶ ἐκ τῶν
γινομένων καταμαθεῖν. τὸ γὰρ ἄρχειν καὶ ἄρχεσθαι
οὐ μόνον τῶν ἀναγκαίων ἀλλὰ καὶ τῶν συμφερόντων
ἐστί, καὶ εὐθὺς ἐκ γενετῆς ἔνια διέστηκε τὰ μὲν
ἐπὶ τὸ ἄρχεσθαι τὰ δ' ἐπὶ τὸ ἄρχειν. καὶ εἴδη
25 πολλὰ καὶ ἀρχόντων καὶ ἀρχομένων ἐστίν (καὶ
ἀεὶ βελτίων ἡ ἀρχὴ ἡ τῶν βελτιόνων ἀρχομένων,
οἷον ἀνθρώπου ἢ θηρίου, τὸ γὰρ ἀποτελούμενον
ἀπὸ τῶν βελτιόνων βέλτιον ἔργον, ὅπου δὲ τὸ μὲν
ἄρχει τὸ δ' ἄρχεται, ἐστί τι τούτων ἔργον)· ὅσα 9
γὰρ ἐκ πλειόνων συνέστηκε καὶ γίνεται ἕν τι
30 κοινόν, εἴτε ἐκ συνεχῶν εἴτ' ἐκ διῃρημένων, ἐν
ἅπασιν ἐμφαίνεται τὸ ἄρχον καὶ τὸ ἀρχόμενον,
καὶ τοῦτο ἐκ τῆς ἁπάσης φύσεως ἐνυπάρχει τοῖς
ἐμψύχοις· καὶ γὰρ ἐν τοῖς μὴ μετέχουσι ζωῆς ἐστί

the slave is not merely the slave of the master **but**
wholly belongs to the master.

7   These considerations therefore make clear the The
nature of the slave and his essential quality : one distinction of ruler
who is a human being belonging by nature not to and ruled
himself but to another is by nature a slave, and a pervades all nature
person is a human being belonging to another if and life.
being a man he is an article of property, and an
article of property is an instrument for action separ-
able from its owner.   But we must next consider
whether or not anyone exists who is by nature of
this character, and whether it is advantageous and
just for anyone to be a slave, or whether on the
8 contrary all slavery is against nature.   And it is not
difficult either to discern the answer by theory or to
learn it empirically.   Authority and subordination
are conditions not only inevitable but also expedient ;
in some cases things are marked out from the moment
of birth to rule or to be ruled.   And there are many
varieties both of rulers and of subjects (and the
higher the type of the subjects, the loftier is the
nature of the authority exercised over them, for
example to control a human being is a higher thing
than to tame a wild beast ; for the higher the type
of the parties to the performance of a function, the
higher is the function, and when one party rules
and another is ruled, there is a function performed
9 between them)—because in every composite thing,
where a plurality of parts, whether continuous or
discrete, is combined to make a single common
whole, there is always found a ruling and a subject
factor, and this characteristic of living things is
present in them as an outcome of the whole of nature,
since even in things that do not partake of life there

1254 a

τις ἀρχή, οἷον ἁρμονίας.¹ ἀλλὰ ταῦτα μὲν ἴσως
ἐξωτερικωτέρας ἐστὶ σκέψεως. τὸ δὲ ζῷον πρῶτον 10
35 συνέστηκεν ἐκ ψυχῆς καὶ σώματος, ὧν τὸ μὲν
ἄρχον ἐστὶ φύσει τὸ δ' ἀρχόμενον. δεῖ δὲ σκοπεῖν
ἐν τοῖς κατὰ φύσιν ἔχουσι μᾶλλον τὸ φύσει, καὶ
μὴ ἐν τοῖς διεφθαρμένοις. διὸ καὶ τὸν βέλτιστα
διακείμενον καὶ κατὰ σῶμα καὶ κατὰ ψυχὴν ἄνθρωπον θεωρητέον, ἐν ᾧ τοῦτο δῆλον· τῶν γὰρ

1254 b μοχθηρῶν ἢ μοχθηρῶς² ἐχόντων δόξειεν ἂν ἄρχειν
πολλάκις τὸ σῶμα τῆς ψυχῆς διὰ τὸ φαύλως καὶ³
παρὰ φύσιν ἔχειν. ἔστι δ' οὖν, ὥσπερ λέγομεν, 11
πρῶτον ἐν ζῴῳ θεωρῆσαι καὶ δεσποτικὴν ἀρχὴν
5 καὶ πολιτικήν· ἡ μὲν γὰρ ψυχὴ τοῦ σώματος
ἄρχει δεσποτικὴν ἀρχήν, ὁ δὲ νοῦς τῆς ὀρέξεως
πολιτικὴν καὶ βασιλικήν· ἐν οἷς φανερόν ἐστιν ὅτι
κατὰ φύσιν καὶ⁴ συμφέρον τὸ ἄρχεσθαι τῷ σώματι
ὑπὸ τῆς ψυχῆς καὶ τῷ παθητικῷ μορίῳ ὑπὸ τοῦ
νοῦ καὶ τοῦ μορίου τοῦ λόγον ἔχοντος, τὸ δ' ἐξ
10 ἴσου ἢ ἀνάπαλιν βλαβερὸν πᾶσιν. πάλιν ἐν 12
ἀνθρώπῳ καὶ τοῖς ἄλλοις ζῴοις ὡσαύτως· τὰ μὲν
γὰρ ἥμερα τῶν ἀγρίων βελτίω τὴν φύσιν, τούτοις
δὲ πᾶσι βέλτιον ἄρχεσθαι ὑπ' ἀνθρώπου, τυγχάνει
γὰρ σωτηρίας οὕτως. ἔτι δὲ τὸ ἄρρεν πρὸς τὸ
θῆλυ φύσει τὸ μὲν κρεῖττον τὸ δὲ χεῖρον, τὸ μὲν
15 ἄρχον τὸ δ' ἀρχόμενον. τὸν αὐτὸν δὲ τρόπον
ἀναγκαῖον εἶναι καὶ ἐπὶ πάντων ἀνθρώπων· ὅσοι 13
μὲν οὖν τοσοῦτον διεστᾶσιν ὅσον ψυχὴ σώματος

---

¹ ἁρμονίαις vel ἐν ἁρμονίαις Richards.
² μοχθηρῶς : φαύλως (Γ ?) Buecheler.
³ φαύλως καὶ secl. idem.   ⁴ ἢ ? Richards.

ᵃ Each 'mode' (Dorian, the modern minor scale, Phrygian
and Lydian, two forms of major) was ruled by its key-note.

20

is a ruling principle, as in the case of a musical scale.[a]
However, this matter perhaps belongs to an investi-
10 gation lying somewhat outside our subject. But in
the first place an animal consists of soul and body, of
which the former is by nature the ruling and the
latter the subject factor. And to discover what is
natural we must study it preferably in things that are
in a natural state, and not in specimens that are de-
generate. Hence in studying man we must consider
a man that is in the best possible condition in regard
to both body and soul, and in him the principle stated
will clearly appear,—since in those that are bad or in
a bad condition it might be thought that the body
often rules the soul because of its vicious and un-
11 natural condition. But to resume—it is in a living
creature, as we say, that it is first possible to discern
the rule both of master and of statesman : the soul
rules the body with the sway of a master, the intelligence the appetites with constitutional or royal rule ;
and in these examples it is manifest that it is natural
and expedient for the body to be governed by the
soul and for the emotional part to be governed by
the intellect, the part possessing reason, whereas
for the two parties to be on an equal footing or in the
12 contrary positions is harmful in all cases. Again, the
same holds good between man and the other animals :
tame animals are superior in their nature to wild
animals, yet for all the former it is advantageous to
be ruled by man, since this gives them security.
Also, as between the sexes, the male is by nature
superior and the female inferior, the male ruler and
the female subject. And the same must also necessarily apply in the case of mankind generally ;
13 therefore all men that differ as widely as the soul

21

1254 b

καὶ ἄνθρωπος θηρίου (διάκεινται δὲ τοῦτον τὸν
τρόπον ὅσων ἐστὶν ἔργον ἡ τοῦ σώματος χρῆσις καὶ
τοῦτ' ἔστ' ἀπ' αὐτῶν βέλτιστον), οὗτοι μέν εἰσι
20 φύσει δοῦλοι, οἷς βέλτιόν ἐστιν ἄρχεσθαι ταύτην
τὴν ἀρχήν, εἴπερ καὶ τοῖς εἰρημένοις. ἔστι γὰρ
φύσει δοῦλος ὁ δυνάμενος ἄλλου εἶναι (διὸ καὶ
ἄλλου ἐστίν) καὶ ὁ κοινωνῶν λόγου τοσοῦτον ὅσον
αἰσθάνεσθαι ἀλλὰ μὴ ἔχειν· τὰ γὰρ ἄλλα ζῷα
οὐ λόγῳ αἰσθανόμενα[1] ἀλλὰ παθήμασιν ὑπηρετεῖ.
25 καὶ ἡ χρεία δὲ παραλλάττει μικρόν· ἡ γὰρ πρὸς 14
τἀναγκαῖα τῷ σώματι βοήθεια γίνεται παρ'
ἀμφοῖν, παρά τε τῶν δούλων καὶ παρὰ τῶν
ἡμέρων ζῴων. βούλεται μὲν οὖν ἡ φύσις καὶ τὰ
σώματα διαφέροντα ποιεῖν τὰ τῶν ἐλευθέρων καὶ
τῶν δούλων, τὰ μὲν ἰσχυρὰ πρὸς τὴν ἀναγκαίαν
30 χρῆσιν, τὰ δ' ὀρθὰ καὶ ἄχρηστα πρὸς τὰς τοιαύτας
ἐργασίας, ἀλλὰ χρήσιμα πρὸς πολιτικὸν βίον (οὗτος
δὲ καὶ γίνεται διῃρημένος εἴς τε τὴν πολεμικὴν
χρείαν καὶ τὴν εἰρηνικήν), συμβαίνει δὲ πολλάκις
καὶ τοὐναντίον, τοὺς μὲν τὰ σώματ' ἔχειν ἐλευθέρων
τοὺς δὲ τὰς ψυχὰς μόνον[2]· ἐπεὶ τοῦτό γε φανερόν, 15
35 ὡς εἰ τοσοῦτον γένοιντο διάφοροι τὸ σῶμα ὅσον
αἱ τῶν θεῶν εἰκόνες, τοὺς ὑπολειπομένους πάντες
φαῖεν ἂν ἀξίους εἶναι τούτοις δουλεύειν. εἰ δ'
ἐπὶ τοῦ σώματος τοῦτ' ἀληθές, πολὺ δικαιό-
τερον ἐπὶ τῆς ψυχῆς τοῦτο διωρίσθαι· ἀλλ' οὐχ
ὁμοίως ῥᾴδιον ἰδεῖν τό τε τῆς ψυχῆς κάλλος καὶ
1255 a τὸ τοῦ σώματος. ὅτι μὲν τοίνυν εἰσὶ φύσει τινὲς

---

[1] πειθόμενα Richards.
[2] μόνον hic ed.; post σῶμα codd.

22

does from the body and the human being from the lower animal (and this is the condition of those whose function is the use of the body and from whom this is the best that is forthcoming)—these are by nature slaves, for whom to be governed by this kind of authority is advantageous, inasmuch as it is advantageous to the subject things already mentioned. For he is by nature a slave who is capable of belonging to another (and that is why he does so belong), and who participates in reason so far as to apprehend it but not to possess it ; for the animals other than man are subservient not to reason, by apprehending it, 14 but to feelings. And also the usefulness of slaves diverges little from that of animals ; bodily service for the necessities of life is forthcoming from both, from slaves and from domestic animals alike. The intention of nature therefore is to make the bodies also of freemen and of slaves different—the latter strong for necessary service, the former erect and unserviceable for such occupations, but serviceable for a life of citizenship (and that again divides into the employments of war and those of peace) ; though as a matter of fact often the very opposite comes about— slaves have the bodies of freemen and freemen the 15 souls only ; since this is certainly clear, that if freemen were born as distinguished in body as are the statues of the gods, everyone would say that those who were inferior deserved to be these men's slaves ; and if this is true in the case of the body, there is far juster reason for this rule being laid down in the case of the soul, but beauty of soul is not so easy to see as beauty of body. It is manifest therefore that there are cases of people of whom some are

Some men fitted by mind and body for slavery,

although because misfits do occur its justice is criticized.

1255 b οἱ μὲν ἐλεύθεροι οἱ δὲ δοῦλοι, φανερόν, οἷς καὶ
συμφέρει τὸ δουλεύειν καὶ δίκαιόν ἐστιν.

Ὅτι δὲ καὶ οἱ τἀναντία φάσκοντες τρόπον τινὰ 16
λέγουσιν ὀρθῶς, οὐ χαλεπὸν ἰδεῖν. διχῶς γὰρ
5 λέγεται τὸ δουλεύειν καὶ ὁ δοῦλος· ἔστι γάρ τις
καὶ κατὰ νόμον δοῦλος καὶ δουλεύων, ὁ γὰρ νόμος
ὁμολογία τίς ἐστιν ἐν ᾗ[1] τὰ κατὰ πόλεμον κρατού-
μενα τῶν κρατούντων εἶναί φασιν.[2] τοῦτο δὴ τὸ
δίκαιον πολλοὶ τῶν ἐν τοῖς νόμοις ὥσπερ ῥήτορα
γράφονται παρανόμων, ὡς δεινὸν εἰ τοῦ βιάσασθαι
10 δυναμένου καὶ κατὰ δύναμιν κρείττονος ἔσται
δοῦλον καὶ ἀρχόμενον τὸ βιασθέν· καὶ τοῖς μὲν
οὕτω δοκεῖ τοῖς δ' ἐκείνως καὶ τῶν σοφῶν. αἴτιον 17
δὲ ταύτης τῆς ἀμφισβητήσεως, καὶ ὃ ποιεῖ τοὺς
λόγους ἐπαλλάττειν, ὅτι τρόπον τινὰ ἀρετὴ τυγ-
χάνουσα χορηγίας καὶ βιάζεσθαι δύναται μάλιστα,
15 καὶ ἔστιν ἀεὶ τὸ κρατοῦν ἐν ὑπεροχῇ ἀγαθοῦ τινός,
ὥστε δοκεῖν μὴ ἄνευ ἀρετῆς εἶναι τὴν βίαν, ἀλλὰ
περὶ τοῦ δικαίου μόνον εἶναι τὴν ἀμφισβήτησιν
(διὰ γὰρ τὸ τοῖς μὲν εὔνοιαν δοκεῖν[3] τὸ δίκαιον
εἶναι, τοῖς δ' αὐτὸ τοῦτο δίκαιον, τὸ τὸν κρείττονα
ἄρχειν)· ἐπεὶ διαστάντων γε χωρὶς τούτων τῶν
20 λόγων οὔτ' ἰσχυρὸν οὐθὲν ἔχουσιν οὔτε πιθανὸν
ἅτεροι λόγοι, ὡς οὐ δεῖ τὸ βέλτιον κατ' ἀρετὴν
ἄρχειν καὶ δεσπόζειν. ὅλως δ' ἀντεχόμενοί τινες 18
ὡς οἷόν τε[4] δικαίου τινός (ὁ γὰρ νόμος δίκαιόν τι)

---

[1] ᾗ ed. Basil.: ᾧ codd. (ἐφ' ᾧ Bernays).
[2] [φασίν] Bernays.
[3] τὸ—εὔνοιαν δοκεῖν Ross: τοῦτο—εὔνοια δοκεῖ codd.
[4] οἷόν τε ed.: οἴονται codd.

---

[a] The difficulty turns on the ambiguity of ἀρετή, (a) moral
goodness, virtue, (b) goodness of any kind, e.g. strength.

24

freemen and the others slaves by nature, and for these slavery is an institution both expedient and just.

16   But at the same time it is not difficult to see that those who assert the opposite are also right in a manner. The fact is that the terms ' slavery ' and ' slave ' are ambiguous ; for there is also such a thing as a slave or a man that is in slavery by law, for the law is a sort of agreement under which the things conquered in war are said to belong to their conquerors. Now this conventional right is arraigned by many jurists just as a statesman is impeached for proposing an unconstitutional measure ; they say that it is monstrous if the person powerful enough to use force, and superior in power, is to have the victim of his force as his slave and subject ; and even among the learned some hold this view, though others 17 hold the other. But the reason of this dispute and what makes the theories overlap is the fact that in a certain manner virtue when it obtains resources has in fact very great power to use force, and the stronger party always possesses superiority in something that is good,[a] so that it is thought that force cannot be devoid of goodness, but that the dispute is merely about the justice of the matter (for it is due to the one party holding that the justification of authority is good-will, while the other identifies justice with the mere rule of the stronger) ; because obviously if these theories be separated apart, the other theories have no force or plausibility at all, implying that the superior in goodness has no claim 18 to rule and be master. But some persons, doing their best to cling to some principle of justice (for the law is a principle of justice), assert that the

Criticism really aimed at legal slavery;

1255 a
τὴν κατὰ πόλεμον δουλείαν τιθέασι δικαίαν· ἅμα
δ' οὔ φασιν, τήν τε γὰρ ἀρχὴν ἐνδέχεται μὴ δι-
25 καίαν εἶναι τῶν πολέμων καὶ τὸν ἀνάξιον δουλεύειν οὐδαμῶς ἂν φαίη τις δοῦλον εἶναι· εἰ δὲ
μή, συμβήσεται τοὺς εὐγενεστάτους εἶναι δοκοῦντας
δούλους εἶναι καὶ ἐκ δούλων ἐὰν συμβῇ πραθῆναι
ληφθέντας. διόπερ αὐτοὺς οὐ βούλονται λέγειν
δούλους, ἀλλὰ τοὺς βαρβάρους. καίτοι ὅταν τοῦτο
30 λέγωσιν, οὐθὲν ἄλλο ζητοῦσιν ἢ τὸ φύσει δοῦλον
ὅπερ ἐξ ἀρχῆς εἴπομεν· ἀνάγκη γὰρ εἶναί τινας
φάναι τοὺς μὲν πανταχοῦ δούλους τοὺς δ' οὐδαμοῦ.
τὸν αὐτὸν δὲ τρόπον καὶ περὶ εὐγενείας· αὐτοὺς μὲν 19
γὰρ οὐ μόνον παρ' αὐτοῖς εὐγενεῖς ἀλλὰ πανταχοῦ
35 νομίζουσιν, τοὺς δὲ βαρβάρους οἴκοι μόνον, ὡς
ὄν τι τὸ μὲν ἁπλῶς εὐγενὲς καὶ ἐλεύθερον τὸ δ'
οὐχ ἁπλῶς, ὥσπερ ἡ Θεοδέκτου Ἑλένη φησὶ

θείων δ' ἀπ' ἀμφοῖν ἔκγονον ῥιζωμάτων
τίς ἂν προσειπεῖν ἀξιώσειεν λάτριν;

ὅταν δὲ τοῦτο λέγωσιν, οὐθενὶ ἀλλ' ἢ ἀρετῇ καὶ
40 κακίᾳ διορίζουσι τὸ δοῦλον καὶ ἐλεύθερον καὶ τοὺς
1255 b εὐγενεῖς καὶ τοὺς δυσγενεῖς· ἀξιοῦσι γάρ, ὥσπερ
ἐξ ἀνθρώπου ἄνθρωπον καὶ ἐκ θηρίων γίνεσθαι
θηρίον, οὕτω καὶ ἐξ ἀγαθῶν ἀγαθόν· ἡ δὲ φύσις
βούλεται μὲν τοῦτο ποιεῖν πολλάκις, οὐ μέντοι
δύναται.

Ὅτι μὲν οὖν ἔχει τινὰ λόγον ἡ ἀμφισβήτησις,

---

* A tragic poet, a friend of Aristotle.

26

enslavement of prisoners of war is just; yet at the *natural slavery implicitly recognized by Common Sense.* same time they deny the assertion, for there is the possibility that wars may be unjust in their origin and one would by no means admit that a man that does not deserve slavery can be really a slave—otherwise we shall have the result that persons reputed of the highest nobility are slaves and the descendants of slaves if they happen to be taken prisoners of war and sold. Therefore they do not mean to assert that Greeks themselves if taken prisoners are slaves, but that barbarians are. Yet when they say this, they are merely seeking for the principles of natural slavery of which we spoke at the outset; for they are compelled to say that there exist certain persons who are essentially slaves everywhere 19 and certain others who are so nowhere. And the same applies also about nobility: our nobles consider themselves noble not only in their own country but everywhere, but they think that barbarian noblemen are only noble in their own country—which implies that there are two kinds of nobility and of freedom, one absolute and the other relative, as Helen says in Theodectes[a]:

> But who would dare to call me menial,
> The scion of a twofold stock divine?

Yet in so speaking they make nothing but virtue and vice the distinction between slave and free, the noble and the base-born; for they assume that just as from a man springs a man and from brutes a brute, so also from good parents comes a good son; but as a matter of fact nature frequently while intending to do this is unable to bring it about.

It is clear therefore that there is some reason for

1255 b

5 καὶ οὐκ εἰσί τινες[1] οἱ μὲν φύσει δοῦλοι οἱ δ'
ἐλεύθεροι, δῆλον· καὶ ὅτι ἔν τισι διώρισται τὸ 20
τοιοῦτον, ὧν συμφέρει τῷ μὲν τὸ δουλεύειν τῷ δὲ
τὸ δεσπόζειν, καὶ δίκαιον καὶ δεῖ τὸ μὲν ἄρχεσθαι
τὸ δ' ἄρχειν ἣν πεφύκασιν ἀρχὴν ἄρχειν, ὥστε
καὶ δεσπόζειν τὸ δὲ κακῶς ἀσυμφόρως ἐστὶν
10 ἀμφοῖν (τὸ γὰρ αὐτὸ συμφέρει τῷ μέρει καὶ τῷ
ὅλῳ καὶ σώματι καὶ ψυχῇ, ὁ δὲ δοῦλος μέρος τι
τοῦ δεσπότου, οἷον ἔμψυχόν τι τοῦ σώματος
κεχωρισμένον δὲ μέρος· διὸ καὶ συμφέρον ἐστί 21
τι καὶ φιλία δούλῳ καὶ δεσπότῃ πρὸς ἀλλήλους
τοῖς φύσει τούτων ἠξιωμένοις, τοῖς δὲ μὴ τοῦτον
15 τὸν τρόπον ἀλλὰ κατὰ νόμον καὶ βιασθεῖσι τοὐναντίον).

Φανερὸν δὲ καὶ ἐκ τούτων ὅτι οὐ ταὐτόν ἐστι
δεσποτεία καὶ πολιτικὴ οὐδὲ πᾶσαι ἀλλήλαις αἱ
ἀρχαί, ὥσπερ τινές φασιν. ἡ μὲν γὰρ ἐλευθέρων
φύσει ἡ δὲ δούλων ἐστίν, καὶ ἡ μὲν οἰκονομικὴ
20 μοναρχία (μοναρχεῖται γὰρ πᾶς οἶκος), ἡ δὲ πολιτικὴ ἐλευθέρων καὶ ἴσων ἀρχή. ὁ μὲν οὖν δεσπό- 22
της οὐ λέγεται κατ' ἐπιστήμην ἀλλὰ τῷ τοιόσδ'
εἶναι, ὁμοίως δὲ καὶ ὁ δοῦλος καὶ ὁ ἐλεύθερος.
ἐπιστήμη δ' ἂν εἴη καὶ δεσποτικὴ καὶ δουλική,

---

[1] εἰσί τινες ed.: εἰσὶν codd.

28

this dispute, and that in some instances it is not the _{Recapitula-}
case that one set are slaves and the other freemen _{tion.}
20 by nature ; and also that in some instances such a
distinction does exist, when slavery for the one and
mastership for the other are. advantageous, and it is
just and proper for the one party to be governed and
for the other to govern by the form of government
for which they are by nature fitted, and therefore
by the exercise of mastership, while to govern badly
is to govern disadvantageously for both parties (for
the same thing is advantageous for a part and for
the whole body or the whole soul, and the slave is a
part of the master—he is, as it were, a part of the
21 body, alive but yet separated from it; hence there
is a certain community of interest and friendship
between slave and master in cases when they have
been qualified by nature for those positions, although
when they do not hold them in that way but by law
and by constraint of force the opposite is the case).

And even from these considerations it is clear that _{Mastership}
the authority of a master over slaves is not the same _{distin-}
_{guished}
as the authority of a magistrate in a republic, nor are _{from}
all forms of government the same, as some assert. _{government}
Republican government controls men who are by _{supervision}
_{of free men,}
nature free, the master's authority men who are by _{of slaves'}
nature slaves ; and the government of a household _{tasks, and}
is monarchy (since every house is governed by a _{acquisition}
_{of slaves.}
single ruler), whereas statesmanship is the govern-
22 ment of men free and equal. The term ' master '
therefore denotes the possession not of a certain
branch of knowledge but of a certain character, and
similarly also the terms ' slave ' and ' freeman.' Yet
there might be a science of mastership and a slave's
science—the latter being the sort of knowledge that

1255 b

δουλικὴ μὲν οἵαν περ ὁ ἐν Συρακούσαις ἐπαίδευεν
25 (ἐκεῖ γὰρ λαμβάνων τις μισθὸν ἐδίδασκε τὰ
ἐγκύκλια διακονήματα τοὺς παῖδας)· εἴη δ' ἂν καὶ
ἐπὶ πλεῖον τῶν τοιούτων μάθησις, οἷον ὀψοποιικὴ
καὶ τἆλλα τὰ τοιαῦτα γένη τῆς διακονίας· ἔστι γὰρ
ἕτερα ἑτέρων τὰ μὲν ἐντιμότερα ἔργα τὰ δ' ἀναγ-
καιότερα, καὶ κατὰ τὴν παροιμίαν

30 δοῦλος πρὸ δούλου, δεσπότης πρὸ δεσπότου.

αἱ μὲν οὖν τοιαῦται πᾶσαι δουλικαὶ ἐπιστῆμαί εἰσι, 23
δεσποτικὴ δ' ἐπιστήμη ἐστὶν ἡ χρηστικὴ δούλων·
ὁ γὰρ δεσπότης οὐκ ἐν τῷ κτᾶσθαι τοὺς δούλους,
ἀλλ' ἐν τῷ χρῆσθαι δούλοις. ἔστι δ' αὕτη ἡ
ἐπιστήμη οὐδὲν μέγα ἔχουσα οὐδὲ σεμνόν· ἃ γὰρ
τὸν δοῦλον ἐπίστασθαι δεῖ ποιεῖν, ἐκεῖνον δεῖ
35 ταῦτα ἐπίστασθαι ἐπιτάττειν. διὸ ὅσοις ἐξουσία
μὴ αὐτοὺς κακοπαθεῖν, ἐπίτροπος λαμβάνει ταύτην
τὴν τιμήν, αὐτοὶ δὲ πολιτεύονται ἢ φιλοσοφοῦσιν.
ἡ δὲ κτητικὴ ἑτέρα ἀμφοτέρων τούτων ἡ δικαία,
οἷον[1] πολεμική τις οὖσα ἢ θηρευτική. περὶ μὲν
οὖν δούλου καὶ δεσπότου τοῦτον διωρίσθω τὸν
40 τρόπον.

1256 a III. Ὅλως δὲ περὶ πάσης κτήσεως καὶ χρη-1
ματιστικῆς θεωρήσωμεν κατὰ τὸν ὑφηγημένον
τρόπον, ἐπείπερ καὶ ὁ δοῦλος τῆς κτήσεως μέρος
τι ἦν. πρῶτον μὲν οὖν ἀπορήσειεν ἄν τις πότερον
5 ἡ χρηματιστικὴ ἡ αὐτὴ τῇ οἰκονομικῇ ἐστιν ἢ
μέρος τι ἢ ὑπηρετική, καὶ εἰ ὑπηρετική, πότερον

---

[1] Richards : οἷον ἡ δικαία codd.

---

[a] Probably from a comedy of Aristotle's contemporary
Philemon.

used to be imparted by the professor at Syracuse (for there used to be a man there who for a fee gave lessons to servants in their ordinary duties); and indeed there might be more advanced scientific study of such matters, for instance a science of cookery and the other such kinds of domestic service—for different servants have different functions, some more honourable and some more menial, and as the proverb says,

Slave before slave and master before master.[a]

23 The slave's sciences then are all the various branches of domestic work; the master's science is the science of employing slaves—for the master's function consists not in acquiring slaves but in employing them. This science however is one of no particular importance or dignity: the master must know how to direct the tasks which the slave must know how to execute. Therefore all people rich enough to be able to avoid personal trouble have a steward who takes this office, while they themselves engage in politics or philosophy. The science of acquiring slaves is different both from their ownership and their direction—that is, the just acquiring of slaves, being like a sort of warfare or hunting. Let this then stand as our definition of slave and master.

1   III. But let us follow our normal method and in-vestigate generally the nature of all kinds of property and the art of getting wealth, inasmuch as we saw the slave to be one division of property. In the first place therefore one might raise the question whether the art of getting wealth is the same as that of house-hold management, or a part of it, or subsidiary to it; and if subsidiary, whether it is so in the sense in which

Business, or the supply of goods: its relation to household management.

31

1256 a

ὡς ἡ κερκιδοποιικὴ τῇ ὑφαντικῇ ἢ ὡς ἡ χαλκουρ-
γικὴ τῇ ἀνδριαντοποιίᾳ (οὐ γὰρ ὡσαύτως ὑπηρετοῦσιν, ἀλλ' ἡ μὲν ὄργανα παρέχει, ἡ δὲ τὴν ὕλην·
λέγω δὲ ὕλην τὸ ὑποκείμενον ἐξ οὗ τι ἀποτελεῖται
10 ἔργον, οἷον ὑφάντῃ μὲν ἔρια, ἀνδριαντοποιῷ δὲ
χαλκόν).

Ὅτι μὲν οὖν οὐχ ἡ αὐτὴ ἡ οἰκονομικὴ τῇ χρη- 2
ματιστικῇ, δῆλον, τῆς μὲν γὰρ τὸ πορίσασθαι, τῆς
δὲ τὸ χρήσασθαι—τίς γὰρ ἔσται ἡ χρησομένη τοῖς
κατὰ τὴν οἰκίαν παρὰ τὴν οἰκονομικήν; πότερον
δὲ μέρος αὐτῆς ἐστί τι ἢ ἕτερον εἶδος, ἔχει διαμ-
15 φισβήτησιν. εἰ γάρ ἐστι τοῦ χρηματιστικοῦ θεωρῆσαι πόθεν χρήματα καὶ κτῆσις ἔσται, ...[1]
ἡ δὲ κτῆσις πολλὰ περιείληφε μέρη καὶ ὁ πλοῦτος,
ὥστε πρῶτον ἡ γεωργικὴ πότερον μέρος τι τῆς
οἰκονομικῆς[2] ἢ ἕτερόν τι γένος; καὶ καθόλου ἡ
περὶ τὴν τροφὴν ἐπιμέλεια καὶ κτῆσις.

20 Ἀλλὰ μὴν εἴδη γε πολλὰ τροφῆς, διὸ καὶ βίοι 3
πολλοὶ καὶ τῶν ζῴων καὶ τῶν ἀνθρώπων εἰσίν·
οὐ γὰρ οἷόν τε ζῆν ἄνευ τροφῆς, ὥστε αἱ διαφοραὶ
τῆς τροφῆς τοὺς βίους πεποιήκασι διαφέροντας
τῶν ζῴων. τῶν τε γὰρ θηρίων τὰ μὲν ἀγελαῖα
τὰ δὲ σποραδικά ἐστιν, ὁποτέρως συμφέρει πρὸς
25 τὴν τροφὴν αὐτοῖς διὰ τὸ τὰ μὲν ζωοφάγα τὰ δὲ
καρποφάγα τὰ δὲ παμφάγα αὐτῶν εἶναι· ὥστε

---

[1] lacunam ? Susemihl.
[2] οἰκονομικῆς Garvey : χρηματιστικῆς codd.

---

[a] Some words seem to have fallen out in the Greek.

the art of making shuttles is subsidiary to the art of weaving or in that in which the art of casting bronze is subsidiary to the making of statues (for the two are not subsidiary in the same way, but shuttle-making supplies tools whereas bronze-founding supplies material—and by material I mean the substance out of which certain work is produced, for example fleeces are material for a weaver and bronze for a statuary).

2 Now it is clear that wealth-getting is not the same art as household management, for the function of the former is to provide and that of the latter to use—for what will be the art that will use the contents of the house if not the art of household management? but whether wealth-getting is a part of the art of household management, or a different sort of science, is open to debate. For if it is the function of the getter of wealth to study the source from which money and property are to be procured, ...[a] But property and riches comprise many divisions; hence first of all is husbandry a division of the house- Husbandry hold art, or is it a different kind of science? and so in general of the superintendence and acquisition of articles of food.

3 But furthermore, there are many sorts of food, Food is owing to which both animals and men have many provided modes of life; for it is impossible to live without by nature; food, so that the differences of food have made the lives of animals different. Among wild animals some are nomadic and others solitary, according to whichever habit is advantageous for their supply of food, because some of them are carnivorous, others graminivorous, and others eat all kinds of food; so that nature has differentiated

1256 a

πρὸς τὰς ῥαστώνας καὶ τὴν αἵρεσιν τὴν τούτων
ἡ φύσις τοὺς βίους αὐτῶν διώρισεν. ἐπεὶ δ' οὐ
ταὐτὸ ἑκάστῳ ἡδὺ κατὰ φύσιν ἀλλ' ἕτερα ἑτέροις,
καὶ αὐτῶν τῶν ζῳοφάγων καὶ τῶν καρποφάγων
οἱ βίοι πρὸς ἄλληλα διεστᾶσιν. ὁμοίως δὲ καὶ 4
30 τῶν ἀνθρώπων, πολὺ γὰρ διαφέρουσιν οἱ τούτων
βίοι. οἱ μὲν οὖν ἀργότατοι νομάδες εἰσίν (ἡ γὰρ
ἀπὸ τῶν ἡμέρων τροφὴ ζῴων ἄνευ πόνου γίνεται
σχολάζουσιν, ἀναγκαίου δ' ὄντος μεταβάλλειν τοῖς
κτήνεσι διὰ τὰς νομὰς καὶ αὐτοὶ ἀναγκάζονται
35 συνακολουθεῖν, ὥσπερ γεωργίαν ζῶσαν γεωργοῦντες)· οἱ δ' ἀπὸ θήρας ζῶσι, καὶ θήρας ἕτεροι ἑτέρας, οἷον οἱ μὲν ἀπὸ λῃστείας, οἱ δ' ἀφ' ἁλιείας
ὅσοι λίμνας καὶ ἕλη καὶ ποταμοὺς ἢ θάλατταν
τοιαύτην προσοικοῦσιν, οἱ δ' ἀπ' ὀρνίθων ἢ θηρίων
ἀγρίων· τὸ δὲ πλεῖστον γένος τῶν ἀνθρώπων ἀπὸ
40 τῆς γῆς ζῇ καὶ τῶν ἡμέρων καρπῶν. οἱ μὲν οὖν 5
βίοι τοσοῦτοι σχεδόν εἰσιν, ὅσοι γε αὐτόφυτον
ἔχουσι τὴν ἐργασίαν καὶ μὴ δι' ἀλλαγῆς καὶ κα-
1256 b πηλείας πορίζονται τὴν τροφήν, νομαδικός γεωργικός λῃστρικός ἁλιευτικός θηρευτικός· οἱ δὲ καὶ
μιγνύντες ἐκ τούτων ἡδέως ζῶσι, προσαναπληροῦν-
τες τὸν ἐνδεέστερον βίον ᾗ τυγχάνει ἐλλείπων πρὸς
5 τὸ αὔταρκες εἶναι, οἷον οἱ μὲν νομαδικὸν ἅμα καὶ
λῃστρικόν, οἱ δὲ γεωργικὸν καὶ θηρευτικόν, ὁμοίως
δὲ καὶ περὶ τοὺς ἄλλους—ὡς ἂν ἡ χρεία συν-
αναγκάζῃ, τοῦτον τὸν τρόπον διάγουσιν. ἡ μὲν 6

---

[a] Perhaps 'slave-raiding,' *cf.* § 9, the appropriation of the
'live tools' that are a part of nature's supplies; but Thucydides (i. 5) speaks of brigandage and piracy as common in
earlier times, and as still deemed respectable professions in
Northern Greece.

their modes of life to suit their facilities and their predilection for those articles of food. And as different kinds of animals by nature relish different sorts of food, and not each kind the same, even within the classes of carnivorous and graminivorous animals their modes of life differ from one another. 4 And similarly in the human race also, for there are wide differences of life among mankind. The idlest men are nomads (for to procure food from domesticated animals involves no toil or industry, but as it is necessary for the herds to move from place to place because of the pastures, the people themselves are forced to follow along with them, as though they were farming a live farm). Other men live from hunting, and different people from different kinds of hunting, for instance some from brigandage,[a] others from fishing—these are those that dwell on the banks of lakes, marshes and rivers or of a sea suitable for fishing,—and others live on wild birds and animals. But the largest class of men live from the 5 land and the fruits of cultivation. This then virtually completes the list of the various modes of life, those at least that have their industry sprung from themselves and do not procure their food by barter and trade—the lives of the herdsman, the husbandman, the brigand, the fisherman, the hunter. Others also live pleasantly by combining some of these pursuits, supplementing the more deficient life where it happens to fall short in regard to being self-sufficing: for instance, some combine a pastoral life and brigandage, others husbandry and hunting, and similarly with the others—they pass their time in such a combination of pursuits as their need 6 compels. Property of this sort then seems to be

35

1256 b

οὖν τοιαύτη κτῆσις ὑπ' αὐτῆς φαίνεται τῆς φύσεως
διδομένη πᾶσιν, ὥσπερ κατὰ τὴν πρώτην γένεσιν
10 εὐθύς, οὕτω καὶ τελειωθεῖσιν. καὶ γὰρ κατὰ τὴν
ἐξ ἀρχῆς γένεσιν τὰ μὲν συνεκτίκτει τῶν ζῴων
τοσαύτην τροφὴν ὡς ἱκανὴν εἶναι μέχρις οὗ ἂν
δύνηται αὐτὸ αὑτῷ πορίζειν τὸ γεννηθέν, οἷον ὅσα
σκωληκοτοκεῖ ἢ ᾠοτοκεῖ· ὅσα δὲ ζῳοτοκεῖ, τοῖς
γεννωμένοις[1] ἔχει τροφὴν ἐν αὑτοῖς μέχρι τινός,
15 τὴν τοῦ καλουμένου γάλακτος φύσιν. ὥστε ὁμοίως
δῆλον ὅτι καὶ γενομένοις οἰητέον τά τε φυτὰ τῶν
ζῴων ἕνεκεν εἶναι καὶ τἆλλα ζῷα τῶν ἀνθρώπων
χάριν, τὰ μὲν ἥμερα καὶ διὰ τὴν χρῆσιν καὶ διὰ
τὴν τροφήν, τῶν δ' ἀγρίων εἰ μὴ πάντα ἀλλὰ τά
γε πλεῖστα τῆς τροφῆς καὶ ἄλλης βοηθείας ἕνεκεν,
20 ἵνα καὶ ἐσθὴς καὶ ἄλλα ὄργανα γίνηται ἐξ αὐτῶν.
εἰ οὖν ἡ φύσις μηθὲν μήτε ἀτελὲς ποιεῖ μήτε μάτην,
ἀναγκαῖον τῶν ἀνθρώπων ἕνεκεν αὐτὰ πάντα
πεποιηκέναι τὴν φύσιν. διὸ καὶ ἡ πολεμικὴ φύσει
κτητική πως ἔσται (ἡ γὰρ θηρευτικὴ μέρος αὐτῆς)
25 ᾗ δεῖ χρῆσθαι πρός τε τὰ θηρία καὶ τῶν ἀνθρώπων
ὅσοι πεφυκότες ἄρχεσθαι μὴ θέλουσιν, ὡς φύσει
δίκαιον τοῦτον ὄντα τὸν πόλεμον.

Ἓν μὲν οὖν εἶδος κτητικῆς κατὰ φύσιν τῆς οἰκονομικῆς μέρος ἐστίν, καθὸ[2] δεῖ ἤτοι ὑπάρχειν ἢ
πορίζειν αὐτὴν ὅπως ὑπάρχῃ ὧν ἐστὶ θησαυρισμὸς

---

[1] γενομένοις codd. cet.
[2] καθὸ Bernays: ὃ codd., ὅτι (quia) Richards, ᾇ (et ᾇ δεῖ—
ὑπάρχειν post 30 οἰκίας tr.) Rassow.

---

[a] Rassow would transpose the clause (with a slight alteration) to give ' of the household art, that is, the acquisition of
those goods capable of accumulation that are necessary for
life and useful for the community of city and household, a

bestowed by nature herself upon all, as immediately upon their first coming into existence, so also when they have reached maturity. For even at the original coming into existence of the young some kinds of animals bring forth with them at birth enough sustenance to suffice until the offspring can provide for itself, for example all the species that bear their young in the form of larvae or in eggs. The viviparous species have sustenance for their offspring inside themselves for a certain period, the substance 7 called milk. So that clearly we must suppose that nature also provides for them in a similar way when grown up, and that plants exist for the sake of animals and the other animals for the good of man, the domestic species both for his service and for his food, and if not all at all events most of the wild ones for the sake of his food and of his supplies of other kinds, in order that they may furnish him both with clothing and with other appliances. If therefore nature makes nothing without purpose or in vain, it follows that nature has made all the animals for the sake of 8 men. Hence even the art of war will by nature be in a manner an art of acquisition (for the art of hunting is a part of it) that is properly employed both against wild animals and against such of mankind as though designed by nature for subjection refuse to submit to it, inasmuch as this warfare is by nature just.

One kind of acquisition therefore in the order of nature is a part of the household art,[a] in accordance with which either there must be forthcoming or else that art must procure to be forthcoming a supply *so moderate acquisition of supplies is the business of the household holder.*

supply of which must be forthcoming or else the art must procure it to be forthcoming.'

87

1256 b

χρημάτων πρὸς ζωὴν ἀναγκαίων καὶ χρησίμων
30 εἰς κοινωνίαν πόλεως ἢ οἰκίας. καὶ ἔοικεν ὅ γ᾽ 9
ἀληθινὸς πλοῦτος ἐκ τούτων εἶναι. ἡ γὰρ τῆς
τοιαύτης κτήσεως αὐτάρκεια πρὸς ἀγαθὴν ζωὴν
οὐκ ἄπειρός ἐστιν, ὥσπερ Σόλων φησὶ ποιήσας

πλούτου δ᾽ οὐθὲν τέρμα πεφασμένον ἀνδράσι κεῖται·

35 κεῖται γὰρ ὥσπερ καὶ ταῖς ἄλλαις τέχναις· οὐδὲν
γὰρ ὄργανον ἄπειρον οὐδεμιᾶς ἐστι τέχνης οὔτε
πλήθει οὔτε μεγέθει, ὁ δὲ πλοῦτος ὀργάνων πλῆθός
ἐστιν οἰκονομικῶν καὶ πολιτικῶν. ὅτι μὲν τοίνυν
ἔστι τις κτητικὴ κατὰ φύσιν τοῖς οἰκονόμοις καὶ
τοῖς πολιτικοῖς, καὶ δι᾽ ἣν αἰτίαν, δῆλον.

40 Ἔστι δὲ γένος ἄλλο κτητικῆς ἣν μάλιστα καλοῦσι, 10
καὶ δίκαιον αὐτὸ καλεῖν, χρηματιστικήν, δι᾽ ἣν
1257 a οὐδὲν δοκεῖ πέρας εἶναι πλούτου καὶ κτήσεως· ἣν
ὡς μίαν καὶ τὴν αὐτὴν τῇ λεχθείσῃ πολλοὶ νομίζουσι διὰ τὴν γειτνίασιν· ἔστι δ᾽ οὔτε ἡ αὐτὴ τῇ
εἰρημένῃ οὔτε πόρρω ἐκείνης. ἔστι δ᾽ ἡ μὲν φύσει
5 ἡ δ᾽ οὐ φύσει αὐτῶν, ἀλλὰ δι᾽ ἐμπειρίας τινὸς καὶ
τέχνης γίνεται μᾶλλον. λάβωμεν δὲ περὶ αὐτῆς
τὴν ἀρχὴν ἐντεῦθεν· ἑκάστου γὰρ κτήματος διττὴ 11
ἡ χρῆσίς ἐστιν, ἀμφότεραι δὲ καθ᾽ αὑτὸ μὲν ἀλλ᾽
οὐχ ὁμοίως καθ᾽ αὑτό, ἀλλ᾽ ἡ μὲν οἰκεία ἡ δ᾽
οὐκ οἰκεία τοῦ πράγματος, οἷον ὑποδήματος ἢ

• Fragment 13 l. 71.

of those goods, capable of accumulation, which are
necessary for life and useful for the community of
9 city or household. And it is of these goods that
riches in the true sense at all events seem to consist.
For the amount of such property sufficient in itself
for a good life is not unlimited, as Solon[a] says that
it is in the verse

But of riches no bound has been fixed or revealed to men;

for a limit has been fixed, as with the other arts,
since no tool belonging to any art is without a limit
whether in number or in size, and riches are a collection of tools for the householder and the statesman.
Therefore that there is a certain art of acquisition
belonging in the order of nature to householders and
to statesmen, and for what reason this is so, is clear.
10 But there is another kind of acquisition that is
specially called wealth-getting, and that is so called
with justice; and to this kind it is due that there
is thought to be no limit to riches and property.
Owing to its affinity to the art of acquisition of which
we spoke, it is supposed by many people to be one
and the same as that; and as a matter of fact, while
it is not the same as the acquisition spoken of, it is
not far removed from it. One of them is natural,
the other is not natural, but carried on rather by
means of a certain acquired skill or art. We may
take our starting-point for its study from the follow-
11 ing consideration: with every article of property
there is a double way of using it; both uses are
related to the article itself, but not related to it in
the same manner—one is peculiar to the thing and
the other is not peculiar to it. Take for example a
shoe—there is its wear as a shoe and there is its use

Trade sprang from barter of household supplies.

10 τε ὑπόδεσις καὶ ἡ μεταβλητική· ἀμφότεραι γὰρ
ὑποδήματος χρήσεις, καὶ γὰρ ὁ ἀλλαττόμενος τῷ
δεομένῳ ὑποδήματος ἀντὶ νομίσματος ἢ τροφῆς
χρῆται τῷ ὑποδήματι ᾗ ὑπόδημα, ἀλλ' οὐ τὴν
οἰκείαν χρῆσιν, οὐ γὰρ ἀλλαγῆς ἕνεκεν γέγονεν.
τὸν αὐτὸν δὲ τρόπον ἔχει καὶ περὶ τῶν ἄλλων
15 κτημάτων· ἔστι γὰρ ἡ μεταβλητικὴ πάντων,
ἀρξαμένη τὸ μὲν πρῶτον ἐκ τοῦ κατὰ φύσιν, τῷ
τὰ μὲν πλείω τὰ δὲ ἐλάττω τῶν ἱκανῶν ἔχειν τοὺς
ἀνθρώπους. ᾗ καὶ δῆλον ὅτι οὐκ ἔστι φύσει τῆς 12
χρηματιστικῆς[1] ἡ καπηλική· ὅσον γὰρ ἱκανὸν αὐτοῖς,
ἀναγκαῖον ἦν ποιεῖσθαι τὴν ἀλλαγήν. ἐν μὲν οὖν
20 τῇ πρώτῃ κοινωνίᾳ (τοῦτο δ' ἐστὶν οἰκία) φανερὸν
ὅτι οὐδέν ἐστιν ἔργον αὐτῆς, ἀλλ' ἤδη πλειόνων[2]
τῆς κοινωνίας οὔσης. οἱ μὲν γὰρ τῶν αὐτῶν[3]
ἐκοινώνουν πάντων, οἱ δὲ κεχωρισμένοι[4] πολλῶν
πάλιν καὶ ἑτέρων, ὧν κατὰ τὰς δεήσεις ἀναγκαῖον[5]
ποιεῖσθαι τὰς μεταδόσεις, καθάπερ ἔτι πολλὰ
25 ποιεῖ καὶ τῶν βαρβαρικῶν ἐθνῶν, κατὰ τὴν ἀλλα-
γήν· αὐτὰ γὰρ τὰ χρήσιμα πρὸς αὐτὰ καταλλάτ-
τονται, ἐπὶ πλέον δ' οὐθέν, οἷον οἶνον πρὸς σῖτον
διδόντες καὶ λαμβάνοντες, καὶ τῶν ἄλλων τῶν
τοιούτων ἕκαστον. ἡ μὲν οὖν τοιαύτη μεταβλη- 13
τικὴ οὔτε παρὰ φύσιν οὔτε χρηματιστικῆς ἐστιν
30 εἶδος οὐδέν, εἰς ἀναπλήρωσιν γὰρ τῆς κατὰ φύσιν
αὐταρκείας ἦν· ἐκ μέντοι ταύτης ἐγένετ' ἐκείνη

---

[1] χρηματιστικῆς] μεταβλητικῆς Bernays.
[2] πλειδνων Richards: πλείονος codd.
[3] αὐτῶν Immisch: αὐτῶν codd.
[4] κεχωρισμένων Immisch.
[5] ἀναγκαῖον ⟨ἦν⟩ Coraes.

as an article of exchange ; for both are ways of using a shoe, inasmuch as even he that barters a shoe for money or food with the customer that wants a shoe uses it as a shoe, though not for the use proper to a shoe, since shoes have not come into existence for the purpose of barter. And the same also holds good about the other articles of property ; for all of them have a use in exchange related to them, which began in the first instance from the natural order of things, because men had more than enough of some things 12 and less than enough of others. This consideration also shows that the art of trade is not by nature a part of the art of wealth-getting *a* ; for the practice of barter was necessary only so far as to satisfy men's own needs. In the primary association therefore (I mean the household) there is no function for trade, but it only arises after the association has become more numerous. For the members of the primitive household used to share commodities that were all their own, whereas on the contrary a group divided into several households participated also in a number of commodities belonging to their neighbours, according to their needs for which they were forced to make their interchanges by way of barter, as also many barbarian tribes do still ; for such tribes do not go beyond exchanging actual commodities for actual commodities, for example giving and taking wine for corn, and so with the various other things 13 of the sort. Exchange on these lines therefore is not contrary to nature, nor is it any branch of the art of wealth-getting, for it existed for the replenishment of natural self-sufficiency ; yet out of it the art of business

a Perhaps Aristotle wrote ' of the art of exchange ': see note 1 on opposite page.

κατὰ λόγον. ξενικωτέρας γὰρ γενομένης[1] τῆς
βοηθείας τῷ εἰσάγεσθαι ὧν ἐνδεεῖς καὶ ἐκπέμπειν
ὧν ἐπλεόναζον, ἐξ ἀνάγκης ἡ τοῦ νομίσματος
ἐπορίσθη χρῆσις. οὐ γὰρ εὐβάστακτον ἕκαστον
35 τῶν κατὰ φύσιν ἀναγκαίων· διὸ πρὸς τὰς ἀλλαγὰς 14
τοιοῦτόν τι συνέθεντο πρὸς σφᾶς αὐτοὺς διδόναι
καὶ λαμβάνειν ὃ τῶν χρησίμων αὐτὸ ὂν εἶχε τὴν
χρείαν εὐμεταχείριστον πρὸς τὸ ζῆν, οἷον σίδηρος
καὶ ἄργυρος κἂν εἴ τι τοιοῦτον ἕτερον, τὸ μὲν πρῶτον ἁπλῶς ὁρισθὲν μεγέθει καὶ σταθμῷ, τὸ δὲ
40 τελευταῖον καὶ χαρακτῆρα ἐπιβαλλόντων ἵνα ἀπο-
λύσῃ τῆς μετρήσεως αὐτούς· ὁ γὰρ χαρακτὴρ
1257 b ἐτέθη τοῦ ποσοῦ σημεῖον. πορισθέντος οὖν ἤδη 15
νομίσματος ἐκ τῆς ἀναγκαίας ἀλλαγῆς θάτερον
εἶδος τῆς χρηματιστικῆς ἐγένετο, τὸ καπηλικόν,
τὸ μὲν πρῶτον ἁπλῶς ἴσως γινόμενον, εἶτα δι᾽
5 ἐμπειρίας ἤδη τεχνικώτερον, πόθεν καὶ πῶς μετα-
βαλλόμενον πλεῖστον ποιήσει κέρδος. διὸ δοκεῖ
ἡ χρηματιστικὴ μάλιστα περὶ τὸ νόμισμα εἶναι,
καὶ ἔργον αὐτῆς τὸ δύνασθαι θεωρῆσαι πόθεν
ἔσται πλῆθος,[2] ποιητικὴ γὰρ[3] εἶναι πλοῦτου[4] καὶ
χρημάτων· καὶ γὰρ τὸν πλοῦτον πολλάκις τιθέασι 16
νομίσματος πλῆθος, διὰ τὸ περὶ τοῦτ᾽ εἶναι τὴν
10 χρηματιστικὴν καὶ τὴν καπηλικήν. ὁτὲ δὲ πάλιν
λῆρος εἶναι δοκεῖ τὸ νόμισμα, καὶ νόμος παντάπασι
φύσει δ᾽ οὐθέν, ὅτι μεταθεμένων τε τῶν χρωμένων
οὐθενὸς ἄξιον, οὔτε χρήσιμον πρὸς οὐδὲν τῶν

---

[1] γενομένης Coraes : γινομένης codd.
[2] πλῆθος χρημάτων codd. : gloss. excisit Gifanius : πλῆθος
αὐτοῦ ? Richards.
[3] γὰρ : δ᾽ Bernays.   [4] πλοῦτου M, τοῦ πλοῦτου cet.

in due course arose. For when they had come to supply themselves more from abroad by importing things in which they were deficient and exporting those of which they had a surplus, the employment of money necessarily came to be devised. For the natural necessaries are not in every case readily portable ;

14 hence for the purpose of barter men made a mutual compact to give and accept some substance of such a sort as being itself a useful commodity was easy to handle in use for general life, iron for instance, silver and other metals, at the first stage defined merely by size and weight, but finally also by impressing on it a stamp in order that this might relieve them of having to measure it ; for the stamp was put on as a token of the amount. So

15 when currency had been now invented as an outcome of the necessary interchange of goods, there came into existence the other form of wealth-getting, trade, which at first no doubt went on in a simple form, but later became more highly organized as experience discovered the sources and methods of exchange that would cause most profit. Hence arises the idea that the art of wealth-getting deals specially with money, and that its function is to be able to discern from what source a large supply can be procured, as this art is supposed to be creative of

16 wealth and riches ; indeed wealth is often assumed to consist of a quantity of money, because money is the thing with which business and trade are employed. But at other times, on the contrary, it is thought that money is nonsense, and entirely a convention but by nature nothing, because when those who use it have changed the currency it is worth nothing, and because it is of no use for any of the necessary needs of life

Money, invented to facilitate exchange, originated Commerce.

Natural wealth limited to needs of the good life (not bodily enjoyment).

1257 b

ἀναγκαίων ἐστὶ καὶ νομίσματος πλουτῶν πολλάκις ἀπορήσει τῆς ἀναγκαίας τροφῆς, καίτοι
15 ἄτοπον τοιοῦτον εἶναι πλοῦτον οὗ εὐπορῶν λιμῷ
ἀπολεῖται, καθάπερ καὶ τὸν Μίδαν ἐκεῖνον μυθολογοῦσι διὰ τὴν ἀπληστίαν τῆς εὐχῆς πάντων αὐτῷ
γιγνομένων τῶν παρατιθεμένων χρυσῶν. διὸ ζη- 1
τοῦσιν ἕτερόν τι τὸν πλοῦτον καὶ τὴν χρηματιστικήν,
ὀρθῶς ζητοῦντες· ἔστι γὰρ ἑτέρα ἡ χρηματιστικὴ
20 καὶ ὁ πλοῦτος ὁ κατὰ φύσιν, καὶ αὕτη μὲν
οἰκονομική, ἡ δὲ καπηλική, ποιητικὴ πλούτου[1]
οὐ πάντως ἀλλ[2] διὰ χρημάτων μεταβολῆς· καὶ
δοκεῖ περὶ τὸ νόμισμα αὕτη εἶναι, τὸ γὰρ νόμισμα
στοιχεῖον καὶ πέρας τῆς ἀλλαγῆς ἐστίν. καὶ
ἄπειρος δὴ οὗτος ὁ πλοῦτος ὁ ἀπὸ ταύτης τῆς
25 χρηματιστικῆς· ὥσπερ γὰρ ἡ ἰατρικὴ τοῦ ὑγιαίνειν
εἰς ἄπειρόν ἐστι καὶ ἑκάστη τῶν τεχνῶν τοῦ τέλους
εἰς ἄπειρον (ὅτι μάλιστα γὰρ ἐκεῖνο βούλονται
ποιεῖν), τῶν δὲ πρὸς τὸ τέλος οὐκ εἰς ἄπειρον
(πέρας γὰρ τὸ τέλος πάσαις), οὕτω καὶ ταύτης
τῆς χρηματιστικῆς οὐκ ἔστι τοῦ τέλους πέρας,
30 τέλος δὲ ὁ τοιοῦτος πλοῦτος καὶ χρημάτων κτῆσις.
τῆς δ' οἰκονομικῆς χρηματιστικῆς[3] ἔστι πέρας· οὐ 18
γὰρ τοῦτο τῆς οἰκονομικῆς ἔργον. διὸ τῇ μὲν
φαίνεται ἀναγκαῖον εἶναι παντὸς πλούτου πέρας,
ἐπὶ δὲ τῶν γινομένων ὁρῶμεν[4] συμβαῖνον τοὺ-

---

[1] Richards : χρημάτων codd.   [2] Richards : ἀλλ' ἢ codd.
[3] χρηματιστικῆς Bojesen : οὐ χρ. codd., αὖ χρ. Bernays.
[4] ὁρῶμεν Sylburg : ὁρῶ codd.

---

[a] *e.g.* on a desert island.
[b] *i.e.* a trader cannot get too much of his goods, any more
than a doctor can make his patient too healthy.

and a man well supplied with money may often ^{a} be destitute of the bare necessities of subsistence, yet it is absurd that wealth should be of such a kind that a man may be well supplied with it and yet die of hunger, like the famous Midas in the story, when owing to the insatiable covetousness of his prayer all the viands served up to him turned into 17 gold. Hence people seek for a different definition of riches and the art of getting wealth, and rightly ; for natural wealth-getting and natural riches are different : natural wealth-getting belongs to household management, whereas the other kind belongs to trade, producing wealth not indiscriminately but by the method of exchanging goods. It is this art of wealth-getting that is thought to be concerned with money, for money is the first element and limit of commerce. And these riches, that are derived from this art of wealth-getting, are truly unlimited ^{b} ; for just as the art of medicine is without limit in respect of health, and each of the arts is without limit in respect of its end (for they desire to produce that in the highest degree possible), whereas they are not without limit as regards the means to their end (for with all of them the end is a limit to the means), so also this wealth-getting has no limit in respect of its end, and its end is riches and the 18 acquisition of goods in the commercial sense. But the household branch of wealth-getting has a limit, inasmuch as the acquisition of money is not the function of household management. Hence from this point of view it appears necessary that there should be a limit to all riches, yet in actual fact we observe that the opposite takes place ; for all

1257 b

ναντίον· πάντες γὰρ εἰς ἄπειρον αὔξουσιν οἱ
35 χρηματιζόμενοι τὸ νόμισμα. αἴτιον δὲ τὸ σύνεγγυς
αὐτῶν. ἐπαλλάττει γὰρ ἡ χρῆσις τοῦ αὐτοῦ οὖσα
ἑκατέρας[1] τῆς χρηματιστικῆς· τῆς γὰρ αὐτῆς ἐστι
κτήσεως χρῆσις,[2] ἀλλ' οὐ κατὰ ταὐτόν, ἀλλὰ τῆς
μὲν ἕτερον τέλος, τῆς δ' ἡ αὔξησις. ὥστε δοκεῖ
τισὶ τοῦτ' εἶναι τῆς οἰκονομικῆς ἔργον, καὶ δια-
40 τελοῦσιν ἢ σῴζειν οἰόμενοι δεῖν ἢ αὔξειν τὴν τοῦ
νομίσματος οὐσίαν εἰς ἄπειρον. αἴτιον δὲ ταύτης 19
τῆς διαθέσεως τὸ σπουδάζειν περὶ τὸ ζῆν ἀλλὰ
1258 a μὴ τὸ εὖ ζῆν· εἰς ἄπειρον οὖν ἐκείνης τῆς ἐπιθυμίας
οὔσης, καὶ τῶν ποιητικῶν ἀπείρων ἐπιθυμοῦσιν.
ὅσοι δὲ καὶ τοῦ εὖ ζῆν ἐπιβάλλονται, τὸ πρὸς τὰς
ἀπολαύσεις τὰς σωματικὰς ζητοῦσιν, ὥστ' ἐπεὶ
5 καὶ τοῦτ' ἐν τῇ κτήσει φαίνεται ὑπάρχειν,[3] πᾶσα
ἡ διατριβὴ περὶ τὸν χρηματισμόν ἐστι, καὶ τὸ
ἕτερον εἶδος τῆς χρηματιστικῆς διὰ τοῦτ' ἐλήλυθεν.
ἐν ὑπερβολῇ γὰρ οὔσης τῆς ἀπολαύσεως, τὴν τῆς
ἀπολαυστικῆς ὑπερβολῆς ποιητικὴν ζητοῦσιν· κἂν
μὴ διὰ τῆς χρηματιστικῆς δύνωνται πορίζειν, δι'
10 ἄλλης αἰτίας τοῦτο πειρῶνται, ἑκάστῃ χρώμενοι
τῶν δυνάμεων οὐ κατὰ φύσιν. ἀνδρείας γὰρ οὐ 20
χρήματα ποιεῖν ἐστιν ἀλλὰ θάρσος, οὐδὲ στρα-
τηγικῆς καὶ ἰατρικῆς, ἀλλὰ τῆς μὲν νίκην τῆς δ'
ὑγίειαν. οἱ δὲ πάσας ποιοῦσι χρηματιστικάς, ὡς

---

[1] ἑκατέρας Ar.: -τέρα cett.
[2] κτήσεως χρῆσις Goettling: χρήσεως κτῆσις codd.
[3] ὑπάρχον Coraes.

46

men engaged in wealth-getting try to increase their money to an unlimited amount. The reason of this is the close affinity of the two branches of the art of business. Their common ground is that the thing that each makes use of is the same; they use the same property, although not in the same way—the one has another end in view, the aim of the other is the increase of the property. Consequently some people suppose that it is the function of household management to increase property, and they are continually under the idea that it is their duty to be either safeguarding their substance in money or

19 increasing it to an unlimited amount. The cause of this state of mind is that their interests are set upon life but not upon the good life; as therefore the desire for life is unlimited, they also desire without limit the means productive of life. And even those who fix their aim on the good life seek the good life as measured by bodily enjoyments, so that inasmuch as this also seems to be found in the possession of property, all their energies are occupied in the business of getting wealth; and owing to this the second kind of the art of wealth-getting has arisen. For as their enjoyment is in excess, they try to discover the art that is productive of enjoyable excess; and if they cannot procure it by the art of wealth-getting, they try to do so by some other means, employing each of the faculties in an unnatural way.

20 For it is not the function of courage to produce wealth, but to inspire daring; nor is it the function of the military art nor of the medical art, but it belongs to the former to bring victory and to the latter to cause health. Yet these people make all these faculties means for the business of providing wealth, in the

47

1258 a

τοῦτο τέλος ὄν, πρὸς δὲ τὸ τέλος ἅπαντα δέον
ἀπαντᾶν.

15 Περὶ μὲν οὖν τῆς τε μὴ ἀναγκαίας χρηματιστικῆς,
καὶ τίς καὶ δι' αἰτίαν τίνα ἐν χρείᾳ ἐσμὲν αὐτῆς,
εἴρηται, καὶ περὶ τῆς ἀναγκαίας, ὅτι ἑτέρα μὲν
αὐτῆς οἰκονομικὴ δὲ κατὰ φύσιν ἡ περὶ τὴν
τροφήν, οὐχ ὥσπερ αὕτη[1] ἄπειρος ἀλλ' ἔχουσα
ὅρον.

Δῆλον δὲ καὶ τὸ ἀπορούμενον ἐξ ἀρχῆς, πότερον 21
20 τοῦ οἰκονομικοῦ καὶ πολιτικοῦ ἐστιν ἡ χρηματιστικὴ ἢ οὔ, ἀλλὰ δεῖ τοῦτο μὲν ὑπάρχειν (ὥσπερ
γὰρ καὶ ἀνθρώπους οὐ ποιεῖ ἡ πολιτικὴ ἀλλὰ
λαβοῦσα παρὰ τῆς φύσεως χρῆται αὐτοῖς, οὕτω καὶ
τροφὴν[2] τὴν φύσιν δεῖ παραδοῦναι γῆν ἢ θάλατ-
25 ταν ἢ ἄλλο τι), ἐκ δὲ τούτων ὡς δεῖ ταῦτα διαθεῖναι
προσήκει τὸν οἰκονόμον. οὐ γὰρ τῆς ὑφαντικῆς
ἔρια ποιῆσαι ἀλλὰ χρήσασθαι αὐτοῖς, καὶ γνῶναι
δὲ τὸ ποῖον χρηστὸν καὶ ἐπιτήδειον ἢ φαῦλον καὶ
ἀνεπιτήδειον. καὶ γὰρ ἀπορήσειεν ἄν τις διὰ τί 22
ἡ μὲν χρηματιστικὴ μόριον τῆς οἰκονομίας ἡ δ'
30 ἰατρικὴ οὐ μόριον, καίτοι δεῖ ὑγιαίνειν τοὺς κατὰ
τὴν οἰκίαν, ὥσπερ ζῆν ἢ ἄλλο τι τῶν ἀναγκαίων.
ἐπεὶ δ' ἔστι μὲν ὡς τοῦ οἰκονόμου καὶ τοῦ ἄρχοντος
καὶ περὶ ὑγιείας ἰδεῖν, ἔστι[3] δ' ὡς οὔ, ἀλλὰ τοῦ
ἰατροῦ, οὕτω καὶ περὶ τῶν χρημάτων ἔστι μὲν ὡς

---

[1] αὕτη Welldon : αὐτὴ codd.
[2] ⟨πρὸς⟩ τροφὴν ? Richards.   [3] ⟨ἐστίν,⟩ ἔστι Welldon.

---

[a] See c. iii. § 1.

belief that wealth is the end and that everything must conspire to the end.

We have therefore discussed both the unnecessary branch of wealth-getting, defining it and also explaining the cause why we require it, and the necessary branch, showing that this branch which has to do with food is different from the unnecessary branch and is by nature a part of household management, not being like that branch unlimited but having a limit.

21 And we can also see the answer to the question raised at the beginning,[a] whether the art of wealth-getting belongs to the householder and the statesman, or whether on the contrary supplies ought to be provided already, since just as statesmanship does not create human beings but having received them from nature makes use of them, so also it is the business of nature to bestow food by bestowing land or sea or something else, while the task of the householder is, starting with these supplies given, to dispose of them in the proper way. For it does not belong to the art of weaving to make fleeces, but to use them, and also to know what sort of fleece is good 22 and suitable or bad and unsuitable. Otherwise the question might be raised, why the getting of wealth is a part of the household art whereas the art of medicine is not a part of it, although the members of the household ought to be healthy, just as they must be alive or fulfil any of the other essential conditions. But inasmuch as although in a way it does belong to the householder and the ruler to see even to health, yet in a way it does not belong to them but to the physician, so also with regard to wealth, although in a way it is the affair of the house-

Natural Business a necessary, subsidiary of Household Management.

49

1258 a

τοῦ οἰκονόμου, ἔστι¹ δ' ὡς οὔ, ἀλλὰ τῆς ὑπηρετικῆς.
35 μάλιστα δέ, καθάπερ εἴρηται πρότερον, δεῖ φύσει
τοῦτο ὑπάρχειν. φύσεως γάρ ἐστιν ἔργον τροφὴν
τῷ γεννηθέντι παρέχειν· παντὶ γάρ, ἐξ οὗ γίνεται,
τροφὴ τὸ λειπόμενόν ἐστιν. διὸ κατὰ φύσιν ἐστὶν
ἡ χρηματιστικὴ πᾶσιν ἀπὸ τῶν καρπῶν καὶ τῶν
ζῴων.

Διπλῆς δ' οὔσης αὐτῆς, ὥσπερ εἴπομεν, καὶ τῆς 23
40 μὲν καπηλικῆς τῆς δ' οἰκονομικῆς, καὶ ταύτης μὲν
1258 b ἀναγκαίας καὶ ἐπαινουμένης, τῆς δὲ μεταβλητικῆς
ψεγομένης δικαίως (οὐ γὰρ κατὰ φύσιν ἀλλ' ἀπ'
ἀλλήλων ἐστίν), εὐλογώτατα μισεῖται ἡ ὀβολο-
στατικὴ διὰ τὸ ἀπ'² αὐτοῦ τοῦ νομίσματος εἶναι
τὴν κτῆσιν καὶ οὐκ ἐφ' ὅπερ ἐπορίσθη· μεταβολῆς
5 γὰρ ἐγένετο χάριν, ὁ δὲ τόκος αὐτὸ ποιεῖ πλέον
(ὅθεν καὶ τοὔνομα τοῦτ' εἴληφεν· ὅμοια γὰρ τὰ
τικτόμενα τοῖς γεννῶσιν αὐτά ἐστιν, ὁ δὲ τόκος
γίνεται νόμισμα ἐκ νομίσματος)· ὥστε καὶ μάλιστα παρὰ φύσιν οὗτος τῶν χρηματισμῶν ἐστίν.

IV. Ἐπεὶ δὲ τὰ πρὸς τὴν γνῶσιν διωρίκαμεν 1
10 ἱκανῶς, τὰ πρὸς τὴν χρῆσιν δεῖ διελθεῖν· πάντα δὲ
τὰ τοιαῦτα τὴν μὲν θεωρίαν ἐλεύθερον ἔχει, τὴν δ'
ἐμπειρίαν ἀναγκαίαν. ἔστι δὲ τῆς χρηματιστικῆς
μέρη χρήσιμα τὸ περὶ τὰ κτήματα³ ἔμπειρον εἶναι,
ποῖα λυσιτελέστατα καὶ ποῦ καὶ πῶς, οἷον ἵππων
κτῆσις ποία τις ἢ βοῶν ἢ προβάτων, ὁμοίως δὲ

---

¹ ⟨ἐστίν,⟩ ἔστι Welldon.
² ὑπ' Bekker : ἐπ' Jackson.
³ κτήνη Bernays.

ᵃ i.e. animals are made of earth and water and live on the products of earth and water.

holder, in a way it is not, but is a matter for the subsidiary art. But best of all, as has been said before, this provision ought to be made in advance by nature. For it is the work of nature to supply nourishment for her offspring, since every creature has for nourishment the residue of the substance from which it springs.ᵃ Hence the business of drawing provision from the fruits of the soil and from animals is natural to all.

23 But, as we said, this art is twofold, one branch *Trade* being of the nature of trade while the other belongs *justly* to the household art; and the latter branch is *disliked;* necessary and in good esteem, but the branch con- *Usury* nected with exchange is justly discredited (for it is *unnatural.* not in accordance with nature, but involves men's taking things from one another). As this is so, usury is most reasonably hated, because its gain comes from money itself and not from that for the sake of which money was invented. For money was brought into existence for the purpose of exchange, but interest increases the amount of the money itself (and this is the actual origin of the Greek word : offspring resembles parent, and interest is money born of money); consequently this form of the business of getting wealth is of all forms the most contrary to nature.

1 IV. And since we have adequately defined the *Outline of* scientific side of the subject, we ought to discuss it *practical* from the point of view of practice ; although, whereas *treatise on* the theory of such matters is a liberal study, the *Trade :* practical pursuit of them is narrowing. The practi- cally useful branches of the art of wealth-getting are first, an expert knowledge of stock, what breeds are most profitable and in what localities and under what conditions, for instance what particular stock in

15 καὶ τῶν λοιπῶν ζώων (δεῖ γὰρ ἔμπειρον εἶναι πρὸς ἄλληλά τε τούτων τίνα λυσιτελέστατα, καὶ ποῖα ἐν ποίοις τόποις, ἄλλα γὰρ ἐν ἄλλαις εὐθηνεῖ χώραις)· εἶτα περὶ γεωργίας, καὶ ταύτης ἤδη ψιλῆς τε καὶ πεφυτευμένης, καὶ μελιττουργίας, καὶ τῶν ἄλλων 20 ζώων τῶν πλωτῶν ἢ πτηνῶν ἀφ' ὅσων ἔστι τυγχάνειν βοηθείας. τῆς μὲν οὖν οἰκειοτάτης χρη-2 ματιστικῆς ταῦτα μόρια καὶ πρῶτα[1]· τῆς δὲ μεταβλητικῆς μέγιστον μὲν ἐμπορία (καὶ ταύτης μέρη τρία, ναυκληρία φορτηγία παράστασις· διαφέρει δὲ τούτων ἕτερα ἑτέρων τῷ τὰ μὲν ἀσφαλέστερα εἶναι 25 τὰ δὲ πλείω πορίζειν τὴν ἐπικαρπίαν), δεύτερον δὲ τοκισμός, τρίτον δὲ μισθαρνία (ταύτης δ' ἡ μὲν τῶν βαναύσων τεχνῶν,[2] ἡ δὲ τῶν ἀτέχνων καὶ τῷ σώματι μόνῳ χρησίμων)· τρίτον δὲ εἶδος χρηματιστικῆς μεταξὺ ταύτης καὶ τῆς πρώτης (ἔχει γὰρ καὶ τῆς κατὰ φύσιν τι μέρος καὶ τῆς μεταβλητικῆς), 30 ὅσα[3] ἀπὸ γῆς καὶ τῶν ἀπὸ γῆς γινομένων ἀκάρπων μὲν χρησίμων δέ, οἷον ὑλοτομία[4] τε καὶ πᾶσα μεταλλευτική· αὕτη δὲ πολλὰ ἤδη περιείληφε γένη, πολλὰ γὰρ εἴδη τῶν ἐκ γῆς μεταλλευομένων ἐστίν. εἰσὶ δὲ[5] τεχνικώταται μὲν τῶν ἐργασιῶν ὅπου 3 ἐλάχιστον τῆς τύχης, βαναυσόταται δ' ἐν αἷς τὰ

---

[1] πρώτης (cf. 25) ? Richards.   [2] τεχνιτῶν Vermehren.
[3] οὖσα Bernays.   [4] ἡ λατομία Thomas Aquinas.
[5] εἰσὶ δὲ—ἀρετῆς post 39 ἐνδιατρίβειν codd. : tr. (et 33 δὴ pro δὲ) Montecatino auctore Susemihl.

---

[a] βάναυσος (said to be from βαῦνος 'furnace,' αὔω 'to dry'), 'artisan' (ranged with farmers, traders, and labourers, as forming the common people 1321 a 6); it acquires the senses of 'cramped in body' (1341 a 7) and 'vulgar in taste' (1337 b 8).

[b] A very probable variant gives 'the quarrying of stone.'

horses or cattle or sheep, and similarly of the other animals also (for the farmer must be an expert as to which of these animals are most profitable compared with one another, and also as to what breeds are most profitable on what sorts of land, since different breeds thrive in different places); secondly, the subject of agriculture, and this again is divided into corn-growing and fruit-farming; also bee-keeping, and the breeding of the other creatures finned and feathered which can be used to furnish supplies.

2 These then are the branches and primary parts of wealth-getting in the most proper sense. Of the kind that deals with exchange, the largest branch is commerce (which has three departments, ship-owning, transport and marketing: these departments differ from each other in the fact that some are safer and others carry larger profits); the second branch is money-lending, and the third labour for hire, one department of which is that of the mechanic[a] arts and the other that of unskilled labourers who are useful only for bodily service. And there is a third form of wealth-getting that lies between the latter and the one placed first, since it possesses an element both of natural wealth-getting and of the sort that employs exchange; it deals with all the commodities that are obtained from the earth and from those fruitless but useful things that come from the earth—examples are the felling of timber[b] and all sorts of mining; and of mining itself there are many classes, since there are many sorts of metals

3 obtained out of the earth. The[c] most scientific of these industries are those which involve the smallest element of chance, the most mechanic those in which

its three branches.

Quarries and mines an inter-mediate class.

[c] In the MSS. this sentence follows the next one.

1258 b

35 σώματα λωβῶνται μάλιστα, δουλικώταται δὲ ὅπου
τοῦ σώματος πλεῖσται χρήσεις, ἀγεννέσταται δὲ
ὅπου ἐλάχιστον προσδεῖ ἀρετῆς. περὶ ἑκάστου δὲ
τούτων καθόλου μὲν εἴρηται καὶ νῦν, τὸ δὲ κατὰ
μέρος ἀκριβολογεῖσθαι χρήσιμον μὲν πρὸς τὰς ἐργασίας, φορτικὸν δὲ τὸ ἐνδιατρίβειν. ἐπεὶ δ᾽ ἐστὶν 4
40 ἐνίοις γεγραμμένα περὶ τούτων, οἷον Χαρητίδῃ τῷ
1259 a Παρίῳ καὶ Ἀπολλοδώρῳ τῷ Λημνίῳ περὶ γεωργίας καὶ ψιλῆς καὶ πεφυτευμένης, ὁμοίως δὲ καὶ
ἄλλοις περὶ ἄλλων, ταῦτα μὲν ἐκ τούτων θεωρείτω
ὅτῳ ἐπιμελές· ἔτι δὲ καὶ τὰ λεγόμενα σποράδην
5 δι᾽ ὧν ἐπιτετυχήκασιν ἔνιοι χρηματιζόμενοι δεῖ
συλλέγειν· πάντα γὰρ ὠφέλιμα ταῦτ᾽ ἐστὶ τοῖς
τιμῶσι τὴν χρηματιστικήν, οἷον καὶ τὸ Θάλεω τοῦ 5
Μιλησίου· τοῦτο γάρ ἐστι κατανόημά τι χρηματιστικόν, ἀλλ᾽ ἐκείνῳ μὲν διὰ τὴν σοφίαν προσ-
άπτουσι, τυγχάνει δὲ καθόλου τι ὄν. ὀνειδιζόντων
10 γὰρ αὐτῷ διὰ τὴν πενίαν ὡς ἀνωφελοῦς τῆς
φιλοσοφίας οὔσης, κατανοήσαντά φασιν αὐτὸν
ἐλαιῶν φορὰν ἐσομένην ἐκ τῆς ἀστρολογίας ἔτι
χειμῶνος ὄντος, εὐπορήσαντα χρημάτων ὀλίγων
ἀρραβῶνας διαδοῦναι τῶν ἐλαιουργίων τῶν τ᾽ ἐν
Μιλήτῳ καὶ Χίῳ πάντων, ὀλίγου μισθωσάμενον ἅτ᾽
15 οὐθενὸς ἐπιβάλλοντος· ἐπειδὴ δ᾽ ὁ καιρὸς ἦκε,
πολλῶν ζητουμένων ἅμα καὶ ἐξαίφνης, ἐκμισθοῦντα
ὃν τρόπον ἠβούλετο πολλὰ χρήματα συλλέξαντα,

---

a Otherwise unknown.
b Also mentioned by Varro and Pliny.
c The author of the Second Book of the pseudo-Aristotelian
Oeconomica seems to have taken this hint.
d The founder of Greek philosophy and mathematics,
and one of the Seven Sages, 6th-5th cent. B.C.

the operatives undergo the greatest amount of bodily degradation, the most servile those in which the most uses are made of the body, and the most ignoble those in which there is the least requirement of virtue as an accessory. But while we have even now given a general description of these various branches, yet a detailed and particular account of them, though useful for the practice of the industries, would be

4 illiberal as a subject of prolonged study. There are books on these subjects by certain authors, for example Charetides [a] of Paros and Apollodorus [b] of Lemnos have written about both agriculture and fruit-farming, and similarly others also on other topics, so these subjects may be studied from these authors by anybody concerned to do so ; but in addition a collection ought also to be made [c] of the scattered accounts of methods that have brought success in business to certain individuals. All these methods are serviceable for those who value wealth-getting,

5 for example the plan of Thales [d] of Miletus, which is a device for the business of getting wealth, but which, though it is attributed to him because of his wisdom, is really of universal application. Thales, so the story goes, because of his poverty was taunted with the uselessness of philosophy ; but from his knowledge of astronomy he had observed while it was still winter that there was going to be a large crop of olives, so he raised a small sum of money and paid round deposits for the whole of the olive-presses in Miletus and Chios, which he hired at a low rent as nobody was running him up ; and when the season arrived, there was a sudden demand for a number of presses at the same time, and by letting them out on what terms he liked he realized a large sum of

Other writers on industries.

Thales and Monopoly.

55

ἐπιδεῖξαι ὅτι ῥᾴδιόν ἐστι πλουτεῖν τοῖς φιλοσόφοις
ἂν βούλωνται, ἀλλ' οὐ τοῦτ' ἐστὶ περὶ ὃ σπουδά-
ζουσιν. Θαλῆς μὲν οὖν λέγεται τοῦτον τὸν τρόπον 6
ἐπίδειξιν ποιήσασθαι τῆς σοφίας· ἔστι δ' ὥσπερ
20 εἴπομεν, καθόλου τὸ τοιοῦτον χρηματιστικόν, ἐάν
τις δύνηται μονοπωλίαν αὑτῷ κατασκευάζειν· διὸ
καὶ τῶν πόλεων ἔνιαι τοῦτον ποιοῦνται τὸν πόρον
ὅταν ἀπορῶσι χρημάτων, μονοπωλίαν γὰρ τῶν
ὠνίων ποιοῦσιν. ἐν Σικελίᾳ δέ τις τεθέντος παρ'
25 αὑτῷ νομίσματος συνεπρίατο πάντα τὸν σίδηρον ἐκ
τῶν σιδηρείων, μετὰ δὲ ταῦτα ὡς ἀφίκοντο ἐκ τῶν
ἐμπορίων οἱ ἔμποροι, ἐπώλει μόνος, οὐ πολλὴν
ποιήσας ὑπερβολὴν τῆς τιμῆς, ἀλλ' ὅμως ἐπὶ τοῖς
30 πεντήκοντα ταλάντοις ἐπέλαβεν ἑκατόν. τοῦτο μὲν 8
οὖν ὁ Διονύσιος αἰσθόμενος τὰ μὲν χρήματα ἐκέλευσεν ἐκκομίσασθαι, μὴ μέντοι γ' ἔτι μένειν ἐν
Συρακούσαις, ὡς πόρους εὑρίσκοντα τοῖς αὑτοῦ[1]
πράγμασιν ἀσυμφόρους. τὸ μέντοι ὅραμα[2] Θάλεω
καὶ τοῦτο[3] ταὐτόν ἐστιν· ἀμφότεροι γὰρ ἑαυτοῖς
35 ἐτέχνασαν γενέσθαι μονοπωλίαν. χρήσιμον δὲ γνωρίζειν ταῦτα καὶ τοῖς πολιτικοῖς· πολλαῖς γὰρ
πόλεσι δεῖ χρηματισμοῦ καὶ τοιούτων πόρων, ὥσπερ
οἰκίᾳ, μᾶλλον δέ· διόπερ τινὲς καὶ πολιτεύονται
τῶν πολιτευομένων ταῦτα μόνον.

V. Ἐπεὶ δὲ τρία μέρη τῆς οἰκονομικῆς ἦν, ἓν 1
μὲν δεσποτική, περὶ ἧς εἴρηται πρότερον, ἓν δὲ
πατρική, τρίτον δὲ γαμική[4]—καὶ γὰρ γυναικὸς

---

[1] αὑτοῦ Susemihl : αὐτοῦ codd.
[2] εὕρημα, θεώρημα, δρᾶμα edd.
[3] Θάλῃ καὶ τούτῳ Γ.   [4] lacunam Conring.

[a] The talent was about £240.
[b] Dionysius the elder, tyrant of Syracuse 405–367 B.C.
[c] Cf. Thucydides οἱ δ' οὐκέτι ἔμειναν ἀλλά . . .

money, so proving that it is easy for philosophers
to be rich if they choose, but this is not what they
6 care about. Thales then is reported to have thus
displayed his wisdom, but as a matter of fact this Government
device of taking an opportunity to secure a monopoly monopolies.
is a universal principle of business; hence even
some states have recourse to this plan as a method
of raising revenue when short of funds : they intro-
7 duce a monopoly of marketable goods. There was a
man in Sicily who used a sum of money deposited with
him to buy up all the iron from the iron foundries,
and afterwards when the dealers came from the
trading-centres he was the only seller, though he
did not greatly raise the price, but all the same he
made a profit of a hundred talents[a] on his capital
8 of fifty. When Dionysius[b] came to know of it he
ordered the man to take his money with him but clear
out of Syracuse on the spot,[c] since he was inventing
means of profit detrimental to the tyrant's own
affairs. Yet really this device is the same as the
discovery of Thales, for both men alike contrived
to secure themselves a monopoly. An acquaintance
with these devices is also serviceable for statesmen, for
many states need financial aid and modes of revenue
like those described, just as a household may, but
in greater degree ; hence some statesmen even
devote their political activity exclusively to finance.
1 V. And since, as we saw,[d] the science of household The
management has three divisions, one the relation of husband's
office
master to slave, of which we have spoken before,[e] one political,
the paternal relation, and the third the conjugal[f]— the father's
royal;

[a] C. ii. init.   [e] C. iii. fin., iv.
[f] The construction of the sentence is interrupted, and never
completed.

1259 a
40 ἄρχειν καὶ τέκνων (ὡς ἐλευθέρων μὲν ἀμφοῖν, οὐ 2
1259 b τὸν αὐτὸν δὲ τρόπον τῆς ἀρχῆς, ἀλλὰ γυναικὸς μὲν
πολιτικῶς, τέκνων δὲ βασιλικῶς)· τό τε γὰρ ἄρρεν
φύσει τοῦ θήλεος ἡγεμονικώτερον (εἰ μή που συνέστηκε παρὰ φύσιν) καὶ τὸ πρεσβύτερον καὶ τέλειον
τοῦ νεωτέρου καὶ ἀτελοῦς. ἐν μὲν οὖν ταῖς πολι-
5 τικαῖς ἀρχαῖς ταῖς πλείσταις μεταβάλλει τὸ ἄρχον
καὶ τὸ ἀρχόμενον (ἐξ ἴσου γὰρ εἶναι βούλεται τὴν
φύσιν καὶ διαφέρειν μηθέν), ὅμως δὲ ὅταν τὸ μὲν
ἄρχῃ τὸ δ᾽ ἄρχηται ζητεῖ διαφορὰν εἶναι καὶ
σχήμασι καὶ λόγοις καὶ τιμαῖς, ὥσπερ καὶ Ἄμασις
εἶπε τὸν περὶ τοῦ ποδανιπτῆρος λόγον· τὸ δ᾽ ἄρρεν
10 ἀεὶ πρὸς τὸ θῆλυ τοῦτον ἔχει τὸν τρόπον. ἡ δὲ
τῶν τέκνων ἀρχὴ βασιλική· τὸ γὰρ γεννῆσαν καὶ
κατὰ φιλίαν ἄρχον καὶ κατὰ πρεσβείαν ἐστίν, ὅπερ
ἐστὶ βασιλικῆς εἶδος ἀρχῆς (διὸ καλῶς Ὅμηρος
τὸν Δία προσηγόρευσεν εἰπὼν

πατὴρ ἀνδρῶν τε θεῶν τε

15 τὸν βασιλέα τούτων ἁπάντων). φύσει γὰρ τὸν
βασιλέα διαφέρειν μὲν δεῖ, τῷ γένει δ᾽ εἶναι τὸν
αὐτόν· ὅπερ πέπονθε τὸ πρεσβύτερον πρὸς τὸ
νεώτερον καὶ ὁ γεννήσας πρὸς τὸ τέκνον.

Φανερὸν τοίνυν ὅτι πλείων ἡ σπουδὴ τῆς οἰκο- 3
νομίας περὶ τοὺς ἀνθρώπους ἢ περὶ τὴν τῶν ἀψύχων
20 κτῆσιν καὶ περὶ τὴν ἀρετὴν τούτων ἢ περὶ τὴν
τῆς κτήσεως, ὃν καλοῦμεν πλοῦτον, καὶ τῶν
ἐλευθέρων μᾶλλον ἢ δούλων.

---

[a] i.e. of the free and equal, 1255 b 20.

[b] Herodotus ii. 172. Amasis king of Egypt was despised by his subjects for his low birth, so he had a statue made out of a gold foot-bath and set it up for them to worship, afterwards explaining to them its lowly origin.　　[c] Il. i. 544.

for it is a part of the household science to rule over
2 wife and children (over both as over freemen, yet not
with the same mode of government,[a] but over the
wife to exercise republican government and over the
children monarchical); for the male is by nature better
fitted to command than the female (except in some
cases where their union has been formed contrary to
nature) and the older and fully developed person than
the younger and immature. It is true that in most
cases of republican government the ruler and the
ruled interchange in turn (for they tend to be on
an equal level in their nature and to have no difference
at all), although nevertheless during the period when
one is ruler and the other ruled they seek to have
a distinction by means of insignia and titles and
honours, just as Amasis made his speech about the
foot-bath[b]; but the male stands in this relationship
to the female continuously. The rule of the father
over the children on the other hand is that of a king;
for the male parent is the ruler in virtue both of
affection and of seniority, which is characteristic
of royal government (and therefore Homer[c] finely
designated Zeus by the words 'father of men and
gods,' as the king of them all). For though in nature
the king must be superior, in race he should be the
same as his subjects, and this is the position of the
elder in relation to the younger and of the father in
relation to the child.
3   It is clear then that household management takes and more
more interest in the human members of the household important
than in its inanimate property, and in the excellence ownership
of these than in that of its property, which we style of goods.
riches, and more in that of its free members than in
that of slaves.

59

Πρῶτον μὲν οὖν περὶ δούλων ἀπορήσειεν ἄν τις,
πότερόν ἐστιν ἀρετή τις δούλου παρὰ τὰς ὀργανικὰς
καὶ διακονικὰς ἄλλη τιμιωτέρα τούτων, οἷον
σωφροσύνη καὶ ἀνδρεία καὶ δικαιοσύνη καὶ[1] τῶν
25 ἄλλων τῶν τοιούτων ἕξεων, ἢ οὐκ ἔστιν οὐδεμία
παρὰ τὰς σωματικὰς ὑπηρεσίας. ἔχει γὰρ ἀπορίαν
ἀμφοτέρως. εἴτε γὰρ ἔστι, τί διοίσουσι τῶν ἐλευθέρων; εἴτε μή ἐστιν, ὄντων ἀνθρώπων καὶ λόγου
κοινωνούντων ἄτοπον. σχεδὸν δὲ ταὐτόν ἐστι τὸ 4
30 ζητούμενον καὶ περὶ γυναικὸς καὶ παιδός, πότερα
καὶ τούτων εἰσὶν ἀρεταί, καὶ δεῖ τὴν γυναῖκα εἶναι
σώφρονα καὶ ἀνδρείαν καὶ δικαίαν, καὶ παῖς ἐστι
καὶ ἀκόλαστος καὶ σώφρων, ἢ οὔ; καὶ καθόλου
δὴ τοῦτ' ἐστὶν ἐπισκεπτέον περὶ ἀρχομένου φύσει
καὶ ἄρχοντος, πότερον ἡ αὐτὴ ἀρετὴ ἢ ἑτέρα. εἰ
35 μὲν γὰρ δεῖ ἀμφοτέρους μετέχειν καλοκἀγαθίας,
διὰ τί τὸν μὲν ἄρχειν δέοι ἂν τὸν δὲ ἄρχεσθαι
καθάπαξ; οὐδὲ γὰρ τῷ μᾶλλον καὶ ἧττον οἷόν τε
διαφέρειν· τὸ μὲν γὰρ ἄρχεσθαι καὶ ἄρχειν εἴδει
διαφέρει, τὸ δὲ μᾶλλον καὶ ἧττον οὐδέν. εἰ δὲ τὸν 5
μὲν δεῖ τὸν δὲ μή, θαυμαστόν· εἴτε γὰρ ὁ ἄρχων
40 μὴ ἔσται σώφρων καὶ δίκαιος, πῶς ἄρξει καλῶς;
1260 a εἴθ' ὁ ἀρχόμενος, πῶς ἀρχθήσεται καλῶς; ἀκόλαστος γὰρ ὢν καὶ δειλὸς οὐθὲν ποιήσει τῶν
προσηκόντων. φανερὸν τοίνυν ὅτι ἀνάγκη μὲν
μετέχειν ἀμφοτέρους ἀρετῆς, ταύτης δ' εἶναι
διαφοράς (ὥσπερ καὶ τῶν φύσει ἀρχομένων).[2]

---

[1] καὶ ⟨ἑκάστη⟩ ? Spengel.
[2] ὥσπερ—ἀρχομένων interpolatum ed. (φύσει ἀρχόντων καὶ
ἀρχομένων cod. Oxon. marg.).

---

[a] Καλοκἄγαθος, 'fine gentleman,' connotes social as well as
moral distinction.

First of all then as to slaves the difficulty might be raised, does a slave possess any other excellence, besides his merits as a tool and a servant, more valuable than these, for instance temperance, courage, justice and any of the other moral virtues, or has he no excellence beside his bodily service? For either way there is difficulty; if slaves do possess moral virtue, wherein will they differ from freemen? or if they do not, this is strange, as they are human 4 beings and participate in reason. And nearly the same is the question also raised about the woman and the child: have they too virtues, and ought a woman to be temperate, brave and just, and can a child be intemperate or temperate, or not? This point therefore requires general consideration in relation to natural ruler and subject: is virtue the same for ruler and ruled, or different? If it is proper for both to partake in nobility of character,[a] how could it be proper for the one to rule and the other to be ruled unconditionally? we cannot say that the difference is to be one of degree, for ruling and being ruled differ in kind, and difference of degree is not a differ- 5 ence in kind at all. Whereas if on the contrary it is proper for the one to have moral nobility but not for the other, this is surprising. For if the ruler is not temperate and just, how will he rule well? And if the ruled, how will he obey well? If intemperate and cowardly he will not perform any of the duties of his position. It is evident therefore that both must possess virtue, but that there are differences in their virtue (as also there are differences between those who are by nature ruled).[b] And of this we

His subjects, slaves— wife and children— have their own virtues.

[b] This clause seems to have been interpolated; one ms. has a marginal correction, ' by nature rulers and ruled.'

5 καὶ τοῦτο εὐθὺς ὑφήγηται περὶ τὴν ψυχήν· ἐν
ταύτῃ γάρ ἐστι φύσει τὸ μὲν ἄρχον τὸ δὲ ἀρχόμενον, ὧν ἑτέραν φαμὲν εἶναι ἀρετήν, οἷον τοῦ
λόγον ἔχοντος καὶ τοῦ ἀλόγου. δῆλον τοίνυν ὅτι 6
τὸν αὐτὸν τρόπον ἔχει καὶ ἐπὶ τῶν ἄλλων. ὥστε
φύσει πλείω τὰ¹ ἄρχοντα καὶ ἀρχόμενα. ἄλλον γὰρ
10 τρόπον τὸ ἐλεύθερον τοῦ δούλου ἄρχει καὶ τὸ ἄρρεν
τοῦ θήλεος καὶ ἀνὴρ παιδός. καὶ πᾶσιν ἐνυπάρχει
μὲν τὰ μόρια τῆς ψυχῆς, ἀλλ' ἐνυπάρχει δια-
φερόντως· ὁ μὲν γὰρ δοῦλος ὅλως οὐκ ἔχει τὸ
βουλευτικόν, τὸ δὲ θῆλυ ἔχει μέν, ἀλλ' ἄκυρον, ὁ
δὲ παῖς ἔχει μέν, ἀλλ' ἀτελές. διὸ² τὸν μὲν 7
15 ἄρχοντα τελέαν ἔχειν δεῖ τὴν διανοητικὴν³ ἀρετήν
(τὸ γὰρ ἔργον ἐστὶν ἁπλῶς τοῦ ἀρχιτέκτονος, ὁ δὲ
λόγος ἀρχιτέκτων), τῶν δ' ἄλλων ἕκαστον ὅσον
ἐπιβάλλει αὐτοῖς.⁴ ὁμοίως τοίνυν ἀναγκαίως ἔχειν
καὶ περὶ τὰς ἠθικὰς ἀρετὰς ὑποληπτέον, δεῖν μὲν
μετέχειν πάντας, ἀλλ' οὐ τὸν αὐτὸν τρόπον, ἀλλ'
20 ὅσον ἑκάστῳ πρὸς τὸ αὑτοῦ ἔργον. ὥστε φανε- 8
ρὸν ὅτι ἐστὶν ἠθικὴ ἀρετὴ τῶν εἰρημένων πάντων,
καὶ οὐχ ἡ αὐτὴ σωφροσύνη γυναικὸς καὶ ἀνδρὸς
οὐδ' ἀνδρεία καὶ δικαιοσύνη, καθάπερ ᾤετο Σωκράτης, ἀλλ' ἡ μὲν ἀρχικὴ ἀνδρεία, ἡ δ' ὑπηρετική,
ὁμοίως δ' ἔχει καὶ περὶ τὰς ἄλλας. δῆλον δὲ τοῦτο
25 καὶ κατὰ μέρος μᾶλλον ἐπισκοποῦσιν· καθόλου γὰρ
οἱ λέγοντες ἐξαπατῶσιν ἑαυτοὺς ὅτι τὸ εὖ ἔχειν

---

¹ πλείω τὰ Ramus : τὰ πλείω codd.
² διὸ—αὐτοῖς hic Thurot, infra post τὸ αὑτοῦ ἔργον codd.
³ διανοητικὴν Thurot : ἠθικὴν codd.
⁴ αὐτοῖς ⟨ἱκανόν⟩ ? Richards.

ᵃ In the mss. this sentence follows the next one, ' We must
suppose—function,' and begins ' Hence the ruler must possess
moral virtue.'

straightway find an indication in connexion with the soul; for the soul by nature contains a part that rules and a part that is ruled, to which we assign different virtues, that is, the virtue of the rational 6 and that of the irrational. It is clear then that the case is the same also with the other instances of ruler and ruled. Hence there are by nature various classes of rulers and ruled. For the free rules the slave, the male the female, and the man the child in a different way. And all possess the various parts of the soul, but possess them in different ways; for the slave has not got the deliberative part at all, and the female has it, but without full authority, while the child has 7 it, but in an undeveloped form. Hence *a* the ruler must possess intellectual virtue in completeness (for any work, taken absolutely, belongs to the master-craftsman, and rational principle is a master-crafts-man); while each of the other parties must have that share of this virtue which is appropriate to them. We must suppose therefore that the same necessarily holds good of the moral virtues: all must partake of them, but not in the same way, but in such measure as is 8 proper to each in relation to his own function. Hence it is manifest that all the persons mentioned have a moral virtue of their own, and that the temperance of a woman and that of a man are not the same, nor their courage and justice, as Socrates thought,*b* but the one is the courage of command, and the other that of subordination, and the case is similar with the other virtues. And this is also clear when we examine the matter more in detail, for it is misleading to give a general definition of virtue, as some do, who say that virtue is being in good condition as regards the

b Plato, *Meno* 74 B ff.

1260 a

τὴν ψυχὴν ἀρετὴ ἢ τὸ ὀρθοπραγεῖν ἤ τι τῶν
τοιούτων· πολὺ γὰρ ἄμεινον λέγουσιν οἱ ἐξαριθ-
μοῦντες τὰς ἀρετάς, ὥσπερ Γοργίας, τῶν οὕτως
ὁριζομένων. διὸ δεῖ, ὥσπερ ὁ ποιητὴς εἴρηκε περὶ
30 γυναικός, οὕτω νομίζειν ἔχειν περὶ πάντων·

γυναικὶ κόσμον ἡ σιγὴ φέρει—

ἀλλ' ἀνδρὶ οὐκέτι τοῦτο. ἐπεὶ δ' ὁ παῖς ἀτελής, 9
δῆλον ὅτι τούτου μὲν καὶ ἡ ἀρετὴ οὐκ αὐτοῦ πρὸς
αὑτόν ἐστιν, ἀλλὰ πρὸς τὸν τέλειον καὶ τὸν ἡγού-
μενον. ὁμοίως δὲ καὶ δούλου πρὸς δεσπότην.

Ἔθεμεν δὲ πρὸς τἀναγκαῖα χρήσιμον εἶναι τὸν
35 δοῦλον, ὥστε δῆλον ὅτι καὶ ἀρετῆς δεῖται μικρᾶς,
καὶ τοσαύτης ὅπως μήτε δι' ἀκολασίαν μήτε διὰ
δειλίαν ἐλλείψει τῶν ἔργων. (ἀπορήσειε δ' ἄν τις, 10
τὸ νῦν εἰρημένον εἰ ἀληθές, ἆρα καὶ τοὺς τεχνίτας
δεήσει ἔχειν ἀρετήν· πολλάκις γὰρ δι' ἀκολασίαν
ἐλλείπουσι τῶν ἔργων. ἢ διαφέρει τοῦτο πλεῖστον;
40 ὁ μὲν γὰρ δοῦλος κοινωνὸς ζωῆς, ὁ δὲ πορρώτερον,
καὶ τοσοῦτον ἐπιβάλλει ἀρετῆς ὅσον περ καὶ
1260 b δουλείας· ὁ γὰρ βάναυσος τεχνίτης ἀφωρισμένην
τινὰ ἔχει δουλείαν, καὶ ὁ μὲν δοῦλος τῶν φύσει,
σκυτοτόμος δ' οὐθεὶς οὐδὲ τῶν ἄλλων τεχνιτῶν.)
φανερὸν τοίνυν ὅτι τῆς τοιαύτης ἀρετῆς αἴτιον εἶναι 11
δεῖ τῷ δούλῳ τὸν δεσπότην, ἀλλ' οὐ¹ τὴν διδα-
5 σκαλικὴν ἔχοντα τῶν ἔργων δεσποτικήν. διὸ

_____

¹ οὐχ ⟨ἢ⟩ Richards.

_____

ᵃ i.e. in Plato, Meno (vide § 7 above), where this sophist
figures as a character in the dialogue ; see also p. 178, note b.
ᵇ Sophocles, Ajax 293.
ᶜ i.e. his excellences as an artisan are the qualities of a
subordinate (his virtues as a human being, apart from his
trade, are not considered).

soul or acting uprightly or the like ; those who enumerate the virtues of different persons separately, as Gorgias does,[a] are much more correct than those who define virtue in that way. Hence we must hold that all of these persons have their appropriate virtues, as the poet said of woman :

> Silence gives grace to woman [b]—

though that is not the case likewise with a man. 9 Also the child is not completely developed, so that manifestly his virtue also is not personal to himself, but relative to the fully developed being, that is, the person in authority over him. And similarly the slave's virtue also is in relation to the master.

And we laid it down that the slave is serviceable for the mere necessaries of life, so that clearly he needs only a small amount of virtue, in fact just enough to prevent him from failing in his tasks 10 owing to intemperance and cowardice. (But the question might be raised, supposing that what has just been said is true, will artisans also need to have virtue ? for they frequently fall short in their tasks owing to intemperance. Or is their case entirely different ? For the slave is a partner in his master's life, but the artisan is more remote, and only so much of virtue falls to his share as of slavery [c]—for the mechanic artisan is under a sort of limited slavery, and whereas the slave is one of the natural classes, no shoemaker or other craftsman belongs to his trade 11 by nature.) It is manifest therefore that the master ought to be the cause to the slave of the virtue proper to a slave, but not as possessing that art of mastership which teaches a slave his tasks. Hence

The slave (and relatively the artisan) needs virtue for his tasks, and the master's admonition supplies it.

65

1260 b

λέγουσιν οὐ καλῶς οἱ λόγου τοὺς δούλους ἀπο-
στεροῦντες καὶ φάσκοντες ἐπιτάξει χρῆσθαι μόνον·
νουθετητέον γὰρ μᾶλλον τοὺς δούλους ἢ τοὺς
παῖδας.

Ἀλλὰ περὶ μὲν τούτων διωρίσθω τὸν τρόπον
τοῦτον· περὶ δὲ ἀνδρὸς καὶ γυναικὸς καὶ τέκνων
10 καὶ πατρός, τῆς τε περὶ ἕκαστον αὐτῶν ἀρετῆς,
καὶ τῆς πρὸς σφᾶς αὐτοὺς ὁμιλίας, τί τὸ καλῶς
καὶ μὴ καλῶς ἐστι καὶ πῶς δεῖ τὸ μὲν εὖ διώκειν
τὸ δὲ κακῶς φεύγειν, ἐν τοῖς περὶ τὰς πολιτείας
ἀναγκαῖον ἐπελθεῖν, ἐπεὶ γὰρ οἰκία μὲν πᾶσα μέρος 12
πόλεως, ταῦτα δ' οἰκίας, τὴν δὲ τοῦ μέρους πρὸς
15 τὴν τοῦ ὅλου δεῖ βλέπειν ἀρετήν, ἀναγκαῖον πρὸς
τὴν πολιτείαν βλέποντας παιδεύειν καὶ τοὺς παῖδας
καὶ τὰς γυναῖκας, εἴπερ τι διαφέρει πρὸς τὸ τὴν
πόλιν εἶναι σπουδαίαν καὶ τοὺς παῖδας εἶναι
σπουδαίους καὶ τὰς γυναῖκας σπουδαίας. ἀναγκαῖον δὲ διαφέρειν· αἱ μὲν γὰρ γυναῖκες ἥμισυ
20 μέρος τῶν ἐλευθέρων, ἐκ δὲ τῶν παίδων οἱ κοινωνοὶ[1]
γίνονται τῆς πολιτείας. ὥστ' ἐπεὶ περὶ μὲν τούτων
διώρισται, περὶ δὲ τῶν λοιπῶν ἐν ἄλλοις λεκτέον,
ἀφέντες ὡς τέλος ἔχοντας τοὺς νῦν λόγους, ἄλλην
ἀρχὴν ποιησάμενοι λέγωμεν, καὶ πρῶτον ἐπισκεψώ-
μεθα περὶ τῶν ἀποφηναμένων περὶ τῆς πολιτείας
τῆς ἀρίστης.

---

[1] οἱ κοινωνοὶ: οἰκονόμοι Susemihl (*dispensatores* Guil.).

[a] Plato, *Laws* 777 E.
[b] As a matter of fact in Books VII., VIII. dealing with
the best constitution this subject is not reached.

those persons are mistaken who deprive the slave of reasoning and tell us to use command only [a] ; for admonition is more properly employed with slaves than with children.

But on these subjects let us conclude our decisions in this manner ; while the question of the virtue severally belonging to man and woman and children and father, and of the right and wrong mode of conducting their mutual intercourse and the proper way of pursuing the good mode and avoiding the bad one, are matters that it will be necessary to follow up in the part of our treatise dealing with the various forms 12 of constitution.[b] For since every household is part of a state, and these relationships are part of the household, and the excellence of the part must have regard to that of the whole, it is necessary that the education both of the children and of the women should be carried on with a regard to the form of the constitution, if it makes any difference as regards the goodness of the state for the children and the women to be good. And it must necessarily make a difference ; for the women are a half of the free population, and the children grow up to be the partners in the government of the state. So that as these questions have been decided, and those that remain must be discussed elsewhere, let us relinquish the present subjects as completed, and make a fresh start in our discourse, and first let us consider those thinkers who have advanced views about the Ideal State.

Ethics of family life and education of children and women deferred.

I. Ἐπεὶ δὲ προαιρούμεθα θεωρῆσαι περὶ τῆς 1
κοινωνίας τῆς πολιτικῆς ἣ κρατίστη πασῶν τοῖς
δυναμένοις ζῆν ὅτι μάλιστα κατ' εὐχήν, δεῖ καὶ
30 τὰς ἄλλας ἐπισκέψασθαι πολιτείας αἷς τε χρῶνταί
τινες τῶν πόλεων τῶν εὐνομεῖσθαι λεγομένων κἂν
εἴ τινες ἕτεραι τυγχάνωσιν ὑπὸ τινῶν εἰρημέναι
καὶ δοκοῦσαι καλῶς ἔχειν, ἵνα τό τ' ὀρθῶς ἔχον
ὀφθῇ καὶ τὸ χρήσιμον, ἔτι δὲ τὸ ζητεῖν τι 'παρ'
35 αὐτὰς ἕτερον μὴ δοκῇ πάντως εἶναι σοφίζεσθαι
βουλομένων, ἀλλὰ διὰ τὸ μὴ καλῶς ἔχειν ταύτας·
τὰς νῦν ὑπαρχούσας, διὰ τοῦτο ταύτην δοκῶμεν
ἐπιβαλέσθαι τὴν μέθοδον.

Ἀρχὴν δὲ πρῶτον ποιητέον ἥπερ πέφυκεν ἀρχὴ 2
ταύτης τῆς σκέψεως. ἀνάγκη γὰρ ἤτοι πάντας
πάντων κοινωνεῖν τοὺς πολίτας, ἢ μηδενός, ἢ τινῶν
μὲν τινῶν δὲ μή. τὸ μὲν οὖν μηδενὸς κοινωνεῖν
40 φανερὸν ὡς ἀδύνατον (ἡ γὰρ πολιτεία κοινωνία τίς
ἐστι, καὶ πρῶτον ἀνάγκη τοῦ τόπου κοινωνεῖν, ὁ
μὲν γὰρ τόπος εἷς ὁ τῆς μιᾶς πόλεως, οἱ δὲ πολῖται
1261 a κοινωνοὶ τῆς μιᾶς πόλεως)· ἀλλὰ πότερον ὅσων

BOOK II

1   I. And since we take for our special consideration
the study of the form of political community that is
the best of all the forms for a people able to pursue
the most ideal mode of life, we must also examine
the other constitutions actually employed by certain
of the states said to be well governed, as well as any
others propounded by certain thinkers and reputed
to be of merit, in order that we may discern what
there is in them that is right and expedient, and also
in order that it may not be thought that to seek for
something different from them springs entirely from
a desire to display ingenuity, but that we may be
thought to enter upon this inquiry because these
forms of constitution that already exist are not
satisfactory.

2   We must first adopt as a starting-point that which
is the natural point of departure for this inquiry.
There are three possible systems of property : either
all the citizens must own everything in common, or
they must own nothing in common, or some things
must be common property and others not. To have
nothing in common is clearly impossible ; for the
state is essentially a form of community, and it must
at any rate have a common locality : a single city
occupies a single site, and the single city belongs
to its citizens in common. But is it better for a city

69

1261 a

ἐνδέχεται κοινωνῆσαι πάντων βέλτιον κοινωνεῖν τὴν
μέλλουσαν οἰκήσεσθαι πόλιν καλῶς, ἢ τινῶν μὲν
τινῶν δ' οὐ βέλτιον; ἐνδέχεται γὰρ καὶ τέκνων
5 καὶ γυναικῶν καὶ κτημάτων κοινωνεῖν τοὺς πολίτας
ἀλλήλοις, ὥσπερ ἐν τῇ Πολιτείᾳ τῇ Πλάτωνος·
ἐκεῖ γὰρ ὁ Σωκράτης φησὶ δεῖν κοινὰ τὰ τέκνα
καὶ τὰς γυναῖκας εἶναι καὶ τὰς κτήσεις. τοῦτο δὴ
πότερον ὡς νῦν οὕτω βέλτιον ἔχειν, ἢ κατὰ τὸν ἐν
τῇ Πολιτείᾳ γεγραμμένον νόμον;

10 Ἔχει δὲ δυσχερείας ἄλλας τε πολλὰς τὸ πάντων 3
εἶναι τὰς γυναῖκας κοινάς, καὶ δι' ἣν αἰτίαν φησὶ
δεῖν νενομοθετῆσθαι τὸν τρόπον τοῦτον ὁ Σωκράτης
οὐ φαίνεται συμβαῖνον ἐκ τῶν λόγων· ἔτι δὲ πρὸς
τὸ τέλος ὅ φησι τῇ πόλει δεῖν ὑπάρχειν, ὡς μὲν
εἴρηται νῦν, ἀδύνατον, πῶς δὲ δεῖ διελεῖν,[1] οὐδὲν
15 διώρισται· λέγω δὲ τὸ μίαν εἶναι τὴν πόλιν πᾶσαν
ὡς ἄριστον ὅτι μάλιστα, λαμβάνει γὰρ ταύτην
ὑπόθεσιν ὁ Σωκράτης.

Καίτοι φανερόν ἐστιν ὡς προϊοῦσα καὶ γινομένη 4
μία μᾶλλον οὐδὲ πόλις ἔσται· πλῆθος γάρ τι τὴν
φύσιν ἐστὶν ἡ πόλις, γινομένη τε μία μᾶλλον οἰκία
20 μὲν ἐκ πόλεως, ἄνθρωπος δ' ἐξ οἰκίας ἔσται,
μᾶλλον γὰρ μίαν τὴν οἰκίαν τῆς πόλεως φαίημεν
ἂν καὶ τὸν ἕνα τῆς οἰκίας· ὥστ' εἰ καὶ δυνατός
τις εἴη τοῦτο δρᾶν, οὐ ποιητέον, ἀναιρήσει γὰρ
τὴν πόλιν. οὐ μόνον δ' ἐκ πλειόνων ἀνθρώπων
ἐστὶν ἡ πόλις, ἀλλὰ καὶ ἐξ εἴδει διαφερόντων. οὐ

[1] δεῖ διελθεῖν MP[2]: διελεῖν Γ.

[a] On the following criticisms see Grote, *Plato*, iii. pp. 211-223.
[b] (1) §§ 3-7 ; (2) § 8-c. ii. § 11 ; (3) c. ii. §§ 11 mid.-13; also (4) other objections c. ii. §§ 15-16.

that is to be well ordered to have community in everything which can possibly be made common property,
or is it better to have some things in common and
others not ? For example, it is possible for the citizens Plato's
to have children, wives and possessions in common with com-
munistic
each other, as in Plato's *Republic*, in which Socrates Republic.
says that there must be community of children, women
and possessions. Well then, which is preferable, the
system that now obtains, or one conforming with
the regulation described in *The Republic* [a] ?

3 Now for all the citizens to have their wives in
common involves a variety of difficulties ; in particular,[b] (1) the object which Socrates advances as
the reason why this enactment should be made
clearly does not follow from his arguments ; also
(2) as a means to the end which he asserts should be
the fundamental object of the city, the scheme as
actually set forth in the dialogue is not practicable ;
yet (3) how it is to be further worked out has been
nowhere definitely stated. I refer to the ideal of
the fullest possible unity of the entire state, which
Socrates takes as his fundamental principle.

4 Yet it is clear that if the process of unification (1) Unity of
advances beyond a certain point, the city will not State not
desirable
be a city at all ; for a state essentially consists because
of a multitude of persons, and if its unification is plurality is
carried beyond a certain point, city will be reduced essential,
to family and family to individual, for we should
pronounce the family to be a more complete unity
than the city, and the single person than the family ;
so that even if any lawgiver were able to unify the
state, he must not do so, for he will destroy it in the
process. And not only does a city consist of a multitude of human beings, it consists of human beings

1261 a

γὰρ γίνεται πόλις ἐξ ὁμοίων. ἕτερον γὰρ συμ-
25 μαχία καὶ πόλις· τὸ μὲν γὰρ τῷ ποσῷ χρήσιμον,
κἂν ᾖ τὸ αὐτὸ τῷ εἴδει (βοηθείας γὰρ χάριν ἡ
συμμαχία πέφυκεν), ὥσπερ ἂν εἰ σταθμὸς πλεῖον
ἑλκύσειε,[1] ἐξ[2] ὧν δὲ δεῖ ἓν γενέσθαι εἴδει δεῖ
διαφέρειν[3] (διοίσει δὲ τῷ τοιούτῳ καὶ πόλις ἔθνους
30 ὅταν μὴ κατὰ κώμας ὦσι κεχωρισμένοι τὸ πλῆθος 5
ἀλλ' οἷον Ἀρκάδες). διόπερ τὸ ἴσον[4] τὸ ἀντι-
πεπονθὸς σῴζει τὰς πόλεις, ὥσπερ ἐν τοῖς Ἠθικοῖς
εἴρηται πρότερον. ἐπεὶ καὶ ἐν τοῖς ἐλευθέροις καὶ
ἴσοις ἀνάγκη τοῦτ' εἶναι· ἅμα γὰρ οὐχ οἷόν τε
πάντας ἄρχειν, ἀλλ' ἢ κατ' ἐνιαυτὸν ἢ κατά τινα
35 ἄλλην τάξιν ἢ χρόνον· καὶ συμβαίνει δὴ τὸν τρόπον
τοῦτον ὥστε πάντας ἄρχειν, ὥσπερ ἂν εἰ μετέβαλλον οἱ σκυτεῖς καὶ οἱ τέκτονες καὶ μὴ οἱ αὐτοὶ ἀεὶ
σκυτοτόμοι καὶ τέκτονες ἦσαν. ἐπεὶ δὲ βέλτιον
οὕτως ἔχειν καὶ τὰ περὶ τὴν κοινωνίαν τὴν πολι- 6
τικήν, δῆλον ὡς τοὺς αὐτοὺς ἀεὶ βέλτιον ἄρχειν, εἰ
1261 b δυνατόν· ἐν οἷς δὲ μὴ δυνατὸν διὰ τὸ τὴν φύσιν ἴσους
εἶναι πάντας, ἅμα δὲ[5] καὶ δίκαιον, εἴτ' ἀγαθὸν εἴτε
φαῦλον τὸ ἄρχειν, πάντας αὐτοῦ μετέχειν, τοῦτο
δὲ μιμεῖται τὸ ἐν μέρει τοὺς ἴσους εἴκειν τὸ ἀνομοίους[6] εἶναι ἐξ ἀρχῆς· οἱ μὲν γὰρ ἄρχουσιν οἱ δ'

---

[1] ἑλκύσειε Coraes: ἑλκύσει, ἑλκύσῃ codd.
[2] ἐξ—διαφέρειν infra post Ἀρκάδες codd.: tr. ed.
[3] εἴδει δεῖ διαφέρειν Buecheler: εἴδει διαφέρει codd. (διαφέρειν M).
[4] [τὸ ἴσον]? (cf. N.E. 1132 b 33) ed.
[5] δὴ Susemihl.
[6] τὸ ἀνομοίους Susemihl: τὸ δ' ὡς ὁμοίους, ὁμοίους τοῖς, ὁμοίως
τοῖς codd. Locum desperatissimum rescripsit Richards
μιμεῖται τὸ ἐν μέρει ἄρχειν τὸ μὴ ἴσους καὶ ὁμοίους εἶναι ἐξ
ἀρχῆς.

differing in kind. A collection of persons all alike classes are
necessary, does not constitute a state. For a city is not the same thing as a league ; a league is of value by its quantity, even though it is all the same in kind (since the essential object of the league is military strength), just as a weight would be worth more if it weighed more, whereas [a] components which are to make up a
5 unity must differ in kind (and it is by this character istic that a city will also surpass a tribe of which the population is not scattered among villages but organized like the Arcadians). Hence reciprocal equality [b] is the preservative of states, as has been said before in *Ethics*. For even among the free and equal this principle must necessarily obtain, since all cannot govern at once : they must hold office for a year at a time or by some other arrangement or period ; and in this manner it does actually come about that all govern, just as all shoemakers would be also carpenters if the shoemakers and the carpenters kept on changing trades instead of the same persons being shoemakers and carpenters
6 always. But since such permanence of function is better for the political community also, it is clear that it is better for the same persons to govern always, if possible ; and among peoples where it is impossible because all the citizens are equal in their nature, yet at the same time it is only just, whether governing is a good thing or a bad, that all should partake in it, then for equals thus to submit to authority in turn imitates their being originally dissimilar [c]; for some govern and others are governed

[a] In the MSS. of the Greek ' whereas—kind ' comes below after ' Arcadian.'   [b] See Additional Note, p. 170.
[c] See Additional Note, p. 171.

5 ἄρχονται παρὰ μέρος, ὥσπερ ἂν ἄλλοι γενόμενοι,
καὶ τὸν αὐτὸν δὴ τρόπον ἀρχόντων ἕτεροι ἑτέρας
ἄρχουσιν ἀρχάς. φανερὸν τοίνυν ἐκ τούτων ὡς 7
οὔτε πέφυκε μίαν οὕτως εἶναι τὴν πόλιν ὥσπερ
λέγουσί τινες, καὶ τὸ λεχθὲν ὡς μέγιστον ἀγαθὸν
ἐν ταῖς πόλεσιν ὅτι τὰς πόλεις ἀναιρεῖ· καίτοι τό
10 γε ἑκάστου ἀγαθὸν σῴζει ἕκαστον.—ἔστι δὲ καὶ
κατ᾽ ἄλλον τρόπον φανερὸν ὅτι τὸ λίαν ἑνοῦν ζητεῖν τὴν πόλιν οὐκ ἔστιν ἄμεινον. οἰκία μὲν γὰρ
αὐταρκέστερον ἑνός, πόλις δ᾽ οἰκίας, καὶ βούλεταί
γ᾽ ἤδη τότε εἶναι πόλις ὅταν αὐτάρκη συμβαίνῃ
τὴν κοινωνίαν εἶναι τοῦ πλήθους· εἴπερ οὖν αἱρετώτερον τὸ αὐταρκέστερον, καὶ τὸ ἧττον ἓν τοῦ
15 μᾶλλον αἱρετώτερον.

'Ἀλλὰ μὴν οὐδ᾽ εἰ τοῦτο ἄριστόν ἐστι, τὸ μίαν 8
ὅτι μάλιστ᾽ εἶναι τὴν κοινωνίαν, οὐδὲ τοῦτ᾽ ἀπο-
δείκνυσθαι φαίνεται κατὰ τὸν λόγον ' ἐὰν πάντες
ἅμα λέγωσι τὸ ἐμὸν καὶ τὸ μὴ ἐμόν'· τοῦτο γὰρ
20 οἴεται ὁ Σωκράτης σημεῖον εἶναι τοῦ τὴν πόλιν
τελέως εἶναι μίαν. τὸ γὰρ πάντες διττόν. εἰ μὲν
οὖν ὡς ἕκαστος, τάχ᾽ ἂν εἴη μᾶλλον ὃ βούλεται
ποιεῖν ὁ Σωκράτης (ἕκαστος γὰρ υἱὸν ἑαυτοῦ φήσει
τὸν αὐτὸν καὶ γυναῖκα δὴ τὴν αὐτήν, καὶ περὶ τῆς
οὐσίας καὶ περὶ ἑκάστου δὴ τῶν συμβαινόντων
25 ὡσαύτως)· νῦν δ᾽ οὐχ οὕτω φήσουσιν οἱ κοιναῖς 9
χρώμενοι ταῖς γυναιξὶ καὶ τοῖς τέκνοις, ἀλλὰ πάντες μέν, οὐχ ὡς ἕκαστος δ᾽ αὐτῶν, ὁμοίως δὲ καὶ

---

[a] The reference is to Plato, *Republic* 462 c. Unity is
secured when everyone thinks that everything belongs
equally to him and to everybody else, *i.e.* everything is
common property.

by turn, as though becoming other persons ; and also
when they hold office in the same way different persons
7 hold different offices. It is clear then from these
considerations that it is not an outcome of nature
for the state to be a unity in the manner in which
certain persons say that it is, and that what has
been said to be the greatest good in states really
destroys states ; yet surely a thing's particular good
acts as its preservative.—Another line of considera- *and
tion also shows that to seek to unify the state ex- numbers
cessively is not beneficial. In point of self-sufficiency give in-
the individual is surpassed by the family and the dependence*
family by the state, and in principle a state is fully
realized only when it comes to pass that the community of numbers is self-suffing ; if therefore the
more self-suffing a community is, the more desirable is its condition, then a less degree of unity is
more desirable than a greater.

8   Again, even granting that it is best for the com- *(2) Unity
munity to be as complete a unity as possible, complete not secured
unity does not seem to be proved by the formula ' if (a) either
all the citizens say " Mine " and " Not mine " at the by com-
same time,' which Socrates *a* thinks to be a sign of the the family,*
city's being completely one. ' All ' is an ambiguous
term. If it means ' each severally,' very likely this *because
would more fully realize the state of things which sense of
Socrates wishes to produce (for in that case every property
citizen will call the same boy his son and also the will be
same woman his wife, and will speak in the same way destroyed,*
of property and indeed of everything that falls to
9 his lot) ; but *ex hypothesi* the citizens, having community of women and children, will not call them
' theirs ' in this sense, but will mean theirs collectively
and not severally, and similarly they will call property

τὴν οὐσίαν πάντες μέν, οὐχ ὡς ἕκαστος δ' αὐτῶν.
ὅτι μὲν τοίνυν παραλογισμός τίς ἐστι τὸ λέγειν
πάντας, φανερόν (τὸ γὰρ πάντες καὶ ἀμφότερα καὶ
80 περιττὰ καὶ ἄρτια διὰ τὸ διττὸν καὶ ἐν τοῖς λόγοις
ἐριστικοὺς ποιεῖ συλλογισμούς)· διὸ ἐστὶ τὸ πάντας τὸ αὐτὸ λέγειν ὡδὶ μὲν καλὸν ἀλλ' οὐ δυνατόν,
ὡδὶ δ' οὐδὲν ὁμονοητικόν. πρὸς δὲ τούτοις ἑτέραν
ἔχει βλάβην τὸ λεγόμενον. ἥκιστα γὰρ ἐπιμελείας
τυγχάνει τὸ πλείστων κοινόν· τῶν γὰρ ἰδίων
85 μάλιστα φροντίζουσιν, τῶν δὲ κοινῶν ἧττον, ἢ ὅσον
ἑκάστῳ ἐπιβάλλει· πρὸς γὰρ τοῖς ἄλλοις ὡς ἑτέρου
φροντίζοντος ὀλιγωροῦσι μᾶλλον, ὥσπερ ἐν ταῖς
οἰκετικαῖς διακονίαις οἱ πολλοὶ θεράποντες ἐνίοτε
χεῖρον ὑπηρετοῦσι τῶν ἐλαττόνων. γίνονται δ' 1
ἑκάστῳ χίλιοι τῶν πολιτῶν υἱοί, καὶ οὗτοι οὐχ
1262 a ὡς ἑκάστου ἀλλὰ τοῦ τυχόντος ὁ τυχὼν ὁμοίως
ἐστὶν υἱός, ὥστε πάντες ὁμοίως ὀλιγωρήσουσιν.

Ἔτι οὕτως ἕκαστος ἐμὸς λέγει τὸν εὖ πράττοντα
τῶν πολιτῶν ἢ κακῶς ὁπόστος τυγχάνει τὸν ἀριθμὸν ὤν, οἷον ἐμὸς ἢ τοῦ δεῖνος, τοῦτον τὸν τρόπον
5 λέγων καθ' ἕκαστον τῶν χιλίων ἢ ὅσων ἡ πόλις
ἐστί, καὶ τοῦτο διστάζων· ἄδηλον γὰρ ᾧ συνέβη
γενέσθαι τέκνον καὶ σωθῆναι γενόμενον. καίτοι 12
πότερον οὕτω κρεῖττον τὸ ἐμὸν λέγειν, ἕκαστον τὸ

' theirs ' meaning the property of them all, not of
each of them severally. We see then that the phrase
' all say ' is equivocal (in fact the words ' all,' ' both,'
' odd,' ' even,' owing to their ambiguity, occasion
argumentative quibbling even in philosophical discussions) ; hence really for ' all ' to say the same
thing is in one sense admirable, although impracticable, but in another sense is not at all a sign of
10 concord. And furthermore, the proposal has another
disadvantage. Property that is common to the
greatest number of owners receives the least attention ; men care most for their private possessions,
and for what they own in common less, or only so
far as it falls to their own individual share ; for in
addition to the other reasons, they think less of it on
the ground that someone else is thinking about it,
just as in household service a large number of
domestics sometimes give worse attendance than a
11 smaller number. And it results in each citizen's
having a thousand sons, and these do not belong to
them as individuals but any child is equally the son
of anyone, so that all alike will regard them with
indifference.

Again, each speaks of one of his fellow-citizens who
is prospering or getting on badly as ' my son ' only
in the sense of the fractional part which he forms
of the whole number, meaning ' mine or so-and-so's,'
indicating by ' so-and-so ' each of the thousand citizens
or whatever the number be of which the state consists,
and even this dubiously, for it is uncertain who has
chanced to have had a son born to him and when born
12 safely reared. Yet which is the better way to use the
word ' mine '—this way, each of two thousand or ten

common
ties and
duties
will be
neglected,

77

1262 a

αὐτὸ ἐμόν[1] προσαγορεύοντα[2] δισχιλίων καὶ μυρίων,
ἢ μᾶλλον ὡς νῦν ἐν ταῖς πόλεσι τὸ ἐμὸν λέγουσιν;
10 ὁ μὲν γὰρ υἱὸν αὑτοῦ ὁ δ᾽ ἀδελφὸν αὑτοῦ προσ-
αγορεύει τὸν αὐτόν, ὁ δ᾽ ἀνεψιὸν ἢ κατ᾽ ἄλλην τινὰ
συγγένειαν ἢ πρὸς αἵματος ἢ κατ᾽ οἰκειότητα καὶ
κηδείαν αὑτοῦ πρῶτον ἢ τῶν αὑτοῦ, πρὸς δὲ τούτοις
ἕτερος[3] φράτορα ἢ φυλέτην. κρεῖττον γὰρ ἴδιον
ἀνεψιὸν εἶναι ἢ τὸν τρόπον τοῦτον υἱόν. οὐ μὴν 13
15 ἀλλ᾽ οὐδὲ διαφυγεῖν δυνατὸν τὸ μή τινας ὑπολαμβάνειν ἑαυτῶν ἀδελφούς τε καὶ παῖδας καὶ πατέρας
καὶ μητέρας· κατὰ γὰρ τὰς ὁμοιότητας αἳ γίνονται
τοῖς τέκνοις πρὸς τοὺς γεννήσαντας ἀναγκαῖον λαμβάνειν περὶ ἀλλήλων τὰς πίστεις. ὅπερ φασὶ καὶ
συμβαίνειν τινὲς τῶν τὰς τῆς γῆς περιόδους πραγ-
20 ματευομένων· εἶναι γάρ τισι τῶν ἄνω Λιβύων
κοινὰς τὰς γυναῖκας, τὰ μέντοι γινόμενα[4] τέκνα
διαιρεῖσθαι κατὰ τὰς ὁμοιότητας. εἰσὶ δέ τινες
καὶ γυναῖκες καὶ τῶν ἄλλων ζῴων, οἷον ἵπποι καὶ
βόες, αἳ σφόδρα πεφύκασιν ὅμοια ἀποδιδόναι τὰ
τέκνα τοῖς γονεῦσιν, ὥσπερ ἡ ἐν Φαρσάλῳ κληθεῖσα
Δικαία ἵππος.
25 Ἔτι δὲ καὶ τὰς τοιαύτας δυσχερείας οὐ ῥᾴδιον 14
εὐλαβηθῆναι τοῖς ταύτην κατασκευάζουσι τὴν
κοινωνίαν, οἷον αἰκίας καὶ φόνους ἀκουσίους, τοὺς
δὲ ἑκουσίους, καὶ μάχας καὶ λοιδορίας· ὧν οὐδὲν
ὅσιόν ἐστι γίνεσθαι πρὸς πατέρας καὶ μητέρας καὶ

---

[1] ἐμὸν Bornemann : ὄνομα Bonitz, μὲν codd.
[2] Bernays : -οντας codd.
[3] ἕτερος Lindau : ἕτερον codd.
[4] γινόμενα (cf. infra b 25) Richards : γενόμενα codd.

thousand people applying it to the same thing, or rather the way in which they say ' mine ' in the actual states now ? for the same person is called ' my son ' by one man and ' my brother ' by another, and another calls him ' nephew,' or by some other relationship, whether of blood or by affinity and marriage, the speaker's own in the first place, or that of his relations ; and in addition someone else calls him ' fellow-clansman ' or ' fellow-tribesman.' For it is better for a boy to be one's own private nephew

13 than one's son in the way described. Moreover it would also be impossible to avoid men's supposing certain persons to be their real brothers and sons and fathers and mothers ; for they would be bound to form their belief about each other by the resemblances which occur between children and parents. This indeed is said by some of those who write of travels round the world[a] actually to occur ; they say that some of the people of Upper Libya have their wives in common, yet the children born are divided among them according to their personal resemblances. And there are some females both of the human race and of the other animals, for instance horses and cattle, who have a strong natural tendency to produce offspring resembling the male parents, as was the case with the mare at Pharsalus named Honest Lady.[b]

family likeness will betray parentage,

14 Moreover it is not easy for those who institute this communism to guard against such objectionable occurrences as outrage, involuntary and in some cases voluntary homicide, fights, abusive language ; all of which are violations of piety when committed

assaults on parents will occur ;

[a] Books of geography, founded on travellers' reports—a famous one by Hecataeus, scoffed at by Herodotus, iv. 36.
[b] Or possibly ' Docile ' (Jackson), *cf.* Xen. *Cyneget.* 7. 4.

1262 a

τοὺς μὴ πόρρω τῆς συγγενείας ὄντας ὥσπερ πρὸς
80 τοὺς ἄπωθεν· ἀλλὰ καὶ πλεῖον συμβαίνειν ἀναγκαῖον ἀγνοούντων ἢ γνωριζόντων, καὶ γενομένων
τῶν μὲν γνωριζόντων ἐνδέχεται τὰς νομιζομένας
γίνεσθαι λύσεις, τῶν δὲ μηδεμίαν. ἄτοπον δὲ καὶ 15
τὸ κοινοὺς ποιήσαντα τοὺς υἱοὺς τὸ συνεῖναι μόνον
ἀφελεῖν τῶν ἐρώντων, τὸ δ᾽ ἐρᾶν μὴ κωλῦσαι,
85 μηδὲ τὰς χρήσεις τὰς ἄλλας, ἃς πατρὶ πρὸς υἱὸν
εἶναι πάντων ἐστὶν ἀπρεπέστατον καὶ ἀδελφῷ πρὸς
ἀδελφόν, ἐπεὶ καὶ τὸ ἐρᾶν μόνον. ἄτοπον δὲ καὶ
τὸ τὴν συνουσίαν ἀφελεῖν δι᾽ ἄλλην μὲν αἰτίαν
μηδεμίαν, ὡς λίαν δ᾽ ἰσχυρᾶς τῆς ἡδονῆς γινο-
μένης· ὅτι δ᾽ ὁ μὲν πατὴρ ἢ υἱός οἱ δ᾽ ἀδελφοὶ
ἀλλήλων, μηθὲν οἴεσθαι διαφέρειν. ἔοικε δὲ μᾶλλον
40 τοῖς γεωργοῖς εἶναι χρήσιμον τὸ κοινὰς εἶναι τὰς
1262 b γυναῖκας καὶ τοὺς παῖδας ἢ τοῖς φύλαξιν· ἧττον
γὰρ ἔσται φιλία κοινῶν ὄντων τῶν τέκνων καὶ τῶν
γυναικῶν, δεῖ δὲ τοιούτους εἶναι τοὺς ἀρχομένους
πρὸς τὸ πειθαρχεῖν καὶ μὴ νεωτερίζειν. ὅλως δὲ 16
5 συμβαίνειν ἀνάγκη τοὐναντίον διὰ τὸν τοιοῦτον
νόμον ὧν προσήκει τοὺς ὀρθῶς κειμένους νόμους
αἰτίους γίνεσθαι, καὶ δι᾽ ἣν αἰτίαν ὁ Σωκράτης
οὕτως οἴεται δεῖν τάττειν τὰ περὶ τὰ τέκνα καὶ
τὰς γυναῖκας. φιλίαν τε¹ γὰρ οἰόμεθα μέγιστον
εἶναι τῶν ἀγαθῶν ταῖς πόλεσιν (οὕτω γὰρ ἂν ἥκιστα
στασιάζοιεν), καὶ τὸ μίαν εἶναι τὴν πόλιν ἐπαινεῖ
10 μάλισθ᾽ ὁ Σωκράτης, ὃ καὶ δοκεῖ κἀκεῖνος εἶναί

¹ τε om. MP, quidem (? γε) Guil.

against fathers, mothers and near relatives as if they were not relatives; but these are bound to occur more frequently when people do not know their relations than when they do, and also, when they do occur, if the offenders know their relationship it is possible for them to have the customary expiations performed, but for those who do not no expiation is possible.

15 Also it is curious that a theorist who makes the sons common property only debars lovers from intercourse and does not prohibit love, nor the other familiarities, which between father and son or brother and brother are most unseemly, since even the fact of love between them is unseemly. And it is also strange that he deprives them of intercourse for no other reason except because the pleasure is too violent; and that he thinks it makes no difference that the parties are in the one case father or son and in the other case brothers of one another. And it seems more serviceable for the Farmers to have this community of wives and sons than the Guardians; for there will be less friendship among them if their children and women are in common, and unfriendliness in the subject classes is a good thing with a view to their being submissive to authority 16 and not making revolution. But speaking generally such a law is bound to bring about the opposite state of things to that which rightly enacted laws ought properly to cause, and because of which Socrates thinks it necessary to make these regulations about the children and women. For we think that friendship is the greatest of blessings for the state, since it is the best safeguard against revolution, and the unity of the state, which Socrates praises most highly, both appears to be and is said by him to be

risk of incest;

(such communism might be useful in the Farmer class)

bond of affection weakened;

81

φησι τῆς φιλίας ἔργον, καθάπερ ἐν τοῖς ἐρωτικοῖς
λόγοις ἴσμεν λέγοντα τὸν Ἀριστοφάνην ὡς τῶν
ἐρώντων διὰ τὸ σφόδρα φιλεῖν ἐπιθυμούντων συμ-
φῦναι[1] καὶ γενέσθαι ἐκ δύο ὄντων ἀμφοτέρους ἕνα·
ἐνταῦθα μὲν οὖν ἀνάγκη ἀμφοτέρους ἐφθάρθαι ἢ 17
15 τὸν ἕνα, ἐν δὲ τῇ πόλει τὴν φιλίαν ἀναγκαῖον
ὑδαρῆ γίνεσθαι διὰ τὴν κοινωνίαν τὴν τοιαύτην,
καὶ ἥκιστα λέγειν[2] τὸν ἐμὸν ἢ υἱὸν πατέρα ἢ
πατέρα υἱόν. ὥσπερ γὰρ μικρὸν γλυκὺ εἰς πολὺ
ὕδωρ μιχθὲν ἀναίσθητον ποιεῖ τὴν κρᾶσιν, οὕτω
συμβαίνει καὶ[3] τὴν οἰκειότητα τὴν πρὸς ἀλλήλους
20 τὴν ἀπὸ τῶν ὀνομάτων τούτων, διαφροντίζειν
ἥκιστα ἀναγκαῖον ὂν ἐν τῇ πολιτείᾳ τῇ τοιαύτῃ ἢ
πατέρα ὡς υἱῶν ἢ υἱὸν ὡς πατρὸς ἢ ὡς ἀδελφοὺς
ἀλλήλων. δύο γάρ ἐστιν ἃ μάλιστα ποιεῖ κήδεσθαι
τοὺς ἀνθρώπους καὶ φιλεῖν, τό τε ἴδιον καὶ τὸ
ἀγαπητόν, ὧν οὐδέτερον οἷόν τε ὑπάρχειν τοῖς οὕτω
25 πολιτευομένοις. ἀλλὰ μὴν καὶ περὶ τοῦ μεταφέρειν 18
τὰ γινόμενα τέκνα τὰ μὲν ἐκ τῶν γεωργῶν καὶ
τεχνιτῶν εἰς τοὺς φύλακας τὰ δ᾽ ἐκ τούτων εἰς
ἐκείνους, πολλὴν ἔχει ταραχὴν τίνα ἔσται τρόπον·
καὶ[4] γινώσκειν ἀναγκαῖον τοὺς διδόντας καὶ μετα-
φέροντας τίσι τίνας διδόασιν. ἔτι δὲ καὶ τὰ πάλαι
30 λεχθέντα μᾶλλον ἐπὶ τούτων ἀναγκαῖον συμβαίνειν,
οἷον αἰκίας ἔρωτας φόνους· οὐ γὰρ ἔτι προσαγορεύσουσιν[5] ἀδελφοὺς καὶ τέκνα καὶ πατέρας

---

[1] συμφυῆναι MPH.
[2] διώκειν H: an δὴ οἰκειοῦν pro λέγειν τὸν ἐμὸν ? Immisch.
[3] κατὰ Lambinus, καὶ κατὰ Bernays.
[4] καὶ ⟨γὰρ⟩ Bernays.
[5] προσαγορεύσουσιν Coraes: -εύουσιν codd.

---

[a] The comic poet, figuring as a character in Plato's
Symposium, see especially 192 c ff.

the effect of friendship, just as we know that Aristophanes [a] in the discourses on love describes how the lovers owing to their extreme affection desire to grow together and both become one instead of being 17 two. In such a union both personalities, or at least one, would be bound to be obliterated ; and in the state friendship would inevitably become diluted in consequence of such association, and the expressions ' my father ' and ' my son ' would quite go out. For just as putting a little sugar into a quantity of water makes the mixture imperceptible, so it also must come about that the mutual relationship based on these names must become imperceptible, since in the republic described by Plato there will be the least possible necessity for people to care for one another as father for sons or as son for father or as brother for brother.   For there are two motives that most cause men to care for things and be fond of them, the sense of ownership and the sense of preciousness ; and neither motive can be present with the citizens 18 of a state so constituted. Again, as to the transference of some of the children at birth from the Farmers and Artisans to the Guardians [b] and of others from the Guardians to the Farmers and Artisans, there is much confusion as to how it is to be done ; and the parents who give the children and the officials who transfer them are bound to know which they give to whom. And again, the things spoken of above are bound to occur even more with these transferred children, such as outrage, love-making and murder ; for the children of the Guardians transferred to the other citizens will no longer speak

reclassing of infants impracticable,

and would increase unnatural crime.

[b] The three classes in Plato's *Republic*.

1226 b

καὶ μητέρας οἵ τε εἰς τοὺς ἄλλους πολίτας δοθέντες
τοὺς φύλακας[1] καὶ πάλιν οἱ παρὰ τοῖς φύλαξιν τοὺς[2]
ἄλλους πολίτας, ὥστ' εὐλαβεῖσθαι τῶν τοιούτων
35 τι πράττειν διὰ τὴν συγγένειαν.

Περὶ μὲν οὖν τῆς περὶ τὰ τέκνα καὶ τὰς γυναῖκας
κοινωνίας διωρίσθω τὸν τρόπον τοῦτον.

II. Ἐχόμενον δὲ τούτων ἐστὶν ἐπισκέψασθαι 1
περὶ τῆς κτήσεως, τίνα τρόπον δεῖ κατασκευά-
ζεσθαι τοῖς μέλλουσι πολιτεύεσθαι τὴν ἀρίστην
40 πολιτείαν, πότερον κοινὴν ἢ μὴ κοινὴν εἶναι τὴν
κτῆσιν. τοῦτο δ' ἄν τις καὶ χωρὶς σκέψαιτο ἀπὸ
τῶν περὶ τὰ τέκνα καὶ τὰς γυναῖκας νενομοθετη-
1263 a μένων· λέγω [δὲ τὰ περὶ τὴν κτῆσιν][3] πότερον,
κἂν ᾖ ἐκεῖνα χωρὶς καθ' ὃν νῦν τρόπον ἔχει πᾶσι,
τάς τε κτήσεις κοινὰς εἶναι βέλτιον καὶ τὰς
χρήσεις . . .,[4] οἷον τὰ μὲν γήπεδα χωρὶς τοὺς δὲ
5 καρποὺς εἰς τὸ κοινὸν φέροντας ἀναλίσκειν (ὅπερ
ἔνια ποιεῖ τῶν ἐθνῶν), ἢ τοὐναντίον τὴν μὲν γῆν
κοινὴν εἶναι καὶ γεωργεῖν κοινῇ, τοὺς δὲ καρποὺς
διαιρεῖσθαι πρὸς τὰς ἰδίας χρήσεις (λέγονται δέ
τινες καὶ τοῦτον τὸν τρόπον κοινωνεῖν τῶν βαρβάρων), ἢ καὶ τὰ γήπεδα καὶ τοὺς καρποὺς κοινούς.
ἑτέρων μὲν οὖν ὄντων τῶν γεωργούντων ἄλλος ἂν 2
10 εἴη τρόπος καὶ ῥάων, αὐτῶν δ' αὑτοῖς διαπονούν-
των τὰ περὶ τὰς κτήσεις πλείους ἂν παρέχοι
δυσκολίας· καὶ γὰρ ἐν ταῖς ἀπολαύσεσι καὶ ἐν τοῖς
ἔργοις μὴ γινομένων ἴσων ἀναγκαῖον ἐγκλήματα

---

[1] τοὺς φύλακας hic Guil.: ante οἵ τε codd. (om. MP).
[2] τοὺς ΓΜΡ: εἰς τοὺς cet.
[3] Susemihl.   [4] lacunam Busse.

---

[a] Something has clearly been lost here, signifying 'or
should there be some limited form of communism?'

84

of the Guardians as brothers and children and fathers and mothers, nor yet will those living among the Guardians so speak of the other classes, so as to be careful not to commit any such offence because of their relationship.

Such therefore may be our decision as to community of children and women.

II. In connexion with this we have to consider the due regulation of property in a community that is to have the best political institutions : should property be owned in common or privately ? This question might indeed be considered separately from the system laid down by law with regard to the children and the women : I mean, even if there be separate families as is now the case with all nations, is it better for both the ownership and the employment of property to be in common . . .,[a] for example, should the farms be separate property but the farm-produce be brought into the common stock for consumption (as is the practice with some non-Greek races) ; or on the contrary should the land be common and farmed in common, but the produce be divided for private use (and this form of communism also is said to prevail among some of the barbarians) ; or should both farms and produce be common property ? Now if the tillers of the soil be of a different class [b] it would work differently and be easier, but if the citizens do the work for themselves, the regulations for the common ownership of property would give more causes for discontent ; for if both in the enjoyment of the produce and in the work of production they prove not equal but unequal, complaints are

(b) nor is unity secured by communism of property : various forms of this.

Under-work and over-consumption.

[a] As in Plato's *Republic*, or like the Helots at Sparta.

1263 a

γίνεσθαι πρὸς τοὺς ἀπολαύοντας μὲν ἢ λαμβάνοντας πολλὰ ὀλίγα δὲ πονοῦντας τοῖς ἐλάττω
15 μὲν λαμβάνουσι πλείω δὲ πονοῦσιν. ὅλως δὲ τὸ
συζῆν καὶ κοινωνεῖν τῶν ἀνθρωπικῶν πάντων
χαλεπόν, καὶ μάλιστα τῶν τοιούτων. δηλοῦσι δ'
αἱ τῶν συναποδήμων κοινωνίαι, σχεδὸν γὰρ οἱ
πλεῖστοι διαφέρονται[1] ἐκ τῶν ἐν ποσὶ καὶ ἐκ
μικρῶν προσκρούοντες ἀλλήλοις· ἔτι δὲ τῶν θερα-
20 πόντων τούτοις μάλιστα προσκρούομεν οἷς πλεῖστα
προσχρώμεθα πρὸς τὰς διακονίας τὰς ἐγκυκλίους.
τὸ μὲν οὖν κοινὰς εἶναι τὰς κτήσεις ταύτας τε καὶ
ἄλλας τοιαύτας ἔχει δυσχερείας, ὃν δὲ νῦν τρόπον
ἔχει καὶ[2] ἐπικοσμηθὲν ἤθεσι καὶ τάξει νόμων ὀρθῶν
οὐ μικρὸν ἂν διενέγκαι· ἕξει γὰρ τὸ ἐξ ἀμφοτέρων
25 ἀγαθόν, λέγω δὲ τὸ ἐξ ἀμφοτέρων τὸ ἐκ τοῦ
κοινὰς εἶναι τὰς κτήσεις καὶ τὸ ἐκ τοῦ ἰδίας. δεῖ
γὰρ πῶς μὲν εἶναι κοινάς, ὅλως δ' ἰδίας. αἱ μὲν
γὰρ ἐπιμέλειαι διῃρημέναι τὰ ἐγκλήματα πρὸς
ἀλλήλους οὐ ποιήσουσιν, μᾶλλον δ'[3] ἐπιδώσουσιν
ὡς πρὸς ἴδιον ἑκάστου προσεδρεύοντος· δι' ἀρετὴν
30 δ' ἔσται πρὸς τὸ χρῆσθαι κατὰ τὴν παροιμίαν
κοινὰ τὰ φίλων. ἔστι δὲ καὶ νῦν τὸν τρόπον τοῦτον
ἐν ἐνίαις πόλεσιν οὕτως ὑπογεγραμμένον ὡς οὐκ
ὂν ἀδύνατον, καὶ μάλιστα ἐν ταῖς καλῶς οἰκου-
μέναις τὰ μὲν ἔστι τὰ δὲ γένοιτ' ἄν· ἰδίαν γὰρ
35 ἕκαστος τὴν κτῆσιν ἔχων τὰ μὲν χρήσιμα ποιεῖ
τοῖς φίλοις τοῖς δὲ χρῆται κοινοῖς,[4] οἷον καὶ ἐν

---

[1] διαφέρονται Coraes: διαφερόμενοι codd.
[2] καὶ om. ΓΜΡ¹Η.
[3] τε ? Susemihl.
[4] κοινοῖς cum 36 ἰδίοις transponendum ? Richards.

• The saying was ascribed to Pythagoras.

bound to arise between those who enjoy or take
much but work little and those who take less but
3 work more. And in general to live together and
share all our human affairs is difficult, and especially to share such things as these. And this is shown
in the partnerships of fellow-travellers, for it may
be said that most of them quarrel because thay
come into collision with one another as a result
of ordinary matters and trifles ; and also we come
into collision most with those of our servants whom
we employ most often for ordinary attendance.
4 Community of property therefore involves these
and other similar difficulties ; and the present system, *Private
if further improved by good morals and by the property
regulation of correct legislation, would be greatly and friendly
superior. For it will possess the merit of both interchange
preferable.*
systems, by which I mean the advantage of property
being common and the advantage of its being private.
For property ought to be common in a sense but
private speaking generally. For the superintendence of properties being divided among the owners
will not cause these mutual complaints, and will
improve the more because each will apply himself
to it as to private business of his own ; while on the
other hand virtue will result in making 'friends'
goods common goods,' as the proverb *a* goes, for the
5 purpose of use. Such a system exists even now
in outline in some states, so it is not deemed impracticable, and especially in the ones that are well-
administered parts of it are realized already and
parts might be realized; for individuals while owning
their property privately put their own possessions
at the service of their friends and make use of their
friends' possessions as common property ; for in-

1263 a

Λακεδαίμονι τοῖς τε δούλοις χρῶνται τοῖς ἀλλήλων
ὡς εἰπεῖν ἰδίοις, ἔτι δ' ἵπποις καὶ κυσίν, κἂν
δεηθῶσιν ἐφοδίων ἐν τοῖς ἀγροῖς¹ κατὰ τὴν χώραν.²
φανερὸν τοίνυν ὅτι βέλτιον εἶναι μὲν ἰδίας τὰς
κτήσεις τῇ δὲ χρήσει ποιεῖν κοινάς· ὅπως δὲ
40 γίνωνται τοιοῦτοι, τοῦ νομοθέτου τοῦτ' ἔργον
ἴδιόν ἐστιν. ἔτι δὲ καὶ πρὸς ἡδονὴν ἀμύθητον
ὅσον διαφέρει τὸ νομίζειν ἴδιόν τι· μὴ γὰρ οὐ
1263 b μάτην τὴν πρὸς αὑτὸν αὐτὸς ἔχει φιλίαν ἕκαστος
ἀλλ' ἔστι τοῦτο φυσικόν. τὸ δὲ φίλαυτον εἶναι
ψέγεται δικαίως· οὐκ ἔστι δὲ τοῦτο τὸ φιλεῖν
ἑαυτὸν ἀλλὰ τὸ μᾶλλον ἢ δεῖ φιλεῖν, καθάπερ καὶ
τὸν φιλοχρήματον, ἐπεὶ φιλοῦσί γε πάντες ὡς
5 εἰπεῖν ἕκαστον τῶν τοιούτων. ἀλλὰ μὴν καὶ τὸ
χαρίσασθαι καὶ βοηθῆσαι φίλοις ἢ ξένοις ἢ ἑταίροις
ἥδιστον· ὃ γίνεται τῆς κτήσεως ἰδίας οὔσης.
ταῦτά τε δὴ οὐ συμβαίνει τοῖς λίαν ἓν ποιοῦσι τὴν
πόλιν, καὶ πρὸς τούτοις ἀναιροῦσιν ἔργα δυοῖν
ἀρεταῖν φανερῶς, σωφροσύνης μὲν τὸ περὶ τὰς
10 γυναῖκας (ἔργον γὰρ καλὸν ἀλλοτρίας οὔσης ἀπ-
έχεσθαι διὰ σωφροσύνην), ἐλευθεριότητος δὲ τὸ
περὶ τὰς κτήσεις (οὔτε γὰρ ἔσται φανερὸς ἐλευ-
θέριος ὢν οὔτε πράξει πρᾶξιν ἐλευθέριον οὐδεμίαν·
ἐν γὰρ τῇ χρήσει τῶν κτημάτων τὸ τῆς ἐλευθεριότητος ἔργον ἐστίν).

15 Εὐπρόσωπος μὲν οὖν ἡ τοιαύτη νομοθεσία, καὶ
φιλάνθρωπος ἂν εἶναι δόξειεν· ὁ γὰρ ἀκροώμενος
ἄσμενος ἀποδέχεται, νομίζων ἔσεσθαι φιλίαν τινὰ
θαυμαστὴν πᾶσι πρὸς ἅπαντας, ἄλλως τε καὶ ὅταν

---

¹ ταῖς ἀγραῖς Busse.   ² θήραν Buecheler.

stance in Sparta people use one another's slaves as
virtually their own, as well as horses and hounds,
and also use the produce in the fields throughout the
country if they need provisions on a journey. It
is clear therefore that it is better for possessions to
be privately owned, but to make them common
property in use ; and to train the citizens to this is
the special task of the legislator. And moreover
to feel that a thing is one's private property makes
an inexpressibly great difference in one's pleasure ;
for the universal feeling of love for oneself is surely
not purposeless, but a natural instinct. Selfishness
on the other hand is justly blamed ; but this is
not to love oneself but to love oneself more than one
ought, just as covetousness means loving money to
excess—since some love of self, money and so on is
practically universal. Moreover, to bestow favours
and assistance on friends or visitors or comrades is
a great pleasure, and a condition of this is the private
ownership of property. These advantages therefore (c) Communism
do not come to those who carry the unification of the would destroy temperance and
state too far ; and in addition to this they manifestly liberality
do away with the practice of two virtues, temperance but not litigiousness
in relation to women (for it is a noble deed to refrain and
from one through temperance when she belongs to covetousness.
another) and liberality in relation to possessions (for
one will not be able to show one's liberality nor perform a single liberal action, since the active exercise
of liberality takes place in the use of possessions).

Such legislation therefore has an attractive appear-
ance, and might be thought to be humane ; for he
who is told about it welcomes it with gladness,
thinking that it will result in a marvellous friendliness
of everybody towards everybody, especially when

1263 b

20 κατηγορῇ τις τῶν νῦν ὑπαρχόντων ἐν ταῖς πολιτείαις κακῶν ὡς γινομένων διὰ τὸ μὴ κοινὴν εἶναι τὴν οὐσίαν, λέγω δὲ δίκας τε πρὸς ἀλλήλους περὶ συμβολαίων καὶ ψευδομαρτυριῶν κρίσεις καὶ πλουσίων κολακείας. ὧν οὐδὲν γίνεται διὰ τὴν ἀκοινωνησίαν ἀλλὰ διὰ τὴν μοχθηρίαν, ἐπεὶ καὶ τοὺς κοινὰ κεκτημένους καὶ κοινωνοῦντας πολλῷ
25 διαφερομένους μᾶλλον ὁρῶμεν ἢ τοὺς χωρὶς τὰς οὐσίας ἔχοντας· ἀλλὰ θεωροῦμεν ὀλίγους τοὺς ἐκ τῶν κοινωνιῶν διαφερομένους πρὸς πολλοὺς συμβάλλοντες τοὺς κεκτημένους ἰδίᾳ τὰς κτήσεις. ἔτι δὲ δίκαιον μὴ μόνον λέγειν ὅσων στερήσονται κακῶν κοινωνήσαντες, ἀλλὰ καὶ ὅσων ἀγαθῶν· φαίνεται δ' εἶναι πάμπαν ἀδύνατος ὁ βίος.

30 Αἴτιον δὲ τῷ Σωκράτει τῆς παρακρούσεως χρὴ νομίζειν τὴν ὑπόθεσιν οὐκ οὖσαν ὀρθήν. δεῖ μὲν γὰρ εἶναί πως μίαν καὶ τὴν οἰκίαν καὶ τὴν πόλιν, ἀλλ' οὐ πάντως. ἔστι μὲν γὰρ ὡς οὐκ ἔσται προϊοῦσα πόλις, ἔστι δ' ὡς ἔσται μέν, ἐγγὺς δ' οὖσα τοῦ μὴ πόλις εἶναι[1] χείρων πόλις, ὥσπερ κἂν
5 εἴ τις τὴν συμφωνίαν ποιήσειεν ὁμοφωνίαν ἢ τὸν ῥυθμὸν βάσιν μίαν. ἀλλὰ δεῖ πλῆθος ὄν, ὥσπερ εἴρηται πρότερον, διὰ τὴν παιδείαν[2] κοινὴν καὶ μίαν ποιεῖν· καὶ τόν γε μέλλοντα παιδείαν εἰσάγειν, καὶ νομίζοντα διὰ ταύτης ἔσεσθαι τὴν πόλιν σπουδαίαν, ἄτοπον τοῖς τοιούτοις οἴεσθαι διορθοῦν,[3]
40 ἀλλὰ μὴ τοῖς ἔθεσι καὶ τῇ φιλοσοφίᾳ καὶ τοῖς νόμοις, ὥσπερ τὰ περὶ τὰς κτήσεις ἐν Λακεδαίμονι

---

[1] εἶναι ⟨ἔσται⟩ Victorius.
[2] τῆς παιδείας (cf. 38) ? Richards.
[3] ⟨δεῖν⟩ διορθοῦν ? Richards.

somebody denounces the evils at present existing in states as due to the fact that wealth is not owned in common—I mean lawsuits between citizens about breach of contract, and trials for perjury, and the flattery of the rich. But the real cause of all these evils is not the absence of communism, but wickedness, since we see far more quarrels occurring among those who own or use property in common than among those who have their estates separate; but we notice that those who quarrel as a result of their partnerships are few when compared with the total number of private owners. And again it is just to state not only all the evils that men will lose by adopting communism, but also all the good things; and life in such circumstances is seen to be utterly impossible.

The cause of Socrates' error must be deemed to be that his fundamental assumption was incorrect. It is certain that in a way both the household and the state should be a unit, but they should not be so in every way. For in one way the state as its unification proceeds will cease to be a state, and in another way, though it continues a state, yet by coming near to ceasing to be one it will be a worse state, just as if one turned a harmony into unison or a rhythm into a single foot. The proper thing is for the state, while being a multitude, to be made a partnership and a unity by means of education, as has been said before; and it is strange that the very philosopher who intends to introduce a system of education and thinks that this will make the city morally good should fancy that he can regulate society by such measures as have been mentioned instead of by manners and culture and laws, just as the legislator introduced

(d) General notes: unity is formed by education; communism has never been untried.

1261 a 18.

91

1264 a καὶ Κρήτῃ τοῖς συσσιτίοις ὁ νομοθέτης ἐκοίνωσεν.
δεῖ δὲ μηδὲ τοῦτο αὐτὸ[1] ἀγνοεῖν, ὅτι χρὴ προσέχειν
τῷ πολλῷ χρόνῳ καὶ τοῖς πολλοῖς ἔτεσιν,[2] ἐν οἷς
οὐκ ἂν ἔλαθεν εἰ ταῦτα καλῶς εἶχεν· πάντα γὰρ
σχεδὸν εὕρηται μέν, ἀλλὰ τὰ μὲν οὐ συνῆκται τοῖς
5 δ᾽ οὐ χρῶνται γινώσκοντες. μάλιστα δ᾽ ἂν γένοιτο
φανερὸν εἴ τις τοῖς ἔργοις ἴδοι τὴν τοιαύτην πολιτείαν κατασκευαζομένην· οὐ γὰρ δυνήσεται μὴ
μερίζων αὐτὰ καὶ χωρίζων ποιῆσαι τὴν πόλιν, τὰ
μὲν εἰς συσσίτια τὰ δὲ εἰς φρατρίας καὶ φυλάς.
ὥστε οὐδὲν ἄλλο συμβήσεται νενομοθετημένον πλὴν
10 μὴ γεωργεῖν τοὺς φύλακας· ὅπερ καὶ νῦν Λακεδαιμόνιοι ποιεῖν ἐπιχειροῦσιν.

Οὐ μὴν ἀλλ᾽ οὐδὲ ὁ τρόπος τῆς ὅλης πολιτείας
τίς ἔσται τοῖς κοινωνοῦσιν οὔτ᾽ εἴρηκεν ὁ Σωκράτης
οὔτε ῥᾴδιον εἰπεῖν. καίτοι σχεδὸν τό γε πλῆθος[3]
τῆς πόλεως τὸ τῶν ἄλλων πολιτῶν γίνεται πλῆθος,
15 περὶ ὧν οὐδὲν διώρισται, πότερον καὶ τοῖς γεωργοῖς
κοινὰς εἶναι δεῖ τὰς κτήσεις ἢ καὶ[4] καθ᾽ ἕκαστον
ἰδίας, ἔτι δὲ καὶ γυναῖκας καὶ παῖδας ἰδίους ἢ
κοινούς. εἰ μὲν γὰρ τὸν αὐτὸν τρόπον κοινὰ πάντα
πάντων, τί διοίσουσιν οὗτοι ἐκείνων τῶν φυλάκων; ἢ τί πλεῖον αὐτοῖς[5] ὑπομένουσι τὴν ἀρχὴν
20 αὐτῶν; ἢ τί μαθόντες ὑπομενοῦσι τὴν ἀρχήν, ἐὰν

---

[1] αὐτὸν ? Richards.   [2] ἔθεσιν. Ar., ἔθνεσιν Bernays.
[3] πλήρωμα ? Richards.   [4] καὶ secl. Susemihl.
[5] Richards : τοῖς codd. (τοῖς ἔχουσι τὴν Greenwood).

community of property in Sparta and Crete by the institution of public messes. And this very point also must not be ignored, that attention must be paid to length of time and to the long period of years, in which it would not have escaped notice if these measures were good ones; for nearly all of them have been discovered already, although some of them have not been collected together and others though brought to knowledge are not put into practice. 11 And their value would become most manifest if one could see such a constitution in actual process of formation; for one will only be able to construct Plato's state by introducing its partitions and dividing up the community into common messes and also into brotherhoods and tribes. So that in the upshot no other regulation will have been enacted except the exemption of the Guardians from the work of agriculture, which is a measure that even now the Spartans attempt to introduce.

Moreover, the working of the constitution as a whole in regard to the members of the state has also not been described by Socrates, nor is it easy to say what it will be. Yet the general mass of the citizens of the other classes make almost the bulk of the state, and about these no definite regulations are laid down, as to whether the Farmers also are to have their property in common or to hold it in private ownership, and also whether community of wives and 12 children is to apply to them or not. For if the Farmers are to have the same complete communism, what will be the difference between them and the Guardian class? or what advantage will they gain by submitting to their government? or what consideration will induce them to submit to the government, unless

(3) Plato's system incomplete. Does communism apply to the Farmers? Objections either way.

93

1264 a

μή τι σοφίζωνται τοιοῦτον οἷον Κρῆτες; ἐκεῖνοι
γὰρ τἆλλα ταὐτὰ τοῖς δούλοις ἐφέντες μόνον ἀπ-
ειρήκασι τὰ γυμνάσια καὶ τὴν τῶν ὅπλων κτῆσιν.
εἰ δὲ καθάπερ ἐν ταῖς ἄλλαις πόλεσι καὶ παρ'
ἐκείνοις ἔσται τὰ τοιαῦτα, τίς ὁ τρόπος ἔσται τῆς
25 κοινωνίας; ἐν μιᾷ γὰρ πόλει δύο πόλεις ἀναγκαῖον
εἶναι, καὶ ταύτας ὑπεναντίας ἀλλήλαις. ποιεῖ γὰρ
τοὺς μὲν φύλακας οἷον φρουρούς, τοὺς δὲ γεωργοὺς
καὶ τοὺς¹ τεχνίτας καὶ τοὺς ἄλλους πολίτας.
ἐγκλήματα δὲ καὶ δίκαι καὶ ὅσα ἄλλα ταῖς πόλεσιν 1
ὑπάρχειν φησὶ κακὰ πάνθ' ὑπάρξει καὶ τούτοις.
30 καίτοι λέγει ὁ Σωκράτης ὡς οὐ πολλῶν δεήσονται
νομίμων διὰ τὴν παιδείαν οἷον ἀστυνομικῶν καὶ
ἀγορανομικῶν καὶ τῶν ἄλλων τῶν τοιούτων, ἀπο-
διδοὺς μόνον τὴν παιδείαν τοῖς φύλαξιν. ἔτι δὲ
κυρίους ποιεῖ τῶν κτημάτων τοὺς γεωργοὺς ἀπο-
φορὰν φέροντας· ἀλλὰ πολὺ μᾶλλον εἰκὸς εἶναι
35 χαλεποὺς καὶ φρονημάτων πλήρεις ἢ τὰς παρ'
ἐνίοις εἱλωτείας τε καὶ πενεστείας καὶ δουλείας.
ἀλλὰ γὰρ εἴτ' ἀναγκαῖα ταῦθ' ὁμοίως εἴτε μή, νῦν 1
γ' οὐδὲν διώρισται, καὶ περὶ τῶν ἐχομένων, τίς ἡ
τούτων τε πολιτεία καὶ παιδεία καὶ νόμοι τίνες.
ἔστι δ' οὔθ' εὑρεῖν ῥᾴδιον, οὔτε τὸ διαφέρον μικρόν,
40 τὸ ποιούς τινας εἶναι² τούτους πρὸς τὸ σῴζεσθαι
1264 b τὴν τῶν φυλάκων κοινωνίαν. ἀλλὰ μὴν εἴ γε τὰς
μὲν γυναῖκας ποιήσει κοινὰς τὰς δὲ κτήσεις ἰδίας,

---

¹ [τοὺς] ? ed.   ² ποίους τινὰς εἶναι ⟨δεῖ⟩ Scaliger.

ᵃ Or (omitting τοὺς before τεχνίτας) 'For Socrates makes
one set of men guardians, a sort of garrison, and another
set farmers and artisans and citizens of the other sorts.'

94

the Guardians adopt some clever device like that of the Cretans ? These have conceded to their slaves all the same rights as they have themselves except that they are forbidden gymnastic exercises and the possession of arms. But if the family life and property of the Farmers are to be such as they are in other states, what will be the form of their community ? There will inevitably be two states in one, and these antagonistic to one another. For Socrates makes the Guardians a sort of garrison, while the Farmers,

3 Artisans and other classes are the citizens.[a] But quarrels and lawsuits and all the other evils which according to Socrates exist in actual states will all be found among his citizens too. Yet he says that owing to their education they will not need many regulations such as city and market by-laws and the other regulations of that sort, although he assigns his education only to the Guardians. Again, he makes the Farmers the masters of the estates, for which they pay rent ; but they are likely to be far more unmanageable and rebellious than the classes of helots, serfs and slaves in certain states to-day.

14 However, whether this communism is to be compulsory for the Farmers in the same way as for the Guardians or whether it is not, has as a matter of fact not been definitely stated anywhere, nor is there any information about the connected questions, what are to be the political functions and the education of the lower classes, and the laws affecting them. But it is not easy to discover the answers to these questions, yet the character of the lower classes is of no small importance for the preservation of the community of the Guardians. But again, if Socrates intends to make the Farmers have their wives in

95

1264 b

τίς οἰκονομήσει ὥσπερ τὰ ἐπὶ τῶν ἀγρῶν οἱ ἄνδρες
αὐτῶν; κἂν εἰ κοιναὶ αἱ κτήσεις καὶ αἱ τῶν
γεωργῶν γυναῖκες . . . .[1]

Ἄτοπον δὲ καὶ τὸ ἐκ τῶν θηρίων ποιεῖσθαι τὴν
5 παραβολήν, ὅτι δεῖ τὰ αὐτὰ ἐπιτηδεύειν τὰς
γυναῖκας τοῖς ἀνδράσιν, οἷς οἰκονομίας οὐδὲν μέτεστιν. ἐπισφαλὲς δὲ καὶ τοὺς ἄρχοντας ὡς καθίστησιν ὁ Σωκράτης· ἀεὶ γὰρ ποιεῖ τοὺς αὐτοὺς
ἄρχοντας, τοῦτο δὲ στάσεως αἴτιον γίνεται καὶ
παρὰ τοῖς μηδὲν ἀξίωμα κεκτημένοις, ἦ που δῆθεν[2]
10 παρά γε θυμοειδέσι καὶ πολεμικοῖς ἀνδράσιν. ὅτι
δ᾽ ἀναγκαῖον αὐτῷ ποιεῖν τοὺς αὐτοὺς ἄρχοντας
φανερόν, οὐ γὰρ ὁτὲ μὲν ἄλλοις ὁτὲ δὲ ἄλλοις
μέμικται ταῖς ψυχαῖς ὁ παρὰ τοῦ θεοῦ χρυσός,
ἀλλ᾽ ἀεὶ τοῖς αὐτοῖς, φησὶ δὲ τοῖς μὲν εὐθὺ γινο-
μένοις μῖξαι χρυσόν, τοῖς δ᾽ ἄργυρον, χαλκὸν δὲ
15 καὶ σίδηρον τοῖς τεχνίταις μέλλουσιν ἔσεσθαι καὶ
γεωργοῖς. ἔτι δὲ καὶ τὴν εὐδαιμονίαν ἀφαιρούμενος
τῶν φυλάκων, ὅλην φησὶ δεῖν εὐδαίμονα ποιεῖν τὴν
πόλιν τὸν νομοθέτην. ἀδύνατον δὲ εὐδαιμονεῖν
ὅλην, μὴ τῶν πλείστων ἢ[3] μὴ πάντων μερῶν ἢ
τινῶν ἐχόντων τὴν εὐδαιμονίαν. οὐ γὰρ τῶν
20 αὐτῶν τὸ εὐδαιμονεῖν ὧνπερ τὸ ἄρτιον· τοῦτο μὲν
γὰρ ἐνδέχεται τῷ ὅλῳ ὑπάρχειν τῶν δὲ μερῶν
μηδετέρῳ, τὸ δὲ εὐδαιμονεῖν ἀδύνατον. ἀλλὰ μὴν
εἰ οἱ φύλακες μὴ εὐδαίμονες, τίνες ἕτεροι; οὐ γὰρ
δὴ οἵ γε τεχνῖται καὶ τὸ πλῆθος τὸ τῶν βαναύσων.

---

[1] lacunam Thurot.
[2] ἦ που δῆθεν Goettling : ἤπουθεν δὴ, εἴπουθεν δὴ codd.
[3] εἰ Victorius.

---

[a] A passage has been lost here.

common but their property private, who is to manage the household in the way in which the women's husbands will carry on the work of the farms ? And if the property and the wives of the Farmers are to be common . . .*a*

It is also strange that Socrates employs the comparison of the lower animals to show that the women are to have the same occupations as the men, considering that animals have no households to manage. Also Socrates' method of appointing the magistrates is not a safe one. For he makes the same persons hold office always ; but this occasions rebellion even among people of no special distinction, much more so then among high-spirited and warlike men. But it is clear that he is compelled to make the same persons govern always, for the god-given admixture of gold in the soul is not bestowed on some at one time and others at another time, but is always in the same men, and Socrates says that at the moment of birth some men receive an admixture of gold and others of silver and those who are to be the Artisans and Farmers an admixture of copper and iron. And again, although he deprives the Guardians of happiness, he says that it is the duty of the lawgiver to make the whole city happy. But it is not possible for the whole to be happy unless most or all of its parts, or some of them, possess happiness. For happiness is not a thing of the same sort as being an even number : that may belong to a whole but not to either of its parts, but happiness cannot belong to the whole and not to its parts. But yet, if the Guardians are not happy, what other class is ? For clearly the Artisans and the general mass of the vulgar classes are not.

(4) Minor objections.

What class will be happy ?

1264 b

Ἡ μὲν οὖν πολιτεία περὶ ἧς ὁ Σωκράτης εἴρηκεν
25 ταύτας τε τὰς ἀπορίας ἔχει καὶ τούτων οὐκ
ἐλάττους ἑτέρας.

III. Σχεδὸν δὲ παραπλησίως καὶ περὶ τοὺς 1
Νόμους ἔχει τοὺς ὕστερον γραφέντας, διὸ καὶ περὶ
τῆς ἐνταῦθα πολιτείας ἐπισκέψασθαι μικρὰ βέλτιον.
καὶ γὰρ ἐν τῇ Πολιτείᾳ περὶ ὀλίγων πάμπαν
30 διώρικεν ὁ Σωκράτης, περί τε γυναικῶν καὶ τέκνων
κοινωνίας, πῶς ἔχειν δεῖ, καὶ περὶ κτήσεως, καὶ
τῆς πολιτείας τὴν τάξιν (διαιρεῖται γὰρ εἰς δύο
μέρη τὸ πλῆθος τῶν οἰκούντων, τὸ μὲν εἰς τοὺς
γεωργοὺς τὸ δὲ εἰς τὸ προπολεμοῦν μέρος, τρίτον
δ' ἐκ τούτων τὸ βουλευόμενον καὶ κύριον τῆς
πόλεως), περὶ δὲ τῶν γεωργῶν καὶ τῶν τεχνιτῶν,
35 πότερον οὐδεμιᾶς ἢ μετέχουσί τινος ἀρχῆς, καὶ
πότερον ὅπλα δεῖ κεκτῆσθαι καὶ τούτους καὶ
συμπολεμεῖν ἢ μή, περὶ τούτων οὐδὲν διώρικεν ὁ
Σωκράτης, ἀλλὰ τὰς μὲν γυναῖκας οἴεται δεῖν
συμπολεμεῖν καὶ παιδείας μετέχειν τῆς αὐτῆς τοῖς
φύλαξιν, τὰ δ' ἄλλα τοῖς ἔξωθεν λόγοις πεπλήρωκε
40 τὸν λόγον καὶ[1] περὶ τῆς παιδείας, ποίαν τινὰ δεῖ
1265 a γίνεσθαι τῶν φυλάκων. τῶν δὲ Νόμων τὸ μὲν 2
πλεῖστον μέρος νόμοι τυγχάνουσιν ὄντες, ὀλίγα δὲ
περὶ τῆς πολιτείας εἴρηκεν, καὶ ταύτην βουλόμενος
κοινοτέραν ποιεῖν ταῖς πόλεσι κατὰ μικρὸν περιάγει
5 πάλιν πρὸς τὴν ἑτέραν Πολιτείαν. ἔξω γὰρ τῆς
τῶν γυναικῶν κοινωνίας καὶ τῆς κτήσεως, τὰ
ἄλλα ταὐτὰ ἀποδίδωσιν ἀμφοτέραις ταῖς πολιτείαις·

---

[1] καὶ—φυλάκων supra post 30 κτήσεως Susemihl.

---

[a] The last clause, 'and about—to have,' has almost certainly been misplaced by a copyist, and should come near the beginning of the sentence, after 'about property.'

The republic discussed by Socrates therefore possesses these difficulties and also others not smaller than these.

1 III. And almost the same holds good of *Laws* also, which was written later, so that it will be advantageous to make some small examination of the constitution described in that book as well. For in *The Republic* Socrates has laid down details about very few matters—regulations about community of wives and children and about property, and the structure of the constitution (for the mass of the population is divided into two parts, one forming the Farmer class and the other the class that defends the state in war, and there is a third class drawn from these latter that forms the council and governs the state), but about the Farmers and the Artisans, whether they are excluded from government or have some part in it, and whether these classes also are to possess arms and to serve in war with the others or not, on these points Socrates has made no decision, but though he thinks that the women ought to serve in war with the Guardians and share the same education, the rest of the discourse he has filled up with external topics, and about the sort of education which 2 it is proper for the Guardians to have.[a] *Laws* on the other hand is mostly a collection of statutes, but the author has said a little about the form of the constitution, and though wishing to make this more suitable for adoption by actual states he brings it round by degrees back to the other form, that of *The Republic*. For except community in wives and property, he assigns all his other regulations in the same form to both states, for he prescribes for both

Plato's Laws; constitution comparable to that of The Republic.

1265 a

καὶ γὰρ παιδείαν τὴν αὐτήν, καὶ τὸ τῶν ἔργων
τῶν ἀναγκαίων ἀπεχομένους ζῆν, καὶ περὶ συσσιτίων ὡσαύτως, πλὴν ἐν ταύτῃ φησὶ δεῖν εἶναι
10 συσσίτια καὶ γυναικῶν, καὶ τὴν μὲν χιλίων τῶν
ὅπλα κεκτημένων, ταύτην δὲ πεντακισχιλίων.

Τὸ μὲν οὖν περιττὸν ἔχουσι πάντες οἱ τοῦ Σω- 3
κράτους λόγοι καὶ τὸ κομψὸν καὶ τὸ καινοτόμον
καὶ τὸ ζητητικόν, καλῶς δὲ πάντα ἴσως χαλεπόν·
ἐπεὶ καὶ τὸ νῦν εἰρημένον πλῆθος δεῖ μὴ λανθάνειν
15 ὅτι χώρας δεήσει τοῖς τοσούτοις Βαβυλωνίας ἢ
τινος ἄλλης ἀπεράντου τὸ πλῆθος, ἐξ ἧς ἀργοὶ
πεντακισχίλιοι θρέψονται καὶ περὶ τούτους γυναικῶν καὶ θεραπόντων ἕτερος ὄχλος πολλαπλάσιος.
δεῖ μὲν οὖν ὑποτίθεσθαι κατ' εὐχήν, μηδὲν μέντοι
ἀδύνατον. λέγεται δ' ὡς δεῖ τὸν νομοθέτην πρὸς 4
20 δύο βλέποντα τιθέναι τοὺς νόμους, πρός τε τὴν
χώραν καὶ τοὺς ἀνθρώπους. ἔτι δὲ καλῶς ἔχει
προσθεῖναι καὶ πρὸς τοὺς γειτνιῶντας τόπους,
εἰ δεῖ τὴν πόλιν ζῆν βίον πολιτικόν[1] (οὐ γὰρ μόνον
ἀναγκαῖόν ἐστιν αὐτὴν τοιούτοις χρῆσθαι πρὸς τὸν
πόλεμον ὅπλοις ἃ χρήσιμα κατὰ τὴν οἰκείαν χώραν
25 ἐστὶν ἀλλὰ καὶ πρὸς τοὺς ἔξω τόπους)· εἰ δέ τις
μὴ τοιοῦτον ἀποδέχεται βίον μήτε τὸν ἴδιον μήτε
τὸν κοινὸν τῆς πόλεως, ὅμως οὐδὲν ἧττον δεῖ
φοβεροὺς εἶναι τοῖς πολεμίοις μὴ μόνον ἐλθοῦσιν
εἰς τὴν χώραν ἀλλὰ καὶ ἀπελθοῦσιν.[2] καὶ τὸ 5

---

[1] πολιτικὸν μὴ μονωτικόν codd. plerique.
[2] ἀπ[ελθ]οῦσιν Bender.

---

[a] A euphemism for an aggressive policy, cf. 1327 b 5.
Some mss. add ' not one of isolation '; this looks like an
explanatory note interpolated.
[b] Perhaps the Greek should be altered to give ' when they
are away from it.'

the same scheme of education, and a life detached from menial tasks, and similarly as regards common meals, except that in the state described in *Laws* he says there are to be common meals for women also, and he makes the Republic consist of a class possessing arms that numbers a thousand, but the state of *Laws* has five thousand.

3 Now it is true that all the discourses of Socrates possess brilliance, cleverness, originality and keenness of inquiry, but it is no doubt difficult to be right about everything : for instance with regard to the size of population just mentioned it must not be overlooked that a territory as large as that of Babylon will be needed for so many inhabitants, or some other country of unlimited extent, to support five thousand men in idleness and another swarm of women and servants around them many times as numerous. It is proper no doubt to assume ideal conditions, but 4 not to go beyond all bounds of possibility. And it is said that in laying down the laws the legislator must have his attention fixed on two things, the territory and the population. But also it would be well to add that he must take into account the neighbouring regions also, if the city is to live a life of active policy,*a* as it will have to use for war not only such arms as are serviceable within its own territory but also such as are serviceable against places outside it ; and if one does not accept such a description whether for the life of the individual or for the common life of the state, yet it is none the less necessary for the citizens to be formidable to their enemies not only when they have entered 5 the country but also when they have left it.*b* Also

Marginal notes: Criticism. Large population needs vast territory. / Neighbouring powers ignored.

1265 a

πλῆθος δὲ τῆς κτήσεως ὁρᾶν δεῖ, μήποτε βέλτιον
ἑτέρως διορίσαι τῷ σαφῶς μᾶλλον· τοσαύτην γὰρ
30 εἶναί φησι δεῖν ὥστε ζῆν σωφρόνως, ὥσπερ ἂν εἴ
τις εἶπεν ὥστε ζῆν εὖ· τοῦτο δ᾽ ἄρ᾽[1] ἐστὶ καθόλου
μᾶλλον, ἐπειδὴ[2] ἔστι σωφρόνως μὲν ταλαιπώρως
δὲ ζῆν. ἀλλὰ βελτίων ὅρος τὸ σωφρόνως κα[ὶ]
ἐλευθερίως (χωρὶς γὰρ ἑκάτερον τὸ μὲν τῷ τρυφᾶ[ν]
ἀκολουθήσει, τὸ δὲ τῷ ἐπιπόνως), ἐπεὶ μόναι γ[ε]
35 εἰσὶν ἕξεις αἱρεταὶ[3] περὶ τὴν τῆς οὐσίας χρῆσι[ν]
αὗται, οἷον οὐσίᾳ πράως ἢ ἀνδρείως χρῆσθαι οὐκ
ἔστιν, σωφρόνως δὲ καὶ ἐλευθερίως ἔστιν, ὥστε
καὶ τὰς ἕξεις[4] ἀναγκαῖον περὶ αὐτὴν εἶναι ταύτας.
ἄτοπον δὲ καὶ τὸ τὰς κτήσεις ἰσάζοντα τὸ περ[ὶ]
40 τὸ πλῆθος τῶν πολιτῶν μὴ κατασκευάζειν, ἀλλ[ὰ]
ἀφεῖναι τὴν τεκνοποιίαν ἀόριστον ὡς ἱκανῶς
1265 b ἀνομαλισθησομένην εἰς τὸ αὐτὸ πλῆθος διὰ τὰς
ἀτεκνίας ὁσωνοῦν γεννωμένων, ὅτι δοκεῖ τοῦτο
καὶ νῦν συμβαίνειν περὶ τὰς πόλεις. δεῖ δὲ
τοῦτ᾽ οὐχ ὁμοίως ἀκριβῶς ἔχειν περὶ τὰς πόλεις[5]
τότε καὶ νῦν· νῦν μὲν γὰρ οὐδεὶς ἀπορεῖ διὰ τὸ
5 μερίζεσθαι τὰς οὐσίας εἰς ὁποσονοῦν πλῆθος, τότε
δ᾽ ἀδιαιρέτων οὐσῶν ἀνάγκη τοὺς παράζυγας
μηδὲν ἔχειν, ἐάν τ᾽ ἐλάττους ὦσι τὸ πλῆθος ἐάν
τε πλείους. μᾶλλον δὲ δεῖν ὑπολάβοι τις ἂν
ὡρίσθαι τῆς οὐσίας τὴν τεκνοποιίαν, ὥστε ἀριθμοῦ
τινὸς μὴ πλείονα γεννᾶν, τοῦτο δὲ τιθέναι τὸ
πλῆθος ἀποβλέποντα πρὸς τὰς τύχας, ἂν συμβαίνῃ

---

[1] δ᾽ ἄρ᾽ ed.: γὰρ codd.
[2] ἐπειδὴ Susemihl: ἔτι δ᾽ codd.
[3] αἱρεταὶ Vettori: ἀρεταὶ codd.
[4] ἕξεις Susemihl: χρήσεις codd.
[5] [περὶ τὰς πόλεις] Bender.

the amount of property requires consideration: ^{Wealth} would it not perhaps be better to define it differently, ^{needed.} by a clearer formula? The writer says that it ought to be sufficiently large for the citizens 'to live a temperate life'—as if one were to say 'to live a good life'; but really that phrase is too general, since it is possible to live temperately yet miserably. But a better definition would be 'to live temperately and liberally' (for if the two are separated a liberal mode of life is liable to slip into luxury and a temperate one into a life of hardship), since surely these are the only desirable qualities relating to the use of wealth—for instance you cannot use wealth gently or bravely, but you can use it temperately and liberally, so that it follows that these are the qualities 6 that have to do with wealth. And it is also strange ^{Birth-} that although equalizing properties the writer does ^{control omitted.} not regulate the number of the citizens, but leaves the birth-rate uncontrolled, on the assumption that it will be sufficiently levelled up to the same total owing to childless marriages, however many children are begotten, because this seems to take place in the states at present. But this ought to be regulated much more in the supposed case than it is now, for now nobody is destitute, because estates are divided among any number, but then, as division of estates will not be allowed, the extra children will necessarily have nothing, whether they are fewer in number or 7 more. And one might think that restriction ought to be put on the birth-rate rather than on property, so as not to allow more than a certain number of children to be produced, and that in fixing their number consideration should be paid to the chances of its happening that some of the children born

1265 b

10 τελευτᾶν τινὰς τῶν γεννηθέντων, καὶ πρὸς τὴν τῶν
ἄλλων ἀτεκνίαν· τὸ δ' ἀφεῖσθαι, καθάπερ ἐν ταῖς
πλείσταις πόλεσι, πενίας ἀναγκαῖον αἴτιον γίνεσθαι
τοῖς πολίταις, ἡ δὲ πενία στάσιν ἐμποιεῖ καὶ
κακουργίαν. Φείδων μὲν οὖν ὁ Κορίνθιος, ὢν
νομοθέτης τῶν ἀρχαιοτάτων, τοὺς οἴκους ἴσους
ᾠήθη δεῖν διαμένειν καὶ τὸ πλῆθος τῶν πολιτῶν,
15 καὶ εἰ τὸ πρῶτον τοὺς κλήρους ἀνίσους εἶχον
πάντες κατὰ μέγεθος· ἐν δὲ τοῖς Νόμοις τούτοις
τοὐναντίον ἐστίν. ἀλλὰ περὶ μὲν τούτων πῶς
οἰόμεθα βέλτιον ἂν ἔχειν, λεκτέον ὕστερον· ἐλλέ-
λειπται δὲ τοῖς Νόμοις τούτοις καὶ τὰ περὶ τοὺς
ἄρχοντας, ὅπως ἔσονται διαφέροντες τῶν ἀρχο-
20 μένων· φησὶ γὰρ δεῖν, ὥσπερ ἐξ ἑτέρου τὸ
στημόνιον ἐρίου γίνεται τῆς κρόκης, οὕτω καὶ
τοὺς ἄρχοντας ἔχειν[1] πρὸς τοὺς ἀρχομένους. ἐπεὶ
δὲ τὴν πᾶσαν οὐσίαν ἐφίησι γίνεσθαι μείζονα
μέχρι πενταπλασίας, διὰ τί τοῦτ' οὐκ ἂν εἴη ἐπὶ
τῆς γῆς μέχρι τινός; καὶ τὴν τῶν οἰκοπέδων δὲ
25 διαίρεσιν δεῖ σκοπεῖν, μή ποτ' οὐ συμφέρῃ πρὸς
οἰκονομίαν· δύο γὰρ οἰκόπεδα ἑκάστῳ ἔνειμε
διελὼν χωρίς, χαλεπὸν δὲ οἰκίας δύο οἰκεῖν. ἡ δὲ
σύνταξις ὅλη βούλεται μὲν εἶναι μήτε δημοκρατία
μήτε ὀλιγαρχία, μέση δὲ τούτων ἣν καλοῦσι
πολιτείαν, ἐκ γὰρ τῶν ὁπλιτευόντων ἐστίν. εἰ
30 μὲν οὖν ὡς κοινοτάτην ταύτην κατασκευάζει ταῖς

---

[1] ed.: ἔχειν δεῖν aut δεῖ codd.

---

[a] Otherwise unknown.

[b] i.e. the estates are equal, and the number of households
fixed, but not the number of citizens.

[c] Laws 734 E f. In weaving cloth the warp (the threads
set up first) must be of strong wool, the woof (the threads
woven across the warp) must be softer.

104

may die, and to the absence of children in the other marriages; but for the matter to be left alone, as it is in most states, is bound to lead to poverty among the citizens, and poverty produces sedition and crime. The Corinthian Phidon[a] in fact, one of the most ancient lawgivers, thought that the households and the citizen population ought to remain at the same numbers, even though at the outset the estates of all were unequal in size; but in Plato's *Laws* the opposite is the case.[b] However, we must say later what we think would be a better system in these matters; but another question omitted in the *Laws* is how the rulers will be different from the classes ruled; the writer prescribes that the rulers are to stand in the same relation to the ruled as the warp of cloth stands to the woof by being made of different wool.[c] And inasmuch as he allows a man's total property to be increased up to five times its original value, for what reason should not an increase in his landed estate be allowed up to a certain point? Also it must be considered whether the proposed separation of homesteads is not inexpedient for household economy—for the writer allotted two homesteads separate from one another to each citizen; but it is difficult to manage two households.[d] And the whole constitution is intended, it is true, to be neither a democracy nor an oligarchy, but of the form intermediate between them which is termed a republic, for the government is constituted from the class that bears arms. If therefore he introduces this constitution as the one most commonly existing

Marginal notes: Difficulties as to ruling caste, and as to personal property, and farms.

Really an oligarchy.

---

[d] The object was to provide a separate establishment for a married son, *Laws* 776 A.

105

1265 b

πόλεσι τῶν ἄλλων πολιτείαν, καλῶς εἴρηκεν ἴσως,
εἰ δ᾽ ὡς ἀρίστην μετὰ τὴν πρώτην πολιτείαν, οὐ
καλῶς· τάχα γὰρ τὴν τῶν Λακώνων ἄν τις ἐπαινέσειε μᾶλλον, ἢ κἂν ἄλλην τινὰ ἀριστοκρατικω-
τέραν. ἔνιοι μὲν οὖν λέγουσιν ὡς δεῖ τὴν ἀρίστην
πολιτείαν ἐξ ἁπασῶν εἶναι τῶν πολιτειῶν μεμιγ-

35 μένην, διὸ καὶ τὴν τῶν Λακεδαιμονίων ἐπαινοῦσιν
(εἶναι γὰρ αὐτὴν οἱ μὲν ἐξ ὀλιγαρχίας καὶ μοναρχίας
καὶ δημοκρατίας φασίν, λέγοντες τὴν μὲν βασιλείαν
μοναρχίαν, τὴν δὲ τῶν γερόντων ἀρχὴν ὀλιγαρχίαν,
δημοκρατεῖσθαι δὲ κατὰ τὴν τῶν ἐφόρων ἀρχὴν

40 διὰ τὸ ἐκ τοῦ δήμου εἶναι τοὺς ἐφόρους, οἱ δὲ τὴν
μὲν ἐφορείαν εἶναι τυραννίδα, δημοκρατεῖσθαι δὲ

1266 a κατά τε τὰ συσσίτια καὶ τὸν ἄλλον βίον τὸν καθ᾽
ἡμέραν)· ἐν δὲ τοῖς Νόμοις εἴρηται τούτοις ὡς δέον
συγκεῖσθαι τὴν ἀρίστην πολιτείαν ἐκ δημοκρατίας
καὶ τυραννίδος, ἃς ἢ τὸ παράπαν οὐκ ἄν τις θείη
πολιτείας ἢ χειρίστας πασῶν. βέλτιον οὖν λέγουσιν

5 οἱ πλείους μιγνύντες· ἡ γὰρ ἐκ πλειόνων συγκειμένη πολιτεία βελτίων. ἔπειτ᾽ οὐδ᾽ ἔχουσα
φαίνεται μοναρχικὸν οὐδέν, ἀλλ᾽ ὀλιγαρχικὰ καὶ
δημοκρατικά, μᾶλλον δ᾽ ἐγκλίνειν βούλεται πρὸς
τὴν ὀλιγαρχίαν. δῆλον δ᾽ ἐκ τῆς τῶν ἀρχόντων
καταστάσεως· τὸ μὲν γὰρ ἐξ αἱρετῶν κληρωτοὺς

---

a Plato wrote 'monarchy,' *Laws* 693 D (*cf.* here § 13, l. 23).
106

of all forms of constitution in the actual states, he
has perhaps made a good proposal, but if he introduces it as the next best to the first form of constitution, it is not a good proposal ; for very likely
one might approve the Spartan constitution more
highly, or perhaps some other form nearer to an
aristocracy. In fact some people assert that the best Different
constitution must be a combination of all the forms to Spartan
of constitution, and therefore praise the constitution constitu-
of Sparta (for some people say that it consists of tion.
oligarchy, monarchy and democracy, meaning that
the kingship is monarchy and the rule of the ephors
oligarchy, but that an element of democracy is
introduced by the rule of the ephors because the
ephors come from the common people ; while others
pronounce the ephorate a tyranny and find an
element of democracy in the public mess-tables and
in the other regulations of daily life). In Plato's
Laws on the other hand it is stated that the best
constitution must consist of a combination of democracy and tyranny,[a] which one might refuse to count
as constitutional governments at all, or else rank
as the worst of all constitutions. A better theory
therefore is put forward by those who intermingle
a larger number of forms, for the constitution composed of a combination of a larger number of forms
is better. In the next place, the constitution in the
Laws proves as a matter of fact not to contain any
element of monarchy at all, but its factors are taken
from oligarchy and democracy, and for the most part
it tends to incline towards oligarchy. This appears
from the regulations for the appointment of the
magistrates ; for their selection by lot from a list
previously elected by vote is a feature common to

1266 a

10 κοινὸν ἀμφοῖν, τὸ δὲ τοῖς μὲν εὐπορωτέροις
ἐπάναγκες ἐκκλησιάζειν εἶναι καὶ φέρειν ἄρχοντας
ἤ τι ποιεῖν ἄλλο τῶν πολιτικῶν, τοὺς δ' ἀφεῖσθαι,
τοῦτο δ' ὀλιγαρχικόν, καὶ τὸ πειρᾶσθαι πλείους
ἐκ τῶν εὐπόρων εἶναι τοὺς ἄρχοντας καὶ τὰς
μεγίστας ἐκ τῶν μεγίστων τιμημάτων. ὀλιγαρχι- 1
15 κὴν δὲ ποιεῖ καὶ τὴν τῆς βουλῆς αἵρεσιν· αἱροῦνται μὲν γὰρ πάντες ἐπάναγκες, ἀλλ' ἐκ¹ τοῦ
πρώτου τιμήματος, εἶτα πάλιν ἴσους ἐκ τοῦ
δευτέρου, εἶτ' ἐκ τῶν τρίτων, πλὴν οὐ πᾶσιν
ἐπάναγκες ἦν τοῖς ἐκ τῶν τρίτων ἢ τετάρτων,
ἐκ δὲ τοῦ τετάρτου² μόνοις ἐπάναγκες τοῖς
πρώτοις καὶ τοῖς δευτέροις· εἶτ' ἐκ τούτων
20 ἴσον ἀφ' ἑκάστου τιμήματος ἀποδεῖξαί φησι δεῖν
ἀριθμόν. ἔσονται δὴ πλείους οἱ ἐκ τῶν μεγίστων
τιμημάτων καὶ βελτίους διὰ τὸ ἐνίους μὴ αἱρεῖσθαι
τῶν δημοτικῶν διὰ τὸ μὴ ἐπάναγκες. ὡς μὲν οὖν 1
οὐκ ἐκ δημοκρατίας καὶ μοναρχίας δεῖ συνιστάναι
τὴν τοιαύτην πολιτείαν, ἐκ τούτων φανερὸν καὶ
25 τῶν ὕστερον ῥηθησομένων ὅταν ἐπιβάλλῃ περὶ τῆς
τοιαύτης πολιτείας ἡ σκέψις· ἔχει δὲ καὶ περὶ τὴν
αἵρεσιν τῶν ἀρχόντων τὸ ἐξ αἱρετῶν αἱρετοὺς
ἐπικίνδυνον, εἰ γάρ τινες συστῆναι θέλουσι καὶ
μέτριοι τὸ πλῆθος, ἀεὶ κατὰ τὴν τούτων αἱρε-
θήσονται βούλησιν.

Τὰ μὲν οὖν περὶ τὴν πολιτείαν τὴν ἐν τοῖς Νόμοις
30 τοῦτον ἔχει τὸν τρόπον.

---

¹ ἀλλὰ ⟨πρῶτον⟩ ἐκ Lambinus.
² Engelhardt: τοῦ τετάρτου τῶν τετάρτων codd.

ᵃ i.e. a better elective body because representative of all
classes.
ᵇ i.e. from voting for the preliminary list from the third and
fourth classes.

both oligarchy and democracy, but the compulsion put upon the richer citizens to attend the assembly and vote for magistrates or perform any other political function, while the others are allowed to do as they like, is oligarchical, as is the endeavour to secure that a majority of the magistrates shall be drawn from the wealthy and that the highest offices shall be filled from the highest of the classes assessed

12 by wealth. But the writer also makes the election of the council oligarchical; for everybody is compelled to elect, but from the first property-class, and then again an equal number from the second class, and then from the members of the third class, except that it was not to be compulsory for all to vote for those to be elected from the members of the third or the fourth class, and to elect from the fourth class was only compulsory for the members of the first and second classes; and afterwards from those thus selected he says that they are to appoint an equal number from each class. Thus those who elect the members from the highest property classes will be more numerous and better,[a] because some of the lower orders will abstain from voting[b] as it is not

13 compulsory. Accordingly that it is not proper to _{Indirect} establish a constitution of this character from a _{election.} blend of democracy and monarchy appears clearly from these considerations, and from what will be said later when our inquiry comes to deal with this class of constitution; also the provision for the election of the rulers from among candidates chosen at a preliminary election is dangerous, for if even a moderate number of people choose to combine into a party, the elections will always go according to their wish.

Such are the points as to the constitution in the *Laws*.

1266 a

IV. Εἰσὶ δέ τινες πολιτεῖαι καὶ ἄλλαι, αἱ μὲν 1
ἰδιωτῶν αἱ δὲ φιλοσόφων καὶ πολιτικῶν, πᾶσαι
δὲ τῶν καθεστηκυιῶν καὶ καθ᾽ ἃς πολιτεύονται
νῦν ἐγγύτερόν εἰσι τούτων ἀμφοτέρων· οὐδεὶς γὰρ
35 οὔτε τὴν περὶ τὰ τέκνα κοινότητα καὶ τὰς γυναῖκας
ἄλλος κεκαινοτόμηκεν οὔτε περὶ τὰ συσσίτια τῶν
γυναικῶν, ἀλλ᾽ ἀπὸ τῶν ἀναγκαίων ἄρχονται
μᾶλλον. δοκεῖ γάρ τισι τὸ περὶ τὰς οὐσίας εἶναι
μέγιστον τετάχθαι καλῶς· περὶ γὰρ τούτων ποιεῖ-
σθαί φασι τὰς στάσεις πάντας. διὸ Φαλέας ὁ 2
40 Χαλκηδόνιος τοῦτ᾽ εἰσήνεγκε πρῶτος· φησὶ γὰρ
δεῖν ἴσας εἶναι τὰς κτήσεις τῶν πολιτῶν· τοῦτο
1266 b δὲ κατοικιζομέναις μὲν εὐθὺς οὐ χαλεπὸν ᾤετο
ποιεῖν, τὰς δ᾽ ἤδη κατοικουμένας ἐργωδέστερον
μέν, ὅμως δὲ τάχιστ᾽ ἂν ὁμαλισθῆναι τῷ τὰς
προῖκας τοὺς μὲν πλουσίους διδόναι μὲν λαμβάνειν
5 δὲ μή, τοὺς δὲ πένητας μὴ διδόναι μὲν λαμβάνειν
δέ. Πλάτων δὲ τοὺς Νόμους γράφων μέχρι μέν
τινος ᾤετο δεῖν ἐᾶν, πλεῖον δὲ τοῦ πενταπλασίαν
εἶναι τῆς ἐλαχίστης μηδενὶ τῶν πολιτῶν ἐξουσίαν
εἶναι κτήσασθαι, καθάπερ εἴρηται καὶ πρότερον. 3

Δεῖ δὲ μηδὲ τοῦτο λανθάνειν τοὺς οὕτω νομοθετοῦντας, ὃ λανθάνει νῦν, ὅτι τὸ τῆς οὐσίας τάττον-
10 τας πλῆθος προσήκει καὶ τῶν τέκνων τὸ πλῆθος
τάττειν· ἐὰν γὰρ ὑπεραίρῃ τῆς οὐσίας τὸ μέγεθος
ὁ τῶν τέκνων ἀριθμός, ἀνάγκη τόν γε νόμον
λύεσθαι, καὶ χωρὶς τῆς λύσεως φαῦλον τὸ πολλοὺς ἐκ πλουσίων γίνεσθαι πένητας· ἔργον γὰρ μὴ

---

^a Otherwise unknown.

110

1 IV. There are also certain other constitutional schemes, some drawn up by amateurs and others by philosophers and statesmen, but all of them are nearer to those which have been actually established and by which states are governed at present than are both of those which have been considered; for nobody else has introduced the innovation of community of children and women, nor that of public meals for the women, but they start rather with the absolute requisites. For some persons think that the right regulation of property is the most important; for the question of property, they say, is universally the cause of party strife. Therefore the Chalcedonian Phaleas[a] was the first who introduced this expedient; 2 for he says that the citizens' estates ought to be equal, and he thought that this would not be difficult to secure at the outset for cities in process of foundation, while in those already settled, although it would be a more irksome task, nevertheless a levelling would most easily be effected by the rich giving dowries but not receiving them and the poor receiving but not giving them. Plato when writing *Laws* thought that up to a certain point inequality ought to be allowed, but that no citizen should be permitted to acquire more land than would make his estate five times the size of the smallest, as has also been said before.

Non-communist theories.

Constitution of Phaleas: property equalized by regulating dowries.

c. iii. § 8.

3 But those who bring in legislation of this sort must also not overlook this point, which is overlooked at present, that when regulating the amount of property legislators ought also to regulate the size of the family; for if the number of children becomes too large for the total property, the law is quite sure to be repealed, and apart from the repeal it is a bad thing that many citizens who were rich should become poor,

νεωτεροποιοὺς εἶναι τοὺς τοιούτους. διότι μὲν οὖν 4
ἔχει τινὰ δύναμιν εἰς τὴν πολιτικὴν κοινωνίαν ἡ
τῆς οὐσίας ὁμαλότης, καὶ τῶν πάλαι τινὲς φαίνονται διεγνωκότες, οἷον καὶ Σόλων ἐνομοθέτησεν,
καὶ παρ' ἄλλοις ἐστὶ νόμος ὃς κωλύει κτᾶσθαι
γῆν ὁπόσην ἂν βούληταί τις· ὁμοίως δὲ καὶ τὴν
οὐσίαν πωλεῖν οἱ νόμοι¹ κωλύουσιν, ὥσπερ ἐν
Λοκροῖς νόμος ἐστὶ μὴ πωλεῖν ἐὰν μὴ φανερὰν
ἀτυχίαν δείξῃ συμβεβηκυῖαν· ἔτι δὲ τοὺς παλαιοὺς
κλήρους διασῴζειν, τοῦτο δὲ λυθὲν καὶ περὶ
Λευκάδα δημοτικὴν ἐποίησε λίαν τὴν πολιτείαν
αὐτῶν, οὐ γὰρ ἔτι συνέβαινεν ἀπὸ τῶν ὡρισμένων
τιμημάτων εἰς τὰς ἀρχὰς βαδίζειν. ἀλλ' ἔστι τὴν 5
ἰσότητα μὲν ὑπάρχειν τῆς οὐσίας, ταύτην δ' ἢ
λίαν εἶναι πολλήν, ὥστε τρυφᾶν, ἢ λίαν ὀλίγην,
ὥστε ζῆν γλίσχρως· δῆλον οὖν ὡς οὐχ ἱκανὸν τὸ
τὰς οὐσίας ἴσας ποιῆσαι τὸν νομοθέτην, ἀλλὰ τοῦ
μέσου στοχαστέον. ἔτι δ' εἴ τις καὶ τὴν μετρίαν
τάξειεν οὐσίαν πᾶσιν, οὐδὲν ὄφελος· μᾶλλον γὰρ
δεῖ τὰς ἐπιθυμίας ὁμαλίζειν ἢ τὰς οὐσίας, τοῦτο
δ' οὐκ ἔστι μὴ παιδευομένοις ἱκανῶς ὑπὸ τῶν 6
νόμων. ἀλλ' ἴσως εἴποι ἂν ὁ Φαλέας ὅτι ταῦτα
τυγχάνει λέγων αὐτός· οἴεται γὰρ δυοῖν τούτοιν
ἰσότητα δεῖν ὑπάρχειν ταῖς πόλεσιν, κτήσεως καὶ
παιδείας. ἀλλὰ τὴν [τε]² παιδείαν ἥτις ἔσται δεῖ
λέγειν, καὶ τὸ μίαν εἶναι καὶ τὴν αὐτὴν οὐδὲν
ὄφελος, ἔστι γὰρ τὴν αὐτὴν μὲν εἶναι καὶ μίαν
ἀλλὰ ταύτην εἶναι τοιαύτην ἐξ ἧς ἔσονται προ-

---

¹ οἱ νόμοι: ἔνιοι Buecheler: ⟨ἐνίους⟩ οἱ νόμοι Richards.
² ed.

for it is difficult for such men not to be advocates
4 of a new order. That a level standard of property
affects the community of the citizens in an important
manner some men even in old times clearly have
recognized ; for example there is the legislation of
Solon, and other states have a law prohibiting the
acquisition of land to any amount that the individual
may desire ; and similarly there is legislation to
prevent the sale of estates, as at Locri there is a law Historic
parallels.
that a man shall not sell unless he can prove that
manifest misfortune has befallen him ; and also there
is legislation to preserve the old allotments, and the
repeal of this restriction at Leucas made the Leu-
cadian constitution excessively democratic, for it came
about that the offices were no longer filled from the
5 established property-qualifications. But it is possible
that equality of estates may be maintained, but their
size may be either too large and promote luxury, or
too small, causing a penurious standard of living ;
it is clear therefore that it is not enough for the lawgiver to make the estates equal, but he must aim at
securing a medium size. And again, even if one
prescribed a moderate property for all, it would be
of no avail, since it is more needful to level men's
desires than their properties, and this can only be
done by an adequate system of education enforced
6 by law. But perhaps Phaleas would say that he Equali-
tarian
education.
himself actually prescribes this, as he considers it
fundamentally necessary for states to have equality
in these two things, property and education. But
the nature of the education needs to be defined : it
is no use merely for it to be one and the same for all,
for it is possible for all to have one and the same
education but for this to be of such a nature as to

113

αἱρετικοὶ τοῦ πλεονεκτεῖν ἢ χρημάτων ἢ τιμῆς ἢ
συναμφοτέρων· ἔτι[1] στασιάζουσιν οὐ μόνον διὰ τὴν
ἀνισότητα τῆς κτήσεως, ἀλλὰ καὶ διὰ τὴν τῶν
40 τιμῶν, τοὐναντίον δὲ περὶ ἑκάτερον· οἱ μὲν γὰρ
1267 a πολλοὶ διὰ τὸ περὶ τὰς κτήσεις ἄνισον, οἱ δὲ
χαρίεντες περὶ τῶν τιμῶν ἐὰν ἴσαι· ὅθεν καὶ

ἐν δὲ ἰῇ τιμῇ ἠμὲν κακὸς ἠδὲ καὶ ἐσθλός.

οὐ μόνον δ' οἱ ἄνθρωποι διὰ τἀναγκαῖα ἀδικοῦσιν,
ὧν ἄκος εἶναι νομίζει τὴν ἰσότητα τῆς οὐσίας,
5 ὥστε μὴ λωποδυτεῖν διὰ τὸ ῥιγοῦν ἢ πεινῆν, ἀλλὰ
καὶ ὅπως χαίρωσι καὶ μὴ ἐπιθυμῶσιν· ἐὰν γὰρ
μείζω ἔχωσιν ἐπιθυμίαν τῶν ἀναγκαίων, διὰ τὴν
ταύτης ἰατρείαν ἀδικήσουσιν· οὐ τοίνυν διὰ ταύτην
μόνον, ἀλλὰ καὶ [ἂν ἐπιθυμοῖεν][2] ἵνα χαίρωσι ταῖς
ἄνευ λυπῶν ἡδοναῖς. τί οὖν ἄκος τῶν τριῶν
10 τούτων; τοῖς μὲν οὐσία βραχεῖα καὶ ἐργασία, τοῖς
δὲ σωφροσύνη· τρίτον δ', εἴ τινες βούλοιντο δι'
αὑτῶν χαίρειν, οὐκ ἂν ἐπιζητοῖεν εἰ μὴ παρὰ
φιλοσοφίας ἄκος, αἱ γὰρ ἄλλαι ἀνθρώπων δέονται.
ἐπεὶ[3] ἀδικοῦσί γε τὰ μέγιστα διὰ τὰς ὑπερβολάς,
ἀλλ' οὐ διὰ τὰ ἀναγκαῖα (οἷον τυραννοῦσιν οὐχ
15 ἵνα μὴ ῥιγῶσιν, διὸ καὶ αἱ τιμαὶ μεγάλαι ἂν ἀπο-
κτείνῃ τις οὐ κλέπτην ἀλλὰ τύραννον)· ὥστε πρὸς
τὰς μικρὰς ἀδικίας βοηθητικὸς μόνον ὁ τρόπος
τῆς Φαλέου πολιτείας. ἔτι τὰ πολλὰ βούλεται

---

[1] ἔτι: ἐπεὶ Spengel.
[2] Bernays: ἀνεῦ ἐπιθυμῶν Bojesen.
[3] ἐπεὶ ⟨δ'⟩ vel ἔτι Rassow.

---

[a] Probably the Greek should be altered to give ' because '
instead of ' moreover.'
[b] *Iliad* ix. 319.

make them desirous of getting more than their share
7 of money or honour or both; moreover [a] civil strife
is caused not only by inequality of property, but also
by inequality of honours, though the two motives
operate in opposite ways—the masses are discon-
tented if possessions are unequally distributed, the
upper classes if honours are equally distributed,
bringing it about that

Noble or base in the like honour stand.[b]

Nor do men do wrong for the sake of the bare necessities only, the sort of wrongdoing for which Phaleas
thinks that equality of substance is a cure—preventing highway robbery by removing the motive of cold
or hunger; men also do wrong to gain pleasure and
to satisfy desire. For if they have a desire above the
bare necessities of existence, they will transgress to
cure this desire; and moreover not because of desire
only, but in order that they may enjoy the pleasures
8 that are not associated with pains. What remedy
then is there for these three classes of offences?
For the first class, a modest competence and work;
for the second, temperance; and as for the third
sort, any people who desired pleasures depending
on themselves could seek no cure for their desires
save that which is derived from philosophy, for the
other pleasures require the aid of fellow-creatures.
Since clearly the greatest transgressions spring from
a desire for superfluities, not for bare necessaries
(for example, men do not become tyrants in order
to avoid shivering with cold, and accordingly high
honours are awarded to one who kills a tyrant, but
not to one who kills a thief); so that the method of
the constitution of Phaleas is efficacious only against
9 the minor social disorders. Again, Phaleas desires to

Equali-
tarianism
ignores
human
passions
and
corruption.

115

1267 a

κατασκευάζειν ἐξ ὧν τὰ πρὸς αὐτοὺς πολιτεύσονται
καλῶς, δεῖ δὲ καὶ πρὸς τοὺς γειτνιῶντας καὶ τοὺς
20 ἔξωθεν πάντας. ἀναγκαῖον ἄρα τὴν πολιτείαν
συντετάχθαι πρὸς τὴν πολεμικὴν ἰσχύν, περὶ ἧς
ἐκεῖνος οὐδὲν εἴρηκεν. ὁμοίως δὲ καὶ περὶ τῆς
κτήσεως· δεῖ γὰρ οὐ μόνον πρὸς τὰς πολιτικὰς
χρήσεις ἱκανὴν ὑπάρχειν, ἀλλὰ καὶ πρὸς τοὺς
ἔξωθεν κινδύνους· διόπερ οὔτε τοσοῦτον δεῖ πλῆθος
25 ὑπάρχειν ὧν οἱ πλησίον καὶ κρείττους ἐπι-
θυμήσουσιν οἱ δ' ἔχοντες ἀμύνειν οὐ δυνήσονται
τοὺς ἐπιόντας, οὔθ' οὕτως ὀλίγην ὥστε μὴ δύνασθαι πόλεμον ὑπενεγκεῖν μηδὲ τῶν ἴσων καὶ τῶν
ὁμοίων. ἐκεῖνος μὲν οὖν οὐδὲν διώρικεν, δεῖ δὲ 10
τοῦτο μὴ λανθάνειν ὅ τι[1] συμφέρει πλῆθος οὐσίας.
30 ἴσως οὖν ἄριστος ὅρος τὸ μὴ λυσιτελεῖν τοῖς
κρείττοσι διὰ τὴν ὑπερβολὴν πολεμεῖν, ἀλλ' οὕτως
ὡς ἂν καὶ μὴ ἐχόντων τοσαύτην οὐσίαν. οἷον
Εὔβουλος Αὐτοφραδάτου μέλλοντος Ἀταρνέα πολι-
ορκεῖν ἐκέλευσεν αὐτὸν σκεψάμενον ἐν πόσῳ χρόνῳ
λήψεται τὸ χωρίον λογίσασθαι τοῦ χρόνου τούτου
35 τὴν δαπάνην, ἐθέλειν γὰρ ἔλαττον τούτου λαβὼν
ἐκλιπεῖν ἤδη τὸν Ἀταρνέα· ταῦτα δ' εἰπὼν ἐποίησε
τὸν Αὐτοφραδάτην σύννουν γενόμενον παύσασθαι
τῆς πολιορκίας. ἔστι μὲν οὖν τι τῶν συμφερόντων 11
τὸ τὰς οὐσίας εἶναι ἴσας τοῖς πολίταις πρὸς τὸ
μὴ στασιάζειν πρὸς ἀλλήλους, οὐ μὴν μέγ' οὐδὲν

---

[1] ὅ τι Stahr: ὅτι codd.

---

[a] A stronghold on the coast of Asia Minor acquired by
Eubulus, a Bithynian banker, when the Persian empire was
breaking up, middle 4th century B.C.; Autophradates was a
Persian general.

frame institutions for the most part which will lead to a right state of affairs in the internal relations of the citizens, but the legislator should also have regard to relations with the neighbouring peoples and with all foreign nations. It is essential therefore for the constitution to be framed with a view to military strength, about which Phaleas has said nothing. And the same is true also about property; for the citizens should not only possess enough to meet their requirements in civic life, but also to encounter the perils that face them from outside; hence they should possess neither so large an amount of wealth that it will be coveted by their neighbours and by stronger states while its possessors will be unable to repel their assailants, nor yet so small an amount as not to be capable of sustaining a war even against equal and similar states. Phaleas, it is true, has laid down no rule at all, but the question must not be overlooked, what amount of wealth is advantageous. Perhaps therefore the best limit to prescribe is that it must not profit a stronger people to make war upon the state because of its excessive wealth, but only just as it might do even if the citizens had not got so much property. For example, when Autophradates was about to lay siege to Atarneus,[a] Eubulus bade him consider how long it would take him to capture the place, and then calculate what his expenditure would be for that period, for he himself was willing for the payment of a smaller sum than that to evacuate Atarneus at once; these words caused Autophradates to ponder and led him to abandon the siege. Now equality of property among the citizens is certainly one of the factors that contribute to the avoidance of party faction; it is not however

Riches tempt attack but poverty weakens defence.

Covetousness can be curbed by education, justice and control.

117

1267 a
40 ὡς εἰπεῖν. καὶ γὰρ ἂν οἱ χαρίεντες ἀγανακτοῖεν
ὡς[1] οὐκ ἴσων ὄντες ἄξιοι, διὸ καὶ φαίνονται πολ-
1267 b λάκις ἐπιτιθέμενοι καὶ στασιάζοντες· ἔτι δ' ἡ
πονηρία τῶν ἀνθρώπων ἄπληστον, καὶ τὸ πρῶτον
μὲν ἱκανὸν διωβολία μόνον, ὅταν δ' ἤδη τοῦτ' ᾖ
πάτριον, ἀεὶ δέονται τοῦ πλείονος, ἕως εἰς ἄπειρον
5 ἔλθωσιν· ἄπειρος γὰρ ἡ τῆς ἐπιθυμίας φύσις, ἧς
πρὸς τὴν ἀναπλήρωσιν οἱ πολλοὶ ζῶσιν. τῶν οὖν
τοιούτων ἀρχή,[2] μᾶλλον τοῦ τὰς οὐσίας ὁμαλίζειν,
τὸ τοὺς μὲν ἐπιεικεῖς τῇ φύσει τοιούτους παρασκευάζειν ὥστε μὴ βούλεσθαι πλεονεκτεῖν, τοὺς
δὲ φαύλους ὥστε μὴ δύνασθαι· τοῦτο δ' ἐστὶν ἂν
10 ἥττους τε ὦσι καὶ μὴ ἀδικῶνται. οὐ καλῶς δ'
οὐδὲ τὴν ἰσότητα τῆς οὐσίας εἴρηκεν· περὶ γὰρ τὴν
τῆς γῆς κτῆσιν ἰσάζει μόνον, ἔστι δὲ καὶ δούλων
καὶ βοσκημάτων πλοῦτος καὶ νομίσματος, καὶ
κατασκευὴ πολλὴ τῶν καλουμένων ἐπίπλων· ἢ
πάντων οὖν τούτων ἰσότητα ζητητέον ἢ τάξιν τινὰ
μετρίαν, ἢ πάντα ἐατέον. φαίνεται δ' ἐκ τῆς
15 νομοθεσίας κατασκευάζων τὴν πόλιν μικράν, εἴ γ'
οἱ τεχνῖται πάντες δημόσιοι ἔσονται καὶ μὴ πλή-
ρωμά τι παρέξονται τῆς πόλεως. ἀλλ' εἴπερ δεῖ
δημοσίους εἶναι, τοὺς τὰ κοινὰ ἐργαζομένους δεῖ
(καθάπερ ἐν Ἐπιδάμνῳ τε καὶ ὡς[3] Διόφαντός ποτε
κατεσκεύαζεν Ἀθήνησι) τοῦτον ἔχειν τὸν τρόπον.

20   Περὶ μὲν οὖν τῆς Φαλέου πολιτείας σχεδὸν ἐκ

---

[1] ὡς MP: ἂν ὡς cet.
[2] ἄκος Schneider: ἀρωγὴ Vermehren.
[3] καὶ ὡς Morel: καὶ codd.

---

[a] Twopence-halfpenny for a seat in the theatre at Athens
paid for citizens by the State after the time of Pericles.
118

a particularly important one. For the upper classes may resent it on the ground that their merits are not equal, owing to which we actually see them often attacking the government and rebelling; and also the baseness of human beings is a thing insatiable, and though at the first a dole of only two obols *a* is enough, yet when this has now become an established custom, they always want more, until they get to an unlimited amount; for appetite is in its nature unlimited, and the majority of mankind live for the satisfaction of appetite. The starting-point in such matters therefore, rather than levelling estates, is to train those that are respectable by nature so that they may not wish for excessive wealth, and to contrive that the base may not be able to do so, and this is secured if they are kept inferior, while not unjustly treated. And also we cannot approve what Phaleas has said about equality of property, for he makes the citizens equal in respect of landed estate only, but wealth also consists in slaves and cattle and money, and there is an abundance of property in the shape of what is called furniture; we must therefore either seek to secure equality or some moderate regulation as regards all these things, or we must permit all forms of wealth. And it is clear from Phaleas's legislation that he makes the citizen-population a small one, inasmuch as all the artisans are to be publicly owned slaves and are not to contribute to the complement of the state. But if it is proper to have public slaves, it is the labourers employed upon the public works who ought to be of that status (as is the case at Epidamnus and as Diophantus once tried to institute at Athens).

These remarks may serve fairly well to indicate

Personal property as well as landed estate needs control.

119

τούτων ἄν τις θεωρήσειεν εἴ τι τυγχάνει καλῶς
εἰρηκὼς ἢ μὴ καλῶς.

V. Ἱππόδαμος δὲ Εὐρυφῶντος Μιλήσιος (ὃς καὶ
τὴν τῶν πόλεων διαίρεσιν εὗρε καὶ τὸν Πειραιᾶ
κατέτεμεν, γενόμενος καὶ περὶ τὸν ἄλλον βίον
25 περιττότερος διὰ φιλοτιμίαν οὕτως ὥστε δοκεῖν
ἐνίοις ζῆν περιεργότερον τριχῶν τε πλήθει καὶ
κόσμῳ πολυτελεῖ,[1] ἔτι δὲ ἐσθῆτος[2] εὐτελοῦς μὲν
ἀλεεινῆς δὲ οὐκ ἐν τῷ χειμῶνι μόνον ἀλλὰ καὶ
περὶ τοὺς θερινοὺς χρόνους, λόγιος δὲ καὶ περὶ
τὴν ὅλην φύσιν εἶναι βουλόμενος) πρῶτος τῶν μὴ
30 πολιτευομένων ἐνεχείρησέ τι περὶ πολιτείας εἰπεῖν
τῆς ἀρίστης. κατεσκεύαζε δὲ τὴν πόλιν τῷ πλήθει
μὲν μυρίανδρον, εἰς τρία δὲ μέρη διῃρημένην·
ἐποίει γὰρ ἓν μὲν μέρος τεχνίτας, ἓν δὲ γεωργούς,
τρίτον δὲ τὸ προπολεμοῦν καὶ τὰ ὅπλα ἔχον.
διῄρει δ' εἰς τρία μέρη τὴν χώραν, τὴν μὲν ἱερὰν
35 τὴν δὲ δημοσίαν τὴν δ' ἰδίαν· ὅθεν μὲν τὰ νομι-
ζόμενα ποιήσουσι πρὸς τοὺς θεούς, ἱεράν, ἀφ' ὧν δ'
οἱ προπολεμοῦντες βιώσονται, κοινήν, τὴν δὲ τῶν
γεωργῶν ἰδίαν. ᾤετο δ' εἴδη καὶ τῶν νόμων εἶναι
τρία μόνον· περὶ ὧν γὰρ αἱ δίκαι γίνονται, τρία
ταῦτ' εἶναι τὸν ἀριθμόν, ὕβριν βλάβην θάνατον.
40 ἐνομοθέτει δὲ καὶ δικαστήριον ἓν τὸ κύριον εἰς ὃ
πάσας ἀνάγεσθαι δεῖν τὰς μὴ καλῶς κεκρίσθαι
δοκούσας δίκας, τοῦτο δὲ κατεσκεύαζεν ἐκ τινῶν
1268 a γερόντων αἱρετῶν. τὰς δὲ κρίσεις ἐν τοῖς δικαστηρίοις οὐ διὰ ψηφοφορίας ᾤετο γίνεσθαι δεῖν,

---

[1] κόσμῳ πολυτελεῖ codd. aliqui: κόμης ΓΜΡ[1].
[2] ἐσθῆτος ⟨χρήσει⟩ ? Richards.

---

[a] Architect and town-planner (see 1330 b 24), c. 475 B.C.
This personal sketch anticipates the manner of Theophrastus.

such merits and defects as may be contained in the constitution of Phaleas.

V. Hippodamus[a] son of Euryphon, a Milesian (who invented the division of cities into blocks and cut up Piraeus, and who also became somewhat eccentric in his general mode of life owing to a desire for distinction, so that some people thought that he lived too fussily, with a quantity of hair[b] and expensive ornaments, and also a quantity of cheap yet warm clothes not only in winter but also in the summer periods, and who wished to be a man of learning in natural science generally), was the first man not engaged in politics who attempted to speak on the subject of the best form of constitution. His system was for a city with a population of ten thousand, divided into three classes ; for he made one class of artisans, one of farmers, and the third the class that fought for the state in war and was the armed class. He divided the land into three parts, one sacred, one public and one private : sacred land to supply the customary offerings to the gods, common land to provide the warrior class with food, and private land to be owned by the farmers. He thought that there are only three divisions of the law, since the matters about which lawsuits take place are three in number—outrage, damage, homicide. He also proposed to establish one supreme court of justice, to which were to be carried up all the cases at law thought to have been decided wrongly, and this court he made to consist of certain selected elders. He held that the verdicts in the courts ought not to be given by ballot, but that each juryman should

Margin notes: Constitution of Hippodamus. Three classes, three areas of land, three divisions of law. Judicial system.

[b] At Sparta men wore their hair long, but at Athens this was the mark of a dandy.

1268 a

ἀλλὰ φέρειν ἕκαστον πινάκιον, ἐν ᾧ γράφειν, εἰ
καταδικάζοι ἁπλῶς, τὴν δίκην, εἰ δ' ἀπολύοι
5 ἁπλῶς, κενόν,[1] εἰ δὲ τὸ μὲν τὸ δὲ μή, τοῦτο δι-
ορίζειν· νῦν γὰρ οὐκ ᾤετο νενομοθετῆσθαι καλῶς,
ἀναγκάζειν γὰρ ἐπιορκεῖν ἢ ταῦτα ἢ ταῦτα δικά-
ζοντας. ἐτίθει δὲ νόμον περὶ τῶν εὑρισκόντων τι
τῇ πόλει συμφέρον, ὅπως τυγχάνωσι τιμῆς, καὶ
τοῖς παισὶ τῶν ἐν τῷ πολέμῳ τελευτώντων ἐκ
δημοσίου γίνεσθαι τὴν τροφήν, ὡς οὔπω τοῦτο
10 παρ' ἄλλοις νενομοθετημένον· ἔστι δὲ καὶ ἐν
Ἀθήναις οὗτος ὁ νόμος νῦν καὶ ἐν ἑτέραις τῶν
πόλεων. τοὺς δ' ἄρχοντας αἱρετοὺς ὑπὸ τοῦ δήμου
εἶναι πάντας, δῆμον δ' ἐποίει τὰ τρία μέρη τῆς
πόλεως· τοὺς δ' αἱρεθέντας ἐπιμελεῖσθαι κοινῶν
καὶ ξενικῶν καὶ ὀρφανικῶν. τὰ μὲν οὖν πλεῖστα
15 καὶ τὰ μάλιστα ἀξιόλογα τῆς Ἱπποδάμου τάξεως
ταῦτ' ἐστίν. ἀπορήσειε δ' ἄν τις πρῶτον μὲν τὴν
διαίρεσιν τοῦ πλήθους τῶν πολιτῶν. οἵ τε γὰρ
τεχνῖται καὶ οἱ γεωργοὶ καὶ οἱ τὰ ὅπλα ἔχοντες
κοινωνοῦσι τῆς πολιτείας πάντες, οἱ μὲν γεωργοὶ
οὐκ ἔχοντες ὅπλα, οἱ δὲ τεχνῖται οὔτε γῆν οὔτε
20 ὅπλα, ὥστε γίνονται σχεδὸν δοῦλοι τῶν τὰ ὅπλα
κεκτημένων. μετέχειν μὲν οὖν πασῶν τῶν τιμῶν
ἀδύνατον (ἀνάγκη γὰρ ἐκ τῶν τὰ ὅπλα ἐχόντων
καθίστασθαι καὶ στρατηγοὺς καὶ πολιτοφύλακας
καὶ τὰς κυριωτάτας ἀρχὰς ὡς εἰπεῖν)· μὴ μετέχοντας δὲ τῆς πολιτείας πῶς οἷόν τε φιλικῶς ἔχειν

---

[1] κενὸν ⟨ἐᾶν⟩ Meier.

bring a tablet on which if he found a simple verdict
of guilty he should write the penalty, and if simply
not guilty leave a blank, but if he found the prisoner
guilty on some counts but not on others he should
state this ; for the present state of the law he thought
unsatisfactory, since it forces jurors to commit perjury
by giving either the one verdict or the other. He pro- Rewards for
posed a law that those who discovered something of political
originality.
advantage to the state should receive honour, and
that the children of those who died in war should War-
have their maintenance from the state, in the belief orphans.
that this had never yet been provided by law among
other people—but as a matter of fact this law exists
at present both at Athens and in others of the cities.
The governing officials were all to be chosen by the Electing
assembly of the people, and this he made to consist assembly.
of the three classes of the city ; and the officials
elected were to superintend the business of the
community and the affairs of foreign residents and
of orphans. These then are the greatest number and
the most noteworthy of the provisions in the system
of Hippodamus. But doubt might be raised first of Criticism
all about the division of the general mass of the of the constitution of
citizens. The artisans, the farmers and the military Hippodamus:
class all participate in the government, though the soldiers
farmers have not got arms and the artisans neither should
be the sole
arms nor land, which makes them almost the slaves citizens;
of those who possess the arms. Therefore for them
to share in all the offices is impossible (for it is inevitable that both military commanders and civic guards
and in general the most important offices should be
appointed from those that have the arms) ; but if
they do not share in the government of the state,
how is it possible for them to be friendly towards the

1268 a

25 πρὸς τὴν πολιτείαν; ἀλλὰ δεῖ κρείττους εἶναι τοὺς
τὰ ὅπλα γε κεκτημένους ἀμφοτέρων τῶν μερῶν.
τοῦτο δ' οὐ ῥᾴδιον μὴ πολλοὺς ὄντας, εἰ δὲ τοῦτ'
ἔσται, τί δεῖ τοὺς ἄλλους μετέχειν τῆς πολιτείας
καὶ κυρίους εἶναι τῆς τῶν ἀρχόντων καταστάσεως;
ἔτι οἱ γεωργοὶ τί χρήσιμοι τῇ πόλει; τεχνίτας
30 μὲν γὰρ ἀναγκαῖον εἶναι (πᾶσα γὰρ δεῖται πόλις
τεχνιτῶν), καὶ δύνανται διαγίγνεσθαι καθάπερ ἐν
ταῖς ἄλλαις πόλεσιν ἀπὸ τῆς τέχνης· οἱ δὲ γεωργοὶ
πορίζοντες μὲν τοῖς τὰ ὅπλα κεκτημένοις τὴν
τροφὴν εὐλόγως ἂν ἦσάν τι τῆς πόλεως μέρος, νῦν
35 δ' ἰδίαν ἔχουσιν καὶ ταύτην ἰδίᾳ γεωργοῦσιν. ἔτι
δὲ τὴν κοινήν, ἀφ' ἧς οἱ προπολεμοῦντες ἕξουσι
τὴν τροφήν, εἰ μὲν αὐτοὶ γεωργήσουσιν, οὐκ ἂν
εἴη τὸ μάχιμον ἕτερον καὶ τὸ γεωργοῦν, βούλεται
δ' ὁ νομοθέτης· εἰ δ' ἕτεροί τινες ἔσονται τῶν τε
τὰ ἴδια γεωργούντων καὶ τῶν μαχίμων, τέταρτον
40 αὖ μόριον ἔσται τοῦτο τῆς πόλεως, οὐδενὸς μετέχον ἀλλ' ἀλλότριον τῆς πολιτείας. ἀλλὰ μὴν εἴ
τις τοὺς αὐτοὺς θήσει τούς τε τὴν ἰδίαν καὶ τοὺς
τὴν κοινὴν γεωργοῦντας, τό τε πλῆθος ἄπορον
1268 b ἔσται τῶν καρπῶν ἐξ ὧν ἕκαστος γεωργήσει δύο
οἰκίαις,[1] καὶ τίνος ἕνεκεν οὐκ εὐθὺς ἀπὸ τῆς γῆς καὶ
τῶν αὐτῶν κλήρων αὐτοῖς τε τὴν τροφὴν λήψονται
καὶ τοῖς μαχίμοις παρέξουσιν; ταῦτα δὴ πάντα
5 πολλὴν ἔχει ταραχήν. οὐ καλῶς δ' οὐδ' ὁ περὶ
τῆς κρίσεως ἔχει νόμος, τὸ κρίνειν ἀξιοῦν διαιροῦντα

[1] Ross: οἰκίας codd.

---

[a] As military posts must be filled by the military class,
civilians will feel excluded and be disaffected; and the
military class may not be strong enough to control them.
Better, then, not to give full citizenship to civilians.

124

6 constitution? But it may be said that the ruling class as possessing the arms is bound to be stronger than both classes. But this is not easy if they are not numerous; and if this be the case, why should the other classes participate in the government and control the appointment of the rulers*? Again, what use are the farmers to the state? artisans there must necessarily be (for every state requires artisans), and they can make a living as in the other states from the practice of their craft; but as for the farmers, although it would have been reasonable for them to be a portion of the state if they provided the class possessing the arms with its food, as it is they have private land of their own and farm it for themselves.

7 And again, if the common land from which those who fight for the state are to have their food is to be farmed by themselves, the military class would not be different from the agricultural, but the legislator intends it to be; while if the cultivators of the common land are to be a different set of people from both those who cultivate the private farms and the soldiers, this will be yet a fourth section of the state, holding no part in it but quite estranged from the government. But yet if one is to make those who cultivate the private and the common land the same people, the amount of the produce from the farms which each man will cultivate will be scanty for two households, and moreover why are they not both to take food for themselves and to supply it to the soldiers direct

8 from the land and from the same allotments? All these points therefore involve much confusion. Also the law about trials is unsatisfactory—the permission for a qualified verdict though the charge in the indict-

land-tenure obscure;

qualified verdicts unworkable;

1268 b

τῆς κρίσεως ἁπλῶς γεγραμμένης, καὶ γίνεσθαι τὸν
δικαστὴν διαιτητήν. τοῦτο δ' ἐν μὲν τῇ διαίτῃ
καὶ πλείοσιν ἐνδέχεται (κοινολογοῦνται γὰρ ἀλλήλοις περὶ τῆς κρίσεως), ἐν δὲ τοῖς δικαστηρίοις
οὐκ ἔστιν, ἀλλὰ καὶ τοὐναντίον τούτῳ τῶν νομο-
10 θετῶν οἱ πολλοὶ παρασκευάζουσιν ὅπως οἱ δικασταὶ
μὴ κοινολογῶνται πρὸς ἀλλήλους. ἔπειτα πῶς οὐκ 9
ἔσται ταραχώδης ἡ κρίσις ὅταν ὀφείλειν μὲν ὁ
δικαστὴς οἴηται μὴ τοσοῦτον δ' ὅσον ὁ δικαζόμενος;
ὁ μὲν γὰρ εἴκοσι μνᾶς, ὁ δὲ δικαστὴς κρινεῖ[1] δέκα
μνᾶς (ἢ ὁ μὲν πλέον ὁ δ' ἔλασσον), ἄλλος δὲ
15 πέντε, ὁ δὲ τέτταρας (καὶ τοῦτον δὴ τὸν τρόπον
δῆλον ὅτι μεριοῦσιν), οἱ δὲ πάντα καταδικάσουσιν,
οἱ δ' οὐδέν· τίς οὖν ὁ τρόπος ἔσται τῆς διαλογῆς
τῶν ψήφων; ἔτι δ' οὐδεὶς ἐπιορκεῖν ἀναγκάζει
τὸν ἁπλῶς ἀποδικάσαντα ἢ καταδικάσαντα, εἴπερ
ἁπλῶς τὸ ἔγκλημα γέγραπται, δικαίως[2]· οὐ γὰρ
20 μηδὲν ὀφείλειν ὁ ἀποδικάσας κρίνει ἀλλὰ τὰς
εἴκοσι μνᾶς· ἀλλ' ἐκεῖνος ἤδη ἐπιορκεῖ ὁ κατα-
δικάσας μὴ νομίζων ὀφείλειν τὰς εἴκοσι μνᾶς.
περὶ δὲ τοῦ τοῖς εὑρίσκουσί τι τῇ πόλει συμφέρον 10
ὡς δεῖ γίνεσθαί τινα τιμήν, οὐκ ἔστιν ἀσφαλὲς τὸ
νομοθετεῖν, ἀλλ' εὐόφθαλμον ἀκοῦσαι μόνον· ἔχει
25 γὰρ συκοφαντίας καὶ κινήσεις, ἂν τύχῃ, πολιτείας.
ἐμπίπτει δ' εἰς ἄλλο πρόβλημα καὶ σκέψιν ἑτέραν·

---

[1] κρινεῖ Bekker : κρίνει codd.   [2] [δικαίως] ? Greenwood.

[a] The mina, 100 drachmas, may be put at £4 (gold).

ment is unqualified, and the conversion of the juror into an arbitrator. A qualified verdict is practicable in an arbitration even when there are several arbitrators, for they confer with one another about their verdict; but it is not practicable in the law-courts, in fact the contrary to this is provided for by most lawgivers, who prohibit consultation between the jurymen. Then the verdict will inevitably be a confused one when the juror thinks that the defendant is liable for damages but not in so large an amount as the plaintiff claims; for the plaintiff will sue for twenty minae *a* and the juror will adjudge ten minae (or the former some larger and the latter some smaller sum), and another juror five minae, and yet another four (and they obviously make fractions like this), while others will award the whole sum, and others nothing; what then will be the method of counting the votes? Again, nobody compels the juror to commit perjury who, as the indictment has been drawn in simple form, gives a simple verdict of acquittal or condemnation, if he gives it justly; for the juror who gives a verdict of acquittal does not give judgement that the defendant owes nothing, but that he does not owe the twenty minae for which he is sued; it is only the juror who gives a verdict condemning the defendant when he does not think that he owes twenty minae who commits perjury. As for the view that an honour ought to be awarded to those who invent something advantageous to the state, legislation to this effect is not safe, but only specious to the ear; for it involves malicious prosecutions and, it may even happen, constitutional upheavals. And the matter leads to another problem and a different inquiry:

reward for political inventions dangerous.

Conservatism v. Reform in general.

1268 b

ἀποροῦσι γάρ τινες πότερον βλαβερὸν ἢ συμφέρον
ταῖς πόλεσι τὸ κινεῖν τοὺς πατρίους νόμους ἂν ᾖ
τις ἄλλος βελτίων. διόπερ οὐ ῥᾴδιον τῷ λεχθέντι
30 ταχὺ συγχωρεῖν, εἴπερ μὴ συμφέρει κινεῖν· ἐνδέχεται δ' εἰσηγεῖσθαί τινας νόμων λύσιν ἢ πολιτείας
ὡς κοινὸν ἀγαθόν. ἐπεὶ δὲ πεποιήμεθα μνείαν, ἔτι 1
μικρὰ περὶ αὐτοῦ διαστείλασθαι βέλτιον, ἔχει γάρ,
ὥσπερ εἴπομεν, ἀπορίαν. καὶ δόξειεν ἂν βέλτιον
εἶναι τὸ κινεῖν· ἐπὶ γοῦν τῶν ἄλλων ἐπιστημῶν
35 τοῦτο συνενήνοχεν, οἷον ἰατρικὴ κινηθεῖσα παρὰ τὰ
πάτρια καὶ γυμναστικὴ καὶ ὅλως αἱ τέχναι πᾶσαι
καὶ αἱ δυνάμεις· ὥστ' ἐπεὶ μίαν τούτων θετέον
καὶ τὴν πολιτικήν, δῆλον ὅτι καὶ περὶ ταύτην
ἀναγκαῖον ὁμοίως ἔχειν. σημεῖον δ' ἂν γεγονέναι
φαίη τις ἐπ' αὐτῶν τῶν ἔργων, τοὺς γὰρ ἀρχαίους
40 νόμους λίαν ἁπλοῦς εἶναι καὶ βαρβαρικούς· ἐσι-
δηροφοροῦντό τε γὰρ οἱ Ἕλληνες καὶ τὰς γυναῖκας
ἐωνοῦντο παρ' ἀλλήλων, ὅσα τε λοιπὰ τῶν ἀρχαίων 1
1269 a ἐστί που νομίμων εὐήθη πάμπαν ἐστίν, οἷον ἐν
Κύμῃ περὶ τὰ φονικὰ νόμος ἐστίν, ἂν πλῆθός τι
παράσχηται μαρτύρων ὁ διώκων τὸν φόνον τῶν
αὑτοῦ συγγενῶν, ἔνοχον εἶναι τῷ φόνῳ τὸν φεύ-
γοντα. ζητοῦσι δ' ὅλως οὐ τὸ πάτριον ἀλλὰ
5 τἀγαθὸν πάντες· εἰκός τε τοὺς πρώτους, εἴτε
128

some persons raise the question whether to alter the traditional laws, supposing another law is better, is harmful or advantageous to states. Hence it is not easy to give a speedy agreement to the above proposal to honour reformers, if really it is disadvantageous to alter the laws ; and a revolutionary legal or constitutional proposal in the interest of the com11 munity is quite possible. And since we have made mention of this question, it will be better if we set out a few further details about it, for, as we said, it involves difficulty. And it might be thought that it would be better for alteration to take place ; at all events in the other fields of knowledge this has proved beneficial—for example, medicine has been improved by being altered from the traditional system, and gymnastic training, and in general all the arts and faculties ; so that since statesmanship also is to be counted as one of these, it is clear that the same thing necessarily holds good in regard to it as well. And it might be said that a sign of this has occurred in the actual events of history, for (one might argue) the laws of ancient times were too simple and uncivilized : the Hellenes, for instance, used both to carry arms and to 12 purchase their wives from one another, and all the survivals of the customs of antiquity existing anywhere are utterly foolish, as for example at Cyme there is a law relating to trials for murder, that if the prosecutor on the charge of murder produces a certain number of his own relatives as witnesses, the defendant is guilty of the murder. And in general all men really seek what is good, not what was customary with their forefathers ; and it is probable that primitive mankind, whether sprung from the

γηγενεῖς ἦσαν εἴτ' ἐκ φθορᾶς τινὸς ἐσώθησαν,
ὁμοίους εἶναι καὶ τοὺς τυχόντας καὶ τοὺς ἀνοήτους,
ὥσπερ καὶ λέγεται κατὰ τῶν γηγενῶν, ὥστ'
ἄτοπον τὸ μένειν ἐν τοῖς τούτων δόγμασιν. πρὸς
δὲ τούτοις οὐδὲ τοὺς γεγραμμένους ἐᾶν ἀκινήτους
βέλτιον. ὥσπερ γὰρ καὶ περὶ τὰς ἄλλας τέχνας,
10 καὶ τὴν πολιτικὴν τάξιν ἀδύνατον ἀκριβῶς πάντα
γραφῆναι· καθόλου γὰρ ἀναγκαῖον γραφῆναι, αἱ δὲ
πράξεις περὶ τῶν καθ' ἕκαστόν εἰσιν. ἐκ μὲν οὖν
τούτων φανερὸν ὅτι κινητέοι καὶ τινὲς καὶ ποτὲ
τῶν νόμων εἰσίν. ἄλλον δὲ τρόπον ἐπισκοποῦσιν
15 εὐλαβείας ἂν δόξειεν εἶναι πολλῆς. ὅταν γὰρ ᾖ τὸ
μὲν βέλτιον μικρόν, τὸ δ' ἐθίζειν εὐχερῶς λύειν
τοὺς νόμους φαῦλον, φανερὸν ὡς ἐατέον ἐνίας
ἁμαρτίας καὶ τῶν νομοθετῶν καὶ τῶν ἀρχόντων·
οὐ γὰρ τοσοῦτον ὠφελήσεται κινήσας ὅσον βλα-
βήσεται τοῖς ἄρχουσιν ἀπειθεῖν ἐθισθείς. ψεῦδος δὲ
20 καὶ τὸ παράδειγμα τὸ περὶ τῶν τεχνῶν· οὐ γὰρ
ὅμοιον τὸ κινεῖν τέχνην καὶ νόμον· ὁ γὰρ νόμος
ἰσχὺν οὐδεμίαν ἔχει πρὸς τὸ πείθεσθαι πλὴν παρὰ
τὸ ἔθος, τοῦτο δ' οὐ γίνεται εἰ μὴ διὰ χρόνου
πλῆθος, ὥστε τὸ ῥᾳδίως μεταβάλλειν ἐκ τῶν
ὑπαρχόντων νόμων εἰς ἑτέρους νόμους καινοὺς
25 ἀσθενῆ ποιεῖν ἐστὶ τὴν τοῦ νόμου δύναμιν. ἔτι
δ' εἰ καὶ κινητέοι, πότερον καὶ πάντες καὶ ἐν
πάσῃ πολιτείᾳ, ἢ οὔ; καὶ πότερον τῷ τυχόντι
ἢ τισίν; ταῦτα γὰρ ἔχει μεγάλην διαφοράν. διὸ

---

[a] So Hesiod, *W.D.* 108, Pindar, *Nem.* 6. 1.
[b] So Plato, *Laws* 676 ff., *Timaeus* 22 ff. Aristotle believed
that man had existed for ever, and that the world had experienced only local cataclysms.

earth [a] or the survivors of some destructive cataclysm, were just like ordinary foolish people, as indeed is actually said of the earth-born race, so that would be absurd for us to abide by their notions. Moreover even written codes of law may with advantage not be left unaltered. For just as in the other arts as well, so with the structure of the state it is impossible that it should have been framed aright in all its details ; for it must of necessity be couched in general terms, but our actions deal with particular things. These considerations then do seem to show that it is proper 13 for some laws sometimes to be altered. But if we consider the matter in another way, it would seem to be a thing that needs much caution. For in cases when the improvement would be small, while it is a bad thing to accustom men to repeal the laws lightly, it is clear that some mistakes both of the legislator and of the magistrate should be passed over ; for the people will not be as much benefited by making an alteration as they will be harmed by becoming accustomed to distrust their rulers. 14 Also the example from the case of the arts is fallacious, as to change the practice of an art is a different thing from altering a law ; for the law has no power to compel obedience beside the force of custom, and custom only grows up in long lapse of time, so that lightly to change from the existing laws to other new laws is to weaken the power of the law. Again, even if alteration of the laws is proper, are all the laws to be open to alteration, and in every form of constitution, or not ? and is any chance person to be competent to introduce alterations or only certain people ? for there is a great difference between these alternatives. Therefore let us abandon this

131

1269 a

νῦν μὲν ἀφῶμεν ταύτην τὴν σκέψιν· ἄλλων γάρ
ἐστι καιρῶν.

VI. Περὶ δὲ τῆς Λακεδαιμονίων πολιτείας καὶ
30 τῆς Κρητικῆς, σχεδὸν δὲ καὶ περὶ τῶν ἄλλων
πολιτειῶν, δύο εἰσὶν αἱ σκέψεις, μία μὲν εἴ τι
καλῶς ἢ μὴ καλῶς πρὸς τὴν ἀρίστην νενομοθέτηται
τάξιν, ἑτέρα δ' εἴ τι πρὸς τὴν ὑπόθεσιν καὶ τὸν
τρόπον ὑπεναντίως[1] τῆς προκειμένης αὐτοῖς
πολιτείας.

Ὅτι μὲν οὖν δεῖ τῇ μελλούσῃ καλῶς πολιτεύε-
35 σθαι τὴν τῶν ἀναγκαίων ὑπάρχειν σχολὴν ὁμολογούμενόν ἐστιν· τίνα δὲ τρόπον ὑπάρχειν, οὐ ῥᾴδιον
λαβεῖν. ἥ τε γὰρ Θετταλῶν πενεστεία πολλάκις
ἐπέθετο τοῖς Θετταλοῖς, ὁμοίως δὲ καὶ τοῖς
Λάκωσιν οἱ Εἵλωτες (ὥσπερ γὰρ ἐφεδρεύοντες
τοῖς ἀτυχήμασι διατελοῦσιν)· περὶ δὲ τοὺς Κρῆτας
40 οὐδέν πω τοιοῦτον συμβέβηκεν. αἴτιον δ' ἴσως τὸ
1269 b τὰς γειτνιώσας πόλεις, καίπερ πολεμούσας ἀλλήλαις, μηδεμίαν εἶναι σύμμαχον τοῖς ἀφισταμέ-
νοις διὰ τὸ μὴ συμφέρειν καὶ αὐταῖς κεκτημέναις
περιοίκους· τοῖς δὲ Λάκωσιν οἱ γειτνιῶντες ἐχθροὶ
5 πάντες ἦσαν, Ἀργεῖοι καὶ Μεσσήνιοι καὶ Ἀρ-
κάδες· ἐπεὶ καὶ τοῖς Θετταλοῖς κατ' ἀρχὰς ἀφ-
ίσταντο διὰ τὸ πολεμεῖν ἔτι τοῖς προσχώροις,
Ἀχαιοῖς καὶ Περραιβοῖς καὶ Μάγνησιν. ἔοικε δὲ
καὶ εἰ μηδὲν ἕτερον, ἀλλὰ τό γε τῆς ἐπιμελείας
ἐργῶδες εἶναι, τίνα δεῖ πρὸς αὐτοὺς ὁμιλῆσαι
τρόπον· ἀνιέμενοί τε γὰρ ὑβρίζουσι καὶ τῶν ἴσων
10 ἀξιοῦσιν ἑαυτοὺς τοῖς κυρίοις, καὶ κακοπαθῶς

---

[1] ⟨ἢ⟩ ὑπεναντίως Scaliger.

inquiry for the present, since it belongs to other occasions.

VI. On the subject of the constitution of Sparta and that of Crete, and virtually in regard to the other forms of constitution also, the questions that arise for consideration are two, one whether their legal structure has any feature that is admirable or the reverse in comparison with the best system, another whether it contains any provision that is really opposed to the fundamental principle and character of the constitution that the founders had in view.

Now it is a thing admitted that a state that is to be well governed must be provided with leisure from menial occupations; but how this is to be provided it is not easy to ascertain. The serf class in Thessaly repeatedly rose against its masters, and so did the Helots at Sparta, where they are like an enemy constantly sitting in wait for the disasters of the Spartiates. Nothing of the kind has hitherto occurred in Crete, the reason perhaps being that the neighbouring cities, even when at war with one another, in no instance ally themselves with the rebels, because as they themselves also possess a serf class this would not be for their interest; whereas the Laconians were entirely surrovnded by hostile neighbours, Argives, Messenians and Arcadians. For with the Thessalians too the serf risings originally began because they were still at war with their neighbours, the Achaeans, Perrhaebi and Magnesians. Also, apart from other drawbacks, the mere necessity of policing their serf class is a troublesome matter— the problem of how intercourse with them is to be carried on: if allowed freedom they grow insolent and claim to be as good as their masters, and if

Spartan Constitution.

Social defects: Helot-system works badly.

133

1269 b

ζῶντες ἐπιβουλεύουσι καὶ μισοῦσιν. δῆλον οὖν ὡς
οὐκ ἐξευρίσκουσι τὸν βέλτιστον τρόπον οἷς τοῦτο
συμβαίνει περὶ τὴν εἰλωτείαν. ἔτι δ' ἡ περὶ τὰς
γυναῖκας ἄνεσις καὶ πρὸς τὴν προαίρεσιν τῆς
πολιτείας βλαβερὰ καὶ πρὸς εὐδαιμονίαν πόλεως·
15 ὥσπερ γὰρ οἰκίας μέρος ἀνὴρ καὶ γυνή, δῆλον ὅτι
καὶ πόλιν ἐγγὺς τοῦ δίχα διῃρῆσθαι δεῖ νομίζειν
εἴς τε τὸ τῶν ἀνδρῶν πλῆθος καὶ τὸ τῶν γυναικῶν,
ὥστ' ἐν ὅσαις πολιτείαις φαύλως ἔχει τὸ περὶ τὰς
γυναῖκας τὸ ἥμισυ τῆς πόλεως εἶναι δεῖ νομίζειν
ἀνομοθέτητον. ὅπερ ἐκεῖ συμβέβηκεν· ὅλην γὰρ
20 τὴν πόλιν ὁ νομοθέτης εἶναι βουλόμενος καρτερικήν,
κατὰ μὲν τοὺς ἄνδρας φανερός ἐστι τοιοῦτος ὤν,
ἐπὶ δὲ τῶν γυναικῶν ἐξημέληκεν· ζῶσι γὰρ ἀκο-
λάστως[1] πρὸς ἅπασαν ἀκολασίαν καὶ τρυφερῶς.
ὥστ' ἀναγκαῖον ἐν τῇ τοιαύτῃ πολιτείᾳ τιμᾶσθαι
25 τὸν πλοῦτον, ἄλλως τε κἂν τύχωσι γυναικοκρατού-
μενοι, καθάπερ τὰ πολλὰ τῶν στρατιωτικῶν καὶ
πολεμικῶν γενῶν, ἔξω Κελτῶν ἢ κἂν εἴ τινες
ἕτεροι φανερῶς τετιμήκασι τὴν πρὸς τοὺς ἄρρενας
συνουσίαν. ἔοικε γὰρ ὁ μυθολογήσας πρῶτος οὐκ
ἀλόγως συζεῦξαι τὸν Ἄρη πρὸς τὴν Ἀφροδίτην·
30 ἢ γὰρ πρὸς τὴν τῶν ἀρρένων ὁμιλίαν ἢ πρὸς τὴν
τῶν γυναικῶν φαίνονται κατακώχιμοι πάντες οἱ
τοιοῦτοι. διὸ παρὰ τοῖς Λάκωσι τοῦθ' ὑπῆρχεν,
καὶ πολλὰ διῳκεῖτο ὑπὸ τῶν γυναικῶν ἐπὶ τῆς
ἀρχῆς αὐτῶν· καίτοι τί διαφέρει γυναῖκας ἄρχειν
ἢ τοὺς ἄρχοντας ὑπὸ τῶν γυναικῶν ἄρχεσθαι;

---

[1] ἀνειμένως ? Richards.

[a] The textual emendation giving 'live without restraint' is
probably correct.

made to live a hard life they plot against them and hate them. It is clear therefore that those whose helot-system works out in this way do not discover the best mode of treating the problem. Again, the freedom in regard to women is detrimental both in regard to the purpose of the constitution and in regard to the happiness of the state. For just as man and wife are part of a household, it is clear that the state also is divided nearly in half into its male and female population, so that in all constitutions in which the position of the women is badly regulated one half of the state must be deemed to have been neglected in framing the law. And this has taken place in the state under consideration, for the law-giver wishing the whole community to be hardy displays his intention clearly in relation to the men, but in the case of the women has entirely neglected the matter ; for they live dissolutely *a* in respect of every sort of dissoluteness, and luxuriously. So that the inevitable result is that in a state thus constituted wealth is held in honour, especially if it is the case that the people are under the sway of their women, as most of the military and warlike races are, except the Celts and such other races as have openly held in honour attachments between males. For it appears that the original teller of the legend had good reason for uniting Ares with Aphrodite, for all men of martial spirit appear to be attracted to the companionship either of male associates or of women. Hence this characteristic existed among the Spartans, and in the time of their empire many things were controlled by the women ; yet what difference does it make whether the women rule or the rulers are ruled by the women ? The result is

5

6

7

Freedom of women : their undue licence, influence, cowardice, lawlessness.

1269 b
85 ταὐτὸ γὰρ συμβαίνει. χρησίμου δ' οὔσης τῆς
θρασύτητος πρὸς οὐδὲν τῶν ἐγκυκλίων, ἀλλ' εἴπερ,
πρὸς τὸν πόλεμον, βλαβερώταται καὶ πρὸς ταῦθ'
αἱ τῶν Λακώνων ἦσαν· ἐδήλωσαν δ' ἐπὶ τῆς τῶν[1]
Θηβαίων ἐμβολῆς, χρήσιμοι μὲν γὰρ οὐδὲν ἦσαν,
ὥσπερ ἐν ἑτέραις πόλεσιν, θόρυβον δὲ παρεῖχον
40 πλείω τῶν πολεμίων. ἐξ ἀρχῆς μὲν οὖν ἔοικε[a]
συμβεβηκέναι τοῖς Λάκωσιν εὐλόγως ἡ τῶν γυ-
1270 a ναικῶν ἄνεσις, ἔξω γὰρ τῆς οἰκείας διὰ τὰς
στρατείας ἀπεξενοῦντο πολὺν χρόνον, πολεμοῦντες
τόν τε πρὸς Ἀργείους πόλεμον καὶ πάλιν τὸν πρὸς
Ἀρκάδας καὶ Μεσσηνίους· σχολάσαντες δὲ αὑτοὺς
5 μὲν παρεῖχον τῷ νομοθέτῃ προωδοπεποιημένους
διὰ τὸν στρατιωτικὸν βίον (πολλὰ γὰρ ἔχει μέρη
τῆς ἀρετῆς), τὰς δὲ γυναῖκας φασὶ μὲν ἄγειν ἐπιχειρῆσαι τὸν Λυκοῦργον ὑπὸ τοὺς νόμους, ὡς δ'
ἀντέκρουον, ἀποστῆναι πάλιν. αἴτιαι μὲν οὖν[b]
εἰσὶν αὗται τῶν γενομένων, ὥστε δῆλον ὅτι καὶ
10 ταύτης τῆς ἁμαρτίας· ἀλλ' ἡμεῖς οὐ τοῦτο σκοποῦμεν, τίνι δεῖ συγγνώμην ἔχειν ἢ μὴ ἔχειν, ἀλλὰ
περὶ τοῦ ὀρθῶς καὶ μὴ ὀρθῶς. τὰ δὲ περὶ τὰς
γυναῖκας ἔχοντα μὴ καλῶς ἔοικεν, ὥσπερ ἐλέχθη
καὶ πρότερον, οὐ μόνον ἀπρέπειάν τινα ποιεῖν τῆς
πολιτείας αὐτῆς καθ' αὑτήν, ἀλλὰ συμβάλλεσθαί
τι πρὸς τὴν φιλοχρηματίαν. μετὰ γὰρ τὰ νῦν[c]
ῥηθέντα τοῖς περὶ τὴν ἀνωμαλίαν τῆς κτήσεως
ἐπιτιμήσειεν ἄν τις. τοῖς μὲν γὰρ αὐτῶν συμβέβηκε κεκτῆσθαι πολλὴν λίαν οὐσίαν, τοῖς δὲ
πάμπαν μικράν· διόπερ εἰς ὀλίγους ἧκεν ἡ χώρα.

---

[1] τῶν om. codd. plurimi.

[a] Under Epaminondas, 369 B.C.

the same. And although bravery is of service for none of the regular duties of life, but if at all, in war, even in this respect the Spartans' women were most harmful; and they showed this at the time of the Theban invasion,[a] for they rendered no useful service, like the women in other states, while they caused more confusion than the enemy. It is true therefore that at the outset the freedom allowed to women at Sparta seems to have come about with good reason, for the Spartans used to be away in exile abroad for long periods on account of their military expeditions, both when fighting the war against the Argives and again during the war against the Arcadians and Messenians, and when they had turned to peaceful pursuits, they handed over themselves to the lawgiver already prepared for obedience by military life (for this has many elements of virtue), but as for the women, though it is said Lycurgus did attempt to bring them under the laws, yet since they resisted he gave it up. So the Spartan women are, it is true, to blame for what took place then and therefore manifestly for the present defect; although for our own part we are not considering who deserves excuse or does not, but what is right or wrong in the constitution as it is. But, as was also said before, errors as regards the status of women seem not only to cause a certain unseemliness in the actual conduct of the state but to contribute in some degree to undue love of money. For next to the things just spoken of one might censure the Spartan institutions with respect to the unequal distribution of wealth. It has come about that some of the Spartans own too much property and some extremely little; owing to which the land

concentration of property and decline of population.

137

1270 a
τοῦτο δὲ καὶ διὰ τῶν νόμων τέτακται φαύλως·
20 ὠνεῖσθαι μὲν γὰρ ἢ πωλεῖν τὴν ὑπάρχουσαν
ἐποίησεν οὐ καλόν, ὀρθῶς ποιήσας, διδόναι δὲ
καὶ καταλείπειν ἐξουσίαν ἔδωκε τοῖς βουλομένοις·
καίτοι τοῦτο συμβαίνειν ἀναγκαῖον ἐκείνως τε καὶ
οὕτως. ἔστι δὲ καὶ τῶν γυναικῶν σχεδὸν τῆς πάσης
χώρας τῶν πέντε μερῶν τὰ δύο, τῶν τ' ἐπικλήρων
25 πολλῶν γινομένων καὶ διὰ τὸ προῖκας διδόναι
μεγάλας· καίτοι βέλτιον ἦν μηδεμίαν ἢ ὀλίγην
ἢ καὶ μετρίαν τετάχθαι.¹ νῦν δ' ἔξεστι δοῦναί
τε τὴν ἐπίκληρον ὅτῳ ἂν βούληται, κἂν ἀποθάνῃ
μὴ διαθέμενος, ὃν ἂν καταλίπῃ κληρονόμον, οὗτος
ᾧ ἂν θέλῃ δίδωσιν. τοιγαροῦν δυναμένης τῆς
30 χώρας χιλίους ἱππεῖς τρέφειν καὶ πεντακοσίους
καὶ ὁπλίτας τρισμυρίους, οὐδὲ χίλιοι τὸ πλῆθος
ἦσαν. γέγονε δὲ διὰ τῶν ἔργων αὐτῶν δῆλον ὅτι
φαύλως αὐτοῖς εἶχε τὰ περὶ τὴν τάξιν ταύτην·
μίαν γὰρ πληγὴν οὐχ ὑπήνεγκεν ἡ πόλις, ἀλλ'
ἀπώλετο διὰ τὴν ὀλιγανθρωπίαν. λέγουσι δ' ὡς
35 ἐπὶ μὲν τῶν προτέρων βασιλέων μετεδίδοσαν τῆς
πολιτείας, ὥστ' οὐ γίνεσθαι τότε ὀλιγανθρωπίαν
πολεμούντων πολὺν χρόνον· καί φασιν εἶναί ποτε
τοῖς Σπαρτιάταις² καὶ μυρίους. οὐ μὴν ἀλλ' εἴτ'
ἐστὶν ἀληθῆ ταῦτα εἴτε μή, βέλτιον τὸ διὰ τῆς
κτήσεως ὠμαλισμένης πληθύειν ἀνδρῶν τὴν πόλιν.

---

¹ hic lacunam Buecheler.
² τοὺς Σπαρτιάτας Buecheler.

ᵃ A clause seems to have been lost: 'Also it would have
been better to regulate by law the marriage of heiresses.'
ᵇ *i.e.* the consequent fall in the number of men rich enough

has fallen into few hands, and this has also been
badly regulated by the laws ; for the lawgiver made
it dishonourable to sell a family's existing estate,
and did so rightly, but he granted liberty to alienate
land at will by gift or bequest ; yet the result that
has happened was bound to follow in the one case
as well as in the other. And also nearly two-fifths
of the whole area of the country is owned by women,
because of the number of women who inherit estates
and the practice of giving large dowries ; yet it
would have been better if dowries had been prohibited by law or limited to a small or moderate
amount [a] ; whereas in fact he is allowed to give an
heiress in marriage to whomever he likes, and if he
dies without having made directions as to this by
will, whoever he leaves as his executor bestows her
upon whom he chooses   As a result of this [b] although
the country is capable of supporting fifteen hundred
cavalry and thirty thousand heavy-armed troopers,
they numbered not even a thousand. And the
defective nature of their system of land-tenure has
been proved by the actual facts of history : the
state did not succeed in enduring a single blow,[c] but
perished owing to the smallness of its population.
They have a tradition that in the earlier reigns they
used to admit foreigners to their citizenship, with
the result that dearth of population did not occur in
those days, although they were at war for a long
period ; and it is stated that at one time the Spartiates numbered as many as ten thousand. However,
whether this is true or not, it is better for a state's
male population to be kept up by measures to equalize

to keep a horse or even to provide themselves with heavy
arms.   [c] The battle of Leuctra, 371 B.C.

139

1270 a
40 ὑπεναντίος δὲ καὶ ὁ περὶ τὴν τεκνοποιίαν νόμος ▮
1270 b πρὸς ταύτην τὴν διόρθωσιν. βουλόμενος γὰρ ὁ
νομοθέτης ὡς πλείστους εἶναι τοὺς Σπαρτιάτας,
προάγεται[1] τοὺς πολίτας ὅτι πλείστους ποιεῖσθαι
παῖδας· ἔστι γὰρ αὐτοῖς νόμος τὸν μὲν γεννήσαντα
τρεῖς υἱοὺς ἄφρουρον εἶναι, τὸν δὲ τέτταρας ἀτελῆ
5 πάντων. καίτοι φανερὸν ὅτι πολλῶν γινομένων,
τῆς δὲ χώρας οὕτω διῃρημένης, ἀναγκαῖον πολλοὺς
γίνεσθαι πένητας.

’Αλλὰ μὴν καὶ τὰ περὶ τὴν ἐφορείαν ἔχει φαύλως· ▮
ἡ γὰρ ἀρχὴ κυρία μὲν αὐτὴ τῶν μεγίστων αὐτοῖς
ἐστίν, γίνονται δ’ ἐκ τοῦ δήμου παντός,[2] ὥστε
10 πολλάκις ἐμπίπτουσιν ἄνθρωποι σφόδρα πένητες
εἰς τὸ ἀρχεῖον, οἳ διὰ τὴν ἀπορίαν ὤνιοι ἦσαν.[3]
ἐδήλωσαν δὲ πολλάκις μὲν καὶ πρότερον, καὶ νῦν
δὲ ἐν τοῖς ’Ανδρίοις· διαφθαρέντες γὰρ ἀργυρίῳ
τινὲς ὅσον ἐφ’ ἑαυτοῖς ὅλην τὴν πόλιν ἀπώλεσαν.
καὶ διὰ τὸ τὴν ἀρχὴν εἶναι λίαν μεγάλην καὶ
15 ἰσοτύραννον δημαγωγεῖν [αὐτοὺς][4] ἠναγκάζοντο
καὶ οἱ βασιλεῖς, ὥστε καὶ ταύτῃ συνεπιβλάπτεσθαι
τὴν πολιτείαν· δημοκρατία γὰρ ἐξ ἀριστοκρατίας
συνέβαινεν. συνέχει μὲν οὖν τὴν πολιτείαν τὸ ▮
ἀρχεῖον τοῦτο—ἡσυχάζει γὰρ ὁ δῆμος διὰ τὸ
μετέχειν τῆς μεγίστης ἀρχῆς, ὥστ’ εἴτε διὰ τὸν
20 νομοθέτην εἴτε διὰ τύχην τοῦτο συμπέπτωκεν, συμ-

---

[1] προάγει Spengel.   [2] παντός Sauppe: πάντες codd.
[3] εἰσίν Richards.   [4] Oncken.

---

[a] The five Ephors, elected for a year by the people, were
the real rulers of Sparta. The two kings were hereditary;
the senate of twenty-eight nobles advised them, and the
Ephors presided at the Assembly of citizens over thirty years
old, who voted on the measures of the Kings and Ephors but

property. The law in relation to parentage is also somewhat adverse to the correction of this evil. For the lawgiver desiring to make the Spartiates as numerous as possible holds out inducements to the citizens to have as many children as possible : for they have a law releasing the man who has been father of three sons from military service, and exempting the father of four from all taxes. Yet it is clear that if a number of sons are born and the land is correspondingly divided there will inevitably come to be many poor men.

Moreover the regulations for the Ephorate *a* are also bad. For this office has absolute control over their most important affairs, but the Ephors are appointed from the entire people, so that quite poor men often happen to get into the office, who owing to their poverty used to be *b* easily bought. This was often manifested in earlier times, and also lately in the affair *c* at Andros ; for certain Ephors were corrupted with money and so far as lay in their power ruined the whole state. And because the office was too powerful, and equal to a tyranny, the kings also were compelled to cultivate popular favour, so that in this way too the constitution was jointly injured, for out of an aristocracy came to be evolved a democracy. Thus this office does, it is true, hold together the constitution—for the common people keep quiet because they have a share in the highest office of state, so that owing to the lawgiver's foresight, or else to accident, the Ephorate is advanta-

Political defects : the Ephorate;

could not discuss them. The small fleet was commanded by a single admiral appointed for a year by the Ephors and not allowed to hold office twice.
b Perhaps the Greek should be altered to give ' are.'
c Unknown.

141

1270 b

φερόντως ἔχει τοῖς πράγμασιν, δεῖ γὰρ τὴν
πολιτείαν τὴν μέλλουσαν σῴζεσθαι πάντα βούλεσθαι τὰ μέρη τῆς πόλεως εἶναι καὶ διαμένειν
κατὰ ταὐτά· οἱ μὲν οὖν βασιλεῖς διὰ τὴν αὑτῶν
τιμὴν οὕτως ἔχουσιν, οἱ δὲ καλοὶ κἀγαθοὶ διὰ τὴν
25 γερουσίαν (ἆθλον γὰρ ἡ ἀρχὴ αὕτη τῆς ἀρετῆς
ἐστίν), ὁ δὲ δῆμος διὰ τὴν ἐφορείαν· καθίσταται
γὰρ ἐξ ἁπάντων—ἀλλ' αἱρετὴν ἔδει τὴν ἀρχὴν 16
εἶναι ταύτην ἐξ ἁπάντων μέν, μὴ τὸν τρόπον δὲ
τοῦτον ὃν νῦν, παιδαριώδης γάρ ἐστι λίαν. ἔτι
δὲ καὶ κρίσεών εἰσι μεγάλων κύριοι, ὄντες οἱ
30 τυχόντες, διόπερ οὐκ αὐτογνώμονας βέλτιον κρίνειν
ἀλλὰ κατὰ τὰ γράμματα καὶ τοὺς νόμους. ἔστι
δὲ καὶ ἡ δίαιτα τῶν ἐφόρων οὐχ ὁμολογουμένη
τῷ βουλήματι τῆς πόλεως[2]· αὕτη[3] μὲν γὰρ ἀνειμένη λίαν ἐστίν, ἐν δὲ τοῖς ἄλλοις μᾶλλον ὑπερβάλλει ἐπὶ τὸ σκληρόν, ὥστε μὴ δύνασθαι καρ-
35 τερεῖν ἀλλὰ λάθρᾳ τὸν νόμον ἀποδιδράσκοντας
ἀπολαύειν τῶν σωματικῶν ἡδονῶν. ἔχει δὲ καὶ 17
τὰ περὶ τὴν τῶν γερόντων ἀρχὴν οὐ καλῶς αὑτοῖς.
ἐπιεικῶν μὲν γὰρ ὄντων καὶ πεπαιδευμένων ἱκανῶς
πρὸς ἀνδραγαθίαν τάχ' ἂν εἴπειέ τις συμφέρειν τῇ
πόλει, καίτοι τό γε διὰ βίου κυρίους εἶναι κρίσεων
40 μεγάλων ἀμφισβητήσιμον (ἔστι γάρ, ὥσπερ καὶ
1271 a σώματος, καὶ διανοίας γῆρας)· τὸν τρόπον δὲ
τοῦτον πεπαιδευμένων ὥστε καὶ τὸν νομοθέτην
αὐτὸν ἀπιστεῖν ὡς οὐκ ἀγαθοῖς ἀνδράσιν, οὐκ
ἀσφαλές. φαίνονται δὲ καὶ καταδωροδοκούμενοι 18
καὶ καταχαριζόμενοι πολλὰ τῶν κοινῶν οἱ κεκοι-

---

[1] κατὰ ταὐτά Bernays: ταύτά, ταῦτα, αὐτά codd.
[2] πολιτείας Scaliger.   [3] αὕτη ΓΜΡ¹Η.

---

[a] There is no clear evidence what the method was.

geous for the conduct of affairs ; for if a constitution is to be preserved, all the sections of the state
must wish it to exist and to continue on the same
lines ; so the kings are in this frame of mind owing to
their own honourable rank, the nobility owing to the
office of the Elders, which is a prize of virtue, and
the common people because of the Ephorate, which
16 is appointed from the whole population—but yet the
Ephorate, though rightly open to all the citizens,
ought not to be elected as it is now, for the method
is too childish.ᵃ And further the Ephors have juris-
diction in lawsuits of high importance, although they
are any chance people, so that it would be better
if they did not decide cases on their own judgement
but by written rules and according to the laws. Also
the mode of life of the Ephors is not in conformity
with the aim of the state, for it is itself too luxurious,
whereas in the case of the other citizens the prescribed life goes too far in the direction of harshness,
so that they are unable to endure it, and secretly
desert the law and enjoy the pleasures of the body.
17 Also their regulations for the office of the Elders are *the Senate :*
not good ; it is true that if these were persons of a
high class who had been adequately trained in manly
valour, one might perhaps say that the institution
was advantageous to the state, although their life-
tenure of the judgeship in important trials is indeed
a questionable feature (for there is old age of mind
as well as of body) ; but as their education has been
on such lines that even the lawgiver himself cannot
trust in them as men of virtue, it is a dangerous
18 institution. And it is known that those who have
been admitted to this office take bribes and betray
many of the public interests by favouritism ; so that

143

νωνηκότες τῆς ἀρχῆς ταύτης· διόπερ βέλτιον αὐτοὺς
μὴ ἀνευθύνους εἶναι, νῦν δ' εἰσίν. δόξειε δ' ἂν ἡ
τῶν ἐφόρων ἀρχὴ πάσας εὐθύνειν τὰς ἀρχάς· τοῦτο
δὲ τῇ ἐφορείᾳ μέγα λίαν τὸ δῶρον, καὶ τὸν τρόπον
οὐ τοῦτον λέγομεν διδόναι δεῖν τὰς εὐθύνας. ἔτι
δὲ καὶ τὴν αἵρεσιν ἣν ποιοῦνται τῶν γερόντων
10 κατά τε τὴν κρίσιν ἐστὶ παιδαριώδης, καὶ τὸ αὐτὸν
αἰτεῖσθαι τὸν ἀξιωθησόμενον τῆς ἀρχῆς οὐκ ὀρθῶς
ἔχει· δεῖ γὰρ καὶ βουλόμενον καὶ μὴ βουλόμενον
ἄρχειν τὸν ἄξιον τῆς ἀρχῆς. νῦν δ' ὅπερ καὶ περὶ
τὴν ἄλλην πολιτείαν ὁ νομοθέτης φαίνεται ποιῶν·
15 φιλοτίμους γὰρ κατασκευάζων τοὺς πολίτας τούτῳ
κέχρηται πρὸς τὴν αἵρεσιν τῶν γερόντων, οὐδεὶς
γὰρ ἂν ἄρχειν αἰτήσαιτο μὴ φιλότιμος ὤν· καίτοι
τῶν ἀδικημάτων τῶν γ'[1] ἑκουσίων τὰ πλεῖστα συμβαίνει σχεδὸν διὰ φιλοτιμίαν καὶ διὰ φιλοχρηματίαν
τοῖς ἀνθρώποις. περὶ δὲ βασιλείας, εἰ μὲν μὴ
20 βέλτιόν ἐστιν ὑπάρχειν ταῖς πόλεσιν ἢ βέλτιον,
ἄλλος ἔστω λόγος· ἀλλὰ μὴν βέλτιόν γε μὴ
καθάπερ νῦν, ἀλλὰ κατὰ τὸν αὑτοῦ βίον ἕκαστον
κρίνεσθαι τῶν βασιλέων. ὅτι δ' ὁ νομοθέτης οὐδ'
αὐτὸς οἴεται δύνασθαι ποιεῖν καλοὺς κἀγαθούς,
δῆλον· ἀπιστεῖ γοῦν ὡς οὐκ οὖσιν ἱκανῶς ἀγαθοῖς
25 ἀνδράσιν· διόπερ ἐξέπεμπον συμπρεσβευτὰς τοὺς
ἐχθρούς, καὶ σωτηρίαν ἐνόμιζον τῇ πόλει εἶναι τὸ
στασιάζειν τοὺς βασιλεῖς. οὐ καλῶς δ' οὐδὲ περὶ
τὰ συσσίτια τὰ καλούμενα φιδίτια νενομοθέτηται

---

[1] ed.: τῶν γ' ἀδικημάτων τῶν aut τῶν γ' ἀδικημάτων codd.

---

[a] *i.e.* the Ephors, two of whom went with the Kings.

it would be better if they were not exempt from having to render an account of their office, but at present they are. And it might be held that the magistracy of the Ephors serves to hold all the offices to account; but this gives altogether too much to the Ephorate, and it is not the way in which, as we maintain, officials ought to be called to account. Again, the procedure in the election of the Elders as a mode of selection is not only childish, but it is wrong that one who is to be the holder of this honourable office should canvass for it, for the man worthy of the office ought to hold it whether he wants to or

19 not. But as it is the lawgiver clearly does the same here as in the rest of the constitution: he makes the citizens ambitious and has used this for the election of the Elders, for nobody would ask for office if he were not ambitious; yet surely ambition and love of money are the motives that bring about almost the greatest part of the voluntary wrongdoing that

20 takes place among mankind. As to monarchy, the *the Kings;* question whether it is not or is an advantageous institution for states to possess may be left to another discussion; but at all events it would be advantageous that kings should not be appointed as they are now, but chosen in each case with regard to their own life and conduct. But it is clear that even the lawgiver himself does not suppose that he can make the kings men of high character: at all events he distrusts them as not being persons of sufficient worth; owing to which the Spartans used to send their enemies *a* with them as colleagues on embassies, and thought that the safety of the state depended on division

21 between the kings. Also the regulations for the *the Messes.* public mess-tables called Phiditia have been badly

145

1271 a

τῷ καταστήσαντι πρῶτον. ἔδει γὰρ ἀπὸ κοινοῦ
μᾶλλον εἶναι τὴν σύνοδον, καθάπερ ἐν Κρήτῃ·
30 παρὰ δὲ τοῖς Λάκωσιν ἕκαστον δεῖ φέρειν, καὶ
σφόδρα πενήτων ἐνίων ὄντων καὶ τοῦτο τὸ ἀνά-
λωμα οὐ δυναμένων δαπανᾶν, ὥστε συμβαίνειν
τοὐναντίον τῷ νομοθέτῃ τῆς προαιρέσεως. βούλεται μὲν γὰρ δημοκρατικὸν εἶναι τὸ κατα-
σκεύασμα τῶν συσσιτίων, γίνεται δ’ ἥκιστα δημο-
35 κρατικὸν οὕτω νενομοθετημένον· μετέχειν μὲν γὰρ
οὐ ῥᾴδιον τοῖς λίαν πένησιν, ὅρος δὲ τῆς πολιτείας
οὗτός ἐστιν αὐτοῖς ὁ πάτριος, τὸν μὴ δυνάμενον
τοῦτο τὸ τέλος φέρειν μὴ μετέχειν αὐτῆς. τῷ δὲ 22
περὶ τοὺς ναυάρχους νόμῳ καὶ ἕτεροί τινες ἐπι-
τετιμήκασιν, ὀρθῶς ἐπιτιμῶντες· στάσεως γὰρ
40 γίνεται αἴτιος, ἐπὶ γὰρ τοῖς βασιλεῦσιν οὖσι
στρατηγοῖς ἀΐδιος ἡ ναυαρχία σχεδὸν ἑτέρα βασιλεία
καθέστηκεν. καὶ ὡδὶ δὲ τῇ ὑποθέσει τοῦ νομο-
1271 b θέτου ἐπιτιμήσειεν ἄν τις, ὅπερ καὶ Πλάτων ἐν
τοῖς Νόμοις ἐπιτετίμηκεν. πρὸς γὰρ μέρος ἀρετῆς
ἡ πᾶσα σύνταξις τῶν νόμων ἐστί, τὴν πολεμικήν·
αὕτη γὰρ χρησίμη πρὸς τὸ κρατεῖν. τοιγαροῦν
ἐσῴζοντο μὲν πολεμοῦντες, ἀπώλλυντο δὲ ἄρξαντες
5 διὰ τὸ μὴ ἐπίστασθαι σχολάζειν μηδὲ ἠσκηκέναι
μηδεμίαν ἄσκησιν ἑτέραν κυριωτέραν τῆς πολεμικῆς. τούτου δὲ ἁμάρτημα οὐκ ἔλαττον· νομί- 23
ζουσι μὲν γὰρ γίνεσθαι τἀγαθὰ τὰ περιμάχητα
δι’ ἀρετῆς μᾶλλον ἢ κακίας, καὶ τοῦτο μὲν καλῶς,
10 ὅτι μέντοι ταῦτα κρείττω τῆς ἀρετῆς ὑπολαμβάνουσιν, οὐ καλῶς. φαύλως δ’ ἔχει καὶ περὶ τὰ
κοινὰ χρήματα τοῖς Σπαρτιάταις· οὔτε γὰρ ἐν τῷ

laid down by their originator. The revenue for
these ought to come rather from public funds, as in
Crete; but among the Spartans everybody has to
contribute, although some of them are very poor and
unable to find money for this charge, so that the
result is the opposite of what the lawgiver purposed.
For he intends the organization of the common
tables to be democratic, but when regulated by the
law in this manner it works out as by no means
democratic; for it is not easy for the very poor to
participate, yet their established regulation for
citizenship is that it is not to belong to one who is
22 unable to pay this tax. The law about the Admirals *the Admirals.*
has been criticized by some other writers also, and
rightly criticized; for it acts as a cause of sedition,
since in addition to the kings who are military commanders the office of Admiral stands almost as
another kingship. Another criticism that may be *General defects:*
made against the fundamental principle of the law- *lack of*
giver is one that Plato has made in the *Laws*. The *training for peace;*
entire system of the laws is directed towards one
part of virtue only, military valour, because this is
serviceable for conquest. Owing to this they remained secure while at war, but began to decline
when they had won an empire, because they did not
know how to live a peaceful life, and had been
trained in no other form of training more important
23 than the art of war. And another error no less
serious than that one is this: they think that the
coveted prizes of life are won by valour more than
by cowardice, and in this they are right, yet they
imagine wrongly that these prizes are worth more
than the valour that wins them. The public finance *bad financial*
of Sparta is also badly regulated: when compelled *system.*

147

1271 b

κοινῷ τῆς πόλεώς ἐστιν οὐδὲν πολέμους μεγάλους
ἀναγκαζομένοις πολεμεῖν, εἰσφέρουσί τε κακῶς,
διὰ γὰρ τὸ τῶν Σπαρτιατῶν εἶναι τὴν πλείστην
15 γῆν οὐκ ἐξετάζουσιν ἀλλήλων τὰς εἰσφοράς. ἀπο-
βέβηκέ τε τοὐναντίον τῷ νομοθέτῃ τοῦ συμ-
φέροντος· τὴν μὲν γὰρ πόλιν πεποίηκεν ἀχρήματον,
τοὺς δ᾿ ἰδιώτας φιλοχρηματους.

Περὶ μὲν οὖν τῆς Λακεδαιμονίων πολιτείας ἐπὶ
τοσοῦτον εἰρήσθω· ταῦτα γάρ ἐστιν ἃ μάλιστ᾿ ἄν
τις ἐπιτιμήσειεν.

20 VII. Ἡ δὲ Κρητικὴ πολιτεία πάρεγγυς μέν ἐστι 1
ταύτης, ἔχει δὲ μικρὰ μὲν οὐ χεῖρον, τὸ δὲ πλεῖον
ἧττον γλαφυρῶς. καὶ γὰρ ἔοικε καὶ λέγεται δὲ
τὰ πλεῖστα μεμιμῆσθαι τὴν Κρητικὴν πολιτείαν ἡ
τῶν Λακώνων, τὰ δὲ πλεῖστα τῶν ἀρχαίων ἧττον
25 διήρθρωται τῶν νεωτέρων. φασὶ γὰρ τὸν Λυκοῦργον, ὅτε τὴν ἐπιτροπείαν τὴν Χαριλάου[1] τοῦ βασιλέως καταλιπὼν ἀπεδήμησεν, τότε τὸν πλεῖστον
διατρῖψαι χρόνον περὶ τὴν Κρήτην διὰ τὴν συγ-
γένειαν· ἄποικοι γὰρ οἱ Λύκτιοι τῶν Λακώνων
ἦσαν, κατέλαβον δ᾿ οἱ πρὸς τὴν ἀποικίαν ἐλθόντες
30 τὴν τάξιν τῶν νόμων ὑπάρχουσαν ἐν τοῖς τότε
κατοικοῦσιν· διὸ καὶ νῦν οἱ περίοικοι τὸν αὐτὸν
τρόπον χρῶνται αὐτοῖς, ὡς κατασκευάσαντος Μίνω
πρώτου τὴν τάξιν τῶν νόμων. δοκεῖ δ᾿ ἡ νῆσος 2
καὶ πρὸς τὴν ἀρχὴν τὴν Ἑλληνικὴν πεφυκέναι καὶ
κεῖσθαι καλῶς· πάσῃ γὰρ ἐπίκειται τῇ θαλάσσῃ,

---

[1] Χαριλάου cod. inf., cf. 1316 a 34 : Χαρίλλου hic cet.

[a] e.g. by Herodotus i. 65.
[b] Posthumous son of Lycurgus's elder brother King Poly-
dectes; cf. 1316 a 34.
[c] Lyctus was an inland city in the east of Crete, not far
from Cnossus.

to carry on wars on a large scale she has nothing in the state treasury, and the Spartiates pay war taxes badly because, as most of the land is owned by them, they do not scrutinize each other's contributions. And the lawgiver has achieved the opposite result to what is advantageous—he has made the state poor and the individual citizen covetous.

So much for a discussion of the constitution of Sparta : for these are the main points in it for criticism.

VII. The Cretan constitution approximates to that of Sparta, but though in a few points it is not worse framed, for the larger part it has a less perfect finish. For the Spartan constitution appears and indeed is actually stated [a] to have been copied in most of its provisions from the Cretan ; and as a rule old things have been less fully elaborated than newer ones. For it is said that when Lycurgus relinquished his post as guardian of King Charilaus [b] and went abroad, he subsequently passed most of his time in Crete because of the relationship between the Cretans and the Spartans; for the Lyctians [c] were colonists from Sparta, and the settlers that went out to the colony found the system of laws already existing among the previous inhabitants of the place ; owing to which the neighbouring villagers even now use these laws in the same manner, in the belief that Minos [d] first instituted this code of laws. Also the island appears to be designed by nature and well situated to be the imperial state, as it lies across the whole of the sea, round which almost

Cretan Constitution.

Model for Lycurgus.

Geographical considerations.

---

[d] Legendary ruler of Crete, son of Zeus and Europa, and after death a judge in the lower world.

149

1271 b
35 σχεδὸν τῶν Ἑλλήνων ἱδρυμένων περὶ τὴν θάλασσαν
πάντων· ἀπέχει γὰρ τῇ μὲν τῆς Πελοποννήσου
μικρόν, τῇ δὲ τῆς Ἀσίας τοῦ περὶ Τριόπιον τόπου
καὶ Ῥόδου. διὸ καὶ τὴν τῆς θαλάσσης ἀρχὴν
κατέσχεν ὁ Μίνως, καὶ τὰς νήσους τὰς μὲν ἐχειρώ-
σατο τὰς δ' ᾤκισεν, τέλος δὲ ἐπιθέμενος τῇ Σικελίᾳ
40 τὸν βίον ἐτελεύτησεν ἐκεῖ περὶ Κάμικον.

Ἔχει δ' ἀνάλογον ἡ Κρητικὴ τάξις πρὸς τὴν
1272 a Λακωνικήν. γεωργοῦσί τε γὰρ τοῖς μὲν οἱ εἵλωτες
τοῖς δὲ Κρησὶν οἱ περίοικοι, καὶ συσσίτια παρ'
ἀμφοτέροις ἐστίν, καὶ τό γε ἀρχαῖον ἐκάλουν οἱ
Λάκωνες οὐ φιδίτια ἀλλ' ἀνδρία, καθάπερ οἱ
Κρῆτες, ᾗ καὶ δῆλον ὅτι ἐκεῖθεν ἐλήλυθεν. ἔτι δὲ
5 τῆς πολιτείας ἡ τάξις· οἱ μὲν γὰρ ἔφοροι τὴν
αὐτὴν ἔχουσι δύναμιν τοῖς ἐν τῇ Κρήτῃ καλου-
μένοις κόσμοις, πλὴν οἱ μὲν ἔφοροι πέντε τὸν ἀριθμὸν οἱ δὲ κόσμοι δέκα εἰσίν· οἱ δὲ γέροντες τοῖς
γέρουσιν οὓς καλοῦσιν οἱ Κρῆτες βουλὴν ἴσοι·
βασιλεία δὲ πρότερον μὲν ἦν, εἶτα κατέλυσαν οἱ
10 Κρῆτες, καὶ τὴν ἡγεμονίαν οἱ κόσμοι τὴν κατὰ
πόλεμον ἔχουσιν· ἐκκλησίας δὲ μετέχουσι πάντες,
κυρία δ' οὐδενός ἐστιν ἀλλ' ἢ συνεπιψηφίσαι τὰ
δόξαντα τοῖς γέρουσι καὶ τοῖς κόσμοις.

Τὰ μὲν οὖν τῶν συσσιτίων ἔχει βέλτιον τοῖς
Κρησὶν ἢ τοῖς Λάκωσιν· ἐν μὲν γὰρ Λακεδαίμονι
15 κατὰ κεφαλὴν ἕκαστος εἰσφέρει τὸ τεταγμένον,
εἰ δὲ μή, μετέχειν νόμος κωλύει τῆς πολιτείας,
καθάπερ εἴρηται καὶ πρότερον, ἐν δὲ Κρήτῃ κοινο-

---

¹ μὲν οἱ (vel μὲν Λάκωσιν οἱ) ed. ; μὲν codd.

all the Greeks are settled; for Crete is only a short distance from the Peloponnese in one direction, and from the part of Asia around Triopium and from Rhodes in the other. Owing to this Minos won the empire of the sea,[a] and made some of the islands subject to him and settled colonies in others, but finally when making an attack on Sicily he ended his life there near Camicus.

The Cretan institutions are on the same lines as those of Sparta: in Sparta the land is tilled by the Helots and in Crete by the serfs; and also both have public mess-tables, and in old days the Spartans called them not 'phiditia' but 'men's messes,' as the Cretans do, which is a proof that they came from Crete. And so also is the system of government; for the Ephors have the same power as the magistrates called Cosmi in Crete, except that the Ephors are five in number and the Cosmi ten; and the Elders at Sparta are equal in number to the Elders whom the Cretans call the Council; and monarchy existed in former times, but then the Cretans abolished it, and the Cosmi hold the leadership in war; and all are members of the Assembly, which has no powers except the function of confirming by vote the resolutions already formed by the Elders and the Cosmi. *Resemblances to Spartan system.*

Now the Cretan arrangements for the public mess-tables are better than the Spartan; for at Sparta each citizen pays a fixed poll-tax, failing which he is prevented by law from taking part in the government, as has been said before; but in Crete the system is more communal, for out of all the crops and cattle *Messes better organized,*

---

[a] See Thucydides i. 4 and 8. The tradition of the wealth of Minos is supported by the recent excavations at Cnossus.

1272 a

τέρως· ἀπὸ πάντων γὰρ τῶν γινομένων καρπῶν
τε καὶ βοσκημάτων δημοσίων καὶ ἐκ τῶν¹ φόρων
οὓς φέρουσιν οἱ περίοικοι τέτακται μέρος τὸ μὲν
20 πρὸς τοὺς θεοὺς καὶ τὰς κοινὰς λειτουργίας, τὸ δὲ
τοῖς συσσιτίοις, ὥστ' ἐκ κοινοῦ τρέφεσθαι πάντας,
καὶ γυναῖκας καὶ παῖδας καὶ ἄνδρας· πρὸς δὲ τὴν
ὀλιγοσιτίαν ὡς ὠφέλιμον πολλὰ πεφιλοσόφηκεν
ὁ νομοθέτης, καὶ πρὸς τὴν διάζευξιν τῶν γυναικῶν ἵνα μὴ πολυτεκνῶσι, τὴν πρὸς τοὺς ἄρρενας
25 ποιήσας ὁμιλίαν, περὶ ἧς εἰ φαύλως ἢ μὴ φαύλως
ἕτερος ἔσται τοῦ διασκέψασθαι καιρός. ὅτι δὴ²
τὰ περὶ τὰ συσσίτια βέλτιον τέτακται τοῖς Κρησὶν
ἢ τοῖς Λάκωσι, φανερόν· τὰ δὲ περὶ τοὺς κόσμους
ἔτι χεῖρον τῶν ἐφόρων. ὃ μὲν γὰρ ἔχει κακὸν τὸ
30 τῶν ἐφόρων ἀρχεῖον, ὑπάρχει καὶ τούτοις, γίνονται
γὰρ οἱ τυχόντες· ὃ δ' ἐκεῖ συμφέρει πρὸς τὴν
πολιτείαν, ἐνταῦθ' οὐκ ἔστιν. ἐκεῖ μὲν γὰρ διὰ
τὸ τὴν αἵρεσιν ἐκ πάντων εἶναι μετέχων ὁ δῆμος
τῆς μεγίστης ἀρχῆς βούλεται μένειν τὴν πολιτείαν·
ἐνταῦθα δ' οὐκ ἐξ ἁπάντων αἱροῦνται τοὺς κόσμους
35 ἀλλ' ἐκ τινῶν γενῶν, καὶ τοὺς γέροντας ἐκ τῶν
κεκοσμηκότων, περὶ ὧν τοὺς αὐτοὺς ἄν τις εἴπειε
λόγους καὶ περὶ τῶν ἐν Λακεδαίμονι γινομένων³·
τὸ γὰρ ἀνυπεύθυνον καὶ τὸ διὰ βίου μεῖζόν ἐστι
γέρας τῆς ἀξίας αὐτοῖς, καὶ τὸ μὴ κατὰ γράμματα ἄρχειν ἀλλ' αὐτογνώμονας ἐπισφαλές. τὸ δ'
40 ἡσυχάζειν μὴ μετέχοντα τὸν δῆμον οὐδὲν σημεῖον

---

¹ ἐκ τῶν ante φόρων Richards, ante δημοσίων codd.
² δὴ Lambinus : δὲ codd.   ³ γερόντων Congreve.

ᵃ This promise is not fulfilled.

152

produced from the public lands, and the tributes paid
by the serfs, one part is assigned for the worship of the
gods and the maintenance of the public services, and
the other for the public mess-tables, so that all the
citizens are maintained from the common funds,
women and children as well as men; and the lawgiver has devised many wise measures to secure the
benefit of moderation at table, and the segregation
of the women in order that they may not bear many
children, for which purpose he instituted association
with the male sex, as to which there will be another
occasion *a* to consider whether it was a bad thing or
a good one. That the regulations for the common
mess-tables therefore are better in Crete than at
Sparta is manifest; but the regulations for the Cosmi
are even worse than those regarding the Ephors.
For the evil attaching to the office of the Ephors censorship
belongs to the Cosmi also, as the post is filled by any worse.
chance persons, while the benefit conferred on the
government by this office at Sparta is lacking in Crete.
At Sparta, as the election is made from all the citizens,
the common people sharing in the highest office
desire the maintenance of the constitution, but in
Crete they do not elect the Cosmi from all the citizens
but from certain clans, and the Elders from those who The Elders.
have held the office of Cosmos, about which regulations
the same comments might be made as about what
takes place at Sparta: their freedom from being
called to account and their tenure for life gives them
greater rank than their merit deserves, and their
administration of their office at their own discretion
and not under the guidance of a written code is
dangerous. And the fact that the common people
quietly tolerate their exclusion is no proof that the

1272 a
τοῦ τετάχθαι καλῶς· οὐδὲν γὰρ λήμματος ἐστὶ
1272 b τοῖς κόσμοις ὥσπερ τοῖς ἐφόροις, πόρρω γ' ἀπ
οἰκοῦσιν ἐν νήσῳ τῶν διαφθερούντων. ἦν δὲ ποι
οῦνται τῆς ἁμαρτίας ταύτης ἰατρείαν, ἄτοπος κα
οὐ πολιτικὴ ἀλλὰ δυναστευτική· πολλάκις γὰ
5 ἐκβάλλουσι συστάντες τινὲς τοὺς κόσμους ἢ τῶ
συναρχόντων αὐτῶν ἢ τῶν ἰδιωτῶν· ἔξεστι δὲ κα
μεταξὺ τοῖς κόσμοις ἀπειπεῖν τὴν ἀρχήν. ταῦτ
δὴ πάντα βέλτιον γίνεσθαι κατὰ νόμον ἢ κατ
ἀνθρώπων βούλησιν· οὐ γὰρ ἀσφαλὴς ὁ κανὼν
πάντων δὲ φαυλότατον τὸ τῆς ἀκοσμίας, ἢ
καθιστᾶσι πολλάκις οἳ ἂν[2] μὴ δίκας βούλωντα
δοῦναι τῶν δυνατῶν[3]· ἢ καὶ δῆλον ὡς ἔχει τ
10 πολιτείας ἡ τάξις, ἀλλ' οὐ πολιτεία ἐστὶν ἀλλ
δυναστεία μᾶλλον. εἰώθασι δὲ διαλαμβάνοντε
τὸν δῆμον καὶ τοὺς φίλους ἀναρχίαν[4] ποιεῖν κα
στασιάζειν καὶ μάχεσθαι πρὸς ἀλλήλους. καίτο
τί διαφέρει τὸ τοιοῦτον ἢ διά τινος χρόνου μηκέτ
15 πόλιν εἶναι τὴν τοιαύτην, ἀλλὰ λύεσθαι τὴν πολι
τικὴν κοινωνίαν;

Ἔστι δ' ἐπικίνδυνος οὕτως ἔχουσα πόλις, τῶ
βουλομένων ἐπιτίθεσθαι καὶ δυναμένων. ἀλλ
καθάπερ εἴρηται, σῴζεται διὰ τὸν τόπον· ξενηλασία
γὰρ τὸ πόρρω πεποίηκεν. διὸ καὶ τὸ τῶν περιοί
κων μένει τοῖς Κρησίν, οἱ δ' εἵλωτες ἀφίσταντα
20 πολλάκις· οὔτε γὰρ ἐξωτερικῆς ἀρχῆς κοινωνοῦσι

---

[1] Richards : λήμματός τι codd.
[2] οἳ ἂν Coraes : ὅταν codd.
[3] τῶν δυνατῶν post 8 ἀκοσμίας codd. (alii hic sed δυναστῶ
vel δικαστῶν.) [4] ἀναρχίαν Bernays : μοναρχίαν codd

---

[a] *i.e.* the defect of the undue restriction of the office.
[b] See 1292 b 10 n.
[c] The mss. give ' bring about a monarchy.'

154

arrangement is a sound one; for the Cosmi unlike *Stability*
the Ephors make no sort of profit, as they live in an *due to position,*
island remote from any people to corrupt them. *not to*
Also the remedy which they employ for this defect[a] *institutions.*
is a curious one, and less characteristic of a republic
7 than of a dynasty[b]: often the Cosmi are expelled
by a conspiracy formed among some of their actual
colleagues or the private citizens; also the Cosmi
are allowed to resign during their term of office.
Now it would be preferable for all these matters to
be regulated by law rather than to be at the discretion of individuals, for that is a dangerous principle.
And the worst expedient of all is that of the suspension
of the office of Cosmi, which is often brought about
by members of the powerful class who wish to escape
being punished; this proves that the constitution
has a republican element, although it is not actually
a republic but rather a dynasty.[b] And the nobles
frequently form parties among the common people
and among their friends and so bring about a suspension of government,[c] and form factions and engage
in war with one another. Yet such a condition of
things really means that for a time such a state is
a state no longer, but the bonds of civil society are
loosened.

And it is a precarious position for a state to be in, *Weakness*
when those who wish to attack it also have the power *proved by history.*
to do so. But, as has been said, it is saved by its
locality; for distance has had the same effect as
alien-acts.[d] A result of this is that with the Cretans
the serf population stands firm, whereas the Helots
often revolt; for the Cretans take no part in foreign

---

[d] Aliens required special permission to reside at Sparta, and
the ephors had powers to expel them for undesirable conduct.

οἱ Κρῆτες, νεωστί τε πόλεμος ξενικὸς διαβέβηκεν
εἰς τὴν νῆσον ὃς πεποίηκε φανερὰν τὴν ἀσθένειαν
τῶν ἐκεῖ νόμων.

Περὶ μὲν οὖν ταύτης εἰρήσθω τοσαῦθ᾽ ἡμῖν τῆς
πολιτείας.

VIII. Πολιτεύεσθαι δὲ δοκοῦσι καὶ Καρχηδόνιοι 1
25 καλῶς καὶ πολλὰ περιττῶς πρὸς τοὺς ἄλλους,
μάλιστα δ᾽ ἔνια παραπλησίως τοῖς Λάκωσιν.
αὗται γὰρ αἱ πολιτεῖαι τρεῖς ἀλλήλαις τε σύνεγγύς
πώς εἰσι καὶ τῶν ἄλλων πολὺ διαφέρουσιν, ἥ τε
Κρητικὴ καὶ ἡ Λακωνικὴ καὶ τρίτη τούτων ἡ
30 Καρχηδονίων. καὶ πολλὰ τῶν τεταγμένων ἔχει
παρ᾽ αὐτοῖς καλῶς· σημεῖον δὲ πολιτείας συν-
τεταγμένης τὸ τὸν δῆμον ἑκούσιον[1] διαμένειν ἐν τῇ
τάξει τῆς πολιτείας, καὶ μήτε στάσιν ὅ τι καὶ ἄξιον
εἰπεῖν γεγενῆσθαι μήτε τύραννον.

Ἔχει δὲ παραπλήσια τῇ Λακωνικῇ πολιτείᾳ τὰ 2
μὲν συσσίτια τῶν ἑταιριῶν τοῖς φιδιτίοις, τὴν δὲ
35 τῶν ἑκατὸν καὶ τεττάρων ἀρχὴν τοῖς ἐφόροις
(πλὴν ὃ οὔ[2] χεῖρον, οἱ μὲν[3] ἐκ τῶν τυχόντων
εἰσί, ταύτην δ᾽ αἱροῦνται τὴν ἀρχὴν ἀριστίνδην),
τοὺς δὲ βασιλεῖς καὶ τὴν γερουσίαν ἀνάλογον τοῖς
ἐκεῖ βασιλεῦσι καὶ γέρουσιν, καὶ βέλτιον δὲ τοὺς
βασιλεῖς μήτε κατὰ τὸ αὐτὸ εἶναι γένος, μηδὲ
40 τοῦτο τὸ τυχόν, εἴτε διαφέρον . . .[4] ἐκ τούτων
αἱρετοὺς μᾶλλον ἢ καθ᾽ ἡλικίαν· μεγάλων γὰρ
1273a κύριοι καθεστῶτες, ἂν εὐτελεῖς ὦσι μεγάλα βλά-

---

[1] ἑκούσιον Spengel: ἔχουσαν codd.
[2] ὃ οὔ Bernays: οὐ codd.   [3] μὲν γὰρ codd. cet. plurimi.
[4] lacunam Conring.

• Clauses seem to have been lost concluding the account

empire, and also the island has only lately been invaded by warfare from abroad, rendering manifest the weakness of the legal system there.

Let this suffice for our discussion of this form of constitution.

VIII. Carthage also appears to have a good consti- Constitu-
tution, with many outstanding features as compared tion of
Carthage.
with those of other nations, but most nearly resembling the Spartan in some points. For these three constitutions are in a way near to one another and are widely different from the others—the Cretan, the Spartan and, thirdly, that of Carthage. Many regulations at Carthage are good ; and a proof that its constitution is well regulated is that the populace willingly remain faithful to the constitutional system, and that neither civil strife has arisen in any degree worth mentioning, nor yet a tyrant.

Points in which the Carthaginian constitution Resem-
resembles the Spartan are the common mess-tables blances to
Sparta.
of its Comradeships corresponding to the Phiditia, and the magistracy of the Hundred and Four corresponding to the Ephors (except one point of superiority—the Ephors are drawn from any class, but the Carthaginians elect this magistracy by merit) ; the kings and the council of Elders correspond to the kings and Elders at Sparta, and it is another superior feature that the Carthaginian kings are not confined to the same family and that one of no particular distinction, and also that if any family distinguishes itself . . .[a] the Elders are to be chosen from these rather than by age ; for as they are put in control of important matters, if they are men of no value they do great

of the appointment of the Kings and turning to the Elders and their selection on grounds of merit and wealth.

πτουσι, καὶ ἔβλαψαν ἤδη τὴν πόλιν τὴν τῶν Λακεδαιμονίων.

Τὰ μὲν οὖν πλεῖστα τῶν ἐπιτιμηθέντων ἂν διὰ
τὰς παρεκβάσεις κοινὰ τυγχάνει πάσαις ὄντα ταῖς
εἰρημέναις πολιτείαις· τῶν δὲ πρὸς τὴν ὑπόθεσιν
5 τῆς ἀριστοκρατίας καὶ τῆς πολιτείας τὰ μὲν εἰς
δῆμον ἐκκλίνει μᾶλλον τὰ δ' εἰς ὀλιγαρχίαν. τοῦ
μὲν γὰρ τὸ μὲν προσάγειν τὸ δὲ μὴ προσάγειν πρὸς
τὸν δῆμον οἱ βασιλεῖς κύριοι μετὰ τῶν γερόντων
ἂν ὁμογνωμονῶσι πάντες, εἰ δὲ μή, καὶ τούτων
10 ὁ δῆμος· ἃ δ' ἂν εἰσφέρωσιν οὗτοι, οὐ διακοῦσαι
μόνον ἀποδιδόασι τῷ δήμῳ τὰ δόξαντα τοῖς ἄρχουσιν, ἀλλὰ κύριοι κρίνειν εἰσί, καὶ τῷ βουλομένῳ
τοῖς εἰσφερομένοις ἀντειπεῖν ἔξεστιν, ὅπερ ἐν ταῖς
ἑτέραις πολιτείαις οὐκ ἔστιν.[1] τὸ δὲ τὰς πενταρχίας
κυρίας οὔσας πολλῶν καὶ μεγάλων ὑφ' αὑτῶν
15 αἱρετὰς εἶναι, καὶ τὴν τῶν ἑκατὸν ταύτας αἱρεῖσθαι
τὴν μεγίστην ἀρχήν, ἔτι δὲ ταύτας πλείονα ἄρχειν
χρόνον τῶν ἄλλων (καὶ γὰρ ἐξεληλυθότες ἄρχουσι
καὶ μέλλοντες) ὀλιγαρχικόν· τὸ δ' ἀμίσθους καὶ
μὴ κληρωτὰς ἀριστοκρατικὸν θετέον, καὶ εἴ τι
τοιοῦτον ἕτερον, καὶ τὸ τὰς δίκας ὑπὸ τῶν[2] ἀρχείων
20 δικάζεσθαι πάσας (καὶ μὴ ἄλλας ὑπ' ἄλλων καθάπερ
ἐν Λακεδαίμονι). παρεκβαίνει δὲ τῆς ἀριστοκρατίας ἡ τάξις τῶν Καρχηδονίων μάλιστα πρὸς

---

[1] ὅπερ—οὐκ ἔστι post δῆμος 10 tr. Wade-Gery.
[2] τινῶν Coraes.

---

[a] i.e. both parties agree to refer or not to refer.
[b] i.e. even when the Kings only or the Elders only desire
reference, it takes place.

harm, and they have already injured the Spartan State.

Now most of the points in the Carthaginian system that would be criticized on the ground of their defects happen to be common to all the constitutions of which we have spoken ; but the features open to criticism as judged by the principle of an aristocracy or republic are some of them departures in the direction of democracy and others in the direction of oligarchy. The reference of some matters and not of others to the popular assembly rests with the kings in consultation with the Elders *Democratic features.* in case they agree unanimously,[a] but failing that, these matters also lie with the people [b] ; and when the kings introduce business in the assembly, they do not merely let the people sit and listen to the decisions that have been taken by their rulers, but the people have the sovereign decision and anybody who wishes may speak against the proposals introduced, a right that does not exist under the other constitutions. The appointment by co-optation of the Boards of *Oligarchic features.* Five which control many important matters, and the election by these boards of the supreme magistracy of the Hundred, and also their longer tenure of authority than that of any other officers (for they are in power after they have gone out of office and before they have actually entered upon it) are oligarchical features ; their receiving no pay and not being chosen by lot and other similar regulations must be set down as aristocratic, and so must the fact that the members of the Boards are the judges in all lawsuits, instead of different suits being tried by different courts as at Sparta. But the Carthaginian system *Plutocracy.* deviates from aristocracy in the direction of oligarchy

1273 a

τὴν ὀλιγαρχίαν κατά τινα διάνοιαν ἢ συνδοκεῖ
τοῖς πολλοῖς· οὐ γὰρ μόνον ἀριστίνδην ἀλλὰ καὶ
πλουτίνδην οἴονται δεῖν αἱρεῖσθαι τοὺς ἄρχοντας,
25 ἀδύνατον γὰρ τὸν ἀποροῦντα καλῶς ἄρχειν καὶ
σχολάζειν. εἴπερ οὖν τὸ μὲν αἱρεῖσθαι πλουτίνδην
ὀλιγαρχικὸν τὸ δὲ κατ᾽ ἀρετὴν ἀριστοκρατικόν,
αὕτη τις ἂν εἴη τάξις τρίτη καθ᾽ ἥνπερ συντέτακται
καὶ τοῖς Καρχηδονίοις τὰ περὶ τὴν πολιτείαν·
αἱροῦνται γὰρ εἰς δύο ταῦτα βλέποντες, καὶ μά-
30 λιστα τὰς μεγίστας, τούς τε βασιλεῖς καὶ τοὺς
στρατηγούς. δεῖ δὲ νομίζειν ἁμάρτημα νομοθέτου
τὴν παρέκβασιν εἶναι τῆς ἀριστοκρατίας ταύτην·
ἐξ ἀρχῆς γὰρ τοῦθ᾽ ὁρᾶν ἐστι τῶν ἀναγκαιοτάτων,
ὅπως οἱ βέλτιστοι δύνωνται σχολάζειν καὶ μηδὲν
35 ἀσχημονεῖν, μὴ μόνον ἄρχοντες ἀλλὰ μηδ᾽ ἰδιωτεύοντες. εἰ δὲ δεῖ βλέπειν καὶ πρὸς εὐπορίαν
χάριν σχολῆς, φαῦλον τὸ τὰς μεγίστας ὠνητὰς
εἶναι τῶν ἀρχῶν, τήν τε βασιλείαν καὶ τὴν στρατηγίαν. ἔντιμον γὰρ ὁ νόμος οὗτος ποιεῖ τὸν πλοῦτον
40 μᾶλλον τῆς ἀρετῆς καὶ τὴν πόλιν ὅλην φιλοχρή-
ματον· ὅ τι δ᾽ ἂν ὑπολάβῃ τίμιον εἶναι τὸ κύριον,
ἀνάγκη καὶ τὴν τῶν ἄλλων πολιτῶν δόξαν ἀκολουθεῖν τούτοις· ὅπου δὲ μὴ μάλιστα ἀρετὴ τιμᾶται,
1273 b ταύτην οὐχ οἷόν τ᾽ εἶναι βεβαίως ἀριστοκρατικὴν
πολιτείαν. ἐθίζεσθαι δ᾽ εὔλογον κερδαίνειν τοὺς
ὠνουμένους, ὅταν δαπανήσαντες ἄρχωσιν· ἄτοπον
γὰρ εἰ πένης μὲν ὢν ἐπιεικὴς δὲ βουλήσεται
κερδαίνειν, φαυλότερος δ᾽ ὢν οὐ βουλήσεται δα-

most signally in respect of a certain idea that is shared by most people ; they think that the rulers should be chosen not only for their merit but also for their wealth, as it is not possible for a poor man to govern well—he has not leisure for his duties. If therefore election by wealth is oligarchical and election by merit aristocratic, this will be a third system, exhibited for instance in the constitution of Carthage, for there elections are made with an eye to these two qualifications, and especially elections to the most important offices, those of the kings and of the generals. But it must be held that this divergence from aristocracy is an error on the part of a lawgiver ; for one of the most important points to keep in view from the outset is that the best citizens may be able to have leisure and may not have to engage in any unseemly occupation, not only when in office but also when living in private life. And if it is necessary to look to the question of means for the sake of leisure, it is a bad thing that the greatest offices of state, the kingship and the generalship, should be for sale. For this law makes wealth more honoured than worth, and renders the whole state avaricious ; and whatever the holders of supreme power deem honourable, the opinion of the other citizens also is certain to follow them, and a state in which virtue is not held in the highest honour cannot be securely governed by an aristocracy. And it is probable that those who purchase office will learn by degrees to make a profit out of it, when they hold office for money spent ; for it would be odd if a man of small means but respectable should want to make a profit but an inferior person when he has spent money to get elected should not want to.

5 πανήσας. διὸ δεῖ τοὺς δυναμένους ἄριστ' ἄρχειν, τούτους ἄρχειν. βέλτιον δ', εἰ καὶ προεῖτο τὴν ἀπορίαν τῶν ἐπιεικῶν ὁ νομοθέτης, ἀλλ' ἀρχόντων γε ἐπιμελεῖσθαι τῆς σχολῆς.

Φαῦλον δ' ἂν δόξειεν εἶναι καὶ τὸ πλείους ἀρχὰς τὸν αὐτὸν ἄρχειν, ὅπερ εὐδοκιμεῖ παρὰ τοῖς 10 Καρχηδονίοις. ἓν γὰρ ὑφ' ἑνὸς ἔργον ἄριστ' ἀποτελεῖται, δεῖ δ' ὅπως γίνηται τοῦθ' ὁρᾶν τὸν νομοθέτην, καὶ μὴ προστάττειν τὸν αὐτὸν αὐλεῖν καὶ σκυτοτομεῖν. ὥσθ' ὅπου μὴ μικρὰ πόλις, πολιτικώτερον πλείονας μετέχειν τῶν ἀρχῶν καὶ δημοτικώτερον· κοινότερόν τε γὰρ καθάπερ εἴπο-15 μεν, καὶ κάλλιον ἕκαστον ἀποτελεῖται τῶν αὐτῶν καὶ θᾶττον. δῆλον δὲ τοῦτο ἐπὶ τῶν πολεμικῶν καὶ τῶν ναυτικῶν· ἐν τούτοις γὰρ ἀμφοτέροις διὰ πάντων ὡς εἰπεῖν διελήλυθε τὸ ἄρχειν καὶ τὸ ἄρχεσθαι.

Ὀλιγαρχικῆς δ' οὔσης τῆς πολιτείας ἄριστα ἐκφεύγουσι τῷ πλουτεῖν, ἀεί τι τοῦ δήμου μέρος 20 ἐκπέμποντες ἐπὶ τὰς πόλεις· τούτῳ γὰρ ἰῶνται καὶ ποιοῦσι μόνιμον τὴν πολιτείαν. ἀλλὰ τοῦτ' ἐστι τύχης ἔργον, δεῖ δὲ ἀστασιάστους εἶναι διὰ τὸν νομοθέτην· νῦν δ', ἂν ἀτυχία γένηταί τις καὶ τὸ πλῆθος ἀποστῇ τῶν ἀρχομένων, οὐδέν ἐστι φάρμακον διὰ τῶν νόμων τῆς ἡσυχίας.

25 Περὶ μὲν οὖν τῆς Λακεδαιμονίων πολιτείας καὶ Κρητικῆς καὶ τῆς Καρχηδονίων, αἵπερ δικαίως εὐδοκιμοῦσι, τοῦτον ἔχει τὸν τρόπον.

---

¹ ἄριστ' ἄρχειν Spengel: ἀρισταρχεῖν codd. (ἄριστα σχολάζειν Richards).   ² ἄριστα ⟨στάσιν⟩ Bernays.

ᵃ Or 'functions remaining the same, each is done better and more quickly.'

Hence the persons who should be in office are those most capable of holding office. And even if the lawgiver neglected to secure comfortable means for respectable people, it would at all events be better that he should provide for their leisure while in office.

And it might also be thought a bad thing for the same person to hold several offices, which is considered a distinction at Carthage. One man one job is the best rule for efficiency, and the lawgiver ought to see that this may be secured, and not appoint the same man to play the flute and make shoes. Hence except in a small city it is better for the state for a larger number to share in the offices and more democratic, for it is fairer to all, as we said, and also functions are performed better and more quickly when separate than when in the same hands.[a] This is clear in military and naval matters ; for in both of these departments command and subordination penetrate throughout almost the whole body.[b] *Official pluralism.*

But the constitution being oligarchical they best escape the dangers by being wealthy, as they constantly send out a portion of the common people to appointments in the cities ; by this means they cure this defect in their system and make it stable. However, this is the achievement of fortune, whereas freedom from civil strife ought to be secured by the lawgiver ; but as it is, suppose some misfortune occurs and the multitude of the subject class revolts, there is no remedy provided by the laws to restore tranquillity. *Emigration to dependencies a safety-valve.*

This then is the character of the Spartan, Cretan and Carthaginian constitutions, which are justly famous.

[b] *i.e.* everyone in command (except the commander-in-chief) has someone of higher rank over him.

1273 b

IX. Τῶν δὲ ἀποφηναμένων τι περὶ πολιτείας
ἔνιοι μὲν οὐκ ἐκοινώνησαν πράξεων πολιτικῶν
οὐδ' ὡντινωνοῦν ἀλλὰ διετέλεσαν ἰδιωτεύοντες τὸν
30 βίον· περὶ ὧν εἴ τι ἀξιόλογον, εἴρηται σχεδὸν
περὶ πάντων. ἔνιοι δὲ νομοθέται γεγόνασιν, οἱ
μὲν ταῖς οἰκείαις πόλεσιν οἱ δὲ καὶ τῶν ὀθνείων
τισί, πολιτευθέντες αὐτοί· καὶ τούτων οἱ μὲν νόμων
ἐγένοντο δημιουργοὶ μόνον, οἱ δὲ καὶ πολιτείας,
οἷον καὶ Λυκοῦργος καὶ Σόλων· οὗτοι γὰρ καὶ
35 νόμους καὶ πολιτείας κατέστησαν. περὶ μὲν οὖν
τῆς Λακεδαιμονίων εἴρηται. Σόλωνα δ' ἔνιοι μὲν
οἴονται νομοθέτην γενέσθαι σπουδαῖον, ὀλιγαρχίαν
τε γὰρ καταλῦσαι λίαν ἄκρατον οὖσαν καὶ δουλεύοντα τὸν δῆμον παῦσαι καὶ δημοκρατίαν καταστῆσαι τὴν πάτριον μίξαντα καλῶς τὴν πολιτείαν·
40 εἶναι γὰρ τὴν μὲν ἐν Ἀρείῳ πάγῳ βουλὴν ὀλιγαρχικόν, τὸ δὲ τὰς ἀρχὰς αἱρετὰς ἀριστοκρατικόν,
τὰ δὲ δικαστήρια δημοτικόν. ἔοικε δὲ Σόλων
1274 a ἐκεῖνα μὲν ὑπάρχοντα πρότερον οὐ καταλῦσαι,
τήν τε βουλὴν καὶ τὴν τῶν ἀρχῶν αἵρεσιν, τὸν δὲ
δῆμον καταστῆσαι τὰ δικαστήρια ποιήσας ἐκ
πάντων. διὸ καὶ μέμφονταί τινες αὐτῷ· λῦσαι
5 γὰρ θάτερα,[1] κύριον ποιήσαντα τὸ δικαστήριον
πάντων, κληρωτὸν ὄν. ἐπεὶ γὰρ τοῦτ' ἴσχυσεν,
ὥσπερ τυράννῳ τῷ δήμῳ χαριζόμενοι τὴν πολιτείαν
εἰς τὴν νῦν δημοκρατίαν κατέστησαν, καὶ τὴν μὲν
ἐν Ἀρείῳ πάγῳ βουλὴν Ἐφιάλτης ἐκόλουσε καὶ

---

[1] Koraes: θάτεραν, θάτερον codd.

164

1 IX. Of those that have put forward views about politics, some have taken no part in any political activities whatever but have passed their whole life as private citizens; and something has been said about almost all the writers of this class about whom there is anything noteworthy. Some on the other hand have been lawgivers, either for their native cities or even for certain foreign peoples, after having themselves been actively engaged in government; and of these some have been framers of laws only, and others of a constitution also, for instance Solon and Lycurgus, who instituted both laws and constitutions. The Spartan constitution has been discussed. 2 As for Solon, he is considered by some people to have been a good lawgiver, as having put an end to oligarchy when it was too unqualified and having liberated the people from slavery and established our traditional democracy with a skilful blending of the constitution: the Council on the Areopagus being an oligarchic element, the elective magistracies aristocratic and the law-courts democratic. And although really in regard to certain of these features, the Council and the election of magistrates, Solon seems merely to have abstained from destroying institutions that existed already, he does appear to have founded the democracy by constituting the jury-3 courts from all the citizens. For this he is actually blamed by some persons, as having dissolved the power of the other parts of the community by making the law-court, which was elected by lot, all-powerful. For as the law-court grew strong, men courted favour with the people as with a tyrant, and so brought the constitution to the present democracy; and Ephialtes and Pericles docked the

165

1274 a

Περικλῆς, τὰ δὲ δικαστήρια μισθοφόρα κατέστησε
10 Περικλῆς, καὶ τοῦτον δὴ τὸν τρόπον ἕκαστος
τῶν δημαγωγῶν προήγαγεν αὔξων εἰς τὴν νῦν
δημοκρατίαν. φαίνεται δ' οὐ κατὰ τὴν Σόλωνος
γενέσθαι τοῦτο προαίρεσιν, ἀλλὰ μᾶλλον ἀπὸ συμπτώματος (τῆς ναυαρχίας¹ γὰρ ἐν τοῖς Μηδικοῖς ὁ
δῆμος αἴτιος γενόμενος ἐφρονηματίσθη καὶ δημα-
15 γωγοὺς ἔλαβε φαύλους ἀντιπολιτευομένων τῶν
ἐπιεικῶν)· ἐπεὶ Σόλων γε ἔοικε τὴν ἀναγκαιοτάτην
ἀποδιδόναι τῷ δήμῳ δύναμιν, τὸ τὰς ἀρχὰς αἱρεῖσθαι καὶ εὐθύνειν (μηδὲ γὰρ τούτου κύριος ὢν ὁ
δῆμος δοῦλος ἂν εἴη καὶ πολέμιος), τὰς δ' ἀρχὰς
ἐκ τῶν γνωρίμων καὶ τῶν εὐπόρων κατέστησε
20 πάσας, ἐκ τῶν πεντακοσιομεδίμνων καὶ ζευγιτῶν
καὶ τρίτου τέλους τῆς καλουμένης ἱππάδος· τὸ δὲ
τέταρτον θητικόν, οἷς οὐδεμιᾶς ἀρχῆς μετῆν.

Νομοθέται δ' ἐγένοντο Ζάλευκός τε Λοκροῖς
τοῖς Ἐπιζεφυρίοις, καὶ Χαρώνδας ὁ Καταναῖος
τοῖς αὑτοῦ πολίταις καὶ ταῖς ἄλλαις ταῖς Χαλκι-
25 δικαῖς πόλεσι ταῖς περὶ Ἰταλίαν καὶ Σικελίαν.
πειρῶνται δέ τινες καὶ συνάγειν, ὡς Ὀνομακρίτου
μὲν γενομένου πρώτου δεινοῦ περὶ νομοθεσίαν,
γυμνασθῆναι δ' αὐτὸν ἐν Κρήτῃ Λοκρὸν ὄντα καὶ
ἐπιδημοῦντα κατὰ τέχνην μαντικήν, τούτου δὲ
γενέσθαι Θάλητα ἑταῖρον, Θάλητος δ' ἀκροατὴν
30 Λυκοῦργον καὶ Ζάλευκον, Ζαλεύκου δὲ Χαρώνδαν.

---

¹ ναυμαχίας Powell.

ᵃ Or 'of the sea-fight,' Salamis.
ᵇ For Solon's classification of the citizens by the annual
income of their estates see *Athenian Constitution*, c. vii.
ᶜ Perhaps 664 B.C.
ᵈ Zephyrium, a promontory in S. Italy.

power of the Council on the Areopagus, while Pericles instituted payment for serving in the law-courts, and in this manner finally the successive leaders of the people led them on by growing stages to the present democracy. But this does not seem to have come about in accordance with the intention of Solon, 4 but rather as a result of accident (for the common people having been the cause of naval victory *a* at the time of the Persian invasion became proud and adopted bad men as popular leaders when the respectable classes opposed their policy); inasmuch as Solon for his part appears to bestow only the minimum of power upon the people, the function of electing the magistrates and of calling them to account (for if even this were not under the control of the populace it would be a mere slave and a foreign enemy), whereas he appointed all the offices from the notable and the wealthy, the Five-hundred-bushel class and the Teamsters and a third property-class called the Knighthood; while the fourth class, the Thetes, were admitted to no office.*b*

5   Laws were given*c* by Zaleucus to the Epizephyrian*d* Locrians and by Charondas *e* of Catana to his fellow-citizens and to the other Chalcidic cities*f* on the coasts of Italy and Sicily. Some persons try to connect Zaleucus and Charondas together *g* : they say that Onomacritus first arose as an able lawgiver, and that he was trained in Crete, being a Locrian and travelling there to practise the art of soothsaying, and Thales became his companion, and Lycurgus and Zaleucus were pupils of Thales, and Charondas of

Notes on various lawgivers.

a See 1252 b 14.
f Colonies from Chalcis in Euboea.
g Or ' try to make a series of legislators.'

1274 a

ἀλλὰ ταῦτα μὲν λέγουσιν ἀσκεπτότερον τῶν χρόνων
ἔχοντες.[1] ἐγένετο δὲ καὶ Φιλόλαος ὁ Κορίνθιος
νομοθέτης Θηβαίοις. ἦν δ' ὁ Φιλόλαος τὸ μὲν
γένος τῶν Βακχιαδῶν, ἐραστὴς δὲ γενόμενος
Διοκλέους τοῦ νικήσαντος Ὀλυμπίασιν, ὡς ἐκεῖνος
35 τὴν πόλιν ἔλιπε διαμισήσας τὸν ἔρωτα τὸν τῆς
μητρὸς Ἀλκυόνης, ἀπῆλθεν εἰς Θήβας, κἀκεῖ τὸν
βίον ἐτελεύτησαν ἀμφότεροι. καὶ νῦν ἔτι δεικνύουσι
τοὺς τάφους αὐτῶν, ἀλλήλοις μὲν εὐσυνόπτους
ὄντας πρὸς δὲ τὴν τῶν Κορινθίων χώραν τὸν μὲν
σύνοπτον τὸν δ' οὐ σύνοπτον·[2] μυθολογοῦσι γὰρ
40 αὐτοὺς οὕτω τάξασθαι τὴν ταφήν, τὸν μὲν Διοκλέα
διὰ τὴν ἀπέχθειαν τοῦ πάθους ὅπως μὴ ἄποπτος
ἔσται ἡ Κορινθία ἀπὸ τοῦ χώματος, τὸν δὲ Φιλό-
1274 b λαον ὅπως ἄποπτος. ᾤκησαν μὲν οὖν διὰ τὴν
τοιαύτην αἰτίαν παρὰ τοῖς Θηβαίοις, νομοθέτης
δ' αὐτοῖς ἐγένετο Φιλόλαος περί τ' ἄλλων τινῶν
καὶ περὶ τῆς παιδοποιίας, οὓς καλοῦσιν ἐκεῖνοι
νόμους θετικούς· καὶ τοῦτ' ἐστὶν ἰδίως ὑπ' ἐκείνου
5 νενομοθετημένον, ὅπως ὁ ἀριθμὸς σῴζηται τῶν
κλήρων. Χαρώνδου δ' ἴδιον μὲν οὐδέν ἐστι πλὴν
αἱ δίκαι τῶν ψευδομαρτυριῶν (πρῶτος γὰρ ἐποίησε
τὴν ἐπίσκηψιν), τῇ δ' ἀκριβείᾳ τῶν νόμων ἐστὶ
γλαφυρώτερος καὶ τῶν νῦν νομοθετῶν. (Φαλέου
δ' ἴδιον ἡ τῶν οὐσιῶν ἀνομάλωσις, Πλάτωνος δ'
10 ἥ τε τῶν γυναικῶν καὶ παίδων καὶ τῆς οὐσίας
κοινότης καὶ τὰ συσσίτια τῶν γυναικῶν, ἔτι δ' ὁ
περὶ τὴν μέθην νόμος, τὸ τοὺς νήφοντας συμ-
ποσιαρχεῖν, καὶ τὴν ἐν τοῖς πολεμικοῖς ἄσκησιν

---

[1] τῶν χρόνων ἔχοντες Susemihl : τῷ χρόνῳ λέγοντες codd.
[2] τὸν—σύνοπτον bis Richards (duce partim Ross): τοῦ—
ϲυνόπτου bis codd.

Zaleucus ; but these stories give too little attention
6 to the dates. Philolaus of Corinth also arose as
lawgiver at Thebes. Philolaus belonged by birth
to the Bacchiad family ; he became the lover of
Diocles the winner *a* at Olympia, but when Diocles
quitted the city because of his loathing for the passion
of his mother Alcyone, he went away to Thebes, and
there they both ended their life. Even now people
still show their tombs, in full view of each other and
one of them fully open to view in the direction of
7 the Corinthian country but the other one not ; for
the story goes that they arranged to be buried in
this manner, Diocles owing to his hatred for his
misfortune securing that the land of Corinth might
not be visible from his tomb, and Philolaus that it
might be from his. It was due then to a reason
of this nature that they went to live at Thebes ; but
Philolaus became the Thebans' lawgiver in regard
to various matters, among others the size of families,
—the laws called by the Thebans laws of adoption ;
about this Philolaus enacted special legislation, in
order that the number of the estates in land might
8 be preserved. There is nothing special in the code
of Charondas except the trials for false witness (for
he was the first to introduce the procedure of de-
nunciation), but in the accuracy of his laws he is
a more finished workman even than the legislators
of to-day. (Peculiar to Phaleas *b* is the measure for
equalizing properties ; to Plato,*c* community of wives
and children and of property, and the common meals
for the women, and also the law about drunkenness,
enacting that sober persons are to be masters of
the drinking-bouts, and the regulation for military

a In 728 B.C.   *b* See c. iv.   *c* Above, cc. i.-iii.

169

1274b

ὅπως ἀμφιδέξιοι γίνωνται κατὰ τὴν μελέτην, ὡς
δέον μὴ τὴν μὲν χρήσιμον εἶναι τοῖν χεροῖν τὴν δὲ
15 ἄχρηστον.) Δράκοντος δὲ νόμοι μέν εἰσι, πολιτείᾳ
δ' ὑπαρχούσῃ τοὺς νόμους ἔθηκεν, ἴδιον δ' ἐν τοῖς
νόμοις οὐδέν ἐστιν ὅ τι καὶ μνείας ἄξιον, πλὴν ἡ
χαλεπότης διὰ τὸ τῆς ζημίας μέγεθος. ἐγένετο
δὲ καὶ Πιττακὸς νόμων δημιουργὸς ἀλλ' οὐ
πολιτείας· νόμος δ' ἴδιος αὐτοῦ τὸ τοὺς μεθύοντας,
20 ἂν τυπτήσωσι, πλείω ζημίαν ἀποτίνειν τῶν νη-
φόντων· διὰ γὰρ τὸ πλείους ὑβρίζειν μεθύοντας
ἢ νήφοντας οὐ πρὸς τὴν συγγνώμην ἀπέβλεψεν,
ὅτι δεῖ μεθύουσιν ἔχειν μᾶλλον, ἀλλὰ πρὸς τὸ
συμφέρον. ἐγένετο δὲ καὶ Ἀνδροδάμας Ῥηγῖνος
νομοθέτης Χαλκιδεῦσι τοῖς ἐπὶ Θρᾴκης, οὗ τὰ[1]
25 περί τε τὰ φονικὰ καὶ τὰς ἐπικλήρους ἐστίν· οὐ μὴν
ἀλλ' ἴδιόν γε οὐδὲν αὐτοῦ λέγειν ἔχοι τις ἄν.

Τὰ μὲν οὖν περὶ τὰς πολιτείας τάς τε κυρίας
καὶ τὰς ὑπό τινων εἰρημένας ἔστω τεθεωρημένα
τὸν τρόπον τοῦτον.

[1] τὰ H: om. cet.

---

[a] Author of the first written code at Athens, 621 B.C.
(though in the *Athenian Constitution*, c. iv., his legislation is
hardly mentioned; he appears there as the framer of the
constitution).

[b] Of Mitylene in Lesbos, one of the Seven Sages, dictator
589-579 B.C.   [c] Otherwise unknown.

[d] Chalcidice, the peninsula in the N. Aegean, was colonized
from Chalcis in Euboea.

ADDITIONAL NOTES

II. i. 5, 1261 a 31. As the best state consists of different
classes, its unity is secured by each citizen giving services
to society and receiving in return benefits proportionate to
his services. Probably τὸ ἴσον is an interpolation (though
Newman explains it as 'the reciprocal rendering of an

170

training to make men by practice ambidextrous, on the ground that it is a mistake to have one of the two hands useful but the other useless.) There are laws of Draco,[a] but he legislated for an existing constitution, and there is nothing peculiar in his laws that is worthy of mention, except their severity in imposing heavy punishment. Pittacus [b] also was a framer of laws, but not of a constitution ; a special law of his is that if men commit an assault when drunk they are to pay a larger fine than those who offend when sober ; because since more men are insolent when drunk than when sober he had regard not to the view that drunken offenders are rightly held less guilty, but to expediency. Androdamas [c] of Rhegium also became lawgiver to the Chalcidians in the direction of Thrace,[d] and to him belong the laws dealing with cases of murder and with heiresses ; however one cannot mention any provision that is peculiar to him.

Let such be our examination of the constitutional schemes actually in force and of those that have been proposed by certain persons.

equal amount of dissimilar things '): omitting τὸ ἴσον, we render ' reciprocity ' and not ' reciprocal equality '; cf. N.E. 1132 b 33, ' In the interchange of services Justice in the form of Reciprocity is the bond that maintains the association : reciprocity, that is, on the basis of proportion, not on the basis of equality.'

II. i. 6, 1261 a 38 ff. The best form of constitution is where there is a superior class that governs continuously —an aristocracy; so where there are no class-distinctions, the next best thing is for all the citizens to take turns in governing and being governed, those in office for the time being forming a sort of aristocracy. Richards's alteration of the text gives ' to take turns to govern is an imitation of original inequality and class-distinction.'

Γ

I. Τῷ περὶ πολιτείας ἐπισκοποῦντι, καὶ τίς ἑκάστη καὶ ποία τις, σχεδὸν πρώτη σκέψις περὶ πόλεως ἰδεῖν, τί ποτ' ἐστὶν ἡ πόλις. νῦν γὰρ
35 ἀμφισβητοῦσιν, οἱ μὲν φάσκοντες τὴν πόλιν πεπραχέναι τὴν πρᾶξιν, οἱ δ' οὐ τὴν πόλιν ἀλλὰ τὴν ὀλιγαρχίαν ἢ τὸν τύραννον· τοῦ δὲ πολιτικοῦ καὶ τοῦ νομοθέτου πᾶσαν ὁρῶμεν τὴν πραγματείαν οὖσαν περὶ πόλιν, ἡ δὲ πολιτεία τῶν τὴν πόλιν οἰκούντων ἐστὶ τάξις τις. ἐπεὶ δ' ἡ πόλις τῶν
40 συγκειμένων καθάπερ ἄλλο τι τῶν ὅλων μὲν συνεστώτων δ' ἐκ πολλῶν μορίων, δῆλον ὅτι πρότερον ὁ πολίτης ζητητέος· ἡ γὰρ πόλις πολιτῶν
1275 a τι πλῆθός ἐστιν, ὥστε τίνα χρὴ καλεῖν πολίτην καὶ τίς ὁ πολίτης ἐστὶ σκεπτέον. καὶ γὰρ ὁ πολίτης ἀμφισβητεῖται πολλάκις· οὐ γὰρ τὸν αὐτὸν ὁμολογοῦσι πάντες εἶναι πολίτην· ἔστι γὰρ ὅστις[1] ἐν δημοκρατίᾳ πολίτης ὢν ἐν ὀλιγαρχίᾳ πολλάκις
5 οὐκ ἔστι πολίτης. τοὺς μὲν οὖν ἄλλως πως τυγχάνοντας ταύτης τῆς προσηγορίας, οἷον τοὺς ποιητοὺς πολίτας, ἀφετέον· ὁ δὲ πολίτης οὐ τῷ

---

[1] Richards : γάρ τις ὃς codd.

[a] So we speak of an action planned and carried by the party in power as an Act of Parliament, and technically as an act of the sovereign.

BOOK III

I. For the student of government, and of the nature and characteristics of the various forms of constitution, almost the first question to consider is in regard to the state : what exactly is the essential nature of a state ? As it is, this is a matter of dispute : a public act is spoken of by some people as the action of the state, others speak of it as the action not of the state but of the oligarchy or the tyrant in power [a]; and we see that the activity of the statesman and lawgiver is entirely concerned with a state as its object, and a constitution is a form of organization of the inhabitants of a state. But a state is a composite thing, in the same sense as any other of the things that are wholes but consist of many parts ; it is therefore clear that we must first inquire into the nature of a citizen ; for a state is a collection of citizens, so that we have to consider who is entitled to the name of citizen, and what the essential nature of a citizen is. For there is often a difference of opinion as to this : people do not all agree that the same person is a citizen ; often somebody who would be a citizen in a democracy is not a citizen under an oligarchy. We need not here consider those who acquire the title of citizen in some exceptional manner, for example those who are citizens by adoption ; and citizenship is not constituted by domicile in a

173

1275 a

οἰκεῖν που πολίτης ἐστίν (καὶ γὰρ μέτοικοι καὶ
δοῦλοι κοινωνοῦσι τῆς οἰκήσεως), οὐδ᾽ οἱ τῶν δικαίων μετέχοντες οὕτως ὥστε καὶ δίκην ὑπέχειν
10 καὶ δικάζεσθαι (τοῦτο γὰρ ὑπάρχει[1] καὶ τοῖς ἀπὸ
συμβόλων κοινωνοῦσιν, καὶ γὰρ ταῦτα τούτοις
ὑπάρχει—πολλαχοῦ μὲν οὖν οὐδὲ τούτων τελέως
οἱ μέτοικοι μετέχουσιν, ἀλλὰ νέμειν ἀνάγκη προστάτην, διὸ ἀτελῶς πως μετέχουσι τῆς τοιαύτης
κοινωνίας), ἀλλὰ[2] καθάπερ καὶ παῖδας τοὺς μήπω
15 δι᾽ ἡλικίαν ἐγγεγραμμένους καὶ τοὺς γέροντας
τοὺς ἀφειμένους φατέον εἶναι μέν πως πολίτας,
οὐχ ἁπλῶς δὲ λίαν ἀλλὰ προστιθέντας τοὺς μὲν
ἀτελεῖς τοὺς δὲ παρηκμακότας ἤ τι τοιοῦτον ἕτερον
(οὐδὲν γὰρ διαφέρει, δῆλον γὰρ τὸ λεγόμενον).
ζητοῦμεν γὰρ τὸν ἁπλῶς πολίτην καὶ μηδὲν ἔχοντα
20 τοιοῦτον ἔγκλημα διορθώσεως δεόμενον, ἐπεὶ καὶ
περὶ τῶν ἀτίμων καὶ φυγάδων ἔστι τὰ τοιαῦτα καὶ
διαπορεῖν καὶ λύειν. πολίτης δ᾽ ἁπλῶς οὐδενὶ τῶν
ἄλλων ὁρίζεται μᾶλλον ἢ τῷ μετέχειν κρίσεως καὶ
ἀρχῆς. τῶν δ᾽ ἀρχῶν αἱ μέν εἰσι διῃρημέναι κατὰ
25 χρόνον, ὥστ᾽ ἐνίας μὲν ὅλως δὶς τὸν αὐτὸν οὐκ
ἔξεστιν ἄρχειν, ἢ διά τινων ὡρισμένων χρόνων· ὁ
δ᾽ ἀόριστος, οἷον ὁ δικαστὴς καὶ ἐκκλησιαστής.
τάχα μὲν οὖν ἂν φαίη τις οὐδ᾽ ἄρχοντας εἶναι τοὺς 5

---

[1] οὕτω γὰρ ἂν ὑπάρχοι (sc. τὸ πολίτην εἶναι) Richards.
[2] [ἀλλὰ] ? Richards.

---

[a] This implies that aged citizens were excused attendance
at the assembly and law-courts, as well as military service.

174

certain place (for resident aliens and slaves share
the domicile of citizens), nor are those citizens who
participate in a common system of justice, conferring
the right to defend an action and to bring one in the
law-courts (for this right belongs also to the parties
under a commercial treaty, as they too can sue and
be sued at law,—or rather, in many places even the
right of legal action is not shared completely by
resident aliens, but they are obliged to produce a
patron, so that they only share in a common legal
procedure to an incomplete degree), but these are
only citizens in the manner in which children who
are as yet too young to have been enrolled in the
list and old men who have been discharged *a* must be
pronounced to be citizens in a sense, yet not quite
absolutely, but with the added qualification of
'under age' in the case of the former and 'super-
annuated' or some other similar term (it makes no
difference, the meaning being clear) in that of the
latter. For we seek to define a citizen in the absolute sense, and one possessing no disqualification
of this nature that requires a correcting term, since
similar difficulties may also be raised, and solved,
about citizens who have been disfranchised or exiled.
A citizen pure and simple is defined by nothing else
so much as by the right to participate in judicial
functions and in office. But some offices of government are definitely limited in regard to time, so that
some of them are not allowed to be held twice by the
same person at all, or only after certain fixed intervals
of time ; other officials are without limit of tenure,
for example the juryman and the member of the
assembly. It might perhaps be said that such
persons are not officials at all, and that the exercise

1275 a

τοιούτους, οὐδὲ μετέχειν διὰ ταῦτ' ἀρχῆς· καίτοι
γελοῖον τοὺς κυριωτάτους ἀποστερεῖν ἀρχῆς.ᵃ
30 ἀλλὰ διαφερέτω μηδέν· περὶ ὀνόματος γὰρ ὁ λόγος·
ἀνώνυμον γὰρ τὸ κοινὸν ἐπὶ δικαστοῦ καὶ ἐκκλησια-
στοῦ τί δεῖ ταῦτ' ἄμφω καλεῖν. ἔστω δὴ διορισμοῦ
χάριν ἀόριστος ἀρχή. τίθεμεν δὴ πολίτας τοὺς
οὕτω μετέχοντας.

Ὁ μὲν οὖν μάλιστ' ἂν ἐφαρμόσας πολίτης² ἐπὶ
πάντας τοὺς λεγομένους πολίτας σχεδὸν τοιοῦτός
35 ἐστιν. δεῖ δὲ μὴ λανθάνειν ὅτι τῶν πραγμάτων
ἐν οἷς τὰ ὑποκείμενα διαφέρει τῷ εἴδει, καὶ τὸ
μὲν αὐτῶν ἐστι πρῶτον τὸ δὲ δεύτερον τὸ δ'
ἐχόμενον, ἢ τὸ παράπαν οὐδ' ἔνεστιν,³ ἢ τοιαῦτα,
τὸ κοινόν, ἢ γλίσχρως. τὰς δὲ πολιτείας ὁρῶμεν
εἴδει διαφερούσας ἀλλήλων, καὶ τὰς μὲν ὑστέρας
1275 b τὰς δὲ προτέρας οὔσας· τὰς γὰρ ἡμαρτημένας καὶ
παρεκβεβηκυίας ἀναγκαῖον ὑστέρας εἶναι τῶν ἀν-
αμαρτήτων (τὰς δὲ παρεκβεβηκυίας πῶς λέγομεν
ὕστερον ἔσται φανερόν). ὥστε καὶ τὸν πολίτην
5 ἕτερον ἀναγκαῖον εἶναι τὸν καθ' ἑκάστην πολιτείαν.
διόπερ ὁ λεχθεὶς ἐν μὲν δημοκρατίᾳ μάλιστ' ἐστὶ
πολίτης, ἐν δὲ ταῖς ἄλλαις ἐνδέχεται μέν, οὐ μὴν
ἀναγκαῖον. ἐν ἐνίαις⁴ γὰρ οὐκ ἔστι δῆμος, οὐδ'
ἐκκλησίαν νομίζουσιν ἀλλὰ⁵ συγκλήτους, καὶ τὰς

---

¹ [ἀρχῆς] ? (sc. τοῦ πολίτας εἶναι) ed.   ² διορισμὸς Richards.
    ³ οὐδ' ἔνεστιν Madvig : οὐδέν ἐστιν.
⁴ ἐν ἐνίαις Coraes : ἐνίαις codd.   ⁵ ἀλλ' ἢ Richards.

ᵃ Or, amending the text, ' and yet that it is absurd to deny
the title of citizen to those—'
    ᵇ The meaning of this abstract principle is most easily seen
from its application here: if states are generically different
from one another, membership of a state, citizenship, can
hardly be a single thing, and come under a single definition.

of these functions does not constitute the holding of office; [a] and yet it is absurd to deny the title of official to those who have the greatest power in the state. But it need not make any difference, as it is only the question of a name, since there is no common name for a juryman and a member of the assembly that is properly applied to both. For the sake of distinction therefore let us call the combination of the two functions ' office ' without limitation. Accordingly we lay it down that those are citizens who ' participate in office ' in this manner.

Such more or less is the definition of ' citizen ' that would best fit with all of those to whom the name is applied. But it must not be forgotten that things in the case of which the things to which they are related differ in kind, one of them being primary, another one secondary and so on, either do not contain a common nature at all, as being what they are, or barely do so.[b] Now we see that constitutions differ from one another in kind, and that some are subsequent and others prior; for erroneous and divergent forms are necessarily subsequent to correct forms (in what sense we employ the terms ' divergent ' of constitutions will appear later). Hence the citizen corresponding to each form of constitution will also necessarily be different. Therefore the definition of a citizen that we have given applies especially to citizenship in a democracy; under other forms of government it may hold good, but will not necessarily do so. For in some states there is no body of common citizens, and they do not have the custom of a popular assembly but councils of specially convened members, and the

(though for non-democratic states this definition must be modified).

177

1275 b

δίκας δικάζουσι κατὰ μέρος, οἷον ἐν Λακεδαίμονι
10 τὰς τῶν συμβολαίων δικάζει τῶν ἐφόρων ἄλλος
ἄλλας, οἱ δὲ γέροντες τὰς φονικάς, ἑτέρα δ' ἴσως
ἀρχή τις ἑτέρας. οὐ τὸν¹ αὐτὸν δὲ τρόπον καὶ περὶ
Καρχηδόνα· πάσας γὰρ ἀρχαί τινες κρίνουσι τὰς
δίκας. ἀλλ' ἔχει γὰρ διόρθωσιν ὁ τοῦ πολίτου
διορισμός. ἐν γὰρ ταῖς ἄλλαις πολιτείαις οὐχ ὁ
15 ἀόριστος ἄρχων ἐκκλησιαστής ἐστι καὶ δικαστής,
ἀλλ' ὁ κατὰ τὴν ἀρχὴν ὡρισμένος· τούτων γὰρ
ἢ πᾶσιν ἢ τισὶν ἀποδέδοται τὸ βουλεύεσθαι καὶ
δικάζειν ἢ περὶ πάντων ἢ περὶ τινῶν. τίς μὲν οὖν
ἐστιν ὁ πολίτης, ἐκ τούτων φανερόν· ᾧ γὰρ ἐξουσία
κοινωνεῖν ἀρχῆς βουλευτικῆς ἢ² κριτικῆς, πολίτην
20 ἤδη λέγομεν εἶναι ταύτης τῆς πόλεως, πόλιν δὲ
τὸ τῶν τοιούτων πλῆθος ἱκανὸν πρὸς αὐτάρκειαν
ζωῆς, ὡς ἁπλῶς εἰπεῖν.

Ὁρίζονται δὲ³ πρὸς τὴν χρῆσιν πολίτην τὸν ἐξ
ἀμφοτέρων πολιτῶν καὶ μὴ θατέρου μόνον, οἷον
πατρὸς ἢ μητρός, οἱ δὲ καὶ τοῦτ' ἐπὶ πλέον ζητοῦσιν, οἷον ἐπὶ πάππους δύο ἢ τρεῖς ἢ πλείους. οὕτω
25 δὴ ὁριζομένων πολιτικῶς καὶ ταχέως,⁴ ἀποροῦσί
τινες τὸν τρίτον ἐκεῖνον ἢ τέταρτον, πῶς ἔσται
πολίτης. Γοργίας μὲν οὖν ὁ Λεοντῖνος, τὰ μὲν
ἴσως ἀπορῶν τὰ δ' εἰρωνευόμενος, ἔφη καθάπερ
ὅλμους εἶναι τοὺς ὑπὸ τῶν ὁλμοποιῶν πεποιημένους, οὕτω καὶ Λαρισαίους τοὺς ὑπὸ τῶν
30 δημιουργῶν πεποιημένους· εἶναι γάρ τινας λαρισο-

---

¹ οὐ τὸν Coraes : τὸν codd.   ² καὶ Ar.
³ δὲ Γ : δὴ codd.   ⁴ πάχεως Camerarius.

---

[a] The negative is a conjectural insertion, cf. 1273 a 20.
[b] Sicilian orator and nihilistic philosopher, visited Athens
427 B.C.

office of trying law-suits goes by sections—for example at Sparta suits for breach of contract are tried by different ephors in different cases, while cases of homicide are tried by the ephors and doubtless other suits by some other magistrate. The same method is not [a] followed at Carthage, where certain magistrates judge all the law-suits. But still, our definition of a citizen admits of correction. For under the other forms of constitution a member of the assembly and of a jury-court is not 'an official' without restriction, but an official defined according to his office ; either all of them or some among them are assigned deliberative and judicial duties either in all matters or in certain matters. What constitutes a citizen is therefore clear from these considerations : we now declare that one who has the right to participate in deliberative or judicial office is a citizen of the state in which he has that right, and a state is a collection of such persons sufficiently numerous, speaking broadly, to secure independence of life.

But in practice citizenship is limited to the child of citizens on both sides, not on one side only, that is, the child of a citizen father or of a citizen mother; and other people carry this requirement further back, for example to the second or the third preceding generation or further. But given this as a practical and hasty definition, some people raise the difficulty, How will that ancestor three or four generations back have been a citizen ? Gorgias [b] of Leontini therefore, partly perhaps in genuine perplexity but partly in jest, said that just as the vessels made by mortar-makers were mortars, so the citizens made by the magistrates were Larisaeans, since some of the magistrates were actually larisa-

Citizenship does not necessarily depend on descent;

179

1275 b

ποιούς.[1] ἔστι δ' ἁπλοῦν· εἰ γὰρ μετεῖχον κατὰ
τὸν ῥηθέντα διορισμὸν τῆς πολιτείας, ἦσαν ἂν
πολῖται· καὶ γὰρ οὐ δυνατὸν ἐφαρμόττειν τὸ ἐκ
πολίτου ἢ ἐκ πολίτιδος ἐπὶ τῶν πρώτων οἰκησάντων
ἢ[2] κτισάντων.

’Αλλ' ἴσως ἐκεῖνοι μᾶλλον ἔχουσιν ἀπορίαν ὅσοι
35 μετέσχον μεταβολῆς γενομένης πολιτείας, οἷον[3]
’Αθήνησιν ἐποίησε Κλεισθένης μετὰ τὴν τῶν
τυράννων ἐκβολήν· πολλοὺς γὰρ ἐφυλέτευσε ξένους
καὶ δούλους μετοίκους. τὸ δ' ἀμφισβήτημα πρὸς
τούτους ἐστὶν οὐ τίς πολίτης, ἀλλὰ πότερον ἀδίκως
ἢ δικαίως. καίτοι κἂν τοῦτό τις ἔτι προσ-
1276 a απορήσειεν, ἆρ' εἰ μὴ δικαίως πολίτης, οὐ πολίτης,
ὡς ταὐτὸ δυναμένου τοῦ τ' ἀδίκου καὶ τοῦ ψευδοῦς.
ἐπεὶ δ' ὁρῶμεν καὶ ἄρχοντάς τινας ἀδίκως, οὓς
ἄρχειν μὲν φήσομεν ἀλλ' οὐ δικαίως, ὁ δὲ πολίτης
ἀρχῇ τινι διωρισμένος ἐστίν (ὁ γὰρ κοινωνῶν τῆς
5 τοιᾶσδε ἀρχῆς πολίτης ἐστίν, ὡς ἔφαμεν), δῆλον
ὅτι πολίτας μὲν εἶναι φατέον καὶ τούτους, περὶ δὲ
τοῦ δικαίως ἢ μὴ δικαίως συνάπτει πρὸς τὴν
εἰρημένην πρότερον ἀμφισβήτησιν. ἀποροῦσι γάρ
τινες πόθ' ἡ πόλις ἔπραξε καὶ πότε οὐχ ἡ πόλις,
οἷον ὅταν ἐξ ὀλιγαρχίας ἢ τυραννίδος γένηται
10 δημοκρατία. τότε γὰρ οὔτε τὰ συμβόλαια ἔνιοι
βούλονται διαλύειν (ὡς οὐ τῆς πόλεως ἀλλὰ τοῦ

---

[1] λαρισαιοποιούς Camerarius. [2] καὶ Richards.
[3] οἷον ⟨οὓς⟩ Richards.

---

[a] Larisa, a city in Thessaly, was famous for the manu-
facture of a kind of kettle called a ' larisa.'
[b] In 509 B.C.
[c] The question, What is a state ? 1274 b 34.

makers.[a] But it is really a simple matter ; for if they possessed citizenship in the manner stated in our definition of a citizen, they were citizens—since it is clearly impossible to apply the qualification of descent from a citizen father or mother to the original colonizers or founders of a city.

But perhaps a question rather arises about those who were admitted to citizenship when a revolution had taken place, for instance such a creation of citizens as that carried out [b] at Athens by Cleisthenes after the expulsion of the tyrants, when he enrolled in his tribes many resident aliens who had been foreigners or slaves. The dispute as to these is not about the fact of their citizenship, but whether they received it wrongly or rightly. Yet even as to this one might raise the further question, whether, if a man is not rightly a citizen, he is a citizen at all, as ' wrongly ' means the same as ' not truly.' But we sometimes see officials governing wrongly, as to whom we shall not deny that they do govern, but shall say that they do not do it rightly, and a citizen is defined by a certain function of government (a citizen, as we said, is one who shares in such and such an office) ; therefore it is clear that even persons wrongly admitted to citizenship are to be pronounced to be citizens, although the question whether they are so rightly or not rightly is connected with the question that was propounded before.[c] For some persons raise the question, When is an occurrence the act of the state and when is it not ? for example, when the government has been altered from oligarchy or tyranny to democracy. In such circumstances some people claim that the new government should not discharge public debts, on the ground that the money

but does revolution, breaking the succession, destroy the identity of the State ?

181

τυράννου λαβόντος) οὔτ' ἄλλα πολλὰ τῶν τοιούτων
ὡς ἐνίας τῶν πολιτειῶν τῷ κρατεῖν οὔσας ἀλλ' οὐ
διὰ τὸ κοινῇ συμφέρον. εἴπερ οὖν καὶ δημοκρα-
15 τοῦνταί τινες κατὰ τὸν τρόπον τοῦτον, ὁμοίως τῆς
πόλεως φατέον εἶναι ταύτης τὰς τῆς πολιτείας
ταύτης πράξεις καὶ τὰς ἐκ τῆς ὀλιγαρχίας καὶ τῆς
τυραννίδος. ἔοικε δ' οἰκεῖος ὁ λόγος εἶναι τῆς
ἀπορίας ταύτης, πῶς ποτε[1] χρὴ λέγειν τὴν πόλιν
εἶναι τὴν αὐτὴν ἢ μὴ τὴν αὐτὴν ἀλλ' ἑτέραν. ἡ
20 μὲν οὖν ἐπιπολαιοτάτη τῆς ἀπορίας ζήτησις περὶ
τὸν τόπον καὶ τοὺς ἀνθρώπους ἐστίν· ἐνδέχεται
γὰρ διαζευχθῆναι τὸν τόπον καὶ τοὺς ἀνθρώπους,
καὶ τοὺς μὲν ἕτερον τοὺς δ' ἕτερον οἰκῆσαι τόπον.
ταύτην μὲν οὖν πραοτέραν θετέον τὴν ἀπορίαν,
πολλαχῶς γὰρ τῆς πόλεως λεγομένης ἐστί πως
25 εὐμάρεια τῆς τοιαύτης ζητήσεως· ὁμοίως δὲ καὶ
τῶν τὸν αὐτὸν τόπον κατοικούντων ἀνθρώπων
πότε δεῖ νομίζειν μίαν εἶναι τὴν πόλιν; οὐ γὰρ
δὴ τοῖς τείχεσιν, εἴη γὰρ ἂν Πελοποννήσῳ περι-
βαλεῖν ἓν τεῖχος· τοιαύτη δ' ἴσως ἐστὶ καὶ
Βαβυλὼν καὶ πᾶσα ἥτις ἔχει περιγραφὴν μᾶλλον
ἔθνους ἢ πόλεως· ἧς γέ φασιν ἑαλωκυίας τρίτην
30 ἡμέραν οὐκ αἰσθέσθαι τι μέρος τῆς πόλεως. ἀλλὰ
περὶ μὲν ταύτης τῆς ἀπορίας εἰς ἄλλον καιρὸν
χρήσιμος ἡ σκέψις (περὶ γὰρ μεγέθους τῆς πόλεως,
τό τε πόσον καὶ πότερον ἔθνος ἓν ἢ πλείω συμ-

---

[1] οἰκεῖός πως—ταύτης, πότε Richards.
[2] τὸν—ἀνθρώπους secl. Susemihl.

---

[a] i.e. πόλις means both (1) ' city ' (and also ' citadel ') and
(2) ' state,' a collection of citizens ; and if the citizens divide
and settle in two different ' cities ' with different governments,
they are clearly not the same ' state ' as before.

was borrowed by the tyrant and not by the state, and should repudiate many other similar claims also, because some forms of government rest upon force and are not aimed at the welfare of the community. 11 If therefore some democracies also are governed in that manner, the acts of the authorities in their case can only be said to be the acts of the state in the same sense as the public acts emanating from an oligarchy or a tyranny are said to be. Akin to this controversy seems to be the subject, What exactly is the principle on which we ought to pronounce a city to be the same city as it was before, or not the same but a different city ? The most obvious mode of inquiring into this difficulty deals with place and people : the place and the people may have been divided, and some may have settled in one place, and some in another. In this form the question must be considered as easier of solution ; for, as ' city ' has several meanings, the inquiry so put is in a way 12 not difficult.ᵃ But it may similarly be asked, Suppose a set of men inhabit the same place, in what circumstances are we to consider their city to be a single city ? Its unity clearly does not depend on the walls, for it would be possible to throw a single wall round the Peloponnesus ; and a case in point perhaps is Babylon, and any other city that has the circuit of a nation rather than of a city ; for it is said that when Babylon was captured a considerable part of the city was not aware of it three days later. But the consideration of this difficulty will be serviceable for another occasion, as the student of politics must not ignore the question, What is the most advantageous size for a city, and should its populations be of one

1276 a

φέρει, δεῖ μὴ λανθάνειν τὸν πολιτικόν)· ἀλλὰ τῶν

35 αὐτῶν¹ κατοικούντων τὸν αὐτὸν τόπον, πότερον
ἕως ἂν ᾖ τὸ γένος ταυτὸ τῶν κατοικούντων τὴν
αὐτὴν εἶναι φατέον πόλιν, καίπερ ἀεὶ τῶν μὲν
φθειρομένων τῶν δὲ γινομένων, ὥσπερ καὶ ποταμοὺς εἰώθαμεν λέγειν τοὺς αὐτοὺς καὶ κρήνας
τὰς αὐτὰς καίπερ ἀεὶ τοῦ μὲν ἐπιγινομένου νάματος

40 τοῦ δ' ὑπεξιόντος, ἢ τοὺς μὲν ἀνθρώπους φατέον
εἶναι τοὺς αὐτοὺς διὰ τὴν τοιαύτην αἰτίαν τὴν δὲ

1276 b πόλιν ἑτέραν; εἴπερ γάρ ἐστι κοινωνία τις ἡ
πόλις, ἔστι δὲ κοινωνία πολιτῶν πολιτείας,² γιγνομένης ἑτέρας τῷ εἴδει καὶ διαφερούσης τῆς
πολιτείας ἀναγκαῖον εἶναι δόξειεν ἂν καὶ τὴν πόλιν

5 εἶναι μὴ τὴν αὐτήν, ὥσπερ γε καὶ χορὸν ὁτὲ μὲν
κωμικὸν ὁτὲ δὲ τραγικὸν ἕτερον εἶναι φαμεν τῶν
αὐτῶν πολλάκις ἀνθρώπων ὄντων, ὁμοίως δὲ καὶ
πᾶσαν ἄλλην κοινωνίαν καὶ σύνθεσιν ἑτέραν ἂν
εἶδος ἕτερον ᾖ τῆς συνθέσεως, οἷον ἁρμονίαν τῶν
αὐτῶν φθόγγων ἑτέραν εἶναι λέγομεν³ ἂν ὁτὲ μὲν

10 ᾖ Δώριος ὁτὲ δὲ Φρύγιος. εἰ δὴ τοῦτον ἔχει τὸν
τρόπον, φανερὸν ὅτι μάλιστα λεκτέον τὴν αὐτὴν
πόλιν εἰς τὴν πολιτείαν βλέποντας· ὄνομα δὲ καλεῖν ἕτερον ἢ ταὐτὸν ἔξεστι καὶ τῶν αὐτῶν κατοικούντων αὐτὴν καὶ πάμπαν ἑτέρων ἀνθρώπων.
εἰ δὲ δίκαιον διαλύειν ἢ μὴ διαλύειν ὅταν εἰς

15 ἑτέραν μεταβάλλῃ πολιτείαν ἡ πόλις, λόγος ἕτερος.

II. Τῶν δὲ νῦν εἰρημένων ἐχόμενόν ἐστιν ἐπι-

---

¹ τῶν ἀνθρώπων Richards.
² πολιτεία Congreve.
³ λέγομεν Alb.: λέγοιμεν codd. (ἑτέραν ἂν εἶναι λέγοιμεν ?
Newman).

3 race or of several ? But are we to pronounce a city, where the same population inhabit the same place, to be the same city so long as the population are of the same race, in spite of the fact that all the time some are dying and others being born, just as it is our custom to say that a river or a spring is the same river or spring although one stream of water is always being added to it and another being withdrawn from it, or are we to say that though the people are the same people for the similar reason of continuity, yet the city is a different city ? For inasmuch as a state is a kind of partnership, and is in fact a partnership of citizens in a government, when the form of the government has been altered and is different it would appear to follow that the state is no longer the same state, just as we say that a chorus which on one occasion acts a comedy and on another a tragedy is a different chorus although it is often composed

4 of the same persons, and similarly with any other common whole or composite structure we say it is different if the form of its structure is different—for instance a musical tune consisting of the same notes we call a different tune if at one time it is played in the Dorian mode and at another in the Phrygian. Therefore if this is the case, it is clear that we must speak of a state as being the same state chiefly with regard to its constitution ; and it is possible for it to be called by the same or by a different designation both when its inhabitants are the same and when they are entirely different persons. But whether a state is or is not bound in justice to discharge its engagements when it has changed to a different constitution, is another subject.

II. The next thing to consider after what has now

185

1276 b

σκέψασθαι πότερον τὴν αὐτὴν ἀρετὴν ἀνδρὸς
ἀγαθοῦ καὶ πολίτου σπουδαίου θετέον ἢ μὴ τὴν
αὐτήν. ἀλλὰ μὴν εἴ γε τοῦτο τυχεῖν δεῖ ζητήσεως,
20 τὴν τοῦ πολίτου τύπῳ τινὶ πρῶτον ληπτέον.
ὥσπερ οὖν ὁ πλωτὴρ εἷς τις τῶν κοινωνῶν ἐστίν,
οὕτω καὶ τὸν πολίτην φαμέν. τῶν δὲ πλωτήρων
καίπερ ἀνομοίων ὄντων τὴν δύναμιν (ὁ μὲν γὰρ
ἐστιν ἐρέτης, ὁ δὲ κυβερνήτης, ὁ δὲ πρωρεύς, ὁ δ'
ἄλλην τιν' ἔχων τοιαύτην ἐπωνυμίαν) δῆλον ὡς ὁ
25 μὲν ἀκριβέστατος ἑκάστου λόγος ἴδιος ἔσται τῆς
ἀρετῆς, ὁμοίως δὲ καὶ κοινός τις ἐφαρμόσει πᾶσιν·
ἡ γὰρ σωτηρία τῆς ναυτιλίας ἔργον ἐστὶν αὐτῶν
πάντων, τούτου γὰρ ἕκαστος ὀρέγεται τῶν πλωτήρων. ὁμοίως τοίνυν καὶ τῶν πολιτῶν, καίπερ 2
ἀνομοίων ὄντων, ἡ σωτηρία τῆς κοινωνίας ἔργον
30 ἐστί, κοινωνία δ' ἐστὶν ἡ πολιτεία, διὸ τὴν ἀρετὴν
ἀναγκαῖον εἶναι τοῦ πολίτου πρὸς τὴν πολιτείαν.
εἴπερ οὖν ἐστὶ πλείω πολιτείας εἴδη, δῆλον ὡς οὐκ
ἐνδέχεται τοῦ σπουδαίου πολίτου μίαν ἀρετὴν
εἶναι τὴν τελείαν· τὸν δ' ἀγαθὸν ἄνδρα φαμὲν κατὰ
μίαν ἀρετὴν εἶναι τὴν τελείαν.[1] ὅτι μὲν οὖν
35 ἐνδέχεται πολίτην ὄντα σπουδαῖον μὴ κεκτῆσθαι
τὴν ἀρετὴν καθ' ἢν σπουδαῖος ἀνήρ, φανερόν. οὐ 3
μὴν ἀλλὰ καὶ κατ' ἄλλον τρόπον ἔστι διαπορoῦντας
ἐπελθεῖν τὸν αὐτὸν λόγον περὶ τῆς ἀρίστης πολιτείας. εἰ γὰρ ἀδύνατον[2] ἐξ ἁπάντων σπουδαίων
ὄντων εἶναι πόλιν, δεῖ δ' ἕκαστον τὸ καθ' αὑτὸν

---

[1] τὸν δ'—τελείαν ΓΡ[1]: om. cet.
[2] δυνατὸν Bernays.

---

[a] Perhaps the Greek should be altered to give ' possible ':
see Additional Note on p. 275.

been said is the question whether we are to hold that the goodness of a good man is the same as that of a good citizen, or not the same. However, if this point really is to receive investigation, we must first ascertain in some general outline what constitutes the excellence of a citizen. Now a citizen we pronounced to be one sort of partner in a community, as is a sailor. And although sailors differ from each other in function—one is an oarsman, another helmsman, another look-out man, and another has some other similar special designation—and so clearly the most exact definition of their excellence will be special to each, yet there will also be a common definition of excellence that will apply alike to all of them ; for security in navigation is the business of them all, since each of the sailors aims at that. Similarly therefore with the citizens, although they are dissimilar from one another, their business is the security of their community, and this community is the constitution, so that the goodness of a citizen must necessarily be relative to the constitution of the state. If therefore there are various forms of constitution, it is clear that there cannot be one single goodness which is the perfect goodness of the good citizen ; but when we speak of a good man we mean that he possesses one single goodness, perfect goodness. Hence it is manifestly possible to be a good citizen without possessing the goodness that constitutes a good man. Moreover it is also feasible to pursue the same topic by raising the question in another manner in relation to the best form of constitution. If it is impossible [a] for a state to consist entirely of good men, and if it is necessary for each person to perform well the work of his position, and

Must a good citizen be a good man?

Not unconditionally ; for civic virtue differs under different constitutions,

and even in the perfect state all good citizens are not good men,

1276 b
40 ἔργον εὖ ποιεῖν, τοῦτο δ' ἀπ' ἀρετῆς, ἐπειδὴ
ἀδύνατον ὁμοίους εἶναι πάντας τοὺς πολίτας, οὐκ
1277 a ἂν εἴη μία ἀρετὴ πολίτου καὶ ἀνδρὸς ἀγαθοῦ· τὴν
μὲν γὰρ τοῦ σπουδαίου πολίτου δεῖ πᾶσιν ὑπάρχειν
(οὕτω γὰρ ἀρίστην ἀναγκαῖον εἶναι τὴν πόλιν), τὴν
δὲ τοῦ ἀνδρὸς τοῦ ἀγαθοῦ ἀδύνατον, εἰ μὴ πάντας
5 ἀναγκαῖον ἀγαθοὺς εἶναι τοὺς ἐν τῇ σπουδαίᾳ
πόλει πολίτας. ἔτι ἐπεὶ ἐξ ἀνομοίων ἡ πόλις—
ὥσπερ ζῷον εὐθὺς ἐκ ψυχῆς καὶ σώματος, καὶ
ψυχὴ ἐκ λόγου καὶ ὀρέξεως, καὶ οἰκία ἐξ ἀνδρὸς
καὶ γυναικὸς καὶ κτῆσις[2] ἐκ δεσπότου καὶ δούλου,
τὸν αὐτὸν τρόπον καὶ πόλις ἐξ ἁπάντων τε τούτων
10 καὶ πρὸς τούτοις ἐξ ἄλλων ἀνομοίων συνέστηκεν
εἰδῶν—, ἀνάγκη μὴ μίαν εἶναι τὴν τῶν πολιτῶν
πάντων ἀρετήν, ὥσπερ οὐδὲ τῶν χορευτῶν κορυ-
φαίου καὶ παραστάτου. διότι μὲν τοίνυν ἁπλῶς
οὐχ ἡ αὐτή, φανερὸν ἐκ τούτων· ἀλλ' ἆρα ἔσται
τινὸς ἡ αὐτὴ ἀρετὴ πολίτου τε σπουδαίου καὶ
ἀνδρὸς σπουδαίου; φαμὲν δὴ τὸν ἄρχοντα τὸν
15 σπουδαῖον ἀγαθὸν εἶναι καὶ φρόνιμον, τὸν δὲ πολιτικὸν ἀναγκαῖον εἶναι φρόνιμον. καὶ τὴν παιδείαν
δ' εὐθὺς ἑτέραν εἶναι λέγουσί τινες τοῦ ἄρχοντος,
ὥσπερ καὶ φαίνονται οἱ τῶν βασιλέων υἱεῖς
ἱππικὴν καὶ πολεμικὴν παιδευόμενοι, καὶ Εὐριπίδης φησὶ

20   μή μοι τὰ κόμψ', ἀλλ' ὧν πόλει δεῖ,

ὡς οὖσάν τινα ἄρχοντος παιδείαν. εἰ δὲ ἡ αὐτὴ

---

[1] ἐπειδὴ ΓΜ : ἐπειδὴ δὲ P[1] : ἐπεὶ δὲ cet. : ἐπεὶ Spengel.
[2] [κτῆσις] Bernays.

---

[a] These words in the Greek are probably an interpolation.
[b] Fragment 16, from *Aeolus*.

to do this springs from goodness, then because it is impossible for all the citizens to be alike, the goodness of a good citizen would not be one and the same as the goodness of a good man; for all ought to possess the goodness of the good citizen (that is a necessary condition of the state's being the best possible), but it is impossible that all should possess the goodness of a good man, if it is not necessary that all the citizens in a good state should be good men. Again, since the state consists of unlike persons— and different citizens just as an animal (to take this instance first) consists have of soul and body, and a soul of reason and appetite, different functions. and a household of husband and wife and [ownership involves] [a] master and slave, in the same manner a state consists of all of these persons and also of others of different classes in addition to these,— it necessarily follows that the goodness of all the citizens is not one and the same, just as among dancers the skill of a head dancer is not the same as that of a subordinate leader. It is clear then from these considerations that the goodness of a good citizen and that of a good man are not the same in general; but will the goodness of a good citizen of a particular sort be the same as that of a good man? Now we say that a good ruler is virtuous and wise, But a good ruler must and that a citizen taking part in politics must be wise. be a good Also some people say that even the education of a man, ruler must be different, as indeed we see that the sons of kings are educated in horsemanship and military exercises, and Euripides says [b]

> No subtleties for me, but what the state
> Requireth—

implying that there is a special education for a ruler.

189

ἀρετὴ ἄρχοντός τε ἀγαθοῦ καὶ ἀνδρὸς ἀγαθοῦ,
πολίτης δ' ἐστὶ καὶ ὁ ἀρχόμενος, οὐχ ἡ αὐτὴ
ἁπλῶς ἂν εἴη πολίτου καὶ ἀνδρός, τινὸς μέντοι
πολίτου· οὐ γὰρ ἡ αὐτὴ ἄρχοντος καὶ πολίτου, καὶ
διὰ τοῦτ' ἴσως Ἰάσων ἔφη πεινῆν ὅτε μὴ τυραννοῖ,
25 ὡς οὐκ ἐπιστάμενος ἰδιώτης εἶναι. ἀλλὰ μὴν
ἐπαινεῖταί γε τὸ δύνασθαι ἄρχειν καὶ ἄρχεσθαι,
καὶ πολίτου δοκεῖ που[1] ἡ ἀρετὴ εἶναι τὸ δύνασθαι
καὶ ἄρχειν καὶ ἄρχεσθαι καλῶς. εἰ οὖν τὴν μὲν
τοῦ ἀγαθοῦ ἀνδρὸς τίθεμεν ἀρχικήν, τὴν δὲ τοῦ
πολίτου ἄμφω, οὐκ ἂν εἴη ἄμφω ἐπαινετὰ ὁμοίως.
30 ἐπεὶ οὖν ποτὲ δοκεῖ[2] ἀμφότερα,[3] καὶ οὐ ταὐτὰ
δεῖν τὸν ἄρχοντα μανθάνειν καὶ τὸν ἀρχόμενον, τὸν
δὲ πολίτην ἀμφότερ' ἐπίστασθαι καὶ μετέχειν
ἀμφοῖν, ...[4] κἀντεῦθεν ἂν κατίδοι τις· ἔστι γὰρ
ἀρχὴ δεσποτική· ταύτην δὲ τὴν περὶ τἀναγκαῖα
λέγομεν, ἃ ποιεῖν ἐπίστασθαι τὸν ἄρχοντ' οὐκ
35 ἀναγκαῖον, ἀλλὰ χρῆσθαι μᾶλλον· θάτερον δὲ καὶ
ἀνδραποδῶδες, λέγω δὲ θάτερον τὸ δύνασθαι καὶ
ὑπηρετεῖν τὰς διακονικὰς πράξεις. δούλου δ' εἴδη
πλείω λέγομεν, αἱ γὰρ ἐργασίαι πλείους. ὧν ἓν
μέρος κατέχουσιν οἱ χερνῆτες· οὗτοι δ' εἰσίν, ὥσπερ
1277 b σημαίνει καὶ τοὔνομ' αὐτούς,[5] οἱ ζῶντες ἀπὸ τῶν
χειρῶν, ἐν οἷς ὁ βάναυσος τεχνίτης ἐστίν. διὸ

---

[1] δοκεῖ που Jackson: δοκίμου codd.
[2] ποτὲ δοκεῖ corruptum: ἀποδέχεσθαι δεῖ Susemihl.
[3] ἄμφω ἕτερα Bernays: ἕτερα Coraes.
[4] lacunam Susemihl.
[5] αὐτὸ Montecatinus.

---

[a] Tyrant of Pherae in Thessaly, assassinated 370 B.C.
[b] Some words seem to have been lost, conveying ' we must
consider how this dual fitness can be acquired,' or possibly

And if the goodness of a good ruler is the same as the goodness of a good man, yet the person ruled is also a citizen, so that the goodness of a citizen in general will not be the same as that of a man, although that of a particular citizen will ; for goodness as a ruler is not the same as goodness as a citizen, and no doubt this is the reason why Jason *a* said that whenever he was not tyrant he felt hungry, meaning that he did not know the art of being a private person. Another point is that we praise the ability to rule and to be ruled, and it is doubtless held that the goodness of a citizen consists in ability both to rule and to be ruled well. If then we lay it down that the goodness of the good man is displayed in ruling, whereas that of the citizen is shown in both capacities, the two capacities cannot be equally laudable. Since therefore both views are sometimes accepted, and it is thought that the ruler and the subject do not have to learn the same arts but that the citizen must know both arts and share in both capacities, ...*b* And it may be discerned from the following illustration : one form of authority is that of a master ; by this we mean the exercise of authority in regard to the necessary work of the house, which it is not necessary for the master to know how to execute, but rather how to utilize ; the other capacity, I mean the ability actually to serve in these menial tasks, is indeed a slave's quality. But we distinguish several kinds of slave, as their employments are several. One department belongs to the handicraftsmen, who as their name implies are the persons that live by their hands, a class that includes the mechanic artisan.

(marginal note: and must have first learnt to obey, as a free man.)

considerably more. But the text at the beginning of the sentence is also corrupt.

1277 b

παρ' ἐνίοις οὐ μετεῖχον οἱ δημιουργοὶ τὸ παλαιὸν
ἀρχῶν, πρὶν δῆμον γενέσθαι τὸν ἔσχατον. τὰ μὲν
οὖν ἔργα τῶν ἀρχομένων οὕτως οὐ δεῖ τὸν ἀγαθὸν
5 οὐδὲ τὸν πολιτικὸν οὐδὲ τὸν πολίτην¹ τὸν ἀγαθὸν
μανθάνειν, εἰ μή ποτε χρείας χάριν αὐτῷ πρὸς
αὐτόν (οὐ γὰρ ἔτι συμβαίνει γίνεσθαι τὸν² μὲν
δεσπότην τὸν² δὲ δοῦλον). ἀλλ' ἔστι τις ἀρχὴ
καθ' ἣν ἄρχει τῶν ὁμοίων τῷ γένει καὶ τῶν
ἐλευθέρων (ταύτην γὰρ λέγομεν εἶναι τὴν πολι-
10 τικὴν ἀρχήν), ἣν δεῖ τὸν ἄρχοντα ἀρχόμενον μαθεῖν
οἷον ἱππαρχεῖν ἱππαρχηθέντα, στρατηγεῖν στρατη-
γηθέντα καὶ ταξιαρχήσαντα καὶ λοχαγήσαντα. διὸ
καὶ λέγεται καὶ τοῦτο καλῶς, ὡς οὐκ ἔστιν εὖ
ἄρξαι μὴ ἀρχθέντα. τούτων δὲ ἀρετὴ μὲν ἑτέρα,
δεῖ δὲ τὸν πολίτην τὸν ἀγαθὸν ἐπίστασθαι καὶ
15 δύνασθαι καὶ ἄρχεσθαι καὶ ἄρχειν, καὶ αὕτη ἀρετὴ
πολίτου, τὸ τὴν τῶν ἐλευθέρων ἀρχὴν ἐπίστασθαι
ἐπ' ἀμφότερα. καὶ ἀνδρὸς δὴ ἀγαθοῦ ἄμφω, καὶ
εἰ ἕτερον εἶδος σωφροσύνης καὶ δικαιοσύνης ἀρχι-
κῆς· καὶ γὰρ ἀρχομένου μὲν ἐλευθέρου δὲ δῆλον
ὅτι οὐ μία ἂν εἴη τοῦ ἀγαθοῦ ἀρετή, οἷον δικαιο-
20 σύνη, ἀλλ' εἴδη ἔχουσα καθ' ἃ ἄρξει καὶ ἄρξεται,
ὥσπερ ἀνδρὸς καὶ γυναικὸς ἑτέρα σωφροσύνη καὶ
ἀνδρεία (δόξαι γὰρ ἂν εἶναι δειλὸς ἀνὴρ εἰ οὕτως
ἀνδρεῖος εἴη ὥσπερ γυνὴ ἀνδρεία, καὶ γυνὴ λάλος³

---

¹ [ἀγαθὸν οὐδὲ τὸν] πολιτικὸν [οὐδὲ τὸν πολίτην] Thurot.
² τότε pro τὸν bis Riese, ὅτε Richards.
³ ἄλλος, ἄλαλος, ἄλλως codd. inf. : ἀκόλαστος Susemihl.

Hence in some states manual labourers were not
admitted to office in old times, before the development of extreme democracy. The tasks of those who
are under this form of authority therefore it is not
proper for the good man or the man fit for citizenship or the good citizen to learn, except for his own
private use occasionally (for then it ceases to be a
case of the one party being master and the other
slave). But there exists a form of authority by
which a man rules over persons of the same race as
himself, and free men (for that is how we describe
political authority), and this the ruler should learn
by being ruled, just as a man should command cavalry
after having served as a trooper, command a regiment after having served in a regiment and been in
command of a company and of a platoon. Hence
there is much truth in the saying that it is impossible
to become a good ruler without having been a subject.
And although the goodness of a ruler and that of a
subject are different, the good citizen must have the
knowledge and the ability both to be ruled and to rule,
and the merit of the good citizen consists in having
a knowledge of the government of free men on both
sides. And therefore both these virtues are characteristic of a good man, even if temperance and
justice in a ruler are of a different kind from temperance and justice in a subject; for clearly a good
man's virtue, for example his justice, will not be one
and the same when he is under government and when
he is free, but it will be of different kinds, one fitting
him to rule and one to be ruled, just as temperance _Male and_
and courage are different in a man and in a woman _female_
virtue.
(for a man would be thought a coward if he were only
as brave as a brave woman, and a woman a chatterer

193

1277 b

εἰ οὕτω κοσμία εἴη ὥσπερ ὁ ἀνὴρ ὁ ἀγαθός· ἐπεὶ
καὶ οἰκονομία ἑτέρα ἀνδρὸς καὶ γυναικός, τοῦ μὲν
25 γὰρ κτᾶσθαι τῆς δὲ φυλάττειν ἔργον ἐστίν). ἡ δὲ
φρόνησις ἄρχοντος ἴδιος ἀρετὴ μόνη· τὰς γὰρ ἄλλας
ἔοικεν ἀναγκαῖον εἶναι κοινὰς καὶ τῶν ἀρχομένων
καὶ τῶν ἀρχόντων, ἀρχομένου δέ γε οὐκ ἔστιν
ἀρετὴ φρόνησις, ἀλλὰ δόξα ἀληθής· ὥσπερ αὐλο-
30 ποιὸς γὰρ ὁ ἀρχόμενος, ὁ δ᾽ ἄρχων αὐλητὴς ὁ
χρώμενος.

Πότερον μὲν οὖν ἡ αὐτὴ ἀρετὴ ἀνδρὸς ἀγαθοῦ
καὶ πολίτου σπουδαίου ἢ ἑτέρα, καὶ πῶς ἡ αὐτὴ
καὶ πῶς ἑτέρα, φανερὸν ἐκ τούτων.

III. Περὶ δὲ τὸν πολίτην ἔτι λείπεταί τις τῶν
ἀποριῶν. ὡς ἀληθῶς γὰρ πότερον πολίτης ἐστὶν
35 ᾧ κοινωνεῖν ἔξεστιν ἀρχῆς, ἢ καὶ τοὺς βαναύσους
πολίτας θετέον; εἰ μὲν οὖν καὶ τούτους θετέον οἷς
μὴ μέτεστιν ἀρχῶν, οὐχ οἷόν τε παντὸς εἶναι πολίτου
τὴν τοιαύτην ἀρετήν, οὗτος γὰρ πολίτης· εἰ δὲ
μηδεὶς τῶν τοιούτων πολίτης, ἐν τίνι μέρει θετέος
ἕκαστος; οὐδὲ γὰρ μέτοικος οὐδὲ ξένος. ἢ διά γε
1278 a τοῦτον τὸν λόγον οὐδὲν φήσομεν συμβαίνειν ἄτοπον;
οὐδὲ γὰρ οἱ δοῦλοι τῶν εἰρημένων οὐδέν, οὐδ᾽ οἱ
ἀπελεύθεροι. τοῦτο γὰρ ἀληθές, ὡς οὐ πάντας
θετέον πολίτας ὧν ἄνευ οὐκ ἂν εἴη πόλις, ἐπεὶ
οὐδ᾽ οἱ παῖδες ὡσαύτως πολῖται καὶ οἱ ἄνδρες, ἀλλ᾽
5 οἱ μὲν ἁπλῶς οἱ δ᾽ ἐξ ὑποθέσεως[1]· πολῖται μὲν
γάρ εἰσιν, ἀλλ᾽ ἀτελεῖς. ἐν μὲν οὖν τοῖς ἀρχαίοις

---

[1] ἐκ προσθέσεως Casaubon.

---

[a] Or perhaps 'for the working-man is a citizen': see
Additional Note p. 275.
[b] Or, with Casaubon's probable correction of the Greek,
'only with a qualification.'

194

if she were only as modest as a good man ; since even the household functions of a man and of a woman are different—his business is to get and hers to keep). And practical wisdom alone of the virtues is a virtue peculiar to a ruler ; for the other virtues seem to be necessary alike for both subjects and rulers to possess, but wisdom assuredly is not a subject's virtue, but only right opinion : the subject corresponds to the man who makes flutes and the ruler to the flute-player who uses them.

The question whether the goodness of a good man is the same as that of a good citizen or different, and how they are the same and how different, is clear from these considerations.

III. But one of the difficulties as to what constitutes a citizen is still left. Is it truly the case that a citizen is a person who has the right to share office in the government, or are the working classes also to be counted citizens ? If these persons also are to be counted who have no share in offices, it is not possible for every citizen to possess the citizen's virtue ; for the true citizen is the man capable of governing.[a] If on the other hand no one of the working people is a citizen, in what class are the various workers to be ranked ? for they are neither resident aliens nor foreigners. Or shall we say that so far as that argument goes no inconsistency results ? for slaves also are not in one of the classes mentioned, nor are freed-men. For it is true that not all the persons indispensable for the existence of a state are to be deemed citizens, since even the sons of citizens are not citizens in the same sense as the adults : the latter are citizens in the full sense, the former only by presumption[b]—they are citizens, but incomplete ones.

Therefore the working classes not citizens in the best state, as they do not hold office.

1278 a

χρόνοις παρ' ἐνίοις ἦν δοῦλον τὸ βάναυσον ἢ
ξενικόν, διόπερ οἱ πολλοὶ τοιοῦτοι καὶ νῦν· ἡ δὲ
βελτίστη πόλις οὐ ποιήσει βάναυσον πολίτην. εἰ
δὲ καὶ οὗτος πολίτης, ἀλλὰ πολίτου ἀρετὴν ἣν
10 εἴπομεν λεκτέον οὐ παντός, οὐδ' ἐλευθέρου μόνον,
ἀλλ' ὅσοι τῶν ἔργων εἰσὶν ἀφειμένοι τῶν ἀναγκαίων.
τῶν δ' ἀναγκαίων¹ οἱ μὲν ἑνὶ λειτουργοῦντες τὰ
τοιαῦτα δοῦλοι, οἱ δὲ κοινοὶ βάναυσοι καὶ θῆτες.
φανερὸν δ' ἐντεῦθεν μικρὸν ἐπισκεψαμένοις πῶς
ἔχει περὶ αὐτῶν[· αὐτὸ γὰρ φανὲν τὸ λεχθὲν ποιεῖ
15 δῆλον].² ἐπεὶ γὰρ πλείους εἰσὶν αἱ πολιτεῖαι, καὶ
εἴδη πολίτου ἀναγκαῖον εἶναι πλείω, καὶ μάλιστα
τοῦ ἀρχομένου πολίτου, ὥστ' ἐν μέν τινι πολιτείᾳ
τὸν βάναυσον ἀναγκαῖον εἶναι καὶ τὸν θῆτα πολίτας,
ἐν τισὶ δ' ἀδύνατον, οἷον εἴ τίς ἐστιν ἣν καλοῦσιν
20 ἀριστοκρατικὴν καὶ ἐν ᾗ κατ' ἀρετὴν αἱ τιμαὶ
δίδονται καὶ κατ' ἀξίαν· οὐ γὰρ οἷόν τ' ἐπιτηδεῦ-
σαι τὰ τῆς ἀρετῆς ζῶντα βίον βάναυσον ἢ θητικόν.
ἐν δὲ ταῖς ὀλιγαρχίαις θῆτα μὲν οὐκ ἐνδέχεται εἶναι
πολίτην (ἀπὸ τιμημάτων γὰρ μακρῶν αἱ μεθέξεις
τῶν ἀρχῶν), βάναυσον δ' ἐνδέχεται· πλουτοῦσι γὰρ
25 καὶ οἱ πολλοὶ τῶν τεχνιτῶν. ἐν Θήβαις δὲ νόμος
ἦν τὸν διὰ³ δέκα ἐτῶν μὴ ἀπεσχημένον τῆς ἀγορᾶς
μὴ μετέχειν ἀρχῆς. ἐν πολλαῖς δὲ πολιτείαις προσ-

¹ ἄλλων Bernays.
² [αὐτὸ—δῆλον] ed.: [φανὲν] vel ⟨τὸ⟩ φανὲν [τὸ λεχθὲν]
Richards.
³ διὰ add. Newman (ἔτη Richards).

* The ill-expressed clause ' for what—clear ' seems almost
certainly to be an interpolation.

In ancient times in fact the artisan class in some states consisted of slaves or aliens, owing to which the great mass of artisans are so even now; and the best-ordered state will not make an artisan a citizen. While if even the artisan is a citizen, then what we said to be the citizen's virtue must not be said to belong to every citizen, nor merely be defined as the virtue of a free man, but will only belong to those who are released from menial occupations. Among menial occupations those who render such services to an individual are slaves, and those who do so for the community are artisans and hired labourers. The state of the case about them will be manifest from what follows when we consider it a little further[, for what has been said when made known itself makes it clear].[a] As there are several forms of constitution, it follows that there are several kinds of citizen, and especially of the citizen in a subject position; hence under one form of constitution citizenship will necessarily extend to the artisan and the hired labourer, while under other forms this is impossible, for instance in any constitution that is of the form entitled aristocratic and in which the honours are bestowed according to goodness and to merit, since a person living a life of manual toil or as a hired labourer cannot practise the pursuits in which goodness is exercised. In oligarchies on the other hand, though it is impossible for a hired labourer to be a citizen (since admission to office of various grades is based on high property-assessments), it is possible for an artisan; for even the general mass of the craftsmen are rich. At Thebes there was a law that no one who had not kept out of trade for the last ten years might be admitted to office. But under many

197

1278 a

ἐφέλκεται καὶ τῶν ξένων ὁ νόμος· ὁ γὰρ ἐκ
πολίτιδος ἔν τισι δημοκρατίαις πολίτης ἐστίν, τὸν
αὐτὸν δὲ τρόπον ἔχει καὶ τὰ περὶ τοὺς νόθους
30 παρὰ πολλοῖς. οὐ μὴν ἀλλ' ἐπεὶ δι' ἔνδειαν τῶν
γνησίων πολιτῶν ποιοῦνται πολίτας τοὺς τοιούτους
(διὰ γὰρ ὀλιγανθρωπίαν οὕτω χρῶνται τοῖς νόμοις),
εὐποροῦντες δὴ¹ ὄχλου κατὰ μικρὸν παραιροῦνται
τοὺς ἐκ δούλου πρῶτον ἢ δούλης, εἶτα τοὺς ἀπὸ
γυναικῶν· τέλος δὲ μόνον τοὺς ἐξ ἀμφοῖν ἀστῶν
35 πολίτας ποιοῦσιν. ὅτι μὲν οὖν εἴδη πλείω πολίτου,
φανερὸν ἐκ τούτων, καὶ ὅτι λέγεται μάλιστα
πολίτης ὁ μετέχων τῶν τιμῶν, ὥσπερ καὶ Ὅμηρος
ἐποίησεν

ὡσεί τιν' ἀτίμητον μετανάστην·

ὥσπερ μέτοικος γάρ ἐστιν ὁ τῶν τιμῶν μὴ μετέχων.
ἀλλ' ἐστὶν² ὅπου τὸ τοιοῦτον ἐπικεκρυμμένον ἐστὶν
40 ἀπάτης χάριν τῶν συνοικούντων.

1278 b

Πότερον μὲν οὖν ἑτέραν ἢ τὴν αὐτὴν θετέον καθ'
ἣν ἀνὴρ ἀγαθός ἐστι καὶ πολίτης σπουδαῖος, δῆλον
ἐκ τῶν εἰρημένων, ὅτι τινὸς μὲν πόλεως ὁ αὐτὸς
τινὸς δ' ἕτερος, κἀκεῖνος οὐ πᾶς ἀλλ' ὁ πολιτικὸς
καὶ κύριος ἢ δυνάμενος εἶναι κύριος, ἢ καθ' αὑτὸν
5 ἢ μετ' ἄλλων, τῆς τῶν κοινῶν ἐπιμελείας.

IV. Ἐπεὶ δὲ ταῦτα διώρισται, τὸ μετὰ ταῦτα

---

¹ δὴ Susemihl: δ' codd.
² ἐστὶν hic Welldon, post συνοικούντων codd.

ᵃ *Iliad* ix. 648, xvi. 59.
ᵇ The mss. give ' But where such exclusion is disguised, it
(this concealment) is for the purpose of deceiving ' etc.

constitutions the law draws recruits even from foreigners; for in some democracies the son of a citizen-mother is a citizen, and the same rule holds good as to base-born sons in many places. Nevertheless, inasmuch as such persons are adopted as citizens owing to a lack of citizens of legitimate birth (for legislation of this kind is resorted to because of under-population), when a state becomes well off for numbers it gradually divests itself first of the sons of a slave father or mother, then of those whose mothers only were citizens, and finally only allows citizenship to the children of citizens on both sides. These facts then show that there are various kinds of citizen, and that a citizen in the fullest sense means the man who shares in the honours of the state, as is implied in the verse of Homer [a]:

> Like to some alien settler without honour,—

since a native not admitted to a share in the public honours is like an alien domiciled in the land. But in some places this exclusion is disguised, for the purpose of deceiving those who are a part of the population.[b]

The answer therefore to the question, Is the goodness that makes a good man to be deemed the same as that which makes a worthy citizen, or different? is now clear from what has been said: in one form of state the good man and the good citizen are the same, but in another they are different, and also in the former case it is not every citizen but only the statesman, the man who controls or is competent to control, singly or with colleagues, the administration of the commonwealth, that is essentially also a good man.

IV. And since these points have been determined,

199

σκεπτέον πότερον μίαν θετέον πολιτείαν ἢ πλείους,
κἂν εἰ πλείους, τίνες καὶ πόσαι καὶ διαφοραὶ τίνες
αὐτῶν εἰσίν. ἔστι δὲ πολιτεία πόλεως τάξις τῶν
10 τε ἄλλων ἀρχῶν καὶ μάλιστα τῆς κυρίας πάντων.
κύριον μὲν γὰρ πανταχοῦ τὸ πολίτευμα τῆς πόλεως,
πολίτευμα δ' ἐστὶν ἡ πολιτεία. λέγω δ' οἷον ἐν
μὲν ταῖς δημοκρατικαῖς κύριος ὁ δῆμος, οἱ δ'
ὀλίγοι τοὐναντίον ἐν ταῖς ὀλιγαρχίαις· φαμὲν δὲ
καὶ πολιτείαν ἑτέραν εἶναι τούτων. τὸν αὐτὸν δὲ
15 τοῦτον ἐροῦμεν λόγον καὶ περὶ τῶν ἄλλων.

Ὑποθετέον δὲ πρῶτον τίνος χάριν συνέστηκε
πόλις καὶ τῆς ἀρχῆς εἴδη πόσα τῆς περὶ ἄνθρωπον
καὶ[1] τὴν κοινωνίαν τῆς ζωῆς.

Εἴρηται δὴ κατὰ τοὺς πρώτους λόγους, ἐν οἷς
περὶ οἰκονομίας διωρίσθη καὶ δεσποτείας, ὅτι
20 φύσει μέν ἐστιν ἄνθρωπος ζῷον πολιτικόν· διὸ καὶ
μηδὲν δεόμενοι τῆς παρ' ἀλλήλων βοηθείας οὐκ
ἔλαττον ὀρέγονται τοῦ συζῆν. οὐ μὴν ἀλλὰ καὶ
τὸ κοινῇ συμφέρον συνάγει, καθ' ὅσον ἐπιβάλλει
μέρος ἑκάστῳ τοῦ ζῆν καλῶς. μάλιστα μὲν οὖν
τοῦτ' ἐστὶ τέλος, καὶ κοινῇ πᾶσι καὶ χωρίς·
συνέρχονται δὲ καὶ τοῦ ζῆν ἕνεκεν αὐτοῦ καὶ
25 συνέχουσι τὴν πολιτικὴν κοινωνίαν,[2] ἴσως γὰρ ἔνεστί
τι τοῦ καλοῦ μόριον καὶ κατὰ τὸ ζῆν αὐτὸ μόνον·
ἂν μὴ τοῖς χαλεποῖς κατὰ τὸν βίον ὑπερβάλλῃ
λίαν, δῆλον δ' ὡς καρτεροῦσι πολλὴν κακοπάθειαν

[1] καὶ: κατὰ Bernays.
[2] καὶ—κοινωνίαν post 26 μόριον codd. cet.

ᵃ 1253 a 1 foll.

the next question to be considered is whether we are to lay it down that there is only one form of constitution or several, and if several, what they are and how many and what are the differences between them. Now a constitution is the ordering of a state in respect of its various magistracies, and especially the magistracy that is supreme over all matters. For the government is everywhere supreme over the state and the constitution is the government. I mean that in democratic states for example the people are supreme, but in oligarchies on the contrary the few are ; and we say that they have a different constitution. And we shall use the same language about the other forms of government also.

We have therefore to determine first the fundamental points, what is the object for which a state exists and how many different kinds of system there are for governing mankind and for controlling the common life.

Now it has been said in our first discourses,[a] in which we determined the principles concerning household management and the control of slaves, that man is by nature a political animal ; and so even when men have no need of assistance from each other they none the less desire to live together. At the same time they are also brought together by common interest, so far as each achieves a share of the good life. The good life then is the chief aim of society, both collectively for all its members and individually ; but they also come together and maintain the political partnership for the sake of life merely, for doubtless there is some element of value contained even in the mere state of being alive, provided that there is not too great an excess on the side of the hardships of life, and it

Constitutions classified.

They vary according to their sovereign.

The true object of the State is the mutual welfare of its members.

1278 b

οἱ πολλοὶ τῶν ἀνθρώπων γλιχόμενοι τοῦ ζῆν, ὡς
30 ἐνούσης τινὸς εὐημερίας ἐν αὐτῷ καὶ γλυκύτητος
φυσικῆς.

'Αλλὰ μὴν καὶ τῆς ἀρχῆς τοὺς λεγομένους
τρόπους ῥᾴδιον διελεῖν· καὶ γὰρ ἐν τοῖς ἐξωτερικοῖς
λόγοις διοριζόμεθα περὶ αὐτῶν πολλάκις. ἡ μὲν
γὰρ δεσποτεία, καίπερ ὄντος κατ' ἀλήθειαν τῷ τε
φύσει δούλῳ καὶ τῷ φύσει δεσπότῃ ταὐτοῦ συμ-
35 φέροντος, ὅμως ἄρχει πρὸς τὸ τοῦ δεσπότου συμφέρον οὐδὲν ἧττον, πρὸς δὲ τὸ τοῦ δούλου κατὰ
συμβεβηκός, οὐ γὰρ ἐνδέχεται φθειρομένου τοῦ
δούλου σῴζεσθαι τὴν δεσποτείαν. ἡ δὲ τέκνων
ἀρχὴ καὶ γυναικὸς [καὶ τῆς οἰκίας πάσης, ἣν δὴ
καλοῦμεν οἰκονομικήν]¹ ἤτοι τῶν ἀρχομένων χάριν
40 ἐστὶν ἢ κοινοῦ τινὸς ἀμφοῖν—καθ' αὑτὸ μὲν τῶν
1279 a ἀρχομένων, ὥσπερ ὁρῶμεν καὶ τὰς ἄλλας τέχνας,
οἷον ἰατρικὴν καὶ γυμναστικήν, κατὰ συμβεβηκὸς
δὲ κἂν αὐτῶν εἶεν· οὐδὲν γὰρ κωλύει τὸν παιδο-
τρίβην ἕνα τῶν γυμναζομένων ἐνίοτ' εἶναι καὶ
αὐτόν, ὥσπερ ὁ κυβερνήτης εἷς ἐστιν ἀεὶ τῶν
5 πλωτήρων· ὁ μὲν οὖν παιδοτρίβης ἢ κυβερνήτης
σκοπεῖ τὸ τῶν ἀρχομένων ἀγαθόν, ὅταν δὲ τούτων
εἷς γένηται καὶ αὐτός, κατὰ συμβεβηκὸς μετέχει
τῆς ὠφελείας, ὁ μὲν γὰρ πλωτήρ, ὁ δὲ τῶν γυμνα-

---

¹ καὶ—πάσης seclusit, ἣν—οἰκονομικήν suspexit Susemihl.

ᵃ Mentioned at 1323 a 22 (and also six times in other
books); they are there appealed to for the tripartite classification of foods which in *Ethics* 1098 b 12 is ascribed to ' current
opinion of long standing and generally accepted by students
of philosophy.' The term may there predenote doctrines
not peculiar to the Peripatetic school.

clear that the mass of mankind cling to life at the
cost of enduring much suffering, which shows that
life contains some measure of well-being and of
sweetness in its essential nature.

And again, the several recognized varieties of government can easily be defined; in fact we frequently discuss them in our external discourses.[a] The authority of a master over a slave, although in truth when both master and slave are designed by nature for their positions their interests are the same, nevertheless governs in the greater degree with a view to the interest of the master, but incidentally with a view to that of the slave, for if the slave deteriorates the position of the master cannot be saved from injury. Authority over children and wife [and over the whole household, which we call the art of household management[b]] is exercised either in the interest of those ruled or for some common interest of both parties,—essentially, in the interest of the ruled, as we see that the other arts also, like medicine and athletic training, are pursued in the interest of the persons upon whom they are practised, although incidentally they may also be in the interest of the practitioners themselves; for nothing prevents the trainer from being on occasions himself also one of the persons in training, just as the pilot is always a member of the crew; so although the trainer or pilot studies the good of those under his authority, when he himself also becomes one among them he incidentally shares the benefit, for the pilot is a sailor in the ship and the trainer can become one of the persons in training

Varieties of authority in private life.

[b] Aristotle can hardly have written this clause, as it includes mastership over slaves.

1279 a

ζομένων εἷς γίνεται παιδοτρίβης ὤν. διὸ καὶ τὰς
πολιτικὰς ἀρχάς, ὅταν ᾖ κατ' ἰσότητα τῶν πολιτῶν
10 συνεστηκυῖα καὶ καθ' ὁμοιότητα, κατὰ μέρος
ἀξιοῦσιν ἄρχειν, πρότερον μέν, ᾗ πέφυκεν, ἀξιοῦντες ἐν μέρει λειτουργεῖν, καὶ σκοπεῖν τινὰ πάλιν
τὸ αὑτοῦ ἀγαθόν ὥσπερ πρότερον αὐτὸς ἄρχων
ἐσκόπει τὸ ἐκείνου συμφέρον· νῦν δὲ διὰ τὰς
ὠφελείας τὰς ἀπὸ τῶν κοινῶν καὶ τὰς ἐκ τῆς
15 ἀρχῆς βούλονται συνεχῶς ἄρχειν, οἷον εἰ συνέβαινεν
ὑγιαίνειν ἀεὶ τοῖς ἄρχουσι νοσακεροῖς οὖσιν· καὶ
γὰρ ἂν οὕτως ἴσως ἐδίωκον τὰς ἀρχάς.

Φανερὸν τοίνυν ὡς ὅσαι μὲν πολιτεῖαι τὸ κοινῇ
συμφέρον σκοποῦσιν, αὗται μὲν ὀρθαὶ τυγχάνουσιν
οὖσαι κατὰ τὸ ἁπλῶς δίκαιον, ὅσαι δὲ τὸ σφέτερον
20 μόνον τῶν ἀρχόντων, ἡμαρτημέναι πᾶσαι καὶ
παρεκβάσεις τῶν ὀρθῶν πολιτειῶν· δεσποτικαὶ
γάρ, ἡ δὲ πόλις κοινωνία τῶν ἐλευθέρων ἐστίν.

Διωρισμένων δὲ τούτων ἐχόμενόν ἐστι τὰς
πολιτείας ἐπισκέψασθαι, πόσαι τὸν ἀριθμὸν καὶ
τίνες εἰσί, καὶ πρῶτον τὰς ὀρθὰς αὐτῶν· καὶ γὰρ
25 αἱ παρεκβάσεις ἔσονται φανεραὶ τούτων διορι-
σθεισῶν. V. ἐπεὶ δὲ πολιτεία μὲν καὶ πολίτευμα
σημαίνει ταὐτόν, πολίτευμα δ' ἐστὶ τὸ κύριον τῶν
πόλεων, ἀνάγκη δ' εἶναι κύριον ἢ ἕνα ἢ ὀλίγους ἢ
τοὺς πολλούς, ὅταν μὲν ὁ εἷς ἢ οἱ ὀλίγοι ἢ οἱ
πολλοὶ πρὸς τὸ κοινὸν συμφέρον ἄρχωσι, ταύτας
30 μὲν ὀρθὰς ἀναγκαῖον εἶναι τὰς πολιτείας, τὰς δὲ
πρὸς τὸ ἴδιον ἢ τοῦ ἑνὸς ἢ τῶν ὀλίγων ἢ τοῦ

6 under his own direction. Hence in regard to the political offices also, when the state is constituted on the principle of equality and of similarity between the citizens, these claim to hold office by turn—in earlier times, under the natural system, claiming to do public services in turn, and for somebody in return to look after their own welfare just as previously they looked after his interest when in office themselves; but nowadays owing to the benefits to be got from public sources and from holding office people wish to be in office continuously, just as if it were the case that those in office although sickly people always enjoyed good health—in which case office would no doubt be much run after by invalids.

7 It is clear then that those constitutions that aim at the common advantage are in effect rightly framed in accordance with absolute justice, while those that aim at the rulers' own advantage only are faulty, and are all of them deviations from the right constitutions; for they have an element of despotism, whereas a city is a partnership of free men.

These matters having been determined the next step is to consider how many forms of constitution there are and what they are; and first to study the right forms of constitution, since the deviations will also become manifest when these are defined.

V. But inasmuch as ' constitution ' means the same as ' government,' and the government is the supreme power in the state, and this must be either a single ruler or a few or the mass of the citizens, in cases when the one or the few or the many govern with an eye to the common interest, these constitutions must necessarily be right ones, while those administered with an eye to the private interest of either the one

Constitutions classified by the number of the sovereign body, and by its selfish or unselfish aim.

205

1279 a πλήθους παρεκβάσεις. ἢ γὰρ οὐ πολίτας φατέον
εἶναι τοὺς μετέχοντας,[1] ἢ δεῖ κοινωνεῖν τοῦ συμ-
φέροντος. καλεῖν δ' εἰώθαμεν τῶν μὲν μοναρ- 2
χιῶν τὴν πρὸς τὸ κοινὸν ἀποβλέπουσαν συμφέρον
35 βασιλείαν, τὴν δὲ τῶν ὀλίγων μὲν πλειόνων δ'
ἑνὸς ἀριστοκρατίαν (ἢ διὰ τὸ τοὺς ἀρίστους ἄρχειν
ἢ διὰ τὸ πρὸς τὸ ἄριστον τῇ πόλει καὶ τοῖς
κοινωνοῦσιν αὐτῆς), ὅταν δὲ τὸ πλῆθος πρὸς τὸ
κοινὸν πολιτεύηται συμφέρον, καλεῖται τὸ κοινὸν
ὄνομα πασῶν τῶν πολιτειῶν, πολιτεία. (συμ- 3
40 βαίνει δ' εὐλόγως· ἕνα μὲν γὰρ διαφέρειν κατ'
ἀρετὴν ἢ ὀλίγους ἐνδέχεται, πλείους δ' ἤδη χαλεπὸν
1279 b ἠκριβῶσθαι πρὸς πᾶσαν ἀρετήν, ἀλλὰ μάλιστα τὴν
πολεμικήν, αὕτη γὰρ ἐν πλήθει γίγνεται· διόπερ
κατὰ ταύτην τὴν πολιτείαν κυριώτατον τὸ προπολεμοῦν, καὶ μετέχουσιν αὐτῆς οἱ κεκτημένοι τὰ
5 ὅπλα.) παρεκβάσεις δὲ τῶν εἰρημένων τυραννὶς 4
μὲν βασιλείας ὀλιγαρχία δὲ ἀριστοκρατίας δημοκρατία δὲ πολιτείας· ἡ μὲν γὰρ τυραννίς ἐστι
μοναρχία πρὸς τὸ συμφέρον τὸ τοῦ μοναρχοῦντος,
ἡ δ' ὀλιγαρχία πρὸς τὸ τῶν εὐπόρων, ἡ δὲ δημοκρατία πρὸς τὸ συμφέρον τὸ τῶν ἀπόρων, πρὸς
10 δὲ τὸ τῷ κοινῷ λυσιτελοῦν οὐδεμία αὐτῶν.

Δεῖ δὲ μικρῷ διὰ μακροτέρων εἰπεῖν τίς ἑκάστη
τούτων τῶν πολιτειῶν ἐστίν· καὶ γὰρ ἔχει τινὰς
ἀπορίας, τῷ δὲ περὶ ἑκάστην μέθοδον φιλοσοφοῦντι

---

[1] ⟨μὴ⟩ μετέχοντας Bernays.

r the few or the multitude are deviations. For either we must not say that those who are part of the state are citizens, or those who are part of the state must share in the advantage of membership. Our customary designation for a monarchy that aims at the common advantage is 'kingship'; for a government of more than one yet only a few 'aristocracy' (either because the best men rule or because they rule with a view to what is best for the state and for its members); while when the multitude govern the state with a view to the common advantage, it is called by the name common to all the forms of constitution, 'constitutional government.' (And this comes about reasonably, since although it is possible for one man or a few to excel in virtue, when the number is larger it becomes difficult for them to possess perfect excellence in respect of every form of virtue, but they can best excel in military valour, for this is found with numbers; and therefore with this form of constitution the class that fights for the state in war is the most powerful, and it is those who possess arms who are admitted to the government.) Deviations from the constitutions mentioned are tyranny corresponding to kingship, oligarchy to aristocracy, and democracy to constitutional government; for tyranny is monarchy ruling in the interest of the monarch, oligarchy government in the interest of the rich, democracy government in the interest of the poor, and none of these forms governs with regard to the profit of the community.

But it is necessary to say at a little greater length what each of these constitutions is; for the question involves certain difficulties, and it is the special mark of one who studies any subject philo-

Oligarchy and Democracy essentially the govern.

1279 b

καὶ μὴ μόνον ἀποβλέποντι πρὸς τὸ πράττειν
15 οἰκεῖόν ἐστι τὸ μὴ παρορᾶν μηδέ τι καταλείπειν
ἀλλὰ δηλοῦν τὴν περὶ ἕκαστον ἀλήθειαν. ἔστι δὲ
τυραννὶς μὲν μοναρχία, καθάπερ εἴρηται, δεσποτικὴ τῆς πολιτικῆς κοινωνίας, ὀλιγαρχία δ' ὅταν
ὦσι κύριοι τῆς πολιτείας οἱ τὰς οὐσίας ἔχοντες,
20 δημοκρατία δὲ τοὐναντίον ὅταν οἱ μὴ κεκτημένοι
πλῆθος οὐσίας ἀλλ' ἄποροι. πρώτη δ' ἀπορία πρὸς
τὸν διορισμόν ἐστιν. εἰ γὰρ εἶεν οἱ πλείους ὄντες
εὔποροι κύριοι τῆς πόλεως, δημοκρατία δ' ἐστὶν
ὅταν ᾖ κύριον τὸ πλῆθος, ὁμοίως δὲ πάλιν κἂν εἴ
που συμβαίνοι[1] τοὺς ἀπόρους ἐλάττους μὲν εἶναι
τῶν εὐπόρων κρείττους δ' ὄντας κυρίους εἶναι τῆς
25 πολιτείας, ὅπου δ' ὀλίγον κύριον πλῆθος ὀλιγαρχίαν εἶναί φασιν, οὐκ ἂν καλῶς δόξειεν διωρίσθαι
περὶ τῶν πολιτειῶν. ἀλλὰ μὴν κἂν εἴ[2] τις
συνθεὶς τῇ μὲν εὐπορίᾳ τὴν ὀλιγότητα τῇ δ'
ἀπορίᾳ τὸ πλῆθος οὕτω προσαγορεύοι τὰς πολιτείας, ὀλιγαρχίαν μὲν ἐν ᾗ τὰς ἀρχὰς ἔχουσιν οἱ
30 εὔποροι ὀλίγοι τὸ πλῆθος ὄντες, δημοκρατίαν δὲ
ἐν ᾗ οἱ ἄποροι πολλοὶ τὸ πλῆθος ὄντες, ἄλλην
ἀπορίαν ἔχει. τίνας γὰρ ἐροῦμεν τὰς ἄρτι λεχ-
θείσας πολιτείας, τὴν ἐν ᾗ πλείους οἱ εὔποροι καὶ
τὴν ἐν[3] ᾗ ἐλάττους οἱ ἄποροι, κύριοι δ' ἑκάτεροι
τῶν πολιτειῶν, εἴπερ μηδεμία ἄλλη πολιτεία παρὰ
35 τὰς εἰρημένας ἐστίν; ἔοικε τοίνυν ὁ λόγος ποιεῖν
δῆλον ὅτι τὸ μὲν ὀλίγους ἢ πολλοὺς εἶναι κυρίους

---

[1] Schneider: συμβαίνει, -η codd.
[2] κἂν εἰ Susemihl: κἂν codd.　　[3] τὴν ἐν ed.: ἐν codd.

[a] i.e. it would be absurd to term government by the people
democracy if the people happened to be very rich, or government by a few oligarchy if the few were poor and the many
whom they governed rich.

208

sophically, and not solely with regard to its practical aspect, that he does not overlook or omit any point, but brings to light the truth about each. Now tyranny, as has been said, is monarchy exerting despotic power over the political community; oligarchy is when the control of the government is in the hands of those that own the properties; democracy is when on the contrary it is in the hands of those that do not possess much property, but are poor. A first difficulty is with regard to the definition. If the majority of the citizens were wealthy and were in control of the state, yet when the multitude is in power it is a democracy, and similarly, to take the other case, if it were to occur somewhere that the poor were fewer than the rich but were stronger than they and accordingly were in control of the government, yet where a small number is in control it is said to be an oligarchy, then it would seem that our definition of the forms of constitution was not a good one.[a] And once again, if one assumed the combination of small numbers with wealth and of multitude with poverty, and named the constitutions thus—one in which the rich being few in number hold the offices, oligarchy: one in which the poor being many in number hold the offices, democracy, —this involves another difficulty. What names are we to give to the constitutions just described—the one in which there are more rich and the one in which the poor are the fewer, and these control their respective governments—if there exists no other form of constitution beside those mentioned? The argument therefore seems to make it clear that for few or many to have power is an accidental feature

ments of the rich and poor, not of the few and many.

209

1279 b

συμβεβηκός ἐστιν, τὸ μὲν ταῖς ὀλιγαρχίαις τὸ δὲ
ταῖς δημοκρατίαις, διὰ τὸ τοὺς μὲν εὐπόρους
ὀλίγους πολλοὺς δ' εἶναι τοὺς ἀπόρους πανταχοῦ
(διὸ καὶ οὐ συμβαίνει τὰς ῥηθείσας αἰτίας γίνεσθαι
40 διαφορᾶς), ᾧ δὲ διαφέρουσιν ἥ τε δημοκρατία καὶ
1280 a ἡ ὀλιγαρχία ἀλλήλων πενία καὶ πλοῦτός ἐστιν·
καὶ ἀναγκαῖον μὲν ὅπου ἂν ἄρχωσι διὰ πλοῦτον,
ἄν τ' ἐλάττους ἄν τε πλείους, εἶναι ταύτην ὀλιγαρχίαν, ὅπου δ' οἱ ἄποροι, δημοκρατίαν, ἀλλὰ συμβαίνει, καθάπερ εἴπομεν, τοὺς μὲν ὀλίγους εἶναι
5 τοὺς δὲ πολλούς, εὐποροῦσι μὲν γὰρ ὀλίγοι τῆς δ'
ἐλευθερίας μετέχουσι πάντες, δι' ἃς αἰτίας ἀμφισβητοῦσιν ἀμφότεροι τῆς πολιτείας.

Ληπτέον δὲ πρῶτον τίνας ὅρους λέγουσι τῆς
ὀλιγαρχίας καὶ δημοκρατίας, καὶ τί τὸ δίκαιον τό
τε ὀλιγαρχικὸν καὶ δημοκρατικόν. πάντες γὰρ
10 ἅπτονται δικαίου τινός, ἀλλὰ μέχρι τινὸς προ-
έρχονται, καὶ λέγουσιν οὐ πᾶν τὸ κυρίως δίκαιον.
οἷον δοκεῖ ἴσον τὸ δίκαιον[1] εἶναι, καὶ ἔστιν, ἀλλ' οὐ
πᾶσιν ἀλλὰ τοῖς ἴσοις· καὶ τὸ ἄνισον δοκεῖ δίκαιον
εἶναι, καὶ γάρ ἐστιν, ἀλλ' οὐ πᾶσιν ἀλλὰ τοῖς
ἀνίσοις· οἱ δὲ τοῦτ' ἀφαιροῦσι, τὸ οἷς, καὶ κρίνουσι
15 κακῶς. τὸ δ' αἴτιον ὅτι περὶ αὐτῶν ἡ κρίσις,
σχεδὸν δ' οἱ πλεῖστοι φαῦλοι κριταὶ περὶ τῶν
οἰκείων. ὥστ' ἐπεὶ τὸ δίκαιον τισίν, καὶ διῄρηται τὸν αὐτὸν τρόπον ἐπί τε τῶν πραγμάτων

---

[1] τὸ ἴσον δίκαιον Victorius.

of oligarchies in the one case and democracies in the other, due to the fact that the rich are few and the poor are many everywhere (so that it is not really the case that the points mentioned constitute a specific difference), but that the real thing in which democracy and oligarchy differ from each other is poverty and wealth; and it necessarily follows that wherever the rulers owe their power to wealth, whether they be a minority or a majority, this is an oligarchy, and when the poor rule, it is a democracy, although it does accidentally happen, as we said, that where the rulers hold power by wealth they are few and where they hold power by poverty they are many, because few men are rich but all men possess freedom, and wealth and freedom are the grounds on which the two classes lay claim to the government.

And first we must ascertain what are stated to be the determining qualities of oligarchy and democracy, and what is the principle of justice under the one form of government and under the other. For all men lay hold on justice of some sort, but they only advance to a certain point, and do not express the principle of absolute justice in its entirety. For instance, it is thought that justice is equality, and so it is, though not for everybody but only for those who are equals; and it is thought that inequality is just, for so indeed it is, though not for everybody, but for those who are unequal; but these partisans strip away the qualification of the persons concerned, and judge badly. And the cause of this is that they are themselves concerned in the decision, and perhaps most men are bad judges when their own interests are in question. Hence inasmuch as 'just' means just for certain persons, and it is divided in the same way in relation to the

The distribution of power. Justice is not the equality of the unequal:

211

1280 a

καὶ οἷς, καθάπερ εἴρηται πρότερον ἐν τοῖς ἠθικοῖς,
τὴν μὲν τοῦ πράγματος ἰσότητα ὁμολογοῦσι, τὴν
20 δὲ οἷς ἀμφισβητοῦσι, μάλιστα μὲν διὰ τὸ λεχθὲν
ἄρτι, διότι κρίνουσι τὰ περὶ αὐτοὺς κακῶς, ἔπειτα
δὲ καὶ διὰ τὸ λέγειν μέχρι τινὸς ἑκατέρους δίκαιόν
τι νομίζουσι[1] δίκαιον λέγειν ἁπλῶς. οἱ μὲν γὰρ
ἂν κατά τι ἄνισοι ὦσιν, οἷον χρήμασιν, ὅλως οἴονται ἄνισοι εἶναι, οἱ δ' ἂν κατά τι ἴσοι, οἷον ἐλευ-
25 θερίᾳ,[2] ὅλως ἴσοι. τὸ δὲ κυριώτατον οὐ λέγουσιν.
εἰ μὲν γὰρ τῶν κτημάτων χάριν ἐκοινώνησαν καὶ
συνῆλθον, τοσοῦτον μετέχουσι τῆς πόλεως ὅσον-
περ καὶ τῆς κτήσεως, ὥσθ' ὁ τῶν ὀλιγαρχικῶν
λόγος δόξειεν ἂν ἰσχύειν (οὐ γὰρ εἶναι δίκαιον
ἴσον μετέχειν τῶν ἑκατὸν μνῶν[3] τὸν εἰσενέγ-
30 καντα μίαν μνᾶν τῷ δόντι τὸ λοιπὸν πᾶν, οὔτε
τῶν ἐξ ἀρχῆς οὔτε τῶν ἐπιγινομένων)· εἰ δὲ μήτε
τοῦ ζῆν μόνον ἕνεκεν ἀλλὰ μᾶλλον τοῦ εὖ ζῆν (καὶ
γὰρ ἂν δούλων καὶ τῶν ἄλλων ζῴων ἦν πόλις,
νῦν δ' οὐκ ἔστι διὰ τὸ μὴ μετέχειν εὐδαιμονίας
μηδὲ τοῦ ζῆν κατὰ προαίρεσιν), μήτε συμμαχίας
ἕνεκεν ὅπως ὑπὸ μηδενὸς ἀδικῶνται, μήτε διὰ τὰς

---

[1] νομίζουσι ⟨τὸ⟩ Spengel.
[2] Sepulveda : ἐλεύθεροι, ἐλευθέριοι codd.
[3] ἑκατὸν ταλάντων Γ.

---

[a] Cf. N.E. v. iii., 1131 a 14-24.
[b] See 1268 b 14 n. ; or read ' 100 talents,' say £24,000
(gold).

things to be distributed and the persons that receive them, as has been said before in *Ethics*,[a] the two parties agree as to what constitutes equality in the thing, but dispute as to what constitutes equality in the person, chiefly for the reason just now stated, because men are bad judges where they themselves are concerned, but also, inasmuch as both parties put forward a plea that is just up to a certain point, they think that what they say is absolutely just. For the one side think that if they are unequal in some respects, for instance in wealth, they are entirely unequal, and the other side think that if they are equal in some respects, for instance in freedom, they are entirely equal. But the most important thing they do not mention. If men formed the community and came together for the sake of wealth, their share in the state is proportionate to their share in the property, so that the argument of the champions of oligarchy would appear to be valid—namely that in a partnership with a capital of 100 minae [b] it would not be just for the man who contributed one mina to have a share whether of the principal or of the profits accruing equal to the share of the man who supplied the whole of the remainder ; but if on the other hand the state was formed not for the sake of life only but rather for the good life (for otherwise a collection of slaves or of lower animals would be a state, but as it is, it is not a state, because slaves [c] and animals have no share in well-being or in purposive life), and if its object is not military alliance for defence against injury by anybody, and it does not exist for the

for the State exists for the sake of the good life,

---

[c] See 1260 a 12, and *N.E.* x. vi., 1177 a 8, 'but no one allows a slave any measure of happiness, any more than a life of his own.'

ἀλλαγὰς καὶ τὴν χρῆσιν τὴν πρὸς ἀλλήλους· καὶ
γὰρ ἂν Τυρρηνοὶ καὶ Καρχηδόνιοι, καὶ πάντες οἷς
ἐστι σύμβολα πρὸς ἀλλήλους, ὡς μιᾶς ἂν πολῖται
πόλεως ἦσαν· εἰσὶ γοῦν αὐτοῖς συνθῆκαι περὶ τῶν
εἰσαγωγίμων καὶ σύμβολα περὶ τοῦ μὴ ἀδικεῖν
40 καὶ γραφαὶ περὶ συμμαχίας· ἀλλ' οὔτ' ἀρχαὶ πᾶσιν
1280 b ἐπὶ τούτοις κοιναὶ καθεστᾶσιν, ἀλλ' ἕτεραι παρ'
ἑκατέροις, οὔτε τοῦ ποίους τινὰς εἶναι δεῖ φροντίζουσιν ἅτεροι τοὺς ἑτέρους, οὐδ' ὅπως μηδεὶς
ἄδικος ἔσται τῶν ὑπὸ τὰς συνθήκας μηδὲ μοχθηρίαν ἕξει μηδεμίαν, ἀλλὰ μόνον ὅπως μηδὲν
5 ἀδικήσουσιν ἀλλήλους. περὶ δ' ἀρετῆς καὶ κακίας
πολιτικῆς διασκοποῦσιν ὅσοι φροντίζουσιν εὐνομίας.
ᾗ καὶ φανερὸν ὅτι δεῖ περὶ ἀρετῆς ἐπιμελὲς εἶναι
τῇ γ' ὡς ἀληθῶς ὀνομαζομένῃ πόλει, μὴ λόγου
χάριν· γίνεται γὰρ ἡ κοινωνία συμμαχία, τῶν
10 ἄλλων[1] τόπῳ διαφέρουσα μόνον τῶν ἄποθεν συμ-
μάχων.[2] καὶ ὁ νόμος συνθήκη καί, καθάπερ ἔφη
Λυκόφρων ὁ σοφιστής, ἐγγυητὴς ἀλλήλοις τῶν
δικαίων, ἀλλ' οὐχ οἷος ποιεῖν ἀγαθοὺς καὶ δικαίους
τοὺς πολίτας. ὅτι δὲ τοῦτον ἔχει τὸν τρόπον
φανερόν. εἰ γάρ τις καὶ συναγάγοι τοὺς τόπους
εἰς ἕν, ὥστε ἅπτεσθαι τὴν Μεγαρέων πόλιν καὶ
15 Κορινθίων τοῖς τείχεσιν, ὅμως οὐ μία πόλις· οὐδ'
εἰ πρὸς ἀλλήλους ἐπιγαμίας ποιήσαιντο, καίτοι
τοῦτο τῶν ἰδίων ταῖς πόλεσι κοινωνημάτων ἐστίν.

---

[1] τῶν ἄλλων : ἄλλως ? Immisch.   [2] συμμαχιῶν Conring.

---

[a] The sentence here breaks off; the inference that should
have formed its conclusion is given in § 15.
[b] Probably a pupil of Gorgias, see 1275 b 26 n.

ake of trade and of business relations [a]—for if so,
Etruscans and Carthaginians and all the people that
have commercial relations with one another would
be virtually citizens of a single state; at all events
they have agreements about imports and covenants
as to abstaining from dishonesty and treaties of
alliance for mutual defence; but they do not have
officials common to them all appointed to enforce
these covenants, but different officials with either
party, nor yet does either party take any concern
as to the proper moral character of the other, nor
attempt to secure that nobody in the states under
the covenant shall be dishonest or in any way immoral,
but only that they shall not commit any wrong
against each other. All those on the other hand who
are concerned about good government do take civic
virtue and vice into their purview. Thus it is also
clear that any state that is truly so called and is not
a state merely in name must pay attention to virtue;
for otherwise the community becomes merely an not merely
alliance, differing only in locality from the other for pro-
alliances, those of allies that live apart. And the intercourse.
law is a covenant or, in the phrase of the sophist
Lycophron,[b] a guarantee of men's just claims on one
another, but it is not designed to make the citizens
virtuous and just. And that this is how the matter
stands is manifest. For if one were actually to bring
the sites of two cities together into one, so that the
city-walls of Megara and those of Corinth were con-
tiguous, even so they would not be one city; nor
would they if they enacted rights of intermarriage
with each other, although intermarriage between
citizens is one of the elements of community which are
characteristic of states. And similarly even if certain

215

1280 b

ὁμοίως δ' οὐδ' εἴ τινες οἰκοῖεν χωρὶς μέν, μὴ
μέντοι τοσοῦτον ἄποθεν ὥστε μὴ κοινωνεῖν, ἀλλ'
εἴησαν αὐτοῖς νόμοι τοῦ μὴ σφᾶς αὐτοὺς ἀδικεῖν
20 περὶ τὰς μεταδόσεις—οἷον εἰ ὁ μὲν εἴη τέκτων ὁ
δὲ γεωργὸς ὁ δὲ σκυτοτόμος ὁ δ' ἄλλο τι τοιοῦτον—,
καὶ τὸ πλῆθος εἶεν μύριοι, μὴ μέντοι κοινωνοῖεν
ἄλλου μηδενὸς ἢ τῶν τοιούτων οἷον ἀλλαγῆς καὶ
συμμαχίας, οὐδ' οὕτω πω πόλις. διὰ τίνα δή
25 ποτ' αἰτίαν; οὐ γὰρ δὴ διὰ τὸ μὴ σύνεγγυς τῆς
κοινωνίας· εἰ γὰρ καὶ συνέλθοιεν οὕτω κοινω-
νοῦντες (ἕκαστος μέντοι χρῶτο τῇ ἰδίᾳ οἰκίᾳ ὥσπερ
πόλει) καὶ σφίσιν αὐτοῖς ὡς ἐπιμαχίας οὔσης
βοηθοῦντες ἐπὶ τοὺς ἀδικοῦντας μόνον, οὐδ' οὕτως
ἂν εἶναι δόξειε πόλις τοῖς ἀκριβῶς θεωροῦσιν,
εἴπερ ὁμοίως ὁμιλοῖεν συνελθόντες καὶ χωρίς.
30 φανερὸν τοίνυν ὅτι ἡ πόλις οὐκ ἔστι κοινωνία
τόπου καὶ τοῦ μὴ ἀδικεῖν σφᾶς αὐτοὺς καὶ τῆς
μεταδόσεως χάριν· ἀλλὰ ταῦτα μὲν ἀναγκαῖον
ὑπάρχειν εἴπερ ἔσται πόλις, οὐ μὴν οὐδ' ὑπαρχόντων τούτων ἁπάντων ἤδη πόλις, ἀλλ' ἡ τοῦ
εὖ ζῆν κοινωνία καὶ ταῖς οἰκίαις καὶ τοῖς γένεσι,
35 ζωῆς τελείας χάριν καὶ αὐτάρκους. οὐκ ἔσται
μέντοι τοῦτο μὴ τὸν αὐτὸν καὶ ἕνα κατοικούντων
τόπον καὶ χρωμένων ἐπιγαμίαις· διὸ κηδεῖαί τ'
ἐγένοντο κατὰ τὰς πόλεις καὶ φρατρίαι καὶ θυσίαι
καὶ διαγωγαὶ τοῦ συζῆν. τὸ δὲ τοιοῦτον φιλίας

people lived in separate places yet not so far apart as not to have intercourse, but had laws to prevent their wronging one another in their interchange of products—for instance, if one man were a carpenter, another a farmer, another a shoemaker and another something else of the kind,—and the whole population numbered ten thousand, but nevertheless they had no mutual dealings in anything else except such things as exchange of commodities and military alliance, even then this would still not be a state. What then exactly is the reason for this ? for clearly it is not because their intercourse is from a distance ; since even if they came together for intercourse of this sort (each nevertheless using his individual house as a city) and for one another's military aid against wrongful aggressors only, as under a defensive alliance, not even then would they seem to those who consider the matter carefully to constitute a state, if they associated on the same footing when they came together as they did when they were apart. It is manifest therefore that a state is not merely the sharing of a common locality for the purpose of preventing mutual injury and exchanging goods. These are necessary pre-conditions of a state's existence, yet nevertheless, even if all these conditions are present, that does not therefore make a state, but a state is a partnership of families and of clans in living well, and its object is a full and independent life. At the same time this will not be realized unless the partners do inhabit one and the same locality and practise intermarriage ; this indeed is the reason why family relationships have arisen throughout the states, and brotherhoods and clubs for sacrificial rites and social recreations. But such organization is pro-

1280 b

ἔργον, ἡ γὰρ τοῦ συζῆν προαίρεσις φιλία· τέλος
40 μὲν οὖν πόλεως τὸ εὖ ζῆν, ταῦτα δὲ τοῦ τέλους
1281 a χάριν. πόλις δὲ ἡ γενῶν καὶ κωμῶν κοινωνία
ζωῆς τελείας καὶ αὐτάρκους,[1] τοῦτο δ᾽ ἐστίν, ὡς
φαμέν, τὸ ζῆν εὐδαιμόνως καὶ καλῶς· τῶν καλῶν
ἄρα πράξεων[2] χάριν θετέον εἶναι τὴν πολιτικὴν
κοινωνίαν, ἀλλ᾽ οὐ τοῦ συζῆν· διόπερ ὅσοι συμ-
5 βάλλονται πλεῖστον εἰς τὴν τοιαύτην κοινωνίαν,
τούτοις τῆς πόλεως μέτεστι πλεῖον ἢ τοῖς κατὰ
μὲν ἐλευθερίαν καὶ γένος ἴσοις ἢ μείζοσι κατὰ δὲ
τὴν πολιτικὴν ἀρετὴν ἀνίσοις, ἢ τοῖς κατὰ πλοῦτον
ὑπερέχουσι κατ᾽ ἀρετὴν δ᾽ ὑπερεχομένοις.

Ὅτι μὲν οὖν πάντες οἱ περὶ τῶν πολιτειῶν
10 ἀμφισβητοῦντες μέρος τι τοῦ δικαίου λέγουσι,
φανερὸν ἐκ τῶν εἰρημένων.

VI. Ἔχει δ᾽ ἀπορίαν τί δεῖ τὸ κύριον εἶναι τῆς
πόλεως. ἢ γάρ τοι τὸ πλῆθος, ἢ τοὺς πλουσίους,
ἢ τοὺς ἐπιεικεῖς, ἢ τὸν βέλτιστον ἕνα πάντων, ἢ
τύραννον. ἀλλὰ ταῦτα πάντα ἔχειν φαίνεται δυσκο-
15 λίαν. τί γάρ; ἂν οἱ πένητες διὰ τὸ πλείους εἶναι
διανέμωνται τὰ τῶν πλουσίων, τοῦτ᾽ οὐκ ἄδικόν
ἐστιν; ἔδοξε γὰρ νὴ Δία τῷ κυρίῳ δικαίως. τὴν
οὖν ἀδικίαν τί χρὴ λέγειν τὴν ἐσχάτην; πάλιν τε,
πάντων ληφθέντων, οἱ πλείους τὰ τῶν ἐλαττόνων
ἂν διανέμωνται, φανερὸν ὅτι φθείρουσι τὴν πόλιν·
20 ἀλλὰ μὴν οὐχ ἥ γ᾽ ἀρετὴ φθείρει τὸ ἔχον αὐτήν,
οὐδὲ τὸ δίκαιον πόλεως φθαρτικόν, ὥστε δῆλον
ὅτι καὶ τὸν νόμον τοῦτον οὐχ οἷόν τ᾽ εἶναι δίκαιον.

[1] αὐτάρκους ⟨χάριν⟩ Scaliger.
[2] πράξεων om. ΓΜΡ[1].

duced by the feeling of friendship, for friendship is the motive of social life ; therefore, while the object of a state is the good life, these things are means to that end. And a state is the partnership of clans and villages in a full and independent life, which in our view constitutes a happy and noble life ; the political fellowship must therefore be deemed to exist for the sake of noble actions, not merely for living in common. Hence those who contribute most to such fellowship have a larger part in the state than those who are their equals or superiors in freedom and birth but not their equals in civic virtue, or than those who surpass them in wealth but are surpassed by them in virtue. *Therefore the absolute right to power is ability to contribute to the good life.*

It is therefore clear from what has been said that all those who dispute about the forms of constitution assert a part of the just principle.

VI. But it is a matter of question what ought to be the sovereign power in the state. Clearly it must be either the multitude, or the rich, or the good, or the one man who is best of all, or a tyrant. But all of these arrangements appear to involve disagreeable consequences. For instance, if the poor take advantage of their greater numbers to divide up the property of the rich, is not this unjust ? No, it may be said, for it was a resolution made by the supreme authority in just form. Then what must be pronounced to be the extreme of injustice ? And again, when everybody is taken into account, suppose the majority share out among themselves the property of the minority, it is manifest that they are destroying the state ; but assuredly virtue does not destroy its possessor, and justice is not destructive of the state, so that it is clear that this principle also cannot *In practice, where is sovereignty to lie? All answers questioned.*

219

1281 a

ἔτι καὶ τὰς πράξεις ὅσας ὁ τύραννος ἔπραξεν
ἀναγκαῖον εἶναι πάσας δικαίας, βιάζεται γὰρ ὢν
κρείττων, ὥσπερ καὶ τὸ πλῆθος τοὺς πλουσίους.

25 ἀλλ᾽ ἆρα τοὺς ἐλάττους δίκαιον ἄρχειν καὶ τοὺς
πλουσίους; ἂν οὖν κἀκεῖνοι ταὐτὰ ποιῶσι καὶ
διαρπάζωσι καὶ ἀφαιρῶνται τὰ κτήματα[1] τοῦ
πλήθους, τοῦτ᾽ ἐστὶ δίκαιον; καὶ θάτερον ἄρα.
ταῦτα μὲν τοίνυν ὅτι πάντα φαῦλα καὶ οὐ δίκαια
φανερόν. ἀλλὰ τοὺς ἐπιεικεῖς ἄρχειν δεῖ καὶ κυρίους

30 εἶναι πάντων; οὐκοῦν ἀνάγκη τοὺς ἄλλους ἀτίμους εἶναι πάντας, μὴ τιμωμένους ταῖς πολιτικαῖς
ἀρχαῖς· τιμὰς γὰρ λέγομεν εἶναι τὰς ἀρχάς, ἀρχόντων δ᾽ αἰεὶ τῶν αὐτῶν ἀναγκαῖον εἶναι τοὺς ἄλλους
ἀτίμους. ἀλλ᾽ ἕνα τὸν σπουδαιότατον ἄρχειν βέλτιον; ἀλλ᾽ ἔτι τοῦτο ὀλιγαρχικώτερον, οἱ γὰρ

35 ἄτιμοι πλείους. ἀλλ᾽ ἴσως φαίη τις ἂν τὸ κύριον
ὅλως ἄνθρωπον εἶναι ἀλλὰ μὴ νόμον φαῦλον, ἔχοντά
γε τὰ συμβαίνοντα πάθη περὶ τὴν ψυχήν. ἂν οὖν
ᾖ νόμος μὲν ὀλιγαρχικὸς δὲ ἢ δημοκρατικός, τι
διοίσει περὶ τῶν ἠπορημένων; συμβήσεται γὰρ
ὁμοίως τὰ λεχθέντα πρότερον.

Περὶ μὲν οὖν τῶν ἄλλων ἔστω τις ἕτερος λόγος·

40 ὅτι δὲ δεῖ κύριον εἶναι μᾶλλον τὸ πλῆθος ἢ τοὺς
ἀρίστους μὲν ὀλίγους δέ, δόξειεν ἂν λύεσθαι[2] καὶ
τιν᾽ ἔχειν ἀπορίαν,[3] τάχα δὲ κἂν ἀλήθειαν. τοὺς

1281 b γὰρ πολλούς, ὧν ἕκαστός ἐστιν οὐ σπουδαῖος
ἀνήρ, ὅμως ἐνδέχεται συνελθόντας εἶναι βελτίους

---

[1] Richards : τὰ κτήματα ἀφαιρῶνται codd.
[2] ἂν εὖ λέγεσθαι Richards.   [3] ἀπολογίαν Wilamowitz.

---

[a] Teehnical term for disfranchisement and loss of civic rights.

be just. Also it follows from it that all the actions done by a tyrant are just, for his use of force is based upon superior strength, as is the compulsion exerted by the multitude against the rich. But is it just that the minority and the rich should rule? Suppose therefore they also act in the same way and plunder and take away the property of the multitude, is this just? If it is, so also is the plunder of the rich by the multitude. It is clear therefore that all these things are bad and not just. But ought the good to rule, and be in control of all classes? If so, then it follows that all the other classes will be dishonoured,[a] if they are not honoured by holding the offices of government; for we speak of offices as honours, and if the same persons are always in office the rest must necessarily be excluded from honour. But is it better for the most virtuous individual to be the ruler? But that is still more oligarchical, for the people excluded from honour will be more numerous. But perhaps some one would say that in any case it is a bad thing for a human being, having in his soul the passions that are the attributes of humanity, to be sovereign, and not the law. Suppose therefore that law is sovereign, but law of an oligarchic or democratic nature, what difference will it make as regards the difficulties that have been raised? for the results described before will come about just the same.

Most of these points therefore must be discussed on another occasion; but the view that it is more proper for the multitude to be sovereign than the few of greatest virtue might be thought to be explicable, and to raise some difficulty but probably to be true. For it is possible that the many, though not individually good men, yet when they come

Qualified approval of limited democracy.

ἐκείνων οὐχ ὡς ἕκαστον ἀλλ' ὡς σύμπαντας, οἷον
τὰ συμφορητὰ δεῖπνα τῶν ἐκ μιᾶς δαπάνης χορη-
γηθέντων· πολλῶν γὰρ ὄντων ἕκαστον μόριον ἔχειν
5 ἀρετῆς καὶ φρονήσεως, καὶ γίνεσθαι συνελθόντας
ὥσπερ ἕνα[1] ἄνθρωπον τὸ πλῆθος πολύποδα καὶ
πολύχειρα καὶ πολλὰς ἔχοντ' αἰσθήσεις, οὕτω καὶ
περὶ τὰ ἤθη καὶ τὴν διάνοιαν. διὸ καὶ κρίνουσιν
ἄμεινον οἱ πολλοὶ καὶ τὰ τῆς μουσικῆς ἔργα καὶ
τὰ τῶν ποιητῶν· ἄλλοι γὰρ ἄλλο τι μόριον, πάντα
10 δὲ πάντες. ἀλλὰ τούτῳ διαφέρουσιν οἱ σπουδαῖοι
τῶν ἀνδρῶν ἑκάστου[2] τῶν πολλῶν, ὥσπερ καὶ τῶν
μὴ καλῶν τοὺς καλούς φασι καὶ τὰ γεγραμμένα
διὰ τέχνης τῶν ἀληθινῶν, τῷ συνῆχθαι τὰ διεσπαρ-
μένα χωρὶς εἰς ἕν, ἐπεὶ κεχωρισμένων γε κάλλιον
15 ἔχειν τοῦ γεγραμμένου τουδὶ μὲν τὸν ὀφθαλμὸν
ἑτέρου δέ τινος ἕτερον μόριον. εἰ μὲν οὖν περὶ
πάντα δῆμον καὶ περὶ πᾶν πλῆθος ἐνδέχεται ταύτην
εἶναι τὴν διαφορὰν τῶν πολλῶν πρὸς τοὺς ὀλίγους
σπουδαίους, ἄδηλον, ἴσως δὲ νὴ Δία δῆλον ὅτι
περὶ ἐνίων ἀδύνατον—ὁ γὰρ αὐτὸς κἂν ἐπὶ τῶν
20 θηρίων ἁρμόσειε λόγος, καίτοι τί διαφέρουσιν ἔνιοι
τῶν θηρίων ὡς ἔπος εἰπεῖν;—ἀλλὰ περί τι πλῆθος
οὐδὲν εἶναι κωλύει τὸ λεχθὲν ἀληθές. διὸ καὶ τὴν
πρότερον εἰρημένην ἀπορίαν λύσειεν ἄν τις διὰ

---

[1] καὶ ὥσπερ γίνεσθαι συνελθεῖν οἷον ἕνα Richards.
[2] ἕκαστοι Thurot.

together may be better, not individually but collectively, than those who are so, just as public dinners to which many contribute are better than those supplied at one man's cost; for where there are many, each individual, it may be argued, has some portion of virtue and wisdom, and when they have come together, just as the multitude becomes a single man with many feet and many hands and many senses, so also it becomes one personality as regards the moral and intellectual faculties. This is why the general public is a better judge of the works of music and those of the poets, because different men can judge a different part of the performance, and all of them all of it. But the superiority of good men over the mass of men individually, like that of handsome men, so it is said, over plain men and of the works of the painter's art over the real objects, really consists in this, that a number of scattered good points have been collected together into one example; since if the features be taken separately, the eye of one real person is more beautiful than that of the man in the picture, and some other feature of somebody else. It is not indeed clear whether this collective superiority of the many compared with the few good men can possibly exist in regard to every democracy and every multitude, and perhaps it may be urged that it is manifestly impossible in the case of some—for the same argument would also apply to animals, yet what difference is there, practically, between some multitudes and animals?—but nothing prevents what has been said from being true about some particular multitude. One might therefore employ these considerations to solve not only the previously stated

τούτων καὶ τὴν ἐχομένην αὐτῆς, τίνων δεῖ κυρίους
εἶναι τοὺς ἐλευθέρους καὶ τὸ πλῆθος τῶν πολιτῶν
25 (τοιοῦτοι δ᾽ εἰσὶν ὅσοι μήτε πλούσιοι μήτε ἀξίωμα
ἔχουσιν ἀρετῆς μηδέν). τὸ μὲν γὰρ μετέχειν
αὐτοὺς τῶν ἀρχῶν τῶν μεγίστων οὐκ ἀσφαλές
(διά τε γὰρ ἀδικίαν καὶ δι᾽ ἀφροσύνην τὰ μὲν
ἀδικεῖν ἀνάγκη[1] τὰ δ᾽ ἁμαρτάνειν αὐτούς), τὸ δὲ
μὴ μεταδιδόναι μηδὲ μετέχειν φοβερόν· ὅταν γὰρ
30 ἄτιμοι πολλοὶ καὶ πένητες ὑπάρχωσι, πολεμίων
ἀναγκαῖον εἶναι πλήρη τὴν πόλιν ταύτην. λείπεται
δὴ τοῦ βουλεύεσθαι καὶ κρίνειν μετέχειν αὐτούς.
διόπερ καὶ Σόλων καὶ τῶν ἄλλων τινὲς νομοθετῶν
τάττουσιν ἐπί τε[2] τὰς ἀρχαιρεσίας καὶ τὰς εὐθύνας
τῶν ἀρχόντων, ἄρχειν δὲ κατὰ μόνας οὐκ ἐῶσιν.
35 πάντες μὲν γὰρ ἔχουσι συνελθόντες ἱκανὴν αἴσθησιν,
καὶ μιγνύμενοι τοῖς βελτίοσι τὰς πόλεις ὠφελοῦσιν,
καθάπερ ἡ μὴ καθαρὰ τροφὴ μετὰ τῆς καθαρᾶς
τὴν πᾶσαν ποιεῖ χρησιμωτέραν τῆς ὀλίγης· χωρὶς
δ᾽ ἕκαστος ἀτελὴς περὶ τὸ κρίνειν ἐστίν. ἔχει
40 δ᾽ ἡ τάξις αὕτη τῆς πολιτείας ἀπορίαν πρώτην
μὲν ὅτι δόξειεν ἂν τοῦ αὐτοῦ εἶναι τὸ κρῖναι τίς
ὀρθῶς ἰάτρευκεν οὗπερ καὶ τὸ ἰατρεῦσαι καὶ
ποιῆσαι ὑγιᾶ τὸν κάμνοντα τῆς νόσου τῆς παρούσης,

οὗτος δ᾽ ἐστὶν ἰατρός· ὁμοίως δὲ τοῦτο καὶ περὶ
τὰς ἄλλας ἐμπειρίας καὶ τέχνας. ὥσπερ οὖν ἰατρὸν
δεῖ διδόναι τὰς εὐθύνας ἐν ἰατροῖς, οὕτω καὶ τοὺς

---

[1] ἀνάγκη Rassow : ἂν codd.
[2] ἐπί τε ⟨ταῦτα αὐτοὺς καὶ ἐπὶ⟩ Wilamowitz.

---

[a] Probably words meaning ' these functions and to ' have
fallen out.
[b] i.e., especially, bran mixed with pure flour.

difficulty but also the related question, over what matters is the authority of the freemen, the mass of the citizens, to extend (using that expression to denote those who are not rich nor possessed of any distinguishing excellence at all)? For it is not safe for them to participate in the highest offices (for injustice and folly would inevitably cause them to act unjustly in some things and to make mistakes in others), but yet not to admit them and for them not to participate is an alarming situation, for when there are a number of persons without political honours and in poverty, the city then is bound to be full of enemies. It remains therefore for them to share the deliberative and judicial functions. For this reason Solon and certain other lawgivers appoint the common citizens to [a] the election of the magistrates and the function of calling them to audit, although they do not allow them to hold office singly. For all when assembled together have sufficient discernment, and by mingling with the better class are of benefit to the state, just as impure food mixed with what is pure [b] makes the whole more nourishing than the small amount of pure food alone ; but separately the individual is immature in judgement. This arrangement of the constitution is however open to question in the first place on the ground that it might be held that the best man to judge which physician has given the right treatment is the man that is himself capable of treating and curing the patient of his present disease, and this is the man who is himself a physician; and that this is the case similarly with regard to the other arts and crafts. Hence just as a court of physicians must judge the work of a physician, so also all other practitioners ought to be called

The people have collective wisdom and wealth;

ἄλλους ἐν τοῖς ὁμοίοις. ἰατρὸς δ᾽ ὅ τε δημιουργὸ
καὶ ὁ ἀρχιτεκτονικὸς καὶ τρίτος ὁ πεπαιδευμένο
5 περὶ τὴν τέχνην (εἰσὶ γάρ τινες τοιοῦτοι καὶ περ
πάσας ὡς εἰπεῖν τὰς τέχνας, ἀποδίδομεν δὲ τ
κρίνειν οὐδὲν ἧττον τοῖς πεπαιδευμένοις ἢ τοῖ
εἰδόσιν). ἔπειτα καὶ περὶ τὴν αἵρεσιν τὸν αὐτὸν ἂ
δόξειεν ἔχειν τρόπον· καὶ γὰρ τὸ ἑλέσθαι ὀρθῶ
10 τῶν εἰδότων ἔργον ἐστίν, οἷον γεωμέτρην τε τῶ
γεωμετρικῶν καὶ κυβερνήτην τῶν κυβερνητικῶι
εἰ γὰρ καὶ περὶ ἐνίων ἔργων καὶ τεχνῶν μετέχουσ
καὶ τῶν ἰδιωτῶν τινές, ἀλλ᾽ οὔ τι τῶν εἰδότων γ
μᾶλλον. ὥστε κατὰ μὲν τοῦτον τὸν λόγον οὐ
ἂν εἴη τὸ πλῆθος ποιητέον κύριον οὔτε τῶν ἀρχ
αἱρεσιῶν οὔτε τῶν εὐθυνῶν. ἀλλ᾽ ἴσως οὐ πάντ
15 ταῦτα λέγεται καλῶς διά τε τὸν πάλαι λόγον, ἂ
ἢ τὸ πλῆθος μὴ λίαν ἀνδραποδῶδες (ἔσται γὰ
ἕκαστος μὲν χείρων κριτὴς τῶν εἰδότων, ἅπαντε
δὲ συνελθόντες ἢ βελτίους ἢ οὐ χείρους), καὶ ὅτ
περὶ ἐνίων οὔτε μόνον ὁ ποιήσας οὔτ᾽ ἄριστ᾽ ἂ
κρίνειεν, ὅσων τἄργα γιγνώσκουσι καὶ οἱ μ
20 ἔχοντες τὴν τέχνην, οἷον οἰκίαν οὐ μόνον ἐστ
γνῶναι τοῦ ποιήσαντος, ἀλλὰ καὶ βέλτιον ὁ χρώ
μενος αὐτῇ κρινεῖ (χρῆται δ᾽ ὁ οἰκονόμος), κα
πηδάλιον κυβερνήτης τέκτονος, καὶ θοίνην ὁ δαιτυ
μὼν ἀλλ᾽ οὐχ ὁ μάγειρος.

Ταύτην μὲν οὖν τὴν ἀπορίαν τάχα δόξειέ τις ἂ

---

[a] See § 4.

to account before their fellows. But 'physician' means both the ordinary practitioner, and the master of the craft, and thirdly, the man who has studied medicine as part of his general education (for in almost all the arts there are some such students, and we assign the right of judgement just as much to cultivated amateurs as to experts). Further the same might be thought to hold good also of the election of officials, for to elect rightly is a task for experts—for example, it is for experts in the science of mensuration to elect a land-surveyor and for experts in navigation to choose a pilot; for even though in some occupations and arts some laymen also have a voice in appointments, yet they certainly do not have more voice than the experts. Hence according to this argument the masses should not be put in control over either the election of magistrates or their audit. But perhaps this statement is not entirely correct, both for the reason stated above,[a] in case the populace is not of too slavish a character (for although each individual separately will be a worse judge than the experts, the whole of them assembled together will be better or at least as good judges), and also because about some things the man who made them would not be the only nor the best judge, in the case of professionals whose products come within the knowledge of laymen also : to judge a house, for instance, does not belong only to the man who built it, but in fact the man who uses the house (that is, the householder) will be an even better judge of it, and a steersman judges a rudder better than a carpenter, and the diner judges a banquet better than the cook.

This difficulty then might perhaps be thought to be

227

1282 a

οὕτω λύειν ἱκανῶς. ἄλλη δ' ἐστὶν ἐχομένη ταύτης
25 δοκεῖ γὰρ ἄτοπον εἶναι τὸ μειζόνων εἶναι κυρίους
τοὺς φαύλους τῶν ἐπιεικῶν, αἱ δ' εὐθῦναι καὶ α
τῶν ἀρχῶν αἱρέσεις εἰσὶ μέγιστον, ἃς ἐν ἐνίαις
πολιτείαις, ὥσπερ εἴρηται, τοῖς δήμοις ἀποδιδόασιν
ἡ γὰρ ἐκκλησία κυρία πάντων τῶν τοιούτων ἐστίν
30 καίτοι τῆς μὲν ἐκκλησίας μετέχουσι καὶ βουλεύουσι
καὶ δικάζουσιν ἀπὸ μικρῶν τιμημάτων καὶ τῆς
τυχούσης ἡλικίας, ταμιεύουσι δὲ καὶ στρατηγοῦσι
καὶ τὰς μεγίστας ἀρχὰς ἄρχουσιν ἀπὸ μεγάλων·
ὁμοίως δή τις ἂν λύσειε καὶ ταύτην τὴν ἀπορίαν—
35 ἴσως γὰρ ἔχει καὶ ταῦτ' ὀρθῶς, οὐ γὰρ ὁ δικαστὴς
οὐδ' ὁ βουλευτὴς οὐδ' ὁ ἐκκλησιαστὴς ἄρχων ἐστίν
ἀλλὰ τὸ δικαστήριον καὶ ἡ βουλὴ καὶ ὁ δῆμος·
τῶν δὲ ῥηθέντων ἕκαστος μόριόν ἐστι τούτων
(λέγω δὲ μόριον[1] τὸν βουλευτὴν καὶ τὸν ἐκκλησια-
στὴν καὶ τὸν δικαστήν). ὥστε δικαίως κύριον μειζόνων τὸ πλῆθος, ἐκ γὰρ πολλῶν ὁ δῆμος καὶ ἡ
10 βουλὴ καὶ τὸ δικαστήριον, καὶ τὸ τίμημα δὲ
πλεῖον τὸ πάντων τούτων ἢ τὸ τῶν καθ' ἕνα καὶ
κατ' ὀλίγους μεγάλας ἀρχὰς ἀρχόντων.

1282 b   Ταῦτα μὲν οὖν διωρίσθω τοῦτον τὸν τρόπον· ἡ
δὲ πρώτη λεχθεῖσα ἀπορία ποιεῖ φανερὸν οὐδὲν
οὕτως ἕτερον ὡς ὅτι δεῖ τοὺς νόμους εἶναι κυρίους
κειμένους ὀρθῶς, τὸν ἄρχοντα δέ, ἄν τε εἷς ἄν τε
πλείους ὦσι, περὶ τούτων εἶναι κυρίους περὶ
5 ὅσων ἐξαδυνατοῦσιν οἱ νόμοι λέγειν ἀκριβῶς διὰ
τὸ μὴ ῥᾴδιον εἶναι καθόλου δηλῶσαι περὶ πάντων

---

[1] [μόριον] ? Richards.

ᵃ Viz. that under any plan some hardships will result, § 1.

11 satisfactorily solved in this way. But there is another
one connected with it: it is thought to be absurd
that the base should be in control over more important
matters than the respectable; but the audits and
elections of magistrates are a very important matter,
yet in some constitutions, as has been said, they are
assigned to the common people, for all such matters
are under the control of the assembly, yet persons
of a low property-assessment and of any age take
part in the assembly and the council and sit on juries,
whereas treasury officials, generals and the holders
of the highest magistracies are drawn from among

2 persons of large property. Now this difficulty also
may be solved in a similar way; for perhaps these
regulations also are sound, since it is not the individual
juryman or councillor or member of the assembly in
whom authority rests, but the court, the council and
the people, while each of the individuals named (I
mean the councillor, the members of assembly and
the juryman) is a part of those bodies. Hence justly
the multitude is sovereign in greater matters, for the
popular assembly, the council and the jury-court are
formed of a number of people, and also the assessed
property of all these members collectively is more than
that of the magistrates holding great offices individually or in small groups.

Let these points therefore be decided in this
manner. But the difficulty first mentioned[a] proves
nothing else so clearly as that it is proper for the laws
when rightly laid down to be sovereign, while the
ruler or rulers in office should have supreme powers
over matters as to which the laws are quite unable to
pronounce with precision because of the difficulty of
making a general rule to cover all cases. We have

and the people should elect and control the magistrates;

but the people must be guided by good laws.

ὁποίους μέντοι τινὰς εἶναι δεῖ τοὺς ὀρθῶς κειμένους
νόμους, οὐδέν πω δῆλον, ἀλλ' ἔτι μένει τὸ πάλαι
διαπορηθέν· ἅμα[1] γὰρ καὶ ὁμοίως ταῖς πολιτείαις ἀνάγκη καὶ τοὺς νόμους φαύλους ἢ σπου-
10 δαίους εἶναι καὶ δικαίους ἢ ἀδίκους (πλὴν τοῦτό
γε φανερόν, ὅτι δεῖ πρὸς τὴν πολιτείαν κεῖσθαι
τοὺς νόμους)· ἀλλὰ μὴν εἰ τοῦτο, δῆλον ὅτι τοὺς
μὲν κατὰ τὰς ὀρθὰς πολιτείας ἀναγκαῖον εἶναι
δικαίους τοὺς δὲ κατὰ τὰς παρεκβεβηκυίας οὐ
δικαίους.

VII. Ἐπεὶ δ' ἐν πάσαις μὲν ταῖς ἐπιστήμαις
15 καὶ τέχναις ἀγαθὸν τὸ τέλος, μέγιστον δὲ καὶ
μάλιστα ἐν τῇ κυριωτάτῃ πασῶν, αὕτη δ' ἐστὶν ἡ
πολιτικὴ δύναμις, ἔστι δὲ τὸ[2] πολιτικὸν ἀγαθὸν
τὸ δίκαιον, τοῦτο δ' ἐστὶ τὸ κοινῇ συμφέρον, δοκεῖ
δὴ[3] πᾶσιν ἴσον τι τὸ δίκαιον εἶναι, καὶ μέχρι γέ
20 τινος ὁμολογοῦσι τοῖς κατὰ φιλοσοφίαν λόγοις ἐν
οἷς διώρισται περὶ τῶν ἠθικῶν· τὶ γὰρ καὶ τισὶ τὸ
δίκαιον, καὶ δεῖν τοῖς ἴσοις ἴσον εἶναί φασιν.
ποίων δ' ἰσότης ἐστὶ καὶ ποίων ἀνισότης δεῖ μὴ
λανθάνειν· ἔχει γὰρ τοῦτ' ἀπορίαν καὶ φιλοσοφίαν
πολιτικήν. ἴσως γὰρ ἂν φαίη τις κατὰ παντὸς
ὑπεροχὴν ἀγαθοῦ δεῖν ἀνίσως νενεμῆσθαι τὰς ἀρ-
25 χάς, εἰ[4] πάντα τὰ λοιπὰ μηδὲν διαφέροιεν ἀλλ'

---

[1] ἅμα Bernays: ἀλλὰ codd., ἀλλὰ γὰρ . . . ἀδίκους post 12
νόμους Congreve.   [2] δὲ τὸ Susemihl: δὲ codd.
[3] δὴ Immisch: δὲ codd.   [4] εἰ ⟨καὶ⟩ ? ed.

---

[a] See 1281 a 36.
[b] Probably this clause should stand after the next, 'though
—constitution' (which will be a parenthesis), and should run
'but ⟨the difficulty is there⟩ for necessarily—states.'
[c] The usual rendering is 'perverted,' but the Greek term
is more neutral.

not however yet ascertained at all what particular character a code of laws correctly laid down ought to possess, but the difficulty raised at the start[a] still remains;[b] for necessarily the laws are good or bad, just or unjust, simultaneously with and similarly to the constitutions of states (though of course it is obvious that the laws are bound to be adapted to the constitution); yet if so, it is clear that the laws in conformity with the correct constitutions must necessarily be just and those in conformity with the divergent[c] forms of constitution unjust.

1   VII. [d]And inasmuch as in all the sciences and arts the End is a good, and the greatest good and good in the highest degree in the most authoritative of all, which is the political faculty, and the good in the political field, that is, the general advantage, is justice, it is therefore thought by all men that justice is some sort of equality, and up to a certain point at all events they agree with the philosophical discourses in which conclusions have been reached about questions of ethics[e]; for justice is a quality of a thing in relation to persons,[f] and they hold that for persons that are equal the thing must be equal. But equality in what characteristics does this mean, and inequality in what? This must be made clear, since this too raises a difficulty, and calls for political

2 philosophy. For perhaps someone might say that the offices of state ought to be distributed unequally according to superiority in every good quality, even if the candidates in all other respects did not differ

Claims to power are birth, wealth, freedom, and above all virtue;

----

[a] What follows is a summary of *Nicomachean Ethics*, I. cc. i., ii.   [e] See also *N.E.* V. c. iii.
[f] Literally, 'the just is (a just) something and (something just) for somebody.'

1232 b

ὅμοιοι τυγχάνοιεν ὄντες· τοῖς γὰρ διαφέρουσιν[1]
ἕτερον εἶναι τὸ δίκαιον καὶ τὸ κατ' ἀξίαν. ἀλλὰ
μὴν εἰ τοῦτ' ἀληθές, ἔσται καὶ κατὰ χρῶμα καὶ
κατὰ μέγεθος καὶ καθ' ὁτιοῦν τῶν ἀγαθῶν πλεον-
30 εξία τις τῶν πολιτικῶν δικαίων τοῖς ὑπερέχουσιν.
ἢ τοῦτο ἐπιπόλαιον τὸ ψεῦδος; φανερὸν δ' ἐπὶ
τῶν ἄλλων ἐπιστημῶν καὶ δυνάμεων· τῶν γὰρ
ὁμοίων αὐλητῶν τὴν τέχνην οὐ δοτέον πλεονεξίαν
τῶν αὐλῶν τοῖς εὐγενεστέροις· οὐδὲν γὰρ αὐλήσουσι
βέλτιον, δεῖ δὲ τῷ κατὰ τὸ ἔργον ὑπερέχοντι διδόναι
35 καὶ τῶν ὀργάνων τὴν ὑπεροχήν. εἰ δὲ μήπω δῆλον
τὸ λεγόμενον, ἔτι μᾶλλον αὐτὸ προαγαγοῦσιν ἔσται[3]
φανερόν. εἰ γὰρ εἴη τις ὑπερέχων μὲν κατὰ τὴν
αὐλητικήν πολὺ δ' ἐλλείπων κατ' εὐγένειαν ἢ κάλλος, εἰ καὶ μεῖζον ἕκαστον ἐκείνων ἀγαθόν ἐστι
τῆς αὐλητικῆς (λέγω δὲ τήν τ' εὐγένειαν καὶ τὸ
40 κάλλος) καὶ κατὰ τὴν ἀναλογίαν ὑπερέχουσι πλέον
τῆς αὐλητικῆς ἢ ἐκεῖνος κατὰ τὴν αὐλητικήν, ὅμως
1283 a τούτῳ δοτέον τοὺς διαφέροντας τῶν αὐλῶν· δεῖ
γὰρ εἰς τὸ ἔργον συμβάλλεσθαι τὴν ὑπεροχὴν καὶ
τοῦ πλούτου καὶ τῆς εὐγενείας, συμβάλλονται δ'
οὐδέν. ἔτι κατά γε τοῦτον τὸν λόγον πᾶν ἀγαθὸν[4]
πρὸς πᾶν ἂν εἴη συμβλητόν. εἰ γὰρ μᾶλλον[2] τὸ τὶ
5 μέγεθος, καὶ ὅλως ἂν τὸ μέγεθος ἐνάμιλλον εἴη
καὶ πρὸς πλοῦτον καὶ πρὸς ἐλευθερίαν· ὥστ' εἰ
πλεῖον ὁδὶ διαφέρει κατὰ μέγεθος ἢ ὁδὶ κατ'
ἀρετήν, καὶ πλεῖον ὑπερέχει[3] ὅλως ἀρετῆς μέγεθος,

---

[1] ⟨ὧδε⟩ διαφέρουσιν ? ed.
[2] ἐνάμιλλον Ingram: καλὸν Richards.
[3] ὑπερέχειν ⟨ἐνδέχεται⟩ ? Susemihl (⟨εἰ⟩ καὶ πλεῖον ὑπερέχει
ὅλως ἀρετὴ μεγέθους Bernays).

232

at all but were exactly alike, because men that are different[a] have different rights and merits. Yet if this is true, those who are superior in complexion or stature or any good quality will have an advantage in respect of political rights. But surely the error here is obvious, and it comes out clearly if we consider the other sciences and faculties. Among flute-players equally good at their art it is not proper to give an advantage in respect of the flutes to those of better birth, for they will not play any better, but it is the superior performers who ought to be given the 3 superior instruments. And if our meaning is not yet plain, it will become still clearer when we have carried the matter further. Suppose someone is superior in playing the flute but much inferior in birth or in good looks, then, even granting that each of these things— birth and beauty—is a greater good than ability to play the flute, and even though they surpass flute-playing proportionately more than the best flute-player surpasses the others in flute-playing, even so the best flute-player ought to be given the outstandingly good flutes; for otherwise superiority both in wealth and in birth ought to contribute to the excellence of the performance, but they do not do 4 so at all. Moreover on this theory every good thing would be commensurable with every other. For if to be of some particular height gave more claim, then height in general would be in competition with wealth and with free birth; therefore if A excels in height more than B does in virtue, and speaking generally size gives more superiority than virtue,[b]

---

[a] *i.e.* different in some good quality.
[b] Perhaps we should rewrite the Greek to give ' even though speaking generally virtue gives more superiority than size.'

1283 a

εἴη ἂν συμβλητὰ πάντα· τοσόνδε γὰρ [μέγεθος]¹
εἰ κρεῖττον τοσοῦδε,² τοσόνδε δῆλον ὡς ἴσον.
10 ἐπεὶ δὲ τοῦτ' ἀδύνατον, δῆλον ὡς καὶ ἐπὶ τῶν 5
πολιτικῶν εὐλόγως οὐ κατὰ πᾶσαν ἀνισότητ' ἀμφισβητοῦσι τῶν ἀρχῶν—εἰ γὰρ οἱ μὲν βραδεῖς οἱ
δὲ ταχεῖς, οὐδὲν διὰ τοῦτο δεῖ τοὺς μὲν πλεῖον
τοὺς δ' ἔλαττον ἔχειν, ἀλλ' ἐν τοῖς γυμνικοῖς ἀγῶσιν
ἡ τούτων διαφορὰ λαμβάνει τὴν τιμήν· ἀλλ' ἐξ
15 ὧν πόλις συνέστηκεν, ἐν τούτοις ἀναγκαῖον ποιεῖσθαι τὴν ἀμφισβήτησιν. διόπερ εὐλόγως ἀντιποιοῦνται τῆς τιμῆς οἱ εὐγενεῖς καὶ ἐλεύθεροι καὶ
πλούσιοι· δεῖ γὰρ ἐλευθέρους τ' εἶναι καὶ τίμημα
φέροντας, οὐ γὰρ ἂν εἴη πόλις ἐξ ἀπόρων πάντων,
ὥσπερ οὐδ' ἐκ δούλων. ἀλλὰ μὴν εἰ δεῖ τούτων, 6
20 δῆλον ὅτι καὶ δικαιοσύνης καὶ τῆς πολιτικῆς³
ἀρετῆς, οὐδὲ γὰρ ἄνευ τούτων οἰκεῖσθαι πόλιν
δυνατόν· πλὴν ἄνευ μὲν τῶν προτέρων ἀδύνατον
εἶναι πόλιν, ἄνευ δὲ τούτων οἰκεῖσθαι καλῶς.

Πρὸς μὲν οὖν τὸ πόλιν εἶναι δόξειεν ἂν ἢ πάντα
ἢ ἔνιά γε τούτων ὀρθῶς ἀμφισβητεῖν, πρὸς μέντοι
25 ζωὴν ἀγαθὴν ἡ παιδεία καὶ ἡ ἀρετὴ μάλιστα
δικαίως ἂν ἀμφισβητοίησαν, καθάπερ εἴρηται καὶ
πρότερον. ἐπεὶ δ' οὔτε πάντων ἴσον ἔχειν⁴ δεῖ
τοὺς ἴσους ἕν τι μόνον ὄντας οὔτε ἄνισον τοὺς
ἀνίσους καθ' ἕν, ἀνάγκη πάσας εἶναι τὰς τοιαύτας
πολιτείας παρεκβάσεις. εἴρηται μὲν οὖν καὶ πρό-
30 τερον ὅτι διαμφισβητοῦσι τρόπον τινὰ δικαίως

¹ [μέγεθος] Susemihl: ἀγαθὸν ? Newman.
² τοσοῦδε ⟨πλούτου⟩ Richards.
³ πολεμικῆς codd. plerique.
⁴ ⟨μετ⟩έχειν Wallies.

ᵃ Doubtless the author meant the other way round, 'for
the slow having less and the fast more political power.'

234

all things would be commensurable ; for if such-and-
such an amount of one thing is better than such-and-
such an amount of another, it is clear that such-and-
such an amount of the one is equal to that amount of
another. But since this is impossible, it is clear that
in politics with good reason men do not claim a right to
office on the ground of inequality of every kind—if one
set of men are slow runners and another fast, this is
no good ground for the one set having more and the
other less ^{a} political power, but the latter's superiority
receives its honour in athletic contests ; but the
claim to office must necessarily be based on superiority
in those things which go to the making of the state.
Hence it is reasonable for the well-born, free and
wealthy to lay claim to honour ; for there must be
free men and tax-payers, since a state consisting
entirely of poor men would not be a state, any more
than one consisting of slaves. But then, granting
there is need of these, it is clear that there is also
need of justice and civic virtue, for these are also
indispensable in the administration of a state ; except
that wealth and freedom are indispensable for a
state's existence, whereas justice and civic virtue are
indispensable for its good administration.

As a means therefore towards a state's existence all for
or at all events some of these factors would seem to education
make a good claim, although as means to a good life form the
education and virtue would make the most just claim, good life,
as has been said also before. On the other hand since c. v. § 15.
those who are equal in one thing only ought not to
have equality in all things nor those unequal as
regards one thing inequality in all, it follows that all
these forms of constitution must be deviations.
Now it has been said before that all make a claim c. v. §§ 8 ff.

1283 a

πάντες, ἁπλῶς δ' οὐ πάντες[1] δικαίως, οἱ πλούσιοι
μὲν ὅτι πλεῖον μέτεστι τῆς χώρας αὐτοῖς, ἡ δὲ
χώρα κοινόν, ἔτι[2] πρὸς τὰ συμβόλαια πιστοὶ μᾶλλον ὡς ἐπὶ τὸ πλέον, οἱ δ' ἐλεύθεροι καὶ εὐγενεῖς
35 ὡς ἐγγὺς ἀλλήλων (πολῖται γὰρ μᾶλλον οἱ γεν-
ναιότεροι τῶν ἀγεννῶν, ἡ δ' εὐγένεια παρ' ἑκάστοις οἴκοι τίμιος), ἔτι διότι βελτίους εἰκὸς τοὺς
ἐκ βελτιόνων, εὐγένεια γάρ ἐστιν ἀρετὴ γένους·
ὁμοίως δὲ[3] φήσομεν δικαίως καὶ τὴν ἀρετὴν ἀμφισβητεῖν, κοινωνικὴν γὰρ ἀρετὴν εἶναί φαμεν τὴν
40 δικαιοσύνην, ᾗ πάσας ἀναγκαῖον ἀκολουθεῖν τὰς
ἄλλας· ἀλλὰ μὴν καὶ οἱ πλείους πρὸς τοὺς ἐλάτ-
τους· καὶ γὰρ κρείττους καὶ πλουσιώτεροι καὶ
βελτίους εἰσὶν ὡς λαμβανομένων τῶν πλειόνων
1283 b πρὸς τοὺς ἐλάττους. ἆρ' οὖν εἰ πάντες εἶεν ἐν μιᾷ
πόλει, λέγω δ' οἷον οἵ τ' ἀγαθοὶ καὶ οἱ πλούσιοι
καὶ εὐγενεῖς, ἔτι δὲ πλῆθος ἄλλο τι πολιτικόν,
πότερον ἀμφισβήτησις ἔσται τίνας ἄρχειν δεῖ ἢ
οὐκ ἔσται; καθ' ἑκάστην μὲν οὖν πολιτείαν τῶν
5 εἰρημένων ἀναμφισβήτητος ἡ κρίσις τίνας ἄρχειν
δεῖ (τοῖς γὰρ κυρίοις διαφέρουσιν ἀλλήλων, οἷον ἡ
μὲν τῷ διὰ πλουσίων ἡ δὲ τῷ διὰ τῶν σπουδαίων
ἀνδρῶν εἶναι, καὶ τῶν ἄλλων ἑκάστη τὸν αὐτὸν
τρόπον)· ἀλλ' ὅμως σκοποῦμεν, ὅταν περὶ τὸν
αὐτὸν ταῦθ' ὑπάρχῃ χρόνον, πῶς διοριστέον.
10 Εἰ δὴ τὸν ἀριθμὸν εἶεν ὀλίγοι πάμπαν οἱ τὴν
ἀρετὴν ἔχοντες, τίνα δεῖ διελεῖν τὸν τρόπον; ἢ τὸ
ὀλίγοι πρὸς τὸ ἔργον δεῖ σκοπεῖν εἰ δυνατοὶ

---

[1] [πάντες] Richards.   [2] ἔτι ⟨ὡς⟩ ? ed.   [3] δὲ Γ : δὴ codd.

hat is in a manner just, though not all a claim that is absolutely just ; the rich claiming because they have a larger share of the land, and the land is common property, and also as being for the most part more faithful to their covenants ; the free and well-born as being closely connected together (for the better-born are citizens to a greater degree than those of low birth, and good birth is in every community held in honour at home), and also because it is probable that the children of better parents will be better, for good birth means goodness of breed ; and we shall admit that virtue also makes an equally just claim, for we hold that justice is social virtue, which necessarily brings all the other virtues in its train ; but moreover the majority have a just claim as compared with the minority, since they are stronger and richer and better if their superior numbers are taken in comparison with the others' inferior numbers. Therefore supposing all were in one city, I mean, that is, the good and the wealthy and noble and also an additional mass of citizens, will there be a dispute, or will there not, as to who ought to govern ? It is true that under each of the forms of constitution that have been mentioned the decision as to who ought to govern is undisputed (for the difference between them lies in their sovereign classes—one is distinguished by being governed by the rich men, one by being governed by the good men, and similarly each of the others) ; but nevertheless we are considering the question how we are to decide between these classes supposing that they all exist in the state at the same period.

If then the possessors of virtue should be quite few in number, how is the decision to be made ? ought we to consider their fewness in relation to the

[marginal notes:] but wealth, birth, numbers also have relative claims, and justify aristocracy and republican government

Difficulties : the end is the good of the community.

1283 b

διοικεῖν τὴν πόλιν ἢ τοσοῦτοι τὸ πλῆθος ὥστ᾽
εἶναι πόλιν ἐξ αὐτῶν; ἔστι δὲ ἀπορία τις πρὸς
ἅπαντας τοὺς διαμφισβητοῦντας περὶ τῶν πολι-
15 τικῶν τιμῶν. δόξαιεν γὰρ ἂν[1] οὐδὲν λέγειν
δίκαιον οἱ διὰ τὸν πλοῦτον ἀξιοῦντες ἄρχειν,
ὁμοίως δὲ καὶ οἱ κατὰ γένος· δῆλον γὰρ ὡς εἴ τις
πάλιν εἷς πλουσιώτερος ἁπάντων ἐστί, δηλόνοτι
κατὰ τὸ αὐτὸ δίκαιον τοῦτον ἄρχειν τὸν ἕνα ἁπάντων δεήσει, ὁμοίως δὲ καὶ τὸν εὐγενείᾳ διαφέροντα
20 τῶν ἀμφισβητούντων δι᾽ ἐλευθερίαν. ταὐτὸ δὲ
τοῦτ᾽ ἴσως συμβήσεται καὶ περὶ τὰς ἀριστοκρατίας ἐπὶ τῆς ἀρετῆς· εἰ γάρ τις εἷς ἀμείνων
ἀνὴρ εἴη τῶν ἄλλων τῶν ἐν τῷ πολιτεύματι
σπουδαίων ὄντων, τοῦτον εἶναι δεῖ κύριον κατὰ
ταὐτὸ δίκαιον. οὐκοῦν εἰ καὶ τὸ πλῆθος εἶναί γε[2]
25 δεῖ κύριον διότι κρείττους εἰσὶ τῶν ὀλίγων, κἂν
εἷς ἢ πλείους μὲν τοῦ ἑνὸς ἐλάττους δὲ τῶν πολλῶν
κρείττους ὦσι τῶν ἄλλων, τούτους ἂν δέοι κυρίους
εἶναι μᾶλλον ἢ τὸ πλῆθος. πάντα δὴ ταῦτ᾽ ἔοικε
φανερὸν ποιεῖν ὅτι τούτων τῶν ὅρων οὐδεὶς ὀρθός
ἐστι καθ᾽ ὃν[3] ἀξιοῦσιν αὐτοὶ μὲν ἄρχειν τοὺς δ᾽
30 ἄλλους ὑπὸ σφῶν ἄρχεσθαι πάντας. καὶ γὰρ δὴ
καὶ πρὸς τοὺς κατ᾽ ἀρετὴν ἀξιοῦντας κυρίους εἶναι
τοῦ πολιτεύματος, ὁμοίως δὲ καὶ τοὺς κατὰ πλοῦτον, ἔχοιεν ἂν λέγειν τὰ πλήθη λόγον τινὰ δίκαιον·
οὐδὲν γὰρ κωλύει ποτὲ τὸ πλῆθος εἶναι βέλτιον τῶν
ὀλίγων καὶ πλουσιώτερον, οὐχ ὡς καθ᾽ ἕκαστον
35 ἀλλ᾽ ὡς ἀθρόους.

Διὸ καὶ πρὸς τὴν ἀπορίαν ἣν ζητοῦσι καὶ προ-

---

[1] γὰρ ἂν Coraes : γὰρ codd.
[2] γ᾽ εἶναι (vel supra κατά γε) Richards.   [3] οὓς ? ed.

ask, and whether they are able to administer the
tate, or sufficiently numerous to constitute a state ? ^{not of the} And there is some difficulty as regards all the rival _{few or the} claimants to political honours. Those who claim to
rule because of their wealth might seem to have no
justice in their proposal, and similarly also those who
claim on the score of birth ; for it is clear that if, to
go a step further, a single individual is richer than all
the others together, according to the same principle
of justice it will obviously be right for this one man to
rule over all, and similarly the man of outstanding
nobility among the claimants on the score of free
birth. And this same thing will perhaps result in
the case of aristocratic government based on virtue ;
for if there be some one man who is better than the
other virtuous men in the state, by the same principle
of justice that man must be sovereign. Accordingly
if it is actually proper for the multitude to be
sovereign because they are better than the few, then
also, if one person or if more than one but fewer
than the many are better than the rest, it would be
proper for these rather than the multitude to be
sovereign. All these considerations therefore seem
to prove the incorrectness of all of the standards
on which men claim that they themselves shall
govern and everybody else be governed by them.
For surely even against those who claim to be
sovereign over the government on account of virtue,
and similarly against those who claim on account of
wealth, the multitudes might be able to advance a
just plea ; for it is quite possible that at some time
the multitude may be collectively better and richer
than the few, although not individually.

Hence it is also possible to meet in this way the

1283 b
βάλλουσί τινες ἐνδέχεται τοῦτον τὸν τρόπον ἀπαντᾶ
(ἀποροῦσι γάρ τινες πότερον τῷ νομοθέτῃ νομο
θετητέον, βουλομένῳ τίθεσθαι τοὺς ὀρθοτάτου
νόμους, πρὸς τὸ τῶν βελτιόνων συμφέρον ἢ πρὸ
40 τὸ τῶν πλειόνων) ὅταν συμβαίνῃ τὸ λεχθέν. τὸ
ὀρθὸν ληπτέον ἴσως, τὸ δ' ἴσως ὀρθὸν πρὸς τὸ τῆ
πόλεως ὅλης συμφέρον καὶ πρὸς τὸ κοινὸν τὸ τῶ
πολιτῶν· πολίτης δὲ κοινῇ μὲν ὁ μετέχων τ
1284 a ἄρχειν καὶ ἄρχεσθαί ἐστι, καθ' ἑκάστην δὲ πολ
τείαν ἕτερος, πρὸς δὲ τὴν ἀρίστην ὁ δυνάμενος κα
προαιρούμενος ἄρχεσθαι καὶ ἄρχειν πρὸς τὸν βίο
τὸν κατ' ἀρετήν.

VIII. Εἰ δέ τίς ἐστιν εἰς τοσοῦτον διαφέρω
κατ' ἀρετῆς ὑπερβολήν, ἢ πλείους μὲν ἑνὸς μ
5 μέντοι δυνατοὶ πλήρωμα παρασχέσθαι πόλεω
ὥστε μὴ συμβλητὴν εἶναι τὴν τῶν ἄλλων ἀρετὴ
πάντων μηδὲ τὴν δύναμιν αὐτῶν τὴν πολιτικὴ
πρὸς τὴν ἐκείνων εἰ πλείους, εἰ δ' εἰς τὴν ἐκείνο
μόνον, οὐκέτι θετέον τούτους μέρος πόλεως· ἀδ
κήσονται γὰρ ἀξιούμενοι τῶν ἴσων, ἄνισοι τοσοῦτο
10 κατ' ἀρετὴν ὄντες καὶ τὴν πολιτικὴν δύναμι
ὥσπερ γὰρ θεὸν ἐν ἀνθρώποις εἰκὸς εἶναι τὸ
τοιοῦτον. ὅθεν δῆλον ὅτι καὶ τὴν νομοθεσία
ἀναγκαῖον εἶναι περὶ τοὺς ἴσους καὶ τῷ γένει κα
τῇ δυνάμει, κατὰ δὲ τῶν τοιούτων οὐκ ἔστι νόμος
αὐτοὶ γάρ εἰσι νόμος· καὶ γὰρ γελοῖος ἂν εἴ
15 νομοθετεῖν τις πειρώμενος κατ' αὐτῶν· λέγοιε
γὰρ ἂν ἴσως ἅπερ Ἀντισθένης ἔφη τοὺς λέοντα

---

[a] At the end of the last sentence, § 12.
[b] Pupil of Socrates and founder of the Cynic sect o
philosophers.
[c] ' Where are your claws and teeth ? '

estion which some persons investigate and put
rward (for some raise the question whether the
gislator desiring to lay down the rightest laws
ould legislate with a view to the advantage of the
etter people or that of the larger number) in cases
hen the situation mentioned[a] occurs. And 'right'
ust be taken in the sense of 'equally right,' and
is means right in regard to the interest of the
hole state and in regard to the common welfare of
e citizens ; and a citizen is in general one who shares
governing and being governed, although he is
fferent according to each form of constitution, but
relation to the best form a citizen is one who has
e capacity and the will to be governed and to govern
ith a view to the life in accordance with virtue.

VIII. But if there is any one man so greatly dis-
nguished in outstanding virtue, or more than one
ut not enough to be able to make up a complete
ate, so that the virtue of all the rest and their
olitical ability is not comparable with that of the
en mentioned, if they are several, or if one, with
is alone, it is no longer proper to count these ex-
eptional men a part of the state ; for they will be
eated unjustly if deemed worthy of equal status,
eing so widely unequal in virtue and in their political
bility : since such a man will naturally be as a god
mong men. Hence it is clear that legislation also
ust necessarily be concerned with persons who are
qual in birth and in ability, but there can be no law
ealing with such men as those described, for they
re themselves a law ; indeed a man would be
diculous if he tried to legislate for them, for prob-
bly they would say what in the story of Antisthenes[b]
e lions said[c] when the hares made speeches in

The safety-valve of Ostracism: its history, and prevalence in all the deviation-forms of state.

241

1284 a

δημηγορούντων τῶν δασυπόδων καὶ τὸ ἴσον ἀξιούν-
των πάντας ἔχειν. διὸ καὶ τίθενται τὸν ὀστρα-
κισμὸν αἱ δημοκρατούμεναι πόλεις διὰ τὴν τοιαύτην αἰτίαν· αὗται γὰρ δὴ δοκοῦσι διώκειν τὴν
20 ἰσότητα μάλιστα πάντων, ὥστε τοὺς δοκοῦντας
ὑπερέχειν δυνάμει διὰ πλοῦτον ἢ πολυφιλίαν ἤ τινα
ἄλλην πολιτικὴν ἰσχὺν ὠστράκιζον καὶ μεθίστασαι
ἐκ τῆς πόλεως χρόνους ὡρισμένους. μυθολογεῖται
δὲ καὶ τοὺς Ἀργοναύτας τὸν Ἡρακλέα καταλιπεῖν διὰ τοιαύτην αἰτίαν· οὐ γὰρ ἐθέλειν αὐτὸ
25 ἄγειν τὴν Ἀργὼ μετὰ τῶν πλωτήρων[1] τῶν ἄλλω
ὡς ὑπερβάλλοντα πολύ. διὸ καὶ τοὺς ψέγοντας
τὴν τυραννίδα καὶ τὴν Περιάνδρου Θρασυβούλῳ
συμβουλίαν οὐχ ἁπλῶς οἰητέον ὀρθῶς ἐπιτιμᾶ
(φασὶ γὰρ τὸν Περίανδρον εἰπεῖν μὲν οὐδὲν πρὸ
τὸν πεμφθέντα κήρυκα περὶ τῆς συμβουλίας, ἀφ
30 αιροῦντα δὲ τοὺς ὑπερέχοντας τῶν σταχύω
ὁμαλῦναι τὴν ἄρουραν· ὅθεν ἀγνοοῦντος μὲν τοῦ
κήρυκος τοῦ γινομένου τὴν αἰτίαν, ἀπαγγείλαντος
δὲ τὸ συμπεσόν, συννοῆσαι τὸν Θρασύβουλον ὅτ
δεῖ τοὺς ὑπερέχοντας ἄνδρας ἀναιρεῖν)· τοῦτο γὰ
οὐ μόνον συμφέρει τοῖς τυράννοις οὐδὲ μόνον ο
35 τύραννοι ποιοῦσιν, ἀλλ' ὁμοίως ἔχει καὶ περὶ τὰς
ὀλιγαρχίας καὶ τὰς δημοκρατίας· ὁ γὰρ ὀστρα-
κισμὸς τὴν αὐτὴν ἔχει δύναμιν τρόπον τινὰ τῷ
κολούειν τοὺς ὑπερέχοντας καὶ φυγαδεύειν. τὸ δ᾽
αὐτὸ καὶ περὶ τὰς πόλεις καὶ τὰ ἔθνη ποιοῦσιν
οἱ κύριοι τῆς δυνάμεως, οἷον Ἀθηναῖοι μὲν περ

---

[1] τῶν πλωτήρων hic Richards, post πολύ codd.

[a] Cf. Apollodorus, Bibliotheca i. 9. 19 τῆς Ἀργοῦς φθεγξαμένη
μὴ δύνασθαι φέρειν τὸ τούτου βάρος. Argo was a live creature
and Athena had built a ' talking timber ' into her cutwater.

the assembly and demanded that all should have equality. This is why democratically governed states institute the system of ostracism, because of a reason of this nature ; for these are the states considered to pursue equality most of all things, so that they used to ostracize men thought to be outstandingly powerful on account of wealth or popularity or some other form of political strength, and used to banish
3 them out of the city for fixed periods of time. And there is a mythical story that the Argonauts left Heracles behind for a similar reason ; for the Argo*a* refused to carry him with the other voyagers because he was so much heavier. Hence also those who blame tyranny and Periander's advice to Thrasybulus*b* must not be thought to be absolutely right in their censure (the story is that Periander made no reply to the herald sent to ask his advice, but levelled the corn-field by plucking off the ears that stood out above the rest ; and consequently, although the herald did not know the reason for what was going on, when he carried back news of what had occurred, Thrasybulus understood that he
4 was to destroy the outstanding citizens) ; for this policy is advantageous not only for tyrants, nor is it only tyrants that use it, but the same is the case with oligarchies and democracies as well ; for ostracism has in a way the same effect as docking off the outstanding men by exile. And the same course is adopted in regard to cities and races by the holders of sovereign power, for example the Athenians so

b Periander was tyrant of Corinth *circa* 626-585 B.C. ; Thrasybulus was tyrant of Miletus. Herodotus v. 92 tells the story with their parts reversed.

1284 a

40 Σαμίους καὶ Χίους καὶ Λεσβίους (ἐπεὶ γὰρ θᾶττον
ἐγκρατῶς ἔσχον τὴν ἀρχήν, ἐταπείνωσαν αὐτοὺς

1284 b παρὰ τὰς συνθήκας), ὁ δὲ Περσῶν βασιλεὺς Μήδους
καὶ Βαβυλωνίους καὶ τῶν ἄλλων τοὺς πεφρονη-
ματισμένους διὰ τὸ γενέσθαι ποτ' ἐπ' ἀρχῆς ἐπ-
έκοπτε πολλάκις. τὸ δὲ πρόβλημα καθόλου περὶ
πάσας ἐστὶ τὰς πολιτείας, καὶ τὰς ὀρθάς· αἱ μὲν
5 γὰρ παρεκβεβηκυῖαι πρὸς τὸ ἴδιον ἀποσκοποῦσαι
τοῦτο δρῶσιν, οὐ μὴν ἀλλὰ περὶ τὰς τὸ κοινὸν
ἀγαθὸν ἐπισκοπούσας τὸν αὐτὸν ἔχει τρόπον.
δῆλον δὲ τοῦτο καὶ ἐπὶ τῶν ἄλλων τεχνῶν καὶ
ἐπιστημῶν· οὔτε γὰρ γραφεὺς ἐάσειεν ἂν τὸν ὑπερβάλλοντα πόδα τῆς συμμετρίας ἔχειν τὸ ζῷον, οὐδ'
10 εἰ διαφέροι τὸ κάλλος, οὔτε ναυπηγὸς πρύμναν ἢ
τῶν ἄλλων τι μορίων τῶν τῆς νεώς, οὐδὲ δὴ
χοροδιδάσκαλος τὸν μεῖζον καὶ κάλλιον τοῦ παντὸς
χοροῦ φθεγγόμενον ἐάσει συγχορεύειν. ὥστε διὰ
τοῦτο μὲν οὐδὲν κωλύει τοὺς μονάρχους συμφωνεῖν
15 ταῖς πόλεσιν, εἰ τῆς οἰκείας ἀρχῆς ὠφελίμου ταῖς
πόλεσιν οὔσης τοῦτο δρῶσιν. διὸ κατὰ τὰς ὁμο-
λογουμένας ὑπεροχὰς ἔχει τι δίκαιον πολιτικὸν ὁ
λόγος ὁ περὶ τὸν ὀστρακισμόν. βέλτιον μὲν οὖν
τὸν νομοθέτην ἐξ ἀρχῆς οὕτω συστῆσαι τὴν πολιτείαν ὥστε μὴ δεῖσθαι τοιαύτης ἰατρείας· δεύτερος
20 δὲ πλοῦς, ἂν συμβῇ, πειρᾶσθαι τοιούτῳ τινὶ διορ-
θώματι διορθοῦν. ὅπερ οὐκ ἐγίγνετο περὶ τὰς
πόλεις, οὐ γὰρ ἔβλεπον πρὸς τὸ τῆς πολιτείας τῆς

---

^a In 440, 424 and 427 B.C. respectively.

244

dealt with the Samians and Chians and Lesbians [a]
(for no sooner did they get a strong hold of their
empire than they humbled them in contravention
of their covenants), and the king of the Persians
frequently used to cut down the numbers of the
Medes and Babylonians and the other races that
had waxed proud because they had once been head
5 of an empire. And the problem applies universally
to all the forms of constitution, even the right forms ;
for while the divergent forms of government do this
because their regard is fixed on their private advantage, nevertheless with the constitutions directed to
the common good the same is the case. And this is
also clear in the field of the other arts and sciences ;
a painter would not let his animal have its foot of
disproportionately large size, even though it was an
exceptionally beautiful foot, nor would a shipbuilder
make the stern or some other part of a ship disproportionately big, nor yet will a trainer of choruses
allow a man who sings louder and more beautifully
6 than the whole band to be a member of it. Hence
as far as this practice goes nothing prevents monarchs
from being in harmony with the cities they rule, if
they resort to it when their own personal rule is
beneficial to the cities. Therefore in relation to
acknowledged superiorities the argument for ostracism has a certain element of political justice. True,
it is better for the lawgiver so to constitute the state
at the outset that it does not need this medicine ;
but the next best course to steer, if occasion arises,
is to endeavour to correct the constitution by some
such method of rectification. But this was not what
happened with the states, for they were not looking
at what was advantageous for their proper constitu-

How far justifiable in the Ideal State?

245

1284 b

οἰκείας συμφέρον, ἀλλὰ στασιαστικῶς ἐχρῶντο
τοῖς ὀστρακισμοῖς. ἐν μὲν οὖν ταῖς παρεκβεβη-
κυίαις πολιτείαις ὅτι μὲν ἰδίᾳ συμφέρει καὶ δίκαιόν
25 ἐστι, φανερόν, ἴσως δὲ καὶ ὅτι οὐχ[1] ἁπλῶς δίκαιον,
καὶ τοῦτο φανερόν· ἀλλ' ἐπὶ τῆς ἀρίστης πολιτείας 7
ἔχει πολλὴν ἀπορίαν, οὐ κατὰ τῶν ἄλλων ἀγαθῶν
τὴν ὑπεροχήν, οἷον ἰσχύος καὶ πλούτου καὶ πολυ-
φιλίας, ἀλλ' ἄν τις γένηται διαφέρων κατ' ἀρετήν,
τί χρὴ ποιεῖν; οὐ γὰρ δὴ φαῖεν ἂν δεῖν ἐκβάλλειν
30 καὶ μεθιστάναι τὸν τοιοῦτον· ἀλλὰ μὴν οὐδ' ἄρχειν
γε τοῦ τοιούτου, παραπλήσιον γὰρ κἂν εἰ τοῦ Διὸς
ἄρχειν ἀξιοῖεν, μερίζοντες τὰς ἀρχάς. λείπεται
τοίνυν, ὅπερ ἔοικε πεφυκέναι, πείθεσθαι τῷ τοιούτῳ
πάντας ἀσμένως, ὥστε βασιλέας εἶναι τοὺς τοιούτους ἀιδίους ἐν ταῖς πόλεσιν.

35 IX. Ἴσως δὲ καλῶς ἔχει μετὰ τοὺς εἰρημένους 1
λόγους μεταβῆναι καὶ σκέψασθαι περὶ βασιλείας·
φαμὲν γὰρ τῶν ὀρθῶν πολιτειῶν μίαν εἶναι ταύτην.
σκεπτέον δὲ πότερον συμφέρει τῇ μελλούσῃ καλῶς
οἰκήσεσθαι καὶ πόλει καὶ χώρᾳ βασιλεύεσθαι, ἢ
40 οὔ, ἀλλ' ἄλλη τις πολιτεία μᾶλλον, ἢ τισὶ μὲν
συμφέρει τισὶ δ' οὐ συμφέρει. δεῖ δὲ πρῶτον
διελέσθαι πότερον ἓν τὸ γένος ἐστὶν αὐτῆς ἢ
1285 a πλείους ἔχει διαφοράς.

Ῥάδιον δὴ τοῦτό γε καταμαθεῖν, ὅτι πλείω τε 2
γένη περιέχει καὶ τῆς ἀρχῆς ὁ τρόπος ἐστὶν οὐχ
εἷς πασῶν. ἡ γὰρ ἐν τῇ Λακωνικῇ πολιτείᾳ δοκεῖ

---

[1] [οὐχ] Bernays.

---

[a] Perhaps ' not ' should be struck out; but if it stands, the
clause refers to § 5 *init.*—in these cases ostracism is practised
only in the interest of those in power.

tion, but their acts of ostracism were done in a revolutionary spirit. In the divergent forms of constitution therefore it is evident that ostracism is advantageous and just under the special constitution, though perhaps 7 it is also evident that it is not *a* just absolutely ; but in the case of the best constitution there is much doubt as to what ought to be done, not as regards superiority in the other things of value, such as strength and wealth and popularity, but in the case of a person becoming exceptionally distinguished for virtue. It certainly would not be said that such a man must be banished and got out of the way ; yet nevertheless no doubt men would not think that they ought to rule over such a man, for that would be the same as if they claimed to rule over Zeus, dividing up his spheres of government. It remains therefore, and this seems to be the natural course, for all to obey such a man gladly, so that men of this sort may be kings in the cities for all time.

1 IX. And perhaps it is well after the subjects that have been discussed to pass over to consider royal government ; for we pronounce this to be one of the correct constitutions. And it has to be considered whether it is advantageous for a city or a country that is to be well administered to be ruled by a king, or whether it is not so but some other constitution is more expedient, or whether royal rule is expedient for some states and not for others. But it is needful to decide first whether there is only one sort of kingship or whether it has several varieties.

2 Now it is at all events easy to discern that kingship includes several kinds, and that the mode of government is not the same in all. For the kingship in the Spartan constitution, which is held to be a typical

Royalty: its varieties:

(1) the Spartan kings;

μὲν εἶναι βασιλεία μάλιστα τῶν κατὰ νόμον, οὐκ
5 ἔστι δὲ κυρία πάντων, ἀλλ' ὅταν ἐξέλθῃ τὴν χώραν
ἡγεμών ἐστι τῶν πρὸς τὸν πόλεμον, ἔτι δὲ τὰ
πρὸς τοὺς θεοὺς ἀποδέδοται τοῖς βασιλεῦσιν.
αὕτη μὲν οὖν ἡ βασιλεία οἷον στρατηγία τις αὐτο-
κρατόρων καὶ ἀΐδιός ἐστιν· κτεῖναι γὰρ οὐ κύριος,
εἰ μὴ ἔν τινι καιρῷ,[1] καθάπερ ἐπὶ τῶν ἀρχαίων
10 ἐν ταῖς πολεμικαῖς ἐξόδοις ἐν χειρὸς νόμῳ· δηλοῖ
δ' Ὅμηρος, ὁ γὰρ Ἀγαμέμνων κακῶς μὲν ἀκούων
ἠνείχετο ἐν ταῖς ἐκκλησίαις, ἐξελθόντων δὲ καὶ
κτεῖναι κύριος ἦν· λέγει γοῦν

ὃν δέ κ' ἐγὼν ἀπάνευθε μάχης . . .

. . . οὔ οἱ
ἄρκιον ἐσσεῖται φυγέειν κύνας ἠδ' οἰωνούς·
πὰρ γὰρ ἐμοὶ θάνατος.

15 ἓν μὲν οὖν τοῦτ' εἶδος βασιλείας, στρατηγία διὰ 3
βίου, τούτων δ' αἱ μὲν κατὰ γένος εἰσὶν αἱ δ'
αἱρεταί· παρὰ ταύτην δ' ἄλλο μοναρχίας εἶδος,
οἷαι παρ' ἐνίοις εἰσὶ βασιλεῖαι τῶν βαρβάρων.
ἔχουσι δ' αὗται τὴν δύναμιν πᾶσαι παραπλησίαν
τυραννίσιν, εἰσὶ δὲ καὶ[2] κατὰ νόμον καὶ πατρικαί·
20 διὰ γὰρ τὸ δουλικώτεροι εἶναι τὰ ἤθη φύσει οἱ
μὲν βάρβαροι τῶν Ἑλλήνων οἱ δὲ περὶ τὴν Ἀσίαν
τῶν περὶ τὴν Εὐρώπην, ὑπομένουσι τὴν δεσποτικὴν
ἀρχὴν οὐδὲν δυσχεραίνοντες. τυραννικαὶ μὲν οὖν
διὰ τὸ τοιοῦτόν εἰσιν, ἀσφαλεῖς δὲ διὰ τὸ πάτριαι

---

[1] καιρῷ (vel ἀνάγκῃ) Richards : βασιλείᾳ (e βασιλεία supra)
codd. (non vertit Ar.).

[2] τυραννίσιν—καὶ Susemihl : lacunas et fragmenta varia
codd.

royalty of the kind guided by law, does not carry sovereignty in all matters, though when a king goes on a foreign expedition he is the leader in all matters relating to the war; and also matters relating to religion have been assigned to the kings. This kingship therefore is a sort of military command vested in generals with absolute powers and held for life; for the king has not authority to put a subject to death, except in some emergency, as in ancient times kings on their military expeditions could kill an offender out of hand, as Homer proves, for Agamemnon endured being reviled in the assemblies but when they were on an expedition had authority to put a man to death: at all events he says

> But whomsoe'er I see far from the fray . . .
> Shall have no hope to fly from dogs and vultures,
> For death is in my hands! [a]

3 This then is one sort of kingship, a lifelong generalship, and some of the kingships of this kind are hereditary, others elective; and by its side there is another sort of monarchy, examples of which are kingships existing among some of the barbarians. The power possessed by all of these resembles that of tyrannies, but they govern according to law and are hereditary; for because the barbarians are more servile in their nature than the Greeks, and the Asiatics than the Europeans, they endure despotic rule without any resentment. These kingships therefore are for these reasons of a tyrannical nature, but they are secure because they are hereditary and

(2) Oriental monarchy;

---

[a] Quoted from *Iliad* ii. 391, but the last line is not in our Homer.

25 καὶ κατὰ νόμον εἶναι. καὶ ἡ φυλακὴ δὲ βασιλικὴ
καὶ οὐ τυραννικὴ διὰ τὴν αὐτὴν αἰτίαν· οἱ γὰρ
πολῖται φυλάττουσιν ὅπλοις τοὺς βασιλεῖς, τοὺς δὲ
τυράννους ξενικόν· οἱ μὲν γὰρ κατὰ νόμον καὶ
ἑκόντων οἱ δ' ἀκόντων ἄρχουσιν, ὥσθ' οἱ μὲν παρὰ
τῶν πολιτῶν οἱ δ' ἐπὶ τοὺς πολίτας ἔχουσι τὴν
30 φυλακήν.   δύο μὲν οὖν εἴδη ταῦτα μοναρχίας·
ἕτερον δ' ὅπερ ἦν ἐν τοῖς ἀρχαίοις Ἕλλησιν, οὓς
καλοῦσιν αἰσυμνήτας. ἔστι δὲ τοῦθ' ὡς ἁπλῶς
εἰπεῖν αἱρετὴ τυραννίς, διαφέρουσα δὲ τῆς βαρ-
βαρικῆς οὐ τῷ μὴ κατὰ νόμον ἀλλὰ τῷ μὴ πάτριος
εἶναι μόνον. ἦρχον δ' οἱ μὲν διὰ βίου τὴν ἀρχὴν
35 ταύτην, οἱ δὲ μέχρι τινῶν ὡρισμένων χρόνων ἢ
πράξεων, οἷον εἵλοντό ποτε Μιτυληναῖοι Πιττακὸν πρὸς τοὺς φυγάδας ὧν προειστήκεσαν Ἀντι-
μενίδης καὶ Ἀλκαῖος ὁ ποιητής. δηλοῖ δ' Ἀλκαῖος
ὅτι τύραννον εἵλοντο τὸν Πιττακὸν ἔν τινι τῶν
σκολιῶν μελῶν· ἐπιτιμᾷ γὰρ ὅτι

τὸν κακοπάτριδα[1]

Πιττακὸν πόλιος[2] τᾶς ἀχόλω[3] καὶ βαρυδαίμονος
1285 b ἐστάσαντο τύραννον μέγ' ἐπαινέοντες ἀολλέες.

αὗται μὲν οὖν εἰσί τε καὶ ἦσαν διὰ μὲν τὸ δεσποτικαὶ εἶναι τυραννικαί,[4] διὰ δὲ τὸ αἱρεταὶ καὶ ἑκόντων
βασιλικαί· τέταρτον δ' εἶδος μοναρχίας βασιλικῆς
5 αἱ κατὰ τοὺς ἡρωϊκοὺς χρόνους ἑκούσιαί τε καὶ
πάτριαι γιγνόμεναι κατὰ νόμον. διὰ γὰρ τὸ τοὺς
πρώτους γενέσθαι τοῦ πλήθους εὐεργέτας κατὰ

---

[1] κακοπατρίδαν Wackernagel.
[2] πόλιος Schneidewin: πόλεως codd.
[3] διχόλω Schmidt.
[4] τυραννικαὶ εἶναι δεσποτικαί codd.: tr. Sepulveda.

4 rule by law. Also their bodyguard is of a royal
and not a tyrannical type for the same reason ; for
kings are guarded by the citizens in arms, whereas
tyrants have foreign guards, for kings rule in accordance with law and over willing subjects, but tyrants
rule over unwilling subjects, owing to which kings
take their guards from among the citizens but
tyrants have them to guard against the citizens.

5 These then are two kinds of monarchy ; while another
is that which existed among the ancient Greeks, the (3) the
type of rulers called *aesymnetae*. This, to put it ^{dictator ;}
simply, is an elective tyranny, and it differs from
the monarchy that exists among barbarians not in
governing without the guidance of law but only in
not being hereditary. Some holders of this type of
monarchy ruled for life, others until certain fixed
limits of time or until certain undertakings were
ended, as for example the people of Mitylene once
elected Pittacus to resist the exiles under the leader-

6 ship of Antimenides and the poet Alcaeus. That they
elected Pittacus [a] as tyrant is proved by Alcaeus in
one of his catches ; for he rebukes the people because

> The base-born Pittacus they did set up
> As tyrant of the meek and luckless city,
> And all did greatly praise him.

These monarchies therefore now and in the past are
of the nature of tyrannies because they are autocratic,
but of the nature of kingships because they are elec-

7 tive and rule over willing subjects. A fourth class of (4) heroic
royal monarchy consists of the hereditary legal king- ^{monarchy ;}
ships over willing subjects in the heroic period. For
because the first of the line had been benefactors of

---

[a] Pittacus held the office 587-579 B.C. He was one of the
Seven Sages. Antimenides and Alcaeus were brothers.

τέχνας ἢ πόλεμον ἢ διὰ τὸ συναγαγεῖν ἢ πορίσαι
χώραν, ἐγίγνοντο βασιλεῖς ἑκόντων καὶ τοῖς παρα-
λαμβάνουσι πάτριοι. κύριοι δ' ἦσαν τῆς τε κατὰ
10 πόλεμον ἡγεμονίας καὶ τῶν θυσιῶν ὅσαι μὴ
ἱερατικαί, καὶ πρὸς τούτοις τὰς δίκας ἔκρινον·
τοῦτο δ' ἐποίουν οἱ μὲν οὐκ ὀμνύοντες οἱ δ'
ὀμνύοντες, ὁ δ' ὅρκος ἦν τοῦ σκήπτρου ἐπανάτασις.
οἱ μὲν οὖν ἐπὶ τῶν ἀρχαίων χρόνων καὶ τὰ κατὰ ᵃ
πόλιν καὶ τὰ ἔνδημα καὶ τὰ ὑπερόρια συνεχῶς
15 ἦρχον· ὕστερον δὲ τὰ μὲν αὐτῶν παριέντων τῶν
βασιλέων τὰ δὲ τῶν ὄχλων παραιρουμένων, ἐν μὲν
ταῖς ἄλλαις πόλεσι θυσίαι κατελείφθησαν τοῖς
βασιλεῦσι μόνον, ὅπου δ' ἄξιον εἰπεῖν εἶναι βασιλείαν, ἐν τοῖς ὑπερορίοις τῶν πολεμικῶν τὴν ἡγεμονίαν μόνον εἶχον.

20 X. Βασιλείας μὲν οὖν εἴδη ταῦτα, τέτταρα τὸν ᵇ
ἀριθμόν, μία μὲν ἡ περὶ τοὺς ἡρωικοὺς χρόνους
(αὕτη δ' ἦν ἑκόντων μέν, ἐπί τισι δ' ὡρισμένοις,
στρατηγὸς γὰρ ἦν καὶ δικαστὴς ὁ βασιλεὺς καὶ
τῶν πρὸς τοὺς θεοὺς κύριος), δευτέρα δ' ἡ βαρ-
βαρική (αὕτη δ' ἐστὶν ἐκ γένους ἀρχὴ δεσποτικὴ
25 κατὰ νόμον), τρίτη δ' ἦν αἰσυμνητείαν προσαγορεύουσιν (αὕτη δ' ἐστὶν αἱρετὴ τυραννίς), τετάρτη
δ' ἡ Λακωνικὴ τούτων (αὕτη δ' ἐστὶν ὡς εἰπεῖν
ἁπλῶς στρατηγία κατὰ γένος ἀΐδιος). αὗται μὲν
οὖν τοῦτον τὸν τρόπον διαφέρουσιν ἀλλήλων.
80 πέμπτον δ' εἶδος βασιλείας ὅταν ᾖ πάντων κύριος
εἷς ὢν ὥσπερ ἕκαστον ἔθνος καὶ πόλις ἑκάστη
τῶν κοινῶν, τεταγμένη κατὰ τὴν οἰκονομικήν·

ᵃ This ritual is mentioned in *Iliad* i. 234, vii. 412, x. 328.
ᵇ The monarchy was reduced to a priesthood at Cyrene
(Herod. iv. 161) and at Ephesus.

the multitude in the arts or in war, or through having drawn them together or provided them with land, these kings used to come to the throne with the consent of the subjects and hand it on to their successors by lineal descent. And they had supreme command in war and control over all sacrifices that were not in the hands of the priestly class, and in addition to these functions they were judges in law-suits ; some gave judgement not on oath and some on oath—the oath was taken by holding up the sceptre.[a] These kings then of ancient times used to govern continuously in matters within the city and in the country and across the frontiers ; but later on when gradually the kings relinquished some of their powers and had others taken from them by the multitudes, in the cities in general only the sacrifices were left to the kings,[b] while where anything that deserves the name of royalty survived the kings only had the command in military expeditions across the frontiers.

X. There are then these kinds of kingship, four in number : one belonging to the heroic times, which was exercised over willing subjects, but in certain limited fields, for the king was general and judge and master of religious ceremonies ; second, the barbarian monarchy, which is an hereditary despotism governing in conformity with law ; third, the rule of the functionary called an *aesymnetes*, which is an elective tyranny ; and fourth among these is the Spartan kingship, which may be described simply as an hereditary generalship held for life. These kingships then differ from one another in this manner. But a fifth kind of kingship is when a single ruler is sovereign over all matters in the way in which each race and each city is sovereign over its common affairs ; this

(5) absolute monarchy.

253

1285 b ὥσπερ γὰρ ἡ οἰκονομικὴ βασιλεία τις οἰκίας
ἐστίν, οὕτως ἡ παμβασιλεία[1] πόλεως καὶ ἔθνους
ἑνὸς ἢ πλειόνων οἰκονομία.

Σχεδὸν δὴ δύο ἐστὶν ὡς εἰπεῖν εἴδη βασιλείας
35 περὶ ὧν σκεπτέον, αὕτη τε καὶ ἡ Λακωνική. τῶν
γὰρ ἄλλων αἱ πολλαὶ μεταξὺ τούτων εἰσίν· ἐλαττόνων μὲν γὰρ κύριοι τῆς παμβασιλείας, πλειόνων
δ' εἰσὶ τῆς Λακωνικῆς. ὥστε τὸ σκέμμα σχεδὸν
περὶ δυοῖν ἐστιν, ἓν μὲν πότερον συμφέρει ταῖς
πόλεσι στρατηγὸν ἀίδιον εἶναι, καὶ τοῦτον ἢ κατὰ
1286 a γένος ἢ κατὰ μέρος,[2] ἢ οὐ συμφέρει, ἓν δὲ πότερον
ἕνα συμφέρει κύριον εἶναι πάντων ἢ οὐ συμφέρει.
τὸ μὲν οὖν περὶ τῆς τοιαύτης στρατηγίας ἐπι-[a]
σκοπεῖν νόμων ἔχει μᾶλλον εἶδος ἢ πολιτείας (ἐν
ἁπάσαις γὰρ ἐνδέχεται γίγνεσθαι τοῦτο ταῖς πολι-
5 τείαις), ὥστ' ἀφείσθω τὴν πρώτην· ὁ δὲ λοιπὸς
τρόπος τῆς βασιλείας πολιτείας εἶδός ἐστιν, ὥστε
περὶ τούτου δεῖ θεωρῆσαι καὶ τὰς ἀπορίας ἐπι-
δραμεῖν τὰς ἐνούσας.

Ἀρχὴ δ' ἐστὶ τῆς ζητήσεως αὕτη, πότερον συμφέρει μᾶλλον ὑπὸ τοῦ ἀρίστου ἀνδρὸς ἄρχεσθαι ἢ
10 ὑπὸ τῶν ἀρίστων νόμων. δοκοῦσι δὴ τοῖς νομίζουσι συμφέρειν βασιλεύεσθαι τὸ καθόλου μόνον
οἱ νόμοι λέγειν ἀλλ' οὐ πρὸς τὰ προσπίπτοντα
ἐπιτάττειν· ὥστ' ἐν ὁποιαοῦν τέχνῃ τὸ κατὰ
γράμματ' ἄρχειν ἠλίθιον (καὶ[3] ἐν Αἰγύπτῳ μετὰ
τὴν τετρήμερον κινεῖν ἔξεστι τοῖς ἰατροῖς, ἐὰν δὲ

---

[1] παμβασιλεία Susemihl (cf. 36): βασιλεία codd.
[2] μέρος: αἵρεσιν codd. aliqui (cf. a 16).
[3] καὶ πως, καὶ ὡς codd. nonnulli (ἠλίθιόν πως καὶ ? Richards).

---

[a] Some MSS. give ' or by election.'
[b] Cf. 1289 a 11 foll.; but the promise of a full discussion
of law is not fulfilled.

monarchy ranges with the rule of a master over a household, for just as the master's rule is a sort of monarchy in the home, so absolute monarchy is domestic mastership over a city, or over a race or several races.

There are therefore, we may say, virtually two kinds of kingship that have been examined, this one and the Spartan. For most of the others lie between these, since with them the king is sovereign over fewer things than under absolute monarchy, but over more than under the Spartan kingship. Hence our inquiry is virtually about two questions, one whether it is expedient or inexpedient for states to have a military commander holding office for life, and that either by descent or by class,[a] and one whether it is expedient or inexpedient for one man to be sovereign over everything. Now the study of a military command of the kind mentioned has more the aspect of a legal than of a constitutional inquiry (for it is possible for this form of office to exist under all constitutions), so let it be dismissed at the first stage[b]; but the remaining mode of kingship is a kind of constitution, so that it is necessary to consider this one and to run over the difficulties that it involves.

And the starting-point of the inquiry is the question whether it is more advantageous to be ruled by the best men or by the best laws. Those of the opinion that it is advantageous to be governed by a king think that laws enunciate only general principles but do not give directions for dealing with circumstances as they arise; so that in an art of any kind it is foolish to govern procedure by written rules (and indeed in Egypt physicians have the right to alter their prescription after four days, although if one of them alters it

The list reduced to two.

The Spartan really a military office.

Absolute monarchy criticized.

Government should be guided by law as a general principle.

1286 a

πρότερον, ἐπὶ τῷ αὑτοῦ κινδύνῳ)· φανερὸν τοίνυν
15 ὡς οὐκ ἔστιν ἡ κατὰ γράμματα καὶ νόμους ἀρίστη
πολιτεία διὰ τὴν αὐτὴν αἰτίαν. ἀλλὰ μὴν κἀκεῖνον
δεῖ ὑπάρχειν τὸν λόγον τὸν καθόλου τοῖς ἄρχουσιν.
κρεῖττον δ᾽ ᾧ μὴ πρόσεστι τὸ παθητικὸν ὅλως ἢ
ᾧ συμφυές· τῷ μὲν οὖν νόμῳ τοῦτο οὐχ ὑπάρχει,
20 ψυχὴν δ᾽ ἀνθρωπίνην ἀνάγκη τοῦτ᾽ ἔχειν πᾶσαν.
ἀλλ᾽ ἴσως ἂν φαίη τις ὡς ἀντὶ τούτου βουλεύσεται
περὶ τῶν καθ᾽ ἕκαστα κάλλιον. ὅτι μὲν τοίνυν
ἀνάγκη νομοθέτην αὐτὸν εἶναι, δῆλον, καὶ κεῖσθαι
νόμους, ἀλλὰ μὴ κυρίους ᾗ παρεκβαίνουσιν, ἐπεὶ
περὶ τῶν γ᾽ ἄλλων εἶναι δεῖ κυρίους· ὅσα δὲ μὴ
25 δυνατὸν τὸν νόμον κρίνειν ἢ ὅλως ἢ εὖ, πότερον
ἕνα τὸν ἄριστον δεῖ ἄρχειν ἢ πάντας; καὶ γὰρ
νῦν συνιόντες δικάζουσι καὶ βουλεύονται καὶ κρίνουσιν, αὗται δ᾽ αἱ κρίσεις εἰσὶ πᾶσαι περὶ τῶν
καθ᾽ ἕκαστον. καθ᾽ ἕνα μὲν οὖν συμβαλλόμενος
ὁστισοῦν ἴσως χείρων· ἀλλ᾽ ἐστὶν ἡ πόλις ἐκ
30 πολλῶν, ὥσπερ δ᾽[1] ἑστίασις συμφορητὸς καλλίων
μιᾶς καὶ ἁπλῆς, διὰ τοῦτο καὶ κρίνει ἄμεινον
ὄχλος πολλὰ ἢ εἷς ὁστισοῦν. ἔτι μᾶλλον ἀδιά-
φθορον τὸ πολύ—καθάπερ[2] ὕδωρ τὸ πλεῖον, οὕτω
καὶ τὸ πλῆθος τῶν ὀλίγων ἀδιαφθορώτερον· τοῦ
δ᾽ ἑνὸς ὑπ᾽ ὀργῆς κρατηθέντος ἤ τινος ἑτέρου
35 πάθους τοιούτου ἀναγκαῖον διεφθάρθαι τὴν κρίσιν,
ἐκεῖ δ᾽ ἔργον ἅμα πάντας ὀργισθῆναι καὶ ἁμαρτεῖν.

---

[1] ὥσπερ δ᾽ ed. : ὥσπερ codd.
[2] καθάπερ ⟨γὰρ⟩ Bekker.

---

a *i.e.* unalterably binding, and not be set aside by special
dispensation of the ruler when deemed to be unjust in some
particular case.
256

efore he does so at his own risk) ; it is clear therefore
at government according to written rules, that is
ws, is not the best, for the same reason. At the
me time, however, rulers ought to be in possession
the general principle before mentioned as well.
nd a thing that does not contain the emotional
ement is generally superior to a thing in which it
innate ; now the law does not possess this factor,
t every human soul necessarily has it. But perhaps Law best
meone might say that in compensation for this a applied by
gle ruler will decide better about particular cases. lective
herefore it is clear that on the one hand the ruler the noble
ust necessarily be a legislator, and that there must or free.
laws laid down, although these must not be
vereign *a* where they go astray—admittedly in all
her cases they ought to be sovereign ; but on the
her hand in matters which it is impossible for the
w either to decide at all or to decide well, ought
e one best man to govern or all the citizens ? As
is, the citizens assembled hear lawsuits and deliber-
e and give judgements, but these judgements are
l on particular cases. Now no doubt any one of
em individually is inferior compared with the best
an, but a state consists of a number of individuals,
d just as a banquet to which many contribute
shes is finer than a single plain dinner, for this
ason in many cases a crowd judges better than
y single person. Also the multitude is more incor-
ptible—just as the larger stream of water is purer,
the mass of citizens is less corruptible than the few ;
d the individual's judgement is bound to be cor-
pted when he is overcome by anger or some other
ch emotion, whereas in the other case it is a difficult
ing for all the people to be roused to anger and go

257

1286 a

ἔστω δὲ τὸ πλῆθος οἱ ἐλεύθεροι, μηδὲν παρὰ τ
νόμον πράττοντες ἀλλ᾽ ἢ περὶ ὧν ἐκλείπειν ἀνα
καῖον αὐτόν. εἰ δὲ δὴ τοῦτο μὴ ῥᾴδιον ἐν πο
λοῖς, ἀλλ᾽ εἰ πλείους εἶεν ἀγαθοὶ καὶ ἄνδρες κ

40 πολῖται, πότερον ὁ εἷς ἀδιαφθορώτερος ἄρχων

1286 b μᾶλλον οἱ πλείους μὲν τὸν ἀριθμὸν ἀγαθοὶ
πάντες; ἢ δῆλον ὡς οἱ πλείους; ἀλλ᾽ οἱ μ
στασιάζουσιν, ὁ δ᾽ εἷς ἀστασίαστος. ἀλλὰ πρ
τοῦτ᾽ ἀντιθετέον ἴσως ὅτι σπουδαῖοι τὴν ψυχ
ὥσπερ κἀκεῖνος ὁ εἷς. εἰ δὴ τὴν μὲν τῶν πλειόν

5 ἀρχὴν ἀγαθῶν δ᾽ ἀνδρῶν πάντων ἀριστοκρατί
θετέον, τὴν δὲ τοῦ ἑνὸς βασιλείαν, αἱρετώτερον
εἴη ταῖς πόλεσιν ἀριστοκρατία βασιλείας, καὶ μετ
δυνάμεως καὶ χωρὶς δυνάμεως οὔσης τῆς ἀρχῆ
ἂν ᾖ λαβεῖν πλείους ὁμοίους. καὶ διὰ τοῦτ᾽ ἴσ
ἐβασιλεύοντο πρότερον, ὅτι σπάνιον ἦν εὑρε
ἄνδρας πολὺ¹ διαφέροντας κατ᾽ ἀρετήν, ἄλλως

10 καὶ τότε μικρὰς οἰκοῦντας πόλεις. ἔτι δ᾽ ἀ
εὐεργεσίας καθίστασαν τοὺς βασιλεῖς, ὅπερ ἐστ
ἔργον τῶν ἀγαθῶν ἀνδρῶν. ἐπεὶ δὲ συνέβαι
γίγνεσθαι πολλοὺς ὁμοίους πρὸς ἀρετήν, οὐκέ
ὑπέμενον ἀλλ᾽ ἐζήτουν κοινόν τι καὶ πολιτεί
καθίστασαν. ἐπεὶ δὲ χείρους γιγνόμενοι ἐχρημα

15 τίζοντο ἀπὸ τῶν κοινῶν, ἐντεῦθέν ποθεν εὔλογ
γενέσθαι τὰς ὀλιγαρχίας· ἔντιμον γὰρ ἐποίησα

¹ πολλοὺς (plures Ar.) Sylburg.

wrong together. But the multitude must consist of the freemen, doing nothing apart from the law except about matters as to which the law must of necessity be deficient. And if this is not indeed easy to ensure in the case of many men, yet if there were a majority of good men and good citizens, would an individual make a more incorruptible ruler or rather those who though the majority in number yet are all good? The majority, is it not obvious? But it will be said that they will split up into factions, whereas with a single ruler this cannot happen. But against this must perhaps be set the fact that they are as virtuous in soul as the single ruler. If then the rule of the majority when these are all good men is to be considered an aristocracy, and that of the one man kingship, aristocracy would be preferable for the states to kingship, whether the royal office be conjoined with military force or without it, if it be possible to get a larger number of men than one who are of similar quality. And it was perhaps only owing to this that kingships existed in earlier times, because it was rare to find men who greatly excelled in virtue, especially as in those days they dwelt in small cities. Moreover they used to appoint their kings on the ground of public service, and to perform this is a task for the good men. But as it began to come about that many men arose who were alike in respect of virtue, they would no longer submit to royalty, but sought for some form of commonwealth, and set up a republican constitution. And as men becoming baser began to make money out of the community, it is reasonable to suppose that some such cause as this occasioned the rise of oligarchies; for they brought wealth into honour.

Normal succession of constitutions in history,

1286 b

τὸν πλοῦτον. ἐκ δὲ τούτων πρῶτον εἰς τυραν
νίδας μετέβαλλον, ἐκ δὲ τῶν τυραννίδων εἰς δημο
κρατίαν· ἀεὶ γὰρ εἰς ἐλάττους ἄγοντες δι' αἰσχρο
κέρδειαν, ἰσχυρότερον τὸ πλῆθος κατέστησαν, ὥστ'
20 ἐπιθέσθαι καὶ γενέσθαι δημοκρατίας. ἐπεὶ δὲ κα
μείζους εἶναι συμβέβηκε τὰς πόλεις, ἴσως οὐδ
ῥᾴδιον ἔτι γίγνεσθαι πολιτείαν ἑτέραν παρὰ δημο
κρατίαν. εἰ δὲ δή τις ἄριστον θείη τὸ βασιλεύεσθα
ταῖς πόλεσιν, πῶς ἕξει τὰ περὶ τῶν τέκνων
πότερον καὶ τὸ γένος δεῖ βασιλεύειν; ἀλλὰ γιγνο
25 μένων ὁποῖοί τινες ἔτυχον βλαβερόν. ἀλλ' ο
παραδώσει κύριος ὢν τοῖς τέκνοις. ἀλλ' οὐκ ἔτ
τοῦτο ῥᾴδιον πιστεῦσαι· χαλεπὸν γάρ, καὶ μείζονο
ἀρετῆς ἢ κατ' ἀνθρωπίνην φύσιν. ἔχει δ' ἀπορία
καὶ περὶ τῆς δυνάμεως, πότερον ἔχειν δεῖ τὸ
30 μέλλοντα βασιλεύειν ἰσχύν τινα περὶ αὐτὸν ᾗ δυνή
σεται βιάζεσθαι τοὺς μὴ βουλομένους πειθαρχεῖν
ἢ πῶς ἐνδέχεται τὴν ἀρχὴν διοικεῖν; εἰ γὰρ κα
κατὰ νόμον εἴη κύριος, μηδὲν πράττων κατὰ τὴ
αὑτοῦ βούλησιν παρὰ τὸν νόμον, ὅμως ἀναγκαῖο
ὑπάρχειν αὐτῷ δύναμιν ᾗ φυλάξει τοὺς νόμους
τάχα μὲν οὖν τὰ περὶ τὸν βασιλέα τὸν τοιοῦτον ο
35 χαλεπὸν διορίσαι· δεῖ γὰρ αὐτὸν μὲν ἔχειν[1] ἰσχύ
εἶναι δὲ τοσαύτην τὴν ἰσχὺν ὥστε ἑκάστου μὲ
καὶ ἑνὸς καὶ συμπλειόνων κρείττω, τοῦ δὲ πλήθου
ἥττω, καθάπερ οἵ τ' ἀρχαῖοι τὰς φυλακὰς ἐδίδοσα

---

[1] ἔχειν μὲν (vel ἰσχὺν μὲν ἔχειν) Richards.

---

[a] *i.e.* more men of consideration went over to the opposition

And from oligarchies they first changed to tyrannies,
and from tyrannies to democracy; for by constantly
bringing the government into fewer hands owing to a
base love of gain, they made the multitude stronger,ª
so that it set upon the oligarchs, and democracies
came into existence. But now that the states have
come to be even greater than they were, perhaps it
is not easy for yet another form of constitution beside
democracy to come into existence. And even if one
held that royal government is best for states, what is
to be the position as regards the king's children? is
the sovereignty to be hereditary? But this will be
disastrous if the king's sons turn out to be like what
some have been. It may be said that the king being
sovereign will not in that case bequeath the throne
to his children. But that is too much to be easy to
believe: it would be difficult for a king to disinherit
his sons, and an act of virtue above the level of human
nature. And there is a difficulty also about the royal
power: ought the man who is to reign as king to
have an armed force about him, by means of which
he will have power to compel those who may be
unwilling to obey, or if not, how is it possible for
him to administer his office? For even if he were a
law-abiding sovereign and never acted according to
his own will against the law, nevertheless it would
be essential for him to have power behind him whereby
to safeguard the laws. Probably therefore it is not
difficult to define the regulations for a king of this
sort: he must have a force of his own, but the force
must be only so large as to be stronger than a single
individual or even several individuals banded together,
but weaker than the multitude, on the principle on
which the men of old times used to assign bodyguards

Heredity may fail.

Need of military force, but its dangers.

1286 b

ὅτε καθισταῖέν τινα τῆς πόλεως ὃν ἐκάλουν αἰσυμνή-
την ἢ τύραννον,[1] καὶ Διονυσίῳ τις, ὅτ' ᾔτει τοὺς
40 φύλακας, συνεβούλευε τοῖς Συρακουσίοις διδόναι
τοσούτους τοὺς φύλακας.

1287 a

XI. Περὶ δὲ τοῦ βασιλέως τοῦ κατὰ τὴν αὑτοῦ
βούλησιν πάντα πράττοντος ὅ τε λόγος ἐφέστηκε
νῦν καὶ ποιητέον τὴν σκέψιν. ὁ μὲν γὰρ κατὰ
νόμον λεγόμενος βασιλεὺς οὐκ ἔστιν εἶδος, καθάπερ
5 εἴπομεν, πολιτείας (ἐν πάσαις γὰρ ὑπάρχειν ἐνδέχεται στρατηγίαν ἀίδιον, οἷον ἐν δημοκρατίᾳ καὶ
ἀριστοκρατίᾳ, καὶ πολλοὶ ποιοῦσιν ἕνα κύριον τῆς
διοικήσεως· τοιαύτη γὰρ ἀρχή τίς ἐστι καὶ περὶ
Ἐπίδαμνον, καὶ περὶ Ὀποῦντα δὲ κατά τι μέρος
ἔλαττον)· περὶ δὲ τῆς παμβασιλείας καλουμένης
10 αὕτη δ' ἐστὶ καθ' ἣν ἄρχει πάντων[2] κατὰ τὴν
ἑαυτοῦ βούλησιν ὁ βασιλεύς. δοκεῖ δέ τισιν οὐδὲ
κατὰ φύσιν εἶναι τὸ κύριον ἕνα πάντων εἶναι τῶν
πολιτῶν ὅπου συνέστηκεν ἐξ ὁμοίων ἡ πόλις· τοῖς
γὰρ ὁμοίοις φύσει τὸ αὐτὸ δίκαιον ἀναγκαῖον καὶ
τὴν αὐτὴν ἀξίαν κατὰ φύσιν εἶναι, ὥστ' εἴπερ καὶ
15 τὸ ἴσην ἔχειν τοὺς ἀνίσους τροφὴν ἢ ἐσθῆτα
βλαβερὸν τοῖς σώμασιν, οὕτως ἔχειν[3] καὶ τὸ περὶ
τὰς τιμάς· ὁμοίως τοίνυν καὶ τὸ ἄνισον τοὺς ἴσους,
διόπερ οὐδένα[4] μᾶλλον ἄρχειν ἢ ἄρχεσθαι δίκαιον,
καὶ τὸ ἀνὰ μέρος τοίνυν ὡσαύτως. τοῦτο δ' ἤδη
νόμος· ἡ γὰρ τάξις νόμος. τὸν ἄρα νόμον ἄρχειν

---

[1] [ἢ τύραννον] Susemihl.   [2] πάντων Jul.: πάντα codd.
[3] ἔχειν Schneider: ἔχει codd.
[4] οὐδένα Bernays: οὐδὲν codd.

---

[a] 'Or tyrant' looks like an incorrect note, see 1285 b 25.
[b] See 1259 a 39 n.   [c] See c. x. § 3.
[d] Durazzo, on the Adriatic.

whenever they appointed somebody as what they termed *aesymnetes* or tyrant [a] of the state, and also, when Dionysius [b] asked for his guards, somebody advised him to give the same number of guards to the citizens of Syracuse.

1 XI. Our discussion has now reached the case of the king who acts in all matters according to his own will, and we must examine this type of royalty. For the so-called constitutional monarchy, as we said,[c] is not a special kind of constitution (since it is possible for a life-long generalship to exist under all constitutions, for example under a democracy and an aristocracy, and many people make one man sovereign over the administration, for instance there is a government of this sort in Epidamnus,[d] and also at Opus [e] to

2 a certain smaller extent); but we have now to discuss what is called Absolute Monarchy, which is the monarchy under which the king governs all men according to his own will Some people think that it is entirely contrary to nature for one person to be sovereign over all the citizens where the state consists of men who are alike ; for necessarily persons alike in nature must in accordance with nature have the same principle of justice and the same value, so that inasmuch as for persons who are unequal to have an equal amount of food or clothing is harmful for their bodies, the same is the case also

3 in regard to honours ; similarly therefore it is wrong for those who are equal to have inequality, owing to which it is just for no one person to govern or be governed more than another, and therefore for everybody to govern and be governed alike in turn. And this constitutes law ; for regulation is law. Therefore

Natural for law to rule administrated by magistrates and supplemented by experts.

[e] Chief town of Locri, near the Straits of Euboea.

1287 a

αἱρετώτερον μᾶλλον ἢ τῶν πολιτῶν ἕνα τινά, κατὰ
τὸν αὐτὸν δὲ λόγον τοῦτον, κἂν εἴ τινας ἄρχειν
βέλτιον, τούτους καταστατέον νομοφύλακας καὶ
ὑπηρέτας τοῖς νόμοις· ἀναγκαῖον γὰρ εἶναί τινας
ἀρχάς, ἀλλ' οὐχ ἕνα τοῦτον εἶναί φασι δίκαιον
ὁμοίων γε ὄντων πάντων. ἀλλὰ μὴν ὅσα γε μὴ 4
δοκεῖ δύνασθαι διορίζειν ὁ νόμος, οὐδ' ἄνθρωπος
25 ἂν δύναιτο γνωρίζειν. ἀλλ' ἐπίτηδες παιδεύσας ὁ
νόμος ἐφίστησι τὰ λοιπὰ 'τῇ δικαιοτάτῃ γνώμῃ'
κρίνειν καὶ διοικεῖν τοὺς ἄρχοντας, ἔτι δ' ἐπανορ-
θοῦσθαι δίδωσιν ὅ τι ἂν δόξῃ πειρωμένοις ἄμεινον
εἶναι τῶν κειμένων. ὁ μὲν οὖν τὸν νοῦν κελεύων
ἄρχειν δοκεῖ κελεύειν ἄρχειν τὸν θεὸν καὶ τὸν
νοῦν μόνους,[1] ὁ δ' ἄνθρωπον κελεύων προστίθησι
καὶ θηρίον· ἥ τε γὰρ ἐπιθυμία τοιοῦτον, καὶ ὁ
θυμὸς ἄρχοντας διαστρέφει καὶ τοὺς ἀρίστους
ἄνδρας. διόπερ ἄνευ ὀρέξεως νοῦς ὁ νόμος ἐστίν.
τὸ δὲ τῶν τεχνῶν εἶναι δοκεῖ παράδειγμα ψεῦδος, 5
ὅτι τὸ κατὰ γράμματα ἰατρεύεσθαι φαῦλον, ἀλλὰ[2]
αἱρετώτερον χρῆσθαι τοῖς ἔχουσι τὰς τέχνας. οἱ
μὲν γὰρ οὐδὲν διὰ φιλίαν παρὰ τὸν λόγον ποιοῦσιν,
ἀλλ' ἄρνυνται τὸν μισθὸν τοὺς κάμνοντας ὑγιά-
σαντες, οἱ δ' ἐν ταῖς πολιτικαῖς ἀρχαῖς πολλὰ πρὸς
ἐπήρειαν καὶ χάριν εἰώθασι πράττειν, ἐπεὶ καὶ
τοὺς ἰατροὺς ὅταν ὑποπτεύωσι πιστευθέντας[3] τοῖς
40 ἐχθροῖς διαφθείρειν διὰ κέρδος, τότε τὴν ἐκ τῶν

---

[1] τὸν νοῦν μόνους cod. Voss. Iul.: τοὺς νόμους cet.
[2] ἀλλὰ καὶ codd. plurimi.
[3] πεισθέντας Schneider.

---

[a] This formula came in the oath taken by the dicasts at
Athens.

[b] i.e. the practical sciences, of which medicine is taken as
an example.

it is preferable for the law to rule rather than any one
of the citizens, and according to this same principle,
even if it be better for certain men to govern, they
must be appointed as guardians of the laws and in
subordination to them; for there must be some
government, but it is clearly not just, men say, for
one person to be governor when all the citizens are
4 alike. It may be objected that any case which the
law appears to be unable to define, a human being
also would be unable to decide. But the law first
specially educates the magistrates for the purpose
and then commissions them to decide and administer
the matters that it leaves over " according to the best
of their judgement," [a] and furthermore it allows them
to introduce for themselves any amendment that experience leads them to think better than the established code. He therefore that recommends that *Law free
the law shall govern seems to recommend that God* *from human
and reason alone shall govern, but he that would* *passions.*
have man govern adds a wild animal also; for
appetite is like a wild animal, and also passion warps
the rule even of the best men. Therefore the law
5 is wisdom without desire. And there seems to be no *Physicians
truth in the analogy which argues from the arts [b]* *may ignore
that it is a bad thing to doctor oneself by book, but* *rules, but
preferable to employ the experts in the arts. For* *they are
free from
bias.*
they never act contrary to principle from motives of
friendship, but earn their fee when (for instance)
they have cured their patients, whereas holders of
political office usually do many things out of spite
and to win favour; since when people suspect even
the physicians of being in the confidence of their
enemies and of trying to make away with them for
gain, in that case they would sooner look up the treat-

1287 a
γραμμάτων θεραπείαν ζητήσαιεν ἂν μᾶλλον. ἀλλὰ 6
1287 b μὴν εἰσάγονταί γ᾽ ἐφ᾽ ἑαυτοὺς οἱ ἰατροὶ κάμνοντες
ἄλλους ἰατροὺς καὶ οἱ παιδοτρίβαι γυμναζόμενοι
παιδοτρίβας, ὡς οὐ δυνάμενοι κρίνειν τὸ ἀληθὲς
διὰ τὸ κρίνειν περί τε οἰκείων καὶ ἐν πάθει ὄντες.
ὥστε δῆλον ὅτι τὸ δίκαιον ζητοῦντες τὸ μέσον
5 ζητοῦσιν· ὁ γὰρ¹ νόμος τὸ μέσον. ἔτι κυριώτεροι
καὶ περὶ κυριωτέρων τῶν κατὰ γράμματα νόμων
οἱ κατὰ τὰ ἔθη εἰσίν, ὥστ᾽ εἰ τῶν κατὰ γράμματα
ἄνθρωπος ἄρχων ἀσφαλέστερος, ἀλλ᾽ οὐ τῶν κατὰ
τὸ ἔθος. ἀλλὰ μὴν οὐδὲ ῥᾴδιον ἐφορᾶν πολλὰ τὸν 7
ἕνα δεήσει ἄρα πλείονας εἶναι τοὺς ὑπ᾽ αὐτοῦ
10 καθισταμένους ἄρχοντας, ὥστε τί διαφέρει τοῦτο
ἐξ ἀρχῆς εὐθὺς ὑπάρχειν ἢ τὸν ἕνα καταστῆσαι
τοῦτον τὸν τρόπον; ἔτι, ὃ καὶ πρότερον εἰρημένον
ἐστίν, εἴπερ ὁ ἀνὴρ ὁ σπουδαῖος, διότι βελτίων,
ἄρχειν δίκαιος, τοῦ δὲ ἑνὸς οἱ δύο ἀγαθοὶ βελτίους·
τοῦτο γάρ ἐστι τὸ

σύν τε δύ᾽ ἐρχομένω

καὶ ἡ εὐχὴ τοῦ Ἀγαμέμνονος,

15   τοιοῦτοι δέκα μοι συμφράδμονες.

εἰσὶ δὲ καὶ νῦν περὶ ἐνίων αἱ ἀρχαὶ κύριαι κρίνειν,
ὥσπερ ὁ δικαστής, περὶ ὧν ὁ νόμος ἀδυνατεῖ
διορίζειν, ἐπεὶ περὶ ὧν γε δυνατός, οὐδεὶς ἀμφισβη-
τεῖ περὶ τούτων ὡς οὐκ ἂν ἄριστα ὁ νόμος ἄρξειε

¹ δὲ Thurot.

---

a Perhaps this should be ' and.'

b *i.e.* the rules of duty and of manners that are customary
but not embodied in legislation : *cf.* 1319 b 40.

c *Iliad* x. 224: the passage goes on καί τε πρὸ ὃ τοῦ
ἐνόησεν | ὅπως κέρδος ἔῃ, 'then one discerneth | Before the
other how advantage lieth.'   *d* *Iliad* ii. 372.

6 ment in the books. Yet certainly physicians themselves call in other physicians to treat them when they are ill, and gymnastic trainers put themselves under other trainers when they are doing exercises, believing that they are unable to judge truly because ^{Customary} they are judging about their own cases and when they are under the influence of feeling. Hence it is ^{judgement.} clear that when men seek for what is just they seek for what is impartial; for ^a the law is that which is impartial. Again, customary laws ^b are more sovereign and deal with more sovereign matters than written laws, so that if a human ruler is less liable to error than written laws, yet he is not less liable to error than the laws of custom. But also it is certainly not ^{To supple-} easy for the single ruler to oversee a multitude of ^{ment the law, several} things; it will therefore be necessary for the officials ^{heads better} appointed by him to be numerous; so that what ^{than one;} difference does it make whether this has been the arrangement immediately from the outset or the single ruler appoints them in this manner? Again, a thing that has also been said before, if the virtuous ^{c. x. § 5 fin.} man justly deserves to rule because he is better, yet two good men are better than one: for that is the meaning of the line ^c

> When two together go—

and of the prayer of Agamemnon ^d

> May ten such fellow-councillors be mine.

And even now the magistrates, like the Athenian dicast, have power to judge certain cases about which the law is unable to give a clear declaration, since nobody disputes that in matters about which it can do so the law would be the best ruler and judge.

καὶ κρίνειν. ἀλλ᾽ ἐπειδὴ τὰ μὲν ἐνδέχεται περι-
20 ληφθῆναι τοῖς νόμοις τὰ δ᾽ ἀδύνατα, ταῦτ᾽ ἐστὶν
ἃ ποιεῖ διαπορεῖν καὶ ζητεῖν πότερον τὸν ἄριστον
νόμον ἄρχειν αἱρετώτερον ἢ τὸν ἄνδρα τὸν ἄριστον.
περὶ ὧν γὰρ βουλεύονται νομοθετῆσαι τῶν ἀδυνάτων ἐστίν. οὐ τοίνυν τοῦτό γ᾽ ἀντιλέγουσιν, ὡς
25 οὐκ ἀναγκαῖον ἄνθρωπον εἶναι τὸν κρινοῦντα περὶ
τῶν τοιούτων, ἀλλ᾽ ὅτι οὐχ ἕνα μόνον ἀλλὰ πολλούς.
κρίνει γὰρ ἕκαστος ἄρχων πεπαιδευμένος ὑπὸ τοῦ
νόμου καλῶς, ἄτοπον δ᾽ ἴσως ἂν εἶναι δόξειεν εἰ
βέλτιον ἴδοι[1] τις δυοῖν ὄμμασι καὶ δυοῖν ἀκοαῖς
κρίνων καὶ πράττων[2] δυσὶ ποσὶ καὶ χεροῖν ἢ πολλοὶ
πολλοῖς, ἐπεὶ καὶ νῦν ὀφθαλμοὺς πολλοὺς οἱ
30 μόναρχοι ποιοῦσιν αὑτῶν καὶ ὦτα καὶ χεῖρας καὶ
πόδας, τοὺς γὰρ τῇ ἀρχῇ καὶ αὑτοῖς[3] φίλους ποιοῦνται συνάρχους. μὴ φίλοι μὲν οὖν ὄντες οὐ ποιήσουσι κατὰ τὴν τοῦ μονάρχου προαίρεσιν· εἰ δὲ
φίλοι κἀκείνου καὶ τῆς ἀρχῆς, ὅ γε φίλος ἴσος καὶ
ὅμοιος, ὥστ᾽ εἰ τούτους οἴεται δεῖν ἄρχειν, τοὺς
35 ἴσους καὶ ὁμοίους ἄρχειν οἴεται δεῖν ὁμοίως.

Ἃ μὲν οὖν οἱ διαμφισβητοῦντες πρὸς τὴν βασιλείαν λέγουσι, σχεδὸν ταῦτ᾽ ἐστίν.

Ἀλλ᾽ ἴσως ταῦτ᾽ ἐπὶ μὲν τινῶν ἔχει τὸν τρόπον
τοῦτον, ἐπὶ δὲ τινῶν οὐχ οὕτως. ἔστι γάρ τι
φύσει δεσποστὸν καὶ ἄλλο βασιλευτὸν καὶ ἄλλο
πολιτικόν, καὶ δίκαιον καὶ συμφέρον ἄλλο ἄλλοις[4]·
40 τυραννικὸν δ᾽ οὐκ ἔστι κατὰ φύσιν, οὐδὲ τῶν ἄλλων

---

[1] ἔχοι Susemihl.
[2] πράττει Conring.
[3] αὑτοῖς Mus. = αὐτοῖ, αὑτοὺς codd.
[4] ἄλλο ἄλλοις add. Richards.

8 But since, although some things can be covered by
the laws, other things cannot, it is the latter that
cause doubt and raise the question whether it is
preferable for the best law to rule or the best man.
For to lay down a law about things that are subjects
for deliberation is an impossibility. Therefore men
do not deny that it must be for a human being to
judge about such matters, but they say that it ought
not to be a single human being only but a number.
For the individual official judges well when he has
9 been instructed by the law, and it would doubtless
seem curious if a person saw better when judging
with two eyes and two organs of hearing and acting
with two feet and hands than many persons with
many, since even as it is monarchs make many eyes
and ears and hands and feet their own, for they adopt
persons that are friendly to their rule and to themselves as their fellow-rulers. Although therefore
if these assistants are not friendly they will not act
in conformity with the monarch's policy, if they are
friends of him and of his rule, well, a friend is one's
equal and like, so that if the monarch thinks that
his friends ought to rule he thinks that people who are
equal to and like himself ought to rule like himself.

This then more or less is the case advanced by
those who argue against kingship.

10 But perhaps, although this is a true account of the
matter in some cases, it does not apply in others. For
there is such a thing as being naturally fitted to be
controlled by a master, and in another case, to be
governed by a king, and in another, to exercise citizenship, and a different government is just and
expedient for different people ; but there is no such
thing as natural fitness for tyranny, nor for any other

and to apply it, safer than subordinates.

But Royalty desirable in cases of exceptional excellence.

269

1287 b

πολιτειῶν ὅσαι παρεκβάσεις εἰσίν, ταῦτα γὰρ
γίγνεται παρὰ φύσιν. ἀλλ' ἐκ τῶν εἰρημένων
1288 a γε φανερὸν ὡς ἐν μὲν τοῖς ὁμοίοις καὶ ἴσοις οὔτε
συμφέρον ἐστὶν οὔτε δίκαιον ἕνα κύριον εἶναι
πάντων, οὔτε μὴ νόμων ὄντων, ἀλλ' αὐτὸν ὡς ὄντα
νόμον, οὔτε νόμων ὄντων, οὔτε ἀγαθὸν ἀγαθῶν
οὔτε μὴ ἀγαθῶν μὴ ἀγαθόν, οὐδ' ἂν κατ' ἀρετὴν
5 ἀμείνων ᾖ, εἰ μὴ τρόπον τινά. τίς δ' ὁ τρόπος,
λεκτέον· εἴρηται δέ πως ἤδη καὶ πρότερον. πρῶτον 11
δὲ διοριστέον τί τὸ βασιλευτὸν καὶ τί τὸ ἀριστοκρατικὸν καὶ τί τὸ πολιτικόν. βασιλευτὸν μὲν
οὖν τὸ τοιοῦτόν ἐστι πλῆθος ὃ πέφυκε φέρειν
γένος ὑπερέχον κατ' ἀρετὴν πρὸς ἡγεμονίαν
10 πολιτικήν, ἀριστοκρατικὸν δὲ[1] ὃ πέφυκε φέρειν
πλῆθος ἄρχεσθαι δυνάμενον τὴν τῶν ἐλευθέρων
ἀρχὴν ὑπὸ τῶν κατ' ἀρετὴν ἡγεμονικῶν πρὸς
πολιτικὴν ἀρχήν, πολιτικὸν δὲ[2] ἐν ᾧ πέφυκεν
ἐγγίνεσθαι πλῆθος πολεμικὸν δυνάμενον ἄρχεσθαι
καὶ ἄρχειν κατὰ νόμον τὸν κατ' ἀξίαν δια-
15 νέμοντα τοῖς εὐπόροις τὰς ἀρχάς. ὅταν οὖν ᾖ 12
γένος ὅλον ἢ καὶ τῶν ἄλλων ἕνα τινὰ συμβῇ
διαφέροντα γενέσθαι κατ' ἀρετὴν τοσοῦτον ὥσθ'
ὑπερέχειν τὴν ἐκείνου τῆς τῶν ἄλλων πάντων, τότε
δίκαιον τὸ γένος εἶναι τοῦτο βασιλικὸν καὶ κύριον
πάντων καὶ βασιλέα τὸν ἕνα τοῦτον. καθάπερ γὰρ
20 εἴρηται πρότερον, οὐ μόνον οὕτως ἔχει κατὰ τὸ
δίκαιον ὃ προφέρειν εἰώθασιν οἱ τὰς πολιτείας

---

[1] δὲ ed.: δὲ πλῆθος codd. (ὃ—πλῆθος secl. Victorius).
[2] δὲ ed.: δὲ πλῆθος codd. (ἐν ᾧ—πολεμικὸν secl. Hercher).

---

[a] The clause translated 'that—populace' some editors
excise as a superfluous insertion.
[b] They also excise 'in which—populace.'

of the forms of government that are divergences, for these come about against nature. But merely from what has been said, it is clear that among people who are alike and equal it is neither expedient nor just for one to be sovereign over all—neither when there are no laws, but he himself is in the place of law, nor when there are laws, neither when both sovereign and subjects are good nor when both are bad, nor yet when the sovereign is superior in virtue, except in a certain manner. What this manner is must be stated ; and in a way it has been 11 stated already even before. But first we must define what constitutes fitness for royal government, what fitness for aristocracy, and what for a republic. A fit subject for royal government is a populace of such a sort as to be naturally capable of producing a family of outstanding excellence for political leadership ; a community fit for aristocracy is one that naturally produces a populace*a* capable of being governed under the form of government fit for free men by those who are fitted by virtue for taking the part of leaders in constitutional government ; a republican community, one in which there naturally grows up a military populace *b* capable of being governed and of governing under a law that distributes the offices among the 12 well-to-do in accordance with merit. When therefore it comes about that there is either a whole family or even some one individual that differs from the other citizens in virtue so greatly that his virtue exceeds that of all the others, then it is just for this family to be the royal family or this individual king, and sovereign over all matters. For, as has been said before, this holds good not only in accordance with the right that is usually brought forward by those

1288 a

καθιστάντες οἵ τε τὰς ἀριστοκρατικὰς καὶ οἱ τὰς
ὀλιγαρχικάς, καὶ πάλιν οἱ τὰς δημοκρατικάς
(πάντες γὰρ καθ᾽ ὑπεροχὴν ἀξιοῦσιν ἀλλ᾽ ὑπεροχὴν
οὐ τὴν αὐτήν), ἀλλὰ «καὶ»¹ κατὰ τὸ πρότερον
25 λεχθέν. οὔτε γὰρ κτείνειν ἢ φυγαδεύειν οὐδ᾽ 11
ὀστρακίζειν δή που τὸν τοιοῦτον πρέπον ἐστίν,
οὔτ᾽ ἀξιοῦν ἄρχεσθαι κατὰ μέρος· οὐ γὰρ πέφυκε
τὸ μέρος ὑπερέχειν τοῦ παντός, τῷ δὲ τηλικαύτην
ὑπερβολὴν ἔχοντι τοῦτο συμβέβηκεν. ὥστε λείπεται
μόνον τὸ πείθεσθαι τῷ τοιούτῳ, καὶ κύριον εἶναι
μὴ ᾗ κατὰ μέρος τοῦτον ἀλλ᾽ ἁπλῶς.

30 Περὶ μὲν οὖν βασιλείας, τίνας ἔχει διαφοράς,
καὶ πότερον οὐ συμφέρει ταῖς πόλεσιν ἢ συμφέρει,
καὶ τίσι, καὶ πῶς, διωρίσθω τὸν τρόπον τοῦτον.

XII. Ἐπεὶ δὲ τρεῖς φαμὲν εἶναι τὰς ὀρθὰς 1
πολιτείας, τούτων δ᾽ ἀναγκαῖον ἀρίστην εἶναι τὴν
ὑπὸ τῶν ἀρίστων οἰκονομουμένην, τοιαύτη δ᾽ ἐστὶν
35 ἐν ᾗ συμβέβηκεν ἢ ἕνα τινὰ συμπάντων ἢ γένος
ὅλον ἢ πλῆθος ὑπερέχον εἶναι κατ᾽ ἀρετήν, τῶν
μὲν ἄρχεσθαι δυναμένων τῶν δ᾽ ἄρχειν πρὸς τὴν
αἱρετωτάτην ζωήν, ἐν δὲ τοῖς πρώτοις ἐδείχθη
λόγοις ὅτι τὴν αὐτὴν ἀναγκαῖον ἀνδρὸς ἀρετὴν
εἶναι καὶ πολίτου τῆς πόλεως τῆς ἀρίστης, φανερὸν
40 ὅτι τὸν αὐτὸν τρόπον καὶ διὰ τῶν αὐτῶν ἀνήρ τε
γίνεται σπουδαῖος καὶ πόλιν συστήσειεν ἄν τις
ἀριστοκρατουμένην² ἢ βασιλευομένην, ὥστ᾽ ἔσται 2

---

¹ ἀλλὰ καὶ ? Γ (immo Guil.).
² ⟨ἀριστ᾽ ἢ⟩ ἀριστοκρατουμένην Buecheler.

ᵃ i.e. the right of merit, c. viii. § 7.
ᵇ Bk. III. cc. ii., iii.
ᶜ Perhaps the Greek should be altered to give " establish a

302

who are founding aristocratic and oligarchic constitutions, and from the other side by those who are
founding democratic ones (for they all make their
claim on the ground of superiority, though not the
same superiority), but it also holds good in accordance
with the right spoken of before.[a]   For it is not seemly
to put to death or banish, nor yet obviously to ostracize, such a man, nor is it seemly to call upon him
to take his turn as a subject ; for it is not in the order
of nature for the part to overtop the whole, but the
man that is so exceptionally outstanding has come
to overtop the whole community. Hence it only
remains for the community to obey such a man, and
for him to be sovereign not in turn but absolutely.

Let this be our answer to the questions as regards
kingship, what are its varieties, and whether it is
disadvantageous for states or advantageous, and for
what states, and under what conditions.

XII. And since we pronounce the right constitutions Recapitula-
to be three, and of these the one governed by the best tion.
men must necessarily be the best, and such is the
one in which it has come about either that some one
man or a whole family or a group of men is superior
in virtue to all the citizens together, the latter being
able to be governed and the former to govern on the
principles of the most desirable life, and since in the
first part of the discourse[b] it was proved that the virtue
of a man and that of a citizen in the best state must
of necessity be the same, it is evident that a man
becomes good in the same way and by the same
means as one might establish an aristocratically or
monarchically governed state,[c] so that it will be

state governed in the best way by an aristocracy or a
monarchy.'

273

1288 b καὶ παιδεία καὶ ἔθη ταὐτὰ σχεδὸν τὰ ποιοῦντα σπουδαῖον ἄνδρα καὶ τὰ ποιοῦντα πολιτικὸν καὶ βασιλικόν.

Διωρισμένων δὲ τούτων περὶ τῆς πολιτείας ἤδη πειρατέον λέγειν τῆς ἀρίστης, τίνα πέφυκε γίνεσθαι 5 τρόπον καὶ καθίστασθαι πῶς. [ἀνάγκη δὴ τὸν μέλλοντα περὶ αὐτῆς ποιήσασθαι τὴν προσήκουσαν σκέψιν. . . .¹]

¹ partem exordii libri VII. admodum uariatam huc transtulerunt codd.

ᵃ The concluding sentence, by whomever written, clearly leads on to the Book that is No. VII. in the mss. and in this edition; and after it the mss. add half the first sentence of that Book, slightly altered. Some editors therefore transfer Books VII. and VIII. here and put Books IV., V. and VI. after them; opinions vary as to the proper order of Books IV., V. and VI. among themselves.

almost the same education and habits that make a man good and that make him capable as a citizen or a king.

These conclusions having been laid down, we must now endeavour to discuss the best form of constitution and to say in what way it is natural for it to come into existence and how it is natural for it to be organized.[a]

ADDITIONAL NOTES

III. ii. 3, 1276 b 38. If we emend the text with Bernays to εἰ γὰρ δύνατον ἐξ ἁπάντων σπουδαίων ὄντων εἶναι πόλιν, the sense is: assuming the possibility of a perfect state, with all its factors the best of their kind, this means that all the population will be good citizens, not that they will all be perfect specimens of the human race, because the state needs citizens of the working classes, etc., and these cannot in the nature of things be perfect human beings.

III. iii. 1, 1277 b 38 οὗτος γὰρ πολίτης. The translation takes πολίτης as subject and οὗτος as predicate (meaning ἔχων τὴν τοιαύτην ἀρετήν, possessing capacity to govern). But possibly the predicate is πολίτης and the subject οὗτος, which then stands for ὁ βάναυσος; if so, the whole sentence means that if the non-official classes are citizens, not all the citizens will possess civic virtue (which is capacity to govern), for the working-man will be a citizen (and he is not capable of governing).

10   I. Ἐν ἁπάσαις ταῖς τέχναις καὶ ταῖς ἐπιστήμαις 1
ταῖς μὴ κατὰ μόριον γινομέναις ἀλλὰ περὶ γένος
ἕν τι τελείαις οὔσαις, μιᾶς ἐστι θεωρῆσαι τὸ περὶ
ἕκαστον γένος[1] ἁρμόττον, οἷον ἄσκησις σώματι
ποία τε ποίῳ συμφέρει καὶ τίς ἀρίστη (τῷ γὰρ
κάλλιστα πεφυκότι καὶ κεχορηγημένῳ τὴν ἀρίστην
15 ἀναγκαῖον ἁρμόττειν), καὶ τίς τοῖς πλείστοις μία
πᾶσιν (καὶ γὰρ τοῦτο τῆς γυμναστικῆς ἐστιν), ἔτι
δ᾽ ἐάν τις μὴ τῆς ἱκνουμένης ἐπιθυμῇ μήθ᾽ ἕξεως
μήτ᾽ ἐπιστήμης τῶν περὶ τὴν ἀγωνίαν, μηδὲν[2]
ἧττον τοῦ παιδοτρίβου καὶ τοῦ γυμναστικοῦ παρασκευάσαι γε[3] καὶ ταύτην ἐστὶ τὴν δύναμιν· ὁμοίως 2
20 δὲ τοῦτο καὶ περὶ ἰατρικὴν καὶ περὶ ναυπηγίαν καὶ
ἐσθῆτα καὶ περὶ πᾶσαν ἄλλην τέχνην ὁρῶμεν συμβαῖνον. ὥστε δῆλον ὅτι καὶ πολιτείαν[a] τῆς αὐτῆς
ἐστὶν ἐπιστήμης τὴν ἀρίστην θεωρῆσαι τίς ἐστι
καὶ ποία τις ἂν οὖσα μάλιστ᾽ εἴη κατ᾽ εὐχὴν μηδενὸς ἐμποδίζοντος τῶν ἐκτός, καὶ τίς τίσιν ἁρμότ-

---

[1] γένος secl. Spengel.
[2] οὐδὲν Bk² (μηδὲν ἧττον cum praecedentibus Immisch, tr. infra post δύναμιν Richards).
[3] γε Coraes (tr. supra, τοῦ γε παιδοτρίβου Richards): τε codd.

---

[a] Transposed as Book VI. by some editors : see p. 274 n.
[b] Perhaps the Greek should be altered to give ' to each individual.'

276

BOOK IV[a]

I. In all the arts and the sciences that are not merely sectional but that in relation to some one class of subject are complete, it is the function of a single art or science to study what is suited to each class,[b] for instance what sort of gymnastic exercise is beneficial for what sort of bodily frame, and what is the best sort (for the best must naturally suit the person of the finest natural endowment and equipment), and also what one exercise taken by all is the best for the largest number (for this is also a question for gymnastic science), and in addition, in case someone desires a habit of body and a knowledge of athletic exercises that are not the ones adapted to him, it is clearly the task of the trainer and gymnastic master to produce this capacity[c] also just as much; and we notice this also happening similarly in regard to medicine, and ship-building, and the making of clothes, and every other craft. Hence it is clear that in the case of the constitution as well it is the business of the same science to study which is the best constitution and what character it must have to be the most ideal if no external circumstance stands in the way, and what constitution is adapted to what

Book IV.
Existing
Constitu-
tions.
Science
studies not
only (1) the
ideal but
also (2) the
best under
given
conditions
or character
or (3) of
resources, or
(4) the best
practicable
on the
average.

[c] *i.e.* a bodily bearing and athletic skill that are not the ones most suited to the pupil's particular physique.

1288 b

25 τουσα (πολλοῖς γὰρ τῆς ἀρίστης τυχεῖν ἴσως
ἀδύνατον, ὥστε τὴν κρατίστην τε ἁπλῶς καὶ τ˙
ἐκ τῶν ὑποκειμένων ἀρίστην οὐ δεῖ λεληθέναι το.
νομοθέτην καὶ τὸν ὡς ἀληθῶς πολιτικόν), ἔτι δὲ
τρίτην τὴν ἐξ ὑποθέσεως (δεῖ γὰρ καὶ τὴν δοθεῖσαν
δύνασθαι θεωρεῖν, ἐξ ἀρχῆς τε πῶς ἂν γένοιτο καὶ
30 γενομένη τίνα τρόπον ἂν σῴζοιτο πλεῖστον χρόνον·
λέγω δ᾽ οἷον εἴ τινι πόλει συμβέβηκε μήτε τὴν
ἀρίστην πολιτείαν πολιτεύεσθαι ἀχορήγητόν τε
εἶναι καὶ τῶν ἀναγκαίων, μήτε τὴν ἐνδεχομένην ἐκ
τῶν ὑπαρχόντων, ἀλλά τινα φαυλοτέραν)· παρὰ
πάντα δὲ ταῦτα τὴν μάλιστα πάσαις ταῖς πόλεσιν
35 ἁρμόττουσαν δεῖ γνωρίζειν, ὡς οἱ πλεῖστοι τῶν
ἀποφαινομένων περὶ πολιτείας, καὶ εἰ τἆλλα λέγουσι
καλῶς, τῶν γε χρησίμων διαμαρτάνουσιν. οὐ γὰρ
μόνον τὴν ἀρίστην δεῖ θεωρεῖν, ἀλλὰ καὶ τὴν
δυνατήν, ὁμοίως δὲ καὶ τὴν ῥᾴω καὶ κοινοτέραν
ἁπάσαις. νῦν δ᾽ οἱ μὲν τὴν ἀκροτάτην καὶ δεο-
40 μένην πολλῆς χορηγίας ζητοῦσι μόνον· οἱ δὲ μᾶλλον κοινήν τινα λέγοντες τὰς ὑπαρχούσας ἀναι-
1289 a ροῦντες πολιτείας τὴν Λακωνικὴν ἤ τινα ἄλλην
ἐπαινοῦσιν· χρὴ δὲ τοιαύτην εἰσηγεῖσθαι τάξιν
ἧς¹ ῥᾳδίως ἐκ τῶν ὑπαρχόντων² καὶ πεισθήσονται
καὶ δυνήσονται κοινωνεῖν,³ ὡς ἔστιν οὐκ ἔλαττον
ἔργον τὸ ἐπανορθῶσαι πολιτείαν ἢ κατασκευάζειν

---

¹ ἧς ed.: ἢν codd.
² ὑπαρχόντων Wilamowitz: ὑπαρχουσῶν codd.
³ κινεῖν MP¹.

ᵃ The fourfold classification given just before is repeated
in rather loose terms in this sentence.
ᵇ The word originally denoted the duty of the wealthy
citizen holding the office of Choregus to supply dresses, etc.,
for the chorus and actors in a drama.

people (since for many it is doubtless impossible to attain the best one, so that the good lawgiver and the true statesman must be acquainted with both the form of constitution that is the highest absolutely and that which is best under assumed conditions), 3) and also thirdly the form of constitution based on a certain supposition (for he must be also capable of considering both how some given constitution could be brought into existence originally and also in what way having been brought into existence it could be preserved for the longest time : I mean for example if it has befallen some state not only not to possess the best constitution and to be unprovided even with the things necessary for it, but also not to have the constitution that is practicable under the 3 circumstances but an inferior one) ; and beside all 4) these matters he must ascertain the form of constitution most suited to all states, since most of those who make pronouncements about the constitution, even if the rest of what they say is good, entirely miss the points of practical utility. For it is proper) to consider [a] not only what is the best constitution but) also what is the one possible of achievement, and) likewise also what is the one that is easier and more) generally shared by all states. But as it is, some students inquire which is the highest form of all even though requiring much material equipment,[b] while those who rather state some general form sweep aside the constitutions actually existing and praise that of Sparta or some other ; but the proper course is to bring forward an organization of such a sort that men will easily be persuaded and be able in the existing circumstances to take part in it, since to reform a constitution is no less a task than to frame

1289 a

ἐξ ἀρχῆς, ὥσπερ καὶ τὸ μεταμανθάνειν τοῦ μανθάνειν ἐξ ἀρχῆς· διὸ πρὸς τοῖς εἰρημένοις καὶ ταῖς
ὑπαρχούσαις πολιτείαις δεῖ δύνασθαι βοηθεῖν τὸν
πολιτικόν, καθάπερ ἐλέχθη καὶ πρότερον. τοῦτο
δὲ ἀδύνατον ἀγνοοῦντα πόσα πολιτείας ἐστὶν εἴδη·
νῦν δὲ μίαν δημοκρατίαν οἴονταί τινες εἶναι καὶ
μίαν ὀλιγαρχίαν, οὐκ ἔστι δὲ τοῦτ' ἀληθές. ὥστε 5
δεῖ τὰς διαφορὰς μὴ λανθάνειν τὰς τῶν πολιτειῶν,
πόσαι, καὶ συντίθενται ποσαχῶς. μετὰ δὲ ταῦτα[1]
τῆς αὐτῆς φρονήσεως ταύτης καὶ νόμους τοὺς
ἀρίστους ἰδεῖν καὶ τοὺς ἑκάστῃ τῶν πολιτειῶν
ἁρμόττοντας. πρὸς γὰρ τὰς πολιτείας τοὺς νόμους
δεῖ τίθεσθαι καὶ τίθενται πάντες, ἀλλ' οὐ τὰς πολιτείας πρὸς τοὺς νόμους· πολιτεία μὲν γάρ ἐστι
τάξις ταῖς πόλεσιν ἡ περὶ τὰς ἀρχάς, τίνα τρόπον
νενέμηνται, καὶ τί τὸ κύριον τῆς πολιτείας καὶ τί
τὸ τέλος ἑκάστης τῆς κοινωνίας ἐστίν, νόμοι δὲ
κεχωρισμένοι τῶν δηλούντων τὴν πολιτείαν, καθ'
οὓς δεῖ τοὺς ἄρχοντας ἄρχειν καὶ φυλάττειν τοὺς
παραβαίνοντας αὐτούς. ὥστε δῆλον ὅτι τὰς δια- 6
φορὰς ἀναγκαῖον καὶ τὸν ἀριθμὸν ἔχειν τῆς πολιτείας ἑκάστης καὶ πρὸς τὰς τῶν νόμων θέσεις·
οὐ γὰρ οἷόν τε τοὺς αὐτοὺς νόμους συμφέρειν ταῖς
ὀλιγαρχίαις οὐδὲ ταῖς δημοκρατίαις πάσαις, εἴπερ
δὴ πλείους[2] καὶ μὴ μία δημοκρατία μηδὲ ὀλιγαρχία
μόνον ἐστίν.

II. Ἐπεὶ δ' ἐν τῇ πρώτῃ μεθόδῳ περὶ τῶν πολι- 1
τειῶν διειλόμεθα τρεῖς μὲν τὰς ὀρθὰς πολιτείας,

---

[1] μετὰ δὲ ταῦτα anon. apud Stahr: μετὰ δὲ codd.
[2] πλείω codd. cet. (εἴπερ εἴδη πλείω Spengel).

* Book III. c. v.

one from the beginning, just as to re-learn a science
is just as hard as to learn it originally ; in addition
therefore to the things mentioned the student of
politics must also be able to render aid to the constitutions that exist already, as was also said before.[a] §§ 2 ff., 3.
But this is impossible if he does not know how many
kinds of constitution there are ; but at present some
people think that there is only one kind of democracy
5 and one kind of oligarchy, but this is not true.   Hence
he must take in view the different varieties of the
constitutions, and know how many there are and
how many are their combinations.   And after this
it needs this same discrimination also to discern the
laws that are the best, and those that are suited to
each of the forms of constitution.   For the laws
should be laid down, and all people lay them down,
to suit the constitutions—the constitutions must not
be made to suit the laws; for a constitution is the
regulation of the offices of the state in regard to the
mode of their distribution and to the question what
is the sovereign power in the state and what is the
object of each community, but laws are distinct
from the principles of the constitution, and regulate
how the magistrates are to govern and to guard
against those who transgress them.   So that clearly
it is necessary to be in possession of the different
varieties of each form of constitution, and the
number of these, even for the purpose of legislation ; for it is impossible for the same laws to be
expedient for all oligarchies or democracies if there
are really several kinds of them, and not one sort
of democracy or oligarchy only.

II. And inasmuch as in our first inquiry [a] about Contents of
the forms of the constitution we classified the right Books IV.,
V., VI.

1289 a

βασιλείαν ἀριστοκρατίαν πολιτείαν, τρεῖς δὲ τὰς
τούτων παρεκβάσεις, τυραννίδα μὲν βασιλείας
30 ὀλιγαρχίαν δὲ ἀριστοκρατίας δημοκρατίαν δὲ
πολιτείας, καὶ περὶ μὲν ἀριστοκρατίας καὶ βασιλείας εἴρηται (τὸ γὰρ περὶ τῆς ἀρίστης πολιτείας
θεωρῆσαι ταὐτὸ καὶ περὶ τούτων ἐστὶν εἰπεῖν τῶν
ὀνομάτων, βούλεται γὰρ ἑκατέρα κατ' ἀρετὴν
συνεστάναι κεχορηγημένην), ἔτι δὲ τί διαφέρουσιν
35 ἀλλήλων ἀριστοκρατία καὶ βασιλεία καὶ πότε δεῖ
βασιλείαν νομίζειν διώρισται πρότερον, λοιπὸν
περὶ πολιτείας διελθεῖν τῆς τῷ κοινῷ προσ-
αγορευομένης ὀνόματι, καὶ περὶ τῶν ἄλλων πολιτειῶν, ὀλιγαρχίας τε καὶ δημοκρατίας καὶ τυραννίδος. φανερὸν μὲν οὖν καὶ τούτων τῶν παρεκ-
βάσεων τίς χειρίστη καὶ δευτέρα τίς. ἀνάγκη
40 γὰρ τὴν μὲν τῆς πρώτης καὶ θειοτάτης παρέκβασιν
εἶναι χειρίστην, τὴν δὲ βασιλείαν ἀναγκαῖον ἢ
1289 b τοὔνομα μόνον ἔχειν οὐκ οὖσαν ἢ διὰ πολλὴν
ὑπεροχὴν εἶναι τὴν τοῦ βασιλεύοντος· ὥστε τὴν
τυραννίδα χειρίστην οὖσαν πλεῖστον ἀπέχειν πολιτείας, δεύτερον δὲ τὴν ὀλιγαρχίαν (ἡ γὰρ ἀριστοκρατία διέστηκεν ἀπὸ ταύτης πολὺ τῆς πολιτείας),
5 μετριωτάτην δὲ τὴν δημοκρατίαν. ἤδη μὲν οὖν
τις ἀπεφήνατο καὶ τῶν πρότερον οὕτως, οὐ μὴν
εἰς ταὐτὸ βλέψας ἡμῖν· ἐκεῖνος μὲν γὰρ ἔκρινε
πασῶν μὲν οὐσῶν ἐπιεικῶν, οἷον ὀλιγαρχίας τε

---

^a *i.e.* πολιτεία, 'polity,' which denotes not only a constitu-
tion of any form, but also (like our term 'constitutiona'
government') a particular form, viz., a republic, *cf.* Bk. III
c. v. § 2.

^b The three forms of constitution last mentioned.

^c *Corruptio optimi pessima,* a Socratic notion: 'the mer

nstitutions as three, kingship, aristocracy and Four constitutions and constitutional government, and the deviations from remain to be ese as three, tyranny from kingship, oligarchy from discussed. istocracy and democracy from constitutional government, and about aristocracy and kingship we have oken (for to study the best constitution is the same Book III. ing as to speak about the forms that bear those cc. ix.-xii. mes, since each of them means a system based on e qualification of virtue equipped with means), d as also the question what constitutes the differ- ce between aristocracy and kingship and when a yal government is to be adopted has been de- ded before, it remains to discuss the form of con- III. xi. 2. itution designated by the name *a* common to them l, and the other forms, oligarchy, democracy and ranny. Now it is manifest also which of these Their order viations *b* is the worst and which the second worst. of merit. r necessarily the deviation from the first and most vine must be the worst,*c* and kingship must of cessity either possess the name only, without ally being kingship, or be based on the outstanding periority of the man who is king; so that tyranny ing the worst form must be the one farthest moved from constitutional government, and olig- chy must be the second farthest (for aristocracy widely separated from that constitution), while mocracy must be the most moderate. An account their relative merits has indeed already been ven also by one of the former writers,*d* though not the same principle as ours; for he inclined to dge that there were good varieties of all the forms,

the best natural gifts, when uneducated, are the worst,'
n. *Mem.* iv. 1. 3.
d Plato, *Politicus* 302 ᴀ ff.

χρηστῆς καὶ τῶν ἄλλων, χειρίστην δημοκρατία
φαύλων δὲ ἀρίστην, ἡμεῖς δὲ ὅλως ταύτας ἐξημαρτι
10 μένας εἶναί φαμεν, καὶ βελτίω μὲν ὀλιγαρχίαν ἄλλ
ἄλλης οὐ καλῶς ἔχειν[1] λέγειν, ἧττον δὲ φαύλη
ἀλλὰ περὶ μὲν τῆς τοιαύτης κρίσεως ἀφείσθ
τὰ νῦν· ἡμῖν δὲ πρῶτον μὲν διαιρετέον πόσαι δι
φοραὶ τῶν πολιτειῶν, εἴπερ ἔστιν εἴδη πλείονα τ
τε δημοκρατίας καὶ τῆς ὀλιγαρχίας, ἔπειτα τ
15 κοινοτάτη, καὶ τίς αἱρετωτάτη μετὰ τὴν ἀρίστ
πολιτείαν, κἂν εἴ τις ἄλλη τετύχηκεν ἀριστοκρατι
καὶ συνεστῶσα καλῶς, ἀλλ' οὐ[2] ταῖς πλείσταις ἁ
μόττουσα πόλεσι, τίς ἐστιν, ἔπειτα καὶ τῶν ἄλλ
τίς τίσιν αἱρετή (τάχα γὰρ τοῖς μὲν ἀναγκαία δημ
κρατία μᾶλλον ὀλιγαρχίας, τοῖς δ' αὕτη μᾶλλ
20 ἐκείνης), μετὰ δὲ ταῦτα τίνα τρόπον δεῖ καθιστάν
τὸν βουλόμενον ταύτας τὰς πολιτείας, λέγω
δημοκρατίας τε καθ' ἕκαστον εἶδος καὶ πάλιν ὀλι
αρχίας, τέλος δέ, πάντων τούτων ὅταν ποιησώμε
συντόμως τὴν ἐνδεχομένην μνείαν, πειρατέον ἐ
ἐλθεῖν τίνες φθοραὶ καὶ τίνες σωτηρίαι τῶν πολ
25 τειῶν καὶ κοινῇ καὶ χωρὶς ἑκάστης, καὶ διὰ τίν
αἰτίας ταῦτα μάλιστα γίνεσθαι πέφυκεν.

III. Τοῦ μὲν οὖν εἶναι πλείους πολιτείας αἴτι
ὅτι πάσης ἐστὶ μέρη πλείω πόλεως τὸν ἀριθμό
πρῶτον μὲν γὰρ ἐξ οἰκιῶν συγκειμένας πάσα
30 ὁρῶμεν τὰς πόλεις, ἔπειτα πάλιν τούτου τ
πλήθους τοὺς μὲν εὐπόρους ἀναγκαῖον εἶναι τοὺ

_____
[1] Richards: ἔχει codd.   [2] οὐ add. Coraes (cf. 1295 a 31 f
284

for instance a good sort of oligarchy and so on, and
that democracy was the worst among these, but the
best among the bad varieties, whereas we say that
the deviations are wholly wrong, and that it is not
right to speak of one form of oligarchy as better than
another, but only as less bad. But let us for the
present dismiss the question of a classification of this
nature. Our business is first to distinguish how many
different forms of the constitutions there are, assuming that there do exist several kinds of democracy
and of oligarchy; next, which form is most general,
and which most desirable after the best constitution,
and also if there exists some other form that is
aristocratic in nature and well constructed but not
fitted to the largest number of cities, which this
is; next, which of the other forms too is desirable
for what people (since probably for some democracy
is necessary more than oligarchy, and for others
oligarchy more than democracy); and after this,
in what way should one proceed who wishes to set
up these constitutions, I mean the various forms of
democracy and of oligarchy; and finally, when as
far as possible we have concisely touched upon all
these questions, we must endeavour to review what
are the agencies that destroy and what are those
that preserve constitutions generally and each variety
of constitution in particular, and what are the causes
by which it is most natural for these events to be
brought about.

III. Now the reason of there being several forms
of constitution is that every city has a considerable
number of parts. For in the first place we see that
all the cities are composed of households, and then
again that of this multitude some must necessarily

1289 b

δ' ἀπόρους τοὺς δὲ μέσους, καὶ τῶν εὐπόρων δὲ
καὶ τῶν ἀπόρων τὸ μὲν ὁπλιτικὸν τὸ δὲ ἄνοπλον.
καὶ τὸν μὲν γεωργικὸν δῆμον ὁρῶμεν ὄντα, τὸν δ'
ἀγοραῖον, τὸν δὲ βάναυσον. καὶ τῶν γνωρίμων
εἰσὶ διαφοραὶ καὶ κατὰ τὸν πλοῦτον καὶ τὰ μεγέθη
35 τῆς οὐσίας (οἷον ἱπποτροφίας, τοῦτο γὰρ οὐ
ῥᾴδιον μὴ πλουτοῦντας ποιεῖν· διόπερ ἐπὶ τῶν
ἀρχαίων χρόνων ὅσαις πόλεσιν ἐν τοῖς ἵπποις ἡ
δύναμις ἦν, ὀλιγαρχίαι παρὰ τούτοις ἦσαν· ἐχρῶντο
δὲ πρὸς τοὺς πολέμους[1] ἵπποις πρὸς[2] τοὺς ἀστυγείτονας, οἷον Ἐρετριεῖς καὶ Χαλκιδεῖς καὶ
40 Μάγνητες οἱ ἐπὶ Μαιάνδρῳ καὶ τῶν ἄλλων πολλοὶ
περὶ τὴν Ἀσίαν). ἔτι πρὸς ταῖς κατὰ πλοῦτον δια-
1290 a φοραῖς ἐστὶν ἡ μὲν κατὰ γένος ἡ δὲ κατ' ἀρετήν,
κἂν εἴ τι δὴ τοιοῦτον ἕτερον εἴρηται πόλεως εἶναι
μέρος ἐν τοῖς περὶ τὴν ἀριστοκρατίαν (ἐκεῖ γὰρ
διειλόμεθα ἐκ πόσων μερῶν ἀναγκαίων ἐστὶ πᾶσα
πόλις)· τούτων γὰρ τῶν μερῶν ὁτὲ μὲν πάντα μετ-
5 έχει τῆς πολιτείας ὁτὲ δ' ἐλάττω ὁτὲ δὲ πλείω.
φανερὸν τοίνυν ὅτι πλείους ἀναγκαῖον εἶναι πολιτείας εἴδει διαφερούσας ἀλλήλων· καὶ γὰρ ταῦτ'
εἴδει διαφέρει τὰ μέρη σφῶν αὐτῶν. πολιτεία μὲν
γὰρ ἡ τῶν ἀρχῶν τάξις ἐστί, ταύτας[3] δὲ διανέμον-
ται πάντες ἢ κατὰ τὴν δύναμιν τῶν μετεχόντων ἢ
10 κατά τιν' αὐτῶν ἰσότητα κοινήν, λέγω δ' οἷον τῶν
ἀπόρων ἢ τῶν εὐπόρων ἢ κοινήν τιν' ἀμφοῖν.[4]
ἀναγκαῖον ἄρα πολιτείας εἶναι τοσαύτας ὅσαι περ

---

[1] πολέμους Γ (cf. 1330 a 18) : πολεμίους codd.
[2] [πρὸς] Immisch (cf. ibid.).
[3] Richards : ταύτην codd.   [4] [ἢ—ἀμφοῖν] Ramus.

ᵃ This clause looks like an interpolation.

be rich and some poor and some between the two, and also of the rich and the poor the former class is heavy-armed and the latter without armour. And we see that one portion of the common people is agricultural, another engaged in trade and another mechanic. And the upper classes have distinctions also corresponding to their wealth and the amounts of their property (for example in a stud of horses— for it is not easy to rear horses without being rich, and this is why in ancient times there were oligarchies in all the states whose strength lay in their cavalry, and they used to use horses for their wars against their neighbours, as for instance did the Eretrians 1306 a 35. and Chalcidians and the people of Magnesia on the Maeander and many of the other Asiatic peoples). Moreover in addition to differences in wealth there is the difference of birth, and that in regard to virtue, and indeed any other similar distinction that in the discussion of aristocracy has been stated to constitute a part of the state (for there we distinguished how many necessary parts there are of which every state must consist); for sometimes all of these parts participate in the constitution and sometimes a smaller or a larger number of them. It is clear therefore that there must necessarily be several forms of constitution differing in kind from one another, inasmuch as these parts differ in kind among themselves. For a constitution means the arrangement of the magistracies, and these all people distribute either according to the power of those who share political rights, or according to some common equality between them, I mean for example between the poor or between the rich, or some equality common to them both.[a] It follows therefore that there are as many forms of

τάξεις κατὰ τὰς ὑπεροχάς εἰσι καὶ κατὰ τὰς διαφορὰς τῶν μορίων. μάλιστα δὲ δοκοῦσιν εἶναι δύο
καθάπερ ἐπὶ τῶν πνευμάτων λέγεται τὰ μὲν βόρεια
τὰ δὲ νότια, τὰ δ᾽ ἄλλα τούτων παρεκβάσεις, οὕτω
καὶ τῶν πολιτειῶν δύο, δῆμος καὶ ὀλιγαρχία· τὴν
γὰρ ἀριστοκρατίαν τῆς ὀλιγαρχίας εἶδος τιθέασιν
ὡς οὖσαν ὀλιγαρχίαν τινά, καὶ τὴν καλουμένην
πολιτείαν δημοκρατίαν,[1] ὥσπερ ἐν τοῖς πνεύμασι
τὸν μὲν ζέφυρον τοῦ βορέου, τὸν δὲ νότον τοῦ
εὔρον. ὁμοίως δ᾽ ἔχει καὶ περὶ τὰς ἁρμονίας, ὥς
φασί τινες· καὶ γὰρ ἐκεῖ τίθενται εἴδη δύο, τὴν
δωριστὶ καὶ τὴν φρυγιστί, τὰ δὲ ἄλλα συντάγματα
τὰ μὲν Δώρια τὰ δὲ Φρύγια καλοῦσιν. μάλιστα μὲ-
οὖν εἰώθασιν οὕτως ὑπολαμβάνειν περὶ τῶν πολι-
τειῶν· ἀληθέστερον δὲ καὶ βέλτιον ὡς ἡμεῖς διείλομεν, δυοῖν ἢ μιᾶς οὔσης τῆς καλῶς συνεστηκυίας
τὰς ἄλλας εἶναι παρεκβάσεις, τὰς μὲν τῆς εὖ κε-
κραμένης [ἁρμονίας][2] τὰς δὲ τῆς ἀρίστης πολιτείας,
ὀλιγαρχικὰς μὲν τὰς συντονωτέρας καὶ δεσποτικωτέρας τὰς δ᾽ ἀνειμένας καὶ μαλακὰς δημοτικάς.

Οὐ δεῖ δὲ τιθέναι δημοκρατίαν, καθάπερ εἰώθασι
τινες νῦν, ἁπλῶς οὕτως, ὅπου κύριον τὸ πλῆθος
(καὶ γὰρ ἐν ταῖς ὀλιγαρχίαις καὶ πανταχοῦ τὸ
πλέον μέρος κύριον), οὐδ᾽ ὀλιγαρχίαν ὅπου κύριοι
ὀλίγοι τῆς πολιτείας. εἰ γὰρ εἶησαν οἱ πάντες
χίλιοι καὶ τριακόσιοι, καὶ τούτων οἱ χίλιοι πλούσιοι,

---

[1] δημοκρατίας Richards: ‹τῆς› δημ. ? ed.
[2] ἁρμονίας secl. Immisch.

---

[a] Aristotle refers to this view in *Meteorologica* 364 a 19
saying that west winds are classed with north and east winds
with south, because wind from the setting sun is cooler and
from the rising sun warmer. He notes that north and south

nstitution as there are modes of arrangement ccording to the superiorities and the differences of e sections. But the forms mostly are thought to be two—just as in the case of the winds we speak of some north and some as south and regard the rest as viations from these,[a] so also of constitutions there e held to be two forms, democracy and oligarchy ; r men reckon aristocracy as a kind of oligarchy cause it is oligarchy of a sort, and what is called nstitutional government as democracy, just as in e case of the winds they reckon the west wind a kind of north wind and the east wind as a nd of south wind. And the case is similar with usical modes, as some people say : for there too they sit two kinds, the Dorian mode and the Phrygian, d call the other scales some of them Dorian d the others Phrygian. For the most part there-re they are accustomed to think in this way about e constitutions ; but it is truer and better to class em as we did, and assuming that there are two well-nstructed forms, or else one, to say that the others e deviations, some from the well-blended constitu-n and the others from the best one, the more tense d masterful constitutions being oligarchic and the laxed and soft ones demotic.

But it is not right to define democracy, as some ople are in the custom of doing now, merely as the nstitution in which the multitude is sovereign (for en in oligarchies and everywhere the majority is vereign) nor oligarchy as the constitution in which ew are sovereign over the government. For if the ole number were thirteen hundred, and a thousand

Usual classification criticized.

c. 11.

Democracy and Oligarchy defined.

nds are the most frequent, *ib.* 361 a 6 ; this may have sug-ted the idea that they were the typical winds.

1290 a
καὶ μὴ μεταδιδοῖεν ἀρχῆς τοῖς τριακοσίοις κ
πένησιν ἐλευθέροις οὖσι καὶ τἆλλα ὁμοίοις, οὐθ
ἂν φαίη δημοκρατεῖσθαι τούτους· ὁμοίως δὲ κ
εἰ πένητες μὲν ὀλίγοι εἶεν, κρείττους δὲ
εὐπόρων πλειόνων ὄντων, οὐδεὶς ἂν ὀλιγαρχ
προσαγορεύσειεν οὐδὲ τὴν τοιαύτην εἰ τοῖς ἄλλο
40 οὖσι πλουσίοις μὴ μετείη τῶν τιμῶν. μᾶλλ
1290 b τοίνυν λεκτέον ὅτι δῆμος μέν ἐστιν ὅταν οἱ ἐλε
θεροι κύριοι ὦσιν ὀλιγαρχία δ' ὅταν οἱ πλούσι
ἀλλὰ συμβαίνει τοὺς μὲν πολλοὺς εἶναι τοὺς
ὀλίγους, ἐλεύθεροι μὲν γὰρ πολλοὶ πλούσιοι
ὀλίγοι. καὶ γὰρ ἂν εἰ κατὰ μέγεθος διενέμον
5 τὰς ἀρχάς, ὥσπερ ἐν Αἰθιοπίᾳ φασί τινες,[2] ἢ κα
κάλλος, ὀλιγαρχία ἦν ἄν, ὀλίγον γὰρ τὸ πλῆθ
καὶ τὸ τῶν καλῶν καὶ τὸ τῶν μεγάλων. οὐ μ
ἀλλ' οὐδὲ τούτοις μόνον ἱκανῶς ἔχει διωρίσ
τὰς πολιτείας ταύτας· ἀλλ' ἐπεὶ πλείονα μόρ
καὶ τοῦ δήμου καὶ τῆς ὀλιγαρχίας εἰσίν, ἔτι δ
10 ληπτέον ὡς οὔτ' ἂν οἱ ἐλεύθεροι ὀλίγοι ὄντ
πλειόνων καὶ μὴ ἐλευθέρων ἄρχωσι δῆμος, οἷ
ἐν Ἀπολλωνίᾳ τῇ ἐν τῷ Ἰονίῳ καὶ ἐν Θήρᾳ (ἐν τ
των γὰρ ἑκατέρα τῶν πόλεων ἐν ταῖς τιμαῖς ἦσ
οἱ διαφέροντες κατ' εὐγένειαν καὶ πρῶτοι κατ
σχόντες τὰς ἀποικίας, ὀλίγοι ὄντες πολλῶν), οὔτ
15 οἱ πλούσιοι διὰ τὸ κατὰ πλῆθος ὑπερέχειν, δῆμο
οἷον ἐν Κολοφῶνι τὸ παλαιόν (ἐκεῖ γὰρ ἐκέκτη
μακρὰν οὐσίαν οἱ πλείους πρὶν γενέσθαι τὸν π

---

¹ πολλοῖς Richards.   ² τινας ? Susemihl.
                      ³ ὀλιγαρχία Bojesen.

ᵃ e.g. Herodotus iii. 20.
ᵇ i.e. those of citizen birth.

of these were rich and did not give the three hundred
poor a share in the government although they were
free-born and like themselves in all other respects,
no one would say that this people was governed
democratically ; and similarly also if there were few
poor, but these more powerful than the rich who were
more numerous, no one would call such a government
a democracy either, if the other citizens being rich
had no share in the honours. Rather therefore ought
we to say that it is a democracy when the free are
sovereign and an oligarchy when the rich are, but
that it comes about that the sovereign class in a
democracy is numerous and that in an oligarchy
small because there are many men of free birth and
few rich. For otherwise, suppose people assigned
the offices by height, as some persons[a] say is done in
Ethiopia, or by beauty, that would be an oligarchy,
because both the handsome and the tall are few in
number. Nevertheless it is not enough to define
these constitutions even by wealth and free birth
only ; but inasmuch as there are more elements than
one both in democracy and in oligarchy, we must add
the further distinction that neither is it a democracy
if the free[b] being few govern the majority who are
not of free birth, as for instance at Apollonia on the
Ionian Gulf and at Thera (for in each of these cities
the offices of honour were filled by the specially
noble families who had been the first settlers of the
colonies, and these were few out of many), nor is it
a democracy[c] if the rich rule because they are in a
majority, as in ancient times at Colophon (for there
the majority of the population owned large property

[c] Perhaps the Greek should be altered here to give 'an
oligarchy.'

291

λεμον τὸν πρὸς Λυδούς), ἀλλ' ἔστι δημοκρατία
μὲν ὅταν οἱ ἐλεύθεροι καὶ ἄποροι πλείους ὄντες
κύριοι τῆς ἀρχῆς ὦσιν, ὀλιγαρχία δ' ὅταν ο[ἱ]
20 πλούσιοι καὶ εὐγενέστεροι ὀλίγοι ὄντες.

Ὅτι μὲν οὖν πολιτεῖαι πλείους, καὶ διὰ τίν' αἰτίαν
εἴρηται· διότι δὲ πλείους τῶν εἰρημένων, καὶ τίνε[ς]
καὶ διὰ τί, λέγωμεν ἀρχὴν λαβόντες τὴν εἰρημένη[ν]
πρότερον. ὁμολογοῦμεν γὰρ οὐχ ἓν μέρος ἀλλὰ
25 πλείω πᾶσαν ἔχειν πόλιν. ὥσπερ οὖν εἰ ζῷου
προῃρούμεθα λαβεῖν εἴδη, πρῶτον ἂν ἀποδιωρί-
ζομεν ὅπερ ἀναγκαῖον πᾶν ἔχειν ζῷον (οἷον ἔνι[α]
τε τῶν αἰσθητηρίων καὶ τὸ τῆς τροφῆς ἐργαστικὸ[ν]
καὶ δεκτικόν, οἷον στόμα καὶ κοιλίαν, πρὸς δ[ὲ]
τούτοις, οἷς κινεῖται μορίοις ἕκαστον αὐτῶν), ε[ἰ]
30 δὲ¹ τοσαῦτα εἴη² μόνον, τούτων δ' εἶεν διαφορα[ὶ]
(λέγω δ' οἷον στόματός τινα πλείω γένη καὶ κοιλία[ς]
καὶ τῶν αἰσθητηρίων, ἔτι δὲ καὶ τῶν κινητικῶ[ν]
μορίων), ὁ τῆς συζεύξεως τῆς τούτων ἀριθμὸς ἐ[ξ]
ἀνάγκης ποιήσει πλείω γένη ζῴων (οὐ γὰρ οἷό[ν]
τε ταὐτὸν ζῷον ἔχειν πλείους στόματος διαφοράς·
35 ὁμοίως δὲ οὐδ' ὤτων), ὥσθ' ὅταν ληφθῶσι τούτω[ν]
πάντες οἱ ἐνδεχόμενοι συνδυασμοὶ ποιήσουσιν εἴδ[η]
ζῴου, καὶ τοσαῦτ' εἴδη τοῦ ζῴου ὅσαπερ α[ἱ]
συζεύξεις τῶν ἀναγκαίων μορίων εἰσίν—τὸν αὐτὸ[ν]
δὴ³ τρόπον καὶ τῶν εἰρημένων πολιτειῶν. καὶ γὰ[ρ]
αἱ πόλεις οὐκ ἐξ ἑνὸς ἀλλ' ἐκ πολλῶν σύγκεινται

---

¹ δὲ Thurot : δὴ aut δεῖ codd.
² εἴη Newman : εἴδη codd.　　³ δὴ Coraes : δὲ codd[d.]

ᵃ See § 1.

efore the war against the Lydians took place), but
t is a democracy when those who are free are in the
majority and have sovereignty over the government,
nd an oligarchy when the rich and more well born
re few and sovereign.

It has then been stated that there are several forms
f constitution, and what is the cause of this ; but
et us take the starting-point that was laid down
efore *a* and say that there are more forms than those
mentioned, and what these forms are, and why they
vary. For we agree that every state possesses not
ne part but several. Therefore just as, in case we
ntended to obtain a classification of animals, we
hould first define the properties necessarily belonging
o every animal (for instance some of the sense-
organs, and the machinery for masticating and for
receiving food, such as a mouth and a stomach,
and in addition to these the locomotive organs of
he various species), and if there were only so many
necessary parts, but there were different varieties
of these (I mean for instance certain various kinds
f mouth and stomach and sensory organs, and also
of the locomotive parts as well), the number of poss-
ble combinations of these variations will necessarily
produce a variety of kinds of animals (for it is not
ossible for the same animal to have several different
orts of mouth, nor similarly of ears either), so that
when all the possible combinations of these are taken
hey will all produce animal species, and there will
e as many species of the animal as there are com-
inations of the necessary parts :—so in the same
vay also we shall classify the varieties of the constitutions that have been mentioned. For states
also are composed not of one but of several parts, as

Eight classes (not four, as Plato) compose the State.

293

1290 b

μερῶν, ὥσπερ εἴρηται πολλάκις. ἐν μὲν οὖν ἐσ[
τὸ περὶ τὴν τροφὴν πλῆθος, οἱ καλούμενοι γεωρ[

1291 a γοί, δεύτερον δὲ τὸ καλούμενον βάναυσον (ἔστι δ[
τοῦτο περὶ τὰς τέχνας ὧν ἄνευ πόλιν ἀδύνατον ο[
κεῖσθαι, τούτων δὲ τῶν τεχνῶν τὰς μὲν ἐξ ἀνάγκη[
ὑπάρχειν δεῖ, τὰς δὲ εἰς τρυφὴν ἢ τὸ καλῶς ζῆ[
5 τρίτον δ' ἀγοραῖον (λέγω δ' ἀγοραῖον τὸ περὶ τὰ[
πράσεις καὶ τὰς ὠνὰς καὶ τὰς ἐμπορίας κα[
καπηλείας διατρῖβον), τέταρτον δὲ τὸ θητικό[
πέμπτον δὲ γένος τὸ προπολεμῆσον, ὃ τούτων οὐθὲ[
ἧττόν ἐστιν ἀναγκαῖον ὑπάρχειν εἰ μέλλουσι μ[
δουλεύσειν τοῖς ἐπιοῦσιν· μὴ γὰρ ἓν τῶν ἀδυνάτω[
ἦ πόλιν ἄξιον εἶναι καλεῖν τὴν φύσει δούλη[
10 αὐτάρκης γὰρ ἡ πόλις τὸ δὲ δοῦλον οὐκ αὐτάρκε[
διόπερ ἐν τῇ πολιτείᾳ κομψῶς τοῦτο, οὐχ ἱκανῶ[
δὲ εἴρηται. φησὶ γὰρ ὁ Σωκράτης ἐκ τεττάρω[
τῶν ἀναγκαιοτάτων πόλιν συγκεῖσθαι, λέγει δ[
τούτους ὑφάντην καὶ γεωργὸν καὶ σκυτοτόμον κα[
15 οἰκοδόμον· πάλιν δὲ προστίθησιν, ὡς οὐχ αὐτάρκω[
τούτων, χαλκέα καὶ τοὺς ἐπὶ τοῖς ἀναγκαίο[
βοσκήμασιν, ἔτι δ' ἔμπορόν τε καὶ κάπηλον. κα[
ταῦτα πάντα γίνεται πλήρωμα τῆς πρώτης πόλεω[
ὡς τῶν ἀναγκαίων γε χάριν πᾶσαν πόλιν συν[
ἑστηκυῖαν ἀλλ' οὐ τοῦ καλοῦ μᾶλλον, ἴσον τ[
δεομένην σκυτέων τε καὶ γεωργῶν· τὸ δὲ προ[
20 πολεμοῦν οὐ πρότερον ἀποδίδωσι μέρος πρὶν ἢ τῆ[
χώρας αὐξομένης καὶ τῆς τῶν πλησίον ἀπτομένη[

---

[a] Plato, *Rep.* ii. 369 B–371 E.
[b] *i.e.* the first sketch of the City-state, *loc. cit.*

has been said often. One of these parts therefore
is the mass of persons concerned with food who are
called farmers, and second is what is called the
mechanic class (and this is the group engaged in the
arts without which it is impossible for a city to be
inhabited, and some of these arts are indispensably
necessary, while others contribute to luxury or noble
living), and third is a commercial class (by which I
mean the class that is engaged in selling and buying
and in wholesale and retail trade), and fourth is the
class of manual labourers, and the fifth class is the
one to defend the state in war, which is no less indispensable than the others if the people are not to
become the slaves of those who come against them ;
for surely it is quite out of the question that it should
be proper to give the name of state to a community
that is by nature a slave, for a state is self-sufficient,
but that which is a slave is not self-sufficient. Therefore the statement made in the *Republic* ^a is witty
but not adequate. For Socrates says that the most
necessary elements of which a state is composed are
four, and he specifies these as a weaver, a farmer, a
shoemaker and a builder ; and then again he adds,
on the ground that these are not self-sufficient, a
copper-smith and the people to look after the necessary live-stock, and in addition a merchant and a
retail trader. These elements together constitute
the full complement of his first city,^b implying that
every city is formed for the sake of the necessaries of
life and not rather for the sake of what is noble, and
that it has equal need of both shoemakers and farmers ;
but the warrior class he does not assign to it until as
the territory is increased and comes into contact
with that of the neighbours they are brought into

εἰς πόλεμον καταστῶσιν. ἀλλὰ μὴν καὶ ἐν τοῖς
τέτταρσι καὶ τοῖς ὁποσοισοῦν κοινωνοῖς ἀναγκαῖον
εἶναί τινα τὸν ἀποδώσοντα καὶ κρινοῦντα τὸ
δίκαιον· εἴπερ οὖν καὶ ψυχὴν ἄν τις θείη ζῴου
25 μόριον μᾶλλον ἢ σῶμα, καὶ πόλεων τὰ τοιαῦτα
μᾶλλον θετέον τῶν εἰς τὴν ἀναγκαίαν χρῆσιν συν-
τεινόντων, τὸ πολεμικὸν καὶ τὸ μετέχον δικαιοσύνης
δικαστικῆς, πρὸς δὲ τούτοις τὸ βουλευόμενον,
ὅπερ ἐστὶ συνέσεως πολιτικῆς ἔργον. καὶ ταῦτ'
εἴτε κεχωρισμένως[1] ὑπάρχει τισὶν εἴτε τοῖς αὐτοῖς,
30 οὐθὲν διαφέρει πρὸς τὸν λόγον· καὶ γὰρ ὁπλιτεύειν
καὶ γεωργεῖν συμβαίνει τοῖς αὐτοῖς πολλάκις.
ὥστε εἴπερ καὶ ταῦτα καὶ ἐκεῖνα θετέα μόρια τῆς
πόλεως, φανερὸν ὅτι τό γε ὁπλιτικὸν ἀναγκαῖόν
ἐστι μόριον τῆς πόλεως. ἕβδομον δὲ τὸ ταῖς οὐσίαις
λειτουργοῦν, ὃ καλοῦμεν εὐπόρους. ὄγδοον δὲ τὸ
35 δημιουργικὸν καὶ τὸ περὶ τὰς ἀρχὰς λειτουργοῦν,
εἴπερ ἄνευ ἀρχόντων ἀδύνατον εἶναι πόλιν· ἀναγκαῖον οὖν εἶναί τινας τοὺς δυναμένους ἄρχειν καὶ
λειτουργοῦντας ἢ συνεχῶς ἢ κατὰ μέρος τῇ πόλει
ταύτην τὴν λειτουργίαν. λοιπὰ δὲ περὶ ὧν τυγχάνομεν διωρικότες ἀρτίως, τὸ βουλευόμενον καὶ
40 τὸ[2] κρῖνον περὶ τῶν δικαίων τοῖς ἀμφισβητοῦσιν.
εἴπερ οὖν ταῦτα δεῖ γίνεσθαι[3] ταῖς πόλεσι καὶ
1291 b καλῶς γίνεσθαι[3] καὶ δικαίως, ἀναγκαῖον καὶ μετ-

---

[1] κεχωρισμένοις ? Richards.　　[2] καὶ τὸ ed.: καὶ codd.
[3] γίνεσθαι ed.: γενέσθαι codd.

---

[a] The first four classes and the military and judicial.

war. But yet even among the four partners or whatever their number be there must necessarily be somebody to assign justice and to judge their claims; inasmuch therefore as one would count the soul of an animal to be more a part of it than the body, so also the factors in states corresponding to the soul must be deemed to be parts of them more than those factors which contribute to necessary utility,—the former being the military class and the class that plays a part in judicial justice, and in addition to these the deliberative class, deliberation being a function of political intelligence. And it makes no difference to the argument whether these functions are held by special classes separately or by the same persons; for it often happens for the same men to be both soldiers and farmers. Hence inasmuch as both groups *a* of classes must be counted parts of the state, it is clear that the heavy-armed soldiery at any rate *b* must be a part of the state. And a seventh class is the one that serves the community by means of its property, the class that we call the rich. And an eighth is the class of public servants, that is, those who serve in the magistracies, inasmuch as without rulers it is impossible for a city to exist; it is therefore necessary that there should be some men who are able to govern and who render this service to the state either continuously or in turn. And there remain the classes which we happen to have defined just before, the deliberative class and the one that judges the claims of litigants. If therefore it is proper for the states to have these functions performed, and well and justly performed, it is necessary

b Lower grades of the forces may be excluded from citizenship, *e.g.* the rowers of the triremes (see below, 1376 b 15).

ἔχοντας εἶναί τινας ἀρετῆς τῆς[1] τῶν πολιτικῶν.[2]
τὰς μὲν οὖν ἄλλας δυνάμεις τοῖς αὐτοῖς ὑπάρχειν
ἐνδέχεσθαι δοκεῖ πολλοῖς, οἷον τοὺς αὐτοὺς εἶναι
τοὺς προπολεμοῦντας καὶ γεωργοῦντας καὶ τεχ-
5 νίτας, ἔτι δὲ τοὺς βουλευομένους τε καὶ κρίνοντας,
ἀντιποιοῦνται δὲ καὶ τῆς ἀρετῆς πάντες καὶ τὰς
πλείστας ἀρχὰς ἄρχειν οἴονται δύνασθαι· ἀλλὰ
πένεσθαι καὶ πλουτεῖν τοὺς αὐτοὺς ἀδύνατον.
διὸ ταῦτα μέρη μάλιστα εἶναι δοκεῖ πόλεως, οἱ
εὔποροι καὶ οἱ ἄποροι. ἔτι δὲ διὰ τὸ ὡς ἐπὶ τὸ
10 πολὺ τοὺς μὲν ὀλίγους εἶναι τοὺς δὲ πολλούς,
ταῦτα ἐναντία μέρη[3] φαίνεται τῶν τῆς πόλεως
μορίων· ὥστε καὶ τὰς πολιτείας κατὰ τὰς ὑπεροχὰς
τούτων καθιστᾶσι, καὶ δύο πολιτεῖαι δοκοῦσιν
εἶναι, δημοκρατία καὶ ὀλιγαρχία.

IV. Ὅτι μὲν οὖν εἰσὶ πολιτεῖαι πλείους, καὶ διὰ
15 τίνας αἰτίας, εἴρηται πρότερον· ὅτι δ᾽ ἐστὶ καὶ
δημοκρατίας εἴδη πλείω καὶ ὀλιγαρχίας, λέγωμεν.
φανερὸν δὲ τοῦτο καὶ ἐκ τῶν εἰρημένων. εἴδη
γὰρ πλείω τοῦ τε δήμου καὶ τῶν λεγομένων
γνωρίμων ἐστίν, οἷον δήμου μὲν εἴδη ἓν μὲν οἱ
γεωργοί, ἕτερον δὲ τὸ περὶ τὰς τέχνας, ἄλλο δὲ τὸ
20 ἀγοραῖον τὸ περὶ ὠνὴν καὶ πρᾶσιν διατρῖβον, ἄλλο
δὲ τὸ περὶ θάλατταν, καὶ τούτου τὸ μὲν πολεμικὸν
τὸ δὲ χρηματιστικὸν τὸ δὲ πορθμευτικὸν τὸ δ᾽
ἁλιευτικόν (πολλαχοῦ γὰρ ἕκαστα τούτων πολύοχλα,

---

[1] ἀρετῆς τῆς Richards: ἀρετῆς codd.
[2] πολιτῶν? Richards.   [3] μόνα Wilamowitz.

---

for there also to be some men possessing virtue in the
5 form of political excellence. Now as to the other
capacities many people think that it is possible for
them to be possessed in combination, for example,
for the same men to be the soldiers that defend the
state in war and the farmers that till the land and
the artizans, and also the councillors and judges, and
indeed all men claim to possess virtue and think
themselves capable of filling most of the offices of
state ; but it is not possible for the same men to
be poor and rich. Hence these seem to be in the
fullest sense the parts of the state, the rich and the
poor. And also the fact that the rich are usually
few and the poor many makes these two among the
parts of the state appear as opposite sections ; so
that the superior claims *a* of these classes are even
made the guiding principles upon which constitutions
are constructed, and it is thought that there are two
forms of constitution, democracy and oligarchy.

Some classes may overlap, but not rich and poor : hence Oligarchy and Democracy thought the chief forms.

IV. That there are then several forms of constitution, and what are the reasons for this, has been
stated before ; let us now say that there are several
varieties both of democracy and of oligarchy. And
this is clear even from what has been said already.
For there are several classes both of the people and
of those called the notables ; for instance classes of
the people are, one the farmers, another the class
dealing with the arts and crafts, another the commercial class occupied in buying and selling and
another the one occupied with the sea—and this
is divided into the classes concerned with naval
warfare, with trade, with ferrying passengers and
with fishing (for each of these classes is extremely
numerous in various places, for instance fishermen

Varieties of Oligarchy and Democracy

1291 b

οἷον ἁλιεῖς μὲν ἐν Τάραντι καὶ Βυζαντίῳ, τριηρικὸν
δὲ ᾿Αθήνησιν, ἐμπορικὸν δὲ ἐν Αἰγίνῃ καὶ Χίῳ,
25 πορθμευτικὸν δ᾿ ἐν[1] Τενέδῳ), πρὸς δὲ τούτοις
τὸ χερνητικὸν καὶ τὸ μικρὰν ἔχον οὐσίαν ὥστε μὴ
δύνασθαι σχολάζειν, ἔτι τὸ μὴ ἐξ ἀμφοτέρων
πολιτῶν ἐλεύθερον, κἂν εἴ τι τοιοῦτον ἕτερον[2]
πλήθους εἶδος· τῶν δὲ γνωρίμων πλοῦτος, εὐγένεια,
ἀρετή, παιδεία καὶ τὰ τούτοις λεγόμενα κατὰ τὴν
30 αὐτὴν διαφοράν.

Δημοκρατία μὲν οὖν ἐστὶ πρώτη μὲν ἡ λεγομένη
μάλιστα κατὰ τὸ ἴσον. ἴσον γάρ φησιν ὁ νόμος
ὁ τῆς τοιαύτης δημοκρατίας τὸ μηδὲν μᾶλλον
ὑπερέχειν[3] τοὺς ἀπόρους ἢ τοὺς εὐπόρους μηδὲ
κυρίους εἶναι ὑποτερουσοῦν ἀλλ᾿ ὁμοίους ἀμφο-
τέρους· εἴπερ γὰρ ἐλευθερία μάλιστ᾿ ἐστὶν ἐν
35 δημοκρατίᾳ, καθάπερ ὑπολαμβάνουσί τινες, καὶ
ἰσότης, οὕτως ἂν εἴη μάλιστα κοινωνούντων
ἁπάντων μάλιστα[4] τῆς πολιτείας ὁμοίως. ἐπεὶ δὲ
πλείων ὁ δῆμος, κύριον δὲ τὸ δόξαν τοῖς πλείοσιν,
ἀνάγκη δημοκρατίαν εἶναι ταύτην. ἓν μὲν οὖν
εἶδος δημοκρατίας τοῦτο, τὸ[5] τὰς ἀρχὰς ἀπὸ
40 τιμημάτων εἶναι, βραχέων δὲ τούτων ὄντων· δεῖ
δὲ τῷ κτωμένῳ ἐξουσίαν εἶναι μετέχειν καὶ
1292 a τὸν ἀποβάλλοντα μὴ μετέχειν. ἕτερον δ᾿ εἶδος
δημοκρατίας τὸ μετέχειν ἅπαντας τοὺς πολίτας
ὅσοι ἀνυπεύθυνοι, ἄρχειν δὲ τὸν νόμον· ἕτερον δὲ
εἶδος δημοκρατίας τὸ πᾶσι μετεῖναι τῶν ἀρχῶν

---

[1] δ᾿ ἐν Susemihl (*autem in* Guil.): ἐν codd.
[2] Sylburg : ἑτέρου codd.
[3] ὑπάρχειν codd. plerique, ἄρχειν Victorius (cf. 1318 a 7).
[4] secl. Coraes.
[5] τὸ Schlosser (cf. 1318 b 6 seq., ed.): ἀλλὰ δὲ τὸ codd.

at Tarentum and Byzantium, navy men at Athens the mercantile class at Aegina and Chios, and the ferryman-class at Tenedos), and in addition to these the hand-working class and the people possessing little substance so that they cannot live a life of leisure, also those that are not free men of citizen parentage on both sides, and any other similar class of common people ; while among the notables wealth, birth, virtue, education, and the distinctions that are spoken of in the same group as these, form the classes.

The first kind of democracy therefore is the one which receives the name chiefly in respect of equality. For the law of this sort of democracy ascribes equality to the state of things in which the poor have no more prominence than the rich, and neither class is sovereign, but both are alike ; for assuming that freedom is chiefly found in a democracy, as some persons suppose, and also equality, this would be so most fully when to the fullest extent all alike share equally in the government. And since the people are in the majority, and a resolution passed by a majority is paramount, this must necessarily be a democracy. This therefore is one kind of democracy, where the offices are held on property-qualifications, but these low ones, although it is essential that the man who acquires the specified amount should have the right to hold office, and the man who loses it should not hold office. And another kind of democracy is for all the citizens that are not open to challenge^a to have a share in office, but for the law to rule ; and another kind of democracy is for all to share in the offices on the mere qualification of

---

^a *i.e.* on the score of birth, *cf.* c. v. § 4.

1292 a

ἐὰν μόνον ᾖ πολίτης, ἄρχειν δὲ τὸν νόμον. ἕτερον
δ' εἶδος δημοκρατίας τἆλλα μὲν εἶναι ταὐτά, κύριον
δ' εἶναι τὸ πλῆθος καὶ μὴ τὸν νόμον· τοῦτο δὲ
γίνεται ὅταν τὰ ψηφίσματα κύρια ᾖ ἀλλὰ μὴ ὁ
νόμος. συμβαίνει δὲ τοῦτο διὰ τοὺς δημαγωγούς.
ἐν μὲν γὰρ ταῖς κατὰ νόμον δημοκρατουμέναις οὐ
γίνεται δημαγωγός, ἀλλ' οἱ βέλτιστοι τῶν πολιτῶν
10 εἰσὶν ἐν προεδρίᾳ· ὅπου δ' οἱ νόμοι μή εἰσι κύριοι,
ἐνταῦθα γίνονται δημαγωγοί· μόναρχος γὰρ ὁ
δῆμος γίνεται σύνθετος εἷς ἐκ πολλῶν, οἱ γὰρ
πολλοὶ κύριοί εἰσιν οὐχ ὡς ἕκαστος ἀλλὰ πάντες.
Ὅμηρος δὲ ποίαν λέγει οὐκ ἀγαθὸν εἶναι πολυ-
κοιρανίην, πότερον ταύτην ἢ ὅταν πλείους ὦσιν
15 οἱ ἄρχοντες ὡς ἕκαστος, ἄδηλον. ὁ δ' οὖν τοιοῦτος
δῆμος ἅτε μόναρχος ὢν ζητεῖ μοναρχεῖν διὰ τὸ
μὴ ἄρχεσθαι ὑπὸ νόμου καὶ γίνεται δεσποτικὸς
ὥστε οἱ κόλακες ἔντιμοι. καὶ ἔστιν ὁ τοιοῦτος
δῆμος ἀνάλογον τῶν μοναρχιῶν τῇ τυραννίδι
διότι[1] καὶ τὸ ἦθος τὸ αὐτό, καὶ ἄμφω δεσποτικὰ
20 τῶν βελτιόνων, καὶ τὰ ψηφίσματα ὥσπερ ἐκεῖ τὰ
ἐπιτάγματα, καὶ ὁ δημαγωγὸς καὶ ὁ κόλαξ οἱ
αὐτοὶ καὶ ἀνάλογον, καὶ μάλιστα δ' ἑκάτεροι παρ'
ἑκατέροις ἰσχύουσιν, οἱ μὲν κόλακες παρὰ τυράννοις, οἱ δὲ δημαγωγοὶ παρὰ τοῖς δήμοις τοῖς τοιούτοις. αἴτιοι δ' εἰσὶ τοῦ εἶναι τὰ ψηφίσματα κύρια
25 ἀλλὰ μὴ τοὺς νόμους οὗτοι, πάντα ἀνάγοντες εἰς
τὸν δῆμον· συμβαίνει γὰρ αὐτοῖς γίνεσθαι μεγάλοις
διὰ τὸ τὸν μὲν δῆμον πάντων εἶναι κύριον τῆς δὲ

---

[1] ed.: διὸ codd.

[a] *Iliad*, ii. 204.

being a citizen, but for the law to rule. Another
kind of democracy is where all the other regulations
are the same, but the multitude is sovereign and not
the law ; and this comes about when the decrees of
the assembly over-ride the law. This state of things
is brought about by the demagogues ; for in the
states under democratic government guided by law
a demagogue does not arise, but the best classes of
citizens are in the most prominent position ; but
where the laws are not sovereign, then demagogues
arise ; for the common people become a single composite monarch, since the many are sovereign not as
individuals but collectively. Yet what kind of democracy Homer [a] means by the words ' no blessing is
the lordship of the many '—whether he means this
kind or when those who rule as individuals are more
numerous, is not clear. However, a people of this
sort, as being monarch, seeks to exercise monarchic
rule through not being ruled by the law, and becomes
despotic, so that flatterers are held in honour. And Demagogy.
a democracy of this nature is comparable to the
tyrannical form of monarchy, because their spirit is
the same, and both exercise despotic control over the
better classes, and the decrees voted by the assembly
are like the commands issued in a tyranny, and the
demagogues and the flatterers are the same people
or a corresponding class, and either set has the
very strongest influence with the respective ruling
power, the flatterers with the tyrants and the demagogues with democracies of this kind. And these
men cause the resolutions of the assembly to be
supreme and not the laws, by referring all things to
the people ; for they owe their rise to greatness to
the fact that the people is sovereign over all things

1292 a

τοῦ δήμου δόξης τούτους, πείθεται γὰρ τὸ πλῆθος
τούτοις. ἔτι δ' οἱ ταῖς ἀρχαῖς ἐγκαλοῦντες τὸν
δῆμόν φασι δεῖν κρίνειν, ὁ δὲ ἀσμένως δέχεται τὴν
30 πρόκλησιν, ὥστε καταλύονται πᾶσαι αἱ ἀρχαί.
εὐλόγως δὲ ἂν δόξειεν ἐπιτιμᾶν ὁ φάσκων τὴν
τοιαύτην εἶναι δημοκρατίαν οὐ πολιτείαν. ὅπου
γὰρ μὴ νόμοι ἄρχουσιν, οὐκ ἔστι πολιτεία, δεῖ γὰρ
τὸν μὲν νόμον ἄρχειν πάντων[1] τῶν δὲ καθ' ἕκαστα
τὰς ἀρχάς, καὶ ταύτην[2] πολιτείαν κρίνειν· ὥστ'
35 εἴπερ ἐστὶ δημοκρατία μία τῶν πολιτειῶν, φανερὸν
ὡς ἡ τοιαύτη κατάστασις, ἐν ᾗ ψηφίσμασι πάντα
διοικεῖται, οὐδὲ δημοκρατία κυρίως, οὐδὲν γὰρ
ἐνδέχεται ψήφισμα εἶναι καθόλου.

Τὰ μὲν οὖν τῆς δημοκρατίας εἴδη διωρίσθω τὸν
τρόπον τοῦτον.

V. Ὀλιγαρχίας δὲ εἴδη ἓν μὲν τὸ ἀπὸ τιμημάτων
40 εἶναι τὰς ἀρχὰς τηλικούτων ὥστε τοὺς ἀπόρους μὴ
μετέχειν πλείους ὄντας, ἐξεῖναι δὲ τῷ κτωμένῳ
1292 b μετέχειν τῆς πολιτείας, ἄλλο δὲ ὅταν ἀπὸ τιμημάτων μακρῶν ὦσιν αἱ ἀρχαὶ καὶ αἱρῶνται αὐτοὶ
τοὺς ἐλλείποντας (ἂν μὲν οὖν ἐκ πάντων τούτων
τοῦτο ποιῶσι, δοκεῖ τοῦτ' εἶναι μᾶλλον ἀριστοκρατικόν, ἐὰν δὲ ἐκ τινῶν ἀφωρισμένων, ὀλιγαρ-
5 χικόν)· ἕτερον δ'[3] εἶδος ὀλιγαρχίας ὅταν παῖς ἀντὶ
πατρὸς εἰσίῃ, τέταρτον δ' ὅταν ὑπάρχῃ τε τὸ[4] νῦν

---

[1] ⟨τῶν καθόλου⟩ πάντων Richards.
[2] Madvig: τὴν codd.
[3] ἕτερον δ' ed.: ἕτερον codd.
[4] τε τὸ ed.: τό τε codd.

while they are sovereign over the opinion of the people, for the multitude believes them. Moreover those who bring charges against the magistrates say that the people ought to judge the suits, and the people receive the invitation gladly, so that all the magistracies are put down. And it would seem to be a reasonable criticism to say that such a democracy is not a constitution at all; for where the laws do not govern there is no constitution, as the law ought to govern all things while the magistrates control particulars, and we ought to judge this to be constitutional government; if then democracy really is one of the forms of constitution, it is manifest that an organization of this kind, in which all things are administered by resolutions of the assembly, is not even a democracy in the proper sense, for it is impossible for a voted resolution to be a universal rule.

Let this be our discussion of the different kinds of democracy.

V. Of the kinds of oligarchy, one is for the magistracies to be appointed from property-assessments so high that the poor who are the majority have no share in the government, but for the man who acquires the requisite amount of property to be allowed to take part in it; another is when the magistracies are filled from high assessments and the magistrates themselves elect to fill vacancies (so that if they do so from all the citizens of this assessment, this appears rather to be of the nature of an aristocracy, but if from a particular section of them, it is oligarchical); another variety of oligarchy is when son succeeds father in office; and a fourth kind is when the hereditary system just mentioned exists

Four kinds of Oligarchy.

305

λεχθὲν καὶ ἄρχῃ μὴ ὁ νόμος ἀλλ' οἱ ἄρχοντες. καὶ
ἔστιν ἀντίστροφος αὕτη ἐν ταῖς ὀλιγαρχίαις ὥσπερ
ἡ τυραννὶς ἐν ταῖς μοναρχίαις καὶ περὶ ἧς τελευταίας εἴπαμεν δημοκρατίας ἐν ταῖς δημοκρατίαις,
10 καὶ καλοῦσι δὴ τὴν τοιαύτην ὀλιγαρχίαν δυναστείαν.
   Ὀλιγαρχίας μὲν οὖν εἴδη τοσαῦτα καὶ δημοκρατίας. οὐ δεῖ δὲ λανθάνειν ὅτι πολλαχοῦ συμβέβηκεν ὥστε τὴν μὲν πολιτείαν τὴν κατὰ τοὺς
νόμους μὴ δημοτικὴν εἶναι, διὰ δὲ τὸ ἦθος καὶ τὴν
15 ἀγωγὴν πολιτεύεσθαι δημοτικῶς, ὁμοίως δὲ πάλιν
παρ' ἄλλοις τὴν μὲν κατὰ τοὺς νόμους εἶναι πολιτείαν δημοτικωτέραν, τῇ δ' ἀγωγῇ καὶ τοῖς ἔθεσιν
ὀλιγαρχεῖσθαι μᾶλλον. συμβαίνει δὲ τοῦτο μάλιστα μετὰ τὰς μεταβολὰς τῶν πολιτειῶν· οὐ γὰρ
εὐθὺς μεταβαίνουσιν ἀλλ' ἀγαπῶσι τὰ πρῶτα
20 μικρὰ πλεονεκτοῦντες παρ' ἀλλήλων, ὥσθ' οἱ μὲν
νόμοι διαμένουσιν οἱ προϋπάρχοντες κρατοῦσι δ'
οἱ μεταβαλόντες[1] τὴν πολιτείαν.
   Ὅτι δ' ἐστὶ τοσαῦτα εἴδη δημοκρατίας καὶ
ὀλιγαρχίας, ἐξ αὐτῶν τῶν εἰρημένων φανερόν ἐστιν.
ἀνάγκη γὰρ ἢ πάντα τὰ εἰρημένα μέρη τοῦ δήμου
25 κοινωνεῖν τῆς πολιτείας, ἢ τὰ μὲν τὰ δὲ μή. ὅταν
μὲν οὖν τὸ γεωργικὸν καὶ τὸ κεκτημένον μετρίαν
οὐσίαν κύριον ᾖ τῆς πολιτείας, πολιτεύονται κατὰ
νόμους· ἔχουσι γὰρ ἐργαζόμενοι ζῆν οὐ δύνανται
δὲ σχολάζειν, ὥστε τὸν νόμον ἐπιστήσαντες ἐκ

---

[1] Richards : μεταβάλλοντες.

---

[a] Government controlled by a few powerful families. C.
Thuc. iii. 62. 4, where the Thebans say, ' In those days ou
state was not governed by an oligarchy that granted equa
justice to all, nor yet by a democracy ; the power was in th
hands of a small cabal (δυναστεία ὀλίγων ἀνδρῶν), than whic

and also the magistrates govern and not the law. This among oligarchies is the form corresponding to tyranny among monarchies and to the form of democracy about which we spoke last among democracies, and indeed oligarchy of this sort has the special name of dynasty.[a]

2 So many therefore are the kinds of oligarchy and of democracy ; but it must not escape notice that in many places it has come about that although the constitution as framed by the laws is not democratic, yet owing to custom and the social system it is democratically administered, and similarly by a reverse process in other states although the legal constitution is more democratic, yet by means of the social system and customs it is carried on rather as an oligarchy. This occurs chiefly after alterations of the constitutions have taken place ; for the people do not change over to the new system immediately but are content at the first stages to gain small advantages from the other party, so that the previously existing laws continue although power is in the hands of the party that changed the constitution. *Non-essential perversions due to circumstances.*

3 And that these various kinds of democracy and oligarchy exist is manifest from the actual things that have been said. For necessarily either all the parts of the population that have been mentioned must have a share in the government, or some and not others. When therefore the farmer class and the class possessed of moderate property is sovereign over the government, they govern according to laws ; for they have a livelihood if they work, but are not able to be at leisure, so that they put the law in *Process of development of the four kinds of Democracy,*

nothing is more opposed to law or to true political order, or more nearly resembles a tyranny ' (Jowett).

ARISTOTLE

1292 b

κλησιάζουσι τὰς ἀναγκαίας[1] ἐκκλησίας· τοῖς δὲ
30 ἄλλοις μετέχειν ἔξεστιν ὅταν κτήσωνται τὸ τίμημα
τὸ διωρισμένον ὑπὸ τῶν νόμων, [2]διὸ πᾶσι τοῖς
κτησαμένοις[3] ἔξεστι μετέχειν· ὅλως μὲν γὰρ τὸ
μὲν μὴ ἐξεῖναι πᾶσιν ὀλιγαρχικόν, τὸ δὲ δὴ ἐξεῖναι[4]
σχολάζειν ἀδύνατον μὴ προσόδων οὐσῶν. τοῦτο
35 μὲν οὖν εἶδος ἓν δημοκρατίας διὰ ταύτας τὰς
αἰτίας. ἕτερον δὲ εἶδος διὰ τὴν ἐχομένην διαίρεσιν[5]· 4
ἔστι γὰρ καὶ πᾶσιν ἐξεῖναι τοῖς ἀνυπευθύνοις κατὰ
τὸ γένος, μετέχειν μέντοι[6] δυναμένους σχολάζειν·
διόπερ ἐν τῇ τοιαύτῃ δημοκρατίᾳ οἱ νόμοι ἄρχουσι,
διὰ τὸ μὴ εἶναι πρόσοδον. τρίτον δ' εἶδος τὸ πᾶσιν
ἐξεῖναι ὅσοι ἂν ἐλεύθεροι ὦσι μετέχειν τῆς πολι-
40 τείας, μὴ μέντοι μετέχειν διὰ τὴν προειρημένην
αἰτίαν, ὥστ' ἀναγκαῖον καὶ ἐν ταύτῃ ἄρχειν τὸν
1293 a νόμον. τέταρτον δὲ εἶδος δημοκρατίας ἡ τελευταία 5
τοῖς χρόνοις ἐν ταῖς πόλεσι γεγενημένη. διὰ
γὰρ τὸ μείζους γεγονέναι πολὺ τὰς πόλεις τῶν
ἐξ ὑπαρχῆς καὶ προσόδων ὑπάρχειν εὐπορίας, μετ-
5 έχουσι μὲν πάντες τῆς πολιτείας διὰ τὴν ὑπεροχὴν
τοῦ πλήθους, κοινωνοῦσι δὲ καὶ πολιτεύονται διὰ
τὸ δύνασθαι σχολάζειν καὶ τοὺς ἀπόρους λαμβάνοντας μισθόν. καὶ μάλιστα δὲ σχολάζει τὸ
τοιοῦτον πλῆθος· οὐ γὰρ ἐμποδίζει αὐτοὺς οὐθὲν
ἡ τῶν ἰδίων ἐπιμέλεια, τοὺς δὲ πλουσίους ἐμποδίζει,

---

[1] ἀναγκαιοτάτας Γ.   [2] διὸ—μετέχειν om. ΓΜΡ[1].
[3] κεκτημένοις ? ed. : κτωμένοις Victorius.
[4] [ἐξεῖναι] Thurot.   [5] Spengel : αἴρεσιν codd.
[6] μέντοι τοὺς Richards.

[a] i.e. revenues from abroad; the poor can only attend often
if paid for attendance, and this can only be financed if the
state has income from tribute or foreign property.

308

control and hold the minimum of assemblies necessary ; and the other persons have the right to take
part when they have acquired the property-assessment
fixed by the laws, so that to take part in the government is open to all who have got that amount of
property ; since for it not to be open to everybody
on any terms at all is a characteristic of oligarchy,
but then on the other hand it is impossible for it to
be open to them to have leisure if there are no
revenues.[a] This then is one kind of democracy for these
4 reasons.   Another kind is due to the distinction that
comes next : it is possible that all the citizens not
liable to objection on the score of birth may have
the right to take part in the assembly, but may
actually take part only when they are able to be at
leisure ; hence in a democracy of this nature the
laws govern because there is no revenue.   A third
kind is when all those who are free men have the
right to take part in the government yet do not
do so because of the aforesaid reason, so that it
follows that in this form of democracy also the law
governs.   And a fourth kind of democracy is the one
that has been the last in point of time to come into
existence in the states.   Because the states have
become much greater than the original ones and
possess large supplies of revenue, while all the
citizens have a share in the government because of
the superiority [b] of the multitude, all actually take
part in it and exercise their citizenship because even
the poor are enabled to be at leisure by receiving
pay.   Indeed the multitude in this kind of state has
a very great deal of leisure, for they are not hampered
at all by the care of their private affairs, but the rich

[b] *Cf.* 1288 a 20 ff.

1293 a

ὥστε πολλάκις οὐ κοινωνοῦσι τῆς ἐκκλησίας οὐδὲ
10 τοῦ δικάζειν. διὸ γίνεται τὸ τῶν ἀπόρων πλῆθος
κύριον τῆς πολιτείας ἀλλ' οὐχ οἱ νόμοι. τὰ μὲν οὖν
τῆς δημοκρατίας εἴδη τοσαῦτα καὶ τοιαῦτα διὰ
ταύτας τὰς ἀνάγκας ἐστίν· τὰ δὲ τῆς ὀλιγαρχίας, 6
ὅταν μὲν πλείους ἔχωσιν οὐσίαν, ἐλάττω δὲ καὶ
μὴ πολλὴν λίαν, τὸ τῆς πρώτης ὀλιγαρχίας εἶδός
15 ἐστιν· ποιοῦσι γὰρ ἐξουσίαν μετέχειν τῷ κτωμένῳ,
καὶ διὰ τὸ πλῆθος εἶναι τῶν μετεχόντων τοῦ
πολιτεύματος ἀνάγκη μὴ τοὺς ἀνθρώπους ἀλλὰ τὸν
νόμον εἶναι κύριον (ὅσῳ γὰρ ἂν πλεῖον ἀπέχωσι
τῆς μοναρχίας, καὶ μήτε τοσαύτην ἔχωσιν οὐσίαν
ὥστε σχολάζειν ἀμελοῦντες[1] μήθ' οὕτως ὀλίγην
20 ὥστε τρέφεσθαι ἀπὸ τῆς πόλεως, ἀνάγκη τὸν
νόμον ἀξιοῦν αὐτοῖς ἄρχειν ἀλλὰ μὴ αὐτούς). ἐὰν 7
δὲ δὴ ἐλάττους ὦσιν οἱ τὰς οὐσίας ἔχοντες ἢ οἱ τὸ
πρότερον, πλείω δέ, τὸ τῆς δευτέρας ὀλιγαρχίας
γίνεται εἶδος· μᾶλλον γὰρ ἰσχύοντες πλεονεκτεῖν
ἀξιοῦσιν, διὸ αὐτοὶ μὲν αἱροῦνται ἐκ τῶν ἄλλων
25 τοὺς εἰς τὸ πολίτευμα βαδίζοντας, διὰ δὲ τὸ μήπω
οὕτως ἰσχυροὶ εἶναι ὥστ' ἄνευ νόμου ἄρχειν, τὸν
νόμον τίθενται τοιοῦτον. ἐὰν δ' ἐπιτείνωσι τῷ 8
ἐλάττονες ὄντες μείζονας οὐσίας ἔχειν, ἡ τρίτη
ἐπίδοσις γίνεται τῆς ὀλιγαρχίας, τὸ δι' αὑτῶν μὲν
τὰς ἀρχὰς ἔχειν, κατὰ νόμον δὲ τὸν κελεύοντα
30 τῶν τελευτώντων διαδέχεσθαι τοὺς υἱεῖς. ὅταν
δὲ ἤδη πολὺ ὑπερτείνωσι ταῖς οὐσίαις καὶ ταῖς
πολυφιλίαις, ἐγγὺς ἡ τοιαύτη δυναστεία μοναρχίας
ἐστίν, καὶ κύριοι γίνονται οἱ ἄνθρωποι ἀλλ' οὐχ

---

[1] ἀμελοῦντες Spengel: -τας codd.

[a] *i.e.* they legalize the recruiting of the ruling class by co-
optation ; or the words may mean ' they make the law ruler.'

are, so that often they take no part in the assembly
nor in judging lawsuits.   Owing to this the multitude
of the poor becomes sovereign over the government,
instead of the laws.   Such in number and in nature
are the kinds of democracy that these causes neces-
6 sarily bring into existence.   To turn to the varieties and of the
of oligarchy, when more men possess property, but four kinds of Oligarchy.
less of it and not a very large amount, this is the first
form of oligarchy ; for they allow the man that
acquires property the right to participate, and because there is a large number of persons participating
in the government it necessarily follows that not the
men but the law is sovereign (for the farther removed
they are from monarchy, and as they have not so
much property as to be idle and neglect it, nor yet
so little as to be kept at the expense of the state,
they are compelled to call upon the law to rule in-
7 stead of ruling themselves).   But then if the owners
of the properties are fewer than those who owned
them previously, and own more, the second form of
oligarchy comes into being ; for as they become
stronger they claim to have a larger share, and therefore they themselves select those from among the rest
of the citizens who go into the government, but as
they are not yet strong enough to rule without law
8 they make the law conform with this.[a]   And if they
carry matters further by becoming fewer and holding
larger properties, there comes about the third advance
in oligarchy, which consists in their keeping the offices
in their own hands, but under a law enacting that
they are to be hereditary.   And when finally they
attain very great pre-eminence by their wealth
and their multitude of friends, a dynasty of this
nature is near to monarchy, and men become

1293 a

ὁ νόμος· καὶ τὸ τέταρτον εἶδος τῆς ὀλιγαρχίας
τοῦτ᾽ ἐστίν, ἀντίστροφον τῷ τελευταίῳ τῆς δημοκρατίας.

35 Ἔτι δ᾽ εἰσὶ δύο πολιτεῖαι παρὰ δημοκρατίαν τε 9
καὶ ὀλιγαρχίαν, ὧν τὴν μὲν ἑτέραν λέγουσί τε
πάντες καὶ εἴρηται τῶν τεττάρων πολιτειῶν εἶδος
ἕν (λέγουσι δὲ τέτταρας μοναρχίαν ὀλιγαρχίαν
δημοκρατίαν τέταρτον δὲ τὴν καλουμένην ἀριστο-
40 κρατίαν)· πέμπτη δ᾽ ἐστὶν ἢ προσαγορεύεται τὸ
κοινὸν ὄνομα πασῶν (πολιτείαν γὰρ καλοῦσιν),
ἀλλὰ διὰ τὸ μὴ πολλάκις γίνεσθαι λανθάνει τοὺς
πειρωμένους ἀριθμεῖν τὰ τῶν πολιτειῶν εἴδη, καὶ
1293 b χρῶνται ταῖς τέτταρσι μόνον (ὥσπερ Πλάτων) ἐν
ταῖς πολιτείαις. ἀριστοκρατίαν μὲν οὖν καλῶς 10
ἔχει καλεῖν περὶ ἧς διήλθομεν ἐν τοῖς πρώτοις
λόγοις (τὴν γὰρ ἐκ τῶν ἀρίστων ἁπλῶς κατ᾽
ἀρετὴν πολιτείαν καὶ μὴ πρὸς ὑπόθεσίν τινα
5 ἀγαθῶν ἀνδρῶν μόνην δίκαιον προσαγορεύειν ἀριστοκρατίαν, ἐν μόνῃ γὰρ ἁπλῶς ὁ αὐτὸς ἀνὴρ καὶ
πολίτης ἀγαθός ἐστιν, οἱ δ᾽ ἐν ταῖς ἄλλαις ἀγαθοὶ
πρὸς τὴν πολιτείαν εἰσὶ τὴν αὑτῶν)· οὐ μὴν ἀλλ᾽
εἰσί τινες αἳ πρός τε τὰς ὀλιγαρχουμένας ἔχουσι
διαφοράς [καὶ καλοῦνται ἀριστοκρατίαι]¹ καὶ πρὸς
10 τὴν καλουμένην πολιτείαν, ὅπου γε μὴ μόνον
πλουτίνδην ἀλλὰ καὶ ἀριστίνδην αἱροῦνται τὰς
ἀρχάς· αὕτη ἡ πολιτεία διαφέρει τε ἀμφοῖν καὶ
ἀριστοκρατικὴ καλεῖται. καὶ γὰρ ἐν ταῖς μὴ
ποιουμέναις κοινὴν ἐπιμέλειαν ἀρετῆς εἰσὶν ὅμως

¹ secl. Jackson.

ᵃ We now pass from the varieties of Oligarchy and of
Democracy to those of the other actually existing constitutions, Aristocracy so-called and Constitutional Government.

312

supreme instead of the law ; and this is the fourth kind of oligarchy, the counterpart of the last kind of democracy.

Furthermore [a] there are two constitutions by the side of democracy and oligarchy, one [b] of which is counted by everybody and has been referred to as one of the four forms of constitution (and the four meant are monarchy, oligarchy, democracy and fourth the form called aristocracy), but there is a fifth, entitled by the common name of them all (for it is called constitutional government), but as it does not often occur it is overlooked by those who try to ennumerate the forms of constitution, and they use the four names only (as does Plato) in the list of constitutions. Now the name of aristocracy is indeed properly given to the constitution that we discussed in our first discourses [c] (for it is right to apply the name ' aristocracy '—' government of the best '—only to the constitution of which the citizens are best in virtue absolutely and not merely good men in relation to some arbitrary standard, for under it alone the same person is a good man and a good citizen absolutely, whereas those who are good under the other constitutions are good relatively to their own form of constitution) ; nevertheless there are also some constitutions that have differences both in comparison with oligarchically governed states and with what is termed constitutional government, inasmuch as in them they elect the officials not only by wealth but also by goodness ; this form of constitution differs from both and is called aristocratic. For even in the states that do not pay any public attention to virtue there are nevertheless

Constitutional Government really a fifth actual form of constitution (cf. 1289 a 26).

Secondary kinds of Aristocracy.

[b] *i.e.* aristocracy.   [c] Bk. III. 1279 a 35 ff., 1286 b 3 ff.

τινὲς οἱ εὐδοκιμοῦντες καὶ δοκοῦντες εἶναι ἐπιεικεῖς.
15 ὅπου οὖν ἡ πολιτεία βλέπει εἴς τε πλοῦτον καὶ
ἀρετὴν καὶ δῆμον, οἷον ἐν Καρχηδόνι, αὕτη ἀρι-
στοκρατική ἐστιν· καὶ ἐν αἷς εἰς τὰ δύο μόνον, οἷον
ἡ Λακεδαιμονίων, εἴς τε¹ ἀρετὴν καὶ δῆμον, καὶ
ἔστι μίξις τῶν δύο τούτων, δημοκρατίας τε καὶ
ἀρετῆς. ἀριστοκρατίας μὲν οὖν παρὰ τὴν πρώτην
20 τὴν ἀρίστην πολιτείαν ταῦτα δύο εἴδη, καὶ τρίτον
ὅσαι τῆς καλουμένης πολιτείας ῥέπουσι πρὸς τὴν
ὀλιγαρχίαν μᾶλλον.

VI. Λοιπὸν δ' ἐστὶν ἡμῖν περί τε τῆς ὀνομα-
ζομένης πολιτείας εἰπεῖν καὶ περὶ τυραννίδος.
ἐτάξαμεν δ' οὕτως οὐκ οὖσαν οὔτε ταύτην παρέκβασιν οὔτε τὰς ἄρτι ῥηθείσας ἀριστοκρατίας, ὅτι
25 τὸ μὲν ἀληθὲς πᾶσαι διημαρτήκασι τῆς ὀρθοτάτης
πολιτείας, ἔπειτα καταριθμοῦνται μετὰ τούτων,
εἰσί τ' αὐτῶν αὗται παρεκβάσεις, ὥσπερ ἐν τοῖς
κατ' ἀρχὴν εἴπομεν. τελευταῖον δὲ περὶ τυραννίδος
εὔλογόν ἐστι ποιήσασθαι μνείαν διὰ τὸ πασῶν
30 ἥκιστα ταύτην εἶναι πολιτείαν, ἡμῖν δὲ τὴν μέθοδον
εἶναι περὶ πολιτείας.

Δι' ἣν μὲν οὖν αἰτίαν τέτακται τὸν τρόπον τοῦτον, εἴρηται· νῦν δὲ δεικτέον ἡμῖν περὶ πολιτείας.
φανερωτέρα γὰρ ὁ δύναμις αὐτῆς διωρισμένων τῶν
περὶ ὀλιγαρχίας καὶ δημοκρατίας· ἔστι γὰρ ἡ
πολιτεία ὡς ἁπλῶς εἰπεῖν μίξις ὀλιγαρχίας καὶ
35 δημοκρατίας. εἰώθασι δὲ καλεῖν τὰς μὲν ἀπο-

¹ τε post ἀρετὴν codd. cet. (sed cf. l. 14 et 1296 b 17).

ᵃ See 1279 b 4 ff. Actual aristocracies are a falling-off
from the Aristocracy and Polity is a decline from Monarchy
and Aristocracy; but they are not deviations in the technical
sense.

some men that are held in high esteem and are thought worthy of respect. Where then the constitution takes in view wealth and virtue as well as the common people, as for instance at Carthage, this is of the nature of an aristocracy ; and so also are the states, in which the constitution, like that of Sparta, takes in view two of these things only, virtue and the common people, and there is a mingling of these two factors, democracy and virtue. These then are two kinds of aristocracy beside the first, which is the best constitution, and a third kind is those instances of what is called constitutional government that incline more in the direction of oligarchy.

VI. It remains for us to speak about what is termed constitutional government and also about tyranny. Though neither the former nor the aristocracies spoken of just now are really deviations, we have classed them thus because in actual truth they have all fallen away from the most correct constitution, and consequently are counted with the deviation-forms, and those are deviations from them, as we said in our remarks at the beginning.[a] Tyranny is reasonably mentioned last because it is the least constitutional of all governments, whereas our investigation is about constitutional government.

Having then stated the reason for this mode of classification, we have now to set forth our view about constitutional government. For its meaning is clearer now that the characteristics of oligarchy and democracy have been defined ; since constitutional government is, to put it simply, a mixture of oligarchy and democracy. But people customarily

Constitutional Government a blend of Oligarchy and Democracy,

1293 b

κλινούσας ὡς πρὸς τὴν δημοκρατίαν πολιτείας, τὰς
δὲ πρὸς τὴν ὀλιγαρχίαν μᾶλλον ἀριστοκρατίας, διὰ
τὸ μᾶλλον ἀκολουθεῖν παιδείαν καὶ εὐγένειαν τοῖς
εὐπορωτέροις, ἔτι δὲ δοκοῦσιν ἔχειν οἱ εὔποροι
ὧν ἕνεκεν οἱ ἀδικοῦντες ἀδικοῦσιν· ὅθεν καὶ καλοὺς

40 κἀγαθοὺς καὶ γνωρίμους τούτους προσαγορεύουσιν.
ἐπεὶ οὖν ἡ ἀριστοκρατία βούλεται τὴν ὑπεροχὴν
ἀπονέμειν τοῖς ἀρίστοις τῶν πολιτῶν, καὶ τὰς
ὀλιγαρχίας εἶναί φασιν ἐκ τῶν καλῶν κἀγαθῶν

1294 a μᾶλλον. δοκεῖ δ᾽ εἶναι τῶν ἀδυνάτων τὸ εὐνομεῖσθαι τὴν μὴ[1] ἀριστοκρατουμένην πόλιν ἀλλὰ
πονηροκρατουμένην, ὁμοίως δὲ καὶ ἀριστοκρατεῖ-
σθαι τὴν μὴ εὐνομουμένην. οὐκ ἔστι δὲ εὐνομία
τὸ εὖ κεῖσθαι τοὺς νόμους μὴ πείθεσθαι δέ. διὸ

5 μίαν μὲν εὐνομίαν ὑποληπτέον εἶναι τὸ πείθεσθαι
τοῖς κειμένοις νόμοις, ἑτέραν δὲ τὸ καλῶς κεῖσθαι
τοὺς νόμους οἷς ἐμμένουσιν (ἔστι γὰρ πείθεσθαι
καὶ κακῶς κειμένοις). τοῦτο δ᾽ ἐνδέχεται διχῶς·
ἢ γὰρ τοῖς ἀρίστοις τῶν ἐνδεχομένων αὐτοῖς ἢ τοῖς
ἁπλῶς ἀρίστοις. δοκεῖ δὲ ἀριστοκρατία μὲν εἶναι

10 μάλιστα τὸ τὰς τιμὰς νενεμῆσθαι κατ᾽ ἀρετήν·
ἀριστοκρατίας μὲν γὰρ ὅρος ἀρετή, ὀλιγαρχίας δὲ
πλοῦτος, δήμου δ᾽ ἐλευθερία (τὸ δ᾽ ὅ τι ἂν δόξῃ
τοῖς πλείοσιν ἐν πάσαις ὑπάρχει, καὶ γὰρ ἐν ὀλιγαρχίᾳ καὶ ἐν ἀριστοκρατίᾳ καὶ ἐν δήμοις ὅ τι ἂν
δόξῃ τῷ πλείονι μέρει τῶν μετεχόντων τῆς πολι-

15 τείας τοῦτ᾽ ἐστὶ κύριον). ἐν μὲν οὖν ταῖς πλείσταις

[1] μὴ hic Thurot: post τὸ codd.

316

give the name of constitutional government only to
those among such mixed constitutions that incline
towards democracy, and entitle those that incline
more towards oligarchy aristocracies, because education and good birth go more with the wealthier
classes, and also the wealthy are thought to have
already the things to get which wrongdoers commit
wrong; owing to which people apply the terms
3 'gentry' and 'notabilities' to the rich. Since *and akin to*
therefore aristocracy means the assignment of the *Aristocracy.*
highest place to the best of the citizens, oligarchies
also are said to be drawn rather from the gentry.
And it seems an impossibility for a city governed
not by the aristocracy but by the base to have well-
ordered government, and similarly also for a city that
has not a well-ordered government to be governed
aristocratically. But to have good laws enacted but
not obey them does not constitute well-ordered
government. Hence one form of good government
must be understood to consist in the laws enacted
being obeyed, and another form in the laws which
the citizens keep being well enacted (for it is possible
to obey badly enacted laws). And for laws to be
well enacted is possible in two ways: they must
either be the best laws possible for the given people
or the best absolutely. But aristocracy in the fullest
sense seems to consist in the distribution of the honours
according to virtue; for virtue is the defining factor
of aristocracy, as wealth is of oligarchy, and freedom
of democracy (while the principle that a decision of
the majority is supreme is found in them all: for
in both oligarchy and aristocracy and democracies
whatever the larger part of those who have a share
in the government decides is supreme). In most

317

1294 a

πόλεσι τοῦτο¹ τῆς πολιτείας εἶδος καλεῖται, μόνον γὰρ
ἡ μίξις στοχάζεται τῶν εὐπόρων καὶ τῶν ἀπόρων,
πλούτου καὶ ἐλευθερίας (σχεδὸν γὰρ² παρὰ τοῖς
πλείστοις οἱ εὔποροι τῶν³ καλῶν κἀγαθῶν δοκοῦσι
κατέχειν χώραν)· ἐπεὶ δὲ τρία ἐστὶ τὰ ἀμφισ- 5
20 βητοῦντα τῆς ἰσότητος τῆς πολιτείας, ἐλευθερία
πλοῦτος ἀρετή (τὸ γὰρ τέταρτον, ὃ καλοῦσιν
εὐγένειαν, ἀκολουθεῖ τοῖς δυσίν, ἡ γὰρ εὐγένειά
ἐστιν ἀρχαῖος πλοῦτος καὶ ἀρετή), φανερὸν ὅτι τὴν
μὲν τοῖν δυοῖν μίξιν, τῶν εὐπόρων καὶ τῶν ἀπόρων,
πολιτείαν λεκτέον, τὴν δὲ τῶν τριῶν ἀριστοκρατίαν
25 μάλιστα τῶν ἄλλων παρὰ τὴν ἀληθινὴν καὶ πρώτην.

Ὅτι μὲν οὖν ἐστὶ καὶ ἕτερα πολιτείας εἴδη παρὰ
μοναρχίαν τε καὶ δημοκρατίαν καὶ ὀλιγαρχίαν,
εἴρηται, καὶ ποῖα ταῦτα, καὶ τί διαφέρουσιν
ἀλλήλων αἵ τ' ἀριστοκρατίαι καὶ αἱ πολιτεῖαι [τῆς
ἀριστοκρατίας]⁴· καὶ ὅτι οὐ πόρρω αὗται ἀλλήλων,
φανερόν.

30 VII. Τίνα δὲ τρόπον γίνεται παρὰ δημοκρατίαν
καὶ ὀλιγαρχίαν ἡ καλουμένη πολιτεία, καὶ πῶς
αὐτὴν δεῖ καθιστάναι, λέγωμεν ἐφεξῆς τοῖς εἰρημένοις. ἅμα δὲ δῆλον ἔσται καὶ οἷς ὁρίζονται τὴν
δημοκρατίαν καὶ τὴν ὀλιγαρχίαν· ληπτέον γὰρ
τὴν τούτων διαίρεσιν, εἶτα ἐκ τούτων ἀφ' ἑκατέρας
35 ὥσπερ σύμβολον λαμβάνοντας συνθετέον. εἰσὶ δὲ
ὅροι τρεῖς τῆς συνθέσεως καὶ μίξεως. ἢ γὰρ
ἀμφότερα ληπτέον ὧν ἑκάτεραι νομοθετοῦσιν, οἷον

---

¹ τοῦτο ed. (cf. 1292 a 33): τὸ codd.   ² γὰρ: δὲ Immisch.
³ ⟨τὴν⟩ τῶν Coraes.   ⁴ [τῆς ἀριστοκρατίας] ed.

ᵃ i.e. in most states that are considered aristocracies.
ᵇ i.e. the more oligarchical form, 1293 b 36.

tates *a* then the name of aristocracy is given to that
orm of constitutional government,*b* for the com-
ination aims only at the well-off and the poor,
vealth and freedom (since in almost the largest
umber of states the rich seem to occupy the place
f the gentry) ; but as there are three things that
laim equal participation in the constitution, freedom,
vealth and virtue (for the fourth, what is called
tobility, accompanies the two latter—nobility means
ncient wealth and virtue), it is manifest that the
nixture of the two factors, the rich and the poor,*c*
ught to be termed constitutional government, while
he mixture of the three factors deserves the name
f aristocracy most of all the various forms of aristo-
racy beside the true and best form.

It has then been stated that other forms of con-
titution also exist besides monarchy, democracy and
ligarchy, and what their characteristics are, and how
he various sorts of aristocracy and of constitutional
overnment differ from one another ; and it is manifest
hat aristocracy and constitutional government are
tot widely apart from one another.

VII. Next to what has been said let us state the
vay in which what is called constitutional government
omes into existence by the side of democracy and
ligarchy, and how it is proper to establish it. At
he same time the defining characteristics of demo-
racy and oligarchy will also be clear ; for we must
grasp the distinction between these and then make
a combination out of them, taking, so to say, a contri-
oution from each. And there are three principles
letermining this combination or mixture. Under Three
one plan we must adopt both features from the legis- forms of
this blend.

e Loosely put for ' wealth and free birth.'

1294 a

περὶ τοῦ δικάζειν—ἐν μὲν γὰρ ταῖς ὀλιγαρχίαις τοῖς
εὐπόροις ζημίαν τάττουσιν ἂν μὴ δικάζωσι τοῖς
40 δ' ἀπόροις οὐδένα μισθόν, ἐν δὲ ταῖς δημοκρατίαις
τοῖς μὲν ἀπόροις μισθὸν τοῖς δ' εὐπόροις οὐδεμίαν
ζημίαν, κοινὸν δὲ καὶ μέσον τούτων ἀμφότερα
1294 b ταῦτα, διὸ καὶ πολιτικόν, μέμικται γὰρ ἐξ ἀμφοῖν.
εἷς μὲν οὖν οὗτος τοῦ συνδυασμοῦ τρόπος· ἕτερος
δὲ τὸ μέσον λαμβάνειν ὧν ἑκάτεροι τάττουσιν, οἷον
ἐκκλησιάζειν οἱ μὲν ἀπὸ τιμήματος οὐθενὸς ἢ
μικροῦ πάμπαν, οἱ δ' ἀπὸ μακροῦ τιμήματος,
5 κοινὸν δέ γε οὐδέτερον ἀλλὰ τὸ μέσον ἑκατέρου
τιμήματος τούτων. τρίτον δ' ἐκ δυοῖν ταγμάτοιν,
τὰ μὲν ἐκ τοῦ ὀλιγαρχικοῦ νόμου τὰ δ' ἐκ τοῦ
δημοκρατικοῦ· λέγω δ' οἷον δοκεῖ δημοκρατικὸν
μὲν εἶναι τὸ κληρωτὰς εἶναι τὰς ἀρχὰς τὸ δ'
αἱρετὰς ὀλιγαρχικόν, καὶ δημοκρατικὸν μὲν τὸ μὴ
10 ἀπὸ τιμήματος ὀλιγαρχικὸν δὲ τὸ ἀπὸ τιμήματος
ἀριστοκρατικὸν τοίνυν καὶ πολιτικὸν τὸ ἐξ ἑκατέρας ἑκάτερον λαβεῖν, ἐκ μὲν τῆς ὀλιγαρχίας τὸ
αἱρετὰς ποιεῖν τὰς ἀρχὰς ἐκ δὲ τῆς δημοκρατίας
τὸ μὴ ἀπὸ τιμήματος. ὁ μὲν οὖν τρόπος τῆς
μίξεως οὗτος· τοῦ δ' εὖ μεμῖχθαι δημοκρατίαν καὶ
15 ὀλιγαρχίαν ὅρος ὅταν ἐνδέχηται λέγειν τὴν αὐτὴν
πολιτείαν δημοκρατίαν καὶ ὀλιγαρχίαν· δῆλον γὰρ
ὅτι τοῦτο πάσχουσιν οἱ λέγοντες[1] διὰ τὸ μεμῖχθαι

---

[1] [οἱ λέγοντες] ? ed.

[a] Perhaps ' the speakers feel ' should be excised.

lative schemes of the two different constitutions :
for example, in regard to the administration of justice,
in oligarchies they institute a fine for the rich if
they do not serve on juries but no pay for the poor
for serving, while in democracies they assign pay for
the poor but no fine for the rich, but a common and
intermediate principle is to have both payment and
fine, and therefore this is a mark of a constitutional
government, since it is a mixture of elements from
both oligarchy and democracy. This then is one mode
of combining the two. Another is to take the middle
course between the regulations of each : for example,
democracies permit membership of the assembly on
no property-qualification at all or a quite small one,
oligarchies on a large property-qualification, but the
combination clearly is to have neither principle, but
one which lies in the middle between either of these
two qualifications. In the third place is a combination
of the two systems, taking some features from the
oligarchical law and some from the democratic ; I
mean, for example, that it is thought to be democratic
for the offices to be assigned by lot, for them to be
elected oligarchic, and democratic for them not to
have a property-qualification, oligarchic to have one ;
therefore it is aristocratic and constitutional to take
one feature from one form and the other from the
other, from oligarchy that offices are to be elected,
and from democracy that this is not to be on a
property-qualification. This then is the mode of
the mixture ; and the mark of a good mixture of Test of
democracy and oligarchy is when it is possible to its merit.
speak of the same constitution as a democracy and
as an oligarchy ; for manifestly the speakers feel *a*
this is so because the mixture is complete, and this is

1294 b

καλῶς, πέπονθε δὲ τοῦτο καὶ τὸ μέσον, ἐμφαίνεται
γὰρ ἑκάτερον ἐν αὐτῷ τῶν ἄκρων. ὅπερ συμβαίνει περὶ τὴν Λακεδαιμονίων πολιτείαν. πολλοὶ
20 γὰρ ἐγχειροῦσι λέγειν ὡς δημοκρατίας οὔσης διὰ
τὸ δημοκρατικὰ πολλὰ τὴν τάξιν ἔχειν, οἷον πρῶτον τὸ περὶ τὴν τροφὴν τῶν παίδων, ὁμοίως γὰρ
οἱ τῶν πλουσίων τρέφονται τοῖς τῶν πενήτων, καὶ
παιδεύονται τὸν τρόπον τοῦτον ὃν ἂν δύναιντο καὶ
τῶν πενήτων οἱ παῖδες, ὁμοίως δὲ καὶ ἐπὶ τῆς
25 ἐχομένης ἡλικίας, καὶ ὅταν ἄνδρες γένωνται, τὸν
αὐτὸν τρόπον, οὐθὲν γὰρ διάδηλος ὁ πλούσιος καὶ
ὁ πένης—οὕτω τὰ περὶ τὴν τροφὴν ταὐτὰ πᾶσιν ἐν
τοῖς συσσιτίοις, καὶ τὴν ἐσθῆτα οἱ πλούσιοι
τοιαύτην οἵαν ἄν τις παρασκευάσαι δύναιτο καὶ
τῶν πενήτων ὁστισοῦν, ἔτι τῷ δύο τὰς μεγίστας
30 ἀρχὰς τὴν μὲν αἱρεῖσθαι τὸν δῆμον, τῆς δὲ μετέχειν (τοὺς μὲν γὰρ γέροντας αἱροῦνται, τῆς δ'
ἐφορείας μετέχουσιν)· οἱ δ' ὀλιγαρχίαν, διὰ τὸ
πολλὰ ἔχειν ὀλιγαρχικά, οἷον τὸ πάσας αἱρετὰς
εἶναι καὶ μηδεμίαν κληρωτήν, καὶ ὀλίγους εἶναι
κυρίους θανάτου καὶ φυγῆς, καὶ ἄλλα τοιαῦτα
35 πολλά. δεῖ δ' ἐν τῇ πολιτείᾳ τῇ μεμιγμένῃ καλῶς
ἀμφότερα δοκεῖν εἶναι καὶ μηδέτερον,[1] καὶ σώ-
ζεσθαι δι' αὑτῆς καὶ μὴ ἔξωθεν, καὶ δι' αὑτῆς μὴ
τῷ πλείους ἔξωθεν[2] εἶναι τοὺς βουλομένους (εἴη
γὰρ ἂν καὶ πονηρᾷ πολιτείᾳ τοῦθ' ὑπάρχον) ἀλλὰ
40 τῷ μηδ' ἂν βούλεσθαι πολιτείαν ἑτέραν μηθὲν τῶν
τῆς πόλεως μορίων ὅλως.

---

[1] μηδέτερον : μὴ θάτερον Boltenstern.   [2] [ἔξωθεν] Thurot.

[a] A conjectural emendation removes this mysterious epi
gram, giving ' and not one of the two (only).'

[b] Or, if ἔξωθεν is an interpolation, ' not merely becaus

the case with the form that lies in the middle, for each of the two extreme forms can be seen in it.
5 This is the case with the constitution of Sparta. For many people endeavour to describe it as being a democracy, because its system has many democratic features, for instance first of all its regulation for the rearing of boys, since the sons of the rich are brought up in the same way as those of the poor, and are educated in a manner in which the sons of the poor also could be educated, and they are also treated similarly at the next age, and in the same manner when they are grown up, for there is nothing that distinguishes the rich man from the poor man—thus the arrangements for food are the same for all at the common messes, and the rich wear clothes such as even any poor man could procure, and also because of the two greatest offices the common people elect to one and share in the other (they elect the Elders and share in the Ephorate) ; but others call it an oligarchy, because it has many oligarchical features, for instance that all the offices are elective and none appointed by lot and few persons have the power to sentence to death and exile, and a number of other such matters. But in a well-constructed mixed constitution both of the two factors, and neither of them,[a] should seem to be present, and it should be kept safe by its own means and not by outside aid, and by its own means not because those who desire its security are more numerous outside it [b] (for even a bad constitution might possess this quality), but because no section of the state whatever would even wish for another constitution.

those (citizens) who wish it to survive are more numerous (than those who do not).'

1294 b

Τίνα μὲν οὖν τρόπον δεῖ καθιστάναι πολιτείαν,
ὁμοίως δὲ καὶ τὰς ὀνομαζομένας ἀριστοκρατίας,
νῦν εἴρηται.

1295 a VIII. Περὶ δὲ τυραννίδος ἦν ἡμῖν λοιπὸν εἰπεῖν, 1
οὐχ ὡς ἐνούσης πολυλογίας περὶ αὐτήν, ἀλλ' ὅπως
λάβῃ τῆς μεθόδου τὸ μέρος, ἐπειδὴ καὶ ταύτην
τίθεμεν τῶν πολιτειῶν τι μέρος. περὶ μὲν οὖν
5 βασιλείας διωρίσαμεν ἐν τοῖς πρώτοις λόγοις, ἐν
οἷς περὶ τῆς μάλιστα λεγομένης βασιλείας ἐποιού-
μεθα τὴν σκέψιν, πότερον ἀσύμφορον ἢ συμφέρει
ταῖς πόλεσιν, καὶ τίνα καὶ πόθεν δεῖ καθιστάναι· 2
καὶ πῶς τυραννίδος δ' εἴδη δύο μὲν διείλομεν ἐν
10 οἷς περὶ βασιλείας ἐπεσκοποῦμεν, διὰ τὸ τὴν
δύναμιν ἐπαλλάττειν πως αὐτῶν καὶ πρὸς τὴν
βασιλείαν, διὰ τὸ κατὰ νόμον εἶναι ἀμφοτέρας ταύτας
τὰς ἀρχάς (ἔν τε γὰρ τῶν βαρβάρων τισὶν αἱροῦνται
αὐτοκράτορας μονάρχους, καὶ τὸ παλαιὸν ἐν τοῖς
ἀρχαίοις Ἕλλησιν ἐγίγνοντό τινες μόναρχοι τὸν
τρόπον τοῦτον, οὓς ἐκάλουν αἰσυμνήτας), ἔχουσι δέ
15 τινας πρὸς ἀλλήλας αὗται διαφοράς, ἦσαν δὲ διὰ
μὲν τὸ κατὰ νόμον βασιλικαὶ καὶ διὰ τὸ μοναρχεῖν
ἑκόντων, τυραννικαὶ δὲ διὰ τὸ δεσποτικῶς ἄρχειν
καὶ κατὰ[1] τὴν αὐτῶν γνώμην. τρίτον δὲ εἶδος
τυραννίδος ἥπερ μάλιστ' εἶναι δοκεῖ τυραννίς,
ἀντίστροφος οὖσα τῇ παμβασιλείᾳ· τοιαύτην δ'
ἀναγκαῖον εἶναι τυραννίδα τὴν μοναρχίαν ἥτις
ἀνυπεύθυνος ἄρχει τῶν ὁμοίων καὶ βελτιόνων

---

[1] καὶ κατὰ Susemihl (*et secundum suam* Guil.): κατὰ codd.

---

a Bk. III. cc. ix.-xii.

The proper way therefore to establish a constitutional government, and similarly also the governments named aristocracies, has now been stated.

1   VIII. It remained for us to speak of tyranny, not Tyranny. because there is much that can be said about it, but in order that it may receive its part in our inquiry, since we rank this also as one among the kinds of constitution. The nature of kingship we have defined in our first discourses,[a] in which we examined the question in relation to the constitution most commonly denoted by the term ' kingship,' whether it is disadvantageous or an advantage to states, and

2 what person ought to be set up as king, and from what source, and by what procedure ; and in the Heroic Monarchs passage in which we were considering kingship we and Aesym- distinguished two kinds of tyranny, because their netae. power in a manner borders upon royalty, because both these forms of rule are in accordance with law (for among some of the barbarians they elect monarchic rulers with autocratic powers, and also in old times among the ancient Greeks some men used to become monarchs of this sort, the rulers called *aesymnetae*), but these two forms of tyranny have certain differences from one another, although they were on the one hand of the nature of royalty because they were in accordance with law and because they exercised monarchic rule over willing subjects, and on the other hand of the nature of a tyranny because they ruled despotically and according to

3 their own judgement. But there is a third kind of Tyranny tyranny which is thought to be tyranny in the fullest proper. degree, being the counterpart of universal kingship ; to this sort of tyranny must necessarily belong a monarchy that exercises irresponsible rule over

1295 a

πάντων πρὸς τὸ σφέτερον αὐτῆς συμφέρον ἀλλὰ
μὴ πρὸς τὸ τῶν ἀρχομένων. διόπερ ἀκούσιος·
οὐθεὶς γὰρ ἑκὼν ὑπομένει τῶν ἐλευθέρων τὴν
τοιαύτην ἀρχήν.

Τυραννίδος μὲν οὖν εἴδη ταῦτα καὶ τοσαῦτα διὰ
τὰς εἰρημένας αἰτίας.

25 IX. Τίς δ' ἀρίστη πολιτεία καὶ τίς ἄριστος βίος 1
ταῖς πλείσταις πόλεσι καὶ τοῖς πλείστοις τῶν
ἀνθρώπων, μήτε πρὸς ἀρετὴν συγκρίνουσι[1] τὴν ὑπὲρ
τοὺς ἰδιώτας μήτε πρὸς παιδείαν ἢ φύσεως δεῖται
καὶ χορηγίας τυχηρᾶς μήτε πρὸς πολιτείαν τὴν κατ'
30 εὐχὴν γινομένην, ἀλλὰ βίον τε τὸν τοῖς πλείστοις
κοινωνῆσαι δυνατὸν καὶ πολιτείαν ἧς τὰς πλείστας
πόλεις ἐνδέχεται μετασχεῖν; καὶ γὰρ ἃς καλοῦσιν 2
ἀριστοκρατίας, περὶ ὧν νῦν εἴπομεν, τὰ μὲν ἐξωτέρω
πίπτουσι ταῖς πλείσταις τῶν πόλεων, τὰ δὲ γειτνιῶσι
τῇ καλουμένῃ πολιτείᾳ, διὸ περὶ ἀμφοῖν ὡς μιᾶς
35 λεκτέον. ἡ δὲ δὴ κρίσις περὶ ἁπάντων τούτων ἐκ
τῶν αὐτῶν στοιχείων ἐστίν. εἰ γὰρ καλῶς ἐν τοῖς
ἠθικοῖς εἴρηται τὸ τὸν εὐδαίμονα βίον εἶναι τὸν κατ'
ἀρετὴν ἀνεμπόδιστον, μεσότητα δὲ τὴν ἀρετήν, τὸν
μέσον ἀναγκαῖον βίον εἶναι βέλτιστον, τῆς ἑκάστοις
ἐνδεχομένης τυχεῖν μεσότητος. τοὺς δὲ αὐτοὺς 3
40 τούτους ὅρους ἀναγκαῖον εἶναι καὶ πόλεως ἀρετῆς
1295 b καὶ κακίας καὶ πολιτείας, ἡ γὰρ πολιτεία βίος τίς
ἐστι πόλεως. ἐν ἁπάσαις δὴ ταῖς πόλεσίν ἐστι
τρία μέρη τῆς πόλεως, οἱ μὲν εὔποροι σφόδρα, οἱ

---

[1] συντείνουσι Richards.

---

[a] Or ' if we do not aim at.'
[b] See 1293 b 7-21, cf. ib. 36—1294 a 25.
[c] N.E. 1101 a 14.

subjects all of the same or of a higher class with a view to its own private interest and not in the interest of the persons ruled. Hence it is held against the will of the subjects, since no free man willingly endures such rule.

These then are the kinds of tyranny and such is their number, for the reasons stated.

1 IX. But what is the best constitution and what is the best mode of life for most cities and most of mankind, if we do not judge by the standard ofᵃ a virtue that is above the level of private citizens or of an education that needs natural gifts and means supplied by fortune, nor by the standard of the ideal constitution, but of a mode of life able to be shared by most men and a constitution possible for most 2 states to attain? For the constitutions called aristocracies, of which we spoke just now,ᵇ in some cases fall somewhat out of the scope of most states, and in others approximate to what is called constitutional government, so that it is proper to speak of these two forms as if they were one. And indeed the decision in regard to all these questions is based on the same elementary principles. For if it has been rightly said in *Ethics*ᶜ that the happy life is the life that is lived without impediment in accordance with virtue, and that virtue is a middle course, it necessarily follows that the middle course of life is the best—such a middle course as it is possible 3 for each class of men to attain. And these same criteria must also necessarily apply to the goodness and badness of a state, and of a constitution—for a constitution is a certain mode of life of a state. In all states therefore there exist three divisions of the state, the very rich, the very poor, and thirdly those

Middle-class government the best practicable.

δὲ ἄποροι σφόδρα, οἱ δὲ τρίτοι οἱ μέσοι τούτων.
ἐπεὶ τοίνυν ὁμολογεῖται τὸ μέτριον ἄριστον καὶ τὸ
5 μέσον, φανερὸν ὅτι καὶ τῶν εὐτυχημάτων ἡ κτῆσις
ἡ μέση βελτίστη πάντων. ῥᾴστη γὰρ τῷ λόγῳ
πειθαρχεῖν, ὑπέρκαλον δὲ ἢ ὑπερίσχυρον ἢ ὑπερ-
ευγενῆ ἢ ὑπερπλούσιον, ἢ τἀναντία τούτοις, ὑπέρ-
πτωχον ἢ ὑπερασθενῆ καὶ σφόδρα ἄτιμον, χαλεπὸν
τῷ λόγῳ ἀκολουθεῖν· γίγνονται γὰρ οἱ μὲν ὑβρισταὶ
10 καὶ μεγαλοπόνηροι μᾶλλον οἱ δὲ κακοῦργοι καὶ
μικροπόνηροι λίαν, τῶν δ' ἀδικημάτων τὰ μὲν
γίγνεται δι' ὕβριν τὰ δὲ διὰ κακουργίαν. ἔτι δ'
ἥκισθ' οὗτοι φυγαρχοῦσι[1] καὶ σπουδαρχοῦσι,[2] ταῦτα
δ' ἀμφότερα βλαβερὰ ταῖς πόλεσιν. πρὸς δὲ τούτοις
15 οἱ μὲν ἐν ὑπεροχαῖς εὐτυχημάτων ὄντες, ἰσχύος καὶ
πλούτου καὶ φίλων καὶ τῶν ἄλλων τῶν τοιούτων,
ἄρχεσθαι οὔτε βούλονται οὔτε ἐπίστανται (καὶ τοῦτ'
εὐθὺς οἴκοθεν ὑπάρχει παισὶν οὖσιν, διὰ γὰρ τὴν
τρυφὴν οὐδ' ἐν τοῖς διδασκαλείοις ἄρχεσθαι σύν-
ηθες αὐτοῖς), οἱ δὲ καθ' ὑπερβολὴν ἐν ἐνδείᾳ
τούτων ταπεινοὶ λίαν· ὥσθ' οἱ μὲν ἄρχειν οὐκ
20 ἐπίστανται ἀλλ' ἄρχεσθαι δουλικὴν ἀρχήν, οἱ δ'
ἄρχεσθαι μὲν οὐδεμιᾷ ἀρχῇ, ἄρχειν δὲ δεσποτικὴν
ἀρχήν. γίγνεται οὖν καὶ δούλων καὶ δεσποτῶν
πόλις, ἀλλ' οὐκ ἐλευθέρων, καὶ τῶν μὲν φθονούντων
τῶν δὲ καταφρονούντων, ἃ πλεῖστον ἀπέχει φιλίας,
καὶ κοινωνίας πολιτικῆς, ἡ γὰρ κοινωνία φιλικόν,

---

[1] Bernays: φιλαρχοῦσι, φυλαρχοῦσι codd.
[2] Coraes: βουλαρχοῦσι codd.

---

[a] The text is an emendation ; some MSS. give ' to rule the
tribe and to rule the council,' but most have ' to love office
and rule the council,' apparently thinking that the verb
translated ' rule the council' meant ' wish office.'

who are between the two. Since then it is admitted that what is moderate or in the middle is best, it is manifest that the middle amount of all of the good 4 things of fortune is the best amount to possess. For this degree of wealth is the readiest to obey reason, whereas for a person who is exceedingly beautiful or strong or nobly born or rich, or the opposite— exceedingly poor or weak or of very mean station, it is difficult to follow the bidding of reason ; for the former turn more to insolence and grand wickedness, and the latter overmuch to malice and petty wickedness, and the motive of all wrongdoing is either insolence or malice. And moreover the middle class are the least inclined to shun office and to covet office,ᵃ and both these tendencies are injurious to 5 states. And in addition to these points, those who have an excess of fortune's goods, strength, wealth, friends and the like, are not willing to be governed and do not know how to be (and they have acquired this quality even in their boyhood from their home-life, which was so luxurious that they have not got used to submitting to authority even in school), while those who are excessively in need of these things are too humble. Hence the latter class do not know how to govern but know how to submit to government of a servile kind, while the former class do not know how to submit to any government, and only know how to govern in the manner of a master. The result is a state consisting of slaves and masters, not of free men, and of one class envious and another contemptuous of their fellows. This condition of affairs is very far removed from friendliness, and from political partnership—for friendliness is an element

25 οὐδὲ γὰρ ὁδοῦ βούλονται κοινωνεῖν τοῖς ἐχθροῖς.
βούλεται δέ γε ἡ πόλις ἐξ ἴσων εἶναι καὶ ὁμοίων
ὅτι μάλιστα, τοῦτο δ' ὑπάρχει μάλιστα τοῖς μέσοις·
ὥστ' ἀναγκαῖον ἄριστα πολιτεύεσθαι ταύτην τὴν
πόλιν ἐστὶν¹ ἐξ ὧν φαμεν φύσει τὴν σύστασιν εἶναι
τῆς πόλεως. καὶ σῴζονται δ' ἐν ταῖς πόλεσιν οὗτοι 7
30 μάλιστα τῶν πολιτῶν· οὔτε γὰρ αὐτοὶ τῶν ἀλλοτρίων
ὥσπερ οἱ πένητες ἐπιθυμοῦσιν, οὔτε τῆς τούτων
ἕτεροι καθάπερ τῆς τῶν πλουσίων οἱ πένητες ἐπι-
θυμοῦσιν· καὶ διὰ τὸ μήτ' ἐπιβουλεύεσθαι μήτ'
ἐπιβουλεύειν ἀκινδύνως διάγουσιν. διὰ τοῦτο καλῶς
ηὔξατο Φωκυλίδης—

πολλὰ μέσοισιν ἄριστα· μέσος θέλω ἐν πόλει
εἶναι.

35 δῆλον ἄρα ὅτι καὶ ἡ κοινωνία ἡ πολιτικὴ ἀρίστη ἡ 8
διὰ τῶν μέσων, καὶ τὰς τοιαύτας ἐνδέχεται εὖ
πολιτεύεσθαι πόλεις ἐν αἷς δὴ πολὺ τὸ μέσον καὶ
κρεῖττον μάλιστα μὲν ἀμφοῖν, εἰ δὲ μή, θατέρου
μέρους, προστιθέμενον γὰρ ποιεῖ ῥοπὴν καὶ κωλύει
γίνεσθαι τὰς ἐναντίας ὑπερβολάς. διόπερ εὐτυχία
40 μεγίστη τοὺς πολιτευομένους οὐσίαν ἔχειν μέσην
1296 a καὶ ἱκανήν, ὡς ὅπου οἱ μὲν πολλὰ σφόδρα κέκτηνται
οἱ δὲ μηθέν, ἢ δῆμος ἔσχατος γίγνεται ἢ ὀλιγαρχία
ἄκρατος ἢ τυραννὶς δι' ἀμφοτέρας τὰς ὑπερβολάς·
καὶ γὰρ ἐκ δημοκρατίας τῆς νεανικωτάτης καὶ ἐξ
5 ὀλιγαρχίας γίνεται τυραννίς, ἐκ δὲ τῶν μέσων καὶ

¹ ἐστὶν om. ΓΜ⁸: ἡ συνέστη Lambinus.

_____

ᵃ Probably Lambinus's alteration of the Greek should be
accepted, giving ' hence that state will necessarily be best
governed which consists of those elements—.'
ᵇ A gnomic poet of Miletus, born 560 B.C.
ᶜ *i.e.* extreme democracy and very limited oligarchy.

of partnership, since men are not willing to be partners with their enemies even on a journey. But surely the ideal of the state is to consist as much as possible of persons that are equal and alike, and this similarity is most found in the middle classes; therefore the middle-class state will necessarily be best constituted in respect of those elements[a] of which we say that the state is by nature composed. And also this class of citizens have the greatest security in the states; for they do not themselves covet other men's goods as do the poor, nor do the other classes covet their substance as the poor covet that of the rich; and because they are neither plotted against nor plotting they live free from danger. Because of this it was a good prayer of Phocylides[b]—

> In many things the middle have the best;
> Be mine a middle station.

It is clear therefore also that the political community administered by the middle class is the best, and that it is possible for those states to be well governed that are of the kind in which the middle class is numerous, and preferably stronger than both the other two classes, or at all events than one of them, for by throwing in its weight it sways the balance and prevents the opposite extremes[c] from coming into existence. Hence it is the greatest good fortune if the men that have political power possess a moderate and sufficient substance, since where some own a very great deal of property and others none there comes about either an extreme democracy or an unmixed oligarchy, or a tyranny may result from both of the two extremes, for tyranny springs from both democracy and oligarchy of the most unbridled kind, but much less often from the middle forms of constitu-

τῶν σύνεγγυς πολὺ ἧττον. τὴν δ' αἰτίαν ὕστερον
ἐν τοῖς περὶ τὰς μεταβολὰς τῶν πολιτειῶν ἐροῦμεν.
ὅτι δ' ἡ μέση βελτίστη, φανερόν· μόνη γὰρ ἀστασίαστος, ὅπου γὰρ πολὺ τὸ διὰ μέσου, ἥκιστα
στάσεις καὶ διαστάσεις γίγνονται τῶν πολιτειῶν.
10 καὶ αἱ μεγάλαι πόλεις ἀστασιαστότεραι διὰ τὴν
αὐτὴν αἰτίαν, ὅτι πολὺ τὸ μέσον· ἐν δὲ ταῖς μικραῖς
ῥᾴδιόν τε διαλαβεῖν εἰς δύο πάντας ὥστε μηθὲν
καταλιπεῖν μέσον, καὶ πάντες σχεδὸν ἄποροι ἢ
εὔποροί εἰσιν. καὶ αἱ δημοκρατίαι δὲ ἀσφαλέστεραι
τῶν ὀλιγαρχιῶν εἰσι καὶ πολυχρονιώτεραι διὰ τοὺς
15 μέσους (πλείους τε γάρ εἰσι καὶ μᾶλλον μετέχουσι
τῶν τιμῶν ἐν ταῖς δημοκρατίαις ἢ ταῖς ὀλιγαρχίαις),
ἐπεὶ ὅταν ἄνευ τούτων τῷ πλήθει ὑπερτείνωσιν οἱ
ἄποροι, κακοπραγία γίνεται καὶ ἀπόλλυνται ταχέως.
σημεῖον δὲ δεῖ νομίζειν καὶ τὸ τοὺς βελτίστους
νομοθέτας εἶναι τῶν μέσων πολιτῶν· Σόλων τε γὰρ
20 ἦν τούτων (δηλοῖ δ' ἐκ τῆς ποιήσεως) καὶ Λυκοῦργος
(οὐ γὰρ ἦν βασιλεύς) καὶ Χαρώνδας καὶ σχεδὸν οἱ
πλεῖστοι τῶν ἄλλων.

Φανερὸν δ' ἐκ τούτων καὶ διότι αἱ πλεῖσται
πολιτεῖαι αἱ μὲν δημοκρατικαί εἰσιν αἱ δ' ὀλιγ-
αρχικαί· διὰ γὰρ τὸ ἐν ταύταις πολλάκις ὀλίγον
25 εἶναι τὸ μέσον, αἰεὶ ὁπότεροι ἂν ὑπερέχωσιν, εἴθ'
οἱ τὰς οὐσίας ἔχοντες εἴθ' ὁ δῆμος, οἱ τὸ μέσον ἐκ-
βαίνοντες καθ' αὑτοὺς ἄγουσι τὴν πολιτείαν, ὥστε
ἢ δῆμος γίγνεται ἢ ὀλιγαρχία. πρὸς δὲ τούτοις
διὰ τὸ στάσεις γίνεσθαι καὶ μάχας πρὸς ἀλλήλους
τῷ δήμῳ καὶ τοῖς εὐπόροις, ὁποτέροις ἂν μᾶλλον

tion and those near to them. The cause of this we will speak of later in our treatment of political 1308 a 1 · 4

9 revolutions. That the middle form of constitution is the best is evident; for it alone is free from faction, since where the middle class is numerous, factions and party divisions among the citizens are least likely to occur. And the great states are more free from faction for the same reason, because the middle class is numerous, whereas in the small states it is easy to divide the whole people into two parties leaving nothing in between, and also almost everybody is needy or wealthy. Also democracies are more secure and more long-lived than oligarchies owing to the citizens of the middle class (for they are more numerous and have a larger share of the honours in democracies than in oligarchies), since when the poor are in a majority without the middle class, adversity

10 sets in and they are soon ruined. And it must be deemed a significant fact that the best lawgivers are from among the middle citizens; for Solon was of that class, as appears from his poetry, and so was Lycurgus 1252 b 14. (for he was not a king) and Charondas and almost the 1271 b 25. greatest number of the other lawgivers.

And these considerations also show the reason why Democracy the constitutions of most states are either demo- and
cratic or oligarchical; owing to the middle class in Oligarchy these states being often a small one, the classes the most usual
diverging from the middle status—whichever of the govern-
two, the owners of the estates or the people, from ments.
time to time has the upper hand—conduct the government on their own lines, so that it becomes

11 either a democracy or an oligarchy. And in addition to this, because factions occur and fights between the people and the wealthy, whichever party happens

1296 a

30 συμβῇ κρατῆσαι τῶν ἐναντίων, οὐ καθιστᾶσι κοινὴν
πολιτείαν οὐδ' ἴσην, ἀλλὰ τῆς νίκης ἆθλον τὴν
ὑπεροχὴν τῆς πολιτείας λαμβάνουσιν, καὶ οἱ μὲν
δημοκρατίαν οἱ δ' ὀλιγαρχίαν ποιοῦσιν. ἔτι δὲ καὶ
τῶν ἐν ἡγεμονίᾳ γενομένων τῆς Ἑλλάδος πρὸς τὴν
παρ' αὑτοῖς ἑκάτεροι πολιτείαν ἀποβλέποντες οἱ
35 μὲν δημοκρατίας ἐν ταῖς πόλεσι καθίστασαν οἱ δ'
ὀλιγαρχίας, οὐ πρὸς τὸ τῶν πόλεων συμφέρον
σκοποῦντες ἀλλὰ πρὸς τὸ σφέτερον αὑτῶν. ὥστε
διὰ ταύτας τὰς αἰτίας ἢ μηδέποτε τὴν μέσην
γίνεσθαι πολιτείαν ἢ ὀλιγάκις καὶ παρ' ὀλίγοις· εἷς
γὰρ ἀνὴρ συνεπείσθη μόνος τῶν πρότερον ἐφ'
40 ἡγεμονίᾳ γενομένων ταύτην ἀποδοῦναι τὴν τάξιν,
1296 b ἤδη δὲ καὶ τοῖς ἐν ταῖς πόλεσιν ἔθος καθέστηκε
μηδὲ βούλεσθαι τὸ ἴσον, ἀλλ' ἢ ἄρχειν ζητεῖν ἢ
κρατουμένους ὑπομένειν.

Τίς μὲν οὖν ἀρίστη πολιτεία, καὶ διὰ τίν' αἰτίαν,
ἐκ τούτων φανερόν· τῶν δ' ἄλλων πολιτειῶν
(ἐπειδὴ πλείους δημοκρατίας καὶ πλείους ὀλιγ-
5 αρχίας φαμὲν εἶναι) ποίαν πρώτην θετέον καὶ
δευτέραν καὶ τοῦτον δὴ τὸν τρόπον ἐχομένην τῷ
τὴν μὲν εἶναι βελτίω τὴν δὲ χείρω, διωρισμένης τῆς
ἀρίστης οὐ χαλεπὸν ἰδεῖν. ἀεὶ[1] γὰρ ἀναγκαῖον
εἶναι βελτίω τὴν ἐγγύτατα ταύτης, χείρω δὲ τὴν
ἀφεστηκυῖαν τοῦ μέσου πλεῖον, ἂν μὴ πρὸς ὑπόθεσιν
10 κρίνῃ τις. λέγω δὲ τὸ πρὸς ὑπόθεσιν, ὅτι πολλάκις

----

[1] ἀεὶ Spengel : δεῖ codd.

----

[a] It is quite uncertain who is meant, possibly Solon or
Theramenes.

to gain the upper hand over its opponents does not establish a common or equal government, but takes the superior share in the government as a prize of victory, and makes it a democracy in the one case and an oligarchy in the other. Moreover each of the two states that in the past held the leadership of Greece took as a pattern the form of government that existed among themselves and set up in the one case democracies and in the other oligarchies in the cities, not considering the interest of the cities but their own advantage. Hence owing to these causes the middle form of constitution either never comes into existence or seldom and in few places; for one man *a* only among the states that have formerly held the leadership was induced to grant this form of organization, and by this time it has become a fixed habit with the people of the separate cities also not even to desire equality, but either to seek to rule or to endure being under a master.

These considerations therefore make it clear which is the best constitution, and why it is the best; and now that the best has been defined, it is not difficult to see, among the other forms of constitution (inasmuch as we pronounce that there are various forms of democracy and various oligarchies), what kind is to be placed first, what second, and what next in this order, by reason of one being better and another worse. For at each stage the form nearest to the best one must necessarily be superior, and the form that is more remote from the middle must be inferior —unless one is judging relatively to given conditions: I make this reservation because it is quite possible that although one form of constitution is

οὔσης ἄλλης πολιτείας αἱρετωτέρας ἐνίοις οὐθὲν
κωλύσει συμφέρειν ἑτέραν μᾶλλον εἶναι πολιτείαν.

X. Τίς δὲ πολιτεία τίσι καὶ ποία συμφέρει ποίοις, 1
ἐχόμενόν ἐστι τῶν εἰρημένων διελθεῖν. ληπτέον δὴ
15 πρῶτον περὶ πασῶν καθόλου ταὐτόν· δεῖ γὰρ
κρεῖττον εἶναι τὸ βουλόμενον μέρος τῆς πόλεως τοῦ
μὴ βουλομένου μένειν τὴν πολιτείαν. ἔστι δὲ πᾶσα
πόλις ἔκ τε τοῦ ποιοῦ καὶ ποσοῦ· λέγω δὲ ποιὸν
μὲν ἐλευθερίαν πλοῦτον παιδείαν εὐγένειαν, ποσὸν
δὲ τὴν τοῦ πλήθους ὑπεροχήν. ἐνδέχεται δὲ τὸ 2
20 μὲν ποιὸν ὑπάρχειν ἑτέρῳ μέρει τῆς πόλεως, ἐξ
ὧν συνέστηκε μερῶν ἡ πόλις, ἄλλῳ δὲ μέρει τὸ
ποσόν, οἷον πλείους τὸν ἀριθμὸν εἶναι τῶν γενναίων
τοὺς ἀγεννεῖς ἢ τῶν πλουσίων τοὺς ἀπόρους, μὴ
μέντοι τοσοῦτον ὑπερέχειν τῷ ποσῷ ὅσον λεί-
πεσθαι τῷ ποιῷ. διὸ ταῦτα πρὸς ἄλληλα συγ-
κριτέον.

25 Ὅπου μὲν οὖν ὑπερέχει τὸ τῶν ἀπόρων πλῆθος
τὴν εἰρημένην ἀναλογίαν, ἐνταῦθα πέφυκεν εἶναι
δημοκρατίαν, καὶ ἕκαστον εἶδος δημοκρατίας κατὰ
τὴν ὑπεροχὴν τοῦ δήμου ἑκάστου, οἷον ἐὰν μὲν τὸ
τῶν γεωργῶν ὑπερτείνῃ πλῆθος, τὴν πρώτην
δημοκρατίαν, ἐὰν δὲ τὸ τῶν βαναύσων καὶ μισθ-
30 αρνούντων, τὴν τελευταίαν, ὁμοίως δὲ καὶ τὰς ἄλλας
τὰς μεταξὺ τούτων· ὅπου δὲ τὸ τῶν εὐπόρων καὶ 3
γνωρίμων μᾶλλον ὑπερτείνει τῷ ποιῷ ἢ λείπεται
τῷ ποσῷ, ἐνταῦθα δὲ ὀλιγαρχίαν, καὶ τῆς ὀλιγαρχίας
τὸν αὐτὸν τρόπον ἕκαστον εἶδος κατὰ τὴν ὑπεροχὴν

---

[a] *i.e.* so as to outbalance their inferiority in quality.
[b] *i.e.* superiority in quality.

preferable it may often be more advantageous for certain people to have another form.

X. The next thing after what has been said is to discuss which constitution is advantageous for which people, and what sort of constitution for what sort of people. Now we must first grasp a general principle that applies equally to all sorts of constitution : it is essential that the part of the state that wishes the constitution to remain should be stronger than the part that does not wish it. But every state consists of both quality and quantity : by quality I mean freedom, wealth, education, good birth, and by quantity the superior numbers of the multitude. And it is possible that, while the quality of the state belongs to one among the parts of which the state consists and its quantity to another part—for example the low-born may be more numerous than the noble or the poor than the rich,—yet the more numerous class may not exceed in quantity as much as they fall behind in quality. Hence these two factors have to be judged in comparison with one another.

Where therefore the multitude of the poor exceeds in the proportion stated,[a] here it is natural for there to be democracy, and each kind of democracy in accordance with the superior number of the common people of each sort, for example if the number of the farming class exceeds, the first sort of democracy, but if that of the common labourers and wage-earners, the last sort, and similarly also with the other sorts that lie between these two ; but where the class of the well-to-do and notable exceeds in quality more than it falls behind in quantity, here it is natural for there to be an oligarchy, and likewise the various kinds of oligarchy according to the degree of superiority [b]

35 τοῦ ὀλιγαρχικοῦ πλήθους. δεῖ δ' ἀεὶ τὸν νομοθέτην
ἐν τῇ πολιτείᾳ προσλαμβάνειν τοὺς μέσους· ἄν τε
γὰρ ὀλιγαρχικοὺς τοὺς νόμους τιθῇ, στοχάζεσθαι
χρὴ τῶν μέσων, ἐάν τε δημοκρατικούς, προσάγεσθαι
τοῖς νόμοις τούτους. ὅπου δὲ τὸ τῶν μέσων
ὑπερτείνει πλῆθος ἢ συναμφοτέρων τῶν ἄκρων
καὶ θατέρου μόνον, ἐνταῦθ' ἐνδέχεται πολιτείαν

1297 a εἶναι μόνιμον· οὐθὲν γὰρ φοβερὸν μή ποτε
συμφωνήσωσιν οἱ πλούσιοι τοῖς πένησιν ἐπ
τούτους· οὐδέποτε γὰρ ἅτεροι βουλήσονται δου
λεύειν τοῖς ἑτέροις, κοινοτέραν δ', ἂν ζητῶσιν
οὐδεμίαν εὑρήσουσιν ἄλλην ταύτης, ἐν μέρει
5 ἄρχειν οὐκ ἂν ὑπομείνειαν διὰ τὴν ἀπιστίαν
πρὸς ἀλλήλους· πανταχοῦ δὲ πιστότατος ὁ δι
αιτητής, διαιτητὴς δ' ὁ μέσος. ὅσῳ δ' ἂν ἄμεινον
ἡ πολιτεία μιχθῇ, τοσούτῳ μονιμωτέρα· δια
μαρτάνουσι δὲ πολλοὶ καὶ τῶν τὰς ἀριστοκρατικὰς
βουλομένων ποιεῖν πολιτείας οὐ μόνον ἐν τῷ
10 πλεῖον νέμειν τοῖς εὐπόροις ἀλλὰ καὶ ἐν τῷ παρα
κρούεσθαι τὸν δῆμον· ἀνάγκη γὰρ χρόνῳ ποτὲ ἐκ
τῶν ψευδῶν ἀγαθῶν ἀληθὲς συμβῆναι κακόν, αἱ
γὰρ πλεονεξίαι τῶν πλουσίων ἀπολλύουσι μᾶλλον
τὴν πολιτείαν ἢ αἱ τοῦ δήμου.

Ἔστι δ' ὅσα προφάσεως χάριν ἐν ταῖς πολι
15 τείαις σοφίζονται πρὸς τὸν δῆμον πέντε τὸν
ἀριθμόν, περὶ ἐκκλησίαν, περὶ τὰς ἀρχάς, περὶ
δικαστήρια, περὶ ὅπλισιν, περὶ γυμνασίαν· περὶ
ἐκκλησίαν μὲν τὸ ἐξεῖναι ἐκκλησιάζειν πᾶσι,
ζημίαν δὲ ἐπικεῖσθαι τοῖς εὐπόροις ἐὰν μὴ ἐκκλη
σιάζωσιν ἢ μόνοις ἢ μείζω πολλῷ· περὶ δὲ τὰς
20 ἀρχὰς τὸ τοῖς μὲν ἔχουσι τίμημα μὴ ἐξεῖναι

---

^a The word is loosely used of this small class.

of the oligarchical multitude.[a] But the lawgiver in his constitution must always take in the middle class ; if he is making the laws of an oligarchical character he must keep the middle class in view, and if democratic, he must legislate so as to bring them in. 4 And where the number of the middle class exceeds both the extreme classes together, or even one of them only, here it is possible for a constitutional government to be lasting; for there is no fear of the rich ever coming to terms with the poor against this numerous middle class ; for neither class will ever wish to be subject to the other, and if they look for another constitution fairer to both than this they will not find one, for they would not endure to take turns to govern because they distrust each other : everywhere it is the arbitrator that is most trusted, and the man in the middle is an arbitrator. And the better the constitution is mixed, the more permanent 5 it is ; and many even of those who want to establish aristocratic forms of constitution make a great mistake not only in giving too large a share to the well-to-do but also in cheating the people ; for false benefits inevitably result ultimately in true evil, as the encroachments of the rich ruin the constitution more than those of the people.

6 The artifices employed in constitutions as a pretext in regard to the people are five in number, and are concerned with the assembly, the magistracies, the law-courts, the bearing of heavy arms, and gymnastic exercises ; in relation to the assembly, the granting to all of the right to attend but the imposition of a fine for non-attendance on the well-to-do only, or a much larger fine on them than others ; in relation to the magistracies, the denial to the

A mixed constitution most permanent.

Safeguards of Oligarchy, Democracy, and the Mixed Constitution.

1297 a

ἐξόμνυσθαι τοῖς δ' ἀπόροις ἐξεῖναι· καὶ περὶ τὰ
δικαστήρια τοῖς μὲν εὐπόροις εἶναι ζημίαν ἂν μὴ
δικάζωσι τοῖς δ' ἀπόροις ἄδειαν, ἢ τοῖς μὲν
μεγάλην τοῖς δὲ μικράν, ὥσπερ ἐν τοῖς Χαρώνδου νόμοις. ἐνιαχοῦ δ' ἔξεστι μὲν πᾶσιν ἀπο- 7
25 γραψαμένοις ἐκκλησιάζειν καὶ δικάζειν, ἐὰν δὲ ἀπο-
γραψάμενοι μήτ' ἐκκλησιάζωσι μήτε δικάζωσιν
ἐπίκεινται μεγάλαι ζημίαι τούτοις, ἵνα διὰ μὲν
τὴν ζημίαν φεύγωσι τὸ ἀπογράφεσθαι διὰ δὲ τὸ
μὴ ἀπογράφεσθαι μὴ δικάζωσι μηδ' ἐκκλησιάζωσιν.
τὸν αὐτὸν δὲ τρόπον καὶ περὶ τοῦ ὅπλα κεκτῆσθαι
30 καὶ τοῦ γυμνάζεσθαι νομοθετοῦσιν· τοῖς μὲν γὰρ
ἀπόροις ἔξεστι μὴ κεκτῆσθαι τοῖς δ' εὐπόροις
ἐπιζήμιον μὴ κεκτημένοις, κἂν μὴ γυμνάζωνται
τοῖς μὲν οὐδεμία ζημία τοῖς δ' εὐπόροις ἐπιζήμιον,
ὅπως οἱ μὲν διὰ τὴν ζημίαν μετέχωσιν οἱ δὲ διὰ
35 τὸ μὴ φοβεῖσθαι μὴ μετέχωσιν. ταῦτα μὲν οὖν
ὀλιγαρχικὰ σοφίσματα τῆς νομοθεσίας, ἐν δὲ 8
ταῖς δημοκρατίαις πρὸς ταῦτ' ἀντισοφίζονται· τοῖς
μὲν γὰρ ἀπόροις μισθὸν πορίζουσιν ἐκκλησιάζουσι
καὶ δικάζουσιν, τοῖς δ' εὐπόροις οὐδεμίαν τάττουσι
ζημίαν. ὥστε φανερὸν ὅτι εἴ τις βούλεται μιγνύναι
40 δικαίως, δεῖ τὰ παρ' ἑκατέροις συνάγειν καὶ τοῖς
μὲν μισθὸν πορίζειν τοῖς δὲ ζημίαν· οὕτω γὰρ ἂν
κοινωνοῖεν ἅπαντες, ἐκείνως δ' ἡ πολιτεία γίγνεται
1297 b τῶν ἑτέρων μόνον. δεῖ δὲ τὴν πολιτείαν εἶναι μὲν

owners of rated property of the right to swear off serving, while the poor have this right ; in relation to the law-courts, the imposition of a fine on the well-to-do if they do not serve on a jury, but no penalty for the poor, or else a large fine for the one class and a small one for the others, as in the laws of Charondas. In some places all have the right to serve in the assembly and on juries after having their names put on a register, but large fines are imposed on those who after so registering fail to attend in either capacity, in order that the fine may cause them to avoid registration and that owing to their not registering they may not serve on juries or in the assembly. They also legislate in the same manner about owning heavy arms and engaging in gymnastic exercises : the poor are not allowed to possess arms, but the well-to-do are liable to a fine if they have not got them, and there is no fine for the former class if they abstain from gymnastics, but the well-to-do are liable to a fine, in order that the one class because of the fine may take part in them and the other because they have no penalty to fear may not. These artifices of legislation then are of an oligarchic nature ; in democracies they introduce contrary devices in regard to these matters : they provide pay for the poor for serving in the assembly and on juries and impose no fine upon the well-to-do for abstaining. Hence it is manifest that if anybody wishes to make a just blend, he must bring together the regulations existing in each of the two forms of constitution, and provide pay for attendance and a fine for non-attendance; for thus all would participate, whereas in the other way the government comes to be in the hands of only one of the two classes. And

1251 b 14.

341

ἐκ τῶν τὰ ὅπλα ἐχόντων μόνον, τοῦ δὲ τιμήματος
τὸ πλῆθος ἁπλῶς μὲν ὁρισαμένους οὐκ ἔστιν
εἰπεῖν τοσοῦτον ὑπάρχειν, ἀλλὰ σκεψαμένους τὸ
5 ποῖον¹ ἐπιβάλλει μακρότατον ὥστε τοὺς μετέχοντας
τῆς πολιτείας εἶναι πλείους τῶν μὴ μετεχόντων,
τοῦτο τάττειν. ἐθέλουσι γὰρ οἱ πένητες καὶ μὴ
μετέχοντες τῶν τιμῶν ἡσυχίαν ἔχειν ἐὰν μὴ
ὑβρίζῃ τις αὐτοὺς μήτε ἀφαιρῆται μηθὲν τῆς
οὐσίας· ἀλλὰ τοῦτο οὐ ῥᾴδιον, οὐ γὰρ ἀεὶ συμβαί-
10 νει χαρίεντας εἶναι τοὺς μετέχοντας τοῦ πολιτεύματος. καὶ εἰώθασι δὲ ὅταν πόλεμος ᾖ ὀκνεῖν ἂν μὴ
λαμβάνωσι τροφὴν ἄποροι δὲ ὦσιν· ἐὰν δὲ πορίζῃ
τις τροφήν, βούλονται πολεμεῖν. ἔστι δ' ἡ πολιτεία
παρ' ἐνίοις οὐ μόνον ἐκ τῶν ὁπλιτευόντων ἀλλὰ
καὶ ἐκ τῶν ὡπλιτευκότων· ἐν Μαλιεῦσι δὲ ἡ μὲν
15 πολιτεία ἦν ἐκ τούτων τὰς δὲ ἀρχὰς ᾑροῦντο ἐκ
τῶν στρατευομένων. καὶ ἡ πρώτη δὲ πολιτεία ἐν
τοῖς Ἕλλησιν ἐγένετο μετὰ τὰς βασιλείας ἐκ τῶν
πολεμούντων, ἡ μὲν ἐξ ἀρχῆς ἐκ τῶν ἱππέων (τὴν
γὰρ ἰσχὺν καὶ τὴν ὑπεροχὴν ἐν τοῖς ἱππεῦσιν ὁ
20 πόλεμος εἶχεν, ἄνευ μὲν γὰρ συντάξεως ἄχρηστον
τὸ ὁπλιτικόν, αἱ δὲ περὶ τῶν τοιούτων ἐμπειρίαι
καὶ τάξεις ἐν τοῖς ἀρχαίοις οὐχ ὑπῆρχον, ὥστ' ἐν
τοῖς ἱππεῦσιν εἶναι τὴν ἰσχύν), αὐξανομένων δὲ
τῶν πόλεων καὶ τῶν ἐν τοῖς ὅπλοις ἰσχυσάντων
μᾶλλον πλείους μετεῖχον τῆς πολιτείας. διόπερ
25 ἃς νῦν καλοῦμεν πολιτείας οἱ πρότερον ἐκάλουν

¹ πόσον Lindau.

although it is proper that the government should be drawn only from those who possess heavy armour, yet it is not possible to define the amount of the property-qualification absolutely and to say that they must possess so much, but only to consider what sort of amount is the highest that is compatible with making those who have a share in the constitution more numerous than those who have not, and to fix that limit. For those who are poor and have no share in the honours are willing to keep quiet if no one insults them or takes away any part of their substance; but this is not easy to secure, for it does not always happen that those who are in the governing class are gentlemen. Also people have a way of being reluctant to serve when there is a war if they do not get rations and are poor men; but if somebody provides food they want to fight. In some states the citizen-body consists not only of those who are serving as heavy-armed soldiers, but also of those who have so served; and at Malea the citizen-body consisted of these, while the magistrates were elected from those who were actually on service. And indeed the earliest form of constitution among the Greeks after the kingships consisted of those who were actually soldiers, the original form consisting of the cavalry (for war had its strength and its pre-eminence in cavalry, since without orderly formation heavy-armed infantry is useless, and the sciences and systems dealing with tactics did not exist among the men of old times, so that their strength lay in their cavalry); but as the states grew and the wearers of heavy armour had become stronger, more persons came to have a part in the government. Hence what we now call constitutional governments the men of

1297 b δημοκρατίας· ἦσαν δὲ αἱ ἀρχαῖαι πολιτεῖαι εὐλόγως 1]
ὀλιγαρχικαὶ καὶ βασιλικαί, δι᾽ ὀλιγανθρωπίαν γὰρ
οὐκ εἶχον πολὺ τὸ μέσον, ὥστ᾽ ὀλίγοι τε ὄντες τὸ
πλῆθος καὶ κατὰ τὴν σύνταξιν μᾶλλον ὑπέμενον
τὸ ἄρχεσθαι.

Διὰ τίνα μὲν οὖν εἰσὶν αἰτίαν αἱ πολιτεῖαι πλείους,
30 καὶ διὰ τί παρὰ τὰς λεγομένας ἕτεραι (δημοκρατία
τε γὰρ οὐ μία τὸν ἀριθμόν ἐστι, καὶ τῶν ἄλλων
ὁμοίως), ἔτι δὲ τίνες αἱ διαφοραὶ καὶ διὰ τίνα
αἰτίαν συμβαίνει, πρὸς δὲ τούτοις τίς ἀρίστη τῶν
πολιτειῶν ὡς ἐπὶ τὸ πλεῖστον εἰπεῖν, καὶ τῶν
ἄλλων ποία ποίοις ἁρμόττει τῶν πολιτειῶν, εἴρηται.

35 XI. Πάλιν δὲ καὶ κοινῇ καὶ χωρὶς περὶ ἑκάστης
λέγωμεν περὶ τῶν ἐφεξῆς, λαβόντες ἀρχὴν τὴι
προσήκουσαν αὐτῶν. ἔστι δὴ τρία μόρια τῶν
πολιτειῶν πασῶν περὶ ὧν δεῖ θεωρεῖν τὸν σπουδαῖον
νομοθέτην ἑκάστῃ τὸ συμφέρον· ὧν ἐχόντων καλῶς
ἀνάγκη τὴν πολιτείαν ἔχειν καλῶς, καὶ τὰς
40 πολιτείας ἀλλήλων διαφέρειν ἐν τῷ διαφέρειν
ἕκαστον τούτων. ἔστι δὲ τῶν τριῶν τούτων ἓν
1298 a μὲν τί[1] τὸ βουλευόμενον περὶ τῶν κοινῶν, δεύτερον
δὲ τὸ περὶ τὰς ἀρχάς, τοῦτο δ᾽ ἐστὶ τίνας[2] δεῖ καὶ[3]
τίνων εἶναι κυρίας, καὶ ποίαν τινὰ δεῖ γίγνεσθαι
τὴν αἵρεσιν αὐτῶν, τρίτον δὲ τί τὸ δικάζον.

Κύριον δ᾽ ἐστὶ τὸ βουλευόμενον περὶ πολέμου

---

[1] μὲν τί Congreve: μέν τι, μέν τοι codd.
[2] ἐστὶ τίνας Wilson: ἐστὶν ἃς codd.
[3] δεῖ ⟨εἶναι⟩ καὶ ? ed.

1 former times called democracies; but the constitutional governments of early days were naturally oligarchical and royal, for owing to the smallness of the populations their middle class was not numerous, so that because of their small numbers as well as in conformity with the structure of the state the middle class more readily endured being in a subject position.

It has then been said what is the reason of there being several forms of constitution, and why there are others besides those designated by name (for there is not one single democracy only, and similarly there are more than one of the other forms), and also what are the differences between them and what is the reason why these differences occur, and in addition to these points, which is the best of the constitutions speaking generally, and of the other constitutions which sort is suited to which sort of people.

XI. And again, let us speak about the points that come next, both generally and with reference to each constitution separately, taking their appropriate starting-point. All forms of constitution then have three factors in reference to which the good lawgiver has to consider what is expedient for each constitution; and if these factors are well-ordered the constitution must of necessity be well-ordered, and the superiority of one constitution over another necessarily consists in the superiority of each of these factors. Of these three factors one is, what is to be the body that deliberates about the common interests, second the one connected with the magistracies, that is, what there are to be and what matters they are to control, and what is to be the method of their election, and a third is, what is to be the judiciary.

The deliberative factor is sovereign about war and

The three elements of government:

345

1298 a
5 καὶ εἰρήνης καὶ συμμαχίας καὶ διαλύσεως, καὶ
περὶ νόμων, καὶ περὶ θανάτου καὶ φυγῆς καὶ
δημεύσεως, καὶ τῶν εὐθυνῶν. ἀναγκαῖον δ᾽ ἤτοι 2
πᾶσι τοῖς πολίταις ἀποδεδόσθαι πάσας ταύτας τὰς
κρίσεις ἢ τισὶ πάσας (οἷον ἀρχῇ τινὶ μιᾷ ἢ πλείοσιν)
ἢ ἑτέραις ἑτέρας ἢ τινὰς μὲν αὐτῶν πᾶσι τινὰς δὲ
τισίν.

10 Τὸ μὲν οὖν πάντας καὶ περὶ ἁπάντων δημοτικόν,
τὴν τοιαύτην γὰρ ἰσότητα ζητεῖ ὁ δῆμος. εἰσὶ δὲ 3
οἱ τρόποι τοῦ πάντας πλείους, εἷς μὲν τὸ κατὰ
μέρος ἀλλὰ μὴ πάντας ἀθρόους (ὥσπερ ἐν τῇ
πολιτείᾳ τῇ Τηλεκλέους ἐστὶ τοῦ Μιλησίου, καὶ
ἐν ἄλλαις δὲ πολιτείαις βουλεύονται αἱ συναρχίαι
15 συνιοῦσαι εἰς δὲ τὰς ἀρχὰς βαδίζουσι πάντες κατὰ
μέρος ἐκ τῶν φυλῶν καὶ τῶν μορίων τῶν ἐλαχίστων
παντελῶς ἕως ἂν διέλθῃ διὰ πάντων), συνιέναι δὲ
μόνον περί τε νόμων θέσεως καὶ τῶν περὶ τῆς
πολιτείας καὶ τὰ παραγγελλόμενα ἀκουσομένους
20 ὑπὸ τῶν ἀρχόντων· ἄλλος δὲ τρόπος τὸ πάντας 4
ἀθρόους, συνιέναι δὲ μόνον πρός τε τὰς ἀρχαιρεσίας [αἱρησομένους][1] καὶ πρὸς τὰς νομοθεσίας
καὶ περὶ πολέμου καὶ εἰρήνης καὶ πρὸς εὐθύνας,
τὰ δ᾽ ἄλλα τὰς ἀρχὰς βουλεύεσθαι τὰς ἐφ᾽ ἑκάστοις
τεταγμένας, αἱρετὰς οὔσας ἐξ ἁπάντων ἢ κληρω-
25 τάς· ἄλλος δὲ τρόπος τὸ περὶ τὰς ἀρχὰς καὶ τὰς
εὐθύνας ἀπαντᾶν τοὺς πολίτας, καὶ περὶ πολέμου

---

[1] Susemihl.

[a] Otherwise unknown.

peace and the formation and dissolution of alliances, and about laws, and about sentences of death and exile and confiscation of property, and about the audits of magistrates. And necessarily either all these decisions must be assigned to all the citizens, or all to some of them (for instance to some one magistracy or to several), or different ones to different magistracies, or some of them to all the citizens and some to certain persons.

(1) The Deliberative: its functions in democracy, oligarchy, aristocracy and republican government.

For all the citizens to be members of the deliberative body and to decide all these matters is a mark of a popular government, for the common people seek for equality of this nature. But there are several modes of such universal membership. One is for the citizens to serve in rotation and not all in a body (as is enacted in the constitution of the Milesian Telecles,[a] and in other constitutions also the boards of magistrates deliberate in joint assemblies but all the citizens enter into the magistracies from the tribes or from the very smallest sections of the citizen-body in rotation until office has gone through the whole body), and for there to be joint assemblies only to consider legislation and reforms of the constitution and to hear the reports submitted by the magistrates. Another mode is for all to assemble in a body, but only for the purpose of electing magistrates, enacting laws, considering the declaration of war and the conclusion of peace and holding the audit of magistrates, but for all other matters to be considered by the magistrates appointed to deal with each respectively and elected by suffrage or by lot from all the citizens. Another mode is for the citizens to meet about the magistracies and the audits and in order to deliberate about declaring war

347

1298 a
βουλευσομένους καὶ συμμαχίας, τὰ δ' ἄλλα τὰς
ἀρχὰς διοικεῖν αἱρετὰς οὔσας, ὅσας ἐνδέχεται,
τοιαῦται δ' εἰσὶν ὅσας ἄρχειν ἀναγκαῖον τοὺς
ἐπισταμένους, τέταρτος δὲ τρόπος τὸ πάντας περὶ
3 πάντων βουλεύεσθαι συνιόντας, τὰς δ' ἀρχὰς περὶ
μηθενὸς κρίνειν ἀλλὰ μόνον προανακρίνειν, ὅνπερ
ἡ τελευταία δημοκρατία νῦν διοικεῖται τρόπον, ἣν
ἀνάλογόν φαμεν εἶναι ὀλιγαρχίᾳ τε δυναστευτικῇ
καὶ μοναρχίᾳ τυραννικῇ. οὗτοι μὲν οὖν οἱ τρόποι
δημοκρατικοὶ πάντες, τὸ δὲ τινὰς περὶ πάντων
35 ὀλιγαρχικόν. ἔχει δὲ καὶ τοῦτο διαφορὰς πλείους.
ὅταν μὲν γὰρ ἀπὸ τιμημάτων μετριωτέρων αἱρετοί
τε ὦσι καὶ πλείους διὰ τὴν μετριότητα τοῦ τιμήματος, καὶ περὶ ὧν ὁ νόμος ἀπαγορεύει μὴ κινῶσιν
ἀλλ' ἀκολουθῶσι, καὶ ἐξῇ κτωμένῳ τὸ τίμημα
μετέχειν, ὀλιγαρχία μὲν πολιτικὴ δ' ἐστὶν ἡ
40 τοιαύτη διὰ τὸ μετριάζειν· ὅταν δὲ μὴ πάντες
1298 b τοῦ βουλεύεσθαι μετέχωσιν ἀλλὰ πρόκριτοι,[1] κατὰ
νόμον δ' ἄρχωσιν ὥσπερ καὶ πρότερον, ὀλιγαρχι-
κόν· ὅταν δὲ καὶ αἱρῶνται αὐτοὶ αὑτοὺς οἱ κύριοι
τοῦ βουλεύεσθαι, καὶ ὅταν παῖς ἀντὶ πατρὸς
εἰσίῃ καὶ κύριοι τῶν νόμων ὦσιν, ὀλιγαρχικὴν[2]
5 ἀναγκαῖον εἶναι τὴν τάξιν ταύτην. ὅταν δὲ τινῶν

---

[1] ἀλλὰ πρόκριτοι Immisch: ἀλλ' αἱρετοί codd.
[2] ὀλιγαρχικωτέραν Garvey, ⟨μᾶλλον⟩ ὀλιγαρχικὴν Spengel.

---

[a] i.e. in an advanced democracy.

and concluding an alliance, but for all other matters
to be dealt with by the magistrates, elected by
suffrage in as many cases as circumstances allow,[a]
and such magistracies are all those which must of
necessity be filled by experts. A fourth mode is for
all to meet in council about all matters, and for the
magistracies to decide about nothing but only to make
preliminary decisions ; this is the mode in which
democracy in its last form is administered at the
present day—the form of democracy which we pronounce to correspond to dynastic oligarchy and to
tyrannical monarchy. These modes then are all of
them democratic. On the other hand for some
persons to deliberate upon all matters is oligarchic.
But this also has several variations. For when the
members of the deliberative body are elected on
comparatively moderate property-qualifications, and
the eligible persons are comparatively numerous
because of the moderateness of the qualification,
and when they do not make changes in things in
which the law forbids it but follow the law, and
when anybody acquiring the property-qualification is
allowed to become a member, a constitution of this
sort is indeed an oligarchy, but one of the nature of
constitutional government, because of its moderation. When on the other hand not everybody thus
qualified participates in deliberation but only certain
persons previously chosen by election, and these
govern in accordance with law as in the former case,
this is oligarchical ; and also when the deliberative
officials are elected by co-optation, and when the
office is hereditary and has supreme control over the
laws, this system is bound to be oligarchical. But
when certain persons control certain matters, for

τινές,[1] οἷον πολέμου μὲν καὶ εἰρήνης καὶ εὐθυνῶν
πάντες τῶν δὲ ἄλλων ἄρχοντες καὶ οὗτοι αἱρετοὶ
μὴ κληρωτοί,[2] ἀριστοκρατία ἢ πολιτεία· ἐὰν
δ' ἐνίων μὲν αἱρετοὶ ἐνίων δὲ κληρωτοί, καὶ
κληρωτοὶ ἢ ἁπλῶς ἢ ἐκ προκρίτων, ἢ κοινῇ
10 αἱρετοὶ καὶ κληρωτοί, τὰ μὲν πολιτείας ἀριστοκρα-
τικῆς ἐστὶ τούτων, τὰ δὲ πολιτείας αὐτῆς.

Διῄρηται μὲν οὖν τὸ βουλευόμενον πρὸς τὰς
πολιτείας τοῦτον τὸν τρόπον, καὶ διοικεῖ[3] ἑκάστη
πολιτεία κατὰ τὸν εἰρημένον διορισμόν· συμφέρει
δὲ δημοκρατίᾳ τῇ[4] μάλιστ' εἶναι δοκούσῃ δημο-
15 κρατίᾳ νῦν (λέγω δὲ τοιαύτην ἐν ᾗ κύριος ὁ δῆμος
καὶ τῶν νόμων ἐστίν) πρὸς τὸ βουλεύεσθαι βέλτιον
τὸ αὐτὸ ποιεῖν ὅπερ ἐπὶ τῶν δικαστηρίων ἐν ταῖς
ὀλιγαρχίαις (τάττουσι γὰρ ζημίαν τούτοις οὓς
βούλονται δικάζειν ἵνα δικάζωσιν, οἱ δὲ δημοτικοὶ
μισθὸν τοῖς ἀπόροις), τοῦτο δὲ καὶ περὶ τὰς
20 ἐκκλησίας ποιεῖν (βουλεύσονται γὰρ βέλτιον κοινῇ
βουλευόμενοι πάντες, ὁ μὲν δῆμος μετὰ τῶν
γνωρίμων, οὗτοι δὲ μετὰ τοῦ πλήθους)· συμφέρει δὲ καὶ τὸ αἱρετοὺς εἶναι τοὺς βουλευομένους
ἢ κληρωτοὺς ἴσως ἐκ τῶν μορίων, συμφέρει δὲ κἂν
ὑπερβάλλωσι πολὺ κατὰ τὸ πλῆθος οἱ δημοτικοὶ
25 τῶν πολιτικῶν[5] ἢ μὴ πᾶσι διδόναι μισθὸν ἀλλ'

---

[1] τινές secl. Camerarius (cum Guilelmi codd. plerisque).
[2] μὴ κληρωτοί ? Newman : ἢ κλ. codd. (secl. Brandis).
[3] disponitur (διοικεῖται ?) Guil. : διοίσει Congreve.
[4] τῇ Coraes : τῇ τε codd.   [5] πολιτῶν ? Richards.

---

[a] The mss. give ' or by lot.'

instance when all the citizens control decisions as to war and peace and the audit of officials while everything else is controlled by magistrates and these are elected by vote, not by lot,[a] the constitution is an aristocracy; while if some matters are controlled by magistrates elected by vote and others by magistrates chosen by lot, and this either directly or from a list previously selected by vote, or if magistrates elected by vote and by lot sit in a joint body, some of these regulations are features of an aristocratic constitution and others of constitutional government itself.

We have then in this way distinguished the different kinds of deliberative body in relation to the forms of constitution, and each form of constitution carries on the administration in accordance with the distinction stated. But for a democracy of the form that at the present day is considered to be democracy in the fullest degree (and I mean one of the sort in which the people is sovereign even over the laws) it is advantageous for the improvement of its deliberative function for it to do the same as is done in oligarchies in the matter of the law-courts (for they enact a fine to compel the attendance on juries of those whom they want to attend, whereas democratic states institute payment for attendance for the benefit of the poor), and also to do this in respect of the assemblies (for they will deliberate better when all are deliberating jointly, the common people when with the notables and these when with the masses), and it is also advantageous for those who deliberate to be elected by vote or by lot equally from the different sections, and, if the men of the people far exceed the political class in number, it is advantageous

351

1298 b

ὅσοι σύμμετροι πρὸς τὸ τῶν γνωρίμων πλῆθος ἢ
ἀποκληροῦν τοὺς πλείους. ἐν δὲ ταῖς ὀλιγαρχίαις 9
ἢ προσαιρεῖσθαί[1] τινας ἐκ τοῦ πλήθους, ἤ, κατα-
σκευάσαντας ἀρχεῖον οἷον ἐν ἐνίαις πολιτείαις
ἐστὶν οὓς καλοῦσι προβούλους καὶ νομοφύλακας,[2]
30 περὶ τούτων χρηματίζειν περὶ ὧν ἂν οὗτοι
προβουλεύσωσιν (οὕτω γὰρ μεθέξει ὁ δῆμος τοῦ
βουλεύεσθαι καὶ λύειν οὐθὲν δυνήσεται τῶν περὶ
τὴν πολιτείαν), ἔτι ἢ ταὐτὰ ψηφίζεσθαι τὸν δῆμον
ἢ μηθὲν ἐναντίον τοῖς εἰσφερομένοις, ἢ τῆς
συμβουλῆς μὲν μεταδιδόναι πᾶσι βουλεύεσθαι δὲ
35 τοὺς ἄρχοντας. καὶ τὸ ἀντικείμενον δὲ τοῦ ἐν
ταῖς πολιτείαις γιγνομένου δεῖ ποιεῖν· ἀποψηφιζό-
μενον μὲν γὰρ κύριον δεῖ ποιεῖν τὸ πλῆθος, κατα-
ψηφιζόμενον δὲ μὴ κύριον, ἀλλ' ἐπαναγέσθω
πάλιν ἐπὶ τοῖς ἄρχοντας· ἐν γὰρ ταῖς πολιτείαις
ἀντεστραμμένως ποιοῦσιν, οἱ γὰρ ὀλίγοι ἀπο-
40 ψηφισάμενοι μὲν κύριοι, καταψηφισάμενοι δὲ οὐ
1299 a κύριοι, ἀλλ' ἐπανάγεται εἰς τοὺς πλείστους αἰεί.

Περὶ μὲν οὖν τοῦ βουλευομένου καὶ τοῦ κυρίου
δὴ τῆς πολιτείας τοῦτον διωρίσθω τὸν τρόπον.

XII. Ἐχομένη δὲ τούτων ἐστὶν ἡ περὶ τὰς
ἀρχὰς διαίρεσις (ἔχει γὰρ καὶ τοῦτο τὸ μόριον τῆς
5 πολιτείας πολλὰς διαφοράς), πόσαι τε ἀρχαὶ καὶ

---

[1] Susemihl: προαιρ. codd.   [2] Coraes: -κας καὶ codd.

---

[a] There were πρόβουλοι at Corinth as well as a βουλή and
an ἐκκλησία; and νομοφύλακες at Sparta, Athens and elsewhere: at Athens they sat with the presidents of the βουλή
and ἐκκλησία to check illegal procedure.

either not to give pay to all but only to as many as
are commensurate with the number of the notables,
or to discard by lot those who exceed this number.
In oligarchies on the other hand it is advantageous
either to co-opt some persons from the multitude,
or to institute an office like the one that exists in
certain constitutional governments under the name
of Preliminary Councillors or Guardians of the Law,[a]
and deal with the matters about which these officials
have held a preliminary deliberation (for thus the
common people will have a share in deliberation and
will not have the power to abolish any part of the
constitution), and then for the people by their vote
either to confirm or at all events not to pass anything
contrary to the resolutions brought before them, or
to allow all to take part in debate but only the
magistrates to frame resolutions; and in fact it
is proper to do just the opposite of what takes
place in constitutionally governed states; for the
common people ought to be given power to vote the
rejection of a measure, but not to vote its ratification, but it should be referred back to the magistrates. In constitutional governments the procedure
is the reverse; the few are competent to vote
the rejection of a resolution but are not competent
to vote its ratification, this being always referred
back to the most numerous body.

Let us then decide in this manner about the deliberative body, which in fact is the sovereign power
in the constitution.

XII. Connected with this subject is the determina- (2) The
tion in regard to the magistracies (for this part of Executive.
the constitution also has many varieties), how many
magistracies there are to be, and what are to be their

1299 a

κύριαι τίνων, καὶ περὶ χρόνου, πόσος ἑκάστης
ἀρχῆς (οἱ μὲν γὰρ ἑξαμήνους, οἱ δὲ δι' ἐλάττονος,
οἱ δ' ἐνιαυσίας, οἱ δὲ πολυχρονιωτέρας ποιοῦσι
τὰς ἀρχάς), καὶ πότερον εἶναι δεῖ τὰς ἀρχὰς ἀιδίους ἢ πολυχρονίους, ἢ μηδέτερον ἀλλὰ πλεονά-
10 κις τοὺς αὐτούς, ἢ μὴ τὸν αὐτὸν δὶς ἀλλ' ἅπαξ
μόνον· ἔτι δὲ περὶ τὴν κατάστασιν τῶν ἀρχῶν, ἐκ
τίνων δεῖ γίνεσθαι καὶ ὑπὸ τίνων καὶ πῶς. περὶ
πάντων γὰρ τούτων δεῖ δύνασθαι διελεῖν κατὰ
πόσους ἐνδέχεται γενέσθαι τρόπους, κἄπειτα προσ-
αρμόσαι ποίαις ποῖοι[1] πολιτείαις συμφέρουσιν.
15 ἔστι δὲ οὐδὲ τοῦτο διορίσαι ῥάδιον, ποίας δεῖ καλεῖ
ἀρχάς· πολλῶν γὰρ ἐπιστατῶν ἡ πολιτικὴ κοινωνία
δεῖται, διόπερ οὐ[2] πάντας οὔτε τοὺς αἱρετοὺς
οὔτε τοὺς κληρωτοὺς ἄρχοντας θετέον, οἷον τοὺς
ἱερεῖς πρῶτον (τοῦτο γὰρ ἕτερόν τι παρὰ τὰς
πολιτικὰς ἀρχὰς θετέον), ἔτι δὲ χορηγοὶ κα
20 κήρυκες, αἱροῦνται δὲ καὶ πρεσβευταί. εἰσὶ δ
αἱ μὲν πολιτικαὶ τῶν ἐπιμελειῶν, ἢ πάντων τῶ
πολιτῶν πρός τινα πρᾶξιν, οἷον στρατηγὸ
στρατευομένων, ἢ κατὰ μέρος, οἷον ὁ γυναικο
νόμος ἢ παιδονόμος· αἱ δ' οἰκονομικαί (πολλάκι
γὰρ αἱροῦνται σιτομέτρας)· αἱ δ' ὑπηρετικαί κα
25 πρὸς ἅς, ἂν εὐπορῶσι, τάττουσι δούλους. μάλιστ
ὧδ' s ἁπλῶς εἰπεῖν ἀρχὰς λεκτέον ταύτας ὅσαι
ἀποδέδοται βουλεύσασθαί τε περὶ τινῶν καὶ κρίνα

---

[1] Ar.: ποῖαι codd. (et nonnulli πολιτεῖαι).
[2] οὐ suppleuit Rassow.

---

[a] Distributions of corn were made at times of scarcity, c
when the state had received a present of corn.

powers, and what their various periods of tenure (for
some people make their magistracies tenable for six
months, others for less, others for a year and others
for a longer period)—shall the magistracies be for life
or for a long period, or if for a shorter term shall the
same people be allowed to hold them several times
or not the same man twice but once only ? and also
as to the appointment of magistrates, who shall be
eligible, who the electors, and what the mode of
election ? For on all these points it is needful to be
able to determine how many modes of procedure are
possible, and then to settle what modes are expedient
for what sorts of constitution. Nor is it easy to decide
to what kinds of office the name of magistracy ought
to be applied ; for the political community requires
a great many officials, owing to which it is not proper
to reckon all of them magistrates, whether elected
by vote or by lot,—for instance first the priests (for
this office must be considered as something different
from the political magistracies), and again there are
leaders of choruses, and heralds, and persons are
also elected as ambassadors. And of the offices
exercising superintendence some are political, and
are exercised either over the whole of the citizens in
regard to some operation—for instance a general
superintends them when serving as soldiers, or over
a section—for instance the superintendent of women
or of children ; while others are economic (for states
often elect officers to dole out corn *a*) ; and others
are subordinate, and are the sort of services to which
people when well off appoint slaves. But the title
of magistracy, to put it simply, is chiefly to be applied
to all those offices to which have been assigned the
duties of deliberating about certain matters and of

1299 a

καὶ ἐπιτάξαι, καὶ μάλιστα τοῦτο, τὸ γὰρ ἐπιτάττειν ἀρχικώτερόν ἐστιν. ἀλλὰ ταῦτα διαφέρει
πρὸς μὲν τὰς χρήσεις οὐθὲν ὡς εἰπεῖν (οὐ γάρ πω
30 κρίσις γέγονεν ἀμφισβητούντων περὶ τοῦ ὀνόματος),
ἔχει δέ τιν' ἄλλην διανοητικὴν πραγματείαν.
ποῖαι δ' ἀρχαὶ καὶ πόσαι ἀναγκαῖαι εἰ ἔσται
πόλις, καὶ ποῖαι ἀναγκαῖαι μὲν οὔ χρήσιμοι δὲ
πρὸς σπουδαίαν πολιτείαν, μᾶλλον ἄν τις ἀπορήσειε πρὸς ἅπασάν τε δὴ πολιτείαν καὶ δὴ καὶ τὰς
35 μικρὰς πόλεις. ἐν μὲν γὰρ δὴ ταῖς μεγάλαις
ἐνδέχεταί τε καὶ δεῖ μίαν τετάχθαι πρὸς ἓν ἔργον
(πολλούς τε γὰρ εἰς τὰ ἀρχεῖα ἐνδέχεται βαδίζειν διὰ τὸ πολλοὺς εἶναι τοὺς πολίτας, ὥστε
τὰς μὲν διαλείπειν πολὺν χρόνον τὰς δ' ἅπαξ
ἄρχειν, καὶ βέλτιον ἕκαστον ἔργον τυγχάνει τῆς
1299 b ἐπιμελείας μονοπραγματούσης ἢ πολυπραγματού-
σης)· ἐν δὲ ταῖς μικραῖς ἀνάγκη συνάγειν εἰς
ὀλίγους πολλὰς ἀρχάς (διὰ γὰρ ὀλιγανθρωπίαν οὐ
ῥᾴδιόν ἐστι πολλοὺς ἐν ταῖς ἀρχαῖς εἶναι· τίνες
γὰρ οἱ τούτους ἔσονται διαδεξόμενοι πάλιν;)
5 δέονται δ' ἐνίοτε τῶν αὐτῶν ἀρχῶν καὶ νόμων
αἱ μικραὶ ταῖς μεγάλαις· πλὴν αἱ μὲν δέονται
πολλάκις τῶν αὐτῶν, ταῖς δ' ἐν πολλῷ χρόνῳ
τοῦτο συμβαίνει. διόπερ οὐθὲν κωλύει πολλὰς
ἐπιμελείας ἅμα προστάττειν (οὐ γὰρ ἐμποδιοῦσιν
ἀλλήλαις), καὶ πρὸς τὴν ὀλιγανθρωπίαν ἀναγκαῖον
10 τὰ ἀρχεῖα οἷον ὀβελισκολύχνια ποιεῖν. ἐὰν οὖν

ᵃ An implement (its exact shape does not appear to be
known), used by soldiers on campaign, here mentioned as
an illustration of one tool serving two purposes, cf. 1252 b 1.

356

acting as judges and of issuing orders, and especially the last, for to give orders is most characteristic of authority. But this question is of virtually no practical importance (for no decision has yet been given, our discussion being merely about the name), although it does admit of some further inquiry of a speculative kind. On the other hand the questions what kinds and what number of magistracies are necessary to constitute a state at all, and what kinds although not necessary are advantageous for a good constitution, are questions that might preferably be discussed, both indeed as regards every form of constitution and particularly in regard to the small states. For it is true that in the large states it is possible and proper for one magistracy to be assigned to one function (for the large number of the citizens makes it possible for many people to enter on an official career, so as to intermit their tenure of some offices for a long time and to hold others only once, and also every task is better attended to if the attention is directed to one thing only than if it is busy with many); but in the small states it is inevitable that many offices must be gathered into few hands (for owing to shortage of man-power it is not easy for many people to be in office, since who will take over the posts as their successors?). But sometimes small states require the same magistracies and laws as large ones; except that the latter require the same persons to serve often, but in the former this only occurs after a long interval. Hence it is possible to assign several duties to one man at the same time (since they will not interfere with one another), and to meet the shortage of man-power it is necessary to make the magistracies like spit-lampholders.[a] If therefore we are able to

357

ἔχωμεν λέγειν πόσας ἀναγκαῖον ὑπάρχειν πάσ
πόλει καὶ πόσας οὐκ ἀναγκαῖον μὲν δεῖ δ' ὑπ
ἄρχειν, ῥᾷον ἄν τις εἰδὼς ταῦτα συνίδοι[1] ποία
ἁρμόττει συνάγειν ἀρχὰς εἰς μίαν ἀρχήν. ἁρ
μόττει δὲ καὶ τοῦτο μὴ λεληθέναι, ποίων[2] δε
15 κατὰ τόπον ἀρχεῖα πολλὰ[3] ἐπιμελεῖσθαι καὶ ποίω
πανταχοῦ μίαν ἀρχὴν εἶναι κυρίαν, οἷον εὐκοσμία
πότερον ἐν ἀγορᾷ μὲν ἀγορανόμον ἄλλον δὲ κατ
ἄλλον τόπον, ἢ πανταχοῦ τὸν αὐτόν· καὶ πότερο
κατὰ τὸ πρᾶγμα δεῖ διαιρεῖν ἢ κατὰ τοὺς ἀνθρώ
πους, λέγω δ' οἷον ἕνα τῆς εὐκοσμίας, ἢ παίδω
20 ἄλλον καὶ γυναικῶν· καὶ κατὰ τὰς πολιτείας δε
πότερον διαφέρει καθ' ἑκάστην καὶ τὸ τῶν ἀρχῶ
γένος ἢ οὐθέν, οἷον ἐν δημοκρατίᾳ καὶ ὀλιγαρχί
καὶ ἀριστοκρατίᾳ καὶ μοναρχίᾳ πότερον αἱ αὐτα
μέν εἰσιν ἀρχαὶ κύριαι, οὐκ ἐξ ἴσων δ' οὐδ' ε
25 ὁμοίως, ἀλλ' ἕτεραι ἐν ἑτέραις (οἷον ἐν μὲν ταῖ
ἀριστοκρατίαις ἐκ πεπαιδευμένων ἐν δὲ ταῖ
ὀλιγαρχίαις ἐκ τῶν πλουσίων ἐν δὲ ταῖς δημο
κρατίαις ἐκ τῶν ἐλευθέρων) ἢ τυγχάνουσι μέν τινε
οὖσαι καὶ κατ' αὐτὰς τὰς διαφορὰς τῶν ἀρχῶ
ἔστι δ' ὅπου συμφέρουσιν αἱ αὐταὶ καὶ ὅπο
διαφέρουσιν (ἔνθα μὲν γὰρ ἁρμόττει μεγάλας
30 ἔνθα δ' εἶναι μικρὰς τὰς αὐτάς). οὐ μὴν ἀλλὰ κα

---

[1] Bojesen : συνάγοι codd. (συνάγοι οἴας ? ed.).
[2] Thurot : ποῖα codd.
[3] Thurot : πολλῶν codd.

say how many magistracies every state must necessarily possess and how many, though not absolutely necessary, it ought to possess, knowing these points one might more easily realize what kinds of magistracies are of a suitable nature to be combined into a single office. And it is suitable for the further question not to be overlooked, what kinds of matters ought to be attended to by a number of officials locally distributed and what ought to be under the authority of one magistrate for all localities, for example should good order be seen to in the market-place by a Controller of the Market and elsewhere by another official, or everywhere by the same one ? and ought the offices to be divided according to the function or according to the persons concerned—I mean, for instance, should there be a single official in control of good order, or a different one for children and for women ? and also under the various constitutions does the nature of the magistracies vary in accordance with each or does it not vary at all—for example in democracy, oligarchy, aristocracy and monarchy are the magistracies the same in their powers, although they are not filled from equal ranks nor from similar classes but are different in different constitutions (for example in aristocracies drawn from the educated, in oligarchies from the wealthy, and in democracies from the free), or although some constitutions happen to be correspondent with the actual differences of their magistracies, yet in other cases are the same magistracies advantageous even where the constitutions differ (for in some places it is suitable for the same magistracies to have large functions and in other places small ones) ? Not but what there are also some offices peculiar to special

1299 b

ἴδιαί τινές εἰσιν, οἷον ἡ τῶν προβούλων. αὕτη
γὰρ οὐ δημοκρατική, βουλὴ δὲ δημοτικόν, δεῖ
μὲν γὰρ εἶναί τι τοιοῦτον ᾧ ἐπιμελὲς ἔσται τοῦ
δήμου προβουλεύειν, ὅπως ἀσχολῶν ἔσται· τοῦτο
δ᾽, ἐὰν ὀλίγοι τὸν ἀριθμὸν ὦσιν, ὀλιγαρχικόν,
35 τοὺς δὲ προβούλους ὀλίγους ἀναγκαῖον εἶναι τὸ
πλῆθος, ὥστ᾽ ὀλιγαρχικόν. ἀλλ᾽ ὅπου ἄμφω
αὗται αἱ ἀρχαί, οἱ πρόβουλοι καθεστᾶσιν ἐπὶ τοῖς
βουλευταῖς· ὁ μὲν γὰρ βουλευτὴς δημοτικόν, ὁ
δὲ πρόβουλος ὀλιγαρχικόν.   καταλύεται δὲ καὶ 9
τῆς βουλῆς ἡ δύναμις ἐν ταῖς τοιαύταις δημο-
1300 a κρατίαις ἐν αἷς αὐτὸς συνιὼν ὁ δῆμος χρηματίζει
περὶ πάντων.   τοῦτο δὲ συμβαίνειν εἴωθεν ὅταν
εὐπορία τις ᾖ μισθοῦ[1] τοῖς ἐκκλησιάζουσιν, σχολά-
ζοντες γὰρ συλλέγονταί τε πολλάκις καὶ ἅπαντα
αὐτοὶ κρίνουσιν.   παιδονόμος δὲ καὶ γυναικονόμος
5 καὶ εἴ τις ἄλλος ἄρχων κύριός ἐστι τοιαύτης
ἐπιμελείας ἀριστοκρατικόν, δημοκρατικὸν δ᾽ οὔ
(πῶς γὰρ οἷόν τε κωλύειν ἐξιέναι τὰς τῶν ἀπόρων;)
οὐδ᾽ ὀλιγαρχικόν (τρυφῶσι γὰρ αἱ τῶν ὀλιγ-
αρχούντων).   ἀλλὰ περὶ μὲν τούτων ἐπὶ τοσοῦτον
10 εἰρήσθω νῦν, περὶ δὲ τὰς τῶν ἀρχῶν καταστάσεις 1
πειρατέον ἐξ ἀρχῆς διελθεῖν. εἰσὶ δ᾽ αἱ διαφοραὶ
ἐν τρισὶν ὅροις, ὧν συντιθεμένων ἀναγκαῖον
πάντας εἰλῆφθαι τοὺς τρόπους. ἔστι δὲ τῶν τριῶν
τούτων ἓν μὲν τίνες οἱ καθιστάντες τὰς ἀρχάς,
δεύτερον δ᾽ ἐκ τίνων, λοιπὸν δὲ τίνα τρόπον.

---

[1] μισθοῦ Spengel: ἢ μισθὸς codd.

---

[a] See 1298 b 29 n.
[b] Or possibly 'from going in processions': Solon made
regulations ταῖς ἐξόδοις τῶν γυναικῶν καὶ τοῖς πένθεσι καὶ ταῖς
ἑορταῖς (Plutarch, *Solon* 21).

forms of constitution, for instance the office of **Preliminary Councillors**.[a] This is undemocratic, although a Council is a popular body, for there is bound to be some body of this nature to have the duty of preparing measures for the popular assembly, in order that it may be able to attend to its business ; but a preparatory committee, if small, is oligarchical, and Preliminary Councillors must necessarily be few in number, so that they are an oligarchical element. But where both of these magistracies exist, the Preliminary Councillors are in authority over the Councillors, since a councillor is a democratic official, but a

9 preliminary councillor is an oligarchic one. Also the power of the Council is weakened in democracies of the sort in which the people in assembly deals with everything itself ; and this usually happens when there is a plentiful supply of pay for those who attend the assembly, for being at leisure they meet frequently and decide all things themselves. But a Superintendent of Children and a Superintendent of Women, and any other magistrates that exercise a similar sort of supervision, are an aristocratic feature, and not democratic (for how is it possible to prevent the wives of the poor from going out of doors [b] ?) nor yet oligarchic (for the wives of oligarchic rulers

10 are luxurious). But let the discussion of these matters go no further at present, and let us attempt to go through from the beginning the question of the ways of appointing the magistrates. The varieties here depend on three determinants, the combinations of which must give all the possible modes. One of these three determining points is, who are the persons who appoint the magistrates ? the second is, from whom ?

Appointment of the Executive : 12 modes and 2 variations.

1300 a

ἑκάστου δὲ τῶν τριῶν τούτων διαφοραὶ τρεῖς
15 εἰσίν· ἢ γὰρ πάντες οἱ πολῖται καθιστᾶσιν ἢ
τινές, καὶ ἢ ἐκ πάντων ἢ ἐκ τινῶν ἀφωρισμένων
(οἷον ἢ τιμήματι ἢ γένει ἢ ἀρετῇ ἤ τινι τοιούτῳ
ἄλλῳ, ὥσπερ ἐν Μεγάροις ἐκ τῶν συγκατελθόντων
καὶ συμμαχεσαμένων πρὸς τὸν δῆμον), καὶ ταῦτα
20 ἢ αἱρέσει ἢ κλήρῳ· πάλιν ταῦτα συνδυαζόμενα, Ι
λέγω δὲ τὰς μὲν τινὲς τὰς δὲ πάντες, καὶ τὰς
μὲν ἐκ πάντων τὰς δ' ἐκ τινῶν, καὶ τὰς μὲν
αἱρέσει τὰς δὲ κλήρῳ. τούτων δ' ἑκάστης
ἔσονται τῆς διαφορᾶς τρόποι τέσσαρες.[1] ἢ γὰρ
πάντες ἐκ πάντων αἱρέσει, ἢ πάντες ἐκ πάντων
25 κλήρῳ—καὶ [ἢ][2] ἐξ ἁπάντων ἢ ὡς ἀνὰ μέρος, οἷον
κατὰ φυλὰς καὶ δήμους καὶ φρατρίας ἕως ἂν
διέλθῃ διὰ πάντων τῶν πολιτῶν,[3] ἢ ἀεὶ ἐξ ἁπάντων,—ἢ καὶ[4] τὰ μὲν οὕτω τὰ δὲ ἐκείνως· πάλιν εἰ
τινὲς οἱ καθιστάντες, ἢ ἐκ πάντων αἱρέσει ἢ ἐκ
πάντων κλήρῳ, ἢ ἐκ τινῶν αἱρέσει ἢ ἐκ τινῶν
30 κλήρῳ, ἢ τὰ μὲν οὕτω τὰ δ' ἐκείνως, λέγω δὲ τὰ
μὲν [ἐκ πάντων][5] αἱρέσει τὰ δὲ κλήρῳ. ὥστε
δώδεκα οἱ τρόποι γίνονται χωρὶς τῶν δύο συν-
δυασμῶν. τούτων δ' αἱ μὲν δύο καταστάσεις
δημοτικαί, τὸ πάντας ἐκ πάντων[6] αἱρέσει ἢ κλήρῳ
[γίνεσθαι][7] ἢ ἀμφοῖν, τὰς μὲν κλήρῳ τὰς δ'
αἱρέσει τῶν ἀρχῶν· τὸ δὲ μὴ πάντας ἅμα μὲν

---

[1] 1300 a 23-b 5 locum vertiginosum viri docti ad libidinem
quisque suam rescripserunt.
[2] Thurot.   [3] πολιτῶν Ar.: πολιτικῶν.
[4] ἢ καὶ Rabe: καὶ ἢ, καὶ codd.   [5] Hayduck.
[6] post πάντων add. καὶ τὸ πάντας ἐκ τινῶν Rabe.
[7] Thurot.

---

[a] It is quite uncertain when this event took place and
362

and last, in what manner ? And of each of these
three determinants there are three variations : either
all the citizens appoint or some, and either from
all or from a certain class (defined for instance by
property-assessment or birth or virtue or some other
such qualification, as at Megara only those were
eligible who returned in a body from exile and fought
together against the common people),[a] and the mode
of appointment may be either by vote or by lot ;
again, these systems may be coupled together—I
mean that some citizens may appoint to some offices
but all to others, and to some offices all citizens may
be eligible but to others only a certain class, and to
some appointment may be by vote but to others by
lot. And of each variation of these determinants
there will be four modes : either all citizens may
appoint from all by vote, or all from all by lot—and
from all either section by section, for instance by
tribes or demes or brotherhoods until the procedure
has gone through all the citizens, or from the whole
number every time,—or else partly in one way and
partly in the other. Again, if the electors are some
of the citizens, they must either appoint from all by
vote, or from all by lot, or from some by vote, or
from some by lot, or partly in one way and partly in
the other—I mean partly by vote and partly by lot.
Hence the modes prove to be twelve, apart from the
two combinations. And among these, two ways of
appointment are democratic—for all to appoint from
all by vote, or by lot, or by both—some offices by lot
and others by vote ; but for not all to be the electors
and for them to appoint simultaneously, and either

whether it is the same as those referred to at 1302 b 30 f.
and 1304 b 34 ff.

1300 a

85 καθιστάναι, ἐξ ἁπάντων δ' ἢ ἔκ τινων, ἢ κλήρῳ ἢ
αἱρέσει ἢ ἀμφοῖν, ἢ τὰς μὲν ἐκ πάντων τὰς δ'
ἔκ τινων ἀμφοῖν (τὸ δὲ ἀμφοῖν λέγω τὰς μὲν
κλήρῳ τὰς δ' αἱρέσει) πολιτικόν. καὶ τὸ τινὰς
ἐκ πάντων τὰς μὲν αἱρέσει καθιστάναι τὰς δὲ
40 κλήρῳ ἢ ἀμφοῖν (τὰς μὲν κλήρῳ τὰς δ' αἱρέσει)
ὀλιγαρχικόν· ὀλιγαρχικώτερον δὲ καὶ τὸ ἐξ ἀμφοῖν.
τὸ δὲ τὰς μὲν ἐκ πάντων τὰς δ' ἔκ τινων πολι-
1300 b τικὸν ἀριστοκρατικῶς, ἢ τὰς μὲν αἱρέσει τὰς δὲ
κλήρῳ. τὸ δὲ τινὰς ἔκ τινων <αἱρέσει>[1] ὀλιγαρχικόν, καὶ τὸ τινὰς ἔκ τινων κλήρῳ (μὴ
γενόμενον δ' ὁμοίως), καὶ τὸ τινὰς ἔκ τινων ἀμφοῖν.
τὸ δὲ τινὰς ἐξ ἁπάντων τότε[2] δὲ ἔκ τινων αἱρέσει
5 πάντας ἀριστοκρατικόν.

Οἱ μὲν οὖν τρόποι τῶν περὶ τὰς ἀρχὰς τοσοῦτοι τὸν ἀριθμόν εἰσι, καὶ διήρηνται κατὰ τὰς
πολιτείας οὕτως· τίνα δὲ τίσι συμφέρει καὶ πῶς
δεῖ γίνεσθαι τὰς καταστάσεις ἅμα ταῖς δυνάμεσι
τῶν ἀρχῶν [καὶ][3] τίνες εἰσὶν ἔσται φανερόν. λέγω
10 δὲ δύναμιν ἀρχῆς οἷον τὴν κυρίαν τῶν προσόδων
καὶ τὴν κυρίαν τῆς φυλακῆς· ἄλλο γὰρ εἶδος
δυνάμεως οἷον στρατηγίας καὶ τῆς τῶν περὶ τὴν
ἀγορὰν συμβολαίων κυρίας.

XIII. Λοιπὸν δὲ τῶν τριῶν τὸ δικαστικὸν εἰπεῖν,
ληπτέον δὲ καὶ τούτων τοὺς τρόπους κατὰ τὴν

---

[1] Lambinus.　　[2] τότε P[2]: τὸ cet.　　[3] [καὶ] om. ΓΜΡ[1].

[a] Perhaps the Greek should be rewritten to give ' for some
to appoint from all either by vote or by lot or by both.'
[b] This insertion by Lambinus seems certain.

from all or from some either by lot or by vote or by both, or some offices from all and others from some by both (by which I mean some by lot and others by vote) is constitutional. And for some to appoint from all, to some offices by vote and to others by lot or by both [a] (to some by lot and to others by vote) is oligarchical; and it is even more oligarchical to 3 appoint from both classes. But to appoint some offices from all and the others from a certain class is constitutional with an aristocratic bias ; or to appoint some by vote and others by lot. And for a certain class to appoint from a certain class ⟨by vote⟩ [b] is oligarchical, and so it is for a certain class to appoint from a certain class by lot (although not working out in the same way), and for a certain class to appoint from a certain class by both methods. And for a certain class to make a preliminary selection from the whole body and then for all to appoint from among certain persons (thus selected) is aristocratic.

So many in number therefore are the modes of appointing to the magistracies, and this is how the modes are classified according to the different constitutions ; and what regulations are advantageous for what people and how the appointments ought to be conducted will be made clear at the same time as we consider what are the powers of the offices. By the power of an office I mean for instance the control of the revenues and the control of the guard ; since a different sort of power belongs for example to a generalship and to the office that controls market contracts.

XIII. Of the three factors of a constitution it (3) The remains to speak of the judiciary, and of judicial Judiciary. bodies also we must consider the various modes, in classified.

365

15 αὐτὴν ὑπόθεσιν. ἔστι δὲ διαφορὰ τῶν δικαστηρίων
ἐν τρισὶν ὅροις, ἐξ ὧν τε καὶ περὶ ὧν καὶ πῶς.
λέγω δὲ ἐξ ὧν μέν, πότερον ἐκ πάντων ἢ ἐκ
τινῶν· περὶ ὧν δέ, πόσα εἴδη δικαστηρίων· τὸ
δὲ πῶς, πότερον κλήρῳ ἢ αἱρέσει. πρῶτον οὖν
διαιρείσθω πόσα εἴδη δικαστηρίων. ἔστι δὲ τὸν
20 ἀριθμὸν ὀκτώ, ἓν μὲν εὐθυντικόν, ἄλλο δὲ εἴ τίς τι
τῶν κοινῶν ἀδικεῖ, ἕτερον ὅσα εἰς τὴν πολιτείαν
φέρει, τέταρτον καὶ ἄρχουσι καὶ ἰδιώταις ὅσα
περὶ ζημιώσεων ἀμφισβητοῦσιν, πέμπτον τὸ περὶ
τῶν ἰδίων συναλλαγμάτων καὶ[1] ἐχόντων μέγεθος,
καὶ παρὰ ταῦτα τό τε φονικὸν καὶ τὸ ξενικὸν
25 (φονικοῦ μὲν οὖν εἴδη, ἄν τ' ἐν τοῖς αὐτοῖς δικα-²
σταῖς ἄν τ' ἐν ἄλλοις, περί τε τῶν ἐκ προνοίας καὶ
περὶ τῶν ἀκουσίων καὶ ὅσα ὁμολογεῖται μὲν
ἀμφισβητεῖται δὲ περὶ τοῦ δικαίου, τέταρτον δὲ
ὅσα τοῖς φεύγουσι φόνου ἐπὶ καθόδῳ ἐπιφέρεται,
οἷον Ἀθήνησι λέγεται καὶ τὸ ἐν Φρεαττοῖ δικα-
30 στήριον, συμβαίνει δὲ τὰ τοιαῦτα ἐν τῷ παντὶ
χρόνῳ ὀλίγα καὶ ἐν ταῖς μεγάλαις πόλεσιν· τοῦ
δὲ ξενικοῦ ἓν μὲν ξένοις πρὸς ξένους, ἄλλο δὲ²
ξένοις πρὸς ἀστούς)· ἔτι δὲ παρὰ πάντα ταῦτα
περὶ τῶν μικρῶν συναλλαγμάτων, ὅσα δραχμιαῖα
καὶ πεντάδραχμα καὶ μικρῷ πλείονος· δεῖ μὲν
35 γὰρ καὶ περὶ τούτων γίνεσθαι κρίσιν, οὐκ ἐμπίπτει
δὲ εἰς δικαστῶν πλῆθος. ἀλλὰ περὶ μὲν τούτων

---

[1] ⟨τῶν⟩ καὶ Richards.   [2] ἄλλο δὲ Richards : ἄλλο codd.

---

[a] *i.e.* men that had been allowed to flee the country when
charged with accidental homicide, and on their return were
accused of another homicide, a wilful murder.

accordance with the same plan. And a difference among judicial courts rests upon three determinants —constituents, sphere of action, and mode of appointment. As to their constituents I mean are the courts drawn from all the citizens or from a certain class? as to sphere of action, how many kinds of courts are there? and as to mode of appointment, are they appointed by lot or by vote? First then let us distinguish how many kinds of courts there are. They are eight in number, one a court of audit, another to deal with offenders against any public interest, another with matters that bear on the constitution, a fourth for both magistrates and private persons in disputes about penalties, fifth the court dealing with private contracts that are on an important scale, and beside these there is (6) the court that tries homicide, and (7) that which hears alien suits (of courts of homicide there are four kinds, whether the jury is the same or different—namely, for cases of deliberate homicide, of involuntary homicide, of homicide admitted but claimed to be justifiable, and fourth to deal with charges of homicide brought against men that have fled from the country for homicide, upon their return,^{a} such as at Athens for instance the Court at Phreatto is said to be, although such cases are of rare occurrence in the whole course of history, even in the great states; and of the aliens' court one branch hears suits of aliens against aliens and another of aliens against citizens); and also beside all of these there are (8) courts to try cases of petty contracts, involving sums of one drachma, five drachmas or a little more—for even these cases have to be tried, though they are not suitable for a numerous jury. But let us dismiss the subject of these petty

1300 b

ἀφείσθω καὶ τῶν φονικῶν καὶ τῶν ξενικῶν, περὶ
δὲ τῶν πολιτικῶν λέγωμεν, περὶ ὧν μὴ γινομένων
καλῶς διαστάσεις γίνονται καὶ τῶν πολιτειῶν αἱ
κινήσεις. ἀνάγκη δ' ἤτοι πάντας περὶ πάντων
40 κρίνειν τῶν διῃρημένων αἱρέσει ἢ κλήρῳ, ἢ
πάντας περὶ πάντων τὰ μὲν κλήρῳ τὰ δ' αἱρέσει,
ἢ περὶ ἐνίων τῶν αὐτῶν τοὺς μὲν κλήρῳ τοὺς δ'
1301 a αἱρετούς. οὗτοι μὲν οὖν οἱ τρόποι τέτταρες τὸν
ἀριθμόν, τοσοῦτοι δ' ἕτεροι καὶ οἱ κατὰ μέρος·
πάλιν γὰρ ἐκ τινων καὶ οἱ δικάζοντες περὶ πάντων
αἱρέσει, ἢ ἐκ τινῶν περὶ πάντων κλήρῳ, ἢ τὰ μὲν
5 κλήρῳ τὰ δὲ αἱρέσει, ἢ ἔνια δικαστήρια περὶ τῶν
αὐτῶν ἐκ κληρωτῶν καὶ αἱρετῶν. οὗτοι μὲν οὖν,
ὥσπερ ἐλέχθησαν, οἱ τρόποι ἀντίστροφοι[1] τοῖς
εἰρημένοις. ἔτι δὲ τὰ αὐτὰ συνδυαζόμενα, λέγω δ'
οἷον τὰ μὲν ἐκ πάντων τὰ δ' ἐκ τινῶν τὰ δ' ἐξ
ἀμφοῖν, οἷον εἰ τοῦ αὐτοῦ δικαστηρίου εἶεν οἱ μὲν
10 ἐκ πάντων οἱ δ' ἐκ τινῶν, καὶ ἢ κλήρῳ ἢ αἱρέσει
ἢ ἀμφοῖν. ὅσους μὲν οὖν ἐνδέχεται τρόπους εἶναι
τὰ δικαστήρια, εἴρηται· τούτων δὲ τὰ μὲν πρῶτα
δημοτικά, ὅσα ἐκ πάντων περὶ[2] πάντων, τὰ δὲ
δεύτερα ὀλιγαρχικά, ὅσα ἐκ τινῶν περὶ πάντων, τὸ
δὲ τρίτα ἀριστοκρατικὰ καὶ πολιτικά, ὅσα τὰ μὲν
15 ἐκ πάντων τὰ δ' ἐκ τινῶν.

---

[1] ἀντίστροφοι suppleuit Newman.
[2] περὶ Susemihl : ἢ περὶ codd.

suits, and the courts for homicide and those for aliens, and let us speak about political trials, which when not well conducted cause party divisions and revolutionary disturbances. And necessarily either all the judges of all the cases that have been classified will be appointed by vote, or by lot, or all in all cases partly by lot and partly by vote, or in some cases some judges will be appointed by lot and others by vote for the same case. These modes then are four in number, and the sectional modes also make as many others ; for here again the judges for all cases may be drawn by vote from a certain class, or for all cases by lot from a certain class, or some courts may be appointed by lot and others by vote, or some courts may be composed of judges chosen by lot and by vote for the same cases. These then are the modes, as was said, corresponding to those mentioned. And there are also the same courts in combination—I mean for example some drawn from the whole body and some from a class and some from both, as for instance if the same court contained some members from the whole body and others from a class, and appointed either by lot or by vote or both. We have then stated all the modes in which it is possible for the courts to be composed ; and of these the first set, drawn from all the citizens and dealing with all cases, are popular, the second, drawn from a certain class to deal with all cases, are oligarchic, and the third, drawn partly from all and partly from a certain class, are suited to an aristocracy and to a constitutional government.

Lawcourts under various constitutions.

E

I. Περὶ μὲν οὖν τῶν ἄλλων ὧν προειλόμεθα
20 σχεδὸν εἴρηται περὶ πάντων· ἐκ τίνων δὲ μεταβάλλουσιν αἱ πολιτεῖαι καὶ πόσων καὶ ποίων, καὶ
τίνες ἑκάστης πολιτείας φθοραί, καὶ ἐκ ποίων
εἰς ποίας μάλιστα μεθίστανται, ἔτι δὲ σωτηρίαι
τίνες καὶ κοινῇ καὶ χωρὶς ἑκάστης εἰσίν, ἔτι δὲ διὰ
τίνων ἂν μάλιστα σώζοιτο τῶν πολιτειῶν ἑκάστη,
25 σκεπτέον ἐφεξῆς τοῖς εἰρημένοις.

Δεῖ δὲ πρῶτον ὑπολαβεῖν τὴν ἀρχήν, ὅτι πολλαὶ
γεγένηνται πολιτεῖαι πάντων μὲν ὁμολογούντων τὸ
δίκαιον καὶ τὸ κατ' ἀναλογίαν ἴσον τούτου δ'
ἁμαρτανόντων (ὥσπερ εἴρηται καὶ πρότερον).
δῆμος μὲν γὰρ ἐγένετο ἐκ τοῦ ἴσους ὁτιοῦν ὄντας
30 οἴεσθαι ἁπλῶς ἴσους εἶναι (ὅτι γὰρ ἐλεύθεροι πάντες
ὁμοίως, ἁπλῶς ἴσοι εἶναι νομίζουσιν), ὀλιγαρχία δὲ
ἐκ τοῦ ἀνίσους ἔν τι ὄντας ὅλως εἶναι ἀνίσους
ὑπολαμβάνειν (κατ' οὐσίαν γὰρ ἄνισοι ὄντες
ἁπλῶς ἄνισοι ὑπολαμβάνουσιν εἶναι). εἶτα οἱ μὲν
ὡς ἴσοι ὄντες πάντων τῶν ἴσων ἀξιοῦσι μετέχειν,

---

[a] Book V. is placed as Book VII. by some editors, as
Book VIII. by others, see Book III. *fin.* note.
[b] For this distinction between broad methods of guarding
against revolution and the practical means by which those
methods can be put into effect Newman compares c. ix. §§ 2 f.,
10 f., iv. ii. 5 *fin.*, vi. i. 1.

370

BOOK V a

Book V.
REVOLU-
TION:
ITS CAUSES
AND
PREVEN-
TION.

1   I. Almost all the other subjects which we intended
to treat have now been discussed. There must
follow the consideration of the questions, what are
the number and the nature of the causes that give
rise to revolutions in constitutions, and what are
the causes that destroy each form of constitution,
and out of what forms into what forms do they
usually change, and again what are the safeguards
of constitutions in general and of each form in particular, and what are the means by which the safe-
guarding of each may best be put into effect.b

2   And we must first assume the starting-point, that
many forms of constitution have come into existence with everybody agreeing as to what is just,
that is proportionate equality, but failing to attain
it (as has also been said before). Thus democracy
arose from men's thinking that if they are equal in
any respect they are equal absolutely (for they suppose that because they are all alike free they are
equal absolutely), oligarchy arose from their assuming that if they are unequal as regards some one
thing they are unequal wholly (for being unequal
in property they assume that they are unequal
3 absolutely); and then the democrats claim as
being equal to participate in all things in equal

1301 a

35 οἱ δ' ὡς ἄνισοι ὄντες πλεονεκτεῖν ζητοῦσιν, τὸ γὰρ
πλεῖον ἄνισον. ἔχουσι μὲν οὖν τι πᾶσαι δίκαιον,
ἡμαρτημέναι δ' ἁπλῶς εἰσίν· καὶ διὰ ταύτην τὴν
αἰτίαν, ὅταν μὴ κατὰ τὴν ὑπόληψιν ἣν ἑκάτεροι
τυγχάνουσιν ἔχοντες μετέχωσι τῆς πολιτείας,
στασιάζουσιν. πάντων δὲ δικαιότατα μὲν ἂν στα-
40 σιάζοιεν, ἥκιστα δὲ τοῦτο πράττουσιν, οἱ κατ'
1301 b ἀρετὴν διαφέροντες· μάλιστα γὰρ εὔλογον ἀνίσους
ἁπλῶς εἶναι τούτους μόνον[1]. εἰσὶ δέ τινες οἳ κατὰ
γένος ὑπερέχοντες οὐκ ἀξιοῦσι τῶν ἴσων αὑτοὺς
διὰ τὴν ἀνισότητα ταύτην· εὐγενεῖς γὰρ εἶναι
δοκοῦσιν οἷς ὑπάρχει προγόνων ἀρετὴ καὶ πλοῦτος.

5 Ἀρχαὶ μὲν οὖν ὡς εἰπεῖν[2] αὗται καὶ πηγαὶ τῶν
στάσεών εἰσιν ὅθεν στασιάζουσιν (διὸ καὶ αἱ μεταβολαὶ γίγνονται διχῶς· ὁτὲ μὲν γὰρ πρὸς τὴν
πολιτείαν, ὅπως ἐκ τῆς καθεστηκυίας ἄλλην μετα-
στήσωσιν, οἷον ἐκ δημοκρατίας ὀλιγαρχίαν ἢ
δημοκρατίαν ἐξ ὀλιγαρχίας, ἢ πολιτείαν καὶ
10 ἀριστοκρατίαν ἐκ τούτων, ἢ ταύτας ἐξ ἐκείνων·
ὁτὲ δ' οὐ πρὸς τὴν καθεστηκυῖαν πολιτείαν, ἀλλὰ
τὴν μὲν κατάστασιν προαιροῦνται τὴν αὐτήν, δι'
αὑτῶν δ' εἶναι βούλονται ταύτην, οἷον τὴν ὀλιγαρχίαν ἢ τὴν μοναρχίαν. ἔτι περὶ τοῦ μᾶλλον καὶ
ἧττον, οἷον ἢ ὀλιγαρχίαν οὖσαν εἰς τὸ μᾶλλον
15 ὀλιγαρχεῖσθαι ἢ εἰς τὸ ἧττον, ἢ δημοκρατίαν
οὖσαν εἰς τὸ μᾶλλον δημοκρατεῖσθαι ἢ εἰς τὸ
ἧττον, ὁμοίως δὲ καὶ ἐπὶ τῶν λοιπῶν πολιτειῶν, ἢ

---

[1] μόνους ? ed.
[2] ⟨πασῶν⟩ ὡς εἰπεῖν vel ὡς εἰπεῖν post πηγαὶ Richards.

shares, while the oligarchs as being unequal seek
to have a larger share, for a larger share is unequal.
All these forms of constitution then have some
element of justice, but from an absolute point of
view they are erroneous ; and owing to this cause,
when each of the two parties has not got the share
in the constitution which accords with the fundamental assumption that they happen to entertain,
class war ensues. And of all men those who excel in
virtue would most justifiably stir up faction, though
they are least given to doing so ; for they alone
can with the fullest reason be deemed absolutely
unequal. And there are some men who being
superior in birth claim unequal rights because of
this inequality ; for persons who have ancestral virtue
and wealth behind them are thought to be noble.

These then roughly speaking are the starting- Aims of
points and sources of factions, which give rise to party revolution.
strife (and revolutions due to this take place in two
ways : sometimes they are in regard to the constitution, and aim at changing from the one established
to another, for instance from democracy to oligarchy,
or to democracy from oligarchy, or from these to
constitutional government and aristocracy, or from
those to these ; but sometimes the revolution is not
in regard to the established constitution, but its
promoters desire the same form of government,
for instance oligarchy or monarchy, but wish it to be
in their own control. Again it may be a question of
degree ; for instance, when there is an oligarchy the
object may be to change to a more oligarchical
government or to a less, or when there is a democracy
to a more or to a less democratic government, and
similarly in the case of the remaining constitutions.

ἵνα ἐπιταθῶσιν ἢ ἀνεθῶσιν. ἔτι πρὸς τὸ μέρος τι
κινῆσαι τῆς πολιτείας, οἷον ἀρχήν τινα καταστῆσαι
ἢ ἀνελεῖν, ὥσπερ ἐν Λακεδαίμονί φασι Λύσανδρόν

20 τινες ἐπιχειρῆσαι καταλῦσαι τὴν βασιλείαν καὶ
Παυσανίαν τὸν βασιλέα τὴν ἐφορείαν· καὶ ἐν
Ἐπιδάμνῳ δὲ μετέβαλεν ἡ πολιτεία κατὰ μόριον,
ἀντὶ γὰρ τῶν φυλάρχων βουλὴν ἐποίησαν, εἰς δὲ
τὴν ἡλιαίαν ἐπάναγκές ἐστιν ἔτι τῶν ἐν τῷ

25 πολιτεύματι βαδίζειν τὰς ἀρχὰς ὅταν ἐπιψηφίζηται
ἀρχή τις· ὀλιγαρχικὸν δὲ καὶ ὁ ἄρχων ὁ εἷς ἦν ἐν
τῇ πολιτείᾳ ταύτῃ). πανταχοῦ γὰρ διὰ τὸ ἄνισον
ἡ στάσις, οὐ μὴ[1] τοῖς ἀνίσοις ὑπάρχει ἀνάλογον
(ἀΐδιος γὰρ βασιλεία ἄνισος ἐὰν ᾖ ἐν ἴσοις)· ὅλως
γὰρ τὸ ἴσον ζητοῦντες στασιάζουσιν. ἔστι δὲ

30 διττὸν τὸ ἴσον, τὸ μὲν γὰρ ἀριθμῷ τὸ δὲ κατ᾽
ἀξίαν ἐστίν—λέγω δὲ ἀριθμῷ μὲν τὸ πλήθει ἢ
μεγέθει ταὐτὸ καὶ ἴσον, κατ᾽ ἀξίαν δὲ τὸ τῷ
λόγῳ· οἷον ὑπερέχει κατ᾽ ἀριθμὸν μὲν ἴσῳ τὰ
τρία τοῖν δυοῖν καὶ ταῦτα τοῦ ἑνός, λόγῳ δὲ
τέτταρα τοῖν δυοῖν καὶ ταῦτα τοῦ ἑνός, ἴσον γὰρ

35 μέρος τὰ δύο τῶν τεττάρων καὶ τὸ ἓν τῶν δυοῖν,
ἄμφω γὰρ ἡμίση.. ὁμολογοῦντες δὲ τὸ ἁπλῶς
εἶναι δίκαιον τὸ κατ᾽ ἀξίαν, διαφέρονται (καθάπερ
ἐλέχθη πρότερον) οἱ μὲν ὅτι ἐὰν κατά τι ἴσοι
ὦσιν ὅλως ἴσοι νομίζουσιν εἶναι, οἱ δ᾽ ὅτι ἐὰν κατά
τι ἄνισοι πάντων ἀνίσων ἀξιοῦσιν ἑαυτούς. διὸ

40 καὶ μάλιστα δύο γίνονται πολιτεῖαι, δῆμος καὶ

---

[1] aut οὖ μὴ aut οὐ μὴν εἰ schol. H: οὐ μὴν codd.

[a] See 1307 a 34 n.

[b] This ethical arithmetic is helped out in Greek by the
fact that, even without the qualification κατ᾽ ἀξίαν, ἴσος often
means 'equal to desert,' fair, just.

[c] See 1301 a 27 ff. and note.

the aim may be either to tighten them up or to relax them. Or again the aim may be to change a certain part of the constitution, for example to establish or abolish a certain magistracy, as according to some accounts Lysander attempted to abolish the kingship at Sparta and the king Pausanias the ephorate [a];

6 and also at Epidamnus the constitution was altered in part, for they set up a council instead of the tribal rulers, and it is still compulsory for the magistrates alone of the class that has political power to come to the popular assembly when an appointment to a magistracy is put to the vote ; and the single supreme magistrate was also an oligarchical feature in this constitution). For party strife is everywhere due to inequality, where classes that are unequal do not receive a share of power in proportion (for a lifelong monarchy is an unequal feature when it exists among equals) ; for generally the motive for factious

7 strife is the desire for equality. But equality is of two kinds, numerical equality and equality according to worth—by numerically equal I mean that which is the same and equal in number or dimension, by equal according to worth that which is equal by proportion [b] ; for instance numerically 3 exceeds 2 and 2 exceeds 1 by an equal amount, but by proportion 4 exceeds 2 and 2 exceeds 1 equally, since 2 and 1 are equal parts of 4 and 2, both being halves. But although men agree that the absolutely just is what is according to worth, they disagree (as was said before [c]) in that some think that if they are equal in something they are wholly equal, and others claim that if they are unequal in something they deserve an unequal share of all things.

8 Owing to this two principal varieties of constitution

1302 a ὀλιγαρχία· εὐγένεια γὰρ καὶ ἀρετὴ ἐν ὀλίγοις, ταῦτα[1] δ' ἐν πλείοσιν· εὐγενεῖς γὰρ καὶ ἀγαθοὶ οὐδαμοῦ ἑκατόν, εὔποροι[2] δὲ πολλαχοῦ.[3] τὸ δὲ ἁπλῶς πάντῃ καθ' ἑκατέραν τετάχθαι τὴν ἰσότητα φαῦλον. φανερὸν δ' ἐκ τοῦ συμβαίνοντος· οὐδεμία 5 γὰρ μόνιμος ἐκ τῶν τοιούτων πολιτειῶν. τούτου δ' αἴτιον ὅτι ἀδύνατον ἀπὸ τοῦ πρώτου καὶ τοῦ ἐν ἀρχῇ ἡμαρτημένου μὴ ἀπαντᾶν εἰς τὸ τέλος κακόν τι. διὸ δεῖ τὰ μὲν ἀριθμητικῇ ἰσότητι χρῆσθαι, τὰ δὲ τῇ κατ' ἀξίαν. ὅμως δὲ ἀσφαλεστέρα καὶ 9 ἀστασίαστος μᾶλλον ἡ δημοκρατία τῆς ὀλιγαρχίας· 10 ἐν μὲν γὰρ ταῖς ὀλιγαρχίαις ἐγγίνονται δύο, ἥ τε πρὸς ἀλλήλους στάσις καὶ ἔτι ἡ πρὸς τὸν δῆμον, ἐν δὲ ταῖς δημοκρατίαις ἡ πρὸς τὴν ὀλιγαρχίαν μόνον, αὐτῷ δὲ πρὸς αὑτὸν ὅ τι καὶ ἄξιον εἰπεῖν οὐκ ἐγγίγνεται τῷ δήμῳ στάσις. ἔτι δὲ ἡ ἐκ τῶν μέσων πολιτεία ἐγγυτέρω τοῦ δήμου ἢ [ἡ][4] τῶν 15 ὀλίγων, ἥπερ ἐστὶν ἀσφαλεστάτη τῶν τοιούτων πολιτειῶν.

II. Ἐπεὶ δὲ σκοποῦμεν ἐκ τίνων αἵ τε στάσεις 1 γίγνονται καὶ αἱ μεταβολαὶ περὶ τὰς πολιτείας, ληπτέον καθόλου πρῶτον τὰς ἀρχὰς καὶ τὰς αἰτίας αὐτῶν. εἰσὶ δὴ σχεδὸν ὡς εἰπεῖν τρεῖς τὸν ἀριθμόν, 20 ἃς διοριστέον καθ' αὑτὰς τύπῳ πρῶτον. δεῖ γὰρ λαβεῖν πῶς τε ἔχοντες στασιάζουσι καὶ τίνων

---

[1] τἀναντία Lambinus.
[2] ἄποροι Γ : εὔποροι δὲ ⟨καὶ ἄποροι⟩ Stahr.
[3] πολλοὶ πολλαχοῦ codd. det.
[4] ἡ om. p² : τῆς Victorius.

---

[a] That is, numbers and wealth.
[b] Perhaps the text should be emended to give ' there are many rich men and poor men in many places.'

come into existence, democracy and oligarchy; for noble birth and virtue are found in few men, but the qualifications specified [a] in more : nowhere are there a hundred men nobly born and good, but there are rich men [b] in many places. But for the constitution to be framed absolutely and entirely according to either kind of equality is bad. And this is proved by experience, for not one of the constitutions formed on such lines is permanent. And the cause of this is that it is impossible for some evil not to occur ultimately from the first and initial error that has been made. Hence the proper course is to employ numerical equality in some things and equality

9 according to worth in others. But nevertheless democracy is safer and more free from civil strife than oligarchy ; for in oligarchies two kinds of strife spring up, faction between different members of the oligarchy and also faction between the oligarchs and the people, whereas in democracies only strife between the people and the oligarchical party occurs, but party strife between different sections of the people itself does not occur to any degree worth mentioning. And again the government formed of the middle classes is nearer to the people than to the few, and it is the safest of the kinds of constitution mentioned.

1 II. And since we are considering what circum- Causes of stances give rise to party factions and revolutions revolution: in constitutions, we must first ascertain their origins and causes generally. They are, speaking roughly, three in number,[c] which we must first define in outline separately. For we must ascertain what state of affairs gives rise to party strife, and for what

[c] Viz. the material, final and efficient causes of revolutions (Jowett).

1302 a

ἕνεκεν καὶ τρίτον τίνες ἀρχαὶ γίνονται τῶν πολιτικῶν ταραχῶν καὶ τῶν πρὸς ἀλλήλους στάσεων.

Τοῦ μὲν οὖν αὐτοὺς ἔχειν πως πρὸς τὴν μεταβολὴν
αἰτίαν καθόλου μάλιστα θετέον περὶ ἧς ἤδη τυγ-
25 χάνομεν εἰρηκότες. οἱ μὲν γὰρ ἰσότητος ἐφιέμενοι
στασιάζουσιν ἂν νομίζωσιν ἔλαττον ἔχειν ὄντες
ἴσοι τοῖς πλεονεκτοῦσιν, οἱ δὲ τῆς ἀνισότητος καὶ
τῆς ὑπεροχῆς ἂν ὑπολαμβάνωσιν ὄντες ἄνισοι μὴ
πλέον ἔχειν ἀλλ' ἴσον ἢ ἔλαττον (τούτων δ' ἔστι 2
μὲν ὀρέγεσθαι δικαίως, ἔστι δὲ καὶ ἀδίκως)· ἐλάτ-
30 τους τε γὰρ ὄντες ὅπως ἴσοι ὦσι στασιάζουσι,
καὶ ἴσοι ὄντες ὅπως μείζους. πῶς μὲν οὖν ἔχοντες
στασιάζουσιν, εἴρηται.

Περὶ ὧν δὲ στασιάζουσιν, ἐστὶ κέρδος καὶ τιμή,
καὶ τἀναντία τούτοις, καὶ γὰρ ἀτιμίαν φεύγοντες
καὶ ζημίαν ἢ ὑπὲρ αὐτῶν ἢ τῶν φίλων στασιάζουσιν
ἐν ταῖς πόλεσιν.

35 Αἱ δ' αἰτίαι καὶ ἀρχαὶ τῶν κινήσεων, ὅθεν αὐτοί 3
τε διατίθενται τὸν εἰρημένον τρόπον καὶ περὶ τῶν
λεχθέντων, ἔστι μὲν ὡς τὸν ἀριθμὸν ἑπτὰ τυγχάνουσιν οὖσαι, ἔστι δ' ὡς πλείους. ὧν δύο μέν ἐστι
ταὐτὰ τοῖς εἰρημένοις, ἀλλ' οὐχ ὡσαύτως· διὰ
κέρδος γὰρ καὶ διὰ τιμὴν καὶ[1] παροξύνονται
40 πρὸς ἀλλήλους οὐχ ἵνα κτήσωνται σφίσιν αὐτοῖς,
1302 b ὥσπερ εἴρηται πρότερον, ἀλλ' ἑτέρους ὁρῶντες
τοὺς μὲν δικαίως τοὺς δ' ἀδίκως πλεονεκτοῦντας
τούτων. ἔτι διὰ ὕβριν, διὰ φόβον, διὰ ὑπεροχήν,

[1] καὶ suppleuit Immisch.

378

objects it is waged, and thirdly what are the origins
of political disorders and internal party struggles.

Now the principal cause, speaking generally, of (1) states of
the citizens being themselves disposed in a certain feeling;
manner towards revolution is the one about which we c. i. §§ 3,
happen to have spoken already. Those that desire 7 fin.
equality enter on party strife if they think that they
have too little although they are the equals of those
who have more, while those that desire inequality or
superiority do so if they suppose that although they
are unequal they have not got more but an equal
amount or less (and these desires may be felt justly,
and they may also be felt unjustly); for when inferior,
people enter on strife in order that they may be equal,
and when equal, in order that they may be greater.
We have therefore said what are the states of feeling
in which men engage in party strife.

The objects about which it is waged are gain and (2) objects;
honour, and their opposites, for men carry on party
faction in states in order to avoid dishonour and loss,
either on their own behalf or on behalf of their friends.

And the causes and origins of the disturbances (3) causes
which occasion the actual states of feeling described and circum-
and their direction to the objects mentioned, accord- stances.
ing to one account happen to be seven in number,
though according to another they are more. Two
of them are the same as those spoken of before § 2 fin.
although not operating in the same way: the
motives of gain and honour also stir men up against
each other not in order that they may get them for
themselves, as has been said before, but because
they see other men in some cases justly and in
other cases unjustly getting a larger share of
them. Other causes are insolence, fear, excessive

379

1302 b

διὰ καταφρόνησιν, διὰ αὔξησιν τὴν παρὰ τὸ ἀνάλογον, ἔτι δὲ ἄλλον τρόπον δι' ἐριθείαν, δι' ὀλι-
5 γωρίαν, διὰ μικρότητα, δι' ἀνομοιότητα. τούτων
δὲ ὕβρις μὲν καὶ κέρδος τίνα ἔχουσι δύναμιν καὶ
πῶς αἴτια σχεδόν ἐστι φανερόν· ὑβριζόντων τε
γὰρ τῶν ἐν ταῖς ἀρχαῖς καὶ πλεονεκτούντων
στασιάζουσι καὶ πρὸς ἀλλήλους[1] καὶ πρὸς τὰς
πολιτείας τὰς διδούσας τὴν ἐξουσίαν· ἡ δὲ πλεονεξία
10 γίνεται ὁτὲ μὲν ἀπὸ τῶν ἰδίων, ὁτὲ δὲ ἀπὸ τῶν
κοινῶν. δῆλον δὲ καὶ ἡ τιμὴ καὶ τί δύναται καὶ
πῶς αἰτία στάσεως· καὶ γὰρ αὐτοὶ ἀτιμαζόμενοι
καὶ ἄλλους ὁρῶντες τιμωμένους στασιάζουσιν·
ταῦτα δὲ ἀδίκως μὲν γίνεται ὅταν παρὰ τὴν ἀξίαν
ἢ τιμῶνταί τινες ἢ ἀτιμάζωνται, δικαίως δὲ ὅταν
15 κατὰ τὴν ἀξίαν. δι' ὑπεροχὴν δέ, ὅταν τις ᾖ τῇ
δυνάμει μείζων (ἢ εἷς ἢ πλείους) ἢ κατὰ τὴν πόλιν
καὶ τὴν δύναμιν τοῦ πολιτεύματος· γίνεσθαι γὰρ
εἴωθεν ἐκ τῶν τοιούτων μοναρχία ἢ δυναστεία.
διὸ ἐνιαχοῦ εἰώθασιν ὀστρακίζειν, οἷον ἐν Ἄργει
καὶ Ἀθήνησιν· καίτοι βέλτιον ἐξ ἀρχῆς ὁρᾶν ὅπως
20 μὴ ἐνέσονται τοσοῦτον ὑπερέχοντες, ἢ ἐάσαντας
γενέσθαι ἰᾶσθαι ὕστερον. διὰ δὲ φόβον στασιάζουσιν οἵ τε ἠδικηκότες, δεδιότες μὴ δῶσι δίκην,
καὶ οἱ μέλλοντες ἀδικεῖσθαι, βουλόμενοι φθάσαι
πρὶν ἀδικηθῆναι, ὥσπερ ἐν Ῥόδῳ συνέστησαν οἱ
γνώριμοι ἐπὶ τὸν δῆμον διὰ τὰς ἐπιφερομένας

---

[1] ἀλλήλους: αὐτοὺς Niemeyer.

[a] The four causes now mentioned are those alluded to just
above (a 38) as in addition to the seven enumerated above,
a 38-b 5.
[b] Cf. 1284 a 18.
[c] Perhaps in 390 B.C., cf. l. 32 f. and 1304 b 27 ff.

predominance, contempt, disproportionate growth
of power; and also other modes of cause [a] are election intrigue, carelessness, pettiness, dissimilarity.
4 Among these motives the power possessed by
insolence and gain, and their mode of operation, is
almost obvious; for when the men in office show
insolence and greed, people rise in revolt against
one another and against the constitutions that
afford the opportunity for such conduct; and greed
sometimes preys on private property and sometimes
on common funds. It is clear also what is the power
of honour and how it can cause party faction; for
men form factions both when they are themselves
dishonoured and when they see others honoured;
and the distribution of honours is unjust when persons
are either honoured or dishonoured against their
deserts, just when it is according to desert. Excessive predominance causes faction, when some
individual or body of men is greater and more powerful than is suitable to the state and the power of the
government; for such are the conditions that usually
result in the rise of a monarchy or dynasty. Owing
to this in some places they have the custom of
temporary banishment,[b] as at Argos and Athens; yet
it would be better to provide from the outset that
there may be no persons in the state so greatly
predominant, than first to allow them to come into
existence and afterwards to apply a remedy. Fear
is the motive of faction with those who have
inflicted wrong and are afraid of being punished,
and also with those who are in danger of suffering
a wrong and wish to act in time before the wrong is
inflicted, as the notables at Rhodes banded together [c]
against the people because of the law-suits that were

381

1302 b

25 δίκας. διὰ καταφρόνησιν δὲ καὶ στασιάζουσι καὶ 6
ἐπιτίθενται, οἷον ἔν τε ταῖς ὀλιγαρχίαις ὅταν
πλείους ὦσιν οἱ μὴ μετέχοντες τῆς πολιτείας
(κρείττους γὰρ οἴονται εἶναι), καὶ ἐν ταῖς δημοκρατίαις οἱ εὔποροι καταφρονήσαντες τῆς ἀταξίας
καὶ ἀναρχίας, οἷον καὶ ἐν Θήβαις μετὰ τὴν ἐν
30 Οἰνοφύτοις μάχην κακῶς πολιτευομένων ἡ δημοκρατία διεφθάρη, καὶ ἡ Μεγαρέων δι' ἀταξίαν καὶ
ἀναρχίαν ἡττηθέντων, καὶ ἐν Συρακούσαις πρὸ τῆς
Γέλωνος τυραννίδος, καὶ ἐν Ῥόδῳ ὁ δῆμος πρὸ
τῆς ἐπαναστάσεως. γίνονται δὲ καὶ δι' αὔξησιν
35 τὴν παρὰ τὸ ἀνάλογον μεταβολαὶ τῶν πολιτειῶν·
ὥσπερ γὰρ σῶμα ἐκ μερῶν σύγκειται καὶ δεῖ
αὐξάνεσθαι ἀνάλογον ἵνα μένῃ συμμετρία, εἰ δὲ
μή, φθείρεται, ὅταν ὁ μὲν πούς τεττάρων πηχῶν
ᾖ τὸ δ' ἄλλο σῶμα δυοῖν σπιθαμαῖν, ἐνίοτε δὲ κἂν
40 εἰς ἄλλου ζῴου μεταβάλλοι μορφὴν εἰ μὴ μόνον
κατὰ τὸ ποσὸν ἀλλὰ καὶ κατὰ τὸ ποιὸν αὐξάνοιτο
1303 a παρὰ τὸ ἀνάλογον, οὕτω καὶ πόλις σύγκειται ἐκ
μερῶν, ὧν πολλάκις λανθάνει τι αὐξανόμενον, οἷον
τὸ τῶν ἀπόρων πλῆθος ἐν ταῖς δημοκρατίαις καὶ
πολιτείαις. συμβαίνει δ' ἐνίοτε τοῦτο καὶ διὰ
5 τύχας, οἷον ἐν Τάραντι ἡττηθέντων καὶ ἀπολο-
μένων πολλῶν γνωρίμων ὑπὸ τῶν Ἰαπύγων μικρὸν
ὕστερον τῶν Μηδικῶν δημοκρατία ἐγένετο ἐκ
πολιτείας, καὶ ἐν Ἄργει τῶν ἐν τῇ ἑβδόμῃ ἀπ-

---

[a] Against Athens, 456 B.C.   [b] See 1300 a 18 n.
[c] 485 B.C.   [d] See l. 23 n.
[e] It is not clear whether what follows refers to a work of
art (cf. 1284 b 8) or is an exaggerated account of a disease;
Galen describes one called σατυρίασις, in which the bones of
the temple swell out like satyrs' horns.
[f] i.e. if, for example, the foot became as hard as a hoof.
382

3 being brought against them. Contempt is a cause of faction and of actual attacks upon the government, for instance in oligarchies when those who have no share in the government are more numerous (for they think themselves the stronger party), and in democracies when the rich have begun to feel contempt for the disorder and anarchy that prevails, as for example at Thebes the democracy was destroyed owing to bad government after the battle of Oenophyta,[a] and that of the Megarians was destroyed when they had been defeated owing to disorder and anarchy,[b] and at Syracuse before the tyranny[c] of Gelo, and at Rhodes[d] the common people had fallen into contempt before the rising against them. Revolutions in the constitutions also take place on account of disproportionate growth; for just as the body[e] is composed of parts, and needs to grow proportionately in order that its symmetry may remain, and if it does not it is spoiled, when the foot is four cubits long and the rest of the body two spans, and sometimes it might even change into the shape of another animal if it increased disproportionately not only in size but also in quality,[f] so also a state is composed of parts, one of which often grows without its being noticed, as for example the number of the poor in democracies and constitutional states. And sometimes this is also brought about by accidental occurrences, as for instance at Tarentum when a great many notables were defeated and killed by the Iapygians a short time after the Persian wars a constitutional government was changed to a democracy, and at Argos when those in the seventh

1303 a

ολομένων ὑπὸ Κλεομένους τοῦ Λάκωνος ἠναγκάσθησαν παραδέξασθαι τῶν περιοίκων τινάς, καὶ ἐν
Ἀθήναις ἀτυχούντων πεζῇ οἱ γνώριμοι ἐλάττους
10 ἐγένοντο διὰ τὸ ἐκ καταλόγου στρατεύεσθαι ὑπὸ
τὸν Λακωνικὸν πόλεμον. συμβαίνει δὲ τοῦτο καὶ[1]
ἐν ταῖς δημοκρατίαις, ἧττον δέ· πλειόνων γὰρ τῶν
εὐπόρων[2] γινομένων ἢ τῶν οὐσιῶν αὐξανομένων
μεταβάλλουσιν εἰς ὀλιγαρχίας καὶ δυναστείας.
μεταβάλλουσι δ᾽ αἱ πολιτεῖαι καὶ ἄνευ στάσεως
15 διά τε τὰς ἐριθείας, ὥσπερ ἐν Ἡραίᾳ (ἐξ αἱρετῶν
γὰρ διὰ τοῦτο ἐποίησαν κληρωτὰς ὅτι ᾑροῦντο τοὺς
ἐριθευομένους), καὶ δι᾽ ὀλιγωρίαν, ὅταν ἐάσωσιν
εἰς τὰς ἀρχὰς τὰς κυρίας παριέναι τοὺς μὴ τῆς
πολιτείας φίλους, ὥσπερ ἐν Ὠρεῷ κατελύθη ἡ
ὀλιγαρχία τῶν ἀρχόντων γενομένου Ἡρακλεοδώρου,
20 ὃς ἐξ ὀλιγαρχίας πολιτείαν καὶ δημοκρατίαν κατ-
εσκεύασεν. ἔτι διὰ τὸ παρὰ μικρόν· λέγω δὲ
παρὰ μικρόν, ὅτι πολλάκις λανθάνει μεγάλη γινομένη μετάβασις τῶν νομίμων, ὅταν παρορῶσι τὸ
μικρόν, ὥσπερ ἐν Ἀμβρακίᾳ μικρὸν ἦν τὸ τίμημα
τέλος δ᾽ ἀπ᾽[3] οὐθενὸς ἦρχον, ὡς ἔγγιον[4] ἢ μηθὲν
25 διαφέρον τοῦ μηθὲν τὸ μικρόν. στασιωτικὸν δὲ
καὶ τὸ μὴ ὁμόφυλον, ἕως ἂν συμπνεύσῃ· ὥσπερ
γὰρ οὐδ᾽ ἐκ τοῦ τυχόντος πλήθους πόλις γίγνεται,

---

[1] καὶ τοῦτο Susemihl.   [2] ἀπόρων ΓΜ.
[3] δ᾽ ἀπ᾽ Aretinus: δ᾽ codd.
[4] ἔγγυς ὄν? vel ἔγγιζον? Immisch (*tanquam propinquum
sit* Guil.).

---

[a] The word to be understood here may be φυλῇ, or possibly
ἡμέρᾳ: the seventh day of the month was sacred to Apollo
especially at Sparta, and one account assigns Cleomenes
victory to that day, in which case the casualties may well
have been known afterwards as 'those who fell on the
seventh.'

tribe ^a had been destroyed by the Spartan Cleomenes the citizens were compelled to admit some of
the surrounding people, and at Athens when they
suffered disasters by land the notables became fewer
because at the time of the war against Sparta the
army was drawn from a muster-roll.^b And this
happens also in democracies, though to a smaller
extent ; for when the wealthy become more numerous or their properties increase, the governments
change to oligarchies and dynasties.^c And revolutions in constitutions take place even without factious
strife, owing to election intrigue, as at Heraea ^d
(for they made their magistrates elected by lot
instead of by vote for this reason, because the people
used to elect those who canvassed) ; and also owing
to carelessness, when people allow men that are not
friends of the constitution to enter into the sovereign
offices, as at Oreus ^e oligarchy was broken up when
Heracleodorus became one of the magistrates, who
in place of an oligarchy formed a constitutional
government, or rather a democracy. Another cause
is alteration by small stages ; by this I mean that
often a great change of institutions takes place unnoticed when people overlook a small alteration, as
in Ambracia the property-qualification was small,
and finally men hold office with none at all, as a little
is near to nothing, or practically the same. Also
difference of race is a cause of faction, until harmony
of spirit is reached ; for just as any chance multitude
of people does not form a state, so a state is not

^b *i.e.* was made up of citizens and not of mercenaries.
^c See 1292 b 10 n.
^d On the Alpheus, in Arcadia.
^e In Euboea ; its secession from Sparta to Athens, 377 B.C.,
was perhaps the occasion of this revolution.

1303 a

οὕτως οὐδ' ἐν τῷ τυχόντι χρόνῳ. διὸ ὅσοι ἤδη
συνοίκους ἐδέξαντο ἢ ἐποίκους οἱ πλεῖστοι ἐστασίασαν, οἷον Τροιζηνίοις Ἀχαιοὶ συνῴκησαν Σύ-
80 βαριν, εἶτα πλείους οἱ Ἀχαιοὶ γενόμενοι ἐξέβαλον
τοὺς Τροιζηνίους, ὅθεν τὸ ἄγος συνέβη τοῖς
Συβαρίταις· καὶ ἐν Θουρίοις Συβαρῖται τοῖς συν-
οικήσασιν, πλεονεκτεῖν γὰρ ἀξιοῦντες ὡς σφετέρας
τῆς χώρας ἐξέπεσον· καὶ Βυζαντίοις οἱ ἔποικοι
ἐπιβουλεύοντες φωραθέντες ἐξέπεσον διὰ μάχης·
85 καὶ Ἀντισσαῖοι τοὺς Χίων φυγάδας εἰσδεξάμενοι
διὰ μάχης ἐξέβαλον· Ζαγκλαῖοι δὲ Σαμίους
ὑποδεξάμενοι ἐξέπεσον καὶ αὐτοί· καὶ Ἀπολ-
λωνιᾶται οἱ ἐν τῷ Εὐξείνῳ πόντῳ ἐποίκους ἐπ-
αγαγόμενοι ἐστασίασαν· καὶ Συρακούσιοι μετὰ τὰ
1303 b τυραννικὰ τοὺς ξένους καὶ τοὺς μισθοφόρους
πολίτας ποιησάμενοι ἐστασίασαν καὶ εἰς μάχην
ἦλθον· καὶ Ἀμφιπολῖται δεξάμενοι Χαλκιδέων
ἐποίκους[1] ἐξέπεσον ὑπὸ τούτων οἱ πλεῖστοι αὐτῶν.
5 (Στασιάζουσι δ' ἐν μὲν ταῖς ὀλιγαρχίαις οἱ
πολλοί, ὡς ἀδικούμενοι ὅτι οὐ μετέχουσι τῶν
ἴσων, καθάπερ εἴρηται πρότερον, ἴσοι ὄντες, ἐν δὲ
ταῖς δημοκρατίαις οἱ γνώριμοι, ὅτι μετέχουσι τῶν
ἴσων οὐκ ἴσοι ὄντες.)

---

[1] Spengel: ἀποίκους codd.

[a] i.e. colonists not from the mother-city, admitted either
at the foundation of the colony or later.

[b] Sybaris, founded 720 B.C., became very wealthy. The
Troezenian population when expelled were received at Croton,
which made war on Sybaris and destroyed it 510 B.C. To
what exactly τὸ ἄγος refers is unknown.

[c] In Lesbos.　　　　　　[d] Later Messana, Messina.

[e] Thrasybulus succeeded his brother Hiero as tyrant in
467 B.C. and fell within a year.

formed in any chance period of time. Hence most of the states that have hitherto admitted joint settlers or additional settlers [a] have split into factions; for example Achaeans settled at Sybaris [b] jointly with Troezenians, and afterwards the Achaeans having become more numerous expelled the Troezenians, which was the cause of the curse that fell on the Sybarites; and at Thurii Sybarites quarrelled with those who had settled there with them, for they claimed to have the larger share in the country as being their own, and were ejected; and at Byzantium the additional settlers were discovered plotting against the colonists and were expelled by force of arms; and the people of Antissa [c] after admitting the Chian exiles expelled them by arms; and the people of Zanclê [d] after admitting settlers from Samos were themselves expelled; and the people of Apollonia on the Euxine Sea after bringing in additional settlers fell into faction; and the Syracusans after the period of the tyrants [e] conferred citizenship on their foreign troops and mercenaries and then faction set in and they came to battle; and the Amphipolitans having received settlers from Chalcis were most of them driven out by them.[f]

(And in oligarchies civil strife is raised by the many, on the ground that they are treated unjustly because they are not admitted to an equal share although they are equal, as has been said before, but in democracies it begins with the notables, because they have an equal share although they are not equal.)[g]

1307 a 27, b 7.

---

[f] *Cf.* 1306 a 2. The exact circumstances are unknown: Amphipolis was colonized from Athens 437 B.C.

[g] This sentence is out of place here, and would fit in better if placed (as it is by Newman) above at 1301 a 39, after στασιάζουσι, or (with other editors) *ib.* b 26.

1303 b

Στασιάζουσι δὲ ἐνίοτε αἱ πόλεις καὶ διὰ τοὺς
τόπους, ὅταν μὴ εὐφυῶς ἔχῃ ἡ χώρα πρὸς τὸ μίαν
εἶναι πόλιν, οἷον ἐν Κλαζομεναῖς οἱ ἐπὶ Χύτρῳ
10 πρὸς τοὺς ἐν νήσῳ, καὶ Κολοφώνιοι καὶ Νοτιεῖς
καὶ Ἀθήνησιν οὐχ ὁμοίως εἰσὶν ἀλλὰ μᾶλλον
δημοτικοὶ οἱ τὸν Πειραιᾶ οἰκοῦντες τῶν τὸ ἄστυ
ὥσπερ γὰρ ἐν τοῖς πολέμοις αἱ διαβάσεις τῶν
ὀχετῶν, καὶ τῶν πάνυ σμικρῶν, διασπῶσι τὰς
φάλαγγας, οὕτως ἔοικε πᾶσα διαφορὰ ποιεῖν
15 διάστασιν. μεγίστη μὲν οὖν ἴσως διάστασις ἀρετὴ
καὶ μοχθηρία, εἶτα πλοῦτος καὶ πενία, καὶ οὕτω
δὴ ἑτέρα ἑτέρας μᾶλλον, ὧν μία καὶ ἡ εἰρημένη
ἐστίν.

III. Γίγνονται μὲν οὖν αἱ στάσεις οὐ περὶ
μικρῶν ἀλλ' ἐκ μικρῶν, στασιάζουσι δὲ περὶ
μεγάλων. μάλιστα δὲ καὶ αἱ μικραὶ ἰσχύουσιν
20 ὅταν ἐν τοῖς κυρίοις γένωνται, οἷον συνέβη καὶ ἐν
Συρακούσαις ἐν τοῖς ἀρχαίοις χρόνοις. μετέβαλε
γὰρ ἡ πολιτεία ἐκ δύο νεανίσκων στασιασάντων
τῶν[2] ἐν ταῖς ἀρχαῖς ὄντων, περὶ ἐρωτικὴν αἰτίαν
θατέρου γὰρ ἀποδημοῦντος ἅτερος[3] ἑταῖρος ὢν
25 τὸν[4] ἐρώμενον αὐτοῦ ὑπεποιήσατο, πάλιν δ'
ἐκεῖνος τούτῳ χαλεπήνας τὴν γυναῖκα αὐτοῦ ἀν-
έπεισεν ὡς αὑτὸν ἐλθεῖν· ὅθεν προσλαμβάνοντες
τοὺς ἐν τῷ πολιτεύματι διεστασίασαν πάντας

---

[1] Χύτρῳ Sylburg.   [2] τῶν suppleuit Richards.
[3] ἅτερος suppleuit Coraes.
[4] τὸν Coraes: τις τὸν codd.

---

[a] Topography uncertain: Clazomenae near Smyrna was
partly on a small island, which Alexander joined to the
mainland with a causeway.

12   Also states sometimes enter on faction for geographical reasons, when the nature of the country is not suited for there being a single city, as for example at Clazomenae ^a the people near Chytrum are in feud with the inhabitants of the island, and the Colophonians and the Notians ^b; and at Athens the population is not uniformly democratic in spirit, but the inhabitants of Piraeus are more so than those of the city. For just as in wars the fording of watercourses, even quite small ones, causes the formations to lose contact, so every difference seems to cause division. Thus perhaps the greatest division is that between virtue and vice, next that between wealth and poverty, and so with other differences in varying degree, one of which is the one mentioned.^c

1   III. Factions arise therefore not about but out of small matters; but they are carried on about great matters. And even the small ones grow extremely violent when they spring up among men of the ruling class, as happened for example at Syracuse in ancient times. For the constitution underwent a revolution as a result of a quarrel that arose ^d between two young men, who belonged to the ruling class, about a love affair. While one of them was abroad the other who was his comrade won over the youth with whom he was in love, and the former in his anger against him retaliated by persuading his wife to come to him; owing to which they stirred up a party struggle among all the people in the state, enlisting them on

Revolutions from petty causes,

---

^b Notium was the port of Colophon.
^c *i.e.* difference of locality.
^d Perhaps under the oligarchy of the Gamori, overthrown by the people and followed by Gelo's tyranny, 485 B.C.

389

1303 b

διόπερ ἀρχομένων εὐλαβεῖσθαι δεῖ τῶν τοιούτων, 2
καὶ διαλύειν τὰς τῶν ἡγεμόνων καὶ δυναμένων
στάσεις· ἐν ἀρχῇ γὰρ γίγνεται τὸ ἁμάρτημα, ἡ δ᾽
30 ἀρχὴ λέγεται ἥμισυ εἶναι παντός, ὥστε καὶ τὸ ἐν
αὐτῇ μικρὸν ἁμάρτημα ἀνάλογόν ἐστι πρὸς τὰ ἐν
τοῖς ἄλλοις μέρεσιν. ὅλως δὲ αἱ τῶν γνωρίμων
στάσεις συναπολαύειν ποιοῦσι καὶ τὴν ὅλην πόλιν,
οἷον ἐν Ἑστιαίᾳ συνέβη μετὰ τὰ Μηδικά, δύο
35 ἀδελφῶν περὶ τῆς πατρῴας[1] νομῆς διενεχθέντων·
ὁ μὲν γὰρ ἀπορώτερος, ὡς οὐκ ἀποφαίνοντος
θατέρου τὴν οὐσίαν οὐδὲ τὸν θησαυρὸν ὃν εὗρεν ὁ
πατήρ, προσηγάγετο[2] τοὺς δημοτικούς, ὁ δ᾽ ἕτερος
ἔχων οὐσίαν πολλὴν τοὺς εὐπόρους. καὶ ἐν 3
Δελφοῖς ἐκ κηδείας γενομένης διαφορᾶς ἀρχὴ
1304 a πασῶν ἐγένετο τῶν στάσεων τῶν ὕστερον· ὁ μὲν
γάρ, οἰωνισάμενός τι σύμπτωμα ὡς ἦλθεν ἐπὶ τὴν
νύμφην, οὐ λαβὼν ἀπῆλθεν, οἱ δ᾽ ὡς ὑβρισθέντες
ἐνέβαλον τῶν ἱερῶν χρημάτων θύοντος κἄπειτα
ὡς ἱερόσυλον ἀπέκτειναν. καὶ περὶ Μιτυλήνην δὲ
5 ἐξ ἐπικλήρων στάσεως γενομένης πολλῶν ἐγένετο
ἀρχὴ κακῶν, καὶ τοῦ πολέμου τοῦ πρὸς Ἀθηναίους
ἐν ᾧ Πάχης ἔλαβε τὴν πόλιν αὐτῶν· Τιμοφάνους
γὰρ τῶν εὐπόρων τινὸς καταλιπόντος δύο θυγα-
τέρας, ὁ περιωσθεὶς καὶ οὐ λαβὼν τοῖς υἱέσιν αὐτοῦ
Δόξανδρος ἦρξε τῆς στάσεως καὶ τοὺς Ἀθηναίους

---

[1] πατρῴων codd. cet. (τῶν π. Victorius).
[2] ed. : προσήγετο codd.

---

* i.e. the ratio of being a half to the whole : a bad start
does as much harm as all the later mistakes put together.

2 their sides. On account of this it is necessary to guard against such affairs at their beginning, and to break up the factions of the leaders and powerful men ; for the error occurs at the beginning, and the beginning as the proverb says is half of the whole, so that even a small mistake at the beginning stands in the same ratio *a* to mistakes at the other stages. And in general the faction quarrels of the notables involve the whole state in the consequences, as happened at Hestiaea *b* after the Persian wars, when two brothers quarrelled about the division of their patrimony ; for the poorer of the two, on the ground that the other would not make a return of the estate and of the treasure that their father had found, got the common people on his side, and the other possessing much property was supported by the rich. And at
3 Delphi the beginning of all the factions that occurred afterwards was when a quarrel arose out of a marriage ; the bridegroom interpreted some chance occurrence when he came to fetch the bride as a bad omen and went away without taking her, and her relatives thinking themselves insulted threw some articles of sacred property into the fire when he was performing a sacrifice and then put him to death as guilty of sacrilege. And also at Mitylene *c* a faction that arose out of some heiresses was the beginning of many misfortunes, and of the war with the Athenians 428-7 b.c. in which Paches captured the city of Mitylene : a wealthy citizen named Timophanes left two daughters, and a man who was rejected in his suit to obtain them for his own sons, Doxander, started the

---

b Also called Oreus, see a 18.
c The revolt of Mitylene 428 b.c. is ascribed to purely political causes by Thucydides (iii. 1-30).

10 παρώξυνε, πρόξενος ὢν τῆς πόλεως. καὶ ἐν 4
Φωκεῦσιν ἐξ ἐπικλήρου στάσεως γενομένης περὶ
Μνασέαν τὸν Μνάσωνος πατέρα καὶ Εὐθυκράτη
τὸν Ὀνομάρχου, ἡ στάσις αὕτη ἀρχὴ τοῦ ἱεροῦ
πολέμου κατέστη τοῖς Φωκεῦσιν. μετέβαλε δὲ
καὶ ἐν Ἐπιδάμνῳ ἡ πολιτεία ἐκ γαμικῶν ὑπο-
15 μνηστευσάμενος γάρ τις θυγατέρα,¹ ὡς ἐζημίωσεν
αὐτὸν ὁ τοῦ ὑπομνηστευθέντος πατὴρ γενόμενος
τῶν ἀρχόντων, ἅτερος συμπαρέλαβε τοὺς ἐκτὸς
τῆς πολιτείας ὡς ἐπηρεασθείς. μεταβάλλουσι δὲ 5
καὶ εἰς ὀλιγαρχίαν καὶ εἰς δῆμον καὶ εἰς πολιτείαν
ἐκ τοῦ εὐδοκιμῆσαί τι ἢ αὐξηθῆναι ἢ ἀρχεῖον ἢ
20 μόριον τῆς πόλεως· οἷον ἡ ἐν Ἀρείῳ πάγῳ βουλὴ
εὐδοκιμήσασα ἐν τοῖς Μηδικοῖς ἔδοξε συντονω-
τέραν ποιῆσαι τὴν πολιτείαν, καὶ πάλιν ὁ ναυτικὸς
ὄχλος γενόμενος αἴτιος τῆς περὶ Σαλαμῖνα νίκης
καὶ διὰ ταύτης τῆς ἡγεμονίας διὰ τὴν κατὰ θάλατταν δύναμιν τὴν δημοκρατίαν ἰσχυροτέραν ἐποίησεν·
25 καὶ ἐν Ἄργει οἱ γνώριμοι εὐδοκιμήσαντες περὶ τὴν
ἐν Μαντινείᾳ μάχην τὴν πρὸς Λακεδαιμονίους
ἐπεχείρησαν καταλύειν τὸν δῆμον· καὶ ἐν Συρα- 6
κούσαις ὁ δῆμος αἴτιος γενόμενος τῆς νίκης τοῦ
πολέμου τοῦ πρὸς Ἀθηναίους ἐκ πολιτείας εἰς
δημοκρατίαν μετέβαλεν· καὶ ἐν Χαλκίδι Φόξον
30 τὸν τύραννον μετὰ τῶν γνωρίμων ὁ δῆμος ἀνελὼν
εὐθὺς εἴχετο τῆς πολιτείας· καὶ ἐν Ἀμβρακίᾳ
πάλιν ὡσαύτως Περίανδρον συνεκβαλὼν τοῖς ἐπι-

---

¹ θυγατέρα om. codd. fere omnes.

ᵃ *i.e.* the fathers of the two suitors for the heiress's hand
turned the quarrel into a faction fight.
ᵇ Perhaps the same event as that referred to 1301 b 21.
ᶜ Unknown.

faction and kept on stirring up the Athenians, whose
4 consul he was at Mitylene. And among the Phocians
when a faction arising out of an heiress sprang up in
connexion with Mnaseas the father of Mnason and
Euthykrates the father of Onomarchus,ᵃ this faction
proved to be the beginning for the Phocians of the
Holy War. At Epidamnus also circumstances relating to a marriage gave rise to a revolution in
the constitutionᵇ; somebody had betrothed his
daughter, and the father of the man to whom he
had betrothed her became a magistrate, and had
to sentence him to a fine ; the other thinking that
he had been treated with insolence formed a party
5 of the unenfranchised classes to assist him. And
also revolutions to oligarchy and democracy and
constitutional government arise from the growth in
reputation or in power of some magistracy or some
section of the state ; as for example the Council on
the Areopagus having risen in reputation during
the Persian wars was believed to have made the
constitution more rigid, and then again the naval
multitude, having been the cause of the victory off
Salamis and thereby of the leadership of Athens due
to her power at sea, made the democracy stronger ;
and at Argos the notables having risen in repute in
connexion with the battle against the Spartans at
Mantinea took in hand to put down the people ; 418 B.C.
6 and at Syracuse the people having been the cause of
the victory in the war against Athens made a revolution from constitutional government to democracy ; 412 B.C.
and at Chalcis the people with the aid of the notables
overthrew the tyrant Phoxus ᶜ and then immediately
seized the government ; and again at Ambracia
similarly the people joined with the adversaries

[margin note beside paragraph 5:] and from party predomin- ance.

393

1304 a

θεμένοις ὁ δῆμος τὸν τύραννον εἰς ἑαυτὸν περι-
έστησε τὴν πολιτείαν. καὶ ὅλως δὴ δεῖ τοῦτο μὴ 7
35 λανθάνειν, ὡς οἱ δυνάμεως αἴτιοι γενόμενοι, καὶ
ἰδιῶται καὶ ἀρχαὶ καὶ φυλαὶ καὶ ὅλως μέρος καὶ
ὁποιονοῦν¹ πλῆθος, στάσιν κινοῦσιν· ἢ γὰρ οἱ τούτοις φθονοῦντες τιμωμένοις ἄρχουσι τῆς στάσεως,
ἢ οὗτοι διὰ τὴν ὑπεροχὴν οὐ θέλουσι μένειν ἐπὶ
τῶν ἴσων. κινοῦνται δ' αἱ πολιτεῖαι καὶ ὅταν
τἀναντία εἶναι δοκοῦντα μέρη τῆς πόλεως ἰσάζῃ
1304 b ἀλλήλοις, οἷον οἱ πλούσιοι καὶ ὁ δῆμος, μέσον δ'
ᾖ μηθὲν ἢ μικρὸν πάμπαν· ἂν γὰρ πολὺ ὑπερέχῃ
ὁποτερονοῦν τῶν μερῶν, πρὸς τὸ φανερῶς κρεῖττον
τὸ λοιπὸν οὐ θέλει κινδυνεύειν. διὸ καὶ οἱ κατ'
5 ἀρετὴν διαφέροντες οὐ ποιοῦσι στάσιν ὡς εἰπεῖν,
ὀλίγοι γὰρ γίγνονται πρὸς πολλούς. καθόλου μὲν
οὖν περὶ πάσας τὰς πολιτείας αἱ ἀρχαὶ καὶ αἰτίαι
τῶν στάσεων καὶ τῶν μεταβολῶν τοῦτον ἔχουσι
τὸν τρόπον.

Κινοῦσι δὲ τὰς πολιτείας ὁτὲ μὲν διὰ βίας ὁτὲ 8
δὲ δι' ἀπάτης· διὰ βίας μὲν ἢ εὐθὺς ἐξ ἀρχῆς
10 ἢ ὕστερον ἀναγκάζοντες· καὶ γὰρ ἡ ἀπάτη διττή·
ὁτὲ μὲν γὰρ ἐξαπατήσαντες τὸ πρῶτον ἑκόντων μεταβάλλουσι τὴν πολιτείαν, εἶθ' ὕστερον βίᾳ
κατέχουσιν ἀκόντων, οἷον ἐπὶ τῶν τετρακοσίων
τὸν δῆμον ἐξηπάτησαν φάσκοντες τὸν βασιλέα

¹ ὁποσονοῦν Richards.

ᵃ 580 B.C.; cf. 1311 a 39 ff.
ᵇ The oligarchy at Athens 411 B.C.

of the tyrant Periander in expelling him and then brought the government round to themselves.[a]

7 And indeed in general it must not escape notice that the persons who have caused a state to win power, whether private citizens or magistrates or tribes, or in general a section or group of any kind, stir up faction ; for either those who envy these men for being honoured begin the faction, or these men owing to their superiority are not willing to remain in a position of equality. And constitutions also or from undergo revolution when what are thought of as party equality. opposing sections of the state become equal to one another, for instance the rich and the people, and there is no middle class or only an extremely small one ; for if either of the two sections becomes much the superior, the remainder is not willing to risk an encounter with its manifestly stronger opponent. Owing to this men who are exceptional in virtue generally speaking do not cause faction, because they find themselves few against many. Universally then in connexion with all the forms of constitution the origins and causes of factions and revolutions are of this nature.

8 The means used to cause revolutions of constitu- Modes of tions are sometimes force and sometimes fraud. revolution. Force is employed either when the revolutionary leaders exert compulsion immediately from the start or later on—as indeed the mode of using fraud is also twofold : sometimes the revolutionaries after completely deceiving the people at the first stage alter the constitution with their consent, but then at a later stage retain their hold on it by force against the people's will : for instance, at the time of the Four Hundred,[b] they deceived the people by saying

395

χρήματα παρέξειν πρὸς τὸν πόλεμον τὸν πρὸς
15 Λακεδαιμονίους, ψευσάμενοι δὲ κατέχειν ἐπειρῶντο
τὴν πολιτείαν· ὀτὲ δὲ ἐξ ἀρχῆς τε πείσαντες καὶ
ὕστερον πάλιν πεισθέντων ἑκόντων ἄρχουσιν αὐτῶν.

Ἁπλῶς μὲν οὖν περὶ πάσας τὰς πολιτείας ἐκ
τῶν εἰρημένων συμβέβηκε γίγνεσθαι τὰς μεταβολάς.

IV. Καθ' ἕκαστον δ' εἶδος πολιτείας ἐκ τούτων 1
20 μερίζοντας τὰ συμβαίνοντα δεῖ θεωρεῖν. αἱ μὲν
οὖν δημοκρατίαι μάλιστα μεταβάλλουσι διὰ τὴν
τῶν δημαγωγῶν ἀσέλγειαν· τὰ μὲν γὰρ ἰδίᾳ
συκοφαντοῦντες τοὺς τὰς οὐσίας ἔχοντας συστρέ-
φουσιν αὐτούς (συνάγει γὰρ καὶ τοὺς ἐχθίστους
ὁ κοινὸς φόβος), τὰ δὲ κοινῇ τὸ πλῆθος ἐπάγοντες.
25 καὶ τοῦτο ἐπὶ πολλῶν ἄν τις ἴδοι γιγνόμενον οὕτως.
καὶ γὰρ ἐν Κῷ ἡ δημοκρατία μετέβαλε πονηρῶν 2
ἐγγενομένων δημαγωγῶν, οἱ γὰρ γνώριμοι συν-
έστησαν· καὶ ἐν Ῥόδῳ, μισθοφοράν τε γὰρ οἱ
δημαγωγοὶ ἐπόριζον καὶ ἐκώλυον ἀποδιδόναι τὰ
ὀφειλόμενα τοῖς τριηράρχοις, οἱ δὲ διὰ τὰς ἐπιφερο-
30 μένας δίκας ἠναγκάσθησαν συστάντες καταλῦσαι
τὸν δῆμον. κατελύθη δὲ καὶ ἐν Ἡρακλείᾳ ὁ
δῆμος μετὰ τὸν ἀποικισμὸν εὐθὺς διὰ τοὺς δημ-
αγωγούς· ἀδικούμενοι γὰρ ὑπ' αὐτῶν οἱ γνώριμοι
ἐξέπιπτον, ἔπειτα ἀθροισθέντες οἱ ἐκπίπτοντες
καὶ κατελθόντες κατέλυσαν τὸν δῆμον. παρα- ?

---

[a] Date unknown.   [b] See 1302 b 23 n.

[c] *i.e.* owed for repairs to the ships, and perhaps also for advances of pay to the crews.

[d] Probably the Pontic Heraclea (*cf.* 1305 b 5, 36, 1306 a 37), founded middle of 6th century B.C., not the Trachinian.

396

that the Persian King would supply money for the war against the Spartans, and after telling them this falsehood endeavoured to keep a hold upon the government ; but in other cases they both persuade the people at the start and afterwards repeat the persuasion and govern them with their consent.

Speaking generally therefore in regard to all the forms of constitution, the causes that have been stated are those from which revolutions have occurred.

IV. But in the light of these general rules we must consider the usual course of events as classified according to each different kind of constitution. In democracies the principal cause of revolutions is the insolence of the demagogues ; for they cause the owners of property to band together, partly by malicious prosecutions of individuals among them (for common fear brings together even the greatest enemies), and partly by setting on the common people against them as a class. And one may see this taking place in this manner in many instances. In Cos the democracy was overthrown [a] when evil demagogues had arisen there, for the notables banded themselves together ; and also in Rhodes,[b] for the demagogues used to provide pay for public services, and also to hinder the payment of money owed [c] to the naval captains, and these because of the lawsuits that were brought against them were forced to make common cause and overthrow the people. And also at Heraclea [d] the people were put down immediately after the foundation of the colony because of the people's leaders ; for the notables being unjustly treated by them used to be driven out, but later on those who were driven out collecting together effected their return and put down the

397

ARISTOTLE

35 πλησίως δὲ καὶ ἡ ἐν Μεγάροις κατελύθη δημο-
κρατία· οἱ γὰρ δημαγωγοί, ἵνα χρήματα ἔχωσι
δημεύειν, ἐξέβαλλον πολλοὺς τῶν γνωρίμων, ἕως
πολλοὺς ἐποίησαν τοὺς φεύγοντας, οἱ δὲ κατιόντες
ἐνίκησαν μαχόμενοι τὸν δῆμον καὶ κατέστησαν
τὴν ὀλιγαρχίαν. συνέβη δὲ ταὐτὸν καὶ περὶ
1305 a Κύμην ἐπὶ τῆς δημοκρατίας ἣν κατέλυσε Θρασύ-
μαχος. σχεδὸν δὲ καὶ ἐπὶ τῶν ἄλλων ἄν τις ἴδοι
θεωρῶν τὰς μεταβολὰς τοῦτον ἐχούσας τὸν τρόπον.
ὁτὲ μὲν γὰρ ἵνα χαρίζωνται ἀδικοῦντες τοὺς
5 γνωρίμους συνιστᾶσιν, ἢ τὰς οὐσίας ἀναδάστους
ποιοῦντες ἢ τὰς προσόδους ταῖς λειτουργίαις, ὁτὲ
δὲ διαβάλλοντες, ἵν' ἔχωσι δημεύειν τὰ κτήματα
τῶν πλουσίων. ἐπὶ δὲ τῶν ἀρχαίων, ὅτε γένοιτο
ὁ αὐτὸς δημαγωγὸς καὶ στρατηγός, εἰς τυραννίδα
μετέβαλλον· σχεδὸν γὰρ οἱ πλεῖστοι τῶν ἀρχαίων
10 τυράννων ἐκ δημαγωγῶν γεγόνασιν. αἴτιον δὲ τοῦ
τότε μὲν γίγνεσθαι νῦν δὲ μή, ὅτι τότε μὲν οἱ
δημαγωγοὶ ἦσαν ἐκ τῶν στρατηγούντων (οὐ γάρ
πω δεινοὶ ἦσαν λέγειν), νῦν δὲ τῆς ῥητορικῆς
ηὐξημένης οἱ δυνάμενοι λέγειν δημαγωγοῦσι μέν,
δι' ἀπειρίαν δὲ τῶν πολεμικῶν οὐκ ἐπιτίθενται,
15 πλὴν εἴ που βραχύ τι γέγονε τοιοῦτον. ἐγίγνοντο
δὲ τυραννίδες πρότερον μᾶλλον ἢ νῦν καὶ διὰ τὸ
μεγάλας ἀρχὰς ἐγχειρίζεσθαί τισιν, ὥσπερ ἐν
Μιλήτῳ ἐκ τῆς πρυτανείας (πολλῶν γὰρ ἦν καὶ

---

[a] See 1300 a 18 ff. n.
[b] An event otherwise unknown.
[c] Perhaps that of Thrasybulus (Hdt. i. 20), 612 B.C.

people. And also the democracy at Megara was
put down in a similar manner [a]; the people's leaders resulting in
oligarchy,
in order to have money to distribute to the people
went on expelling many of the notables, until they
made the exiles a large body, and these came back
and defeated the people in a battle and set up the
oligarchy. And the same thing happened also at
Cyme in the time of the democracy which Thrasy-
machus put down,[b] and in the case of other states
also examination would show that revolutions take
place very much in this manner. Sometimes they
make the notables combine by wronging them in
order to curry favour, causing either their estates to
be divided up or their revenues by imposing public
services, and sometimes by so slandering them that
they may have the property of the wealthy to con-
fiscate. And in old times whenever the same man
became both leader of the people and general, they
used to change the constitution to a tyranny; for
almost the largest number of the tyrants of early
days have risen from being leaders of the people.
And the reason why this used to happen then but
does not do so now is because then the leaders of
the people were drawn from those who held the
office of general (for they were not yet skilled in
oratory), but now when rhetoric has developed the
able speakers are leaders of the people, but owing to
their inexperience in military matters they are not
put in control of these, except in so far as something
of the kind has taken place to a small extent in some
places. And tyrannies also used to occur in former
times more than they do now because important
offices were entrusted to certain men, as at Miletus a
tyranny [c] arose out of the presidency (for the president

1305 a

μεγάλων κύριος ὁ πρύτανις). ἔτι δὲ διὰ τὸ μὴ
μεγάλας εἶναι τότε τὰς πόλεις ἀλλ' ἐπὶ τῶν ἀγρῶν
20 οἰκεῖν τὸν δῆμον ἄσχολον ὄντα πρὸς τοῖς ἔργοις,
οἱ προστάται τοῦ δήμου, ὅτε πολεμικοὶ γένοιντο,
τυραννίδι ἐπετίθεντο. πάντες δὲ τοῦτο ἔδρων
ὑπὸ τοῦ δήμου πιστευθέντες, ἡ δὲ πίστις ἦν ἡ
ἀπέχθεια ἡ πρὸς τοὺς πλουσίους, οἷον Ἀθήνησί
25 τε Πεισίστρατος στασιάσας πρὸς τοὺς πεδιακούς,
καὶ Θεαγένης ἐν Μεγάροις τῶν εὐπόρων τὰ κτήνη
ἀποσφάξας, λαβὼν παρὰ τὸν ποταμὸν ἐπινέμοντας,
καὶ Διονύσιος κατηγορῶν Δαφναίου καὶ τῶν
πλουσίων ἠξιώθη τῆς τυραννίδος, διὰ τὴν ἔχθραν
πιστευθεὶς ὡς δημοτικὸς ὤν. μεταβάλλουσι δὲ
καὶ ἐκ τῆς πατρίας δημοκρατίας εἰς τὴν νεωτάτην·
30 ὅπου γὰρ αἱρεταὶ μὲν αἱ ἀρχαί, μὴ ἀπὸ τιμημάτων
δέ, αἱρεῖται δὲ ὁ δῆμος, δημαγωγοῦντες οἱ σπουδ-
αρχιῶντες εἰς τοῦτο καθιστᾶσιν ὥστε[1] κύριον
εἶναι τὸν δῆμον καὶ τῶν νόμων. ἄκος δὲ τοῦ ἢ
μὴ γίνεσθαι ἢ τοῦ γίνεσθαι ἧττον τὸ τὰς φυλὰς
φέρειν τοὺς ἄρχοντας ἀλλὰ μὴ πάντα τὸν δῆμον.
35 Τῶν μὲν οὖν δημοκρατιῶν αἱ μεταβολαὶ γίγνονται
πᾶσαι σχεδὸν διὰ ταύτας τὰς αἰτίας.

V. Αἱ δ' ὀλιγαρχίαι μεταβάλλουσι διὰ[2] δύο
μάλιστα τρόπους τοὺς φανερωτάτους, ἕνα μὲν ἐὰι
ἀδικῶσι τὸ πλῆθος· πᾶς γὰρ ἱκανὸς γίνεται προ-
40 στάτης, μάλιστα δ' ὅταν ἐξ αὐτῆς συμβῇ τῆς
ὀλιγαρχίας γίνεσθαι τὸν ἡγεμόνα, καθάπερ ἐι
Νάξῳ Λύγδαμις, ὃς καὶ ἐτυράννησεν ὕστερον τῶι
1305 b Ναξίων. ἔχει δὲ καὶ ἡ ἐξ ἄλλων ἀρχὴ στάσεω;

---

[1] ὥστε ed.: ὡς codd.   [2] κατὰ Richards.

[a] Dionysius the elder, see 1259 a 29 n.

had control of many important matters). And moreover, because the cities in those times were not large
but the common people lived on their farms busily
engaged in agriculture, the people's champions when
they became warlike used to aim at tyranny. And
they all used to do this when they had acquired the
confidence of the people, and their pledge of confidence was their enmity towards the rich, as at Athens
Pisistratus made himself tyrant by raising up a party 650 B.C.
against the men of the plain, and Theagenes at
Megara by slaughtering the cattle of the well-to-do 625 B.C.
which he captured grazing by the river, and Dionysius ^a established a claim to become tyrant when he
accused Daphnaeus and the rich, since his hostility
to them caused him to be trusted as a true man of the
people. And revolutions also take place from the *or in*
ancestral form of democracy to one of the most *extreme democracy.*
modern kind ; for where the magistracies are elec-
tive, but not on property-assessments, and the people
elect, men ambitious of office by acting as popular
leaders bring things to the point of the people's
being sovereign even over the laws. A remedy to
prevent this or to reduce its extent is for the tribes to
elect the magistrates, and not the people collectively.

These then are the causes through which almost
all the revolutions in democracies take place.

V. Oligarchies undergo revolution principally *Revolutions*
through two ways that are the most obvious. One *in oligarchies :*
is if they treat the multitude unjustly ; for anybody *(i.) caused*
makes an adequate people's champion, and especi- *from outside ;*
ally so when their leader happens to come from the
oligarchy itself, like Lygdamis at Naxos, who afterwards actually became tyrant of the Naxians. *c. 540 B.C.*
Faction originating with other people also has

διαφοράς. ὁτὲ μὲν γὰρ ἐξ αὐτῶν τῶν εὐπόρων, οὐ
τῶν ὄντων δ' ἐν ταῖς ἀρχαῖς, γίγνεται κατάλυσις,
ὅταν ὀλίγοι σφόδρα ὦσιν οἱ ἐν ταῖς τιμαῖς, οἷον
⁵ ἐν Μασσαλίᾳ καὶ ἐν Ἴστρῳ καὶ ἐν Ἡρακλείᾳ καὶ
ἐν ἄλλαις πόλεσι συμβέβηκεν· οἱ γὰρ μὴ μετέχοντες
τῶν ἀρχῶν ἐκίνουν, ἕως μετέλαβον οἱ πρεσβύτεροι
πρότερον τῶν ἀδελφῶν, ὕστερον δ' οἱ νεώτεροι
πάλιν (οὐ γὰρ ἄρχουσιν ἐνιαχοῦ μὲν ἅμα πατήρ
τε καὶ υἱός, ἐνιαχοῦ δὲ ὁ πρεσβύτερος καὶ ὁ νεώ-
¹⁰ τερος ἀδελφός). καὶ ἔνθα μὲν πολιτικωτέρα ἐγένετο ἡ ὀλιγαρχία, ἐν Ἴστρῳ δ' εἰς δῆμον ἀπ-
ετελεύτησεν, ἐν Ἡρακλείᾳ δ' ἐξ ἐλαττόνων εἰς ἑξα-
κοσίους ἦλθεν. μετέβαλε δὲ καὶ ἐν Κνίδῳ ἡ ὀλιγαρχία ⁵
στασιασάντων τῶν γνωρίμων αὐτῶν πρὸς αὐτοὺς διὰ
τὸ ὀλίγους μετέχειν καὶ καθάπερ εἴρηται, εἰ πατήρ,
¹⁵ υἱὸν μὴ μετέχειν, μηδ', εἰ πλείους ἀδελφοί, ἀλλ' ἢ
τὸν πρεσβύτατον· ἐπιλαβόμενος γὰρ στασιαζόντων
ὁ δῆμος καὶ λαβὼν προστάτην ἐκ τῶν γνωρίμων, ἐπιθέμενος ἐκράτησεν· ἀσθενὲς γὰρ τὸ στασιάζον. καὶ ⁵
ἐν Ἐρυθραῖς δὲ ἐπὶ τῆς τῶν Βασιλιδῶν ὀλιγαρχίας ἐν
²⁰ τοῖς ἀρχαίοις χρόνοις, καίπερ καλῶς ἐπιμελομένων
τῶν ἐν τῇ πολιτείᾳ, ὅμως διὰ τὸ ὑπ' ὀλίγων ἄρχεσθαι ἀγανακτῶν ὁ δῆμος μετέβαλε τὴν πολιτείαν.

Κινοῦνται δ' αἱ ὀλιγαρχίαι ἐξ αὐτῶν καὶ διὰ
φιλονεικίαν δημαγωγούντων (ἡ δημαγωγία δὲ

---

[a] The contrasted case, of dissolution of oligarchy arising
from the people, should follow, but is omitted.

[b] Cf. 1321 a 29 ff.

[c] Near the mouth of the Danube.   [d] See 1304 b 31 n.

[e] Perhaps not the same as the one mentioned at 1306 b 3.

[f] Just west of Smyrna.   The family name implies a claim
to royal ancestry.

[g] This sentence is interrupted by a parenthesis and is
resumed in § 6, 'And revolutions in oligarchy also—'.

various ways of arising. Sometimes when the honours of office are shared by very few, dissolution originates from the wealthy themselves,[a] but not those that are in office, as for example has occurred at Marseilles,[b] at Istrus,[c] at Heraclea,[d] and in other states; for those who did not share in the magistracies raised disturbances until as a first stage the older brothers were admitted, and later the younger ones again (for in some places a father and a son may not hold office together, and in others an elder and a younger brother may not). At Marseilles the oligarchy became more constitutional, while at Istrus it ended in becoming democracy, and in Heraclea the government passed from a smaller number to six hundred. At Cnidus also there was a revolution[e] of the oligarchy caused by a faction formed by the notables against one another, because few shared in the government, and the rule stated held, l. 8 ff. that if a father was a member a son could not be, nor if there were several brothers could any except the eldest; for the common people seized the opportunity of their quarrel and, taking a champion from among the notables, fell upon them and conquered them, for a party divided against itself is weak. Another case was at Erythrae,[f] where at the time of the oligarchy of the Basilidae in ancient days, although the persons in the government directed affairs well, nevertheless the common people were resentful because they were governed by a few, and brought about a revolution of the constitution.

On the other hand, oligarchies are overthrown (2) arising from within themselves both[g] when from motives owing to of rivalry they play the demagogue (and this dem- demagogy.

403

1305 b

διττή, ἡ μὲν ἐν αὐτοῖς τοῖς ὀλίγοις, ἐγγίνεται γὰρ
25 δημαγωγὸς κἂν πάνυ ὀλίγοι ὦσιν—οἷον ἐν τοῖς
τριάκοντα Ἀθήνησιν οἱ περὶ Χαρικλέα ἴσχυσαν
τοὺς τριάκοντα δημαγωγοῦντες, καὶ ἐν τοῖς τετρα-
κοσίοις οἱ περὶ Φρύνιχον τὸν αὐτὸν τρόπον—, ἡ δ᾽[1]
ὅταν τὸν ὄχλον δημαγωγῶσιν οἱ ἐν τῇ ὀλιγαρχίᾳ
ὄντες, οἷον ἐν Λαρίσῃ οἱ πολιτοφύλακες διὰ τὸ
30 αἱρεῖσθαι αὐτοὺς τὸν ὄχλον ἐδημαγώγουν, καὶ ἐν
ὅσαις ὀλιγαρχίαις οὐχ οὗτοι[2] αἱροῦνται τὰς ἀρχὰς
ἐξ ὧν οἱ ἄρχοντές εἰσιν ἀλλ᾽ αἱ μὲν ἀρχαὶ ἐκ
τιμημάτων μεγάλων εἰσὶν ἢ ἑταιριῶν αἱροῦνται
δ᾽ οἱ ὁπλῖται ἢ ὁ δῆμος, ὅπερ ἐν Ἀβύδῳ συνέβαινεν, καὶ ὅπου τὰ δικαστήρια μὴ ἐκ τοῦ πολι-
35 τεύματός ἐστιν—δημαγωγοῦντες γὰρ πρὸς τὰς
κρίσεις μεταβάλλουσι τὴν πολιτείαν, ὅπερ καὶ ἐν
Ἡρακλείᾳ ἐγένετο τῇ ἐν τῷ Πόντῳ—, ἔτι δ᾽
ὅταν ἔνιοι εἰς ἐλάττους ἕλκωσι τὴν ὀλιγαρχίαν,
οἱ γὰρ τὸ ἴσον ζητοῦντες ἀναγκάζονται βοηθὸν
ἐπαγαγέσθαι τὸν δῆμον). γίγνονται δὲ μεταβολαὶ
40 τῆς ὀλιγαρχίας καὶ ὅταν ἀναλώσωσι τὰ ἴδια
ζῶντες ἀσελγῶς· καὶ γὰρ οἱ τοιοῦτοι καινοτομεῖν
ζητοῦσι, καὶ ἢ τυραννίδι ἐπιτίθενται αὐτοὶ ἢ
1306 a κατασκευάζουσιν ἕτερον (ὥσπερ Ἱππαρῖνος Διονύσιον ἐν Συρακούσαις, καὶ ἐν Ἀμφιπόλει ᾧ
ὄνομα ἦν Κλεότιμος τοὺς ἐποίκους τοὺς Χαλκιδέων
ἤγαγε καὶ ἐλθόντων διεστασίασεν αὐτοὺς πρὸς
τοὺς εὐπόρους, καὶ ἐν Αἰγίνῃ ὁ τὴν πρᾶξιν τὴν

---

[1] ἡ δ᾽ ed.: ἡ codd.   [2] αὐτοὶ ? Richards.

---

[a] See 1304 b 12 n.   [b] See 1275 b 29 n.
[c] *i.e.* (apparently) where membership is not confined to the
class eligible for the magistracies.   [d] See 1304 b 31 n.
[e] See 1259 a 29 n.   [f] See 1303 b 2 n.

404

agogy is of two sorts, one among the oligarchs themselves, for a demagogue can arise among them even when they are a very small body,—as for instance in the time of the Thirty at Athens, the party of Charicles rose to power by currying popularity with the Thirty, and in the time of the Four Hundred [a] the party of Phrynichus rose in the same way,—the other when the members of the oligarchy curry popularity with the mob, as the Civic Guards at Larisa [b] courted popularity with the mob because it elected them, and in all the oligarchies in which the magistracies are not elected by the class from which the magistrates come but are filled from high property-grades or from political clubs while the electors are the heavy-armed soldiers or the common people, as used to be the case at Abydos, and in places where the jury-courts are not made up from the government [c]—for there members of the oligarchy by courting popular favour with a view to their trials cause a revolution of the constitution, as took place at Heraclea on the Euxine [d] ; and a further instance is when some men try to narrow down the oligarchy to a smaller number, for those who seek equality are forced to bring in the people as a helper.) And revolutions in oligarchy also take place when they squander their private means by riotous living ; for also men of this sort seek to bring about a new state of affairs, and either aim at tyranny themselves or suborn somebody else (as Hipparinus put forward Dionysius [e] at Syracuse, and at Amphipolis [f] a man named Cleotimus led the additional settlers that came from Chalcis and on their arrival stirred them up to sedition against the wealthy, and in Aegina

404 B.C.

or to extravagance

405

1306 a

5 πρὸς Χάρητα πράξας ἐνεχείρησε μεταβαλεῖν τὴν πολιτείαν διὰ· τοιαύτην αἰτίαν)· ὁτὲ μὲν οὖν ἐπιχειροῦσί τι κινεῖν, ὁτὲ δὲ κλέπτουσι τὰ κοινά, ὅθεν πρὸς αὑτοὺς στασιάζουσιν ἢ οὗτοι ἢ[1] οἱ πρὸς τούτους μαχόμενοι κλέπτοντας, ὅπερ ἐν Ἀπολλωνίᾳ

10 συνέβη τῇ ἐν τῷ Πόντῳ. ὁμονοοῦσα δὲ ὀλιγαρχία οὐκ εὐδιάφθορος ἐξ αὑτῆς· σημεῖον δὲ ἡ ἐν Φαρσάλῳ πολιτεία, ἐκεῖνοι γὰρ ὀλίγοι ὄντες πολλῶν κύριοί εἰσι διὰ τὸ χρῆσθαι σφίσιν αὐτοῖς καλῶς. καταλύονται δὲ καὶ ὅταν ἐν τῇ ὀλιγαρχίᾳ ἑτέραν ὀλιγαρχίαν ἐμποιῶσιν. τοῦτο δ᾽ ἐστὶν ὅταν τοῦ

15 παντὸς πολιτεύματος ὀλίγου ὄντος τῶν μεγίστων ἀρχῶν μὴ μετέχωσιν οἱ ὀλίγοι πάντες· ὅπερ ἐν Ἤλιδι συνέβη ποτέ, τῆς πολιτείας γὰρ δι᾽ ὀλίγων οὔσης τῶν γερόντων ὀλίγοι πάμπαν ἐγίνοντο διὰ τὸ ἀϊδίους εἶναι ἐνενήκοντα ὄντας, τὴν δ᾽ αἵρεσιν δυναστευτικὴν εἶναι καὶ ὁμοίαν τῇ τῶν ἐν Λακεδαίμονι γερόντων.

20 Γίγνεται δὲ μεταβολὴ τῶν ὀλιγαρχικῶν καὶ ἐν πολέμῳ καὶ ἐν εἰρήνῃ· ἐν μὲν πολέμῳ διὰ τὴν πρὸς τὸν δῆμον ἀπιστίαν στρατιώταις ἀναγκαζομένων χρῆσθαι (ᾧ γὰρ ἂν ἐγχειρίσωσιν, οὗτος πολλάκις γίγνεται τύραννος, ὥσπερ ἐν Κορίνθῳ Τιμοφάνης, ἂν δὲ πλείους, οὗτοι αὑτοῖς περιποιοῦνται δυνα-

25 στείαν), ὁτὲ δὲ ταῦτα δεδιότες μεταδιδόασι τῷ

---

[1] ὅθεν ἢ αὐτοὶ πρὸς αὐτοὺς στασιάζουσιν ἢ Richards.

---

[a] *i.e.* he had squandered his fortune in riotous living; thi deal with the Athenian general may have been in 367 B.C.

[b] *i.e.* both of the lower classes and of the subject cities.

[c] *i.e.* the small governing body.

[d] *i.e.* like a *dynasteia*, favourable to the interest of a few very wealthy families; see 1292 b 10 n.

[e] Corinth was at war with Argos *c.* 350 B.C. Timophane

the man who carried out the transactions with
Chares attempted to cause a revolution in the con-
7 stitution for a reason of this sort [a]) ; so sometimes
they attempt at once to introduce some reform, at
other times they rob the public funds and in consequence either they or those who fight against them
in their peculations stir up faction against the government, as happened at Apollonia on the Black Sea.
On the other hand, harmonious oligarchy does not
easily cause its own destruction ; and an indication
of this is the constitutional government at Pharsalus, for there the ruling class though few are
masters of many men [b] because on good terms with
8 one another. Also oligarchical governments break *or to*
up when they create a second oligarchy within the *further ex-*
oligarchy. This is when, although the whole citizen *clusiveness.*
class is small, its few members are not all admitted to
the greatest offices ; this is what once occurred in
Elis, for the government being in the hands of a few,
very few men used to become members of the Elders,[c]
because these numbering ninety held office for life,
and the mode of election was of a dynastic type [d] and
resembled that of the Elders at Sparta.

Revolutions of oligarchies occur both during war *Internal*
and in time of peace—during war since the oligarchs *weaknesses.*
are forced by their distrust of the people to employ
mercenary troops (for the man in whose hands they
place them often becomes tyrant, as Timophanes
did at Corinth,[e] and if they put several men in
command, these win for themselves dynastic power),
and when through fear of this they give a share in
the constitution to the multitude, the oligarchy falls

was killed by his brother the famous Timoleon, in order to
restore constitutional government.

1306 a

πλήθει τῆς πολιτείας, διὰ τὸ ἀναγκάζεσθαι τῷ
δήμῳ χρῆσθαι· ἐν δὲ τῇ εἰρήνῃ διὰ τὴν ἀπιστίαν
τὴν πρὸς ἀλλήλους ἐγχειρίζουσι τὴν φυλακὴν
στρατιώταις καὶ ἄρχοντι μεσιδίῳ, ὃς ἐνίοτε γίνεται
30 κύριος ἀμφοτέρων, ὅπερ συνέβη ἐν Λαρίσῃ ἐπὶ
τῆς τῶν Ἀλευαδῶν ἀρχῆς τῶν[1] περὶ Σῖμον καὶ ἐν
Ἀβύδῳ ἐπὶ τῶν ἑταιριῶν ὧν ἦν μία ἡ Ἰφιάδου.
γίνονται δὲ στάσεις καὶ ἐκ τοῦ περιωθεῖσθαι 10
ἑτέρους ὑφ' ἑτέρων τῶν ἐν τῇ ὀλιγαρχίᾳ αὐτῶν
καὶ καταστασιάζεσθαι κατὰ γάμους ἢ δίκας, οἷον
35 ἐκ γαμικῆς μὲν αἰτίας αἱ εἰρημέναι πρότερον, καὶ
τὴν ἐν Ἐρετρίᾳ δ' ὀλιγαρχίαν τὴν τῶν ἱππέων
Διαγόρας κατέλυσεν ἀδικηθεὶς περὶ γάμον, ἐκ
δὲ δικαστηρίου κρίσεως ἡ ἐν Ἡρακλείᾳ στάσις
ἐγένετο καὶ ἡ[2] ἐν Θήβαις, ἐπ' αἰτίᾳ μοιχείας
δικαίως μὲν στασιωτικῶς δὲ ποιησαμένων τὴν
1306 b κόλασιν τῶν μὲν ἐν Ἡρακλείᾳ κατ' Εὐρυτίωνος
τῶν δ' ἐν Θήβαις κατ' Ἀρχίου· ἐφιλονείκησαν γὰρ
αὐτοὺς[3] οἱ ἐχθροὶ ὥστε δεθῆναι ἐν ἀγορᾷ ἐν τῷ
κύφωνι. πολλαὶ δὲ καὶ διὰ τὸ ἄγαν δεσποτικὰς 1
εἶναι τὰς ὀλιγαρχίας ὑπὸ τῶν ἐν τῇ πολιτείᾳ τινῶν
5 δυσχερανάντων κατελύθησαν, ὥσπερ ἡ ἐν Κνίδῳ
καὶ ἡ ἐν Χίῳ ὀλιγαρχία. γίγνονται δὲ καὶ ἀπὸ
συμπτώματος μεταβολαὶ καὶ τῆς καλουμένης
πολιτείας καὶ τῶν ὀλιγαρχιῶν ἐν ὅσαις ἀπὸ τιμή-

---

[1] τῶν non vertit Guil.: τοῖς Niemeyer.
[2] καὶ ⟨ἡ⟩ ? Newman: καὶ codd.
[3] αὐτοῖς L. & S.: αὐτοὺς codd. (tr. post δεθῆναι Richards).

---

[a] A probable emendation of the Greek gives 'happened
at Larisa to Simus and his party at the time of the government of the Aleuadae.' This family were hereditary rulers
of Larisa (see also 1275 b 29 ff. n., and 1305 b 29 ff.).

because they are compelled to make use of the common people; during peace, on the other hand, because of their distrust of one another they place their protection in the hands of mercenary troops and a magistrate between the two parties, who sometimes becomes master of both, which happened at Larisa in the time of the government of the Aleuadae led by Simus,[a] and at Abydos in the time of the 1305 b 33 political clubs of which that of Iphiades was one.

10 And factions arise also in consequence of one set of Internal the members of the oligarchy themselves being pushed quarrels. aside by another set and being driven into party strife in regard to marriages or law-suits; examples of such disorders arising out of a cause related to marriage are the instances spoken of before, and also 1303 b 38 ff the oligarchy of the knights at Eretria was put down [b] by Diagoras when he had been wronged in respect of a marriage, while the faction at Heraclea and that at Thebes arose out of a judgement of a law-court, when the people at Heraclea justly but factiously enforced the punishment against Eurytion on a charge of adultery and those at Thebes did so against Archias; for their personal enemies stirred up party feeling against them so as to get them bound in 11 the pillory in the market-place. Also many governments have been put down by some of their members who had become resentful because the oligarchies were too despotic; this is how the oligarchies fell at Cnidus [c] and at Chios. And revolutions also occur Fall in value from an accident, both in what is called a consti- of money. tutional government and in those oligarchies in

---

[b] Possibly before the Persian wars. See 1289 b 36 ff. The two following cases are unrecorded elsewhere.
[c] See 1305 b 13 n.

1306 b

ματος βουλεύουσι καὶ δικάζουσι καὶ τὰς ἄλλας
ἀρχὰς ἄρχουσιν. πολλάκις γὰρ[1] τὸ ταχθὲν πρῶτον
10 τίμημα πρὸς τοὺς παρόντας καιρούς, ὥστε μετέχειν ἐν μὲν τῇ ὀλιγαρχίᾳ ὀλίγους ἐν δὲ τῇ πολιτείᾳ
τοὺς μέσους, εὐετηρίας[2] γιγνομένης δι᾽ εἰρήνην ἢ
δι᾽ ἄλλην τιν᾽ εὐτυχίαν συμβαίνει πολλαπλασίου
γίγνεσθαι τιμήματος ἀξίας τὰς αὐτὰς κτήσεις,
ὥστε πάντας πάντων μετέχειν, ὁτὲ μὲν ἐκ προσ-
15 αγωγῆς καὶ κατὰ μικρὸν γινομένης τῆς μεταβολῆς
καὶ λανθανούσης, ὁτὲ δὲ καὶ θᾶττον.

Αἱ μὲν οὖν ὀλιγαρχίαι μεταβάλλουσι καὶ στασιά- 12
ζουσι διὰ τοιαύτας αἰτίας (ὅλως δὲ καὶ αἱ δημοκρατίαι καὶ ὀλιγαρχίαι ἐξίστανται ἐνίοτε οὐκ εἰς τὰς
ἐναντίας πολιτείας ἀλλ᾽ εἰς τὰς ἐν τῷ αὐτῷ γένει,
20 οἷον ἐκ τῶν ἐννόμων δημοκρατιῶν καὶ ὀλιγαρχιῶν
εἰς τὰς κυρίους καὶ ἐκ τούτων εἰς ἐκείνας).

VI. Ἐν δὲ ταῖς ἀριστοκρατίαις γίγνονται αἱ 1
στάσεις αἱ μὲν διὰ τὸ ὀλίγους τῶν τιμῶν μετέχειν
(ὅπερ εἴρηται κινεῖν καὶ τὰς ὀλιγαρχίας, διὰ τὸ
25 καὶ τὴν ἀριστοκρατίαν ὀλιγαρχίαν εἶναί πως, ἐν
ἀμφοτέραις γὰρ ὀλίγοι οἱ ἄρχοντες—οὐ μέντοι
διὰ ταὐτὸν ὀλίγοι—ἐπεὶ δοκεῖ γε διὰ ταῦτα καὶ ἡ
ἀριστοκρατία ὀλιγαρχία εἶναι). μάλιστα δὲ τοῦτο
συμβαίνειν ἀναγκαῖον ὅταν ᾖ τι[3] πλῆθος τῶν
πεφρονηματισμένων ὡς ὁμοίων[4] κατ᾽ ἀρετήν (οἷον
30 ἐν Λακεδαίμονι οἱ λεγόμενοι Παρθενίαι—ἐκ τῶν

---

[1] γὰρ ⟨εἰ καὶ ἱκανὸν⟩ Richards.
[2] εὐετηρίας ⟨δὲ⟩ Immisch.
[3] τι Congreve: τὸ codd.
[4] ὁμοίων Lambinus: ὅμοιον codd.

---

[a] See 1306 a 13 ff.

which membership of the council and the law-courts and tenure of the other offices are based on a property-qualification. For often the qualification first having been fixed to suit the circumstances of the time, so that in an oligarchy a few may be members and in a constitutional government the middle classes, when peace or some other good fortune leads to a good harvest it comes about that the same properties become worth many times as large an assessment, so that all the citizens share in all the rights, the change sometimes taking place gradually and little by little and not being noticed, but at other times more quickly.

Such then are the causes that lead to revolutions and factions in oligarchies (and generally, both democracies and oligarchies are sometimes altered not into the opposite forms of constitution but into ones of the same class, for instance from legitimate democracies and oligarchies into autocratic ones and from the latter into the former).

VI. In aristocracies factions arise in some cases because few men share in the honours (which has also been said [a] to be the cause of disturbances in oligarchies, because an aristocracy too is a sort of oligarchy, for in both those who govern are few—although the reason for this is not the same in both —since this does cause it to be thought that aristocracy is a form of oligarchy). And this is most bound to come about when there is a considerable number of people who are proud-spirited on the ground of being equals in virtue (for example the clan called the Maidens' Sons [b] at Sparta—for

Faction in aristocracy due to (1) monopoly of honours,

[b] Said to be descended from irregular unions authorized in order to keep up the population during the First Messenian War. They founded Taranto 708 B.C.

1306 b

ὁμοίων γὰρ ἦσαν,—οὓς φωράσαντες ἐπιβουλεύσαν-
τας ἀπέστειλαν Τάραντος οἰκιστάς)· ἢ ὅταν τινὲς 2
ἀτιμάζωνται μεγάλοι ὄντες καὶ μηθενὸς ἥττους
κατ᾽ ἀρετὴν ὑπὸ τινῶν ἐντιμοτέρων (οἷον Λύσανδρος
ὑπὸ τῶν βασιλέων)· ἢ ὅταν ἀνδρώδης τις ὢν μὴ
35 μετέχῃ τῶν τιμῶν (οἷον Κινάδων ὁ τὴν ἐπ᾽ Ἀγησιλάου[1] συστήσας ἐπίθεσιν ἐπὶ τοὺς Σπαρτιάτας).
ἔτι ὅταν οἱ μὲν ἀπορῶσι λίαν οἱ δ᾽ εὐπορῶσιν
(καὶ μάλιστα ἐν τοῖς πολέμοις τοῦτο γίνεται,
συνέβη δὲ καὶ τοῦτο ἐν Λακεδαίμονι ὑπὸ τὸν
Μεσσηνιακὸν πόλεμον—δῆλον δὲ [καὶ τοῦτο][2] ἐκ
1307 a τῆς Τυρταίου ποιήσεως τῆς καλουμένης Εὐνομίας·
θλιβόμενοι γάρ τινες διὰ τὸν πόλεμον ἠξίουν
ἀνάδαστον ποιεῖν τὴν χώραν). ἔτι ἐάν τις μέγας
ᾖ καὶ δυνάμενος ἔτι μείζων εἶναι, ἵνα μοναρχῇ
(ὥσπερ ἐν Λακεδαίμονι δοκεῖ Παυσανίας ὁ στρα-
5 τηγήσας κατὰ τὸν Μηδικὸν πόλεμον καὶ ἐν
Καρχηδόνι Ἄννων).

Λύονται δὲ μάλιστα αἵ τε πολιτεῖαι καὶ αἱ
ἀριστοκρατίαι διὰ τὴν ἐν αὐτῇ τῇ πολιτείᾳ τοῦ
δικαίου παρέκβασιν. ἀρχὴ γὰρ τὸ μὴ μεμῖχθαι
καλῶς ἐν μὲν τῇ πολιτείᾳ δημοκρατίαν καὶ ὀλιγαρχίαν ἐν δὲ τῇ ἀριστοκρατίᾳ ταῦτά τε καὶ τὴν
10 ἀρετήν, μάλιστα δὲ τὰ δύο (λέγω δὲ τὰ δύο δῆμον

---

[1] Ἀγησιλάου Schneider: -λάῳ codd.
[2] Verrall (καὶ non vertit Guil.).

---

[a] King Pausanias II. checked Lysander after his conquest
of Athens in 403 B.C., and King Agesilaus thwarted him on
the expedition into Asia Minor in 396.

[b] His conspiracy against the Ὅμοιοι in 398 B.C. was discovered and he was executed.

they were descended from the Equals—whom the
Spartans detected in a conspiracy and sent away
to colonize Tarentum); or when individuals although
great men and inferior to nobody in virtue are
treated dishonourably by certain men in higher
honour (for example Lysander by the kings[a]); or
when a person of manly nature has no share in the
honours (for example Cinadon,[b] who got together the
attack upon the Spartans in the reign of Agesilaus).
Faction in aristocracies also arises when some of the (2) or of
well-born are too poor and others too rich (which wealth,
happens especially during wars, and this also occurred at Sparta at the time of the Messenian War
—as appears from the poem of Tyrtaeus entitled
Law and Order; for some men being in distress
because of the war put forward a claim to carry out
a re-division of the land of the country). Also if a (3) or one
man is great and capable of being yet greater, he man aiming
stirs up faction in order that he may be sole ruler monarchy.
(as Pausanias who commanded the army through
the Persian war seems to have done at Sparta, and
Hanno[c] at Carthage).

But the actual overthrow of both constitutional Revolutions
governments and aristocracies is mostly due to a in politics
deviation from justice in the actual framework of oligarchy,
the constitution. For what starts it in the case of a in aristo-
constitutional government is that it does not contain cracies de-
a good blend of democracy and oligarchy ; and in the mocracy.
case of an aristocracy it is the lack of a good blend
of those two elements and of virtue, but chiefly of
the two elements (I mean popular government and

---

[c] Perhaps Hanno who fought in Sicily against the elder
Dionysius *c.* 400 B.C.

1307 a

καὶ ὀλιγαρχίαν), ταῦτα γὰρ αἱ πολιτεῖαί τε
πειρῶνται μιγνύναι καὶ αἱ πολλαὶ τῶν καλουμένων
ἀριστοκρατιῶν. διαφέρουσι γὰρ τῶν ὀνομαζο-
μένων πολιτειῶν αἱ ἀριστοκρατίαι τούτῳ, καὶ διὰ
τοῦτ᾽ εἰσὶν αἱ μὲν ἧττον αἱ δὲ μᾶλλον μόνιμοι

15 αὐτῶν· τὰς γὰρ ἀποκλινούσας μᾶλλον πρὸς τὴν
ὀλιγαρχίαν ἀριστοκρατίας καλοῦσιν, τὰς δὲ πρὸς
τὸ πλῆθος πολιτείας, διόπερ ἀσφαλέστεραι αἱ
τοιαῦται τῶν ἑτέρων εἰσίν, κρεῖττόν τε γὰρ τὸ
πλεῖον καὶ μᾶλλον ἀγαπῶσιν ἴσον ἔχοντες, οἱ δ᾽
ἐν ταῖς εὐπορίαις, ἂν ἡ πολιτεία διδῷ τὴν ὑπεροχήν,

20 ὑβρίζειν ζητοῦσι καὶ πλεονεκτεῖν. ὅλως δ᾽ ἐφ᾽
ὁπότερον ἂν ἐγκλίνῃ ἡ πολιτεία, ἐπὶ τοῦτο¹
μεθίσταται ἑκατέρων τὸ σφέτερον αὐξανόντων,
οἷον ἡ μὲν πολιτεία εἰς δῆμον ἀριστοκρατία δ᾽
εἰς ὀλιγαρχίαν, ἢ εἰς τἀναντία, οἷον ἡ μὲν ἀριστοκρατία εἰς δῆμον (ὡς ἀδικούμενοι γὰρ περισπῶσιν

25 εἰς τοὐναντίον οἱ ἀπορώτεροι) αἱ δὲ πολιτεῖαι
εἰς ὀλιγαρχίαν (μόνον γὰρ μόνιμον τὸ κατ᾽ ἀξίαν
ἴσον καὶ τὸ ἔχειν τὰ αὑτῶν). συνέβη δὲ τὸ
εἰρημένον ἐν Θουρίοις· διὰ μὲν γὰρ τὸ ἀπὸ πλείονος
τιμήματος εἶναι τὰς ἀρχὰς εἰς ἔλαττον μετέβη καὶ

30 εἰς ἀρχεῖα πλείω, διὰ δὲ τὸ τὴν χώραν ὅλην τοὺς
γνωρίμους συγκτήσασθαι παρὰ τὸν νόμον (ἡ γὰρ

___

¹ τοῦτο (uel ὁπότερα) Spengel: ταῦτα codd.

___

ᵃ i.e. their mode of blending oligarchy and democracy.
ᵇ The writer loosely speaks of aristocracies and polities
as a single class, differing only in degree of concentration of
power in the hands of the upper classes.
ᶜ i.e. from aristocracy to democracy. Possibly these
events occurred after the defeat of Athens at Syracuse in
413 B.C., when the Athenian party at Thurii was banished

414

ligarchy), for both constitutional governments and
most of the constitutions that are called aristocracies
aim at blending these. For this [a] is the point of distinction between aristocracies and what are called
constitutional governments, and it is owing to this
that some of them [b] are less and others more
stable; for the constitutions inclining more towards
oligarchy men call aristocracies and those inclining
more to the side of the multitude constitutional
governments, owing to which those of the latter sort
are more secure than the others, for the greater
number is the stronger, and also are men more content when they have an equal amount, whereas the
owners of wealthy properties, if the constitution
gives them the superior position, seek to behave
insolently and to gain money. And speaking
broadly, to whichever side the constitution leans,
that is the side to which it shifts as either of the two
parties increases its own side—a constitutional
government shifts to democracy and an aristocracy
to oligarchy, or to the opposite extremes, that is,
aristocracy to democracy (for the poorer people
feeling they are unjustly treated pull it round to
the opposite) and constitutional governments to
oligarchy (for the only lasting thing is equality in
accordance with desert and the possession of what is
their own). And the change mentioned [c] came about
at Thurii, for because the property-qualification for
honours was too high, the constitution was altered to
a lower property-qualification and to a larger number
of official posts, but because the notables illegally
bought up the whole of the land (for the constitution

Lysias 835 D). The events in § 8 were perhaps in the
fourth century.

1307 a

πολιτεία ὀλιγαρχικωτέρα ἦν, ὥστε ἐδύναντο πλεο
εκτεῖν). . . .[1] ὁ δὲ δῆμος γυμνασθεὶς ἐν τῷ πολέμ
τῶν φρουρῶν ἐγένετο κρείττων, ἕως ἀφεῖσαν τ
χώρας ὅσοι πλείω ἦσαν ἔχοντες.

Ἔτι διὰ τὸ πάσας τὰς ἀριστοκρατικὰς πολιτεί
35 ὀλιγαρχικὰς εἶναι μᾶλλον πλεονεκτοῦσιν οἱ γνω
ριμοι (οἷον καὶ ἐν Λακεδαίμονι εἰς ὀλίγους
οὐσίαι ἔρχονται)· καὶ ἔξεστι ποιεῖν ὅ τι ἂν θέλω
τοῖς γνωρίμοις μᾶλλον, καὶ κηδεύειν ὅτῳ θέλωσ
(διὸ καὶ ἡ Λοκρῶν πόλις ἀπώλετο ἐκ τῆς πρ
Διονύσιον κηδείας, ὃ ἐν δημοκρατίᾳ οὐκ
40 ἐγένετο, οὐδ' ἂν ἐν ἀριστοκρατίᾳ εὖ μεμιγμέν
1307 b μάλιστα δὲ λανθάνουσιν αἱ ἀριστοκρατίαι μετ
βάλλουσαι τῷ λύεσθαι κατὰ μικρόν, ὅπερ εἴρητ
ἐν τοῖς πρότερον καθόλου κατὰ πασῶν τ
πολιτειῶν, ὅτι αἴτιον τῶν μεταβολῶν καὶ
μικρόν ἐστιν· ὅταν γάρ τι προῶνται τῶν πρ
5 τὴν πολιτείαν, μετὰ τοῦτο καὶ ἄλλο μικρῷ μεῖζ
εὐχερέστερον κινοῦσιν, ἕως ἂν πάντα κινήσω
τὸν κόσμον. συνέβη δὲ τοῦτο καὶ ἐπὶ τῆς Θ
ρίων πολιτείας. νόμου γὰρ ὄντος διὰ πέντε ἐτ
στρατηγεῖν, γενόμενοί τινες πολεμικοὶ τ
νεωτέρων καὶ παρὰ τῷ πλήθει τῶν φρουρ
10 εὐδοκιμοῦντες, καταφρονήσαντες τῶν ἐν τοῖς πρά
μασι καὶ νομίζοντες ῥᾳδίως κατασχήσειν, τοῦτ
τὸν νόμον λύειν ἐπεχείρησαν πρῶτον, ὥστ' ἐξεῖ
τοὺς αὐτοὺς συνεχῶς στρατηγεῖν, ὁρῶντες τ
δῆμον αὐτοὺς χειροτονήσοντα προθύμως. οἱ

---

[1] lacunam vel vitium Schneider.

---

[a] Probably a clause meaning ' civil strife ensued ' has be
lost.

was too oligarchical, so that they were able to grasp
at wealth) . . .[a] And the people having been trained
in the war overpowered the guards, until those who
were in the position of having too much land relinquished it.

Besides, as all aristocratic constitutions are inclined towards oligarchy, the notables grasp at
wealth (for example at Sparta the estates are coming
into a few hands) ; and the notables have more power
to do what they like, and to form marriage connexions
with whom they like (which was the cause of the
fall of the state of Locri, as a result of the marriage
with Dionysius,[b] which would not have taken place
in a democracy, nor in a well-blended aristocracy). Small
And aristocracies are most liable to undergo revolu- reforms
tion unobserved, through gradual relaxation, just as revolution.
it has been said in what has gone before about all 1303 a 20 ff.
forms of constitution in general, that even a small
change may cause a revolution. For when they give
up one of the details of the constitution, afterwards
they also make another slightly bigger change more
readily, until they alter the whole system. This
occurred for instance with the constitution of Thurii.
There was a law that the office of general could be
held at intervals of four years, but some of the
younger men, becoming warlike and winning high
repute with the mass of the guards, came to despise
the men engaged in affairs, and thought that they
could easily get control ; so first they tried to repeal
the law referred to, so as to enable the same persons
to serve as generals continuously, as they saw that
the people would vote for themselves with enthusiasm.

[b] See 1259 a 28 n. He married in 397 B.C. the daughter
of a Locrian citizen, who bore him the younger Dionysius.

1307 b

ἐπὶ τούτῳ τεταγμένοι τῶν ἀρχόντων, οἱ καλούμενοι
15 σύμβουλοι, ὁρμήσαντες τὸ πρῶτον ἐναντιοῦσθαι
συνεπείσθησαν, ὑπολαμβάνοντες τοῦτον κινήσαν-
τας τὸν νόμον ἐάσειν τὴν ἄλλην πολιτείαν,
ὕστερον δὲ βουλόμενοι κωλύειν ἄλλων κινουμένων
οὐκέτι πλέον ἐποίουν οὐθέν, ἀλλὰ μετέβαλεν ἡ
τάξις πᾶσα τῆς πολιτείας εἰς δυναστείαν τῶν
ἐπιχειρησάντων νεωτερίζειν.

20 Πᾶσαι δ' αἱ πολιτεῖαι λύονται ὁτὲ μὲν ἐξ
αὑτῶν ὁτὲ δ' ἔξωθεν, ὅταν ἐναντία πολιτεία ἢ ἥ
πλησίον ἢ πόρρω μὲν ἔχουσα δὲ δύναμιν. ὅπερ
συνέβαινεν ἐπ' Ἀθηναίων καὶ Λακεδαιμονίων· οἱ
μὲν γὰρ Ἀθηναῖοι πανταχοῦ τὰς ὀλιγαρχίας οἱ
δὲ Λάκωνες τοὺς δήμους κατέλυον.

25 Ὅθεν μὲν οὖν αἱ μεταβολαὶ γίγνονται τῶν
πολιτειῶν καὶ αἱ στάσεις, εἴρηται σχεδόν.

VII. Περὶ δὲ σωτηρίας καὶ κοινῇ καὶ χωρὶ
ἑκάστης πολιτείας ἐχόμενόν ἐστιν εἰπεῖν. πρῶτο
μὲν οὖν δῆλον ὅτι εἴπερ ἔχομεν δι' ὧν φθείροντα
αἱ πολιτεῖαι ἔχομεν καὶ δι' ὧν σώζονται· τῶν γὰ
30 ἐναντίων τἀναντία ποιητικά, φθορᾷ δὲ σωτηρί
ἐναντίον. ἐν μὲν οὖν ταῖς εὖ κεκραμέναις πολι
τείαις, εἴπερ[1] ἄλλο τι δεῖ τηρεῖν ὅπως μηθὲ
παρανομῶσι, καὶ μάλιστα τὸ μικρὸν φυλάττει
λανθάνει γὰρ παραδυομένη ἡ παρανομία,[2] ὥσπε
τὰς οὐσίας αἱ μικραὶ δαπάναι δαπανῶσι πολλάκι
35 γινόμεναι· λανθάνει γὰρ ἡ δαπάνη[3] διὰ τὸ μ

---

[1] εἴπερ Richards: ὥσπερ codd.
[2] παραδυομένη ἡ παρανομία (ex Plat. de rep. 424 D) M⁸P⁵
ὑπεισδύουσα ἡ παράβασις cet.
[3] δαπάνη: ἀπάτη M⁸, μετάβασις Par.

And though the magistrates in charge of this matter, called the Councillors, at first made a movement to oppose them, they were won over, believing that after repealing this law they would allow the rest of the constitution to stand ; but later, though they wished to prevent them when other laws were being repealed, they could no longer do anything more, but the whole system of the constitution was converted into a dynasty of the men who had initiated the innovations.

And constitutions of all forms are broken up sometimes from movements initiating from within themselves, but sometimes from outside, when there is an opposite form of constitution either near by or a long way off yet possessed of power. This used to happen in the days of the Athenians and the Spartans ; the Athenians used to put down oligarchies everywhere and the Spartans democracies. *Foreign intervention.*

We have then approximately stated the causes that give rise to revolutions in the constitutions of states and to party factions.

VII. The next thing to speak about is security both in general and for each form of constitution separately. First then it is clear that if we know the causes by which constitutions are destroyed we also know the causes by which they are preserved ; for opposites create opposites, and destruction is the opposite of security. In well-blended constitutions therefore, if care must be taken to prevent men from committing any other breach of the law, most of all must a small breach be guarded against, for transgression of the law creeps in unnoticed, just as a small expenditure occurring often ruins men's estates ; for the expense is not noticed because it *Stability of constitutions. General safeguards.*

1307 b

ἀθρόα γίγνεσθαι, παραλογίζεται γὰρ ἡ διάνοια
ὑπ' αὐτῶν, ὥσπερ ὁ σοφιστικὸς λόγος 'εἰ ἕκαστον
μικρόν, καὶ πάντα.' τοῦτο δ' ἔστι μὲν ὥς, ἔστι
δ' ὡς οὔ· τὸ γὰρ ὅλον καὶ τὰ πάντα οὐ μικρὸν
ἀλλὰ σύγκειται ἐκ μικρῶν. μίαν μὲν οὖν φυλα-
40 κὴν πρὸς ταύτην τὴν ἀρχὴν δεῖ ποιεῖσθαι, ἔπειτα
1308 a μὴ πιστεύειν τοῖς σοφίσματος χάριν πρὸς τὸ πλῆθος
συγκειμένοις, ἐξελέγχεται γὰρ ὑπὸ τῶν ἔργων
(ποῖα δὲ λέγομεν τῶν πολιτειῶν σοφίσματα, πρότερον εἴρηται). ἔτι δ' ὁρᾶν ὅτι ἔνιαι μένουσιν οὐ
5 μόνον ἀριστοκρατίαι ἀλλὰ καὶ ὀλιγαρχίαι οὐ διὰ
τὸ ἀσφαλεῖς εἶναι τὰς πολιτείας ἀλλὰ διὰ τὸ εὖ
χρῆσθαι τοὺς ἐν ταῖς ἀρχαῖς γινομένους καὶ τοῖς
ἔξω τῆς πολιτείας καὶ τοῖς ἐν τῷ πολιτεύματι, τοὺς
μὲν μὴ μετέχοντας τῷ μὴ ἀδικεῖν καὶ τῷ τοὺς
ἡγεμονικοὺς αὐτῶν εἰσάγειν εἰς τὴν πολιτείαν καὶ
τοὺς μὲν φιλοτίμους μὴ ἀδικεῖν εἰς ἀτιμίαν τοὺς
10 δὲ πολλοὺς εἰς κέρδος, πρὸς αὐτοὺς δὲ καὶ τοὺς
μετέχοντας τῷ χρῆσθαι ἀλλήλοις δημοτικῶς. ὁ
γὰρ ἐπὶ τοῦ πλήθους ζητοῦσιν οἱ δημοτικοὶ τὸ
ἴσον, τοῦτ' ἐπὶ τῶν ὁμοίων οὐ μόνον δίκαιον ἀλλὰ
καὶ συμφέρον ἐστίν. διὸ ἐὰν πλείους ὦσιν ἐν τῷ
πολιτεύματι, πολλὰ συμφέρει τῶν δημοτικῶν νομο-
15 θετημάτων, οἷον τὸ ἑξαμήνους τὰς ἀρχὰς εἶναι
ἵνα πάντες οἱ ὅμοιοι μετέχωσιν· ἔστι γὰρ ὥσπερ
δῆμος ἤδη οἱ ὅμοιοι (διὸ καὶ ἐν τούτοις ἐγγίγνονται
δημαγωγοὶ πολλάκις, ὥσπερ εἴρηται πρότερον)·
ἔπειθ' ἧττον εἰς δυναστείας ἐμπίπτουσιν αἱ ὀλιγ-

---

does not come all at once, for the mind is led astray
by the repeated small outlays, just like the sophistic
puzzle, ' if each is little, then all are a little.' *a* This is
true in one way but in another it is not; for the
whole or total is not little, but made up of little
parts. One thing therefore that we must guard
against is this beginning; and the next point is that
we must not put faith in the arguments strung together for the sake of tricking the multitude, for they
are refuted by the facts (and what sort of constitutional
sophistries we refer to has been said before). And 1274 a 14 ff.
again we must observe that not only some aristocracies but also some oligarchies endure not because
the constitutions are secure but because those who
get in the offices treat both those outside the constitution and those in the government well, on the
one hand by not treating those who are not members
of it unjustly and by bringing their leading men into
the constitution and not wronging the ambitious
ones in the matter of dishonour or the multitude in
the matter of gain, and on the other hand, in relation
to themselves and those who are members, by treating
one another in a democratic spirit. For that equality
which men of democratic spirit seek for in the case
of the multitude is not only just but also expedient
in the case of their compeers. Hence if there are
a greater number in the governing class, many of
the legislative enactments of a democratic nature
are advantageous, for example for the offices to be
tenable for six months, to enable all the compeers to
participate in them; for the compeers in this case are
as it were the people (owing to which demagogues often
arise even among them, as has been said already), 1306 a 24.
and also oligarchies and aristocracies fall into dyn-

421

1308 a

αρχίαι καὶ ἀριστοκρατίαι (οὐ γὰρ ὁμοίως ῥάδιον
20 κακουργῆσαι ὀλίγον χρόνον ἄρχοντας καὶ πολύν,
ἐπεὶ διὰ τοῦτο ἐν ταῖς ὀλιγαρχίαις καὶ δημοκρατίαις γίγνονται τυραννίδες· ἢ γὰρ οἱ μέγιστοι
ἐν ἑκατέρᾳ ἐπιτίθενται τυραννίδι, ἔνθα μὲν οἱ δημαγωγοὶ ἔνθα δ' οἱ δυνάσται, ἢ οἱ τὰς μεγίστας
ἔχοντες ἀρχάς, ὅταν πολὺν χρόνον ἄρχωσιν). σῴ- 5
25 ζονται δ' αἱ πολιτεῖαι οὐ μόνον διὰ τὸ πόρρω
εἶναι τῶν διαφθειρόντων ἀλλ' ἐνίοτε καὶ διὰ τὸ
ἐγγύς, φοβούμενοι γὰρ διὰ χειρῶν ἔχουσι μᾶλλον
τὴν πολιτείαν· ὥστε δεῖ τοὺς τῆς πολιτείας
φροντίζοντας φόβους παρασκευάζειν, ἵνα φυλάτ-
τωσι καὶ μὴ καταλύσωσι ὥσπερ νυκτερινὴν φυλα-
30 κὴν τὴν τῆς πολιτείας τήρησιν, καὶ τὸ πόρρω
ἐγγὺς ποιεῖν. ἔτι τὰς τῶν γνωρίμων φιλονεικίας
καὶ στάσεις καὶ διὰ τῶν νόμων πειρᾶσθαι δεῖ
φυλάττειν, καὶ τοὺς ἔξω τῆς φιλονεικίας ὄντας
πρὶν παρειληφέναι καὶ αὐτούς, ὡς τὸ ἐν ἀρχῇ
γινόμενον κακὸν γνῶναι οὐ τοῦ τυχόντος ἀλλὰ
35 πολιτικοῦ ἀνδρός. πρὸς δὲ τὴν διὰ τὰ τιμήματα
γιγνομένην μεταβολὴν ἐξ ὀλιγαρχίας καὶ πολιτείας,
ὅταν συμβαίνῃ τοῦτο μενόντων μὲν τῶν αὐτῶν
τιμημάτων εὐπορίας δὲ νομίσματος γιγνομένης,
συμφέρει τοῦ τιμήματος ἐπισκοπεῖν τοῦ κοινοῦ τὸ
40 πλῆθος πρὸς τὸ παρελθόν, ἐν ὅσαις μὲν πόλεσι
τιμῶνται κατ' ἐνιαυτόν, κατὰ τοῦτον τὸν χρόνον,
1308 b ἐν δὲ ταῖς μείζοσι διὰ τριετηρίδος ἢ πενταετηρίδος,
κἂν ᾖ πολλαπλάσιον ἢ πολλοστημόριον τοῦ πρότερον ἐν ᾧ αἱ τιμήσεις κατέστησαν τῆς πολι-

---

^a This modifies 1207 a 31.

asties less (for it is not so easy to do wrongs when in
office for a short time as when in for a long time, since
it is long tenure of office that causes tyrannies to
spring up in oligarchies and democracies ; for either
those who are the greatest men in either sort of state
aim at tyranny, in the one sort the demagogues and
in the other the dynasts, or those who hold the
greatest offices, when they are in office for a long time).
5 And constitutions are kept secure not only through
being at a distance from destroyers but sometimes also
through being near them,^a for when they are afraid
the citizens keep a closer hold on the government ;
hence those who take thought for the constitution
must contrive causes of fear, in order that the citizens
may keep guard and not relax their vigilance for the
constitution like a watch in the night, and they must
make the distant near. Again, they must also
endeavour to guard against the quarrels and party
struggles of the notables by means of legislation,
and to keep out those who are outside the quarrel
before they too have taken it over ; since to
discern a growing evil at the commencement is not
any ordinary person's work but needs a statesman.
And to deal with the revolution from oligarchy and
constitutional government that arises because of the
property-qualifications, when this occurs while the
rates of qualification remain the same but money is
becoming plentiful, it is advantageous to examine the
total amount of the rated value of the community
as compared with the past amount, in states where
the assessment is made yearly, over that period, and
three years or five years ago in the larger states, and
if the new total is many times larger or many times
smaller than the former one at the time when

1308 b

τείας, νόμον εἶναι καὶ τὰ τιμήματα ἐπιτείνειν ἢ
5 ἀνιέναι, ἐὰν μὲν ὑπερβάλλῃ ἐπιτείνοντας κατὰ τὴν
πολλαπλασίωσιν, ἐὰν δ' ἐλλείπῃ ἀνιέντας καὶ
ἐλάττω ποιοῦντας τὴν τίμησιν. ἐν[1] γὰρ ταῖς
ὀλιγαρχίαις καὶ ταῖς πολιτείαις μὴ ποιούντων,
οὕτως μὲν[2] ἔνθα μὲν ὀλιγαρχίαν ἔνθα δὲ δυναστείαν
γίγνεσθαι συμβαίνει, ἐκείνως δὲ ἐκ μὲν πολιτείας
10 δημοκρατίαν ἐκ δ' ὀλιγαρχίας πολιτείαν ἢ δῆμον.
κοινὸν δὲ καὶ ἐν δήμῳ καὶ ὀλιγαρχίᾳ [καὶ ἐν
μοναρχίᾳ][3] καὶ πάσῃ πολιτείᾳ μήτ' αὐξάνειν[4] λίαν
μηθένα παρὰ τὴν συμμετρίαν ἀλλὰ μᾶλλον πειρᾶσθαι μικρὰς καὶ πολυχρονίους διδόναι τιμὰς ἢ
ταχὺ[5] μεγάλας (διαφθείρονται γάρ, καὶ φέρειν οὐ
15 παντὸς ἀνδρὸς εὐτυχίαν), εἰ δὲ μή, μή τοί γ'
ἀθρόας δόντας ἀφαιρεῖσθαι πάλιν ἀθρόας ἀλλ' ἐκ
προσαγωγῆς· καὶ μάλιστα μὲν πειρᾶσθαι τοῖς
νόμοις οὕτως ἄγειν ὥστε μηθένα ἐγγίγνεσθαι πολὺ
ὑπερέχοντα δυνάμει μήτε φίλων μήτε χρημάτων,
εἰ δὲ μή, ἀποδημητικὰς ποιεῖσθαι τὰς παραστάσεις
20 αὐτῶν. ἐπεὶ δὲ καὶ διὰ τοὺς ἰδίους βίους νεωτερί-
ζουσιν, δεῖ ἐμποιεῖν ἀρχήν τινα τὴν ἐποψομένην
τοὺς ζῶντας ἀσυμφόρως πρὸς τὴν πολιτείαν, ἐν
μὲν δημοκρατίᾳ πρὸς τὴν δημοκρατίαν, ἐν δὲ
ὀλιγαρχίᾳ πρὸς τὴν ὀλιγαρχίαν, ὁμοίως δὲ καὶ
τῶν ἄλλων πολιτειῶν ἑκάστῃ. καὶ τὸ εὐημεροῦν

---

[1] ἐν Susemihl: ἐν μὲν codd.
[2] Niemeyer: μὲν οὕτως codd.
[3] om. codd. cet.   [4] αὐξάνειν ⟨δεῖν⟩ ? ed.
[5] ταχὺ vix sanum: breviter et Guil., βραχὺ καὶ Susemihl,
βραχυχρονίους καὶ Sepulveda.

---

[a] i.e. if the total valuation has decreased.
[b] i.e. if the total has increased.
[c] Some MSS. and many editors omit these words.

424

the rates qualifying for citizenship were fixed, it is advantageous that there should be a law for the magistrates correspondingly to tighten up or to relax the rates, tightening them up in proportion to the ratio of increase if the new total rated value exceeds the old, and relaxing them and making the qualification lower if the new total falls below the old. For in oligarchies and constitutional states, when they do not do this, in the one case *a* the result is that in the latter an oligarchy comes into existence and in the former a dynasty, and in the other case *b* a constitutional government turns into a democracy and an oligarchy into a constitutional government or a government of the people. But it is a policy common to democracy and oligarchy [and to monarchy],*c* and every form of constitution not to raise up any man too much beyond due proportion, but rather to try to assign small honours and of long tenure or great ones quickly *d* (for officials grow corrupt, and not every man can bear good fortune), or if not, at all events not to bestow honours in clusters and take them away again in clusters, but by a gradual process; and best of all to try so to regulate people by the law that there may be nobody among them specially pre-eminent in power due to friends or wealth, or, failing this, to cause their periods out of office to be spent abroad. And since men also cause revolutions through their private lives, some magistracy must be set up to inspect those whose mode of living is unsuited to the constitution—unsuited to democracy in a democracy, to oligarchy in an oligarchy, and similarly for each of the other forms of constitution.

d The text should probably be emended ' with a short tenure.'

δὲ τῆς πόλεως ἀνὰ μέρος φυλάττεσθαι διὰ τὰς
αὐτὰς αἰτίας· τούτου δ' ἄκος τὸ αἰεὶ τοῖς ἀντικει-
μένοις μορίοις ἐγχειρίζειν τὰς πράξεις καὶ τὰς ἀρχὰς
(λέγω δ' ἀντικεῖσθαι τοὺς ἐπιεικεῖς τῷ πλήθει
καὶ τοὺς ἀπόρους τοῖς εὐπόροις), καὶ τὸ πειρᾶσθαι ἢ συμμιγνύναι τὸ τῶν ἀπόρων πλῆθος
30 καὶ τὸ τῶν εὐπόρων ἢ τὸ μέσον αὔξειν (τοῦτο
γὰρ διαλύει τὰς διὰ τὴν ἀνισότητα στάσεις).
μέγιστον δὲ ἐν πάσῃ πολιτείᾳ τὸ καὶ τοῖς νόμοις
καὶ τῇ ἄλλῃ οἰκονομίᾳ οὕτω τετάχθαι ὥστε μὴ
εἶναι τὰς ἀρχὰς κερδαίνειν. τοῦτο δὲ μάλιστα ἐν
ταῖς ὀλιγαρχικαῖς δεῖ τηρεῖν· οὐ γὰρ οὕτως ἀγανα-
35 κτοῦσιν εἰργόμενοι τοῦ ἄρχειν οἱ πολλοί (ἀλλὰ
καὶ χαίρουσιν ἐάν τις ἐᾷ πρὸς τοῖς ἰδίοις σχολάζειν) ὡς ἐὰν οἴωνται τὰ κοινὰ κλέπτειν τοὺς
ἄρχοντας, τότε δ' ἀμφότερα λυπεῖ, τό τε τῶν
τιμῶν μὴ μετέχειν καὶ τὸ τῶν κερδῶν. μοναχῶς
δὲ καὶ ἐνδέχεται ἅμα εἶναι δημοκρατίαν καὶ
40 ἀριστοκρατίαν, εἰ τοῦτο κατασκευάσειέ τις· ἐν-
1309 a δέχοιτο γὰρ ἂν καὶ τοὺς γνωρίμους καὶ τὸ πλῆθος
ἔχειν ἃ βούλονται ἀμφοτέρους· τὸ μὲν γὰρ ἐξεῖναι
πᾶσιν ἄρχειν δημοκρατικόν τὸ δὲ τοὺς γνωρίμους
εἶναι ἐν ταῖς ἀρχαῖς ἀριστοκρατικόν, τοῦτο δ'
5 ἔσται ὅταν μὴ ᾖ κερδαίνειν ἀπὸ τῶν ἀρχῶν· οἱ
γὰρ ἄποροι οὐ βουλήσονται ἄρχειν τῷ μηδὲν
κερδαίνειν, ἀλλὰ πρὸς τοῖς ἰδίοις εἶναι μᾶλλον, οἱ
δ' εὔποροι δυνήσονται διὰ τὸ μηδὲν προσδεῖσθαι
τῶν κοινῶν· ὥστε συμβήσεται τοῖς μὲν ἀπόροις γί-

And also sectional prosperity in the state must be guarded against for the same reasons ; and the way to avert this is always to entrust business and office to the opposite sections (I mean that the respectable are opposite to the multitude and the poor to the wealthy), and to endeavour either to mingle together the multitude of the poor and that of the wealthy or to increase the middle class (for this dissolves party

9 factions due to inequality). And in every form of constitution it is a very great thing for it to be so framed both by its laws and by its other institutions that it is impossible for the magistracies to make a profit. And this has most to be guarded against in oligarchies ; for the many are not so much annoyed at being excluded from holding office (but in fact they are glad if somebody lets them have leisure to spend on their own affairs) as they are if they think that the magistrates are stealing the common funds, but then both things annoy them, exclusion from the honours of office and exclusion from its profits.

10 And indeed the sole way in which a combination of democracy and aristocracy is possible is if someone could contrive this arrangement *a* ; for it would then be possible for the notables and also the multitude both to have what they want ; for it is the democratic principle for all to have the right to hold office and the aristocratic one for the offices to be filled by the notables, and this will be the case when it is impossible to make money from office ; for the poor will not want to hold office because of making nothing out of it, but rather to attend to their own affairs, while the wealthy will be able to hold office because they have no need to add to their resources from the public funds ; so that the result will be that the poor

1309 a

γνεσθαι εὐπόροις διὰ τὸ διατρίβειν πρὸς τοῖς ἔργοις,
τοῖς δὲ γνωρίμοις μὴ ἄρχεσθαι ὑπὸ τῶν τυχόντων.

10 τοῦ μὲν οὖν μὴ κλέπτεσθαι τὰ κοινὰ ἡ παράδοσις
γιγνέσθω τῶν χρημάτων παρόντων πάντων τῶν
πολιτῶν, καὶ ἀντίγραφα κατὰ φρατρίας καὶ λόχους
καὶ φυλὰς τιθέσθωσαν· τοῦ δὲ ἀκερδῶς ἄρχειν
τιμὰς εἶναι δεῖ νενομοθετημένας τοῖς εὐδοκιμοῦσιν.

15 δεῖ δ' ἐν μὲν ταῖς δημοκρατίαις τῶν εὐπόρων
φείδεσθαι, μὴ μόνον τῷ τὰς κτήσεις μὴ ποιεῖν
ἀναδάστους, ἀλλὰ μηδὲ τοὺς καρπούς (ὃ ἐν ἐνίαις
τῶν πολιτειῶν λανθάνει γιγνόμενον), βέλτιον δὲ καὶ
βουλομένους κωλύειν λειτουργεῖν τὰς δαπανηρὰς

20 μὲν μὴ χρησίμους δὲ λειτουργίας, οἷον χορηγίας
καὶ λαμπαδαρχίας καὶ ὅσαι ἄλλαι τοιαῦται· ἐν
δ' ὀλιγαρχίᾳ τῶν ἀπόρων ἐπιμέλειαν ποιεῖσθαι
πολλήν, καὶ τὰς ἀρχὰς ἀφ' ὧν λήμματα τούτοις
ἀπονέμειν, κἄν τις ὑβρίσῃ τῶν εὐπόρων εἰς τούτους, μείζω τὰ ἐπιτίμια εἶναι ἢ ἂν σφῶν αὐτῶν,
καὶ τὰς κληρονομίας μὴ κατὰ δόσιν εἶναι ἀλλὰ

25 κατὰ γένος, μηδὲ πλειόνων ἢ μιᾶς τὸν αὐτὸν
κληρονομεῖν, οὕτω γὰρ ἂν ὁμαλώτεραι αἱ οὐσίαι
εἶεν καὶ τῶν ἀπόρων εἰς εὐπορίαν ἂν καθίσταιντο
πλείους. συμφέρει δὲ καὶ ἐν δημοκρατίᾳ καὶ ἐν
ὀλιγαρχίᾳ τῶν ἄλλων ἢ ἰσότητα ἢ προεδρίαν
νέμειν τοῖς ἧττον κοινωνοῦσι τῆς πολιτείας, ἐν

30 μὲν δήμῳ τοῖς εὐπόροις ἐν δ' ὀλιγαρχίᾳ τοῖς
ἀπόροις, πλὴν ὅσαι ἀρχαὶ κύριαι τῆς πολιτείας,

---

[a] Groups of citizens normally three to a tribe, supposed
to be based on relationship.

[b] Originally a military, later a civil classification.

will become well-off through spending their time upon their work, and the notables will not be governed by any casual persons. Therefore to prevent peculation of the public property, let the transfer of the funds take place in the presence of all the citizens, and let copies of the lists be deposited for each brotherhood,[a] company [b] and tribe ; and to get men to hold office without profit there must be honours assigned by law to officials of good repute. And in democracies it is necessary to be sparing of the wealthy not only by not causing properties to be divided up, but not incomes either (which under some constitutions takes place unnoticed), and it is better to prevent men from undertaking costly but useless public services like equipping choruses and torch-races [c] and all other similar services, even if they wish to ; in an oligarchy on the other hand it is necessary to take much care of the poor, and to allot to them the offices of profit, and the penalty if one of the rich commits an outrage against them must be greater than if it is done by one of themselves,[d] and inheritance must not go by bequest but by family, and the same man must not inherit more than one estate, for so estates would be more on a level, and more of the poor would establish themselves as prosperous. And it is expedient both in a democracy and in an oligarchy to assign to those who have a smaller share in the government—in a democracy to the wealthy and in an oligarchy to the poor—either equality or precedence in all other things excepting the supreme offices of state ; but

Constitu-
tional safe-
guards in
democracies
and in
oligarchie

[c] Equipping the chorus and actors for tragedies and comedies and providing for the ceremonial torch-races were public services borne by individuals at Athens.

[d] Or possibly ' than if he does it against one of his own class.'

1309 a

ταύτας δὲ τοῖς ἐκ τῆς πολιτείας ἐγχειρίζειν μόνοις
ἢ πλείοσιν.

Τρία δέ τινα χρὴ ἔχειν τοὺς μέλλοντας ἄρξειν
τὰς κυρίας ἀρχάς, πρῶτον μὲν φιλίαν πρὸς τὴν
35 καθεστῶσαν πολιτείαν, ἔπειτα δύναμιν μεγίστην
τῶν ἔργων τῆς ἀρχῆς, τρίτον δ' ἀρετὴν καὶ
δικαιοσύνην ἐν ἑκάστῃ πολιτείᾳ τὴν πρὸς τὴν
πολιτείαν (εἰ γὰρ μὴ ταὐτὸν τὸ δίκαιον κατὰ
πάσας τὰς πολιτείας, ἀνάγκη καὶ τῆς δικαιοσύνης
εἶναι διαφοράς). ἔχει δ' ἀπορίαν, ὅταν μὴ συμβαίνῃ
40 ταῦτα πάντα περὶ τὸν αὐτόν, πῶς χρὴ ποιεῖσθαι
1309 b τὴν αἵρεσιν[1]· οἷον εἰ στρατηγικὸς μέν τις εἴη
πονηρὸς δὲ καὶ μὴ τῇ πολιτείᾳ φίλος, ὁ δὲ δίκαιος
καὶ φίλος,[2] πῶς δεῖ ποιεῖσθαι τὴν αἵρεσιν; ἔοικε
δὲ δεῖν βλέπειν εἰς δύο, τίνος πλεῖον μετέχουσι
πάντες καὶ τίνος ἔλαττον. διὸ ἐν στρατηγίᾳ μὲν
5 εἰς τὴν ἐμπειρίαν μᾶλλον τῆς ἀρετῆς, ἔλαττον γὰρ
στρατηγίας μετέχουσι, τῆς δ' ἐπιεικείας πλεῖον·
ἐν δὲ φυλακῇ καὶ ταμιείᾳ τἀναντία, πλείονος γὰρ
ἀρετῆς δεῖται ἢ ὅσην οἱ πολλοὶ ἔχουσιν, ἡ δὲ
ἐπιστήμη κοινὴ πᾶσιν. ἀπορήσειε δ' ἄν τις κἂν
10 δύναμις ὑπάρχῃ καὶ τῆς πολιτείας[3] φιλία, τί δεῖ
τῆς ἀρετῆς; ποιήσει γὰρ τὰ συμφέροντα καὶ τὰ
δύο. ἢ ὅτι ἐνδέχεται τοὺς τὰ δύο ταῦτα ἔχοντας
ἀκρατεῖς εἶναι, ὥστε καθάπερ καὶ αὑτοῖς οὐχ
ὑπηρετοῦσιν εἰδότες καὶ φιλοῦντες αὑτούς, οὕτω

---

[1] αἵρεσιν corr. cod. inferior: διαίρεσιν cet.
[2] φίλος μὴ στρατηγικὸς δὲ codd. nonnulli.
[3] καὶ post πολιτείας codd., tr. Stahr.

these should be entrusted to those prescribed by the constitution exclusively, or to them for the most part.

4 There are some three qualities which those who are to hold the supreme magistracies ought to possess, first, loyalty to the established constitution, next, very great capacity to do the duties of the office, and third, virtue and justice—in each constitution the sort of justice suited to the constitution (for if the rules of justice are not the same under all constitutions, it follows that there must be differences in the nature of justice also). It is a difficult question how the choice ought to be made when it happens that all these qualities are not found in the same person ; for instance, if one man is a good military commander but a bad man and no friend of the constitution, and the other is just and loyal, how should 5 the choice be made ? It seems that two things ought to be considered, what is the quality of which all men have a larger share, and what the one of which all have a smaller share ? Therefore in the case of military command one must consider experience more than virtue, for men have a smaller share of military experience and a larger share of moral goodness ; but in the case of a trusteeship or a stewardship the opposite, for these require more virtue than most men possess, but the knowledge required is common to all men. And somebody might raise the question, why is virtue needed if both capacity and loyalty to the constitution are forthcoming, as even these two qualities will do what is suitable ? May not the answer be, because those who possess these two qualities may possibly lack self-control, so that just as they do not serve themselves well although they know how to and

431

1309 b

καὶ πρὸς τὸ κοινὸν οὐθὲν κωλύει ἔχειν ἐνίους,
ἁπλῶς δέ, ὅσα ἐν τοῖς νόμοις ὡς συμφέροντα λέ-
15 γομεν ταῖς πολιτείαις, ἅπαντα ταῦτα σῴζει τὰς
πολιτείας, καὶ τὸ πολλάκις εἰρημένον μέγιστον
στοιχεῖον, τὸ τηρεῖν ὅπως κρεῖττον ἔσται τὸ
βουλόμενον τὴν πολιτείαν πλῆθος τοῦ μὴ βουλομένου. παρὰ πάντα δὲ ταῦτα δεῖ μὴ λανθάνειν,
ὃ νῦν λανθάνει τὰς παρεκβεβηκυίας πολιτείας, τὸ
20 μέσον· πολλὰ γὰρ τῶν δοκούντων δημοτικῶν λύει
τὰς δημοκρατίας καὶ τῶν ὀλιγαρχικῶν τὰς ὀλιγαρχίας. οἱ δ', οἰόμενοι ταύτην εἶναι μίαν ἀρετήν,
ἕλκουσιν εἰς τὴν ὑπερβολήν, ἀγνοοῦντες ὅτι
καθάπερ ῥίς ἐστι παρεκβεβηκυῖα μὲν τὴν εὐθύτητα
τὴν καλλίστην πρὸς τὸ γρυπὸν ἢ τὸ σιμὸν ἀλλ'
25 ὅμως ἔτι καλὴ καὶ χάριν ἔχουσα πρὸς τὴν ὄψιν,
οὐ μὴν ἀλλ' ἐὰν ἐπιτείνῃ τις ἔτι μᾶλλον εἰς τὴν
ὑπερβολήν, πρῶτον μὲν ἀποβαλεῖ τὴν μετριότητα
τοῦ μορίου τέλος δ' οὕτως ὥστε μηδὲ ῥῖνα
ποιήσει φαίνεσθαι διὰ τὴν ὑπεροχὴν καὶ τὴν
ἔλλειψιν τῶν ἐναντίων (τὸν αὐτὸν δὲ τρόπον ἔχει
30 καὶ περὶ τῶν ἄλλων μορίων), συμβαίνει δὴ τοῦτο
καὶ περὶ τὰς ἄλλας πολιτείας· καὶ γὰρ ὀλιγαρχίαν
καὶ δημοκρατίαν ἔστιν ὥστ' ἔχειν ἱκανῶς, καίπερ
ἐξεστηκυίας τῆς βελτίστης τάξεως, ἐὰν δέ τις
ἐπιτείνῃ μᾶλλον ἑκατέραν αὐτῶν, πρῶτον μὲν
χείρω ποιήσει τὴν πολιτείαν, τέλος δ' οὐδὲ πολι-
35 τείαν. διὸ δεῖ τοῦτο μὴ ἀγνοεῖν τὸν νομοθέτην

ᵃ See 1279 a 20.

although they love themselves, so possibly in some cases they may behave in this way in regard to the 6 community also? And broadly, whatever provisions in the laws we describe as advantageous to constitutions, these are all preservative of the constitutions, and so is the supreme elementary principle that has been often stated, that of taking precautions that the section desirous of the constitution shall be stronger in number than the section not desirous of it. And beside all these matters one thing must not be overlooked which at present is overlooked by the deviation-forms *a* of constitution —the middle party; for many of the institutions thought to be popular destroy democracies, and many of those thought oligarchical destroy oligarchies. 7 But the adherents of the deviation-form, thinking that this form is the only right thing, drag it to excess, not knowing that just as there can be a nose that although deviating from the most handsome straightness towards being hooked or snub nevertheless is still beautiful and agreeable to look at, yet all the same, if a sculptor carries it still further in the direction of excess, he will first lose the symmetry of the feature and finally will make it not even look like a nose at all, because of its excess and deficiency in the two opposite qualities (and the same is the case also in regard to the other parts of the body), so this is what happens about constitutions likewise; for it is possible for an oligarchy and a democracy to be satisfactory although they have diverged from the best structure, but if one strains either of them further, first he will make the constitution worse, and finally he will make it not a constitution at all. Therefore the legislator and the statesman must not fail to

moderate differences of wealth,

433

1809 b

καὶ τὸν πολιτικόν, ποῖα σῴζει τῶν δημοτικῶν καὶ
ποῖα φθείρει τὴν δημοκρατίαν, καὶ ποῖα τῶν
ὀλιγαρχικῶν τὴν ὀλιγαρχίαν· οὐδετέραν μὲν γὰρ
ἐνδέχεται αὐτῶν εἶναι καὶ διαμένειν ἄνευ τῶν
εὐπόρων καὶ τοῦ πλήθους, ἀλλ᾽ ὅταν ὁμαλότης
40 γένηται τῆς οὐσίας, ἄλλην ἀνάγκη εἶναι ταύτην
1310 a τὴν πολιτείαν, ὥστε φθείροντες τοῖς καθ᾽ ὑπεροχὴν
νόμοις φθείρουσι τὰς πολιτείας. ἁμαρτάνουσι δὲ
καὶ ἐν ταῖς δημοκρατίαις καὶ ἐν ταῖς ὀλιγαρχίαις,
ἐν μὲν ταῖς δημοκρατίαις οἱ δημαγωγοί, ὅπου τὸ
5 πλῆθος κύριον τῶν νόμων· δύο γὰρ ποιοῦσιν ἀεὶ
τὴν πόλιν μαχόμενοι τοῖς εὐπόροις, δεῖ δὲ τοὐναντίον αἰεὶ δοκεῖν λέγειν ὑπὲρ εὐπόρων,[1] ἐν δὲ ταῖς
ὀλιγαρχίαις ὑπὲρ τοῦ δήμου τοὺς ὀλιγαρχικούς,
καὶ τοὺς ὅρκους ἐναντίους ἢ νῦν ὀμνύναι τοὺς
ὀλιγαρχικούς, νῦν μὲν γὰρ ἐν ἐνίαις ὀμνύουσι "καὶ
10 τῷ δήμῳ κακόνους ἔσομαι καὶ βουλεύσω ὅ τι ἂν
ἔχω κακόν," χρὴ δὲ καὶ ὑπολαμβάνειν καὶ ὑπο-
κρίνεσθαι τοὐναντίον, ἐπισημαινομένους ἐν τοῖς
ὅρκοις ὅτι "οὐκ ἀδικήσω τὸν δῆμον." μέγιστον
δὲ πάντων τῶν εἰρημένων πρὸς τὸ διαμένειν τὰς
πολιτείας, οὗ νῦν ὀλιγωροῦσι πάντες, τὸ παιδεύε-
15 σθαι πρὸς τὰς πολιτείας. ὄφελος γὰρ οὐθὲν τῶν
ὠφελιμωτάτων νόμων καὶ συνδεδοξασμένων ὑπὸ
πάντων τῶν πολιτευομένων, εἰ μὴ ἔσονται εἰθι-
σμένοι καὶ πεπαιδευμένοι ἐν τῇ πολιτείᾳ, εἰ μὲν
οἱ νόμοι δημοτικοί, δημοτικῶς, εἰ δ᾽ ὀλιγαρχικοί,

---

[1] τῶν εὐπόρων cod. inferior.

[a] The 'scoffing anapaestic cadence' of this oath has been
noted. In 411 B.C. the democratic reaction at Athens swore

know what sort of democratic institutions save and what destroy a democracy, and what sort of oligarchical institutions an oligarchy; for neither constitution can exist and endure without the well-to-do and the multitude, but when an even level of property comes about, the constitution resulting must of necessity be another one, so that when men destroy these classes by laws carried to excess they destroy the constitutions. And a mistake is made both in democracies and in oligarchies—in democracies by the demagogues, where the multitude is supreme over the laws; for they always divide the state into two by fighting with the well-to-do, but they ought on the contrary always to pretend to be speaking on behalf of men that are well-to-do, while in democracies the oligarchical statesmen ought to pretend to be speaking on behalf of the people, and the oligarchics ought to take oath in terms exactly opposite to those which they use now, for at present in some oligarchies they swear, ' And I will be hostile to the people and will plan whatever evil I can against them," [a] but they ought to hold, and to act the part of holding, the opposite notion, declaring in their oaths, " I will not wrong the people." But the greatest of all the means spoken of to secure the stability of constitutions is one that at present all people despise: it is a system of education suited to the constitutions. For there is no use in the most valuable laws, ratified by the unanimous judgement of the whole body of citizens, if these are not trained and educated in the constitution, popularly if the laws are popular, oligarchically if they are oligarchical;

and above all, education.

' to be enemies of the Four Hundred and to hold no parley with them.'

1310 a

ὀλιγαρχικῶς· εἴπερ γάρ ἐστιν ἐφ' ἑνὸς ἀκρασία,
20 ἔστι καὶ ἐπὶ πόλεως. ἔστι δὲ τὸ πεπαιδεῦσθαι
πρὸς τὴν πολιτείαν οὐ τοῦτο, τὸ ποιεῖν οἷς χαίρουσιν
οἱ ὀλιγαρχοῦντες ἢ οἱ δημοκρατίαν βουλόμενοι,
ἀλλ' οἷς δυνήσονται οἱ μὲν ὀλιγαρχεῖν οἱ δὲ δημοκρατεῖσθαι. νῦν δ' ἐν μὲν ταῖς ὀλιγαρχίαις οἱ
τῶν ἀρχόντων υἱοὶ τρυφῶσιν, οἱ δὲ τῶν ἀπόρων
25 γίγνονται γεγυμνασμένοι καὶ πεπονηκότες, ὥστε
καὶ βούλονται μᾶλλον καὶ δύνανται νεωτερίζειν·
ἐν δὲ ταῖς δημοκρατίαις ταῖς μάλιστα εἶναι
δοκούσαις δημοκρατικαῖς τοὐναντίον τοῦ συμ-
φέροντος καθέστηκεν. αἴτιον δὲ τούτου ὅτι κακῶς
ὁρίζονται τὸ ἐλεύθερον (δύο γάρ ἐστιν οἷς ἡ
δημοκρατία δοκεῖ ὡρίσθαι, τῷ τὸ πλεῖον εἶναι
30 κύριον καὶ τῇ ἐλευθερίᾳ)· τὸ μὲν γὰρ δίκαιον
ἴσον[1] δοκεῖ εἶναι, ἴσον δ' ὅ τι ἂν δόξῃ τῷ πλήθει
τοῦτ' εἶναι κύριον, ἐλεύθερον δὲ [καὶ ἴσον][2] τὸ ὅ τι
ἂν βούληταί τις ποιεῖν· ὥστε ζῇ ἐν ταῖς τοιαύταις
δημοκρατίαις ἕκαστος ὡς βούλεται, καὶ εἰς ὃ
χρῄζων, ὡς φησὶν Εὐριπίδης. τοῦτο δ' ἐστὶ
35 φαῦλον· οὐ γὰρ δεῖ οἴεσθαι δουλείαν εἶναι τὸ ζῆν
πρὸς τὴν πολιτείαν ἀλλὰ σωτηρίαν.

Ἐξ ὧν μὲν οὖν αἱ πολιτεῖαι μεταβάλλουσι καὶ
φθείρονται καὶ διὰ τίνων σῴζονται καὶ διαμένουσιν,
ὡς ἁπλῶς εἰπεῖν τοσαῦτά ἐστιν.

VIII. Λείπεται δ' ἐπελθεῖν καὶ περὶ μοναρχίας,
40 ἐξ ὧν τε φθείρεται καὶ δι' ὧν σῴζεσθαι πέφυκεν.
1310 b σχεδὸν δὲ παραπλήσια τοῖς εἰρημένοις περὶ τὰς
πολιτείας ἐστὶ καὶ τὰ συμβαίνοντα περὶ τὰς

---

[1] ἴσον ante δίκαιον Richards.
[2] Spengel.

[a] Fragment 883, from an unknown play.

for there is such a thing as want of self-discipline in a state, as well as in an individual. But to have been educated to suit the constitution does not mean to do the things that give pleasure to the adherents of oligarchy or to the supporters of democracy, but the things that will enable the former to govern oligarchically and the latter to govern themselves democratically. But at present in the oligarchies the sons of the rulers are luxurious, and the sons of the badly-off become trained by exercise and labour, so that they are both more desirous of reform and more able to bring it about ; while in the democracies thought to be the most democratic the opposite of what is expedient has come about. And the cause of this is that they define liberty wrongly (for there are two things that are thought to be defining features of democracy, the sovereignty of the majority and liberty) ; for justice is supposed to be equality, and equality the sovereignty of whatever may have been decided by the multitude, and liberty doing just what one likes. Hence in democracies of this sort everybody lives as he likes, and ' unto what end he listeth,' as Euripides ^a says. But this is bad ; for to live in conformity with the constitution ought not to be considered slavery but safety.

This therefore, speaking broadly, is a list of the things that cause the alteration and the destruction of constitutions, and of those that cause their security and continuance.

VIII. It remains to speak of monarchy, the causes that destroy it and the natural means of its preservation. And the things that happen about royal governments and tyrannies are almost similar to those that have been narrated about constitu-

Stability of monarchies.

437

1310 b

βασιλείας καὶ τὰς τυραννίδας. ἡ μὲν γὰρ βασιλεία
κατὰ τὴν ἀριστοκρατίαν ἐστίν, ἡ δὲ τυραννὶς ἐξ
ὀλιγαρχίας τῆς ὑστάτης σύγκειται καὶ δημοκρατίας·
5 διὸ δὴ καὶ βλαβερωτάτη τοῖς ἀρχομένοις ἐστίν
ἅτε ἐκ δυοῖν συγκειμένη κακῶν καὶ τὰς παρεκβάσεις καὶ τὰς ἁμαρτίας ἔχουσα τὰς παρ' ἀμφοτέρων τῶν πολιτειῶν. ὑπάρχει δ' ἡ γένεσις εὐθὺς
ἐξ ἐναντίων ἑκατέρᾳ τῶν μοναρχιῶν· ἡ μὲν γὰρ
10 βασιλεία πρὸς βοήθειαν τὴν ἀπὸ τοῦ δήμου[1] τοῖς
ἐπιεικέσι γέγονεν, καὶ καθίσταται βασιλεὺς ἐκ τῶν
ἐπιεικῶν καθ' ὑπεροχὴν ἀρετῆς ἢ πράξεων τῶν
ἀπὸ τῆς ἀρετῆς, ἢ καθ' ὑπεροχὴν τοιούτου γένους, ὁ
δὲ τύραννος ἐκ τοῦ δήμου καὶ τοῦ πλήθους ἐπὶ
τοὺς γνωρίμους, ὅπως ὁ δῆμος ἀδικῆται μηθὲν
ὑπ' αὐτῶν. φανερὸν δ' ἐκ τῶν συμβεβηκότων·
15 σχεδὸν γὰρ οἱ πλεῖστοι τῶν τυράννων γεγόνασιν
ἐκ δημαγωγῶν ὡς εἰπεῖν, πιστευθέντες ἐκ τοῦ
διαβάλλειν τοὺς γνωρίμους. αἱ μὲν γὰρ τοῦτον
τὸν τρόπον κατέστησαν τῶν τυραννίδων ἤδη τῶν
πόλεων ηὐξημένων, αἱ δὲ πρὸ τούτων ἔκ [τε]
τῶν βασιλέων παρεκβαινόντων τὰ πάτρια καὶ
20 δεσποτικωτέρας ἀρχῆς ὀρεγομένων, αἱ δ' ἐκ τῶν
αἱρετῶν ἐπὶ τὰς κυρίας ἀρχάς (τὸ γὰρ ἀρχαῖον οἱ
δῆμοι καθίστασαν πολυχρονίους τὰς δημιουργίας
καὶ τὰς θεωρίας), αἱ δ' ἐκ τῶν ὀλιγαρχιῶν αἱρου-
μένων ἕνα τινὰ κύριον ἐπὶ τὰς μεγίστας ἀρχάς·
πᾶσι γὰρ ὑπῆρχε τοῖς τρόποις τούτοις τὸ κατεργά-
25 ζεσθαι ῥᾳδίως, εἰ μόνον βουληθεῖεν, διὰ τὸ δύναμιν

---

[1] ἐπὶ τὸν δῆμον Rassow.   [2] [τε] om. cod. inferior.

[a] Cf. 1296 a 3, 1312 b 35.

[b] Here δημιουργία means 'magistracy' generally; δημιουργός
was the title of a special officer in some Peloponnesian states.

tional governments. For royal government corre- Royalty and
tyranny.
sponds with aristocracy, while tyranny is a combina-
tion of the last form of oligarchy [a] and of democracy ;
and for that very reason it is most harmful to
its subjects, inasmuch as it is a combination of two
bad things, and is liable to the deviations and errors
2 that spring from both forms of constitution. And
these two different sorts of monarchy have their
origins from directly opposite sources ; royalty has
come into existence for the assistance of the distinguished against the people, and a king is appointed
from those distinguished by superiority in virtue
or the actions that spring from virtue, or by superiority in coming from a family of that character, while
a tyrant is set up from among the people and the
multitude to oppose the notables, in order that the
people may suffer no injustice from them. And this
is manifest from the facts of history. For almost the
greatest number of tyrants have risen, it may be said,
from being demagogues, having won the people's
confidence by slandering the notables. For some
tyrannies were set up in this manner when the states
had already grown great, but others that came
before them arose from kings departing from the
ancestral customs and aiming at a more despotic
rule, and others from the men elected to fill the
supreme magistracies (for in old times the peoples
used to appoint the popular officials [b] and the sacred
embassies [c] for long terms of office), and others from
oligarchies electing some one supreme official for
the greatest magistracies. For in all these methods
they had it in their power to effect their purpose
easily, if only they wished, because they already

[c] Official missions to religious games and to oracles.

1310 b

προϋπάρχειν τοῖς μὲν βασιλικῆς ἀρχῆς τοῖς δὲ
τὴν τῆς τιμῆς, οἷον Φείδων μὲν περὶ Ἄργος καὶ
ἕτεροι τύραννοι κατέστησαν βασιλείας ὑπαρχούσης,
οἱ δὲ περὶ τὴν Ἰωνίαν καὶ Φάλαρις ἐκ τῶν
τιμῶν, Παναίτιος δ' ἐν Λεοντίνοις καὶ Κύψελος ἐν
80 Κορίνθῳ καὶ Πεισίστρατος Ἀθήνησι καὶ Διονύσιος
ἐν Συρακούσαις καὶ ἕτεροι τὸν αὐτὸν τρόπον ἐκ
δημαγωγίας. καθάπερ οὖν εἴπομεν, ἡ βασιλεία 5
τέτακται κατὰ τὴν ἀριστοκρατίαν· κατ' ἀξίαν
γάρ ἐστιν, ἢ κατ' ἰδίαν ἀρετὴν ἢ κατὰ γένους ἢ
κατ' εὐεργεσίας ἢ κατὰ ταῦτά τε καὶ δύναμιν.
85 ἅπαντες γὰρ εὐεργετήσαντες ἢ δυνάμενοι τὰς
πόλεις ἢ τὰ ἔθνη εὐεργετεῖν ἐτύγχανον τῆς τιμῆς
ταύτης, οἱ μὲν κατὰ πόλεμον κωλύσαντες δουλεύειν,
ὥσπερ Κόδρος, οἱ δ' ἐλευθερώσαντες, ὥσπερ
Κῦρος, ἢ κτίσαντες ἢ κτησάμενοι χώραν, ὥσπερ
οἱ Λακεδαιμονίων βασιλεῖς καὶ Μακεδόνων καὶ
40 Μολοττῶν. βούλεται δ' ὁ βασιλεὺς εἶναι φύλαξ,
1311 a ὅπως οἱ μὲν κεκτημένοι τὰς οὐσίας μηθὲν ἄδικον
πάσχωσιν ὁ δὲ δῆμος μὴ ὑβρίζηται μηθέν, ἡ δὲ
τυραννίς, ὥσπερ εἴρηται πολλάκις, πρὸς οὐδὲν
ἀποβλέπει κοινὸν εἰ μὴ τῆς ἰδίας ὠφελείας χάριν·
5 ἔστι δὲ σκοπὸς τυραννικὸς μὲν τὸ ἡδὺ βασιλικὸς
δὲ τὸ καλόν. διὸ καὶ τῶν πλεονεκτημάτων τὰ
μὲν χρήματα[1] τυραννικὰ τὰ δ' εἰς τιμὴν βασιλικὰ
μᾶλλον· καὶ φυλακὴ βασιλικὴ μὲν πολιτική, τυραν-

---

[1] χρημάτων Γ: ⟨εἰς⟩ χρήματα ? Susemihl.

---

[a] Perhaps c. 750 B.C.
[b] e.g. Thrasybulus, tyrant of Miletus, 612 B.C.
[c] Tyrant of Agrigentum 572 B.C.
[d] See 1305 a 23 n.   [e] See 1259 a 28 n.

possessed the power of royal rule in the one set of cases and of their honourable office in the other, for example Phidon in Argos [a] and others became tyrants when they possessed royal power already, while the Ionian tyrants [b] and Phalaris [c] rose from offices of honour, and Panaetius at Leontini and 608 B.C. Cypselus at Corinth and Pisistratus [d] at Athens and 655 B.C. Dionysius [e] at Syracuse and others in the same manner from the position of demagogue. Therefore, as we said, royalty is ranged in correspondence with aristo- § 1. cracy, for it goes by merit, either by private virtue or by family or by services or by a combination of these things and ability. For in every instance this honour fell to men after they had conferred benefit or because they had the ability to confer benefit on their cities or their nations, some having prevented their enslavement in war, for instance Codrus,[f] others having set them free, for instance Cyrus,[g] or having settled or acquired territory, for instance the kings of Sparta and Macedon and the Molossians.[h] And a king wishes to be a guardian, to protect the owners of estates from suffering injustice and the people from suffering insult, but tyranny, as has repeatedly been said, pays regard to no common interest unless for the sake of its private benefit; and the aim of tyranny is what is pleasant, that of royalty what is noble. Hence even in their requisitions money is the aim of tyrants but rather marks of honour that of kings; and a king's body-guard consists of citizens, a tyrant's of foreign

[f] The usual tradition was that Codrus was already king when he saved Athens by sacrificing his life.

[g] Cyrus liberated Persia from the Median empire 559 B.C.

[h] Neoptolemus, son of Achilles, conquered the Molossi and became their king.

1311 a

νικὴ δὲ διὰ ξένων. ὅτι δ᾽ ἡ τυραννὶς ἔχει κακὰ 7
καὶ τὰ τῆς δημοκρατίας καὶ τὰ τῆς ὀλιγαρχίας,
φανερόν· ἐκ μὲν ὀλιγαρχίας τὸ τὸ τέλος εἶναι
πλοῦτον (οὕτω γὰρ καὶ διαμένειν ἀναγκαῖον μόνως
τήν τε φυλακὴν καὶ τὴν τρυφήν) καὶ τὸ τῷ πλήθει
μηδὲν πιστεύειν (διὸ καὶ τὴν παραίρεσιν ποιοῦνται
τῶν ὅπλων, καὶ τὸ κακοῦν τὸν ὄχλον καὶ τὸ ἐκ
τοῦ ἄστεος ἀπελαύνειν καὶ διοικίζειν ἀμφοτέρων
κοινόν, καὶ τῆς ὀλιγαρχίας καὶ τῆς τυραννίδος),
ἐκ δημοκρατίας δὲ τὸ πολεμεῖν τοῖς γνωρίμοις καὶ
διαφθείρειν λάθρα καὶ φανερῶς καὶ φυγαδεύειν ὡς
ἀντιτέχνους καὶ πρὸς τὴν ἀρχὴν ἐμποδίους. ἐκ
γὰρ τούτων συμβαίνει γίγνεσθαι καὶ τὰς ἐπιβουλάς,
τῶν μὲν ἄρχειν αὐτῶν βουλομένων, τῶν δὲ μὴ
δουλεύειν. ὅθεν καὶ τὸ Περιάνδρου πρὸς Θρασύβουλον συμβούλευμά ἐστιν, ἡ τῶν ὑπερεχόντων
σταχύων κόλουσις, ὡς δέον ἀεὶ τοὺς ὑπερέχοντας
τῶν πολιτῶν ἀναιρεῖν. καθάπερ οὖν σχεδὸν 8
ἐλέχθη,[1] τὰς αὐτὰς ἀρχὰς δεῖ νομίζειν περί τε τὰς
πολιτείας εἶναι τῶν μεταβολῶν καὶ περὶ τὰς
μοναρχίας· διά τε γὰρ ἀδικίαν καὶ διὰ φόβον καὶ
διὰ καταφρόνησιν ἐπιτίθενται πολλοὶ τῶν ἀρχομένων ταῖς μοναρχίαις, τῆς δὲ ἀδικίας μάλιστα[2]
δι᾽ ὕβριν, ἐνίοτε δὲ καὶ διὰ τὴν τῶν ἰδίων στέρησιν.
ἔστι δὲ καὶ τὰ τέλη ταὐτὰ καθάπερ κἀκεῖ καὶ περὶ
τὰς τυραννίδας καὶ τὰς βασιλείας· μέγεθος γὰρ
ὑπάρχει πλούτου καὶ τιμῆς τοῖς μονάρχοις, ὧν

---

[1] σχεδὸν post ἐλέχθη Spengel (om. ΓΜΡ¹).
[2] μάλιστα ⟨μὲν⟩ ? ed.

---

[a] See 1284 a 26 n.

mercenaries. And it is manifest that tyranny has the evils of both democracy and oligarchy; it copies oligarchy in making wealth its object (for inevitably that is the only way in which the tyrant's body-guard and his luxury can be kept up) and in putting no trust in the multitude (which is why they resort to the measure of stripping the people of arms, and why ill-treatment of the mob and its expulsion from the city and settlement in scattered places is common to both forms of government, both oligarchy and tyranny), while it copies democracy in making war on the notables and destroying them secretly and openly and banishing them as plotting against it and obstructive to its rule. For it is from them that counter-movements actually spring, some of them wishing themselves to rule, and others not to be slaves. Hence comes the advice of Periander to Thrasybulus,[a] his docking of the prominent corn-stalks, meaning that the prominent citizens must always be made away with.

Therefore, as was virtually stated,[b] the causes of revolutions in constitutional and in royal governments must be deemed to be the same; for subjects in many cases attack monarchies because of unjust treatment and fear and contempt, and among the forms of unjust treatment most of all because of insolence, and sometimes the cause is the seizure of private property. Also the objects aimed at by the revolutionaries in the case both of tyrannies and of royal governments are the same as in revolts against constitutional government; for monarchs possess great wealth and great honour, which are

Attacks on tyrants from personal motives.

[b] This has not been stated, but can be inferred from what precedes.

1311 a
ἐφίενται πάντες. τῶν δ' ἐπιθέσεων αἱ μὲν ἐπ
τὸ σῶμα γίγνονται τῶν ἀρχόντων αἱ δ' ἐπὶ τὴ
ἀρχήν. αἱ μὲν οὖν δι' ὕβριν ἐπὶ τὸ σῶμα· τῆς δ
ὕβρεως οὔσης πολυμεροῦς, ἕκαστον αὐτῶν αἴτιον
35 γίγνεται τῆς ὀργῆς, τῶν δ' ὀργιζομένων σχεδὸ
οἱ πλεῖστοι τιμωρίας χάριν ἐπιτίθενται ἀλλ' οὐ
ὑπεροχῆς· οἷον ἡ μὲν τῶν Πεισιστρατιδῶν δι
τὸ προπηλακίσαι μὲν τὴν Ἁρμοδίου ἀδελφήν, ἐπ
ηρεάσαι δ' Ἁρμόδιον (ὁ μὲν[1] γὰρ Ἁρμόδιος διὰ τὴ
ἀδελφὴν ὁ δ' Ἀριστογείτων διὰ τὸν Ἁρμόδιον
40 ἐπεβούλευσαν δὲ καὶ Περιάνδρῳ τῷ ἐν Ἀμβρακί
1311 b τυράννῳ διὰ τὸ συμπίνοντα μετὰ τῶν παιδικῶ
ἐρωτῆσαι αὐτὸν εἰ ἤδη ἐξ αὐτοῦ κύει), ἡ δὲ Φιλίππο
ὑπὸ Παυσανίου διὰ τὸ ἐᾶσαι ὑβρισθῆναι αὐτὸ
ὑπὸ τῶν περὶ Ἄτταλον, καὶ ἡ Ἀμύντου το
μικροῦ ὑπὸ Δέρδα[2] διὰ τὸ καυχήσασθαι εἰς τὴ
5 ἡλικίαν αὐτοῦ, καὶ ἡ τοῦ εὐνούχου Εὐαγόρᾳ τ
Κυπρίῳ, διὰ γὰρ τὸ τὴν γυναῖκα παρελέσθαι τὸ
υἱὸν αὐτοῦ ἀπέκτεινεν ὡς ὑβρισμένος. πολλα
δ' ἐπιθέσεις γεγένηνται καὶ διὰ τὸ εἰς τὸ σῶμ
αἰσχύνεσθαι τῶν μονάρχων τινάς· οἷον καὶ
Κραταίου εἰς Ἀρχέλαον· ἀεὶ γὰρ βαρέως εἶχε πρὸ
10 τὴν ὁμιλίαν, ὥστε ἱκανὴ καὶ ἐλάττων ἐγένετ
πρόφασις, ἢ διότι τῶν θυγατέρων οὐδεμίαν ἔδωκε
ὁμολογήσας αὐτῷ, ἀλλὰ τὴν μὲν προτέραν κατ
εχόμενος ὑπὸ πολέμου πρὸς Σίρραν[3] καὶ Ἀρράβαιο
ἔδωκε τῷ βασιλεῖ τῷ τῆς Ἐλιμείας, τὴν δὲ νεω

---

[1] μὲν om. mg. H.
[2] Ἀμύντου ὑπὸ Δέρδα [τοῦ μικροῦ] Thompson.
[3] Ἴρραν Paton (sic Plutarchus et Strabo).

---

[a] See 1304 a 31 n.
[b] A Macedonian youth of family, who murdered Phili
336 B.C. Attalus was the uncle of Philip's wife Cleopatra.

desired by all men. And in some cases the attack is aimed at the person of the rulers, in others at their office. Risings provoked by insolence are aimed against the person; and though insolence has many varieties, each of them gives rise to anger, and when men are angry they mostly attack for the sake of revenge, not of ambition. For example the attack on the Pisistratidae took place because they 510 B.C. outraged Harmodius's sister and treated Harmodius with contumely (for Harmodius attacked them because of his sister and Aristogiton because of Harmodius, and also the plot was laid against Periander the tyrant in Ambracia *a* because when drinking with his favourite he asked him if he was yet with child by him), and the attack on Philip by Pausanias *b* was because he allowed him to be insulted by Attalus and his friends, and that on Amyntas the Little *c* by Derdas because he mocked at his youth, and the attack of the eunuch on Evagoras of Cyprus was for revenge, for he murdered him as being insulted, 347 B.C. because Evagoras's son had taken away his wife. And many risings have also occurred because of shameful personal indignities committed by certain monarchs. One instance is the attack of Crataeas on Archelaus *d*; for he was always resentful of the association, so that even a smaller excuse became sufficient, or perhaps it was because he did not give him the hand of one of his daughters after agreeing to do so, but gave the elder to the king of Elimea when hard pressed in a war against Sirras and Arrabaeus, and

c Perhaps the adjective should be transferred to Derdas and expunged as an interpolated note. The persons referred to are uncertain.

d King of Macedon 413-399 B.C. Euripides went to reside at his court 408 B.C. and died there 406 B.C. at the age of 75.

τέραν τῷ υἱεῖ Ἀμύντᾳ οἰόμενος οὕτως ἂν ἐκεῖνο
15 ἥκιστα διαφέρεσθαι καὶ τὸν ἐκ τῆς Κλεοπάτρας
ἀλλὰ τῆς γε ἀλλοτριότητος ὑπῆρχεν ἀρχὴ τ
βαρέως φέρειν πρὸς τὴν ἀφροδισιαστικὴν χάρι
συνεπέθετο δὲ καὶ Ἑλλανοκράτης ὁ Λαρισαῖο
διὰ τὴν αὐτὴν αἰτίαν· ὡς γὰρ χρώμενος αὐτοῦ τ
ἡλικίᾳ οὐ κατῆγεν ὑποσχόμενος, δι' ὕβριν καὶ ο
20 δι' ἐρωτικὴν ἐπιθυμίαν ᾤετ' εἶναι τὴν γεγενημένη
ὁμιλίαν. Πύθων δὲ καὶ Ἡρακλείδης οἱ Αἴνι
Κότυν διέφθειραν τῷ πατρὶ τιμωροῦντες, Ἀδάμα
δ' ἀπέστη Κότυος διὰ τὸ ἐκτμηθῆναι παῖς ὢν ὑπ
αὐτοῦ, ὡς ὑβρισμένος. πολλοὶ[1] δὲ καὶ διὰ τὸ εἰ
τὸ σῶμα αἰκισθῆναι πληγαῖς ὀργισθέντες οἱ μὲ
25 διέφθειραν οἱ δ' ἐνεχείρησαν ὡς ὑβρισθέντες, κα
τῶν περὶ τὰς ἀρχὰς καὶ βασιλικὰς δυναστείας, οἷο
ἐν Μιτυλήνῃ τοὺς Πενθιλίδας Μεγακλῆς περιόντα
καὶ τύπτοντας ταῖς κορύναις ἐπιθέμενος μετὰ τῶ
φίλων ἀνεῖλεν, καὶ ὕστερον Σμέρδις Πενθίλο
30 πληγὰς λαβὼν καὶ παρὰ τῆς γυναικὸς ἐξελκυσθεὶ
διέφθειρεν. καὶ τῆς Ἀρχελάου δ' ἐπιθέσεω
Δεκάμνιχος ἡγεμὼν ἐγένετο, παροξύνων τοὺ
ἐπιθεμένους πρῶτος· αἴτιον δὲ τῆς ὀργῆς ὅτ
αὐτὸν ἐξέδωκε μαστιγῶσαι Εὐριπίδῃ τῷ ποιητῇ
ὁ δ' Εὐριπίδης ἐχαλέπαινεν εἰπόντος τι αὐτοῦ εἰ
35 δυσωδίαν τοῦ στόματος. καὶ ἄλλοι δὲ πολλοὶ δι
τοιαύτας αἰτίας οἱ μὲν ἀνῃρέθησαν οἱ δ' ἐπεβου
λεύθησαν. ὁμοίως δὲ καὶ διὰ φόβον· ἐν γάρ τ

---

[1] πολλοὺς Richards.

---

[a] King of Thrace 382-358 B.C.
[b] The ruling family in the early oligarchy there, claimin
descent from Penthilus, an illegitimate son of Orestes.

the younger to his son Amyntas, thinking that thus Amyntas would be least likely to quarrel with his son by Cleopatra; but at all events Crataeas's estrangement was primarily caused by resentment because of the love affair. And Hellanocrates of Larisa also joined in the attack for the same reason; for because while enjoying his favours Archelaus would not restore him to his home although he had promised to do so, he thought that the motive of the familiarity that had taken place had been insolence and not passionate desire. And Pytho and Heraclides of Aenus made away with Cotys[a] to avenge their father, and Adamas revolted from Cotys because he had been mutilated by him when a boy, on the ground of the insult. And also many men when enraged by the indignity of corporal chastisement have avenged the insult by destroying or attempting to destroy its author, even when a magistrate or member of a royal dynasty. For example when the Penthilidae[b] at Mitylene went about striking people with their staves Megacles with his friends set on them and made away with them, and afterwards Smerdis when he had been beaten and dragged out from his wife's presence killed Penthilus. Also Decamnichus took a leading part in §11 above the attack upon Archelaus, being the first to stir on the attackers; and the cause of his anger was that he had handed him over to Euripides the poet to flog, Euripides being angry because he had made a remark about his breath smelling. And many others also for similar reasons have been made away with or plotted against. And similarly also from the motive of fear; for this was one of the

447

1311 b

τοῦτο τῶν αἰτίων ἦν, ὥσπερ καὶ περὶ[1] τὰς πολιτείας, καὶ περὶ[1] τὰς μοναρχίας· οἷον Ξέρξην Ἀρταπάνης φοβούμενος τὴν διαβολὴν τὴν περὶ Δαρεῖον, ὅτι ἐκρέμασεν οὐ κελεύσαντος Ξέρξου

40 ἀλλ' οἰόμενος συγγνώσεσθαι ὡς ἀμνημονοῦντα διὰ

1312 a τὸ δειπνεῖν. αἱ δὲ διὰ καταφρόνησιν, ὥσπερ Σαρδανάπαλλον ἰδών τις ξαίνοντα μετὰ τῶν γυναικῶν (εἰ ἀληθῆ ταῦτα οἱ μυθολογοῦντες λέγουσιν, εἰ δὲ μὴ ἐπ' ἐκείνου, ἀλλ' ἐπ' ἄλλου γε ἂν γένοιτο ἀληθές), καὶ Διονυσίῳ τῷ ὑστέρῳ Δίων ἐπέθετο

5 διὰ τὸ καταφρονεῖν, ὁρῶν τούς τε πολίτας οὕτως ἔχοντας καὶ αὐτὸν ἀεὶ μεθύοντα. καὶ τῶν φίλων δέ τινες ἐπιτίθενται διὰ καταφρόνησιν· διὰ γὰρ τὸ πιστεύεσθαι καταφρονοῦσιν ὡς λήσοντες. καὶ οἱ οἰόμενοι δύνασθαι κατασχεῖν τὴν ἀρχὴν τρόπον

10 τινὰ διὰ τὸ καταφρονεῖν ἐπιτίθενται· ὡς δυνάμενοι γὰρ καὶ καταφρονοῦντες τοῦ κινδύνου διὰ τὴν δύναμιν ἐπιχειροῦσι ῥᾳδίως, ὥσπερ οἱ στρατηγοῦντες τοῖς μονάρχοις, οἷον Κῦρος Ἀστυάγῃ καὶ τοῦ βίου καταφρονῶν καὶ τῆς δυνάμεως διὰ τὸ τὴν μὲν δύναμιν ἐξηργηκέναι αὐτὸν δὲ τρυφᾶν, καὶ Σεύ-

15 θης ὁ Θρᾷξ Ἀμαδόκῳ στρατηγὸς ὤν. οἱ δὲ καὶ διὰ πλείω τούτων ἐπιτίθενται, οἷον καὶ καταφρονοῦντες καὶ διὰ κέρδος, ὥσπερ Ἀριοβαρζάνη

---

[1] καὶ περί ed.: καὶ codd.

[a] Captain of Xerxes' body-guard.
[b] Last king of the Assyrian empire at Nineveh.
[c] Tyrant of Syracuse 367-356 and 346-343 B.C., cf. 1312 a 34 ff.
[d] The last king of Media, reigned 594-559 B.C.

causes we mentioned in the case of monarchies, § 6. as also in that of constitutional governments; c. ii. § 5. for instance Artapanes[a] killed Xerxes fearing the charge about Darius, because he had hanged him when Xerxes had ordered him not to but he had thought that he would forgive him because he would forget, as he had been at dinner. And other attacks on monarchs have been on account of contempt, as somebody killed Sardanapallus[b] when he saw him combing his hair with his women (if this story told by the narrators of legends is true—and if it did not happen with Sardanapallus, it might quite well be true of somebody else), and Dion attacked the younger Dionysius[c] because he despised him, when he saw the citizens despising him and the king himself always drunk. And contempt has led some even of the friends of monarchs to attack them, for they despise them for trusting them and think they will not be found out. And contempt is in a manner the motive of those who attack monarchs thinking that they are able to seize the government; for they make the attempt with a light heart, feeling that they have the power and because of their power despising the danger, as generals commanding the armies attack their monarchs; for instance Cyrus attacked Astyages[d] when he despised both his mode of life and his power, because his power had waned and he himself was living luxuriously, and the Thracian Seuthes attacked Amadocus[e] when his general. Others again attack monarchs for more than one of these motives, for instance both because they despise them and for the sake of gain, as

[e] Both these Thracian kings became allies of Athens 390 B.C., but the event referred to may be later.

449

1312 a

Μιθριδάτης. μάλιστα[1] δὲ διὰ ταύτην τὴν αἰτίαν
ἐγχειροῦσιν οἱ τὴν φύσιν μὲν θρασεῖς τιμὴν δ
ἔχοντες πολεμικὴν παρὰ τοῖς μονάρχοις· ἀνδρείι
20 γὰρ δύναμιν ἔχουσα θράσος ἐστίν, δι᾽ ἃς ἀμφοτέρα
ὡς ῥᾳδίως κρατήσοντες ποιοῦνται τὰς ἐπιθέσεις
τῶν δὲ διὰ φιλοτιμίαν ἐπιτιθεμένων ἕτερος τρόπο
ἐστὶ τῆς αἰτίας παρὰ τοὺς εἰρημένους πρότερον
οὐ γὰρ ὥσπερ ἔνιοι τοῖς τυράννοις ἐπιχειροῦσιι
ὁρῶντες κέρδη τε μεγάλα καὶ τιμὰς μεγάλας οὖσα
25 αὐτοῖς, οὕτω καὶ τῶν διὰ φιλοτιμίαν ἐπιτιθεμένων
ἕκαστος προαιρεῖται κινδυνεύειν· ἀλλ᾽ ἐκεῖνοι μὲ
διὰ τὴν εἰρημένην αἰτίαν, οὗτοι δ᾽, ὥσπερ κἂ
ἄλλης τινὸς γενομένης πράξεως περιττῆς καὶ δι
ἣν ὀνομαστοὶ γίγνονται καὶ γνώριμοι τοῖς ἄλλοις
οὕτω καὶ τοῖς μονάρχοις ἐγχειροῦσιν οὐ κτήσασθα
30 βουλόμενοι μοναρχίαν ἀλλὰ δόξαν. οὐ μὴν ἀλλ
ἐλάχιστοί γε τὸν ἀριθμὸν εἰσιν οἱ διὰ ταύτην τὴ
αἰτίαν ὁρμῶντες· ὑποκεῖσθαι γὰρ δεῖ τὸ το
σωθῆναι μηδὲν φροντίζειν ἂν μὴ μέλλῃ κατα
σχήσειν τὴν πρᾶξιν· οἷς ἀκολουθεῖν μὲν δεῖ τὴ
Δίωνος ὑπόληψιν, οὐ ῥᾴδιον δ᾽ αὐτὴν ἐγγενέσθα
35 πολλοῖς· ἐκεῖνος γὰρ μετ᾽ ὀλίγων ἐστράτευσεν ἐπ
Διονύσιον οὕτως ἔχειν φάσκων ὡς ὅποι[2] περ ἃ
δύναται προελθεῖν ἱκανὸν αὐτῷ τοσοῦτον μετασχεῖ
τῆς πράξεως, οἷον εἰ μικρὸν ἐπιβάντα τῆς γῆ
εὐθὺς συμβαίη τελευτῆσαι τοῦτον[3] καλῶς ἔχει
αὐτῷ τὸν θάνατον.

40 Φθείρεται δὲ τυραννὶς ἕνα μὲν τρόπον, ὥσπε

---

[1] μάλιστα—20 ἐπιθέσεις post 6 μεθύοντα traicienda Newman.
[2] ὅποι Thompson : ὅπου codd.   [3] τὸν βίον, τοῦτον P

---

* Perhaps Mithridates II., who succeeded his fathe
Ariobarzanes as satrap of Pontus 336 B.C.

Mithridates [a] attacked Ariobarzanes. [b] And it is men of bold nature and who hold a military office with monarchs who most often make the attempt for this reason; for courage possessing power is boldness, and they make their attacks thinking that with courage and power they will easily prevail. But with those whose attack is prompted by ambition the motive operates in a different way from those spoken of before; some men attack tyrants because they see great profits and great honours belonging to them, but that is not the reason that in each case leads the persons who attack from motives of ambition to resolve on the venture; those others are led by the motive stated, but these attack monarchs from a wish to gain not monarchy but glory, just as they would wish to take part in doing any other uncommon deed that makes men famous and known to their fellows. Not but what those who make the venture from this motive are very few indeed in number, for underlying it there must be an utter disregard of safety, if regard for safety is not to check the enterprise; they must always have present in their minds the opinion of Dion, although it is not a 4 above. easy for many men to have it; Dion marched with a small force against Dionysius, saying that his feeling was that, whatever point he might be able to get to, it would be enough for him to have had that much share in the enterprise—for instance, if it should befall him to die as soon as he had just set foot in the country, that death would satisfy him.

And one way in which tyranny is destroyed, as is

[b] This sentence may have been shifted by mistake from the end of § 14 above.

1312 b καὶ τῶν ἄλλων ἑκάστη πολιτειῶν, ἔξωθεν, ἐὰν
ἐναντία τις ᾖ πολιτεία κρείττων (τὸ μὲν γὰρ
βούλεσθαι δῆλον ὡς ὑπάρξει διὰ τὴν ἐναντιότητα
τῆς προαιρέσεως, ἃ δὲ βούλονται, δυνάμενοι πράττουσι πάντες), ἐναντίαι δ' αἱ πολιτεῖαι, δῆμος μὲν
5 τυραννίδι καθ' Ἡσίοδον ὡς ' κεραμεῖ κεραμεύς '
(καὶ γὰρ ἡ δημοκρατία ἡ τελευταία τυραννίς
ἐστιν), βασιλεία δὲ καὶ ἀριστοκρατία διὰ τὴν
ἐναντιότητα τῆς πολιτείας (διὸ Λακεδαιμόνιοι
πλείστας κατέλυσαν τυραννίδας καὶ Συρακούσιοι
κατὰ τὸν χρόνον ὃν ἐπολιτεύοντο καλῶς)· ἕνα δ' ἐξ
10 αὑτῆς, ὅταν οἱ μετέχοντες στασιάζωσιν, ὥσπερ
ἡ τῶν περὶ Γέλωνα καὶ νῦν ἡ τῶν περὶ Διονύσιον,
ἡ μὲν Γέλωνος Θρασυβούλου τοῦ Ἱέρωνος ἀδελφοῦ
τὸν υἱὸν τοῦ Γέλωνος δημαγωγοῦντος καὶ πρὸς
ἡδονὰς ὁρμῶντος ἵν' αὐτὸς ἄρχῃ, τῶν δ' οἰκείων
συστησάντων¹ ἵνα μὴ ἥ ᾖ τυραννὶς ὅλως καταλυθῇ
15 ἀλλὰ Θρασύβουλος, οἱ δὲ συστάντες αὐτῶν² ὡς
καιρὸν ἔχοντες ἐξέβαλον ἅπαντας αὐτούς· Διονύσιον
δὲ Δίων στρατεύσας κηδεστὴς ὤν, καὶ προσλαβὼν
τὸν δῆμον, ἐκεῖνον ἐκβαλὼν διεφθάρη. δύο δὲ
οὐσῶν αἰτιῶν δι' ἃς μάλιστ' ἐπιτίθενται ταῖς
τυραννίσι, μίσους καὶ καταφρονήσεως, θάτερον
20 μὲν ἀεὶ τούτων ὑπάρχει⁴ τοῖς τυράννοις, τὸ μῖσος

---

¹ συστάντων ΓΜΡ²: στασιασάντων Richards.
² μὴ ᾖ ed.: μὴ codd.
³ ⟨μετ'⟩ αὐτῶν Susemihl: tr. post 13 ⟨ἡ⟩ τυραννὶς Richards.
⁴ ἀεὶ τούτων ὑπάρχει Richards: δεῖ τ. ὑπάρχειν codd.

ᵃ *Works and Days* 25 καὶ κεραμεὺς κεραμεῖ κοτέει καὶ τέκτονι
τέκτων, ' two of a trade never agree.'
ᵇ Tyrant of Syracuse 485-478 B.C., succeeded by hi
452

each of the other forms of constitution also, is from Foreign attacks on without, if some state with an opposite constitution tyrants. is stronger (for the wish to destroy it will clearly be present in such a neighbour because of the opposition of principle, and all men do what they wish if they have the power)—and the constitutions opposed to tyranny are, on the one hand democracy, which is opposed to it as (in Hesiod's phrase *a*) ' potter to potter,' because the final form of democracy is tyranny, and on the other hand royalty and aristocracy are opposed to tyranny because of the opposite nature of their constitutional structure (owing to which the Spartans put down a very great many tyrannies, and so did the Syracusans at the period when they were governed well). But one way is from within itself, Family feuds. when the partners in it fall into discord, as the tyranny of the family of Gelo *b* was destroyed, and in modern times *c* that of the family of Dionysius *d*— Gelo's, when Thrasybulus the brother of Hiero paid court to the son of Gelo and urged him into indulgences in order that he himself might rule, and the son's connexions banded together a body of confederates in order that the tyranny might not be put down entirely but only Thrasybulus, but their confederates seizing the opportunity expelled them all; Dionysius was put down by Dion, his relative, who got the people on to his side and expelled him, but was afterwards killed. There are two causes that chiefly Motives lead men to attack tyranny, hatred and contempt; the former, hatred, attaches to tyrants always, but it is

brother Hiero who died 467. Gelo's son is unknown. *Cf.* 1315 b 35 ff.

c 356 B.C., a good many years before this book was written.
d See 1312 a 4 n.

1312 b

ἐκ δὲ τοῦ καταφρονεῖσθαι πολλαὶ γίνονται τῶν
καταλύσεων. σημεῖον δέ· τῶν μὲν γὰρ κτησα-
μένων οἱ πλεῖστοι καὶ διεφύλαξαν τὰς ἀρχάς, οἱ
δὲ παραλαβόντες εὐθὺς ὡς εἰπεῖν ἀπολλύασι
πάντες, ἀπολαυστικῶς γὰρ ζῶντες εὐκαταφρόνητοί
25 τε γίγνονται καὶ πολλοὺς καιροὺς παραδιδόασι τοῖς
ἐπιτιθεμένοις. μόριον δέ τι τοῦ μίσους καὶ τὴν
ὀργὴν δεῖ τιθέναι, τρόπον γάρ τινα τῶν αὐτῶν
αἰτία γίνεται πράξεων. πολλάκις δὲ καὶ πρακτικω-
τερον τοῦ μίσους· συντονώτερον γὰρ ἐπιτίθενται
30 διὰ τὸ μὴ χρῆσθαι λογισμῷ τὸ πάθος (μάλιστα
δὲ συμβαίνει τοῖς θυμοῖς ἀκολουθεῖν διὰ τὴν ὕβριν
δι' ἣν αἰτίαν ἥ τε τῶν Πεισιστρατιδῶν κατελύθη
τυραννὶς καὶ πολλαὶ τῶν ἄλλων), ἀλλὰ μᾶλλον τὸ
μῖσος· ἡ μὲν γὰρ ὀργὴ μετὰ λύπης πάρεστιν, ὥστ'
οὐ ῥάδιον λογίζεσθαι, ἡ δ' ἔχθρα ἄνευ λύπης. ὡς
35 δ' ἐν κεφαλαίοις εἰπεῖν, ὅσας αἰτίας εἰρήκαμεν
τῆς τε ὀλιγαρχίας τῆς ἀκράτου καὶ τελευταίας καὶ
τῆς δημοκρατίας τῆς ἐσχάτης, τοσαύτας καὶ τῆς
τυραννίδος θετέον· καὶ γὰρ αὗται τυγχάνουσιν
οὖσαι διαιρεταὶ[1] τυραννίδες. βασιλεία δ' ὑπὸ μὲν
40 τῶν ἔξωθεν ἥκιστα φθείρεται, διὸ καὶ πολυχρόνιός
ἐστιν· ἐξ αὑτῆς δ' αἱ πλεῖσται φθοραὶ συμβαίνουσιν.

1313 a φθείρεται δὲ κατὰ δύο τρόπους, ἕνα μὲν στασιασάντων τῶν μετεχόντων τῆς βασιλείας, ἄλλον
δὲ τρόπον τυραννικώτερον πειρωμένων διοικεῖν
ὅταν εἶναι κύριοι πλειόνων ἀξιῶσι καὶ παρὰ τὸν
νόμον. οὐ γίγνονται δ' ἔτι βασιλεῖαι νῦν, ἀλλ'
5 ἄν περ γίγνωνται μοναρχίαι,[2] τυραννίδες μᾶλλον

---

[1] αἱρεταὶ codd. nonnulli.
[2] μοναρχίαι Spengel: μοναρχίαι καὶ codd.

their being despised that causes their downfall in many cases. A proof of this is that most of those that have won tyrannies have also kept their offices to the end, but those that have inherited them almost all lose them at once; for they live a life of indulgence, and so become despicable and also give many opportunities to their attackers. And also anger must be counted as an element in the hatred felt for them, for in a way it occasions the same actions. And often it is even more active than hatred, since angry men attack more vigorously because passion does not employ calculation (and insolence most frequently causes men to be led by their angry tempers, which was the cause of the fall of the tyranny of the Pisistratidae and many others), but hatred calculates more; for anger brings with it an element of pain, making calculation difficult, but enmity is not accompanied by pain. And to speak summarily, all the things that we have mentioned as causing the downfall of unmixed and extreme oligarchy and of the last form of democracy must be counted as destructive of tyranny as well, since extreme oligarchy and democracy are in reality divided^a tyrannies. Royal government on the other hand is very seldom destroyed by external causes, so that it is long-lasting; but in most cases its destruction arises out of itself. And it is destroyed in two ways, one when those who participate in it quarrel, and another when the kings try to administer the government too tyrannically, claiming to exercise sovereignty in more things and contrary to the law. Royal governments do not occur any more now, but if ever monarchies

1311 a 37.

Fall of kings.

---

^a *i.e.* divided among several persons, 'put into commission.'

1313 a
διὰ τὸ τὴν βασιλείαν ἑκούσιον μὲν ἀρχὴν εἶναι
μειζόνων δὲ κυρίαν, πολλοὺς δ' εἶναι τοὺς ὁμοίους
καὶ μηδένα διαφέροντα τοσοῦτον ὥστε ἀπαρτίζειν
πρὸς τὸ μέγεθος καὶ τὸ ἀξίωμα τῆς ἀρχῆς· ὥστε
διὰ μὲν τοῦτο ἑκόντες οὐχ ὑπομένουσιν, ἂν δὲ δι'
10 ἀπάτης ἄρξῃ τις ἢ βίας, ἤδη δοκεῖ τοῦτο εἶναι
τυραννίς. ἐν δὲ ταῖς κατὰ γένος βασιλείαις τιθέναι
δεῖ τῆς φθορᾶς αἰτίαν πρὸς ταῖς εἰρημέναις καὶ τὸ
γίνεσθαι πολλοὺς εὐκαταφρονήτους καὶ τὸ δύναμιν
μὴ κεκτημένους τυραννικὴν ἀλλὰ βασιλικὴν τιμὴν
ὑβρίζειν· ῥᾳδία γὰρ ἐγίνετο ἡ κατάλυσις, μὴ
15 βουλομένων γὰρ εὐθὺς οὐκ ἔσται βασιλεύς, ἀλλ'
ὁ τύραννος καὶ μὴ βουλομένων.

Φθείρονται μὲν οὖν αἱ μοναρχίαι διὰ ταύτας καὶ
τοιαύτας ἑτέρας αἰτίας.

IX. Σῴζονται δὲ δῆλον[1] ὡς ἁπλῶς μὲν εἰπεῖν
ἐκ τῶν ἐναντίων, ὡς δὲ καθ' ἕκαστον, τῷ τὰς μὲν
20 βασιλείας ἄγειν ἐπὶ τὸ μετριώτερον. ὅσῳ γὰρ ἂν
ἐλαττόνων ὦσι κύριοι, πλείω χρόνον ἀναγκαῖον
μένειν πᾶσαν τὴν ἀρχήν, αὐτοί τε γὰρ ἧττον γίνονται δεσποτικοὶ καὶ τοῖς ἤθεσιν ἴσοι μᾶλλον καὶ
ὑπὸ τῶν ἀρχομένων φθονοῦνται ἧττον. διὰ γὰρ
τοῦτο καὶ ἡ περὶ Μολοττοὺς πολὺν χρόνον βασιλεία διέμεινεν, καὶ ἡ Λακεδαιμονίων διὰ τὸ ἐξ

---

[1] δῆλον ⟨ὅτι⟩ Vahlen.

do occur they are rather tyrannies, because royalty is government over willing subjects but with sovereignty over greater matters, but men of equal quality are numerous and no one is so outstanding as to fit the magnitude and dignity of the office; so that for this reason the subjects do not submit willingly, and if a man has made himself ruler by deception or force, then this is thought to be a tyranny. In cases of hereditary royalty we must also set down as a cause of their destruction, in addition to those mentioned, the fact that hereditary kings often become despicable, and that although possessing not the power of a tyrant but the dignity of a king they commit insolent outrages; for the deposition of kings used to be easy, since a king will at once cease to be king if his subjects do not wish him to be, whereas a tyrant will still be tyrant even though his subjects do not wish it.

These causes then and others of the same nature are those that bring about the destruction of monarchies.

IX. On the other hand it is clear that monarchies, speaking generally, are preserved in safety as a result of the opposite causes to those by which they are destroyed. But taking the different sorts of monarchy separately—royalties are preserved by bringing them into a more moderate form; for the fewer powers the kings have, the longer time the office in its entirety must last, for they themselves become less despotic and more equal to their subjects in temper, and their subjects envy them less. For this was the cause of the long persistence of the Molossian royalty, and that of Sparta has continued because the office was from the beginning divided

Preservatives of royalty.

457

1313 a
ἀρχῆς τε εἰς δύο μέρη διαιρεθῆναι τὴν ἀρχήν, καὶ
πάλιν Θεοπόμπου μετριάσαντος τοῖς τε ἄλλοις καὶ
τὴν τῶν ἐφόρων ἀρχὴν ἐπικαταστήσαντος· τῆς γὰρ
δυνάμεως ἀφελὼν ηὔξησε τῷ χρόνῳ τὴν βασιλείαν,
ὥστε τρόπον τινὰ ἐποίησεν οὐκ ἐλάττονα ἀλλὰ
80 μείζονα αὐτήν. ὅπερ καὶ πρὸς τὴν γυναῖκα ἀπο-
κρίνασθαί φασιν αὐτόν, εἰποῦσαν εἰ μηδὲν αἰ-
σχύνεται τὴν βασιλείαν ἐλάττω παραδιδοὺς τοῖς
υἱέσιν ἢ παρὰ τοῦ πατρὸς παρέλαβεν· " οὐ δῆτα "
φάναι· " παραδίδωμι γὰρ πολυχρονιωτέραν."

Αἱ δὲ τυραννίδες σῴζονται κατὰ δύο τρόπους
85 τοὺς ἐναντιωτάτους. ὧν ἅτερός ἐστιν ὁ παραδεδο-
μένος καὶ καθ' ὃν διοικοῦσιν οἱ πλεῖστοι τῶν τυράννων τὴν ἀρχήν· τούτων δὲ τὰ πολλά φασι
καταστῆσαι Περίανδρον τὸν Κορίνθιον, πολλὰ δὲ
καὶ παρὰ τῆς τῶν Περσῶν ἀρχῆς ἔστι τοιαῦτα
λαβεῖν. ἔστι δὲ τά τε πάλαι λεχθέντα πρὸς
40 σωτηρίαν, ὡς οἷόν τε,[1] τῆς τυραννίδος, τὸ τοὺς
ὑπερέχοντας κολούειν καὶ τοὺς φρονηματίας ἀν-
1313 b αιρεῖν, καὶ μήτε συσσίτια ἐᾶν μήτε ἑταιρίαν μήτε
παιδείαν μήτε ἄλλο μηθὲν τοιοῦτον, ἀλλὰ πάντα
φυλάττειν ὅθεν εἴωθε γίνεσθαι δύο, φρόνημά τε
καὶ πίστις, καὶ μήτε σχολὰς μήτε ἄλλους συλλόγους
5 ἐπιτρέπειν γίνεσθαι σχολαστικούς, καὶ πάντα
ποιεῖν ἐξ ὧν ὅτι μάλιστα ἀγνῶτες ἀλλήλοις ἔσονται
πάντες (ἡ γὰρ γνῶσις πίστιν ποιεῖ μᾶλλον πρὸς
ἀλλήλους)· καὶ τὸ τοὺς ἐπιδημοῦντας ἀεὶ φανεροὺς

---

[1] ὡς οἴονται ? Bekker (ὡς οἷόν τε post 41 ὑπερέχοντας vel
alio transp. Richards).

---

[a] King of Sparta c. 770-720 B.C.   [b] See 1284 a 26 n.
[c] The phrases cover Plato's gatherings in the Academy,
Aristotle's in the Peripatos of the Lyceum, and other meet-

into two halves, and because it was again limited in various ways by Theopompus,[a] in particular by his instituting the office of the ephors to keep a check upon it; for by taking away some of the kings' power he increased the permanence of the royal office, so that in a manner he did not make it less but greater. This indeed as the story goes is what he said in reply to his wife, when she asked if he felt no shame in bequeathing the royal power to his sons smaller than he had inherited it from his father: "Indeed I do not," he is said to have answered, "for I hand it on more lasting."

Tyrannies on the other hand are preserved in two extremely opposite ways. One of these is the traditional way and the one in which most tyrants administer their office. Most of these ordinary safeguards of tyranny are said to have been instituted by Periander[b] of Corinth, and also many such devices may be borrowed from the Persian empire. These are both the measures mentioned some time back to secure the safety of a tyranny as far as possible—the lopping off of outstanding men and the destruction of the proud,—and also the prohibition of common meals and club-fellowship and education and all other things of this nature, in fact the close watch upon all things that usually engender the two emotions of pride and confidence, and the prevention of the formation of study-circles and other conferences for debate,[c] and the employment of every means that will make people as much as possible unknown to one another (for familiarity increases mutual confidence); and for the people in the city to be always

Preservatives of tyrannies: (a) repression and precautions;

1313 a 16 ff.

ings for the intellectual use of leisure in gymnasia, palaestrae and leschae.

1313 b

εἶναι καὶ διατρίβειν περὶ θύρας (οὕτω γὰρ ὃ
ἥκιστα λανθάνοιεν τί πράττουσι, καὶ φρονεῖν ὃ
ἐθίζοιντο μικρὸν αἰεὶ δουλεύοντες)· καὶ τᾶλλα ὅσ
10 τοιαῦτα Περσικὰ καὶ βάρβαρα τυραννικά ἐστ
(πάντα γὰρ ταὐτὸν δύναται)· καὶ τὸ μὴ λανθάνε
πειρᾶσθαι ὅσα τυγχάνει τις λέγων ἢ πράττων τῶ
ἀρχομένων, ἀλλ᾽ εἶναι κατασκόπους, οἷον περ
Συρακούσας αἱ ποταγωγίδες καλούμεναι, καὶ οὗ
ὠτακουστὰς ἐξέπεμπεν Ἱέρων ὅπου τις εἴη συ
15 ουσία καὶ σύλλογος (παρρησιάζονταί τε γὰρ ἧττο
φοβούμενοι τοὺς τοιούτους, κἂν παρρησιάζωντ
λανθάνουσιν ἧττον)· καὶ τὸ διαβάλλειν ἀλλήλο
καὶ συγκρούειν καὶ φίλους φίλοις καὶ τὸν δῆμ
τοῖς γνωρίμοις καὶ τοὺς πλουσίους ἑαυτοῖς. κα
τὸ πένητας ποιεῖν τοὺς ἀρχομένους τυραννικό
20 ὅπως μήτε² φυλακὴ³ τρέφηται καὶ πρὸς τῷ κα
ἡμέραν ὄντες ἄσχολοι ὦσιν ἐπιβουλεύειν. παρά
δειγμα δὲ τούτου αἵ τε πυραμίδες αἱ περὶ Αἴγυπτο
καὶ τὰ ἀναθήματα⁴ τῶν Κυψελιδῶν καὶ το
Ὀλυμπιείου⁵ ἡ οἰκοδόμησις ὑπὸ τῶν Πεισι
στρατιδῶν, καὶ τῶν περὶ Σάμον, ἔργα⁶ Πολυκράτει
25 (πάντα γὰρ ταῦτα δύναται ταὐτόν, ἀσχολίαν κα
πενίαν τῶν ἀρχομένων)· καὶ ἡ εἰσφορὰ τῶν τελῶ
οἷον ἐν Συρακούσαις (ἐν πέντε γὰρ ἔτεσιν ἐπ

---

¹ οὓς Coraes: τοὺς codd. (ὠτακουστὰς οὓς M¹).
² μήτε: ἤ τε Victorius (μήτε—καὶ secl. Richards).
³ φυλακὴ: δύναμις Thurot.   ⁴ τὸ ἀνάθημα τὸ Cobet.
⁵ Ὀλυμπιείου anonymus: Ὀλυμπίου codd.
⁶ ἔργων τὰ Coraes.

ᵃ Apparently this means a citizen force side by side with
the tyrant's mercenaries; a variant gives 'in order that the
(tyrant's) guard may be kept.'

visible and to hang about the palace-gates (for thus
there would be least concealment about what they
are doing, and they would get into a habit of being
humble from always acting in a servile way) ; and all
the other similar devices of Persian and barbarian
tyranny (for all have the same effect) ; and to try
not to be uninformed about any chance utterances
or actions of any of the subjects, but to have spies
like the women called 'provocatrices' at Syracuse and
the 'sharp-ears' that used to be sent out by Hiero
wherever there was any gathering or conference (for
when men are afraid of spies of this sort they keep a
check on their tongues, and if they do speak freely
4 are less likely not to be found out) ; and to set men
at variance with one another and cause quarrels
between friend and friend and between the people
and the notables and among the rich. And it is a
device of tyranny to make the subjects poor, so that
a guard *a* may not be kept, and also that the people
being busy with their daily affairs may not have
leisure to plot against their ruler. Instances of this
are the pyramids in Egypt and the votive offerings
of the Cypselids,*b* and the building of the temple of
Olympian Zeus by the Pisistratidae *c* and of the
temples at Samos, works of Polycrates *d* (for all these
undertakings produce the same effect, constant
occupation and poverty among the subject people) ;
5 and the levying of taxes, as at Syracuse (for in the

---

b Cypselus and his son Periander (1310 b 29 n., 1284 a 26 n.)
dedicated a colossal statue of Zeus at Olympia and other
monuments there and at Delphi.

c Pisistratus is said to have begun the temple of Olympian
Zeus at Athens, not finished till the time of Hadrian.

d Tyrant of Samos, d. 522 B.C.

1313 b Διονυσίου τὴν οὐσίαν ἅπασαν εἰσενηνοχέναι συνέβαινεν). ἔστι δὲ καὶ πολεμοποιὸς ὁ τύραννος,
ὅπως ἄσχολοί τε ὦσι καὶ ἡγεμόνος ἐν χρείᾳ δια-
30 τελῶσιν ὄντες. καὶ ἡ μὲν βασιλεία σῴζεται διὰ
τῶν φίλων, τυραννικὸν δὲ τὸ μάλιστ' ἀπιστεῖν τοῖς
φίλοις, ὡς βουλομένων μὲν πάντων δυναμένων δὲ
μάλιστα τούτων.[1] καὶ τὰ περὶ τὴν δημοκρατίαν 6
δὲ γιγνόμενα τὴν τελευταίαν τυραννικὰ πάντα,
35 γυναικοκρατία τε περὶ τὰς οἰκίας ἵν' ἐξαγγέλλωσι
κατὰ τῶν ἀνδρῶν, καὶ δούλων ἄνεσις διὰ τὴν αὐτὴν
αἰτίαν· οὔτε γὰρ ἐπιβουλεύουσιν οἱ δοῦλοι καὶ αἱ
γυναῖκες τοῖς τυράννοις, εὐημεροῦντάς τε ἀναγκαῖον εὔνους εἶναι καὶ ταῖς τυραννίσι καὶ τοῖς
δημοκρατίαις (καὶ γὰρ ὁ δῆμος εἶναι βούλεται
μόναρχος). διὸ καὶ ὁ κόλαξ παρ' ἀμφοτέροις
40 ἔντιμος, παρὰ μὲν τοῖς δήμοις ὁ δημαγωγός (ἔστι
γὰρ ὁ δημαγωγὸς τοῦ δήμου κόλαξ), παρὰ δὲ τοῖς
1314 a τυράννοις οἱ ταπεινῶς ὁμιλοῦντες, ὅπερ ἐστὶν
ἔργον κολακείας. καὶ γὰρ διὰ τοῦτο πονηρόφιλον[2]
ἡ τυραννίς· κολακευόμενοι γὰρ χαίρουσιν, τοῦτο
δ' οὐδ' ἂν εἷς ποιήσειε φρόνημα ἔχων ἐλεύθερον,
ἀλλὰ φιλοῦσιν οἱ ἐπιεικεῖς, ἢ οὐ κολακεύουσιν.
5 καὶ χρήσιμοι οἱ πονηροὶ εἰς τὰ πονηρά, ἥλῳ γὰρ 7
ὁ ἧλος, ὥσπερ ἡ παροιμία. καὶ τὸ μηδενὶ χαίρειν 7
σεμνῷ μηδ' ἐλευθέρῳ τυραννικόν· αὐτὸν γὰρ εἶναι
μόνον ἀξιοῖ τοιοῦτον ὁ τύραννος, ὁ δ' ἀντισεμνυ-

---

[1] τούτων αὐτὸν καθελεῖν codd. nonnulli.
[2] φιλοπόνηρον Immisch.

---

[a] See 1259 a 28 n.   [b] Cf. 1309 b 27 ff.
[c] The proverb ἥλῳ ἧλος ἐκκρούεται usually meant driving
out something by a thing of the same kind ('set a thief to

reign of Dionysius ^a the result of taxation used to be that in five years men had contributed the whole of their substance). Also the tyrant is a stirrer-up of war, with the deliberate purpose of keeping the people busy and also of making them constantly in need of a leader. Also whereas friends are a means of security to royalty, it is a mark of a tyrant to be extremely distrustful of his friends, on the ground that, while all have the wish, these chiefly have the power. Also the things that occur in connexion with the final form of democracy ^b are all favourable to tyranny—dominance of women in the homes, in order that they may carry abroad reports against the men, and lack of discipline among the slaves, for the same reason ; for slaves and women do not plot against tyrants, and also, if they prosper under tyrannies, must feel well-disposed to them, and to democracies as well (for the common people also wishes to be sole ruler). Hence also the flatterer is in honour with both—with democracies the demagogue (for the demagogue is a flatterer of the people), and with the tyrants those who associate with them humbly, which is the task of flattery. In fact owing to this tyranny is a friend of the base ; for tyrants enjoy being flattered, but nobody would ever flatter them if he possessed a free spirit—men of character love their ruler, or at all events do not flatter him. And the base are useful for base business, for nail is driven out by nail, as the proverb goes.^c And it is a mark of a tyrant to dislike anyone that is proud or free-spirited ; for the tyrant claims for himself alone the right to bear that character, and the man who

catch a thief '), not as here the execution of evil designs by appropriate agents.

νόμενος καὶ ἐλευθεριάζων ἀφαιρεῖται τὴν ὑπεροχὴν
καὶ τὸ δεσποτικὸν τῆς τυραννίδος· μισοῦσιν οὖν
10 ὥσπερ καταλύοντας τὴν ἀρχήν. καὶ τὸ χρῆσθαι
συσσίτοις καὶ συνημερευταῖς ξενικοῖς μᾶλλον ἢ
πολιτικοῖς τυραννικόν, ὡς τοὺς μὲν πολεμίους
τοὺς δ' οὐκ ἀντιποιουμένους. ταῦτα καὶ τὰ
τοιαῦτα τυραννικὰ μὲν καὶ σωτήρια τῆς ἀρχῆς,
οὐθὲν δ' ἐλλείπει μοχθηρίας. ἔστι δ' ὡς εἰπεῖν
15 πάντα ταῦτα περιειλημμένα τρισὶν εἴδεσιν· στοχάζεται γὰρ ἡ τυραννὶς τριῶν, ἑνὸς μὲν τοῦ μικρὰ
φρονεῖν τοὺς ἀρχομένους (οὐδενὶ γὰρ ἂν μικρό-
ψυχος ἐπιβουλεύσειεν), δευτέρου δὲ τοῦ διαπιστεῖν
ἀλλήλοις (οὐ καταλύεται γὰρ πρότερον τυραννὶς
πρὶν ἢ πιστεύσουσί τινες αὑτοῖς, διὸ καὶ τοῖς
20 ἐπιεικέσι πολεμοῦσιν ὡς βλαβεροῖς πρὸς τὴν ἀρχὴν
οὐ μόνον διὰ τὸ μὴ ἀξιοῦν ἄρχεσθαι δεσποτικῶς
ἀλλὰ καὶ διὰ τὸ πιστοὺς καὶ ἑαυτοῖς καὶ τοῖς
ἄλλοις εἶναι καὶ μὴ καταγορεύειν μήτε ἑαυτῶν μήτε
τῶν ἄλλων)· τρίτον δ' ἀδυναμία τῶν πραγμάτων
25 (οὐθεὶς γὰρ ἐπιχειρεῖ τοῖς ἀδυνάτοις, ὥστε οὐδὲ
τυραννίδα καταλύειν μὴ δυνάμεως ὑπαρχούσης).
εἰς οὓς μὲν οὖν ὅρους ἀνάγεται τὰ βουλεύματα[1] τῶν
τυράννων, οὗτοι τρεῖς τυγχάνουσιν ὄντες· πάντα
γὰρ ἀναγάγοι τις ἂν τὰ τυραννικὰ πρὸς ταύτας
τὰς ὑποθέσεις, τὰ μὲν ὅπως μὴ πιστεύωσιν ἀλλήλοις, τὰ δ' ὅπως μὴ δύνωνται, τὰ δ' ὅπως μικρὸν
φρονῶσιν.
30 Ὁ μὲν οὖν εἷς τρόπος δι' οὗ γίνεται σωτηρία
ταῖς τυραννίσι τοιοῦτός ἐστιν. ὁ δ' ἕτερος σχεδὸν
ἐξ ἐναντίας ἔχει τοῖς εἰρημένοις τὴν ἐπιμέλειαν.

---

[1] Richards : βουλήματα codd.

[a] i.e. do not claim to be respected as his equals.

meets his pride with pride and shows a free spirit
robs tyranny of its superiority and position of
mastery ; tyrants therefore hate the proud as under-
mining their authority. And it is a mark of a tyrant
to have men of foreign extraction rather than
citizens as guests at table and companions, feeling
that citizens are hostile but strangers make no claim
against him.[a] These and similar habits are characteristic of tyrants and preservative of their office,
8 but they lack no element of baseness. And broadly
speaking, they are all included under three heads ;
for tyranny aims at three things, one to keep its
subjects humble (for a humble-spirited man would
not plot against anybody), second to have them
continually distrust one another (for a tyranny is not
destroyed until some men come to trust each other,
owing to which tyrants also make war on the respectable, as detrimental to their rule not only because
of their refusal to submit to despotic rule, but also
because they are faithful to one another and to the
other citizens, and do not inform against one another
nor against the others) ; and the third is lack of
power for political action (since nobody attempts
impossibilities, so that nobody tries to put down a
9 tyranny if he has not power behind him). These
then in fact are the three aims to which the plans
of tyrants are directed ; for all the measures taken
by tyrants one might class under these principles—
some are designed to prevent mutual confidence
among the subjects, others to curtail their power,
and others to make them humble-spirited.

10 Such then is the nature of one method by which *(b) concilia-*
security is obtained for tyrannies. The other tries *tory
methods.*
to operate in a manner almost the opposite of the

465

1314 a
ἔστι δὲ λαβεῖν αὐτὸν ἐκ τῆς φθορᾶς τῆς τῶν βασι-
λειῶν. ὥσπερ γὰρ τῆς βασιλείας εἷς τρόπος τῆς
φθορᾶς τὸ ποιεῖν τὴν ἀρχὴν τυραννικωτέραν, οὕτω
35 τῆς τυραννίδος σωτηρία ποιεῖν αὐτὴν βασιλικω-
τέραν, ἓν φυλάττοντα μόνον, τὴν δύναμιν, ὅπως
ἄρχῃ μὴ μόνον βουλομένων ἀλλὰ καὶ μὴ βουλο-
μένων· προϊέμενος γὰρ καὶ τοῦτο προῖεται καὶ
τὸ τυραννεῖν. ἀλλὰ τοῦτο μὲν ὥσπερ ὑπόθεσιν
δεῖ μένειν, τὰ δ' ἄλλα τὰ μὲν ποιεῖν τὰ δὲ δοκεῖν
40 ὑποκρινόμενον τὸ[1] βασιλικὸν καλῶς. πρῶτον μὲν
1314 b [τοῦ δοκεῖν][2] φροντίζειν τῶν κοινῶν, μήτε δα-
πανῶντα δωρεὰς τοιαύτας ἐφ' αἷς τὰ πλήθη χαλε-
παίνουσιν, ὅταν ἀπ' αὐτῶν μὲν λαμβάνωσιν ἐργαζο-
μένων καὶ πονούντων γλίσχρως, διδῶσι δ' ἑταίραις
5 καὶ ξένοις καὶ τεχνίταις ἀφθόνως, λόγον τε ἀπο-
διδόντα τῶν λαμβανομένων καὶ δαπανωμένων,
ὅπερ ἤδη πεποιήκασί τινες τῶν τυράννων (οὕτω
γὰρ ἄν τις διοικῶν οἰκονόμος ἀλλ' οὐ τύραννος
εἶναι δόξειεν, οὐ δεῖ δὲ φοβεῖσθαι μή ποτε ἀπορήσῃ
χρημάτων κύριος ὢν τῆς πόλεως· ἀλλὰ τοῖς γ'
10 ἐκτοπίζουσι τυράννοις ἀπὸ τῆς οἰκείας καὶ συμφέρει
τοῦτο μᾶλλον ἢ καταλιπεῖν ἀθροίσαντας, ἧττον
γὰρ ἂν οἱ φυλάττοντες ἐπιτιθεῖντο τοῖς πράγμασιν·
εἰσὶ δὲ φοβερώτεροι τῶν τυράννων τοῖς ἀπο-
δημοῦσιν οἱ φυλάττοντες τῶν πολιτῶν, οἱ μὲν
γὰρ συναποδημοῦσιν οἱ δὲ ὑπομένουσιν)· ἔπειτα
15 τὰς εἰσφορὰς καὶ τὰς λειτουργίας δεῖ φαίνεσθαι τῆς
τε οἰκονομίας ἕνεκα συνάγοντα κἄν ποτε δεηθῇ
χρῆσθαι πρὸς τοὺς πολεμικοὺς καιρούς, ὅλως τε

---

[1] τὸ ΓΗ: τὸν cet.
[2] Spengel (δοκεῖν codd. nonnulli).

devices mentioned. And it can be ascertained from considering the downfall of royal governments. For just as one mode of destroying royalty is to make its government more tyrannical, so a mode of securing tyranny is to make it more regal, protecting one thing only, its power, in order that the ruler may govern not only with the consent of the subjects but even without it; for if he gives up this, he also gives up his position as tyrant. But while this must stand as a fundamental principle, in all his other actions real or pretended he should cleverly

11 play the part of royalty. The first step is to be careful of the public funds, not squandering presents such as the multitudes resent, when tyrants take money from the people themselves while they toil and labour in penury and lavish it on mistresses and foreigners and craftsmen, and also rendering account of receipts and expenditure, as some tyrants have done already (for this careful management would make a ruler seem a steward of the state and not a tyrant, and he need not be afraid of ever being at a loss for funds while he is master

12 of the state; on the contrary, for those tyrants who go abroad on foreign campaigns this is actually more expedient than to leave their money there collected into one sum, for there is less fear of those guarding it making an attempt on power; since for tyrants campaigning abroad the keepers of the treasury are more to be feared than the citizens, for the citizens go abroad with him but the others stay at home). Secondly he must be seen to collect his taxes and benevolences for purposes of administration and to meet his occasional requirements for military emergencies, and generally must pose as

1814 b

αὑτὸν παρασκευάζειν φύλακα καὶ ταμίαι ὡς
κοινῶν ἀλλὰ μὴ ὡς ἰδίων· καὶ φαίνεσθαι μὴ 13
χαλεπὸν ἀλλὰ σεμνόν, ἔτι δὲ τοιοῦτον ὥστε μὴ
20 φοβεῖσθαι τοὺς ἐντυγχάνοντας ἀλλὰ μᾶλλον αἰδεῖ-
σθαι, τούτου μέντοι τυγχάνειν οὐ ῥᾴδιον ὄντα
εὐκαταφρόνητον, διὸ δεῖ κἂν μὴ τῶν ἄλλων ἀρετῶν
ἐπιμέλειαν ποιῆται ἀλλὰ τῆς πολεμικῆς,[1] καὶ δόξαν
ἐμποιεῖν περὶ αὑτοῦ τοιαύτην· ἔτι δὲ μὴ μόνον
αὐτὸν φαίνεσθαι μηθένα τῶν ἀρχομένων ὑβρίζοντα,
25 μήτε νέον μήτε νέαν, ἀλλὰ μηδ' ἄλλον μηδένα τῶν
περὶ αὑτόν, ὁμοίως δὲ καὶ τὰς οἰκείας ἔχειν γυναῖκας πρὸς τὰς ἄλλας, ὡς καὶ διὰ γυναικῶν ὕβρεις
πολλαὶ τυραννίδες ἀπολώλασιν· περί τε τὰς ἀπο- 14
λαύσεις τὰς σωματικὰς τοὐναντίον ποιεῖν ἢ νῦν
τινὲς τῶν τυράννων ποιοῦσιν (οὐ γὰρ μόνον εὐθὺς
80 ἕωθεν τοῦτο δρῶσιν καὶ συνεχῶς πολλὰς ἡμέρας,
ἀλλὰ καὶ φαίνεσθαι τοῖς ἄλλοις βούλονται τοῦτο
πράττοντες ἵν' ὡς εὐδαίμονας καὶ μακαρίους
θαυμάσωσιν), ἀλλὰ μάλιστα μὲν μετριάζειν τοῖς
τοιούτοις, εἰ δὲ μή, τό γε φαίνεσθαι τοῖς ἄλλοις
διαφεύγειν (οὔτε γὰρ εὐεπίθετος οὔτ' εὐκατα-
85 φρόνητος ὁ νήφων ἀλλ' ὁ μεθύων, οὐδ' ὁ ἄγρυπνος
ἀλλ' ὁ καθεύδων)· τοὐναντίον τε ποιητέον τῶν 15
πάλαι λεχθέντων σχεδὸν πάντων, κατασκευάζειν
γὰρ δεῖ καὶ κοσμεῖν τὴν πόλιν ὡς ἐπίτροπον ὄντα
καὶ μὴ τύραννον· ἔτι δὲ τὰ πρὸς τοὺς θεοὺς φαίνε-
40 σθαι ἀεὶ σπουδάζοντα διαφερόντως (ἧττόν τε γὰρ
φοβοῦνται τὸ παθεῖν τι παράνομον ὑπὸ τῶν τοιού-
1315 a των, ἐὰν δεισιδαίμονα νομίζωσιν εἶναι τὸν ἄρχοντα
καὶ φροντίζειν τῶν θεῶν, καὶ ἐπιβουλεύουσιν ἧττον
ὡς συμμάχους ἔχοντι καὶ τοὺς θεούς), δεῖ δ' ἄνευ

[1] πολεμικῆς Madvig : πολιτικῆς codd.

uardian and steward as it were of a public fund and
ot a private estate. And his bearing must not be
arsh but dignified, and also such as to inspire not
:ar but rather respect in those who encounter him,
hough this is not easy to achieve if he is a contempt-
ble personality; so that even if he neglects the other
irtues he is bound to cultivate military valour, and to
aake himself a reputation as a soldier. And further-
aore not only must he himself be known not to out-
age any of his subjects, either boy or girl, but so
lso must everybody about him, and also their wives
aust similarly show respect towards the other women,
nce even the insolences of women have caused the
all of many tyrannies. And in regard to bodily
njoyments he must do the opposite of what some
yrants do now (for they not only begin their de-
aucheries at daybreak and carry them on for many
ays at a time, but also wish to be seen doing so by
ae public, in order that people may admire them as
rtunate and happy), but best of all he must be
aoderate in such matters, or if not, he must at all
vents avoid displaying his indulgences to his fellows
or not the sober man but the drunkard is easy to
ttack and to despise, not the wakeful man but the
eeper). And he must do the opposite of almost all
ae things mentioned some time back, for he must 1313 a 19-25.
y out and adorn the city as if he were a trustee and
ot a tyrant. And further he must be seen always to
e exceptionally zealous as regards religious observ-
aces (for people are less afraid of suffering any
legal treatment from men of this sort, if they think
aat their ruler has religious scruples and pays regard
• the gods, and also they plot against him less,
ainking that he has even the gods as allies), though

1315 a

ἀβελτηρίας φαίνεσθαι τοιοῦτον· τούς τε ἀγαθο
5 περί τι γιγνομένους τιμᾶν οὕτως ὥστε μὴ νομίζε
ἄν ποτε τιμηθῆναι μᾶλλον ὑπὸ τῶν πολιτ
αὐτονόμων ὄντων· καὶ τὰς μὲν τοιαύτας τιμ
ἀπονέμειν αὐτόν, τὰς δὲ κολάσεις δι' ἑτέρ
ἀρχόντων καὶ δικαστηρίων.[1] κοινὴ δὲ φυλα
πάσης μοναρχίας τὸ μηθένα ποιεῖν ἕνα μέγαν, ἀλ
10 εἴπερ, πλείους (τηρήσουσι γὰρ ἀλλήλους), ἐὰν
ἄρα τινὰ δέη ποιῆσαι μέγαν, μή τοι τό γε ἦθ
θρασύν (ἐπιθετικώτατον γὰρ τὸ τοιοῦτον ἦθ
περὶ πάσας τὰς πράξεις)· κἂν τῆς δυνάμεώς τι
δοκῇ παραλύειν, ἐκ προσαγωγῆς τοῦτο δρᾶν κ
μὴ πᾶσαν ἀθρόαν[2] ἀφαιρεῖσθαι τὴν ἐξουσίαν. ἔ
15 δὲ πάσης μὲν ὕβρεως εἴργεσθαι, παρὰ πάσας
δυοῖν, τῆς τε εἰς τὰ σώματα κολάσεως[3] καὶ τ
εἰς τὴν ἡλικίαν. μάλιστα δὲ ταύτην ποιητέον τ
εὐλάβειαν περὶ τοὺς φιλοτίμους· τὴν μὲν γὰρ
τὰ χρήματα ὀλιγωρίαν οἱ φιλοχρήματοι φέρου
βαρέως, τὴν δ' εἰς[4] ἀτιμίαν οἵ τε φιλότιμοι καὶ
20 ἐπιεικεῖς τῶν ἀνθρώπων. διόπερ ἢ μὴ χρῆσ
δεῖ τοῖς τοιούτοις, ἢ τὰς μὲν κολάσεις πατρικ
φαίνεσθαι ποιούμενον καὶ μὴ δι' ὀλιγωρίαν, τὰς
πρὸς τὴν ἡλικίαν ὁμιλίας δι' ἐρωτικὰς αἰτίας ἀλ
μὴ δι' ἐξουσίαν, ὅλως δὲ τὰς δοκούσας ἀτιμ
ἐξωνεῖσθαι μείζοσι τιμαῖς. τῶν δ' ἐπιχειρούντ
25 ἐπὶ τὴν τοῦ σώματος διαφθορὰν οὗτοι φοβερώτα
καὶ δέονται πλείστης φυλακῆς ὅσοι μὴ προαιροῦν

---

[1] ἀρχόντων καὶ δικαστηρίων secl. Oncken.
[2] ed. : ἀθρόον codd.
[3] κολάσεως secl. Schneider.
[4] εἰς secl. Spengel.

e should not display a foolish religiosity. And he
ust pay such honour to those who display merit in
ny matter that they may think that they could never
e more honoured by the citizens if they were in-
ependent; and honours of this kind he should bestow
a person, but inflict his punishments by the agency
f other magistrates and law-courts. And it is a
rotection common to every sort of monarchy to make
o one man great, but if necessary to exalt several
or they will keep watch on one another), and if
fter all the ruler has to elevate an individual, at all
vents not take a man of bold spirit (for such a char-
cter is most enterprising in all undertakings); and
he thinks fit to remove somebody from his power,
o do this by gradual stages and not take away the
hole of his authority at once. And again he should
arefully avoid all forms of outrage, and two beyond
ll, violent bodily punishments and outrage of the
oung. And this caution must especially be exer-
ised in relation to the ambitious, for while to be
lighted in regard to property annoys the lovers
f wealth, slights that involve dishonour are what
en of honourable ambition and high character
esent. Hence the tyrant should either not con-
ort with men of this kind, or appear to inflict his
unishments paternally and not because of contempt,
nd to indulge in the society of the young for reasons
f passion, not because he has the power, and in
eneral he should buy off what are thought to be
ishonours by greater honours. And among those
ho make attempts upon the life of a ruler the most
rmidable and those against whom the greatest
recaution is needed are those that are ready to

471

1315 a

περιποιεῖσθαι τὸ ζῆν διαφθείραντες. διὸ μάλιστ
εὐλαβεῖσθαι δεῖ τοὺς ὑβρίζεσθαι νομίζοντας
αὐτοὺς ἢ ὧν κηδόμενοι τυγχάνουσιν· ἀφειδ
γὰρ ἑαυτῶν ἔχουσιν οἱ διὰ θυμὸν ἐπιχειροῦντε
30 καθάπερ καὶ Ἡράκλειτος εἶπε, χαλεπὸν φάσκ
εἶναι θυμῷ μάχεσθαι, ψυχῆς γὰρ ὠνεῖσθαι. ἐπ
δ᾽ αἱ πόλεις ἐκ δύο συνεστήκασι μορίων, ἔκ τε τ
ἀπόρων ἀνθρώπων καὶ τῶν εὐπόρων, μάλιστα μ
ἀμφοτέρους ὑπολαμβάνειν δεῖ σῴζεσθαι διὰ τ
35 ἀρχὴν καὶ τοὺς ἑτέρους ὑπὸ τῶν ἑτέρων ἀδικεῖσθ
μηδέν, ὁπότεροι δ᾽ ἂν ὦσι κρείττους τούτους ἰδίο
μάλιστα ποιεῖσθαι τῆς ἀρχῆς, ὡς ἂν ὑπάρξῃ τοῦ
τοῖς πράγμασιν οὔτε δούλων ἐλευθέρωσιν ἀνάγ
ποιεῖσθαι τὸν τύραννον οὔτε ὅπλων παραίρεσ
40 ἱκανὸν γὰρ θάτερον μέρος πρὸς τῇ δυνάμει προσ
θέμενον ὥστε κρείττους εἶναι τῶν ἐπιτιθεμέν
περίεργον δὲ τὸ λέγειν καθ᾽ ἕκαστον τῶν τοιούτ
ὁ γὰρ σκοπὸς φανερός, ὅτι δεῖ μὴ τυραννικ
1315 b ἀλλ᾽ οἰκονόμον καὶ βασιλικὸν εἶναι φαίνεσθαι τ
ἀρχομένοις καὶ μὴ σφετεριστὴν ἀλλ᾽ ἐπίτροπ
καὶ τὰς μετριότητας τοῦ βίου διώκειν, μὴ τ
ὑπερβολάς, ἔτι δὲ τοὺς μὲν γνωρίμους καθομιλ
5 τοὺς δὲ πολλοὺς δημαγωγεῖν. ἐκ γὰρ τούτ
ἀναγκαῖον οὐ μόνον τὴν ἀρχὴν εἶναι καλλίω κ
ζηλωτοτέραν τῷ βελτιόνων ἄρχειν καὶ μὴ τ
ταπεινωμένων μηδὲ μισούμενον καὶ φοβούμεν
διατελεῖν, ἀλλὰ καὶ τὴν ἀρχὴν εἶναι[1] πολυχρονι
τέραν, ἔτι δ᾽ αὐτὸν διακεῖσθαι κατὰ τὸ ἦθος ἤτ

---

[1] τὴν ἀρχὴν εἶναι secl. Coraes.

---

[a] The natural philosopher of Ephesus, *fl. c.* 513 B.
known as ὁ σκοτεινός for his epigrammatic obscurity.

sacrifice their lives if they can destroy him. Hence the greatest care must be taken to guard against those who think that insolent outrage is being done either to themselves or to those who happen to be under their care ; for men attacking under the influence of anger are reckless of themselves, as Heraclitus ^a also observed when he said that anger is hard to combat because it buys its wish with life. And since states consist of two parts, the poor people and the rich, the most important thing is for both to think that they owe their safety to the government and for it to prevent either from being wronged by the other, but whichever class is the stronger, this must be made to be entirely on the side of the government, as, if this support for the tyrant's interests is secured, there is no need for him to institute a liberation of slaves or a disarming of the citizens, for one of the two parts of the state added to his power will be enough to make him and them stronger than their attackers. But to discuss each of such matters separately is superfluous ; for the thing to aim at is clear, that it is necessary to appear to the subjects to be not a tyrannical ruler but a steward and a royal governor, and not an appropriator of wealth but a trustee, and to pursue the moderate things of life and not its extravagances, and also to make the notables one's comrades and the many one's followers. For the result of these methods must be that not only the tyrant's rule will be more honourable and more enviable because he will rule nobler subjects and not men that have been humiliated, and will not be continually hated and feared, but also that his rule will endure longer, and moreover that he himself in his personal character

10 καλῶς πρὸς ἀρετὴν ἢ¹ ἡμίχρηστον ὄντα, καὶ μὴ
πονηρὸν ἀλλ᾽ ἡμιπόνηρον.

Καίτοι πασῶν ὀλιγοχρονιώτεραι τῶν πολι
τειῶν εἰσιν ὀλιγαρχία καὶ τυραννίς. πλεῖστον γὰ
ἐγένετο χρόνον ἡ περὶ Σικυῶνα τυραννίς, ἡ τῶ
Ὀρθαγόρου παίδων καὶ αὐτοῦ Ὀρθαγόρου, ἔτ
15 δ᾽ αὕτη διέμεινεν ἑκατόν. τούτου δ᾽ αἴτιον ὅτ
τοῖς ἀρχομένοις ἐχρῶντο μετρίως καὶ πολλὰ τοῖ
νόμοις ἐδούλευον, καὶ διὰ τὸ πολεμικὸς γενέ
σθαι Κλεισθένης οὐκ ἦν εὐκαταφρόνητος,² καὶ τ
πολλὰ ταῖς ἐπιμελείαις ἐδημαγώγουν. λέγεται γοῦ
20 Κλεισθένης τὸν ἀποκρίναντα τῆς νίκης αὐτὸν ὡ
ἐστεφάνωσεν· ἔνιοι δ᾽ εἰκόνα φασὶν εἶναι τοῦ κρ
ναντος οὕτω τὸν ἀνδριάντα τὸν ἐν τῇ ἀγορᾷ καθ
ἥμενον. φασὶ δὲ καὶ Πεισίστρατον ὑπομεῖναί ποτ
προσκληθέντα δίκην εἰς Ἄρειον πάγον. δευτέρ
δὲ ἡ³ περὶ Κόρινθον ἡ τῶν Κυψελιδῶν· καὶ γὰ
αὕτη διετέλεσεν ἔτη τρία καὶ ἑβδομήκοντα καὶ ἑ
25 μῆνας, Κύψελος μὲν γὰρ ἐτυράννησεν ἔτη τριά
κοντα, Περίανδρος δὲ τετταράκοντα καὶ τέτταρα⁴
Ψαμμήτιχος δ᾽ ὁ Γορδίου⁵ τρία ἔτη. τὰ δ᾽ αὐτ
ταῦτὰ καὶ ταύτης· ὁ μὲν γὰρ Κύψελος δημ
αγωγὸς ἦν καὶ κατὰ τὴν ἀρχὴν διετέλεσεν ἀδορ
φόρητος, Περίανδρος δ᾽ ἐγένετο μὲν τυραννικό
30 ἀλλὰ πολεμικός. τρίτη δ᾽ ἡ τῶν Πεισιστρατιδ(

---

¹ ἢ ⟨ὡς⟩ ? Richards.
² καὶ διὰ—εὐκαταφρόνητος infra post 23 πάγον Richards.
³ δὲ ἡ ed. : δὲ codd.
⁴ τέτταρα: ἥμισυ edd. arithmetices gratia.
⁵ Γόργου Susemihl.

ᵃ Oligarchy is not mentioned in what follows, and t
context deals with the forms of monarchy. Tyranny is i
cluded among the constitutions at 1312 a 40, but not els
474

will be nobly disposed towards virtue, or at all events half-virtuous, and not base but only half-base.

Nevertheless oligarchy and tyranny *a* are less Historical lasting than any of the constitutional governments. examples. For the longest-lived was the tyranny at Sicyon, that of the sons *b* of Orthagoras and of Orthagoras himself, and this lasted a hundred years.*c* The cause of this was that they treated their subjects moderately and in many matters were subservient to the laws, and Cleisthenes because he was a warlike man was not easily despised, and in most things they kept the lead of the people by looking after their interests. At all events it is said that Cleisthenes placed a wreath on the judge who awarded the victory away from him, and some say that the statue of a seated figure in the market-place is a statue of the man who gave this judgement. And they say that Pisistratus *d* also once submitted to a summons for trial before the Areopagus. And the second longest is the tyranny at Corinth, that of the Cypselids,*e* for even this lasted seventy-three and a half years, as Cypselus was tyrant for thirty years, Periander for forty-four,*f* and Psammetichus son of Gordias for three years. And the reasons for the permanence of this tyranny also are the same : Cypselus was a leader of the people and continuously throughout his period of office dispensed with a bodyguard ; and although Periander became tyrannical, yet he was warlike. The third longest tyranny is that of

here in this Book. Some editors bracket ll. 19-29 as spurious or out of place.
b *i.e.* descendants ; Cleisthenes was his grandson.
c From 670 B.C.   *d* See 1305 a 23 n.   *e* From 655 B.C.
f The Greek may be corrected to ' forty and a half ' to give the stated total.

^{1315 b} Ἀθήνησιν, οὐκ ἐγένετο δὲ συνεχής· δὶς γ
ἔφυγε Πεισίστρατος τυραννῶν, ὥστ᾽ ἐν ἔτε
τριάκοντα καὶ τρισὶν ἑπτακαίδεκα ἔτη τούτ
ἐτυράννευσεν, ὀκτωκαίδεκα δὲ οἱ παῖδες, ὥστε
πάντα ἐγένετο ἔτη τριάκοντα καὶ πέντε. τῶν
35 λοιπῶν ἡ περὶ¹ Ἱέρωνα καὶ Γέλωνα περὶ Συρ
κούσας,² ἔτη δ᾽ οὐδ᾽ αὕτη πολλὰ διέμεινεν, ἀλ
τὰ σύμπαντα δυοῖν δέοντα εἴκοσι· Γέλων μὲν γ
ἑπτὰ τυραννεύσας τῷ ὀγδόῳ τὸν βίον ἐτελεύτησε
δέκα δ᾽ Ἱέρων, Θρασύβουλος δὲ τῷ ἑνδεκά
μηνὶ ἐξέπεσεν. αἱ δὲ πολλαὶ τῶν τυραννίδ
ὀλιγοχρόνιαι πᾶσαι γεγόνασι παντελῶς.

40 Τὰ μὲν οὖν περὶ τὰς πολιτείας καὶ τὰ περὶ τ
μοναρχίας, ἐξ ὧν τε φθείρονται καὶ πάλιν σῴζο
^{1316 a} ται, σχεδὸν εἴρηται περὶ πάντων.

X. Ἐν δὲ τῇ Πολιτείᾳ λέγεται μὲν πε
τῶν μεταβολῶν ὑπὸ τοῦ Σωκράτους, οὐ μέντ
λέγεται καλῶς· τῆς τε γὰρ ἀρίστης πολιτείας κ
πρώτης οὔσης οὐ λέγει τὴν μεταβολὴν ἰδί
5 φησὶ γὰρ αἴτιον εἶναι τὸ μὴ μένειν μηθὲν ἀλλ᾽
τινι περιόδῳ μεταβάλλειν, ἀρχὴν δ᾽ εἶναι τούτ
ὧν ἐπίτριτος πυθμὴν πεμπάδι συζυγεὶς δ
ἁρμονίας παρέχεται, λέγων ὅταν ὁ τοῦ διαγρά
ματος ἀριθμὸς τούτου γένηται στερεός, ὡς τ
φύσεώς ποτε φυούσης φαύλους καὶ κρείττους τ
10 παιδείας, τοῦτο μὲν οὖν αὐτὸ λέγων ἴσως
κακῶς (ἐνδέχεται γὰρ εἶναί τινας οὓς παιδευθῆ

---

¹ ἡ ⟨τῶν⟩ περὶ Bojesen.
² ἐν Συρακούσαις Schneider : παρὰ Συρακουσίοις Sylburg.

---

^a See 1305 a 23 n.   ^b See 1312 b 12 n.
^c Plato, *Republic*, Bks. VIII., IX. init. ; the mathemati

the Pisistratidae at Athens, but it was not continuous; for while Pisistratus *a* was tyrant he twice fled into exile, so that in a period of thirty-three years he was tyrant for seventeen years out of the total, and his sons for eighteen years, so that the whole duration of their rule was thirty-five years. Among the remaining tyrannies is the one connected with Hiero and Gelo *b* at Syracuse, but even this did not last many years, but only eighteen in all, for Gelo after being tyrant for seven years ended his life in the eighth, and Hiero ruled ten years, but Thrasybulus was expelled after ten months. And the usual tyrannies have all of them been of quite short duration.

The causes therefore of the destruction of constitutional governments and of monarchies and those again of their preservation have almost all of them been discussed.

X. The subject of revolutions is discussed by Socrates in the *Republic,c* but is not discussed well. For his account of revolution in the constitution that is the best one and the first does not apply to it particularly. He says that the cause is that nothing is permanent but everything changes in a certain cycle, and that change has its origin in those numbers ' whose basic ratio 4 : 3 linked with the number 5 gives two harmonies,'—meaning whenever the number of this figure becomes cubed,—in the belief that nature sometimes engenders men that are evil, and too strong for education to influence—speaking perhaps not ill as far as this particular dictum goes (for it is possible that there are some

Plato on revolution criticized.

formula for the change from Aristocracy to Timocracy quoted here occurs at 546 c—see Adam's note there.

καὶ γενέσθαι σπουδαίους ἄνδρας ἀδύνατον), ἀλλ'
αὕτη τί ἂν ἴδιος εἴη μεταβολὴ τῆς ὑπ' ἐκείνου
λεγομένης ἀρίστης πολιτείας μᾶλλον ἢ τῶν ἄλλων
πασῶν καὶ τῶν γιγνομένων πάντων; καὶ διά γε¹
15 τοῦ² χρόνου, δι' ὃν λέγει πάντα μεταβάλλειν, καὶ
τὰ μὴ ἅμα ἀρξάμενα γίγνεσθαι ἅμα μεταβάλλει,
οἷον εἰ τῇ προτέρᾳ ἡμέρᾳ ἐγένετο τῆς τροπῆς,
ἅμα ἆρα μεταβάλλει; πρὸς δὲ τούτοις διὰ τίν'
αἰτίαν ἐκ ταύτης εἰς τὴν Λακωνικὴν μεταβάλλει;
πλεονάκις γὰρ εἰς τὴν ἐναντίαν μεταβάλλουσι πᾶσαι
20 αἱ πολιτεῖαι ἢ τὴν σύνεγγυς. ὁ δ' αὐτὸς λόγος καὶ
περὶ τῶν ἄλλων μεταβολῶν· ἐκ γὰρ τῆς Λακωνικῆς, φησί, μεταβάλλει εἰς τὴν ὀλιγαρχίαν, ἐκ δὲ
ταύτης εἰς δημοκρατίαν, εἰς τυραννίδα δὲ ἐκ δημοκρατίας. καίτοι καὶ ἀνάπαλιν μεταβάλλουσιν, οἷον
ἐκ δήμου εἰς ὀλιγαρχίαν, καὶ μᾶλλον ἢ εἰς μον-
25 αρχίαν. ἔτι δὲ τυραννίδος οὐ λέγει οὔτ' εἰ ἔσται
μεταβολὴ οὔτ' εἰ μὴ ἔσται, ⟨οὔτ' εἰ ἔσται,⟩³ διὰ τίν'
αἰτίαν καὶ εἰς ποίαν πολιτείαν· τούτου δ' αἴτιον
ὅτι οὐ ῥᾳδίως ἂν εἶχε λέγειν, ἀόριστον γάρ, ἐπεὶ
κατ' ἐκεῖνον δεῖ εἰς τὴν πρώτην καὶ τὴν ἀρίστην,
οὕτω γὰρ ἂν ἐγίγνετο συνεχὲς καὶ κύκλος, ἀλλὰ
30 μεταβάλλει καὶ εἰς τυραννίδα τυραννίς, ὥσπερ ἡ
Σικυῶνος ἐκ τῆς Μύρωνος εἰς τὴν Κλεισθένους,

¹ γε corr. cod. inf.: τε codd.
² ⟨τὸ⟩ τοῦ Thompson.
³ Casaubon (potius οὐδ' ed.).

ᵃ Timocracy, Plato, *Republic* 545 A.
ᵇ See 1315 b 13 n.

persons incapable of being educated and becoming men of noble character), but why should this process of revolution belong to the constitution which Socrates speaks of as the best, more than to all the other forms of constitution, and to all men that come into existence ? and why merely by the operation of time, which he says is the cause of change in all things, do even things that did not begin to exist simultaneously change simultaneously ? for instance, if a thing came into existence the day before the completion of the cycle, why does it yet change simultaneously with everything else ? And in addition to these points, what is the reason why the republic changes from the constitution mentioned into the Spartan form [a] ? For all constitutions more often change into the opposite form than into the one near them. And the same remark applies to the other revolutions as well. For from the Spartan constitution the state changes, he says, to oligarchy, and from this to democracy, and from democracy to tyranny. Yet revolutions also occur the other way about, for example from democracy to oligarchy, and more often so than from democracy to monarchy. Again as to tyranny he does not say whether it will undergo revolution or not, nor, if it will, what will be the cause of it, and into what sort of constitution it will change ; and the reason for this is that he would not have found it easy to say, for it is irregular ; since according to him tyranny ought to change into the first and best constitution, for so the process would be continuous and a circle, but as a matter of fact tyranny also changes into tyranny, as the constitution of Sicyon [b] passed from the tyranny of Myron to that of Cleisthenes, and into

479

1316 a
καὶ εἰς ὀλιγαρχίαν, ὥσπερ ἡ ἐν Χαλκίδι ἡ Ἀντι-
λέοντος, καὶ εἰς δημοκρατίαν, ὥσπερ ἡ τῶν
Γέλωνος ἐν Συρακούσαις, καὶ εἰς ἀριστοκρατίαν,
ὥσπερ ἡ Χαριλάου ἐν Λακεδαίμονι [καὶ ἐν Καρχη-
25 δόνι].[1] καὶ εἰς τυραννίδα μεταβάλλει ἐξ ὀλιγαρχίας, 4
ὥσπερ ἐν Σικελίᾳ σχεδὸν αἱ πλεῖσται τῶν ἀρχαίων,
ἐν Λεοντίνοις εἰς τὴν Παναιτίου τυραννίδα καὶ ἐν
Γέλᾳ εἰς τὴν Κλεάνδρου καὶ ἐν Ῥηγίῳ εἰς τὴν
Ἀναξιλάου καὶ ἐν ἄλλαις πολλαῖς πόλεσιν ὡσαύτως.
40 ἄτοπον δὲ καὶ τὸ οἴεσθαι εἰς ὀλιγαρχίαν διὰ τοῦτο
μεταβάλλειν ὅτι φιλοχρήματοι καὶ χρηματισταὶ[2]

1316 b
οἱ ἐν ταῖς ἀρχαῖς, ἀλλ᾽ οὐχ ὅτι οἱ πολὺ ὑπερέχοντες ταῖς οὐσίαις οὐ δίκαιον οἴονται εἶναι ἴσον
μετέχειν τῆς πόλεως τοὺς κεκτημένους μηθὲν τοῖς
κεκτημένοις· ἐν πολλαῖς τε ὀλιγαρχίαις οὐκ ἔξεστι
5 χρηματίζεσθαι, ἀλλὰ νόμοι εἰσὶν οἱ κωλύοντες, ἐν
Καρχηδόνι δὲ δημοκρατουμένῃ[3] χρηματίζονται καὶ
οὔπω μεταβεβλήκασιν. ἄτοπον δὲ καὶ τὸ φάναι
δύο πόλεις εἶναι τὴν ὀλιγαρχικήν, πλουσίων καὶ
πενήτων. τί γὰρ αὕτη[4] μᾶλλον τῆς Λακωνικῆς
πέπονθεν ἢ ὁποιασοῦν ἄλλης οὗ μὴ πάντες κέκτην-
10 ται ἴσα ἢ μὴ πάντες ὁμοίως εἰσὶν ἀγαθοὶ ἄνδρες;
οὐδενὸς δὲ πενεστέρου γενομένου ἢ πρότερον
οὐθὲν ἧττον μεταβάλλουσιν εἰς δῆμον ἐξ ὀλιγ-

---

[1] secl. ? Susemihl : om. cod. inferior.
[2] ⟨φιλο⟩χρηματισταὶ e Platone Spengel.
[3] ἀριστοκρατουμένῃ Schneider : τιμοκρατουμένῃ ? Newman.
[4] αὕτη ⟨τοῦτο⟩ Richards.

---

[a] Unknown, cf. 1304 a 29 n.
[b] See 1302 b 33 n.   [c] See 1271 b 26 n.

oligarchy, as did that of Antileon *a* at Chalcis, and into democracy, as that of the family of Gelo *b* at Syracuse, and into aristocracy, as that of Charilaus *c* at Sparta 4 [and as at Carthage].*d* And constitutions change from oligarchy to tyranny, as did almost the greatest number of the ancient oligarchies in Sicily, at Leontini to the tyranny of Panaetius,*e* at Gelo to that of Cleander, at Rhegium to that of Anaxilaus,*f* and in many other cities similarly. And it is also a strange idea that revolutions into oligarchy take place because the occupants of the offices are lovers of money and engaged in money-making, but not because owners of much more than the average amount of property think it unjust for those who do not own any property to have an equal share in the state with those who do ; and in many oligarchies those in office are not allowed to engage in business, but there are laws preventing it, whereas in Carthage, which has a democratic government,*g* the magistrates go in for business, and they have not yet had a revolution. And it is also a strange remark *h* that the oligarchical state is two states, one of rich men and one of poor men. For what has happened to this state rather than to the Spartan or any other sort of state where all do not own an equal amount of wealth or where all are not equally good men ? and when nobody has become poorer than he was before, none the less revolution takes place from oligarchy to democracy

d This clause seems an interpolation ; *cf.* b 6.

e See 1310 b 29 n.

f Unknown. Reggio is situated in relation to Sicily as Calais is to England.

g Apparently this clause also is an interpolation, or ' democratic ' is a copyist's mistake for ' oligarchic ' or ' timocratic,' see 1272 b 24 ff.   *h* Plato, *Republic* 551 D.

1316 b

ἀρχίας ἂν γένωνται πλείους οἱ ἄποροι, καὶ ἐκ
δήμου εἰς ὀλιγαρχίαν, ἐὰν κρεῖττον ᾖ τοῦ πλήθους
τὸ εὔπορον καὶ οἱ μὲν ἀμελῶσιν οἱ δὲ προσέχωσι
15 τὸν νοῦν. πολλῶν τε οὐσῶν αἰτιῶν δι' ὧν γίγνονται αἱ μεταβολαί, οὐ λέγει ἀλλ' ἢ¹ μίαν, ὅτι ἀσω-
τευόμενοι κατατοκιζόμενοι² γίγνονται πένητες, ὡς
ἐξ ἀρχῆς πλουσίων ὄντων πάντων ἢ τῶν πλείστων·
τοῦτο δ' ἐστὶ ψεῦδος, ἀλλ' ὅταν μὲν τῶν ἡγεμόνων
τινὲς ἀπολέσωσι τὰς οὐσίας, καινοτομοῦσιν, ὅταν
20 δὲ τῶν ἄλλων, οὐθὲν γίγνεται δεινόν· καὶ μεταβάλλουσιν οὐθὲν μᾶλλον οὐδὲ τότε³ εἰς δῆμον ἢ εἰς
ἄλλην πολιτείαν. ἔτι δὲ κἂν τιμῶν μὴ μετέχωσιν
κἂν ἀδικῶνται ἢ ὑβρίζωνται, στασιάζουσι καὶ μεταβάλλουσι τὰς πολιτείας, κἂν μὴ καταδαπανήσωσι
τὴν οὐσίαν . . .⁴ διὰ τὸ ἐξεῖναι ὅ τι ἂν βούλωνται
25 ποιεῖν· οὗ αἰτίαν τὴν ἄγαν ἐλευθερίαν εἶναί φησιν
πλειόνων δ' οὐσῶν ὀλιγαρχιῶν καὶ δημοκρατιῶν,
ὡς μιᾶς οὔσης ἑκατέρας λέγει τὰς μεταβολὰς ὁ
Σωκράτης.

---

¹ ἀλλ' ἢ Richards : ἀλλὰ codd.
² ⟨καὶ⟩ κατατοκιζόμενοι Lambinus.
³ οὐδὲ τότε Camotius : οὐδέποτε.
⁴ lacunam Schneider.

ᵃ Some words appear to be lost here ; what follows refers
to democracy, cf. Plato, Republic 587 ʙ.

f the men of no property become more numerous,
and from democracy to oligarchy if the wealthy
class is stronger than the multitude and the latter
neglect politics but the former give their mind to
them. And although there are many causes through
which revolutions in oligarchies occur, he mentions
only one—that of men becoming poor through riotous
living, by paying away their money in interest on
loans—as if at the start all men or most men were
rich. But this is not true, but although when
some of the leaders have lost their properties they
stir up innovations, when men of the other classes
are ruined nothing strange happens; and even
when such a revolution does occur it is no more
likely to end in a democracy than in another form
of constitution. And furthermore men also form
factions and cause revolutions in the constitution if
they are not allowed a share of honours, and if they
are unjustly or insolently treated, even if they have
not run through all their property . . . a because of
being allowed to do whatever they like; the cause
of which he states to be excessive liberty. And
although there are several forms of oligarchy and
of democracy, Socrates speaks of the revolutions
that occur in them as though there were only one
form of each.

ADDITIONAL NOTE

V. vii. 2, 1307 b 37 (p. 421). This is the *sorites* fallacy;
add to one stone another, and another, and another—when
do they make a heap (σωρός)? and take away stone after
stone—when do they cease to be a heap? Horace's 'ratio
ruentis acerui' (*Epistles* ii. 1. 47).

I. Πόσαι μὲν οὖν διαφοραὶ καὶ τίνες τοῦ τε [a]
βουλευτικοῦ καὶ κυρίου τῆς πολιτείας καὶ τῆς
περὶ τὰς ἀρχὰς τάξεως καὶ περὶ δικαστηρίων, καὶ
ποῖα πρὸς ποίαν συντέτακται πολιτείαν, ἔτι δὲ
35 περὶ φθορᾶς τε καὶ σωτηρίας τῶν πολιτειῶν ἐκ
ποίων τε γίνεται καὶ διὰ τίνας αἰτίας, εἴρηται
πρότερον. ἐπεὶ δὲ τετύχηκεν εἴδη πλείω δημοκρατίας ὄντα καὶ τῶν ἄλλων ὁμοίως πολιτειῶν,
ἅμα τε περὶ ἐκείνων εἴ τι λοιπὸν οὐ χεῖρον ἐπισκέψασθαι καὶ τὸν οἰκεῖον καὶ τὸν συμφέροντα
40 τρόπον ἀποδοῦναι πρὸς ἑκάστην. ἔτι δὲ καὶ τὰς
συναγωγὰς αὐτῶν τῶν εἰρημένων ἐπισκεπτέον
1317 a πάντων τῶν τρόπων· ταῦτα γὰρ συνδυαζόμενα
ποιεῖ τὰς πολιτείας ἐπαλλάττειν, ὥστε ἀριστοκρατίας τε ὀλιγαρχικὰς εἶναι καὶ πολιτείας δημο-
κρατικωτέρας. λέγω δὲ τοὺς συνδυασμοὺς οὓς
δεῖ μὲν ἐπισκοπεῖν οὐκ ἐσκεμμένοι δ' εἰσὶ νῦν,
5 οἷον ἂν τὸ μὲν[1] βουλευόμενον καὶ τὸ περὶ τὰς ἀρχαιρεσίας ὀλιγαρχικῶς ᾖ συντεταγμένον τὰ δὲ περὶ

---

[1] τὸ μὲν ⟨περὶ τὸ⟩ Spengel.

---

[a] Book VII. in some editions, Book VIII. in others.
[b] Book IV., 1297 b 35 ff.
[c] Book V.
[d] 1318 b—1319 a 6.
[e] These topics do not occur in the extant work.

BOOK VI [a]

1 I. We have already discussed [b] how many and what are the varieties of the deliberative body or sovereign power in the state, and of the system of magistracies and of law-courts, and which variety is adapted to which form of constitution, and also [c] the destruction of constitutions and their preservation, from what sort of people they originate and what are their causes. But as a matter of fact since there have come into existence several kinds of democracy and similarly of the other forms of constitution, it will be well at the same time to consider [d] any point that remains about these varieties, and also determine the mode of organization appropriate and advantageous **2** for each. And further we must also investigate [e] the combinations of all the modes of organizing the actual departments of state that have been mentioned,[f] for these modes when coupled together make the constitutions overlap, so as to produce oligarchical aristocracies and republics inclining towards democracy. I refer to the combinations which ought to be investigated but have not at present been studied, for example if the deliberative body and the system of electing magistrates are organized oligarchically

[f] *i.e.* the deliberative, executive and judicial, see 1297 **b** 41 ff.

τὰ δικαστήρια ἀριστοκρατικῶς, ἢ ταῦτα μὲν καὶ τ
περὶ τὸ βουλευόμενον ὀλιγαρχικῶς ἀριστοκρατι
κῶς δὲ τὸ περὶ τὰς ἀρχαιρεσίας, ἢ κατ᾽ ἄλλο
10 τινὰ τρόπον μὴ πάντα συντεθῇ τὰ τῆς πολιτεία
οἰκεῖα.

Ποία μὲν οὖν δημοκρατία πρὸς ποίαν ἁρμόττε
πόλιν, ὡσαύτως δὲ καὶ ποία τῶν ὀλιγαρχιῶ
ποίῳ πλήθει, καὶ τῶν λοιπῶν δὲ πολιτειῶν τί
συμφέρει τίσιν, εἴρηται πρότερον· ὅμως δ᾽ ἐπε
δεῖ[1] γενέσθαι δῆλον μὴ μόνον ποία τούτων τῶ
15 πολιτειῶν ἀρίστη ταῖς[2] πόλεσιν ἀλλὰ καὶ πῶ
δεῖ κατασκευάζειν καὶ ταύτας καὶ τὰς ἄλλας, ἐπ
ἔλθωμεν συντόμως. καὶ πρῶτον περὶ δημοκρατία
εἴπωμεν· ἅμα γὰρ καὶ περὶ τῆς ἀντικειμένη
πολιτείας φανερόν, αὕτη δ᾽ ἐστὶν ἣν καλοῦσί τινε
ὀλιγαρχίαν.

Ληπτέον δὲ πρὸς ταύτην τὴν μέθοδον πάντα τ
20 δημοτικὰ καὶ τὰ δοκοῦντα ταῖς δημοκρατίαι
ἀκολουθεῖν· ἐκ γὰρ τούτων συντιθεμένων τὰ τῆ
δημοκρατίας εἴδη γίνεσθαι συμβαίνει, καὶ πλείου
δημοκρατίας μιᾶς εἶναι καὶ διαφόρους. δύο γά
εἰσιν αἰτίαι δι᾽ ἅσπερ αἱ δημοκρατίαι πλείου
εἰσί, πρῶτον μὲν ἡ λεχθεῖσα πρότερον, ὅτι διά
25 φοροι οἱ δῆμοι (γίνεται γὰρ τὸ μὲν γεωργικὸν πλῆθο
τὸ δὲ βάναυσον καὶ θητικόν, ὧν τοῦ πρώτου τῷ
δευτέρῳ προσλαμβανομένου καὶ τοῦ τρίτου πάλι
τοῖς ἀμφοτέροις οὐ μόνον διαφέρει τῷ βελτίω

---

[1] δ᾽ ἐπεὶ δεῖ duce Lambino ed.: δὲ δεῖ codd.
[2] ἀρίστη ταῖς: αἱρετὴ ποίαις Spengel.

---

but the regulations as to the law-courts aristocratically, or these and the structure of the deliberative body oligarchically and the election of magistracy aristocratically, or if in some other manner not all the parts of the constitution are appropriately combined.

3 Now it has been stated before [a] what kind of democracy is suited to what kind of state, and similarly which of the kinds of oligarchy is suited to what kind of populace, and also which of the remaining constitutions is advantageous for which people ; but nevertheless since it must not only be made clear which variety of these constitutions is best for states, but also how both these best varieties and the other forms must be established, let us briefly pursue the subject. And first let us speak about democracy ; for at the same time the facts will also become clear about the opposite form of constitution, that is, the constitution which some people call oligarchy.[b]

4 And for this inquiry we must take into view all the features that are popular and that are thought to go with democracies ; for it comes about from combinations of these that the kinds of democracy are formed, and that there are different democracies and more than one sort. In fact there are two causes for there being several kinds of democracy, first the one stated before, the fact that the populations are different (for we find one multitude engaged in agriculture and another consisting of handicraftsmen and day-labourers, and when the first of these is added to the second and again the third to both of them it not only makes a difference in that the

Varieties of democracy :

due to varieties of population

---

[b] ' Rule of the few,' *i.e.* the few rich, but the name is not exact, for in aristocracy also the rulers are few.

1317 a

καὶ χείρω γίνεσθαι τὴν δημοκρατίαν ἀλλὰ καὶ τῷ
μὴ τὴν αὐτήν), δευτέρα δὲ περὶ ἧς νῦν λέγομεν.

30 τὰ γὰρ ταῖς δημοκρατίαις ἀκολουθοῦντα καὶ
δοκοῦντα εἶναι τῆς πολιτείας οἰκεῖα ταύτης ποιεῖ
συντιθέμενα τὰς δημοκρατίας ἑτέρας· τῇ μὲν γὰρ
ἐλάττω τῇ δ' ἀκολουθήσει πλείονα τῇ δ' ἅπαντα
ταῦτα. χρήσιμον δ' ἕκαστον αὐτῶν γνωρίζειν
πρός τε τὸ κατασκευάζειν ἣν ἄν τις αὐτῶν τύχῃ

35 βουλόμενος, καὶ πρὸς τὰς διορθώσεις. ζητοῦσι
μὲν γὰρ οἱ τὰς πολιτείας καθιστάντες ἅπαντα τὰ
οἰκεῖα συναγαγεῖν πρὸς τὴν ὑπόθεσιν, ἁμαρτάνουσι
δὲ τοῦτο ποιοῦντες, καθάπερ ἐν τοῖς περὶ τὰς
φθορὰς καὶ τὰς σωτηρίας τῶν πολιτειῶν εἴρηται
πρότερον. νυνὶ δὲ τὰ ἀξιώματα καὶ τὰ ἤθη καὶ
ὧν ἐφίενται λέγωμεν.

40 Ὑπόθεσις μὲν οὖν τῆς δημοκρατικῆς πολιτείας
ἐλευθερία· τοῦτο γὰρ λέγειν εἰώθασιν, ὡς ἐν μόνῃ

1317 b τῇ πολιτείᾳ ταύτῃ μετέχοντας ἐλευθερίας, τούτου
γὰρ στοχάζεσθαί φασι πᾶσαν δημοκρατίαν. ἐλευθερίας δὲ ἓν μὲν τὸ ἐν μέρει ἄρχεσθαι καὶ ἄρχειν·
καὶ γὰρ τὸ δίκαιον τὸ δημοτικὸν τὸ ἴσον ἔχειν ἐστὶ

5 κατ' ἀριθμὸν ἀλλὰ μὴ κατ' ἀξίαν, τούτου δ' ὄντος
τοῦ δικαίου τὸ πλῆθος ἀναγκαῖον εἶναι κύριον καὶ
ὅ τι ἂν δόξῃ τοῖς πλείοσι τοῦτ' εἶναι τέλος[1] καὶ
τοῦτ' εἶναι[2] τὸ δίκαιον, φασὶ γὰρ δεῖν ἴσον ἔχειν
ἕκαστον τῶν πολιτῶν· ὥστε ἐν ταῖς δημοκρατίαις
συμβαίνει κυριωτέρους εἶναι τοὺς ἀπόρους τῶν
εὐπόρων, πλείους γάρ εἰσι κύριον δὲ τὸ τοῖς

---

[1] εἶναι καὶ τέλος codd. cett.
[2] καὶ τοῦτ' εἶναι post 7 πολιτῶν Richards.

quality of the democracy becomes better or worse but also by its becoming different in kind); and the second cause is the one about which we now speak.

For the institutions that go with democracies and seem to be appropriate to this form of constitution make the democracies different by their combinations; for one form of democracy will be accompanied by fewer, another by more, and another by all of them. And it is serviceable to ascertain each of them both for the purpose of instituting whichever of these kinds of democracy one happens to wish and for the purpose of amending existing ones. For people setting up constitutions seek to collect together all the features appropriate to their fundamental principle, but in so doing they make a mistake, as has been said before in the passage dealing with the causes of the destruction and the preservation of constitutions. And now let us state the postulates, the ethical characters and the aims of the various forms of democracy.

Now a fundamental principle of the democratic form of constitution is liberty—that is what is usually asserted, implying that only under this constitution do men participate in liberty, for they assert this as the aim of every democracy. But one factor of liberty is to govern and be governed in turn; for the popular principle of justice is to have equality according to number, not worth, and if this is the principle of justice prevailing, the multitude must of necessity be sovereign and the decision of the majority must be final and must constitute justice, for they say that each of the citizens ought to have an equal share; so that it results that in democracies the poor are more powerful than the rich, because there are more of them and whatever is decided by the majority

and of constitutional structure.

1309 b 18 ff.

Democracy is based on liberty to govern in turn and to live as you like.

10 πλείοσι δόξαν. ἐν μὲν οὖν τῆς ἐλευθερίας σημεῖον 7
τοῦτο ὂν τίθενται πάντες οἱ δημοτικοὶ τῆς πολιτείας ὅρον, ἐν δὲ τὸ ζῆν ὡς βούλεταί τις· τοῦτο
γὰρ τῆς ἐλευθερίας ἔργον¹ εἶναί φασιν, εἴπερ τοῦ
δούλου ὄντος τὸ ζῆν μὴ ὡς βούλεται. τῆς μὲν
οὖν δημοκρατίας ὅρος οὗτος δεύτερος· ἐντεῦθεν δ'
15 ἐλήλυθε τὸ μὴ ἄρχεσθαι, μάλιστα μὲν ὑπὸ μηθενός,
εἰ δὲ μή, κατὰ μέρος· καὶ συμβάλλεται ταύτῃ
πρὸς τὴν ἐλευθερίαν τὴν κατὰ τὸ ἴσον.² τούτων δ' 8
ὑποκειμένων καὶ τοιαύτης οὔσης τῆς ἀρχῆς, τὰ
τοιαῦτα δημοτικά· τὸ αἱρεῖσθαι τὰς ἀρχὰς πάντας
20 ἐκ πάντων, τὸ ἄρχειν πάντας μὲν ἑκάστου ἕκαστον
δ' ἐν μέρει πάντων, τὸ κληρωτὰς εἶναι τὰς ἀρχὰς
ἢ πάσας ἢ ὅσαι μὴ ἐμπειρίας δέονται καὶ τέχνης,
τὸ μὴ ἀπὸ τιμήματος μηθενὸς εἶναι τὰς ἀρχὰς
ἢ ὅτι μικροτάτου, τὸ μὴ δὶς τὸν αὐτὸν ἄρχειν
μηδεμίαν ἢ ὀλιγάκις ἢ ὀλίγας ἔξω τῶν κατὰ
25 πόλεμον, τὸ ὀλιγοχρονίους τὰς ἀρχὰς ἢ πάσας ἢ
ὅσας ἐνδέχεται, τὸ δικάζειν πάντας καὶ³ ἐκ πάντων,
καὶ⁴ περὶ πάντων ἢ περὶ τῶν πλείστων καὶ τῶν
μεγίστων καὶ τῶν κυριωτάτων, οἷον περὶ εὐθυνῶν
καὶ πολιτείας καὶ τῶν ἰδίων συναλλαγμάτων, τὸ
30 τὴν ἐκκλησίαν κυρίαν εἶναι πάντων ἀρχὴν δὲ
μηδεμίαν μηθενὸς ἢ ὅτι ὀλιγίστων, ἢ τῶν μεγίστων βουλὴν κυρίαν⁵ (τῶν δ' ἀρχῶν δημοτικώτατον ᵃ
βουλὴ ὅπου μὴ μισθοῦ εὐπορία πᾶσιν· ἐνταῦθα
γὰρ ἀφαιροῦνται καὶ ταύτης τῆς ἀρχῆς τὴν δύναμιν,
εἰς αὑτὸν γὰρ ἀνάγει τὰς κρίσεις πάσας ὁ δῆμος

---

¹ v.l. τὸ ἔργον : τοῦτον ? ed. et ὅρον ? Richards.
² [καὶ—ἴσον] ? ed.   ³ καὶ : ἢ Γ.   ⁴ [καὶ] Wilamowitz.
⁵ βουλὴν κυρίαν Immisch : κυρίαν codd.

ᵃ This clause is obscure : perhaps it is an interpolation.

is sovereign. This then is one mark of liberty which all democrats set down as a principle of the constitution. And one is for a man to live as he likes ; for they say that this is the function of liberty, inasmuch as to live not as one likes is the life of a man that is a slave. This is the second principle of democracy, and from it has come the claim not to be governed, preferably not by anybody, or failing that, to govern and be governed in turns ; and this is the way in which the second principle contributes to equalitarian liberty.[a] And these principles having been laid down and this being the nature of democratic government, the following institutions are democratic in character : election of officials by all from all ; government of each by all, and of all by each in turn ; election by lot either to all magistracies or to all that do not need experience and skill ; no property-qualification for office, or only a very low one ; no office to be held twice, or more than a few times, by the same person, or few offices except the military ones ; short tenure either of all offices or of as many as possible ; judicial functions to be exercised by all citizens, that is by persons selected from all, and on all matters, or on most and the greatest and most important, for instance the audit of official accounts, constitutional questions, private contracts ; the assembly to be sovereign over all matters, but no official over any or only over extremely few ; or else a council to be sovereign over the most important matters (and a council is the most democratic of magistracies in states where there is not a plentiful supply of pay for everybody—for where there is, they deprive even this office of its power, since the people draws all the trials to itself when it has plenty

*Character-
istics and
details of
democracy*

491

1317 b

εὐπορῶν μισθοῦ, καθάπερ εἴρηται πρότερον ἐν τ[

μεθόδῳ τῇ πρὸ ταύτης), ἔπειτα τὸ μισθοφορεῖ

35 μάλιστα μὲν πάντας, ἐκκλησίαν δικαστήρια ἀρχάς

εἰ δὲ μή, τὰς ἀρχὰς καὶ τὰ δικαστήρια καὶ τὴ[

βουλὴν καὶ τὰς ἐκκλησίας τὰς κυρίας, ἢ τῶ[

ἀρχῶν ἃς ἀνάγκη συσσιτεῖν μετ᾽ ἀλλήλων. ἔτ[

ἐπειδὴ ὀλιγαρχία καὶ γένει καὶ πλούτῳ καὶ παιδεί[

40 ὁρίζεται, τὰ δημοτικὰ δοκεῖ τἀναντία τούτω[

εἶναι, ἀγένεια πενία βαναυσία. ἐπὶ δὲ τῶν ἀρχῶ[

1318 a τὸ μηδεμίαν ἀίδιον εἶναι· ἐὰν δέ τις καταλειφθῇ[

ἐξ ἀρχαίας μεταβολῆς, τό γε[1] περιαιρεῖσθαι τὴ[

δύναμιν αὐτῆς καὶ ἐξ αἱρετῶν κληρωτοὺς ποιεῖν.

Τὰ μὲν[2] οὖν κοινὰ ταῖς δημοκρατίαις ταῦτ᾽

ἐστί· συμβαίνει δ᾽ ἐκ τοῦ δικαίου τοῦ ὁμο-

5 λογουμένου εἶναι δημοκρατικοῦ (τοῦτο δ᾽ ἐστὶ τ[

ἴσον ἔχειν ἅπαντας κατ᾽ ἀριθμόν) ἡ μάλιστ᾽ εἶνα[

δοκοῦσα δημοκρατία καὶ δῆμος. ἴσον γὰρ τὸ μηθὲ[

μᾶλλον ἄρχειν τοὺς ἀπόρους ἢ τοὺς εὐπόρους

μηδὲ κυρίους εἶναι μόνους ἀλλὰ πάντας ἐξ ἴσο[

[κατ᾽ ἀριθμόν][3]· οὕτω γὰρ ἂν ὑπάρχειν νομίζοιε[

10 τήν τ᾽ ἰσότητα τῇ πολιτείᾳ καὶ τὴν ἐλευθερίαν

τὸ δὲ μετὰ τοῦτο ἀπορεῖται, πῶς ἕξουσι τ[

ἴσον; πότερον δεῖ τὰ τιμήματα διελεῖν χιλίοις[4] τ[

τῶν πεντακοσίων καὶ τοὺς χιλίους ἴσον δύνασθα[

τοῖς πεντακοσίοις; ἢ οὐχ οὕτω δεῖ τιθέναι τὴ[

---

[1] τό γε Coraes : τότε codd.
[2] τὰ μὲν—b 5 φροντίζουσιν secl. Susemihl.   [3] ed.
[4] διελεῖν ⟨ἰσοῦντα τοῖς⟩ χιλίοις ? Richards.

---

[a] Book IV. 1299 b 38 ff. (Books IV. and V. are regarded

as forming one treatise.)

[b] i.e. owing to the nature of their duties, and by genera[l]

custom.

of pay, as has been said before in the treatise preceding this one [a]) ; also payment for public duties, preferably in all branches, assembly, law-courts, magistracies, or if not, for the magistracies, the law-courts, council and sovereign assemblies, or for those magistracies which are bound [b] to have common messtables. Also inasmuch as oligarchy is defined by birth, wealth and education, the popular qualifications are thought to be the opposite of these, low birth, poverty, vulgarity. And in respect of the magistracies it is democratic to have none tenable for life, and if any life-office has been left after an ancient revolution, at all events to deprive it of its power and to substitute election by lot for election by vote.

[c] These then are the features common to democracies. But what is thought to be the extreme form of democracy and of popular government comes about as a result of the principle of justice that is admitted to be democratic, and this is for all to have equality according to number. For it is equality for the poor to have no larger share of power than the rich, and not for the poor alone to be supreme but for all to govern equally ; for in this way they would feel that the constitution possessed both equality and liberty. But the question follows, how will they have equality? are the property-assessments of five hundred citizens to be divided among a thousand and the thousand to have equal power to the five hundred [d] ? or is

Equality according to number and to wealth.

---

[c] The rest of the chapter is most obscure, and its authenticity is questioned.

[d] *i.e.* two groups of voters, with equal total wealth and total voting-power, but one group twice as numerous as the other, so that a man in the rich group has two votes and one in the poor group one, the former being on the average twice as rich as the latter.

15 κατὰ τοῦτο ἰσότητα, ἀλλὰ διελεῖν μὲν οὕτως,
ἔπειτα ἐκ τῶν πεντακοσίων ἴσους λαβόντα καὶ ἐκ
τῶν χιλίων, τούτους κυρίους εἶναι τῶν αἱρέσεων[1]
καὶ τῶν δικαστηρίων; πότερον οὖν αὕτη ἡ πολιτεία δικαιοτάτη κατὰ τὸ δημοτικὸν δίκαιον, ἢ
μᾶλλον ἡ κατὰ τὸ πλῆθος; φασὶ γὰρ οἱ δημοτικοὶ
20 τοῦτο δίκαιον ὅ τι ἂν δόξῃ τοῖς πλείοσιν, οἱ δ᾽
ὀλιγαρχικοὶ ὅ τι ἂν δόξῃ τῇ πλείονι οὐσίᾳ, κατὰ
πλῆθος γὰρ οὐσίας φασὶ κρίνεσθαι δεῖν. ἔχει δ᾽
ἀμφότερα ἀνισότητα καὶ ἀδικίαν· εἰ μὲν γὰρ ὅ τι
ἂν οἱ ὀλίγοι, τυραννίς, καὶ γὰρ ἐὰν εἷς ἔχῃ πλείω
τῶν ἄλλων εὐπόρων, κατὰ τὸ ὀλιγαρχικὸν δίκαιον
25 ἄρχειν δίκαιος μόνος· εἰ δ᾽ ὅ τι ἂν οἱ πλείους κατ᾽
ἀριθμόν, ἀδικήσουσι δημεύοντες τὰ τῶν πλουσίων
καὶ ἐλαττόνων, καθάπερ εἴρηται πρότερον. τίς ἂν
οὖν εἴη ἰσότης ἣν ὁμολογήσουσιν ἀμφότεροι, σκεπτέον ἐξ ὧν ὁρίζονται δικαίων ἀμφότεροι. λέγουσι
γὰρ ὡς ὅ τι ἂν δόξῃ τοῖς πλείοσι τῶν πολιτῶν
30 τοῦτ᾽ εἶναι δεῖ κύριον. ἔστω δὴ τοῦτο, μὴ μέντοι
πάντως, ἀλλ᾽ ἐπειδὴ δύο μέρη τετύχηκεν ἐξ ὧν ἡ
πόλις, πλούσιοι καὶ πένητες, ὅ τι ἂν ἀμφοτέροις
δόξῃ ἢ τοῖς πλείοσι τοῦτο κύριον ἔστω, ἐὰν δὲ
τἀναντία δόξῃ, ὅ τι ἂν οἱ πλείους καὶ ὧν τὸ

---

[1] αἱρέσεων Camotius: διαιρέσεων codd.

- i.e. 'equality in proportion to number.'
- i.e. 'one man one vote.'
- i.e. apparently, more than the property of all the others
put together.   d 1281 a 14.

equality on this principle *a* not to be arranged in his manner, but the division into classes to be on his system, but then an equal number to be taken from the five hundred and from the thousand and these to control the elections and the law-courts? Is this then the justest form of constitution in accordance with popular justice, or is it rather one that goes by counting heads? *b* For democrats say that justice is whatever seems good to the larger number, but advocates of oligarchy think that it is whatever seems good to the owners of the larger amount of property, for they say that the decision ought to go by amount of property. But both views involve inequality and injustice; for if the will of the few is to prevail, this means a tyranny, since if one man owns more than the other rich men, *c* according to the oligarchic principle of justice it is just for him to rule alone; whereas if the will of the numerical majority is to prevail, they will do injustice by confiscating the property of the rich minority, as has been said before. *d* What form of equality therefore would be one on which both parties will agree must be considered in the light of the principles of justice as defined by both sets. For they say that whatever seems good to the majority of the citizens ought to be sovereign. Let us then accept this principle, yet not wholly without qualification, but inasmuch as fortune has brought into existence two component parts of the state, rich and poor, let any resolution passed by both classes, or by a majority of each, be sovereign, but if the two classes carry opposite resolutions, let the decision of the majority, in the sense of the group whose total property-assessment is the larger, prevail: for instance, if

The claim of wealth.

495

1318 a

τίμημα πλεῖον· οἷον οἱ μὲν δέκα οἱ δ᾽ εἴκοσιν
35 ἔδοξε δὲ τῶν μὲν πλουσίων τοῖς ἐξ τῶν δ᾽ ἀπορω-
τέρων τοῖς πεντεκαίδεκα, προσγεγένηνται τοῖς μὲν
πένησι τέτταρες τῶν πλουσίων τοῖς δὲ πλουσίοις
πέντε τῶν πενήτων· ὁποτέρων οὖν τὸ τίμημα
ὑπερτείνει συναριθμουμένων ἀμφοτέρων ἑκατέροις
τοῦτο κύριον. ἐὰν δὲ ἴσοι συμπέσωσι, κοινὴν
40 εἶναι ταύτην νομιστέον ἀπορίαν, ὥσπερ νῦν ἐὰν δίχα
1318 b ἡ ἐκκλησία γένηται ἢ τὸ δικαστήριον· ἢ γὰρ
ἀποκληρωτέον ἢ ἄλλο τι τοιοῦτον ποιητέον. ἀλλὰ
περὶ μὲν τοῦ ἴσου καὶ τοῦ δικαίου, κἂν ᾖ πάνυ
χαλεπὸν εὑρεῖν τὴν ἀλήθειαν περὶ αὐτῶν, ὅμως
5 ῥᾷον τυχεῖν ἢ συμπεῖσαι τοὺς δυναμένους πλεον-
εκτεῖν· ἀεὶ γὰρ ζητοῦσι τὸ ἴσον καὶ τὸ δίκαιον οἱ
ἥττους, οἱ δὲ κρατοῦντες οὐδὲν φροντίζουσιν.

II. Δημοκρατιῶν δ᾽ οὐσῶν τεττάρων βελτίστη
μὲν ἡ πρώτη τάξει, καθάπερ ἐν τοῖς πρὸ τούτων
ἐλέχθη λόγοις· ἔστι δὲ καὶ ἀρχαιοτάτη πασῶν
αὕτη, λέγω δὲ πρώτην ὥσπερ ἄν τις διέλοι τοὺς
10 δήμους. βέλτιστος γὰρ δῆμος ὁ γεωργικός ἐστιν,
ὥστε καὶ ποιεῖν[1] ἐνδέχεται δημοκρατίαν ὅπου ζῇ
τὸ πλῆθος ἀπὸ γεωργίας ἢ νομῆς. διὰ μὲν γὰρ τὸ
μὴ πολλὴν οὐσίαν ἔχειν ἄσχολος, ὥστε μὴ πολλάκις ἐκκλησιάζειν, διὰ δὲ τὸ[2] ἔχειν τἀναγκαῖα

---

[1] ⟨χρήστην⟩ ποιεῖν (cf. 1319 a 34) Richards.
[2] τὸ Bojesen : τὸ μὴ codd.

---

[a] If the rich citizens are on the average twice as wealthy
as the poor (§ 11), and therefore a rich man has two votes to
a poor man's one, when 6 rich and 5 poor vote one way,
and 15 poor and 4 rich the other, the division is 17 to 23, and
the view of the latter party, which is carried, represents a
larger total of wealth but a larger proportion of poor men.
[b] Cf. IV., 1291 b 30-41, 1292 b 25-33.

496

there are ten rich citizens and twenty poor ones, and
opposite votes have been cast by six of the rich on
one side and by fifteen of the less wealthy on the
other, four of the rich have sided with the poor and
five of the poor with the rich ; then the side that has
the larger total property when the assessments of
both classes on either side are added together carries
4 the voting.*a* But if the totals fall out exactly equal,
this is to be deemed an *impasse* common to both sides,
as it is at present if the assembly or law-court is
exactly divided ; either a decision must be made by
casting lots or some other such device must be adopted.
But on questions of equality and justice, even though
it is very difficult to discover the truth about them,
nevertheless it is easier to hit upon it than to persuade
people that have the power to get an advantage to
agree to it ; equality and justice are always sought
by the weaker party, but those that have the upper
hand pay no attention to them.

1 II. There being four kinds of democracy, the best Agricultural
is the one that stands first in structure, as was said democracy
in the discourses preceding these *b* ; it is also the the best.
oldest of them all, but by first I mean first as it were
in a classification of the kinds of common people.
The best common people are the agricultural population, so that it is possible to introduce democracy
as well as other forms of constitution where the multitude lives by agriculture or by pasturing cattle.
For owing to their not having much property they
are busy, so that they cannot often meet in the
assembly, while owing to their having *c* the necessaries of life they pass their time attending to their

---

c The MSS. give ' not having,' but editors do not explain
how in that case people would avoid starvation.

1318 b

πρὸς τοῖς ἔργοις διατρίβουσι καὶ τῶν ἀλλοτρίων
15 οὐκ ἐπιθυμοῦσιν, ἀλλ' ἥδιον τὸ ἐργάζεσθαι τοῖ
πολιτεύεσθαι καὶ ἄρχειν, ὅπου ἂν μὴ ᾖ λήμματα
μεγάλα ἀπὸ τῶν ἀρχῶν· οἱ γὰρ πολλοὶ μᾶλλον
ὀρέγονται τοῦ κέρδους ἢ τῆς τιμῆς. σημεῖον δέ·
καὶ γὰρ τὰς ἀρχαίας τυραννίδας ὑπέμενον καὶ τὰς
ὀλιγαρχίας ὑπομένουσιν, ἐάν τις αὐτοὺς ἐργά-
20 ζεσθαι μὴ κωλύῃ μηδ' ἀφαιρῆται μηθέν· ταχέως
γὰρ οἱ μὲν πλουτοῦσιν αὐτῶν οἱ δ' οὐκ ἀποροῦσιν.
ἔτι δὲ τὸ κυρίους εἶναι τοῦ ἑλέσθαι καὶ εὐθύνειν
ἀναπληροῖ τὴν ἔνδειαν εἴ τι φιλοτιμίας ἔχουσιν,
ἐπεὶ παρ' ἐνίοις δήμοις, κἂν μὴ μετέχωσι τῆς
αἱρέσεως τῶν ἀρχῶν ἀλλά τινες αἱρετοὶ κατὰ
25 μέρος ἐκ πάντων, ὥσπερ ἐν Μαντινείᾳ, τοῦ δὲ
βουλεύεσθαι κύριοι ὦσιν, ἱκανῶς ἔχει τοῖς πολλοῖς
(καὶ δεῖ νομίζειν καὶ τοῦτ' εἶναι σχῆμά τι δημοκρατίας, ὥσπερ ἐν Μαντινείᾳ ποτ' ἦν). διὸ δὴ καὶ
συμφέρον ἐστὶ τῇ πρότερον ῥηθείσῃ δημοκρατίᾳ
καὶ ὑπάρχειν εἴωθεν, αἱρεῖσθαι μὲν τὰς ἀρχὰς καὶ
30 εὐθύνειν καὶ δικάζειν πάντας, ἄρχειν δὲ τὰς
μεγίστας αἱρετοὺς καὶ ἀπὸ τιμημάτων, τὰς
μείζους ἀπὸ μειζόνων, ἢ καὶ ἀπὸ τιμημάτων
μὲν μηδεμίαν, ἀλλὰ τοὺς δυναμένους. ἀνάγκη δὲ
πολιτευομένους οὕτω πολιτεύεσθαι καλῶς (αἵ τε[1]
γὰρ ἀρχαὶ ἀεὶ διὰ τῶν βελτίστων ἔσονται τοῦ
35 δήμου βουλομένου καὶ τοῖς ἐπιεικέσιν οὐ φθονοῦν-
τος), καὶ τοῖς ἐπιεικέσι καὶ γνωρίμοις ἀρκοῦσαν

---

[1] τε ante καλῶς transposuit Richards.

farmwork and do not covet their neighbours' goods,
but find more pleasure in working than in taking part
in politics and holding office, where the profits to be
made from the offices are not large ; for the mass of
mankind are more covetous of gain than of honour.
And this is indicated by the fact that men endured
the tyrannies of former times, and endure oligarchies,
if a ruler does not prevent them from working or rob
them ; for then some of them soon get rich and the
others free from want. And also, if they have any
ambition, to have control over electing magistrates
and calling them to account makes up for the lack
of office, since in some democracies even if the people
have no part in electing the magistrates but these
are elected by a special committee selected in turn
out of the whole number, as at Mantinea, yet if they
have the power of deliberating on policy, the multitude are satisfied. (And this too must be counted as
one form of democracy, on the lines on which it once
existed at Mantinea.) Indeed it is for this reason
that it is advantageous for the form of democracy
spoken of before, and is a customary institution in it,
for all the citizens to elect the magistrates and call
them to account, and to try law-suits, but for the
holders of the greatest magistracies to be elected and
to have property-qualifications, the higher offices
being elected from the higher property-grades, or else
for no office to be elected on a property-qualification,
but for officials to be chosen on the ground of
capacity. And a state governed in this way is bound
to be governed well (for the offices will always be
administered by the best men with the consent of the
people and without their being jealous of the upper
classes), and this arrangement is certain to be satis-

1318 b

εἶναι ταύτην τὴν τάξιν, ἄρξονται γὰρ οὐχ ὑπ'
ἄλλων χειρόνων, καὶ ἄρξουσι δικαίως διὰ τὸ τῶν
εὐθυνῶν εἶναι κυρίους ἑτέρους· τὸ γὰρ ἐπανα-
κρέμασθαι καὶ μὴ πᾶν ἐξεῖναι ποιεῖν ὅ τι ἂν δόξῃ
40 συμφέρον ἐστίν, ἡ γὰρ ἐξουσία τοῦ πράττειν ὅ τι

1319 a ἂν ἐθέλῃ τις οὐ δύναται φυλάττειν τὸ ἐν ἑκάστῳ
τῶν ἀνθρώπων φαῦλον. ὥστε ἀναγκαῖον συμβαίνειν ὅπερ ἐστὶν ὠφελιμώτατον ἐν ταῖς πολιτείαις,
ἄρχειν τοὺς ἐπιεικεῖς ἀναμαρτήτους ὄντας μηδὲν
ἐλαττουμένου τοῦ πλήθους. ὅτι μὲν οὖν αὕτη τῶν
5 δημοκρατιῶν ἀρίστη, φανερόν, καὶ διὰ τίν' αἰτίαν,
ὅτι διὰ τὸ ποιόν τινα εἶναι τὸν δῆμον.

Πρὸς δὲ τὸ κατασκευάζειν γεωργὸν[1] τὸν δῆμον
τῶν τε νόμων τινὲς τῶν παρὰ[2] πολλοῖς κειμένων
τὸ ἀρχαῖον χρήσιμοι πάντως,[3] ἢ τὸ ὅλως μὴ
ἐξεῖναι κεκτῆσθαι πλείω γῆν μέτρου τινὸς ἢ
10 ἀπό τινος τόπου πρὸς τὸ ἄστυ καὶ τὴν πόλιν·
ἦν δὲ τό γε ἀρχαῖον ἐν πολλαῖς πόλεσι νενομοθετημένον μηδὲ πωλεῖν ἐξεῖναι τοὺς πρώτους
κλήρους· ἔστι δὲ καὶ ὃν λέγουσιν Ὀξύλου νόμον
εἶναι τοιοῦτόν τι δυνάμενος, τὸ μὴ δανείζειν εἴς
τι μέρος τῆς ὑπαρχούσης ἑκάστῳ γῆς), νῦν δὲ
5 δεῖ διορθοῦν καὶ τῷ Ἀφυταίων νόμῳ, πρὸς γὰρ
ὃ λέγομεν ἐστὶ χρήσιμος· ἐκεῖνοι γὰρ καίπερ
ὄντες πολλοὶ κεκτημένοι δὲ γῆν ὀλίγην ὅμως
πάντες γεωργοῦσιν, τιμῶνται γὰρ οὐχ ὅλας τὰς

---

[1] γεωργικὸν Richards.
[2] παρὰ Madvig: παρὰ τοῖς codd.
[3] Coraes: πάντες codd.

---

[a] Leader of the Heraclidae in their invasion of the Peloponnese, and afterwards king of Elis.
[b] Aphȳtis was on the Isthmus of Pallene in Macedonia.

factory for the upper classes and notables, for they
will not be under the government of others inferior
to themselves, and they will govern justly because
a different class will be in control of the audits—
4 since it is expedient to be in a state of suspense
and not to be able to do everything exactly as seems
good to one, for liberty to do whatever one likes
cannot guard against the evil that is in every man's
character.   Hence there necessarily results the condition of affairs that is the most advantageous in the
government of states—for the upper classes to govern
without doing wrong, the common people not being
deprived of any rights.   It is manifest therefore that
this is the best of the forms of democracy, and why
this is so—namely, because in it the common people
are of a certain kind.

5   For the purpose of making the people an agri- Provision
cultural community, not only were some of the laws of small
that were enacted in many states in early times holdings.
entirely serviceable, prohibiting the ownership of
more than a certain amount of land under any conditions or else of more than a certain amount lying
between a certain place and the citadel or city (and
in early times at all events in many states there was
even legislation prohibiting the sale of the original
allotments ;   and there is a law said to be due to
Oxylus *a* with some similar provision, forbidding loans
secured on a certain portion of a man's existing
estate), but at the present day it would also be well
to introduce reform by means of the law of the
Aphytaeans, as it is serviceable for the purpose
of which we are speaking ; the citizens of Aphytis *b*
although numerous and possessing a small territory
nevertheless are all engaged in agriculture, for they

1819 a

κτήσεις, ἀλλὰ κατὰ τηλικαῦτα μόρια διαιροῦντες ὥστ᾽ ἔχειν ὑπερβάλλειν ταῖς τιμήσεσι καὶ τοὺς πένητας.

20 Μετὰ δὲ τὸ γεωργικὸν πλῆθος βέλτιστος δῆμός ἐστιν ὅπου νομεῖς εἰσὶ καὶ ζῶσιν ἀπὸ βοσκημάτων· πολλὰ γὰρ ἔχει τῇ γεωργίᾳ παραπλησίως, καὶ τὰ πρὸς τὰς πολεμικὰς πράξεις μάλισθ᾽ οὗτοι γεγυμνασμένοι τὰς ἕξεις καὶ χρήσιμοι τὰ σώματα καὶ δυνάμενοι θυραυλεῖν. τὰ δ᾽ ἄλλα

25 πλήθη πάντα σχεδὸν ἐξ ὧν αἱ λοιπαὶ δημοκρατίαι συνεστᾶσι πολλῷ φαυλότερα τούτων· ὁ γὰρ βίος φαῦλος, καὶ οὐθὲν ἔργον μετ᾽ ἀρετῆς ὧν μεταχειρίζεται τὸ πλῆθος τό τε τῶν βαναύσων καὶ τὸ τῶν ἀγοραίων ἀνθρώπων καὶ τὸ θητικόν, ἔτι δὲ διὰ τὸ περὶ τὴν ἀγορὰν καὶ τὸ ἄστυ κυ-

80 λίεσθαι πᾶν τὸ τοιοῦτον γένος ὡς εἰπεῖν ῥᾳδίως ἐκκλησιάζει· οἱ δὲ γεωργοῦντες διὰ τὸ διεσπάρθαι κατὰ τὴν χώραν οὔτ᾽ ἀπαντῶσιν οὔθ᾽ ὁμοίως δέονται τῆς συνόδου ταύτης. ὅπου δὲ καὶ συμβαίνει τὴν χώραν τὴν θέσιν ἔχειν τοιαύτην ὥστε τὴν χώραν πολὺ τῆς πόλεως ἀπηρτῆσθαι, ῥᾴδιον

85 καὶ δημοκρατίαν ποιεῖσθαι χρηστὴν καὶ πολιτείαν, ἀναγκάζεται γὰρ τὸ πλῆθος ἐπὶ τῶν ἀγρῶν ποιεῖσθαι τὰς ἀποικίας· ὥστε δεῖ, κἂν ἀγοραῖος ὄχλος ᾖ, μὴ ποιεῖν[1] ἐν ταῖς δημοκρατίαις ἐκκλησίας[2] ἄνευ τοῦ κατὰ τὴν χώραν πλήθους.

Πῶς μὲν οὖν δεῖ κατασκευάζειν τὴν βελτίστην

[1] ἐπιπολάζειν vel πλεονάζειν Immisch.
[2] Lambinus: δημοκρατικαῖς ἐκκλησίαις codd.

---

[a] No satisfactory explanation seems to have been suggested of what this means.

[b] i.e. in a largely agricultural democracy, even though

502

are assessed not on the whole of their estates, but on divisions of them so small that even the poor can exceed the required minimum in their assessments.[a]

After the agricultural community the best kind of democracy is where the people are herdsmen and get their living from cattle ; for this life has many points of resemblance to agriculture, and as regards military duties pastoral people are in a very well trained condition and serviceable in body and capable of living in the open. But almost all the other classes of populace, of which the remaining kinds of democracy are composed, are very inferior to these, for their mode of life is mean, and there is no element of virtue in any of the occupations in which the multitude of artisans and market-people and the wage-earning class take part, and also owing to their loitering about the market-place and the city almost all people of this class find it easy to attend the assembly ; whereas the farmers owing to their being scattered over the country do not attend, and have not an equal desire for this opportunity of meeting. And where it also happens that the lie of the land is such that the country is widely separated from the city, it is easy to establish a good democracy and also a good constitutional government, for the multitude is forced to live at a distance on the farms ; and so, even if there is a crowd that frequents the market-place, it is best in democracies not to hold assemblies without the multitude scattered over the country.[b]

It has then been stated how the best and first

The three inferior democracies

there may be a considerable idle population, which would attend frequent assemblies, it is best to hold them infrequently, so as to secure the attendance of the farmers.

40 καὶ πρώτην δημοκρατίαν εἴρηται· φανερὸν δὲ καὶ
1319 b πῶς τὰς ἄλλας· ἑπομένως γὰρ δεῖ παρεκβαίνειν
καὶ τὸ χεῖρον ἀεὶ πλῆθος χωρίζειν. τὴν δὲ τελευταίαν, διὰ τὸ πάντας κοινωνεῖν, οὔτε πάσης ἐστὶ
πόλεως φέρειν οὔτε ῥᾴδιον διαμένειν μὴ τοῖς
νόμοις καὶ τοῖς ἔθεσιν εὖ συγκειμένην (ἃ δὲ
5 φθείρειν συμβαίνει καὶ ταύτην καὶ τὰς ἄλλας
πολιτείας, εἴρηται πρότερον τὰ πλεῖστα σχεδόν)
πρὸς δὲ τὸ καθιστάναι ταύτην τὴν δημοκρατίαν
καὶ τὸν δῆμον ποιεῖν ἰσχυρὸν εἰώθασιν οἱ προ-
εστῶτες προσλαμβάνειν ὡς πλείστους καὶ ποιεῖν
πολίτας μὴ μόνον τοὺς γνησίους ἀλλὰ καὶ τοὺς
10 νόθους καὶ τοὺς ἐξ ὁποτερουοῦν πολίτου, λέγω δὲ
οἷον πατρὸς ἢ μητρός· ἅπαν γὰρ οἰκεῖον τοῦτο
τῷ τοιούτῳ δήμῳ μᾶλλον. εἰώθασι μὲν οὖν οἱ
δημαγωγοὶ κατασκευάζειν οὕτως· δεῖ μέντοι προσλαμβάνειν μέχρις ἂν ὑπερτείνῃ τὸ πλῆθος τῶν
15 γνωρίμων καὶ τῶν μέσων καὶ τούτου μὴ πέρα
προβαίνειν· ὑπερβάλλοντες γὰρ ἀτακτοτέραν τε
ποιοῦσι τὴν πολιτείαν, καὶ τοὺς γνωρίμους πρὸς
τὸ χαλεπῶς ὑπομένειν τὴν δημοκρατίαν παρ-
οξύνουσι μᾶλλον, ὅπερ συνέβη τῆς στάσεως αἴτιον
γενέσθαι περὶ Κυρήνην· ὀλίγον μὲν γὰρ πονηρὸν
20 παρορᾶται, πολὺ δὲ γινόμενον ἐν ὀφθαλμοῖς
μᾶλλόν ἐστιν. ἔτι δὲ καὶ τὰ τοιαῦτα κατασκευά-
σματα χρήσιμα πρὸς τὴν δημοκρατίαν τὴν τοιαύτην οἷς Κλεισθένης τε Ἀθήνησιν ἐχρήσατο βουλόμενος αὐξῆσαι τὴν δημοκρατίαν καὶ περὶ Κυρήνην

---

[a] In Book V.

[b] In N. Africa. Diodorus (xiv. 34) describes a revolution
there in 401 B.C., when five hundred of the rich were put to
death and others fled, but after a battle a compromise was
arranged.
504

kind of democracy is to be organized, and it is clear
how we ought to organize the other kinds also. For
they must diverge in a corresponding order, and at
each stage we must admit the next inferior class.
9 The last kind of democracy, because all the popula- *The last
tion share in the government, it is not within the* and worst
power of every state to endure, and it is not easy *democracy
for it to persist if it is not well constituted in its laws
and customs (but the things that result in destroying
both this state and the other forms of constitution
have been nearly all of them spoken of before*[a]).
With a view to setting up this kind of democracy
and making the people powerful their leaders usually
acquire as many supporters as possible and admit to
citizenship not only the legitimate children of citizens
but also the base-born and those of citizen-birth on
one side, I mean those whose father or mother is a
citizen; for all this element is specially congenial to a
democracy of this sort. Popular leaders therefore *Dem-
regularly introduce such institutions; they ought how-* agogues.
ever only to go on adding citizens up to the point
where the multitude outnumbers the notables and
the middle class and not to go beyond that point;
for if they exceed it they make the government
more disorderly, and also provoke the notables
further in the direction of being reluctant to endure
the democracy, which actually took place and caused
the revolution at Cyrene[b]; for a small base element
is overlooked, but when it grows numerous it is more
in evidence. A democracy of this kind will also
find useful such institutions as were employed by
Cleisthenes[c] at Athens when he wished to increase
the power of the democracy, and by the party setting

[c] See 1275 b 36 n.

1319 b οἱ τὸν δῆμον καθιστάντες· φυλαί τε γὰρ ἕτεραι
ποιητέαι πλείους καὶ φρατρίαι, καὶ τὰ τῶν ἰδίων
25 ἱερῶν συνακτέον εἰς ὀλίγα καὶ κοινά, καὶ πάντα
σοφιστέον ὅπως ἂν ὅτι μάλιστα ἀναμιχθῶσι
πάντες ἀλλήλοις αἱ δὲ συνήθειαι διαζευχθῶσιν
αἱ πρότερον. ἔτι δὲ καὶ τὰ τυραννικὰ κατα- 1.
σκευάσματα δημοτικὰ δοκεῖ πάντα, λέγω δ' οἷον
ἀναρχία τε δούλων (αὕτη δ' ἂν εἴη μέχρι του
30 συμφέρουσα) καὶ γυναικῶν καὶ παίδων, καὶ τὸ
ζῆν ὅπως τις βούλεται παρορᾶν· πολὺ γὰρ ἔσται
τὸ τῇ τοιαύτῃ πολιτείᾳ βοηθοῦν, ἥδιον γὰρ τοῖς
πολλοῖς τὸ ζῆν ἀτάκτως ἢ τὸ σωφρόνως.

III. Ἔστι δὲ [ἔργον][1] τοῦ νομοθέτου καὶ τῶν ▶
βουλομένων συνιστάναι τινὰ τοιαύτην πολιτείαν
35 οὐ τὸ καταστῆσαι μέγιστον ἔργον οὐδὲ μόνον, ἀλλ'
ὅπως σῴζηται μᾶλλον· μίαν γὰρ ἢ δύο ἢ τρεῖς
ἡμέρας οὐ χαλεπὸν μεῖναι πολιτευομένους ὁπωσοῦν.
διὸ δεῖ περὶ ὧν τεθεώρηται πρότερον, τίνες σωτηρίαι καὶ φθοραὶ τῶν πολιτειῶν, ἐκ τούτων πειρᾶσθαι κατασκευάζειν τὴν ἀσφάλειαν, εὐλαβουμέ-
40 νους μὲν τὰ φθείροντα, τιθεμένους δὲ τοιούτους
1320 a νόμους καὶ τοὺς ἀγράφους καὶ τοὺς γεγραμμένους
οἳ περιλήψονται μάλιστα τὰ σῴζοντα τὰς πολιτείας, καὶ μὴ νομίζειν τοῦτ' εἶναι δημοτικὸν μηδ'
ὀλιγαρχικὸν ὃ ποιήσει τὴν πόλιν ὅτι μάλιστα
δημοκρατεῖσθαι ἢ ὀλιγαρχεῖσθαι, ἀλλ' ὃ πλεῖστον
5 χρόνον. οἱ δὲ νῦν δημαγωγοὶ χαριζόμενοι τοῖς

---

[1] Scaliger.

up the democracy at Cyrene; different tribes and
brotherhoods must be created outnumbering the
old ones, and the celebrations of private religious
rites must be grouped together into a small number
of public celebrations, and every device must be
employed to make all the people as much as possible
intermingled with one another, and to break up the
previously existing groups of associates. Moreover
the characteristics of a tyranny also are all thought
to be democratic, I mean for instance licence among
slaves, which may really be advantageous for the
popular party up to a point, and among women
and children, and indulgence to live as one likes; a
constitution of this sort will have a large number of
supporters, as disorderly living is pleasanter to the
mass of mankind than sober living.

III. But it is not the greatest or only task of the Safe-
legislator or of those who desire to construct a consti- guards of
tution of this kind merely to set it up, but rather to democracy.
ensure its preservation; for it is not difficult for any
form of constitution to last for one or two or three
days. We must therefore employ the results obtained in the inquiries that we have made already [a]
into the causes of the preservation and the destruction of constitutions, and attempt in the light of
those results to establish the safety of the state,
carefully avoiding the things that cause destruction,
and enacting such laws both written and unwritten
as shall best compass the results preservative of
constitutions, and not think that a measure is democratic or oligarchic which will cause the state to
be democratically or oligarchically governed in the
greatest degree, but which will cause it to be so
governed for the longest time. But the demagogues

1320 a δήμοις πολλὰ δημεύουσι διὰ τῶν δικαστηρίων. διὸ δεῖ πρὸς ταῦτα ἀντιπράττειν τοὺς κηδομένους τῆς πολιτείας, νομοθετοῦντας μηδὲν εἶναι δημόσιον τῶν καταδικαζομένων καὶ φερόμενον[1] πρὸς τὸ κοινόν, ἀλλ' ἱερόν· οἱ μὲν γὰρ ἀδικοῦντες

10 οὐδὲν ἧττον εὐλαβεῖς ἔσονται (ζημιώσονται γὰρ ὁμοίως), ὁ δ' ὄχλος ἧττον καταψηφιεῖται τῶν κρινομένων λήψεσθαι μηθὲν μέλλων. ἔτι δὲ τὰς γινομένας δημοσίας δίκας ὡς ὀλιγίστας ἀεὶ ποιεῖν, μεγάλοις ἐπιτιμίοις τοὺς εἰκῇ γραφομένους κωλύοντας· οὐ γὰρ τοὺς δημοτικοὺς ἀλλὰ τοὺς γνωρίμους

15 εἰώθασιν εἰσάγειν, δεῖ δὲ καὶ ταύτῃ τῇ[2] πολιτείᾳ πάντας μάλιστα μὲν εὔνους εἶναι τοὺς πολίτας, εἰ δὲ μή, μή τοί γε ὡς πολεμίους νομίζειν τοὺς κυρίους. ἐπεὶ δ' αἱ τελευταῖαι δημοκρατίαι πολυάνθρωποί τέ εἰσι καὶ χαλεπὸν ἐκκλησιάζειν ἀμίσθους, τοῦτο δ' ὅπου πρόσοδοι μὴ τυγχάνουσιν οὖσαι

20 πολέμιον τοῖς γνωρίμοις (ἀπό τε γὰρ εἰσφορᾶς καὶ δημεύσεως ἀναγκαῖον γίνεσθαι καὶ δικαστηρίων φαύλων, ἃ πολλὰς ἤδη δημοκρατίας ἀνέτρεψεν)— ὅπου μὲν οὖν πρόσοδοι μὴ τυγχάνουσιν οὖσαι, δεῖ ποιεῖν ὀλίγας ἐκκλησίας, καὶ δικαστήρια πολλῶν μὲν ὀλίγας δ' ἡμέρας (τοῦτο γὰρ φέρει μὲν

25 καὶ πρὸς τὸ μὴ φοβεῖσθαι τοὺς πλουσίους τὰς δαπάνας κἂν[3] οἱ μὲν εὔποροι μὴ λαμβάνωσι δικαστικὸν οἱ δ' ἄποροι, φέρει δὲ καὶ πρὸς τὸ κρίνε-

---

[1] Bernays: φερομένων ΓΡ[1]: φερόντων cet.
[2] ταύτῃ τῇ Immisch: τῇ codd.
[3] κἂν Immisch: ἐὰν.

508

of to-day to court the favour of the peoples often use the law-courts to bring about confiscations of property. Hence those who are caring for the safety of the constitution must counteract this by enacting that nothing belonging to persons condemned at law shall be confiscated and liable to be carried to the public treasury, but that their property shall be consecrated to the service of religion ; for malefactors will be no less on their guard, as they will be punished just the same, while the mob will less often vote guilty against men on trial when it is not going to get anything out of it. Also they must always make the public trials that occur as few as possible, checking those who bring indictments at random by big penalties ; for they do not usually indict men of the people but notables, whereas even with this form of constitution it is desirable for all the citizens if possible to be friendly to the state, or failing that, at all events not to think of their rulers as enemies. And inasmuch as the ultimate forms of democracy tend to have large populations and it is difficult for their citizens to sit in the assembly without pay, and this in a state where there do not happen to be revenues is inimical to the notables (for pay has to be obtained from a property-tax and confiscation, and from corruption of the law-courts, which has caused the overthrow of many democracies before now),—where therefore there happen to be no revenues, few meetings of the assembly must be held, and the law-courts must consist of many members but only sit a few days (for this not only contributes to the rich not being in fear of the cost of the system even if the well-off do not take the pay and only the poor do, but also leads to far greater efficiency in the

1320 a

σθαι τὰς δίκας πολὺ βέλτιον, οἱ γὰρ εὔποροι
πολλὰς μὲν ἡμέρας οὐκ ἐθέλουσιν ἀπὸ τῶν ἰδίων
ἀπεῖναι, βραχὺν δὲ χρόνον ἐθέλουσιν), ὅπου δ' εἰσὶ
30 πρόσοδοι, μὴ ποιεῖν ὃ νῦν οἱ δημαγωγοὶ ποιοῦσιν
(τὰ γὰρ περιόντα νέμουσιν, λαμβάνουσι δὲ ἅμα
καὶ πάλιν δέονται τῶν αὐτῶν, ὁ τετρημένος γάρ
ἐστι πίθος ἡ τοιαύτη βοήθεια τοῖς ἀπόροις), ἀλλὰ
δεῖ τὸν ἀληθινῶς δημοτικὸν ὁρᾶν ὅπως τὸ πλῆθος
μὴ λίαν ἄπορον ᾖ· τοῦτο γὰρ αἴτιον τοῦ μοχθηρὰν
35 εἶναι τὴν δημοκρατίαν. τεχναστέον οὖν ὅπως ἂν
εὐπορία γένοιτο χρόνιος. ἐπεὶ δὲ[1] συμφέρει τοῦτο
καὶ τοῖς εὐπόροις, τὰ μὲν ἀπὸ τῶν προσόδων
γινόμενα συναθροίζοντας ἀθρόα χρὴ διανέμειν τοῖς
ἀπόροις, μάλιστα μὲν εἴ τις δύναται τοσοῦτον
ἀθροίζων[2] ὅσον εἰς γῃδίου κτῆσιν, εἰ δὲ μή, πρὸς
1320 b ἀφορμὴν ἐμπορίας καὶ γεωργίας, καὶ εἰ μὴ πᾶσι
δυνατόν, ἀλλὰ κατὰ φυλὰς ἤ τι μέρος ἕτερον ἐν
μέρει διανέμειν, ἐν δὲ τούτῳ πρὸς τὰς ἀναγκαίας
συνόδους τοὺς εὐπόρους εἰσφέρειν τὸν μισθὸν
5 ἀφιεμένους τῶν ματαίων λειτουργιῶν. τοιοῦτον
δέ τινα τρόπον Καρχηδόνιοι πολιτευόμενοι φίλον
κέκτηνται τὸν δῆμον· ἀεὶ γάρ τινας ἐκπέμποντες
τοῦ δήμου πρὸς τὰς περιοικίδας ποιοῦσιν εὐπόρους.
χαριέντων δ' ἐστὶ καὶ νοῦν ἐχόντων γνωρίμων κα
διαλαμβάνοντας τοὺς ἀπόρους ἀφορμὰς διδόντας
τρέπειν ἐπ' ἐργασίας. καλῶς δ' ἔχει μιμεῖσθα
10 καὶ τὰ Ταραντίνων· ἐκεῖνοι γὰρ κοινὰ ποιοῦντες τὲ

[1] ἐπειδὴ Immisch (post εὐπόροις interpuncto).
[2] ἀθροίζειν cod. inferior.

---

[a] The fifty daughters of Danaus were married to thei
cousins, and all but one murdered their husbands on the
bridal night, and were punished in Hades by having to pou
water into the jar described.

510

rial of law-suits, for the well-to-do, though not wishing to be away from their private affairs for many days, are willing to leave them for a short time), while where there are revenues men must not do what the popular leaders do now (for they use the surplus for doles, and people no sooner get them than they want the same doles again, because this way of helping the poor is the legendary jar with a hole in it [a]), but the truly democratic statesman must study how the multitude may be saved from extreme poverty ; for this is what causes democracy to be corrupt. Measures must therefore be contrived that may bring about lasting prosperity. And since this is advantageous also for the well-to-do, the proper course is to collect all the proceeds of the revenues into a fund and distribute this in lump sums to the needy, best of all, if one can, in sums large enough for acquiring a small estate, or, failing this, to serve as capital for trade or husbandry, and if this is not possible for all, at all events to distribute the money by tribes or some other division of the population in turn, while in the meantime the well-to-do must contribute pay for attendance at the necessary assemblies, being themselves excused from useless public services. By following some such policy as this the Carthaginians have won the friendship of the common people ; for they constantly send out some of the people to the surrounding territories and so make them well-off. And if the notables are men of good feeling and sense they may also divide the needy among them in groups and supply them with capital to start them in businesses. It is also a good plan to imitate the policy [b] of the Tarentines. They

[b] Cf. 1263 a 35.

κτήματα τοῖς ἀπόροις ἐπὶ τὴν χρῆσιν εὔνουν παρασκευάζουσι τὸ πλῆθος· ἔτι δὲ τὰς ἀρχὰς πάσας
ἐποίησαν διττάς, τὰς μὲν αἱρετὰς τὰς δὲ κληρωτάς,
τὰς μὲν κληρωτὰς ὅπως ὁ δῆμος αὐτῶν μετέχῃ,
τὰς δ' αἱρετὰς ἵνα πολιτεύωνται βέλτιον. ἔστι δὲ
15 τοῦτο ποιῆσαι καὶ τῆς αὐτῆς ἀρχῆς[1] μερίζοντας
τοὺς μὲν κληρωτοὺς τοὺς δ' αἱρετούς.

Πῶς μὲν οὖν δεῖ τὰς δημοκρατίας κατασκευάζειν, εἴρηται.

IV. Σχεδὸν δὲ καὶ περὶ τὰς ὀλιγαρχίας πῶς δεῖ
φανερὸν ἐκ τούτων. ἐκ τῶν ἐναντίων γὰρ δεῖ
20 συνάγειν, ἑκάστην ὀλιγαρχίαν πρὸς τὴν ἐναντίαν
δημοκρατίαν ἀναλογιζόμενον, τὴν μὲν εὔκρατον
μάλιστα τῶν ὀλιγαρχιῶν καὶ πρώτην — αὕτη δ'
ἐστὶν ἡ σύνεγγυς τῇ καλουμένῃ πολιτείᾳ, ᾗ δεῖ τὰ
τιμήματα διαιρεῖν, τὰ μὲν ἐλάττω τὰ δὲ μείζω
ποιοῦντας, ἐλάττω μὲν ἀφ' ὧν τῶν ἀναγκαίων
25 μεθέξουσιν ἀρχῶν, μείζω δ' ἀφ' ὧν τῶν κυ-
ριωτέρων· τῷ τε κτωμένῳ τὸ τίμημα μετέχειν
ἐξεῖναι τῆς πολιτείας, τοσοῦτον εἰσαγομένους τοῦ
δήμου πλῆθος διὰ τοῦ τιμήματος μεθ' οὗ κρείτ-
τονες ἔσονται τῶν μὴ μετεχόντων· ἀεὶ δὲ δεῖ
παραλαμβάνειν ἐκ τοῦ βελτίονος δήμου τοὺς
30 κοινωνούς. ὁμοίως δὲ καὶ τὴν ἐχομένην ὀλιγαρχίαν ἐπιτείνοντας δεῖ μικρὸν κατασκευάζειν.
τῇ δ' ἀντικειμένῃ τῇ τελευταίᾳ δημοκρατίᾳ, τῇ

---

[1] Γ: ἀρχῆς αὐτῆς codd.

---

[a] This seems to mean that the land was in private owner
ship, but that there was some system of poor-relief, to pro
vide for the destitute out of the produce.

[b] In contrast with the first and best form of democracy
c. ii. *init.*

get the goodwill of the multitude by making property communal for the purpose of use by the needy [a] ; also they have divided the whole number of their magistracies into two classes, one elected by vote and the other filled by lot,—the latter to ensure that the people may have a share in them, and the former to improve the conduct of public affairs. And it is also possible to effect this by dividing the holders of the same magistracy into two groups, one appointed by lot and the other by vote.

We have then said how democracies should be organized.

IV. It is also fairly clear from these considerations how oligarchies ought to be organized. We must infer them from their opposites, reasoning out each form of oligarchy with reference to the form of democracy opposite to it, starting with the most well-blended and first form of oligarchy [b]—and this is the one near to what is called a constitutional government, and for it the property-qualifications must be divided into one group of smaller properties and another of larger ones, smaller properties qualifying their owners for the indispensable offices and larger ones for the more important ; and a person owning the qualifying property must be allowed to take a share in the government,—introducing by the assessment a large enough number of the common people to secure that with them the governing class will have a majority over those excluded ; and persons to share in the government must constantly be brought in from the better class of the common people. And the next form of oligarchy also must be constructed in a similar way with a slight tightening up of the qualification. But the form of oligarchy that stands

Oligarchy: its best and worst forms.

513

1320 b

δυναστικωτάτη καὶ τυραννικωτάτη τῶν ὀλιγαρχιῶν
ὅσῳ περ χειρίστη τοσούτῳ δεῖ πλείονος φυλακῆς·
ὥσπερ γὰρ τὰ μὲν σώματα εὖ διακείμενα πρὸ
35 ὑγίειαν καὶ πλοῖα τὰ πρὸς ναυτιλίαν καλῶς ἔχοντ
τοῖς πλωτῆρσιν ἐπιδέχεται πλείους ἁμαρτίας ὥστ
μὴ φθείρεσθαι δι' αὐτάς, τὰ δὲ νοσερῶς ἔχοντ
τῶν σωμάτων καὶ τὰ τῶν πλοίων ἐκλελυμένα κα
πλωτήρων τετυχηκότα φαύλων οὐδὲ τὰς μικρὰ
δύναται φέρειν ἁμαρτίας, οὕτω καὶ τῶν πολιτειῶ
1321 a αἱ χείρισται πλείστης δέονται φυλακῆς. τὰς μὲ
οὖν δημοκρατίας ὅλως ἡ πολυανθρωπία σῴζει
τοῦτο γὰρ ἀντίκειται πρὸς τὸ δίκαιον τὸ κατὰ τὴ
ἀξίαν· τὴν δ' ὀλιγαρχίαν δῆλον ὅτι τοὐναντίο
ὑπὸ τῆς εὐταξίας δεῖ τυγχάνειν τῆς σωτηρίας.

5 Ἐπεὶ δὲ τέτταρα μέν ἐστι μέρη μάλιστα το
πλήθους, γεωργικὸν βάναυσον ἀγοραῖον θητικόν,
τέτταρα δὲ τὰ χρήσιμα πρὸς πόλεμον, ἱππικὸ
ὁπλιτικὸν ψιλὸν ναυτικόν, ὅπου μὲν συμβέβηκε τὴ
χώραν εἶναι ἱππάσιμον, ἐνταῦθα μὲν εὐφυῶς ἔχε
10 κατασκευάζειν τὴν ὀλιγαρχίαν ἰσχυράν (ἡ γὰρ
σωτηρία τοῖς οἰκοῦσι διὰ ταύτης ἐστὶ τῆς δυνάμεως, αἱ δ' ἱπποτροφίαι τῶν μακρὰς οὐσίας
κεκτημένων εἰσίν), ὅπου δ' ὁπλῖτιν,[1] τὴν ἐχομένη
ὀλιγαρχίαν (τὸ γὰρ ὁπλιτικὸν τῶν εὐπόρων ἐστ
μᾶλλον ἢ τῶν ἀπόρων), ἡ δὲ ψιλὴ δύναμις κα
15 ναυτικὴ δημοκρατικὴ[2] πάμπαν. νῦν μὲν οὖν ὅπου
τοιοῦτον πολὺ πλῆθός ἐστιν, ὅταν διαστῶσι, πολ-

---

[1] Lambinus: ὁπλίτην codd.
[2] cod. inf.: δημοτικὴ cet.

opposite to the last form of democracy, the most autocratic and tyrannical of the oligarchies, in as far as it is the worst requires a correspondingly great amount of safe guarding. For just as human bodies in a good state of health and ships well equipped with their crews for a voyage admit of more mistakes without being destroyed thereby, but bodies of a morbid habit and vessels strained in their timbers and manned with bad crews cannot endure even the smallest mistakes, so also the worst constitutions need the most safe-guarding. Democracies therefore generally speaking are kept safe by the largeness of the citizen-body, for this is the antithesis of justice according to desert; but oligarchy on the contrary must manifestly obtain its security by means of good organization.

And since the mass of the population falls principally into four divisions, the farming class, artisans, retail traders and hired labourers, and military forces are of four classes, cavalry, heavy infantry, light infantry and marines, in places where the country happens to be suitable for horsemanship, there natural conditions favour the establishment of an oligarchy that will be powerful (for the security of the inhabitants depends on the strength of this element, and keeping studs of horses is the pursuit of those who own extensive estates); and where the ground is suitable for heavy infantry, conditions favour the next form of oligarchy (for heavy infantry is a service for the well-to-do rather than the poor); but light infantry and naval forces are an entirely democratic element. As things are therefore, where there is a large multitude of this class, when party strife occurs the oligarchs often get the worst of

Safeguards of oligarchy: military organization.

λάκις ἀγωνίζονται χεῖρον· δεῖ δὲ πρὸς τοῦτο φάρμακον παρὰ τῶν πολεμικῶν λαμβάνειν στρατηγῶν
οἳ συνδυάζουσι πρὸς τὴν ἱππικὴν δύναμιν καὶ τὴν
ὁπλιτικὴν τὴν ἁρμόττουσαν τῶν ψιλῶν. ταύτῃ

20 δ' ἐπικρατοῦσιν ἐν ταῖς διαστάσεσιν οἱ δῆμοι τῶν
εὐπόρων, ψιλοὶ γὰρ ὄντες πρὸς ἱππικὴν καὶ ὁπλιτικὴν ἀγωνίζονται ῥᾳδίως. τὸ μὲν οὖν ἐκ τούτων
καθιστάναι ταύτην τὴν δύναμιν ἐφ' ἑαυτοὺς ἐστι
καθιστάναι, δεῖ δὲ διῃρημένης τῆς ἡλικίας, καὶ τῶν
μὲν ὄντων πρεσβυτέρων τῶν δὲ νέων, ἔτι μὲν

25 ὄντας νέους τοὺς αὑτῶν υἱεῖς διδάσκεσθαι τὰς
κούφας καὶ τὰς ψιλὰς ἐργασίας, ἐκκεκριμένους δ'
ἐκ παίδων ἀθλητὰς εἶναι αὐτοὺς τῶν ἔργων. τὴν
δὲ μετάδοσιν γίνεσθαι τῷ πλήθει τοῦ πολιτεύματος
ἤτοι καθάπερ εἴρηται πρότερον, τοῖς τὸ τίμημα
κτωμένοις, ἢ καθάπερ Θηβαίοις, ἀποσχομένοις

30 χρόνον τινὰ τῶν βαναύσων ἔργων, ἢ καθάπερ ἐν
Μασσαλίᾳ, κρίσιν ποιουμένους τῶν ἀξίων τῶν[1] ἐν
τῷ πολιτεύματι καὶ τῶν ἔξωθεν. ἔτι δὲ καὶ ταῖς
ἀρχαῖς ταῖς κυριωτάταις, ἃς δεῖ τοὺς ἐν τῇ
πολιτείᾳ κατέχειν, δεῖ προσκεῖσθαι λειτουργίας,
ἵν' ἑκὼν ὁ δῆμος μὴ μετέχῃ καὶ συγγνώμην ἔχῃ

35 τοῖς ἄρχουσιν ὡς μισθὸν πολὺν διδοῦσι τῆς ἀρχῆς.
ἁρμόττει δὲ θυσίας τε εἰσιόντας ποιεῖσθαι μεγαλο-
πρεπεῖς καὶ κατασκευάζειν τι τῶν κοινῶν, ἵνα
τῶν περὶ τὰς ἑστιάσεις μετέχων ὁ δῆμος καὶ τὴν
πόλιν ὁρῶν κοσμουμένην τὰ μὲν ἀναθήμασι τὰ δὲ

---

[1] τοὺς Niemeyer.

[a] *i.e.* by superior mobility.   [b] § 1, 1320 b 25 f
[c] If the text is correct it seems to mean that the list was
revised from time to time and some old names taken off and
new ones put on.

the struggle; and a remedy for this must be adopted from military commanders, who combine with their cavalry and heavy infantry forces a contingent of light infantry. And this is the way [a] in which the common people get the better over the well-to-do in outbreaks of party strife: being unencumbered they fight easily against cavalry and 5 heavy infantry. Therefore to establish this force out of this class is to establish it against itself, but the right plan is for the men of military age to be separated into a division of older and one of younger men, and to have their own sons while still young trained in the exercises of light and unarmed troops, and for youths selected from among the boys to be themselves trained in active operations. And the bestowal of a share in the government upon the multitude should either go on the lines stated before,[b] and be made to those who acquire the property-qualification, or as at Thebes, to people after they have abstained for a time from mechanic industries, or as at Marseilles, by making a selection among members of the governing classes and those outside 6 it of persons who deserve [c] inclusion. And furthermore the most supreme offices also, which must be retained by those within the constitution, must have expensive duties attached to them, in order that the common people may be willing to be excluded from them, and may feel no resentment against the ruling class, because it pays a high price for office. And it fits in with this that they should offer splendid sacrifices and build up some public monument on entering upon office, so that the common people sharing in the festivities and seeing the city decorated both with votive offerings and with buildings

517

1321 a
οἰκοδομήμασιν ἄσμενος ὁρᾷ μένουσαν τὴν πολιτείαν·
40 συμβήσεται δὲ καὶ τοῖς γνωρίμοις εἶναι μνημεῖα
τῆς δαπάνης. ἀλλὰ τοῦτο νῦν οἱ περὶ τὰς ὀλιγαρχίας οὐ ποιοῦσιν ἀλλὰ τοὐναντίον, τὰ λήμματα
γὰρ ζητοῦσιν οὐχ ἧττον ἢ τὴν τιμήν· διόπερ εὖ
1321 b ἔχει λέγειν ταύτας εἶναι δημοκρατίας μικράς.

Πῶς μὲν οὖν χρὴ καθιστάναι τὰς δημοκρατίας
καὶ τὰς ὀλιγαρχίας, διωρίσθω τὸν τρόπον τοῦτον.

V. Ἀκόλουθον δὲ τοῖς εἰρημένοις ἐστὶ τὸ διῃρῆ-
5 σθαι καλῶς τὰ περὶ τὰς ἀρχάς, πόσαι καὶ τίνες καὶ
τίνων, καθάπερ εἴρηται καὶ πρότερον. τῶν μὲν
γὰρ ἀναγκαίων ἀρχῶν χωρὶς ἀδύνατον εἶναι πόλιν
τῶν δὲ πρὸς εὐταξίαν καὶ κόσμον ἀδύνατον οἰκεῖσθαι καλῶς. ἔτι δ᾽ ἀναγκαῖον ἐν μὲν ταῖς μικραῖς
10 ἐλάττους εἶναι τὰς ἀρχάς ἐν δὲ ταῖς μεγάλαις
πλείους, ὥσπερ τυγχάνει πρότερον εἰρημένον·
ποίας οὖν ἁρμόττει συνάγειν καὶ ποίας χωρίζειν
δεῖ μὴ λανθάνειν. πρῶτον μὲν οὖν ἐπιμέλεια τῶν
ἀναγκαίων ἡ περὶ τὴν ἀγοράν, ἐφ᾽ ᾗ δεῖ τιν᾽
ἀρχὴν εἶναι τὴν ἐφορῶσαν περί τε τὰ συμβόλαια
15 καὶ τὴν εὐκοσμίαν· σχεδὸν γὰρ ἀναγκαῖον πάσαις
ταῖς πόλεσι τὰ μὲν ὠνεῖσθαι τὰ δὲ πωλεῖν πρὸς
τὴν ἀλλήλων ἀναγκαίαν χρείαν, καὶ τοῦτ᾽ ἐστὶ
ὑπογυιότατον πρὸς αὐτάρκειαν, δι᾽ ἣν δοκοῦσι
εἰς μίαν πολιτείαν συνελθεῖν. ἑτέρα δὲ ἐπιμέλεια
20 ταύτης ἐχομένη καὶ σύνεγγυς ἡ τῶν περὶ τὸ ἄστυ
δημοσίων καὶ ἰδίων, ὅπως εὐκοσμία ᾖ καὶ τῶ

---

[a] The phrase suggests that in a democracy public duties
are chiefly undertaken for their emoluments.
[b] Book IV. 1297 b 35 ff., 1299 a 3 ff.
[c] Cf. c. iv. § 1.   [d] Book IV. 1299 b 30 ff.
518

may be glad to see the constitution enduring; **and** an additional result will be that the notables will have memorials of their outlay. But at present the members of oligarchies do not adopt this course but the opposite, for they seek the gains of office just as much as the honour; hence these oligarchies are well described as miniature democracies.[a]

Let this then be a description of the proper way to organize the various forms of democracy and of oligarchy.

1 V. As a consequence of what has been said there follow satisfactory conclusions to the questions concerning magistracies—how many and what they should be and to whom they should belong, as has also been said before.[b] For without the indispensable[c] magistracies a state cannot exist, while without those that contribute to good order and seemliness it cannot be well governed. And furthermore the magistracies are bound to be fewer in the small states and more numerous in the large ones, as in fact has been said before[d]; it must therefore be kept in view what kinds of magistracies it is desirable to combine and **2** what kinds to keep separate. First among the indispensable services is the superintendence of the market, over which there must be an official to superintend contracts and good order; since it is a necessity for almost all states that people shall sell some things and buy others according to one another's necessary requirements, and this is the readiest means of securing self-sufficiency, which seems to be the reason for men's having united into **3** a single state. Another superintendency connected very closely with this one is the curatorship of public and private properties in the city, to secure good

OFFICES OF GOVERN-MENT (c. v.).

(1) The in-dispensable offices: super-intendent of markets;

super-intendent of streets and buildings;

519

πιπτόντων οἰκοδομημάτων καὶ ὁδῶν σωτηρία καὶ
διόρθωσις, καὶ τῶν ὁρίων τῶν πρὸς ἀλλήλους,
ὅπως ἀνεγκλήτως ἔχωσιν, καὶ ὅσα τούτοις ἄλλα
τῆς ἐπιμελείας ὁμοιότροπα. καλοῦσι δ' ἀστυνομίαν
οἱ πλεῖστοι τὴν τοιαύτην ἀρχήν, ἔχει δὲ μόρια
25 πλείω τὸν ἀριθμόν, ὧν ἑτέρους ἐφ' ἕτερα καθιστᾶσιν ἐν ταῖς πολυανθρωποτέραις πόλεσιν, οἷον
τειχοποιοὺς καὶ κρηνῶν ἐπιμελητὰς καὶ λιμένων
φύλακας. ἄλλη δ' ἀναγκαία τε καὶ παραπλησία
ταύτῃ· περὶ τῶν αὐτῶν μὲν γάρ, ἀλλὰ περὶ τὴν
χώραν ἐστὶ καὶ [τὰ]¹ περὶ τὰ ἔξω τοῦ ἄστεος·
30 καλοῦσι δὲ τοὺς ἄρχοντας τούτους οἱ μὲν ἀγρονόμους οἱ δ' ὑλωρούς. αὗται μὲν οὖν ἐπιμέλειαι
εἰσι τούτων τρεῖς, ἄλλη δ' ἀρχὴ πρὸς ἣν αἱ πρόσοδοι τῶν κοινῶν ἀναφέρονται, παρ' ὧν φυλαττόν-
των μερίζονται πρὸς ἑκάστην διοίκησιν· καλοῦσι
δ' ἀποδέκτας τούτους καὶ ταμίας. ἑτέρα δ' ἀρχὴ
35 πρὸς ἣν ἀναγράφεσθαι δεῖ τά τε ἴδια συμβόλαια
καὶ τὰς κρίσεις τὰς² ἐκ τῶν δικαστηρίων· παρὰ
δὲ τοῖς αὐτοῖς τούτοις καὶ τὰς γραφὰς τῶν δικῶν
γίνεσθαι δεῖ καὶ τὰς εἰσαγωγάς. ἐνιαχοῦ μὲν οὖν
μερίζουσι καὶ ταύτην εἰς πλείους, ἔστι δ' οὗ³
μία κυρία τούτων πάντων· καλοῦνται δὲ ἱερο-
μνήμονες καὶ ἐπιστάται καὶ μνήμονες καὶ τούτοις
40 ἄλλα ὀνόματα σύνεγγυς. μετὰ δὲ ταύτην ἐχομένη
μὲν ἀναγκαιοτάτη δὲ σχεδὸν καὶ χαλεπωτάτη τῶν
ἀρχῶν ἐστὶν ἡ περὶ τὰς πράξεις τῶν καταδικασθέν-

---

¹ om. Γ. ² τὰς inseruit Wilamowitz.
³ δ' οὖ Thurot: δὲ codd.

order and the preservation and rectification of falling buildings and roads, and of the bounds between different persons' estates, so that disputes may not arise about them, and all the other duties of superintendence similar to these. An office of this nature is in most states entitled that of City-controller, but it has several departments, each of which is filled by separate officials in the states with larger populations, for instance Curators of Walls, Superintendents of Wells, Harbours-guardians. And another office also is indispensable and closely akin to these, for it controls the same matters but deals with the country and the regions outside the city ; and these magistrates are called in some places Land-controllers and in others Custodians of Forests. These then are three departments of control over these matters, while another office is that to which the revenues of the public funds are paid in, the officials who guard them and by whom they are divided out to the several administrative departments ; these magistrates are called Receivers and Stewards. Another magistracy is the one that has to receive a written return of private contracts and of the verdicts of the lawcourts ; and with these same officials the registration of legal proceedings and their institution have also to take place. In some states this office also is divided into several, but there are places where one magistracy controls all these matters ; and these officials are called Sacred Recorders, Superintendents, Recorders, and other names akin to these. And after these is the office connected with it but perhaps the most indispensable and most difficult of all, the one concerned with the execution of judgement upon persons cast in suits and those posted as de-

super-intendent of farms ;

revenue officers ;

recorders ;

penal executive officers.

1322 a τῶν καὶ τῶν προτιθεμένων κατὰ τὰς ἐγγραφὰς
καὶ περὶ τὰς φυλακὰς τῶν σωμάτων. χαλεπὴ
μὲν οὖν ἐστι διὰ τὸ πολλὴν ἔχειν ἀπέχθειαν, ὥστε
ὅπου μὴ μεγάλα ἔστι κερδαίνειν, οὔτ' ἄρχειν
ὑπομένουσιν αὐτὴν οὔθ' ὑπομείναντες ἐθέλουσι
5 πράττειν κατὰ τοὺς νόμους· ἀναγκαία δ' ἐστίν,
ὅτι οὐδὲν ὄφελος γίνεσθαι μὲν δίκας περὶ τῶν
δικαίων ταύτας δὲ μὴ λαμβάνειν τέλος, ὥστ' εἰ
μὴ γιγνομένων κοινωνεῖν ἀδύνατον ἀλλήλοις, καὶ
πράξεων μὴ γιγνομένων. διὸ βέλτιον μὴ μίαν
εἶναι ταύτην τὴν ἀρχὴν ἀλλ' ἄλλους ἐξ ἄλλων
10 δικαστηρίων, καὶ περὶ τὰς προθέσεις τῶν ἀνα-
γεγραμμένων ὡσαύτως πειρᾶσθαι διαιρεῖν, ἔτι δ'
ἔνια πράττεσθαι καὶ τὰς[1] ἀρχὰς τάς τε ἄλλας καὶ
τὰς τῶν ἔνων[2] μᾶλλον τὰς νέας, καὶ τὰς[1] τῶν
ἐνεστώτων ἑτέρας καταδικασάσης ἑτέραν εἶναι τὴν
πραττομένην, οἷον ἀστυνόμους τὰς[1] παρὰ τῶν
15 ἀγορανόμων, τὰς[1] δὲ παρὰ τούτων ἑτέρους. ὅσῳ
γὰρ ἂν ἐλάττων ἀπέχθεια ἐνῇ τοῖς πραττομένοις,
τοσούτῳ μᾶλλον λήψονται τέλος αἱ πράξεις· τὸ
μὲν οὖν τοὺς αὐτοὺς εἶναι τοὺς καταδικάσαντας
καὶ πραττομένους ἀπέχθειαν ἔχει διπλῆν, τὸ δὲ
περὶ πάντων τοὺς αὐτοὺς πολεμίους πᾶσιν ποιεῖ[3].
πολλαχοῦ δὲ διῄρηται καὶ ἡ φυλάττουσα πρὸς
20 τὴν πραττομένην, οἷον Ἀθήνησιν ἡ[4] τῶν ἕνδεκα

---

[1] quater pro τὰς Niemeyer τά.
[2] ἔνων Scaliger : νέων codd.
[3] ποιεῖ inseruit mg. cod. inf. (post αὐτοὺς Welldon).
[4] ἡ inseruit Coraes.

---

faulters according to the lists, and with the custody
of prisoners. This is an irksome office because it
involves great unpopularity, so that where it is not
possible to make a great deal of profit out of it men
will not undertake it, or when they have undertaken
it are reluctant to carry out its functions according
to the laws ; but it is necessary, because there is no
use in trials being held about men's rights when the
verdicts are not put into execution, so that if when
no legal trial of disputes takes place social intercourse is impossible, so also is it when judgements
are not executed. Hence it is better for this magistracy not to be a single office but to consist of several
persons drawn from different courts, and it is desirable
similarly to try to divide up the functions connected
with the posting up of people registered as public
debtors, and further also in some cases for the sentences to be executed by magistrates, especially by
the newly elected ones preferably in suits tried by
the outgoing ones, and in those tried by men actually
in office for the magistrate executing the sentence
to be different from the one that passed it, for instance the City-controllers to execute the judgements
passed on from the Market-controllers and other
magistrates those passed on by the City-controllers.
For the less odium involved for those who execute
the judgements, the more adequately the judgements
will be carried out ; so for the same magistrates to
have imposed the sentence and to execute it involves
a twofold odium, and for the same ones to execute
it in all cases makes them the enemies of everybody.
And in many places also the office of keeping custody
of prisoners, for example at Athens the office of the
magistrates known as the Eleven,^a is separate from

1322 a

καλουμένων.[1] διὸ βέλτιον καὶ ταύτην χωρίζειν,
καὶ τὸ[2] σόφισμα ζητεῖν καὶ περὶ ταύτην. ἀναγκαία
μὲν γάρ ἐστιν οὐχ ἧττον τῆς εἰρημένης, συμβαίνει
δὲ τοὺς μὲν ἐπιεικεῖς φεύγειν μάλιστα ταύτην τὴν
ἀρχήν, τοὺς δὲ μοχθηροὺς οὐκ ἀσφαλὲς ποιεῖν
25 κυρίους· αὐτοὶ γὰρ δέονται φυλακῆς μᾶλλον
ἄλλων[3] ἢ φυλάττειν ἄλλους δύνανται. διὸ δεῖ μὴ
μίαν ἀποτεταγμένην ἀρχὴν εἶναι πρὸς αὐτοῖς μηδὲ
συνεχῶς τὴν αὐτήν, ἀλλὰ τῶν τε νέων, ὅπου τις
ἐφήβων ἢ φρουρῶν ἐστι τάξις, καὶ τῶν ἀρχῶν δεῖ
κατὰ μέρη ποιεῖσθαι τὴν ἐπιμέλειαν ἑτέρους.

30 Ταύτας μὲν οὖν τὰς ἀρχὰς ὡς ἀναγκαιοτάτας
θετέον εἶναι πρώτας, μετὰ δὲ ταύτας τὰς ἀναγκαίας μὲν οὐθὲν ἧττον, ἐν σχήματι δὲ μείζονι
τεταγμένας, καὶ γὰρ ἐμπειρίας καὶ πίστεως δέονται
πολλῆς· τοιαῦται δ᾽ εἶεν αἵ τε περὶ τὴν φυλακὴν
τῆς πόλεως, καὶ ὅσαι τάττονται πρὸς τὰς πολε-
35 μικὰς χρείας. δεῖ δὲ καὶ ἐν εἰρήνῃ καὶ ἐν πολέμῳ
πυλῶν τε καὶ τειχῶν φυλακῆς ὁμοίως ἐπιμελητὰς
εἶναι καὶ ἐξετάσεως καὶ συντάξεως τῶν πολιτῶν.
ἔνθα μὲν οὖν ἐπὶ πᾶσι τούτοις ἀρχαὶ πλείους εἰσίν,
ἔνθα δ᾽ ἐλάττους, οἷον ἐν ταῖς μικραῖς πόλεσι μία
περὶ πάντων. καλοῦσι δὲ στρατηγοὺς καὶ πολεμ-
1322 b άρχους τοὺς τοιούτους. ἔτι δὲ κἂν ὦσιν ἱππεῖς
ἢ ψιλοὶ ἢ τοξόται ἢ ναυτικόν, καὶ ἐπὶ τούτων
ἑκάστων ἐνίοτε καθίστανται ἀρχαί, αἳ καλοῦνται

---

[1] οἷον . . . καλουμένων secl. Susemihl.
[2] καί τι mg. cod. inf.
[3] μᾶλλον ἄλλων ed. (*aliorum magis* Guil.): ἄλλων M :
μᾶλλον cet.

---

[a] At Athens and elsewhere young citizens from eighteen
to twenty were enrolled in training corps for military instruction; these served as police and home troops.

the magistracy that executes sentences. It is better therefore to keep this also separate, and to attempt the same device with regard to this as well. For though it is no less necessary than the office of which I spoke, yet in practice respectable people avoid it most of all offices, while it is not safe to put it into the hands of the base, for they themselves need others to guard them instead of being able to keep guard over others. Hence there must not be one magistracy specially assigned to the custody of prisoners nor must the same magistracy perform this duty continuously, but it should be performed by the young, in places where there is a regiment of cadets[a] or guards, and by the magistrates, in successive sections.

These magistracies therefore must be counted first as supremely necessary, and next to them must be put those that are not less necessary but are ranked on a higher grade of dignity, because they require much experience and trustworthiness ; in this class would come the magistracies concerned with guarding the city and those assigned to military requirements. And both in peace and in war it is equally necessary for there to be magistrates to superintend the guarding of gates and walls and the inspection and drill of the citizen troops. In some places therefore there are more magistracies assigned to all these duties, and in others fewer—for instance in the small states there is one to deal with all of them. And the officers of this sort are entitled Generals or War-lords. And moreover if there are also cavalry or light infantry or archers or a navy, sometimes a magistracy is appointed to have charge of each of these arms also, and they carry the titles

(2) The higher offices : military officers ;

525

ναυαρχίαι καὶ ἱππαρχίαι καὶ ταξιαρχίαι, καὶ κατὰ
μέρος δὲ αἱ ὑπὸ ταύτας τριηραρχίαι καὶ λοχαγίαι
5 καὶ φυλαρχίαι καὶ ὅσα τούτων μόρια. τὸ δὲ πᾶν
ἕν τι τούτων ἐστὶν εἶδος, ἐπιμελείας[1] πολεμικῶν.
περὶ μὲν οὖν ταύτην τὴν ἀρχὴν ἔχει τὸν τρόπον 10
τοῦτον· ἐπεὶ δὲ ἔνιαι τῶν ἀρχῶν, εἰ καὶ μὴ πᾶσαι,
διαχειρίζουσι πολλὰ τῶν κοινῶν, ἀναγκαῖον ἑτέραν
10 εἶναι τὴν ληψομένην λογισμὸν καὶ προσευθυνοῦ-
σαν, αὐτὴν μηθὲν διαχειρίζουσαν ἕτερον· καλοῦσι
δὲ τούτους οἱ μὲν εὐθύνους οἱ δὲ λογιστὰς οἱ
δὲ ἐξεταστὰς οἱ δὲ συνηγόρους. παρὰ πάσας δὲ
ταύτας τὰς ἀρχὰς ἡ μάλιστα κυρία πάντων ἐστίν·
ἡ γὰρ αὐτὴ πολλάκις ἔχει τὸ τέλος καὶ τὴν
εἰσφοράν,[2] ἣ[3] προκάθηται τοῦ πλήθους ὅπου
15 κύριός ἐστιν ὁ δῆμος· δεῖ γὰρ εἶναι τὸ συνάγον
τὸ κύριον κύριον[4] τῆς πολιτείας. καλεῖται δὲ
ἔνθα μὲν[5] πρόβουλοι διὰ τὸ προβουλεύειν, ὅπου
δὲ πλῆθός ἐστι, βουλὴ μᾶλλον. αἱ μὲν οὖν πολιτικαὶ τῶν ἀρχῶν σχεδὸν τοσαῦταί τινές εἰσιν· ἄλλο 11
δ' εἶδος ἐπιμελείας ἡ περὶ τοὺς θεούς, οἷον ἱερεῖς
20 τε καὶ ἐπιμεληταὶ τῶν περὶ τὰ ἱερὰ τοῦ σῴζεσθαί
τε τὰ ὑπάρχοντα καὶ ἀνορθοῦσθαι τὰ πίπτοντα τῶν
οἰκοδομημάτων καὶ τῶν ἄλλων ὅσα τέτακται πρὸς
τοὺς θεούς. συμβαίνει δὲ τὴν ἐπιμέλειαν ταύτην
ἐνιαχοῦ μὲν εἶναι μίαν, οἷον ἐν ταῖς μικραῖς

---

[1] ἐπιμέλεια Lambinus.   [2] ἐφορείαν ΓΜΡ[1].
[3] ἢ Μ : ἡ cet.   [4] κύριον κύριον ed. : κύριον codd.
[5] μὲν ⟨νομοφύλακες ἔνθα δὲ⟩ Schneider.

of Admiral, Cavalry-commander and Taxiarch, and also the divisional commissions subordinate to these of Captains of Triremes, Company-commanders and Captains of Tribes, and all the subdivisions of these commands. But the whole of this sort of officers constitute a single class, that of military command. This then is how the matter stands in regard to this office; but inasmuch as some of the magistracies, if not all, handle large sums of public money, there must be another office to receive an account and subject it to audit, which must itself handle no other business; and these officials are called Auditors by some people, Accountants by others, Examiners by others and Advocates by others. And by the side of all these offices is the one that is most supreme over all matters, for often the same magistracy has the execution of business that controls its introduction, or presides over the general assembly in places where the people are supreme; for the magistracy that convenes the sovereign assembly is bound to be the sovereign power in the state. It is styled in some places the Preliminary Council because it considers business in advance, but where there is a democracy[a] it is more usually called a Council. This more or less completes the number of the offices of a political nature; but another kind of superintendence is that concerned with divine worship; in this class are priests and superintendents of matters connected with the temples, the preservation of existing buildings and the restoration of those that are ruinous, and the other duties relating to the gods. In practice this superintendence in some places forms a single office, for instance in

auditors;

the Council;

religious officials.

---

[a] *Cf.* 1323 a 9 below. Apparently πλῆθός ἐστι stands for τὸ πλῆθος κύριόν ἐστι, but editors quote no parallel.

1322 b

πόλεσιν, ἐνιαχοῦ δὲ πολλὰς καὶ κεχωρισμένας τῆς
25 ἱερωσύνης, οἷον ἱεροποιοὺς καὶ ναοφύλακας καὶ
ταμίας τῶν ἱερῶν χρημάτων. ἐχομένη δὲ ταύτης
ἡ πρὸς τὰς θυσίας ἀφωρισμένη τὰς κοινὰς πάσας
ὅσας μὴ τοῖς ἱερεῦσιν ἀποδίδωσιν ὁ νόμος ἀλλ'
ἀπὸ τῆς κοινῆς ἑστίας ἔχουσι τὴν τιμήν· καλοῦσι
δ' οἱ μὲν ἄρχοντας τούτους οἱ δὲ βασιλεῖς οἱ δὲ
30 πρυτάνεις. αἱ μὲν οὖν ἀναγκαῖαι ἐπιμέλειαί εἰσι
περὶ τούτων, ὡς εἰπεῖν συγκεφαλαιωσαμένους, περί
τε τὰ δαιμόνια καὶ τὰ πολεμικὰ καὶ περὶ τὰς
προσόδους καὶ περὶ τὰ ἀναλισκόμενα, καὶ περὶ
ἀγορὰν καὶ περὶ τὸ ἄστυ καὶ λιμένας καὶ τὴν
χώραν, ἔτι τὰ περὶ τὰ δικαστήρια καὶ συναλλαγ-
35 μάτων ἀναγραφὰς καὶ πράξεις καὶ φυλακάς, καὶ
ἐπὶ λογισμούς[1] τε καὶ ἐξετάσεις, καὶ πρὸς εὐθύνας
τῶν ἀρχόντων, καὶ τέλος αἱ περὶ τὸ βουλευόμενόν
εἰσι περὶ τῶν[2] κοινῶν. ἰδίᾳ δὲ ταῖς σχολαστι-
κωτέραις καὶ μᾶλλον εὐημερούσαις πόλεσιν, ἔτι
δὲ φροντιζούσαις εὐκοσμίας, γυναικονομία νομο-
1323 a φυλακία παιδονομία γυμνασιαρχία, πρὸς δὲ τούτοις
περὶ ἀγῶνας ἐπιμέλεια γυμνικοὺς καὶ Διονυσια-
κοὺς κἂν εἴ τινας ἑτέρας συμβαίνει τοιαύτας
γίνεσθαι θεωρίας. τούτων δ' ἔναι φανερῶς εἰσὶν
οὐ δημοτικαὶ τῶν ἀρχῶν, οἷον γυναικονομία καὶ
5 παιδονομία· τοῖς γὰρ ἀπόροις ἀνάγκη χρῆσθαι καὶ
γυναιξὶ καὶ παισὶν ὥσπερ ἀκολούθοις διὰ τὴν
ἀδουλίαν. τριῶν δ' οὐσῶν ἀρχῶν καθ'[3] ἃς αἱροῦν-
ταί τινες ἀρχὰς τὰς κυρίους, νομοφυλάκων προ-

---

[1] πὶ λογισμούς Spengel (*circa ratiocinationes* Guil.):
ἐπιλογισμούς codd.

[2] περὶ τῶν Richards: τῶν codd.   [3] [καθ'] Heinsius.

the small cities, but in others it belongs to a number of officials who are not members of the priesthood, for example Sacrificial Officers and Temple-guardians and Stewards of Sacred Funds. And connected with this is the office devoted to the management of all the public festivals which the law does not assign to the priests but the officials in charge of which derive their honour from the common sacrificial hearth, and these officials are called in some places Archons, in 12 others Kings and in others Presidents. To sum up therefore, the necessary offices of superintendence deal with the following matters : institutions of religion, military institutions, revenue and expenditure, control of the market, citadel, harbours and country, also the arrangements of the law-courts, registration of contracts, collection of fines, custody of prisoners, supervision of accounts and inspections, and the auditing of officials, and lastly the offices connected with the body that deliberates about 13 public affairs. On the other hand, peculiar to the states that have more leisure and prosperity, and also pay attention to public decorum, are the offices of Superintendent of Women, Guardian of the Laws, Superintendent of Children, Controller of Physical Training, and in addition to these the superintendence of athletic and Dionysiac contests and of any similar displays that happen to be held. Some of these offices are obviously not of a popular character, for instance that of Superintendent of Women and of Children ; for the poor having no slaves are forced to employ their women and children as servants. There are three offices which in some states supervise the election of the chief magistrates—Guardians of the Laws, Preliminary Councillors and Council ; of

(3) Other officials (in wealthy states).

529

βούλων βουλῆς, οἱ μὲν νομοφύλακες ἀριστοκρα
τικόν, ὀλιγαρχικὸν δ' οἱ πρόβουλοι, βουλὴ δὲ δημο-
10 τικόν. περὶ μὲν οὖν τῶν ἀρχῶν ὡς ἐν τύπῳ
σχεδὸν εἴρηται περὶ πασῶν.

these the Guardians of the Laws are an aristocratic institution, the Preliminary Councillors oligarchic, and a Council democratic.

We have now therefore spoken in outline about almost all the offices of state.

Η

I.

Περὶ πολιτείας ἀρίστης τὸν μέλλοντα ποιήσασθαι τὴν προσήκουσαν ζήτησιν ἀνάγκη διορίσασθαι
πρῶτον τίς αἱρετώτατος βίος. ἀδήλου γὰρ ὄντος
τούτου καὶ τὴν ἀρίστην ἀναγκαῖον ἄδηλον εἶναι
πολιτείαν, ἄριστα γὰρ πράττειν προσήκει τοὺς
ἄριστα πολιτευομένους ἐκ τῶν ὑπαρχόντων αὐτοῖς,
ἐὰν μή τι γίγνηται παράλογον. διὸ δεῖ πρῶτον
ὁμολογεῖσθαι τίς ὁ πᾶσιν ὡς εἰπεῖν αἱρετώτατος
βίος, μετὰ δὲ τοῦτο πότερον κοινῇ καὶ χωρὶς ὁ
αὐτὸς ἢ ἕτερος. νομίσαντας οὖν ἱκανῶς πολλὰ
λέγεσθαι καὶ τῶν ἐν τοῖς ἐξωτερικοῖς λόγοις περὶ
τῆς ἀρίστης ζωῆς, καὶ νῦν χρηστέον αὐτοῖς. ὡς
ἀληθῶς γὰρ πρός γε μίαν διαίρεσιν οὐδεὶς ἀμφισβητήσειεν ἂν ὡς οὐ τριῶν οὐσῶν μερίδων, τῶν
τε ἐκτὸς καὶ τῶν ἐν τῷ σώματι καὶ τῶν ἐν τῇ
ψυχῇ, πάντα ταῦτα ὑπάρχειν τοῖς μακαρίοις χρή.[1]
οὐδεὶς γὰρ ἂν φαίη μακάριον τὸν μηθὲν μόριον
ἔχοντα ἀνδρείας μηδὲ σωφροσύνης μηδὲ δικαιοσύνης μηδὲ φρονήσεως, ἀλλὰ δεδιότα μὲν τὰς
παραπετομένας μυίας, ἀπεχόμενον δὲ μηθενός, ἂν

---

[1] δεῖ Victorius.

---

a Book IV. in some editions.
b Cf. c. iii. § 6. It is debated whether the phrase refers
to Aristotle's own popular writings, or to those of other
532

BOOK VII [a]

I. The student who is going to make a suitable investigation of the best form of constitution must necessarily decide first of all what is the most desirable mode of life. For while this is uncertain it is also bound to be uncertain what is the best constitution, since it is to be expected that the people that have the best form of government available under their given conditions will fare the best, exceptional circumstances apart. Hence we must first agree what life is most desirable for almost all men, and after that whether the same life is most desirable both for the community and for the individual, or a different one. Believing therefore in the adequacy of much of what is said even in extraneous discourses [b] on the subject of the best life, let us make use of these pronouncements now. For as regards at all events one classification of things good, putting them in three groups, external goods, goods of the soul and goods of the body, assuredly nobody would deny that the ideally happy are bound to possess all three. For nobody would call a man ideally happy that has not got a particle of courage nor of temperance nor of justice nor of wisdom, but is afraid of the flies that flutter by him, cannot refrain from any of the most

Book VII.
THE BEST
CONSTITU-
TION.

cc. i.-iii.
Résumé of
Nic. Ethics.
The best
state gives
the best
life.

Goods of
mind, body
and estate:
the first
the highest,

philosophers, or to discussions of the subject in ordinary intercourse.

1323 a
ἐπιθυμήσῃ τοῦ φαγεῖν ἢ πιεῖν, τῶν ἐσχάτων,
ἕνεκα δὲ τεταρτημορίου διαφθείροντα τοὺς φιλτά-
τους [φίλους],[1] ὁμοίως δὲ καὶ τὰ περὶ τὴν διάνοιαν
οὕτως ἄφρονα καὶ διεψευσμένον ὥσπερ τι παιδίον
ἢ μαινόμενον. ἀλλὰ ταῦτα μὲν λεγόμενα [ὥσπερ][2]

35 πάντες ἂν συγχωρήσειαν, διαφέρονται δ' ἐν τῷ
ποσῷ καὶ ταῖς ὑπεροχαῖς. τῆς μὲν γὰρ ἀρετῆς
ἔχειν ἱκανὸν εἶναι νομίζουσιν ὁποσονοῦν, πλούτου
δὲ καὶ χρημάτων καὶ δυνάμεως καὶ δόξης καὶ
πάντων τῶν τοιούτων εἰς ἄπειρον ζητοῦσι τὴν
ὑπερβολήν. ἡμεῖς δὲ αὐτοῖς ἐροῦμεν ὅτι ῥᾴδιον

40 μὲν περὶ τούτων καὶ διὰ τῶν ἔργων λαμβάνειν[3]
τὴν πίστιν, ὁρῶντας ὅτι κτῶνται καὶ φυλάττουσιν
οὐ τὰς ἀρετὰς τοῖς ἐκτὸς ἀλλ' ἐκεῖνα ταύταις,

1323 b καὶ τὸ ζῆν εὐδαιμόνως, εἴτ' ἐν τῷ χαίρειν ἐστὶν εἴτ'
ἐν ἀρετῇ τοῖς ἀνθρώποις εἴτ' ἐν ἀμφοῖν, ὅτι μᾶλλον
ὑπάρχει τοῖς τὸ ἦθος μὲν καὶ τὴν διάνοιαν κεκο-
σμημένοις εἰς ὑπερβολὴν περὶ δὲ τὴν ἔξω κτῆσιν

5 τῶν ἀγαθῶν μετριάζουσιν ἢ τοῖς ἐκεῖνα μὲν
κεκτημένοις πλείω τῶν χρησίμων ἐν δὲ τούτοις
ἐλλείπουσιν. οὐ μὴν ἀλλὰ καὶ κατὰ τὸν λόγον
σκοπουμένοις εὐσύνοπτόν ἐστιν. τὰ μὲν γὰρ
ἐκτὸς ἔχει πέρας, ὥσπερ ὄργανόν τι (πᾶν δὲ
τὸ χρήσιμον εἴς τι[4]), ὧν τὴν ὑπερβολὴν ἢ
βλάπτειν ἀναγκαῖον ἢ μηθὲν ὄφελος εἶναι[5] τοῖς

10 ἔχουσιν· τῶν δὲ περὶ ψυχὴν ἕκαστον ἀγαθῶν,
ὅσῳ περ ἂν ὑπερβάλλῃ, τοσούτῳ μᾶλλον χρήσιμον
εἶναι,[6] εἰ δεῖ καὶ τούτοις ἐπιλέγειν μὴ μόνον τ

---

[1] Coraes.   [2] Richards: ἁπλῶς Bernays.
[3] Vahlen: διαβαίνειν ΓΜΡ[1]: διαλαμβάνειν cet.
[4] εἴς τι Vahlen: ἐστιν codd. (⟨ἀλλήλων⟩ ἐστίν Richards).
[5] εἶναι ΓΜΡ[1]: εἶναι αὐτῶν cett.

outrageous actions in order to gratify a desire to eat
or to drink, ruins his dearest friends for the sake of
a farthing, and similarly in matters of the intellect
also is as senseless and mistaken as any child or
lunatic. But although these are propositions which
when uttered everybody would agree to, yet men
differ about amount and degrees of value. They
think it is enough to possess however small a quantity
of virtue, but of wealth, riches, power, glory and
everything of that kind they seek a larger and larger
amount without limit. We on the other hand shall
tell them that it is easy to arrive at conviction on
these matters in the light of the actual facts, when one
sees that men do not acquire and preserve the virtues
by means of these external goods, but external goods
by means of the virtues, and that whether the life
of happiness consists for man in enjoyment or in
virtue or in both, it is found in larger measure with
those who are of surpassingly high cultivation in
character and intellect but only moderate as regards
the external acquisition of goods, than with those
who own more than they can use of the latter but
are deficient in the former. Not but what the truth because
is also easily seen if we consider the matter in the they are
light of reason. For external goods have a limit, as (1) ends,
as any instrument (and everything useful is useful (2) psychic,
for something), so an excessive amount of them must and (3) the
necessarily do harm, or do no good, to its possessor; others are
whereas with any of the goods of the soul, the more means.
abundant it is, the more useful it must be—if even
to goods of the soul not only the term ' noble ' but

---

⁶ χρήσιμον [εἶναι], ⟨χρὴ⟩ χρήσιμον εἶναι, χρήσιμόν ἐστι edd.
sed fortasse ἀναγκαῖον intelligendum).

1323 b

καλὸν ἀλλὰ καὶ τὸ χρήσιμον. ὅλως τε δῆλον ὡ
ἀκολουθεῖν φήσομεν τὴν διάθεσιν τὴν ἀρίστη
ἑκάστου πράγματος πρὸς ἄλληλα κατὰ τὴν ὑπερ
15 οχὴν ἥνπερ εἴληφε διάστασιν ὧν φαμὲν αὐτὰ
εἶναι διαθέσεις ταύτας. ὥστ᾽ εἴπερ ἐστὶν ἡ ψυχ
καὶ τῆς κτήσεως καὶ τοῦ σώματος τιμιώτερον κα
ἁπλῶς καὶ ἡμῖν, ἀνάγκη καὶ τὴν διάθεσιν τὴ
ἀρίστην ἑκάστου ἀνάλογον τούτων ἔχειν. ἔτι δ
20 τῆς ψυχῆς ἕνεκεν ταῦτα πέφυκεν αἱρετὰ καὶ δε
πάντας αἱρεῖσθαι τοὺς εὖ φρονοῦντας, ἀλλ᾽ οὐ
ἐκείνων ἕνεκεν τὴν ψυχήν. ὅτι μὲν οὖν ἑκάστ
τῆς εὐδαιμονίας ἐπιβάλλει τοσοῦτον ὅσον πε
ἀρετῆς καὶ φρονήσεως καὶ τοῦ πράττειν κατὰ ταύ
τας, ἔστω συνωμολογημένον ἡμῖν, μάρτυρι τε
θεῷ χρωμένοις, ὃς εὐδαίμων μέν ἐστι καὶ μακάριος
25 δι᾽ οὐθὲν δὲ τῶν ἐξωτερικῶν ἀγαθῶν ἀλλὰ δ
αὐτὸν αὐτὸς καὶ τῷ ποιός τις εἶναι τὴν φύσιν· ἐπε
καὶ τὴν εὐτυχίαν τῆς εὐδαιμονίας διὰ ταῦτ
ἀναγκαῖον ἑτέραν εἶναι, τῶν μὲν γὰρ ἐκτὸ
ἀγαθῶν τῆς ψυχῆς αἴτιον ταὐτόματον καὶ ἡ τύχ
δίκαιος δ᾽ οὐδεὶς οὐδὲ σώφρων ἀπὸ τύχης οὐδ
30 διὰ τὴν τύχην ἐστίν. ἐχόμενον δ᾽ ἐστὶ καὶ τῶ
αὐτῶν λόγων δεόμενον καὶ πόλιν εὐδαίμονα τὴ
ἀρίστην εἶναι καὶ πράττουσαν καλῶς. ἀδύνατο
δὲ καλῶς πράττειν τοῖς μὴ τὰ καλὰ πράττουσι
οὐθὲν δὲ καλὸν ἔργον οὔτ᾽ ἀνδρὸς οὔτε πόλεω

ᵃ e.g. the finest man excels the finest monkey to the degr
in which the species man excels the species monkey.
ᵇ Aristotle taught that some events are the result of th
undesigned interaction of two lines of causation in nature
design; he denoted this (1) in general, by 'the automatic
or self-acting (represented in Latin by *sponte,* spontaneous
(2) as concerning man, by 'fortune.'

also the term ' useful ' can be properly applied. And broadly, it is clear that we shall declare that the best condition of each particular thing, comparing things with one another, corresponds in point of superiority to the distance that subsists between the things of which we declare these conditions themselves to be conditions.[a] Hence inasmuch as our soul is a more valuable thing both absolutely and relatively to ourselves than either our property or our body, the best conditions of these things must necessarily stand in the same relation to one another as the things themselves do. Moreover it is for the sake of the soul that these goods are in their nature desirable, and that all wise men must choose them, not the soul for the sake of those other things. Let us then take it as agreed between us that to each man there falls just so large a measure of happiness as he achieves of virtue and wisdom and of virtuous and wise action : in evidence of this we have the case of God, who is happy and blessed, but is so on account of no external goods, but on account of himself, and by being of a certain quality in his nature ; since it is also for this reason that prosperity is necessarily different from happiness—for the cause of goods external to the soul is the spontaneous and fortune,[b] but nobody is just or temperate as a result of or owing to the action of fortune. And connected is a truth requiring the same arguments to prove it, that it is also the best state, and the one that does well,[c] that is happy. But to do well is impossible save for those who do good actions, and there is no good action either of a

Virtue and wisdom give happiness to a man.

[c] The common play on the ambiguity of ' do well,' meaning either ' prosper ' or ' act rightly.'

ARISTOTLE

χωρὶς ἀρετῆς καὶ φρονήσεως· ἀνδρεία δὲ πόλεως
καὶ δικαιοσύνη καὶ φρόνησις[1] τὴν αὐτὴν ἔχει
35 δύναμιν καὶ μορφὴν ὧν μετασχὼν ἕκαστος τῶν
ἀνθρώπων λέγεται δίκαιος καὶ[2] φρόνιμος καὶ
σώφρων.

Ἀλλὰ γὰρ ταῦτα μὲν ἐπὶ τοσοῦτον ἔστω πεφροι-
μιασμένα τῷ λόγῳ· οὔτε γὰρ μὴ θιγγάνειν αὐτῶν
δυνατόν, οὔτε πάντας τοὺς οἰκείους ἐπεξελθεῖν
ἐνδέχεται λόγους, ἑτέρας γάρ ἐστιν ἔργον σχολῆς
40 ταῦτα. νῦν δ᾽ ὑποκείσθω τοσοῦτον, ὅτι βίος μὲν
ἄριστος, καὶ χωρὶς ἑκάστῳ καὶ κοινῇ ταῖς πόλεσιν,
1324 a ὁ μετὰ ἀρετῆς κεχορηγημένης ἐπὶ τοσοῦτον ὥστε
μετέχειν τῶν κατ᾽ ἀρετὴν πράξεων, πρὸς δὲ τοὺς
ἀμφισβητοῦντας, ἐάσαντας ἐπὶ τῆς νῦν μεθόδου,
διασκεπτέον ὕστερον, εἴ τις τοῖς εἰρημένοις τυγχάνει μὴ πειθόμενος.

5 II. Πότερον δὲ τὴν εὐδαιμονίαν τὴν αὐτὴν εἶναι
φατέον ἑνός τε ἑκάστου τῶν ἀνθρώπων καὶ
πόλεως ἢ μὴ τὴν αὐτὴν λοιπόν ἐστιν εἰπεῖν.
φανερὸν δὲ καὶ τοῦτο· πάντες γὰρ ἂν ὁμολογήσειαν
εἶναι τὴν αὐτήν· ὅσοι γὰρ ἐν πλούτῳ τὸ ζῆν εὖ
τίθενται ἐφ᾽ ἑνός, οὗτοι καὶ τὴν πόλιν ὅλην ἐὰν
10 ᾖ πλουσία μακαρίζουσιν, ὅσοι τε τὸν τυραννικὸν
βίον μάλιστα τιμῶσιν, οὗτοι καὶ πόλιν τὴν πλείστων
ἄρχουσαν εὐδαιμονεστάτην ἂν εἶναι φαῖεν· εἴ τε
τις τὸν ἕνα δι᾽ ἀρετὴν ἀποδέχεται, καὶ πόλιν
εὐδαιμονεστέραν φήσει τὴν σπουδαιοτέραν. ἀλλὰ
ταῦτ᾽ ἤδη δύο ἐστὶν ἃ δεῖται σκέψεως, ἓν μὲ
15 πότερος αἱρετώτερος βίος, ὁ διὰ τοῦ συμπολιτεύε-

---

[1] φρόνησις ⟨καὶ σωφροσύνη⟩ Coraes.
[2] καὶ ⟨ἀνδρεῖος καὶ⟩ Coraes.

---

[a] *Eth. Nic.* i. 1099 a 32, x. 1179 a 4 ff.

..an or of a state without virtue and wisdom ; and
..urage, justice and wisdom belonging to a state have
..e same meaning and form as have those virtues
..hose possession bestows the titles of just and wise
..nd temperate on an individual human being.

These remarks however must suffice by way of preface provided a
sufficiency
of worldly
goods.
.. our discourse : for neither is it possible to abstain
..om touching on these subjects altogether, nor is it
..asible to follow out all the arguments that are ger-
..ane to them, for that is the business of another
..urse of study. For the present let us take it as estab-
..shed that the best life, whether separately for an in-
..ividual or collectively for states, is the life conjoined
..ith virtue furnished with sufficient means for taking
..art in virtuous actions[a]; while objections to this
..osition we must pass over in the course of the present
..quiry, and reserve them for future consideration, if
..nyone is found to disagree with what has been said.

II. On the other hand it remains to say whether True also
of the State.
..e happiness of a state is to be pronounced the same
.. that of each individual man, or whether it is
..fferent. Here too the answer is clear : everybody
..ould agree that it is the same ; for all those who
..ase the good life upon wealth in the case of the
..dividual, also assign felicity to the state as a whole
.. it is wealthy ; and all who value the life of the
..rant highest, would also say that the state which
..les the widest empire is the happiest ; and if any-
..dy accepts the individual as happy on account of
..rtue, he will also say that the state which is the
..tter morally is the happier. But there now arise
..ese two questions that require consideration :
..rst, which mode of life is the more desirable, the
..fe of active citizenship and participation in politics,

1324 a

σθαι καὶ κοινωνεῖν πόλεως ἢ μᾶλλον ὁ ξενικὸς
καὶ τῆς πολιτικῆς κοινωνίας ἀπολελυμένος, ἔτι
δὲ τίνα πολιτείαν θετέον καὶ ποίαν διάθεσιν πόλεως ἀρίστην, εἴτε πᾶσιν ὄντος αἱρετοῦ κοινωνεῖν
20 πόλεως εἴτε καὶ τισὶ μὲν μὴ τοῖς δὲ πλείστοις
ἐπεὶ δὲ τῆς πολιτικῆς διανοίας καὶ θεωρίας τοῦτ'
ἐστὶν ἔργον, ἀλλ' οὐ τὸ περὶ ἕκαστον αἱρετόν·
ἡμεῖς δὲ ταύτην προηρήμεθα νῦν τὴν σκέψιν, ἐκείν
μὲν[1] πάρεργον ἂν εἴη, τοῦτο δ' ἔργον τῆς μεθόδο
ταύτης.

Ὅτι μὲν οὖν ἀναγκαῖον εἶναι πολιτείαν ἀρίστη
ταύτην καθ' ἣν τάξιν κἂν ὁστισοῦν ἄριστα πράττο
25 καὶ ζῴη μακαρίως φανερόν ἐστιν· ἀμφισβητεῖτα
δὲ παρ' αὐτῶν τῶν ὁμολογούντων τὸν μετ' ἀρετῆ
εἶναι βίον αἱρετώτατον πότερον ὁ πολιτικὸς κα
πρακτικὸς βίος αἱρετὸς ἢ μᾶλλον ὁ πάντων τῶ
ἐκτὸς ἀπολελυμένος, οἷον θεωρητικός τις, ὃν μόνο
τινές φασιν εἶναι φιλόσοφον.[2] σχεδὸν γὰρ τούτου
30 τοὺς δύο βίους τῶν ἀνθρώπων οἱ φιλοτιμότατο
πρὸς ἀρετὴν φαίνονται προαιρούμενοι καὶ τῶ
προτέρων καὶ τῶν νῦν, λέγω δὲ δύο τόν τε πολι
τικὸν καὶ τὸν φιλόσοφον. διαφέρει δὲ οὐ μικρο
ποτέρως ἔχει τὸ ἀληθές· ἀνάγκη γὰρ τόν γε[3] ε
φρονοῦντα πρὸς τὸν βελτίω σκοπὸν συντάττεσθα
35 καὶ τῶν ἀνθρώπων ἕκαστον καὶ κοινῇ τὴν πολι
τείαν. νομίζουσι δ' οἱ μὲν τὸ τῶν πέλας ἄρχει
δεσποτικῶς μὲν γιγνόμενον μετ' ἀδικίας τινὸ
εἶναι τῆς μεγίστης, πολιτικῶς δὲ τὸ μὲν ἄδικο

[1] μὲν γὰρ codd. plurimi.
[2] φιλόσοφοι Jackson : φιλοσόφου Richards.
[3] γε Spengel : τε codd.

* Perhaps the Greek should be altered to give ' whic
alone is said to be desirable by some philosophers.'

540

or rather the life of an alien and that of detachment from the political partnership ; next, what constitution and what organization of a state is to be deemed the best,—either on the assumption that to take an active part in the state is desirable for everybody, or that it is undesirable for some men although desirable for most. But as it is the latter question that is the business of political study and speculation, and not the question of what is desirable for the individual, and as it is the investigation of politics that we have now taken up, the former question would be a side issue, and the latter is the business of political inquiry.

Now it is clear that the best constitution is the system under which anybody whatsoever would be best off and would live in felicity ; but the question is raised even on the part of those who agree that the life accompanied by virtue is the most desirable, whether the life of citizenship and activity is desirable or rather a life released from all external affairs, for example some form of contemplative life, which is said by some to be the only life that is philosophic.[a] For it is manifest that these are the two modes of life principally chosen by the men most ambitious of excelling in virtue, both in past times and at the present day—I mean the life of politics and the life of philosophy. And it makes no little difference which way the truth lies ; for assuredly the wise are bound to arrange their affairs in the direction of the better goal—and this applies to the state collectively as well as to the individual human being. Some persons think that empire over one's neighbours, if despotically exercised, involves a definite injustice of the greatest kind, and if constitutionally, although

The active v. the contemplative life for the individual.

541

1324 a

οὐκ ἔχειν, ἐμπόδιον δὲ ἔχειν τῇ περὶ αὐτὸν
εὐημερίᾳ· τούτων δ' ὥσπερ ἐξ ἐναντίας ἕτεροι
40 τυγχάνουσι δοξάζοντες, μόνον γὰρ ἀνδρὸς τὸν
πρακτικὸν εἶναι βίον καὶ πολιτικόν, ἐφ'[1] ἑκάστης
γὰρ ἀρετῆς οὐκ εἶναι πράξεις μᾶλλον τοῖς ἰδιώταις
1324 b ἢ τοῖς τὰ κοινὰ πράττουσι καὶ πολιτευομένοις.
οἱ μὲν οὖν οὕτως ὑπολαμβάνουσιν, οἱ δὲ τὸν
δεσποτικὸν καὶ τυραννικὸν τρόπον τῆς πολιτείας
εἶναι μόνον εὐδαίμονά φασιν· παρ' ἐνίοις δὲ καὶ
5 τῆς πολιτείας οὗτος ὅρος καὶ τῶν[2] νόμων ὅπως
δεσπόζωσι τῶν πέλας. διὸ καὶ τῶν πλείστων
νομίμων χύδην ὡς εἰπεῖν κειμένων παρὰ τοῖς
πλείστοις, ὅμως εἴ πού τι πρὸς ἓν οἱ νόμοι βλέπουσι,
τοῦ κρατεῖν στοχάζονται πάντες, ὥσπερ ἐν Λακεδαίμονι καὶ Κρήτῃ πρὸς τοὺς πολέμους συντέτακται σχεδὸν ἥ τε παιδεία καὶ τὸ τῶν νόμων πλῆθος·
10 ἔτι δ' ἐν τοῖς ἔθνεσι πᾶσι τοῖς δυναμένοις πλεονεκτεῖν ἡ τοιαύτη τετίμηται δύναμις, οἷον ἐν Σκύθαις καὶ Πέρσαις καὶ Θραξὶ καὶ Κελτοῖς. ἐν
ἐνίοις γὰρ καὶ νόμοι τινές εἰσι παροξύνοντες πρὸς
τὴν ἀρετὴν ταύτην, καθάπερ ἐν Καρχηδόνι φασὶ
τὸν ἐκ τῶν κρίκων κόσμον λαμβάνειν ὅσας ἂν
15 στρατεύσωνται στρατείας· ἦν δέ ποτε καὶ περὶ
Μακεδονίαν νόμος τὸν μηθένα ἀπεκταγκότα πολέμιον ἄνδρα περιεζῶσθαι τὴν φορβειάν· ἐν δὲ
Σκύθαις οὐκ ἐξῆν πίνειν ἐν ἑορτῇ τινι σκύφον
περιφερόμενον τῷ μηθένα ἀπεκταγκότι πολέμιον·
ἐν δὲ τοῖς Ἴβηρσιν, ἔθνει πολεμικῷ, τοσούτους τὸν

[1] ἀφ' Richards.
[2] καὶ τῶν Congreve (δ' οὗτος καὶ τῶν νόμων καὶ τῆς πολιτείας
ὅρος ΓΜ, et sic cum παιδείας pro πολιτείας Busse): τῶν codd.

it carries no injustice, yet is a hindrance to the
ruler's own well-being; but others hold almost the
opposite view to these—they think that the life of
action and citizenship is the only life fit for a man,
since with each of the virtues its exercise in actions
is just as possible for men engaged in public affairs
and in politics as for those who live a private life.
Some people then hold the former view, while others Imperialism
declare that the despotic and tyrannical form of for the
State.
constitution alone achieves happiness; and in some
states it is also the distinctive aim of the constitution
and the laws to enable them to exercise despotic
rule over their neighbours. Hence even though
with most peoples most of the legal ordinances have
been laid down virtually at random, nevertheless if
there are places where the laws aim at one definite
object, that object is in all cases power, as in Sparta
and Crete both the system of education and the mass
of the laws are framed in the main with a view to
war; and also among all the non-Hellenic nations
that are strong enough to expand at the expense of
others, military strength has been held in honour, for
example, among the Scythians, Persians, Thracians
and Celts. Indeed among some peoples there are
even certain laws stimulating military valour; for
instance at Carthage, we are told, warriors receive
the decoration of armlets of the same number as
the campaigns on which they have served; and at
one time there was also a law in Macedonia that a
man who had never killed an enemy must wear his
halter instead of a belt. Among Scythian tribes at
a certain festival a cup was carried round from which
a man that had not killed an enemy was not allowed
to drink. Among the Iberians, a warlike race, they

1324 b

20 ἀριθμὸν ὀβελίσκους καταπηγνύουσι περὶ τὸν τάφον
ὅσους ἂν διαφθείρῃ τῶν πολεμίων· καὶ ἕτερα δὴ
παρ' ἑτέροις ἐστὶ τοιαῦτα πολλά, τὰ μὲν νόμοις
κατειλημμένα τὰ δὲ ἔθεσιν.

Καίτοι δόξειεν ἂν ἄγαν ἄτοπον ἴσως εἶναι τοῖς
βουλομένοις ἐπισκοπεῖν, εἰ τοῦτ' ἐστὶν ἔργον τοῦ
25 πολιτικοῦ, τὸ δύνασθαι θεωρεῖν ὅπως ἄρχῃ καὶ
δεσπόζῃ τῶν πλησίον καὶ βουλομένων καὶ μὴ
βουλομένων. πῶς γὰρ ἂν εἴη τοῦτο πολιτικὸν ἢ
νομοθετικὸν ὅ γε μηδὲ νόμιμόν ἐστιν; οὐ νόμιμον
δὲ τὸ μὴ μόνον δικαίως ἀλλὰ καὶ ἀδίκως ἄρχειν,
κρατεῖν δ' ἔστι καὶ μὴ δικαίως. ἀλλὰ μὴν οὐδ'
30 ἐν ταῖς ἄλλαις ἐπιστήμαις τοῦτο ὁρῶμεν· οὔτε γὰρ
τοῦ ἰατροῦ οὔτε τοῦ κυβερνήτου ἔργον ἐστὶ τὸ ἢ
πεῖσαι ἢ βιάσασθαι τοῦ μὲν τοὺς θεραπευομένους
τοῦ δὲ τοὺς πλωτῆρας. ἀλλ' ἐοίκασιν οἱ πολλοὶ
τὴν δεσποτικὴν πολιτικὴν[1] οἴεσθαι εἶναι, καὶ ὅπερ
αὑτοῖς ἕκαστοι οὔ φασιν εἶναι δίκαιον οὐδὲ συμφέρον, τοῦτ' οὐκ αἰσχύνονται πρὸς τοὺς ἄλλους
35 ἀσκοῦντες· αὐτοὶ μὲν γὰρ παρ' αὑτοῖς τὸ δικαίως
ἄρχειν ζητοῦσι, πρὸς δὲ τοὺς ἄλλους οὐδὲν μέλει
τῶν δικαίων. ἄτοπον δὲ εἰ μὴ φύσει τὸ μὲν
δεσποστόν ἐστι τὸ δὲ οὐ δεσποστόν,[2] ὥστε εἴπερ
ἔχει τὸν τρόπον τοῦτον, οὐ δεῖ πάντων πειρᾶσθαι
δεσπόζειν, ἀλλὰ τῶν δεσποστῶν,[3] ὥσπερ οὐδὲ
40 θηρεύειν ἐπὶ θοίνην ἢ θυσίαν ἀνθρώπους, ἀλλὰ τὸ
πρὸς τοῦτο θηρευτόν· ἔστι δὲ θηρευτὸν ὃ ἂν ἄγριον
1325 a ᾖ ἐδεστὸν ζῷον. ἀλλὰ μὴν εἴη γ' ἂν καὶ καθ'

---

[1] τὴν πολιτικὴν δεσποτικήν ? Richards.
[2] δεσποστόν (bis) Stahr: δεσπόζον (bis) codd.
[3] Lambinus: δεσποτῶν codd.

---

[a] Or perhaps ' pointed stones.'

fix small spits *a* in the earth round a man's grave corresponding in number to the enemies he has killed. So with other races there are many other practices of a similar kind, some established by law and others by custom.

Nevertheless those who wish to examine the matter closely might perhaps think it exceedingly strange that it should be the business of a statesman to be able to devise means of holding empire and mastery over the neighbouring peoples whether they desire it or not. How can that be worthy of a statesman or lawgiver which is not even lawful ? and government is not lawful when it is carried on not only justly but also unjustly—and superior strength may be unjustly exercised. Moreover we do not see this in the other sciences either : it is no part of a physician's or ship-captain's business to use either persuasion or compulsion upon the patients in the one case and the crew *b* in the other. Yet most peoples seem to think that despotic rule is statesmanship, and are not ashamed to practise towards others treatment which they declare to be unjust and detrimental for themselves ; for in their own internal affairs they demand just government, yet in their relations with other peoples they pay no attention to justice. Yet it is strange if there is not a natural distinction between peoples suited to be despotically ruled and those not suited ; so that if this is so, it is not proper to attempt to exercise despotic government over all people, but only over those suited for it, just as it is not right to hunt human beings for food or sacrifice, but only the game suitable for this purpose, that is, such wild creatures as are good to eat. And more-

Qualifications.

b Or perhaps ' the passengers.'

545

ἑαυτὴν μία πόλις εὐδαίμων, ἢ πολιτεύεται δηλον
ὅτι καλῶς, εἴπερ ἐνδέχεται πόλιν οἰκεῖσθαί πο
καθ' ἑαυτὴν νόμοις χρωμένην σπουδαίοις, ἧ
τῆς πολιτείας ἡ σύνταξις οὐ πρὸς πόλεμον οὐδ
5 πρὸς τὸ κρατεῖν ἔσται τῶν πολεμίων· μηθὲν γὰ
ὑπαρχέτω τοιοῦτον. δῆλον ἄρα ὅτι πάσας τὰ
πρὸς τὸν πόλεμον ἐπιμελείας καλὰς μὲν θετέον
οὐχ ὡς τέλος δὲ πάντων ἀκρόταταν ἀλλ' ἐκείνο
χάριν ταύτας. τοῦ δὲ νομοθέτου τοῦ σπουδαίο
10 ἐστὶ τὸ θεάσασθαι πόλιν καὶ γένος ἀνθρώπων κα
πᾶσαν ἄλλην κοινωνίαν, ζωῆς ἀγαθῆς πῶς μεθ
ἕξουσι καὶ τῆς ἐνδεχομένης αὐτοῖς εὐδαιμονίας
διοίσει μέντοι τῶν ταττομένων ἔνια νομίμων· κα
τοῦτο τῆς νομοθετικῆς ἐστιν ἰδεῖν, ἐάν τινες ὑπ
ἄρχωσι γειτνιῶντες, ποῖα πρὸς ποίους ἀσκητέον ἢ
πῶς τοῖς καθήκουσι πρὸς ἑκάστους χρηστέον.

Ἀλλὰ τοῦτο μὲν κἂν ὕστερον τύχοι τῆς προσ
15 ηκούσης σκέψεως, πρὸς τί τέλος δεῖ τὴν ἀρίστη
πολιτείαν συντείνειν.

III. Πρὸς δὲ τοὺς ὁμολογοῦντας μὲν τὸν μετ
ἀρετῆς εἶναι βίον αἱρετώτατον διαφερομένους δ
περὶ τῆς χρήσεως αὐτοῦ, λεκτέον ἡμῖν πρὸς ἀμφο
τέρους αὐτούς (οἱ μὲν γὰρ ἀποδοκιμάζουσι τὰ
πολιτικὰς ἀρχάς, νομίζοντες τὸν[2] τοῦ ἐλευθέρο
20 βίον ἕτερόν τινα εἶναι τοῦ πολιτικοῦ καὶ πάντω
αἱρετώτατον, οἱ δὲ τοῦτον ἄριστον, ἀδύνατον γὰ
τὸν μηθὲν πράττοντα πράττειν εὖ, τὴν δ' εὐπρα
γίαν καὶ τὴν εὐδαιμονίαν εἶναι ταὐτόν), ὅτι τὰ μὲ
ἀμφότεροι λέγουσιν ὀρθῶς τὰ δ' οὐκ ὀρθῶς, οἱ μὲ

---

[1] ἢ: καὶ ? Richards.   [2] Spengel: τόν τε codd.

[a] See cc. xiii., xiv.
[b] On the ambiguous use of 'do well' see 1323 b 32 n.

over it is possible even for a single state in isolation to be happy, that is one that is well governed, inasmuch as it is conceivable that a state might be carried on somewhere in isolation, enjoying good laws, and in such a state the system of the constitution will not be framed for the purpose of war or of overpowering its enemies—for we are to suppose everything to do with war to be excluded. It is evident therefore that while all military pursuits are to be deemed honourable, they are not so as being the ultimate end of all things but as means to that end. And it is the business of the good lawgiver to study how a state, a race of men or any other community is to partake of the good life and the happiness possible for them. Some however of the regulations laid down will vary ; and in case there exist any neighbour peoples, it is the business of the legislative art to consider what sort of exercises should be practised in relation to what sort of neighbours or how the state is to adopt the regulations that are suitable in relation to each.

War only a means.

But this question of the proper end for the best constitutions to aim at may receive its due consideration later.[a]

III. We turn to those who, while agreeing that the life of virtue is the most desirable, differ about the way in which that life should be pursued. Some disapprove of holding office in the state, thinking that the life of the free man is different from the life of politics and is the most desirable of any ; whereas others think the political life the best life, for they argue that it is impossible for the man who does nothing to do well, and doing well and happiness are the same thing.[b] To these two parties we must reply that both are partly right and partly wrong. The

The active life for man and State.

547

1325 a

ὅτι ὁ τοῦ ἐλευθέρου βίος τοῦ δεσποτικοῦ ἀμείνω
25 τοῦτο γὰρ ἀληθές, οὐθὲν γὰρ τό γε δούλῳ,
δοῦλος, χρῆσθαι σεμνόν, ἡ γὰρ ἐπίταξις ἡ περ
τῶν ἀναγκαίων οὐδενὸς μετέχει τῶν καλῶν· τ
μέντοι νομίζειν πᾶσαν ἀρχὴν εἶναι δεσποτεία
οὐκ ὀρθόν, οὐ γὰρ ἔλαττον διέστηκεν ἡ τῶν ἐλει
θέρων ἀρχὴ τῆς τῶν δούλων ἢ αὐτὸ τὸ φύσ
30 ἐλεύθερον τοῦ φύσει δούλου. διώρισται δὲ πε
αὐτῶν ἱκανῶς ἐν τοῖς πρώτοις λόγοις. τὸ δ
μᾶλλον ἐπαινεῖν τὸ ἀπρακτεῖν τοῦ πράττειν οὐ
ἀληθές· ἡ γὰρ εὐδαιμονία πρᾶξίς ἐστιν, ἔτι δὲ πολ
λῶν καὶ καλῶν τέλος ἔχουσιν αἱ τῶν δικαίων κ
σωφρόνων πράξεις. καίτοι τάχ' ἂν ὑπολάβοι τ
35 τούτων οὕτω διωρισμένων ὅτι τὸ κύριον εἶν
πάντων ἄριστον, οὕτω γὰρ ἂν πλείστων κ
καλλίστων κύριος εἴη πράξεων· ὥστε οὐ δεῖν[1] τ
δυνάμενον ἄρχειν παριέναι τῷ πλησίον, ἀλλ
μᾶλλον ἀφαιρεῖσθαι, καὶ μήτε πατέρα παίδων μή
παῖδας πατρὸς μήθ' ὅλως φίλον φίλου μηθέ
40 ὑπόλογον ποιεῖσθαι[2] μηδὲ πρὸς τοῦτο φροντίζει
τὸ γὰρ ἄριστον αἱρετώτατον, τὸ δ' εὖ πράττε
ἄριστον. τοῦτο μὲν οὖν ἀληθῶς ἴσως λέγουσι
1325 b εἴπερ ὑπάρξει τοῖς ἀποστεροῦσι καὶ βιαζομένοις τ
τῶν ὄντων αἱρετώτατον. ἀλλ' ἴσως οὐχ οἷόν τ
ὑπάρχειν, ἀλλ' ὑποτίθενται τοῦτο ψεῦδος. οὐ γὰ
ἔτι καλὰς τὰς πράξεις ἐνδέχεται εἶναι τῷ μ
διαφέροντι τοσοῦτον ὅσον ἀνὴρ γυναικὸς ἢ πατ

---

[1] Susemihl: δεῖ codd.
[2] ὑπόλογον ποιεῖσθαι Madvig: ὑπολογεῖν codd. (v.ll. ὑπ
λογεῖν, ὑπολογίζειν).

548

former are right in saying that the life of the free
man is better than the life of mastership, for this is
true—there is nothing specially dignified in employing a slave, as a slave, for giving orders about
2 menial duties has in it nothing of nobility ; yet to
think that all government is exercising the authority
of a master is a mistake, for there is as wide a difference
between ruling free men and ruling slaves as there is
between the natural freeman and the natural slave
themselves. But these things have been adequately
decided in the first discourses.ª But to praise
inaction more highly than action is an error, for
happiness is an activity, and further the actions of the
just and temperate have in them the realization of
3 much that is noble. Yet on the strength of these *Power must*
decisions somebody might perhaps suppose that the *be based*
highest good is to be the master of the world, since *on virtue*
thus one would have the power to compass the
greatest number and the noblest kind of actions, and
therefore it is not the duty of the man that is capable
of ruling to surrender office to his neighbour, but
rather to take it from him, and no account must be
taken by father of sons nor by sons of father nor in
general by one friend of another, and no heed must
be paid to them in comparison with this ; for the
best thing is the most to be desired, and to do well
4 is the best thing. Now this statement is perhaps
true if it is the case that the most desirable of existing
things will belong to men that use robbery and
violence. But perhaps it cannot belong to them, and
this is a false assumption. For a man's acts can no
longer be noble if he does not excel as greatly as
a man excels a woman or a father his children or

● *i.e.* Book I.

5 τέκνων ἢ δεσπότης δούλων, ὥστε ὁ παραβαίνων
οὐθὲν ἂν τηλικοῦτον κατορθώσειεν ὕστερον ὅσον
ἤδη παρεκβέβηκε τῆς ἀρετῆς· τοῖς γὰρ ὁμοίοις τὸ
καλὸν καὶ τὸ δίκαιον ἐν τῷ ἐν¹ μέρει, τοῦτο
γὰρ ἴσον καὶ ὅμοιον, τὸ δὲ μὴ ἴσον τοῖς ἴσοις καὶ
τὸ μὴ ὅμοιον τοῖς ὁμοίοις παρὰ φύσιν, οὐδὲν δὲ
10 τῶν παρὰ φύσιν καλόν. διὸ κἂν ἄλλος τις ᾖ
κρείττων κατ' ἀρετὴν καὶ κατὰ δύναμιν τὴν
πρακτικὴν τῶν ἀρίστων, τούτῳ καλὸν ἀκολουθεῖν
καὶ τούτῳ πείθεσθαι δίκαιον· δεῖ δ' οὐ μόνον
ἀρετὴν ἀλλὰ καὶ δύναμιν ὑπάρχειν καθ' ἣν ἔσται
πρακτικός. ἀλλ' εἰ ταῦτα λέγεται καλῶς καὶ τὴν 5
15 εὐδαιμονίαν εὐπραγίαν θετέον, καὶ κοινῇ πάσης
πόλεως ἂν εἴη καὶ καθ' ἕκαστον ἄριστος βίος ὁ
πρακτικός. ἀλλὰ τὸν πρακτικὸν οὐκ ἀναγκαῖον
εἶναι πρὸς ἑτέρους, καθάπερ οἴονταί τινες, οὐδὲ
τὰς διανοίας εἶναι μόνας ταύτας πρακτικὰς τὰς
τῶν ἀποβαινόντων χάριν γιγνομένας ἐκ τοῦ
20 πράττειν, ἀλλὰ πολὺ μᾶλλον τὰς αὐτοτελεῖς καὶ
τὰς αὑτῶν ἕνεκεν θεωρίας καὶ διανοήσεις· ἡ γὰρ
εὐπραξία τέλος, ὥστε καὶ πρᾶξίς τις. μάλιστα δὲ
καὶ πράττειν λέγομεν κυρίως καὶ τῶν ἐξωτερικῶν
πράξεων τοὺς ταῖς διανοίαις ἀρχιτέκτονας. ἀλλὰ
μὴν οὐδ' ἀπρακτεῖν ἀναγκαῖον τὰς καθ' αὑτὰς
25 πόλεις ἱδρυμένας καὶ ζῆν οὕτω προηρημένας·
ἐνδέχεται γὰρ κατὰ μέρη καὶ τοῦτο συμβαίνειν,
πολλαὶ γὰρ κοινωνίαι πρὸς ἄλληλα τοῖς μέρεσι
τῆς πόλεώς εἰσιν. ὁμοίως δὲ τοῦτο ὑπάρχει καὶ

¹ τῷ ἐν Thurot: τῷ codd.

a Cf. 1323 b 32 n., 1325 a 21.

a master his slaves, so that one who transgresses cannot afterwards achieve anything sufficient to rectify the lapse from virtue that he had already committed ; because for equals the noble and just consists in their taking turns, since this is equal and alike, but for those that are equal to have an unequal share and those that are alike an unlike share is contrary to nature, and nothing contrary to nature is noble. Hence in case there is another person who is our superior in virtue and in practical capacity for the highest functions, him it is noble to follow and him it is just to obey ; though he must possess not only virtue but also capacity that will render him capable of action. But if these things are well said, and if happiness is to be defined as well-doing, the active life is the best life both for the whole state collectively and for each man individually. But the active life is not necessarily active in relation to other men, as some people think, nor are only those processes of thought active that are pursued for the sake of the objects that result from action, but far more those speculations and thoughts that have their end in themselves and are pursued for their own sake ; for the end is to do well, and therefore is a certain form of action.[a] And even with actions done in relation to external objects we predicate action in the full sense chiefly of the master-craftsmen who direct the action by their thoughts. Moreover with cities also, those that occupy an isolated situation and pursue a policy of isolation are not necessarily inactive ; for state activities also can be sectional, since the sections of the state have many common relations with one another. And this is also possible similarly in the

[marginal note: Internal activity of state higher than external.]

1325 b

καθ᾽ ἑνὸς ὁτουοῦν τῶν ἀνθρώπων· σχολῇ γὰρ ἂν ὁ
θεὸς εἶχε[1] καλῶς καὶ πᾶς ὁ κόσμος, οἷς οὐκ εἰσὶν
30 ἐξωτερικαὶ πράξεις παρὰ τὰς οἰκείας τὰς αὐτῶν.

Ὅτι μὲν οὖν τὸν αὐτὸν βίον ἀναγκαῖον εἶναι τὸν
ἄριστον ἑκάστῳ τε τῶν ἀνθρώπων καὶ κοινῇ ταῖς
πόλεσι καὶ τοῖς ἀνθρώποις,[2] φανερόν ἐστιν.

IV. Ἐπεὶ δὲ πεφροιμίασται τὰ νῦν εἰρημένα
περὶ αὐτῶν, καὶ περὶ τὰς ἄλλας πολιτείας ἡμῖν
35 τεθεώρηται πρότερον, ἀρχὴ τῶν λοιπῶν εἰπεῖν
πρῶτον ποίας τινὰς δεῖ τὰς ὑποθέσεις εἶναι περὶ
τῆς μελλούσης κατ᾽ εὐχὴν συνεστάναι πόλεως. οὐ
γὰρ οἷόν τε πολιτείαν γενέσθαι τὴν ἀρίστην ἄνευ
συμμέτρου χορηγίας. διὸ δεῖ πολλὰ προϋπο-
τεθεῖσθαι καθάπερ εὐχομένους, εἶναι μέντοι μηθὲν
40 τούτων ἀδύνατον. λέγω δὲ οἷον περί τε πλήθους
πολιτῶν καὶ χώρας. ὥσπερ γὰρ καὶ τοῖς ἄλλοις
δημιουργοῖς, οἷον ὑφάντῃ καὶ ναυπηγῷ, δεῖ τὴν
1326 a ὕλην ὑπάρχειν ἐπιτηδείαν οὖσαν πρὸς τὴν ἐργασίαν (ὅσῳ γὰρ ἂν αὐτὴ τυγχάνῃ παρεσκευασμένη
βέλτιον, ἀνάγκη καὶ τὸ γιγνόμενον ὑπὸ τῆς τέχνης
εἶναι κάλλιον), οὕτω καὶ τῷ πολιτικῷ καὶ τῷ
5 νομοθέτῃ δεῖ τὴν οἰκείαν ὕλην ὑπάρχειν ἐπι-
τηδείως ἔχουσαν. ἔστι δὲ πολιτικῆς χορηγίας
πρῶτον τό τε πλῆθος τῶν ἀνθρώπων, πόσους τε
καὶ ποίους τινὰς ὑπάρχειν δεῖ φύσει, καὶ κατὰ τὴν
χώραν ὡσαύτως, πόσην τε εἶναι καὶ ποίαν τινὰ
ταύτην. οἴονται μὲν οὖν οἱ πλεῖστοι προσήκειν
μεγάλην εἶναι τὴν εὐδαίμονα πόλιν· εἰ δὲ τοῦτ᾽
10 ἀληθές, ἀγνοοῦσι ποία μεγάλη καὶ ποία μικρὰ

---

[1] ed. : ἔχοι codd.
[2] ἀνθρώποις : ἄλλοις ? Coraes : πολίταις Richards.

---

[a] This seems to refer to Books IV.-VI.   [b] Cf. 1288 b 39 n.

case of any individual human being ; for otherwise God and the whole universe could hardly be well circumstanced, since they have no external activities by the side of their own private activities.

It is therefore manifest that the same life must be the best both for each human being individually and for states and mankind collectively.

IV. And as we have prepared the way by this prefatory discussion of the subject, and have previously studied all the other forms of constitution,[a] the starting-point for the remainder of our subject is first to specify the nature of the conditions that are necessary in the case of the state that is to be constituted in the ideally best manner. For the best constitution cannot be realized without suitable equipment.[b] We must therefore posit as granted in advance a number of as it were ideal conditions, although none of these must be actually impossible. I mean for instance in reference to number of citizens and territory. All other craftsmen, for example a weaver or a shipwright, have to be supplied with their material in a condition suitable for their trade, for the better this material has been prepared, the finer is bound to be the product of their craft ; so also the statesman and the lawgiver ought to be furnished with their proper material in a suitable condition. Under the head of material equipment for the state there first come the questions as to a supply of population—what precisely ought to be its number and what its natural character ? and similarly in regard to the territory, what is to be its particular size and nature ? Most people imagine that the prosperous state must be a great state ; but granted the truth of this, they fail to realize in what quality the

Structure of Ideal State.

A. External conditions : (1) size of population ;

πόλις· κατ' ἀριθμοῦ γὰρ πλῆθος τῶν ἐνοικούντων
κρίνουσι τὴν μεγάλην, δεῖ δὲ μᾶλλον μὴ εἰς τὸ
πλῆθος εἰς δὲ δύναμιν ἀποβλέπειν. ἔστι γάρ τι
καὶ πόλεως ἔργον, ὥστε τὴν δυναμένην τοῦτο
μάλιστ' ἀποτελεῖν, ταύτην οἰητέον εἶναι μεγίστην,
15 οἷον Ἱπποκράτην οὐκ ἄνθρωπον ἀλλ' ἰατρὸν εἶναι
μείζω φήσειεν ἄν τις τοῦ διαφέροντος κατὰ τὸ
μέγεθος τοῦ σώματος. οὐ μὴν ἀλλὰ κἂν εἰ δεῖ
κρίνειν πρὸς τὸ πλῆθος ἀποβλέποντας, οὐ κατὰ τὸ
τυχὸν πλῆθος τοῦτο ποιητέον[1] (ἀναγκαῖον γὰρ ἐν
ταῖς πόλεσιν ἴσως ὑπάρχειν καὶ δούλων ἀριθμὸν
20 πολλῶν καὶ μετοίκων καὶ ξένων), ἀλλ' ὅσοι
πόλεώς εἰσι μέρος καὶ ἐξ ὧν συνίσταται πόλις
οἰκείων μορίων· ἡ γὰρ τούτων ὑπεροχὴ τοῦ
πλήθους μεγάλης πόλεως σημεῖον, ἐξ ἧς δὲ
βάναυσοι μὲν ἐξέρχονται πολλοὶ τὸν ἀριθμὸν
ὁπλῖται δὲ ὀλίγοι, ταύτην ἀδύνατον εἶναι μεγάλην·
25 οὐ γὰρ ταὐτὸν μεγάλη τε πόλις καὶ πολυάνθρωπος.
ἀλλὰ μὴν καὶ τοῦτό γε ἐκ τῶν ἔργων φανερόν,
ὅτι χαλεπόν, ἴσως δ' ἀδύνατον, εὐνομεῖσθαι τὴν
λίαν πολυάνθρωπον. τῶν γοῦν δοκουσῶν πολιτεύεσθαι καλῶς οὐδεμίαν ὁρῶμεν οὖσαν ἀνειμένην
πρὸς τὸ πλῆθος. τοῦτο δὲ δῆλον καὶ διὰ τῆς τῶν
30 λόγων πίστεως. ὅ τε γὰρ νόμος τάξις τίς ἐστι, καὶ
τὴν εὐνομίαν ἀναγκαῖον εὐταξίαν εἶναι· ὁ δὲ λίαν
ὑπερβάλλων ἀριθμὸς οὐ δύναται μετέχειν τάξεως,
θείας γὰρ δὴ τοῦτο δυνάμεως ἔργον, ἥτις καὶ τόδε
συνέχει τὸ πᾶν. [2]διὸ καὶ πόλιν ἧς μετὰ μεγέθους

---

[1] Camerarius: οἰητέον codd. (cf. 14).

[2] διὸ—ἀναγκαῖον infra post ἐπεὶ—γίνεσθαι codd.: transp.
Boecker.

---

[a] In the mss. this clause follows the next.

greatness or smallness of a state consists : they judge a great state by the numerical magnitude of the population, but really the more proper thing to look at is not numbers but efficiency. For a state like other things has a certain function to perform, so that it is the state most capable of performing this function that is to be deemed the greatest, just as one would pronounce Hippocrates to be greater, not as a human being but as a physician, than somebody 4 who surpassed him in bodily size. All the same, even if it be right to judge the state by the test of its multitude, this ought not to be done with regard to the multitude of any and every class (for states are doubtless bound to contain a large number of slaves and resident aliens and foreigners), but the test should be the number of those who are a portion of the state—the special parts of which a state consists. It is superiority in the number of these that indicates a great state ; a state that sends forth to war a large number of the baser sort and a small number of heavy-armed soldiers cannot possibly be a great state—for a great state is not the same thing as a state with a large population. But certainly experience also shows that it is difficult and perhaps impossible for a state with too large a population to have good legal government. At all events we see that none of the states reputed to be well governed is without some restriction in regard to numbers. The evidence of theory proves the same point. Law is a form of order, and good law must necessarily mean good order ; but an excessively large number cannot participate in order : to give it order would surely be a task for divine power, which holds even this universe together. ^a Hence that state also must

1326 a
35 ὁ λεχθεὶς ὅρος ὑπάρχει, ταύτην εἶναι καλλίστην
ἀναγκαῖον· ἐπεὶ τό γε καλὸν ἐν πλήθει καὶ 6
μεγέθει εἴωθε γίνεσθαι, ἀλλ' ἔστι τι καὶ πόλεσι
μεγέθους μέτρον, ὥσπερ καὶ τῶν ἄλλων πάντων,
ζῴων φυτῶν ὀργάνων· καὶ γὰρ τούτων ἕκαστον
οὔτε λίαν μικρὸν οὔτε κατὰ μέγεθος ὑπερβάλλον
ἕξει τὴν αὑτοῦ δύναμιν, ἀλλ' ὁτὲ μὲν ὅλως
40 ἐστερημένον ἔσται τῆς φύσεως, ὁτὲ δὲ φαύλως
ἔχον, οἷον πλοῖον σπιθαμιαῖον μὲν οὐκ ἔσται
πλοῖον ὅλως, οὐδὲ δυοῖν σταδίοιν, εἰς δέ τι μέγεθος
1326 b ἐλθὸν ὁτὲ μὲν διὰ σμικρότητα φαύλην ποιήσει τὴν
ναυτιλίαν ὁτὲ δὲ διὰ τὴν ὑπερβολήν. ὁμοίως δὲ καὶ
πόλις ἡ μὲν ἐξ ὀλίγων λίαν οὐκ αὐτάρκης (ἡ δὲ
πόλις αὐτάρκες), ἡ δὲ ἐκ πολλῶν ἄγαν ἐν τοῖς μὲν
5 ἀναγκαίοις αὐτάρκης, ὥσπερ ⟨δ'⟩[1] ἔθνος, ἀλλ' οὐ
πόλις, πολιτείαν γὰρ οὐ ῥᾴδιον ὑπάρχειν—τίς γὰρ
στρατηγὸς ἔσται τοῦ λίαν ὑπερβάλλοντος πλήθους;
ἢ τίς κῆρυξ μὴ Στεντόρειος; διὸ πρώτην μὲν
εἶναι πόλιν ἀναγκαῖον τὴν ἐκ τοσούτου πλήθους
ὃ πρῶτον πλῆθος αὔταρκες πρὸς τὸ εὖ ζῆν ἐστι
κατὰ τὴν πολιτικὴν κοινωνίαν. ἐνδέχεται δὲ καὶ
10 τὴν ταύτης ὑπερβάλλουσαν κατὰ πλῆθος εἶναι
μείζω πόλιν· ἀλλὰ τοῦτ' οὐκ ἔστιν, ὥσπερ εἴπομεν,
ἀόριστον, τίς δ' ἐστὶν ὁ τῆς ὑπερβολῆς ὅρος, ἐκ
τῶν ἔργων ἰδεῖν ῥᾴδιον. εἰσὶ γὰρ αἱ πράξεις τῆς
πόλεως τῶν μὲν ἀρχόντων τῶν δ' ἀρχομένων,

---

[1] ὥσπερ ⟨δ'⟩ vel ⟨αὐτάρκης δ'⟩ ὥσπερ Jackson.

---

[a] *i.e.* presumably an Ethnos in the usual sense, a community composed of villages loosely bound together by
relationship and trade, and united for defence, but not
for political life; not an Ethnos of associated cities.

necessarily be the most beautiful with whose magnitude is combined the above-mentioned limiting principle ; for certainly beauty is usually found in number and magnitude, but there is a due measure of magnitude for a city-state as there also is for all other things—animals, plants, tools ; each of these if too small or excessively large will not possess its own proper efficiency, but in the one case will have entirely lost its true nature and in the other will be in a defective condition ; for instance, a ship a span long will not be a ship at all, nor will a ship a quarter of a mile long, and even when it reaches a certain size, in the one case smallness and in the other excessive largeness will make it sail badly. Similarly a state consisting of too few people will not be self-sufficing (which is an essential quality of a state), and one consisting of too many, though self-sufficing in the mere necessaries, will be so in the way in which a nation [a] is, and not as a state, since it will not be easy for it to possess constitutional government—for who will command its over-swollen multitude in war ? or who will serve as its herald, unless he have the lungs of a Stentor ? It follows that the lowest limit for the existence of a state is when it consists of a population that reaches the minimum number that is self-sufficient for the purpose of living the good life after the manner of a political community. It is possible also for one that exceeds this one in number to be a greater state, but, as we said, this possibility of increase is not without limit, and what the limit of the state's expansion is can easily be seen from practical considerations. The activities of the state are those of the rulers and those of the persons ruled, and the work of a ruler is to direct the ad-

ἄρχοντος δ' ἐπίταξις καὶ κρίσις ἔργον· πρὸς δὲ τὸ
15 κρίνειν περὶ τῶν δικαίων καὶ πρὸς τὸ τὰς ἀρχὰς
διανέμειν κατ' ἀξίαν ἀναγκαῖον γνωρίζειν ἀλλήλους ποῖοί τινές εἰσι τοὺς πολίτας, ὡς ὅπου τοῦτο
μὴ συμβαίνει γίγνεσθαι, φαύλως ἀνάγκη γίγνεσθαι
τὰ περὶ τὰς ἀρχὰς καὶ τὰς κρίσεις· περὶ ἀμφότερα
20 γὰρ οὐ δίκαιον αὐτοσχεδιάζειν, ὅπερ ἐν τῇ πολυ-
ανθρωπίᾳ τῇ λίαν ὑπάρχει φανερῶς. ἔτι δὲ ξένοις
καὶ μετοίκοις ῥᾴδιον μεταλαμβάνειν τῆς πολιτείας·
οὐ γὰρ χαλεπὸν τὸ λανθάνειν διὰ τὴν ὑπερβολὴν
τοῦ πλήθους. δῆλον τοίνυν ὡς οὗτός ἐστι πόλεως
ὅρος ἄριστος, ἡ μεγίστη τοῦ πλήθους ὑπερβολὴ
25 πρὸς αὐτάρκειαν ζωῆς εὐσύνοπτος. περὶ μὲν οὖν
μεγέθους πόλεως διωρίσθω τὸν τρόπον τοῦτον.

V. Παραπλησίως δὲ καὶ τὰ περὶ τῆς χώρας
ἔχει. περὶ μὲν γὰρ τοῦ ποίαν τινά, δῆλον ὅτι τὴν
αὐταρκεστάτην πᾶς τις ἂν ἐπαινέσειεν (τοιαύτην
δ' ἀναγκαῖον εἶναι τὴν παντοφόρον, τὸ γὰρ πάντα
30 ὑπάρχειν καὶ δεῖσθαι μηθενὸς αὔταρκες)· πλήθει
δὲ καὶ μεγέθει τοσαύτην ὥστε δύνασθαι τοὺς οἰκοῦντας ζῆν σχολάζοντας ἐλευθερίως ἅμα καὶ
σωφρόνως. τοῦτον δὲ τὸν ὅρον εἰ καλῶς ἢ μὴ
καλῶς λέγομεν, ὕστερον ἐπισκεπτέον ἀκριβέστερον,
ὅταν ὅλως περὶ κτήσεως καὶ τῆς περὶ τὴν οὐσίαν
35 εὐπορίας συμβαίνῃ ποιεῖσθαι μνείαν, πῶς δεῖ καὶ
τίνα τρόπον ἔχειν πρὸς τὴν χρῆσιν αὐτῆς.[1] πολλαὶ

---

[1] αὐτῆς Richards.

---

[a] This promise is not fulfilled in the work as it has come
down to us.

[b] The distinction seems to be between owning (or perhaps
getting) wealth and using it; but a probable emendation of
the Greek gives ' how we ought to stand in relation to its
employment.'

ministration and to judge law-suits ; but in order to decide questions of justice and in order to distribute the offices according to merit it is necessary for the citizens to know each other's personal characters, since where this does not happen to be the case the business of electing officials and trying law-suits is bound to go badly ; haphazard decision is unjust in both matters, and this must obviously prevail in an excessively numerous community. Also in such a community it is easy for foreigners and resident aliens to usurp the rights of citizenship, for the excessive number of the population makes it not difficult to escape detection. It is clear therefore that the best limiting principle for a state is the largest expansion of the population with a view to self-sufficiency that can well be taken in at one view.

Such may be our conclusion on the question of the size of the state.

V. Very much the same holds good about its (2) extent territory. As to the question what particular kind and nature of land it ought to have, it is clear that everybody of territory would command that which is most self-sufficing (and such is necessarily that which bears every sort of produce, for self-sufficiency means having a supply of everything and lacking nothing). In extent and magnitude the land ought to be of a size that will enable the inhabitants to live a life of liberal and at the same time temperate leisure. Whether this limiting principle is rightly or wrongly stated must be considered more precisely later on,[a] when we come to raise the general subject of property and the ownership of wealth,—how and in what way it ought to be related to its actual employment [b] ; about this question there are many

1326 b

γὰρ περὶ τὴν σκέψιν ταύτην εἰσὶν ἀμφισβητήσεις
διὰ τοὺς ἕλκοντας ἐφ' ἑκατέραν τοῦ βίου τὴν ὑπερβολήν, τοὺς μὲν ἐπὶ τὴν γλισχρότητα τοὺς δὲ ἐπὶ
τὴν τρυφήν. τὸ δ' εἶδος τῆς χώρας οὐ χαλεπὸν
40 εἰπεῖν (δεῖ δ' ἔνια πείθεσθαι καὶ τοῖς περὶ τὴν
στρατηγίαν ἐμπείροις), ὅτι χρὴ μὲν τοῖς[1] πολεμίοις

1327 a εἶναι δυσέμβολον αὐτοῖς δ' εὐέξοδον, ἔτι δ',
ὥσπερ τὸ πλῆθος τὸ τῶν ἀνθρώπων εὐσύνοπτον
ἔφαμεν εἶναι δεῖν, οὕτω καὶ τὴν χώραν, τὸ δ'
εὐσύνοπτον τὸ εὐβοήθητον εἶναι τὴν χώραν ἐστίν.
5 τῆς δὲ πόλεως τὴν θέσιν εἰ χρὴ ποιεῖν κατ' εὐχήν,
πρός τε τὴν θάλατταν προσήκει κεῖσθαι καλῶς
πρός τε τὴν χώραν. εἷς μὲν ὁ λεχθεὶς ὅρος, δεῖ
γὰρ πρὸς τὰς ἐκβοηθείας κοινὴν εἶναι τῶν τόπων
ἁπάντων· ὁ δὲ λοιπὸς πρὸς τὰς τῶν γιγνομένων
καρπῶν παραπομπάς, ἔτι δὲ τῆς περὶ ξύλα ὕλης
10 κἂν εἴ τινα ἄλλην ἐργασίαν ἡ χώρα τυγχάνοι
κεκτημένη τοιαύτην, εὐπαρακόμιστον.[2]

Περὶ δὲ τῆς πρὸς τὴν θάλατταν κοινωνίας,
πότερον ὠφέλιμος ταῖς εὐνομουμέναις πόλεσιν ἢ
βλαβερά, πολλὰ τυγχάνουσιν ἀμφισβητοῦντες· τό
τε γὰρ ἐπιξενοῦσθαί τινας ἐν ἄλλοις τεθραμμένους
15 νόμοις ἀσύμφορον εἶναί φασι πρὸς τὴν εὐνομίαν,
καὶ τὴν πολυανθρωπίαν, γίνεσθαι μὲν γὰρ ἐκ τοῦ
χρῆσθαι τῇ θαλάσσῃ διαπέμποντας καὶ δεχομένους
ἐμπόρων πλῆθος, ὑπεναντίαν δ' εἶναι πρὸς τὸ
πολιτεύεσθαι καλῶς. ὅτι μὲν οὖν, εἰ ταῦτα μὴ
συμβαίνει, βέλτιον καὶ πρὸς ἀσφάλειαν καὶ πρὸς

----

[1] τοῖς μὲν Richards.
[2] ⟨τὸ⟩ εὐπαρακόμιστον ? Immisch.

----

[a] At the beginning of § 2.

controversies, owing to those that draw us towards either extreme of life, the one school towards
2 parsimony and the other towards luxury. The proper configuration of the country it is not difficult to state (though there are some points on which the advice of military experts also must be taken) : on the one hand it should be difficult for enemies to invade and easy for the people themselves to march out from, and in addition, on the other hand, the same thing holds good of the territory that we said about the size of the population—it must be well able to be taken in at one view, and that means being a country easy for military defence. As to the site (3) Site of of the city, if it is to be ideally placed, it is proper for city. it to be well situated with regard both to the sea and to the country. One defining principle is that mentioned above ^a—the city must be in communication with all parts of the territory for the purpose of sending out military assistance ; and the remaining principle is that it must be easily accessible for the conveyance to it of the agricultural produce, and also of timber-wood and any other such material that the country happens to possess.

3 As to communication with the sea it is in fact much Proximity debated whether it is advantageous to well-ordered to sea, states or harmful. It is maintained that the visits advantages of persons brought up under other institutions are and disadvantages detrimental to law and order, and so also is a swollen advantages. population, which grows out of sending out abroad and receiving in a number of traders, but is un-
4 favourable to good government. Now it is not difficult to see that, if these consequences are avoided, it is advantageous in respect of both security and the supply of necessary commodities

561

20 εὐπορίαν τῶν ἀναγκαίων μετέχειν τὴν πόλιν καὶ
τὴν χώραν τῆς θαλάττης, οὐκ ἄδηλον. καὶ γὰρ
πρὸς τὸ ῥᾷον φέρειν τοὺς πολέμους[1] εὐβοηθήτους
εἶναι δεῖ κατ' ἀμφότερα τοὺς σωθησομένους, καὶ
κατὰ γῆν καὶ κατὰ θάλατταν· καὶ πρὸς[2] τὸ βλάψαι
τοὺς ἐπιτιθεμένους, εἰ μὴ κατ' ἄμφω δυνατόν,
25 ἀλλὰ κατὰ θάτερον ὑπάρξει μᾶλλον ἀμφοτέρων
μετέχουσιν. ὅσα τ' ἂν μὴ τυγχάνῃ παρ' αὐτοῖς[3]
ὄντα, δέξασθαι ταῦτα καὶ τὰ πλεονάζοντα τῶν
γιγνομένων ἐκπέμψασθαι τῶν ἀναγκαίων ἐστίν·
αὐτῇ γὰρ ἐμπορικήν, ἀλλ' οὐ τοῖς ἄλλοις δεῖ
εἶναι τὴν πόλιν· οἱ δὲ παρέχοντες σφᾶς αὐτοὺς
30 πᾶσιν ἀγορὰν προσόδου χάριν ταῦτα πράττουσιν,
ἣν δὲ μὴ δεῖ πόλιν τοιαύτης μετέχειν πλεονεξίας,
οὐδ' ἐμπόριον δεῖ κεκτῆσθαι τοιοῦτον. ἐπεὶ δὲ
καὶ νῦν ὁρῶμεν πολλαῖς ὑπάρχοντα[4] καὶ χώραις
καὶ πόλεσιν ἐπίνεια καὶ λιμένας εὐφυῶς κείμενα
πρὸς τὴν πόλιν, ὥστε μήτε τὸ αὐτὸ νέμειν[5] ἄστυ
35 μήτε πόρρω λίαν ἀλλὰ κρατεῖσθαι τείχεσι καὶ
τοιούτοις ἄλλοις ἐρύμασι, φανερὸν ὡς εἰ μὲν
ἀγαθόν τι συμβαίνει γίγνεσθαι διὰ τῆς κοινωνίας
αὐτῶν, ὑπάρξει τῇ πόλει τοῦτο τὸ ἀγαθόν, εἰ δέ
τι βλαβερόν, φυλάξασθαι ῥᾴδιον τοῖς νόμοις φρά-
ζοντας καὶ διορίζοντας τίνας οὐ δεῖ καὶ τίνας ἐπι-
40 μίσγεσθαι δεῖ πρὸς ἀλλήλους. περὶ δὲ τῆς ναυτικῆς
δυνάμεως, ὅτι μὲν βέλτιστον ὑπάρχειν μέχρι τινὸς
πλήθους, οὐκ ἄδηλον (οὐ γὰρ μόνον αὐτοῖς ἀλλὰ
καὶ τῶν πλησίον τισὶ δεῖ καὶ φοβεροὺς εἶναι καὶ

---

[1] Sylburg : πολεμίους codd. [2] [πρὸς] e 21 Richards.
[3] ed. : αὐτοῖς codd. [4] Welldon : ὑπάρχον codd.
[5] τὸ αὐτὸ νέμειν : αὐτὸ νέμειν τὸ ? ed. (*ipsum* Guil.).

that the city and the country should have access to the sea. With a view to enduring wars more easily people that are to be secure must be capable of defensive operations on both elements, land and sea, and with a view to striking at assailants, even if it be not possible on both elements, yet to do so on one or the other will be more in the power of people that have access to both. And the importation of commodities that they do not happen to have in their own country and the export of their surplus products are things indispensable ; for the state ought to engage in commerce for its own interest, but not for the interest of the foreigner. People that Foreign trade. throw open their market to the world do so for the sake of revenue, but a state that is not to take part in that sort of profit-making need not possess a great commercial port. But since even now we see many countries and cities possessing sea-ports and harbours conveniently situated with regard to the city, so as not to form part of the same town ^a and yet not to be too far off, but commanded by walls and other defence-works of the kind, it is manifest that if any advantage does result through the communication of city with port the state will possess this advantage, and if there is any harmful result it is easy to guard against it by means of laws stating and regulating what persons are not and what persons are to have intercourse with one another. On the question of naval forces, there is no doubt Navy. that to possess them up to a certain strength is most desirable (for a state ought to be formidable, and also capable of the defence of not only its own people

<hr>

^a Perhaps the Greek should be altered to give ' part of the town itself.'

1327 b δύνασθαι βοηθεῖν, ὥσπερ κατὰ γῆν, καὶ κατὰ
θάλατταν)· περὶ δὲ πλήθους ἤδη καὶ μεγέθους τῆς
δυνάμεως ταύτης πρὸς τὸν βίον ἀποσκεπτέον τῆς
5 πόλεως· εἰ μὲν γὰρ ἡγεμονικὸν καὶ πολιτικὸν
ζήσεται βίον, ἀναγκαῖον καὶ ταύτην τὴν δύναμιν
ὑπάρχειν πρὸς τὰς πράξεις σύμμετρον. τὴν δὲ
πολυανθρωπίαν τὴν γιγνομένην περὶ τὸν ναυτικὸν
ὄχλον οὐκ ἀναγκαῖον ὑπάρχειν ταῖς πόλεσιν· οὐθὲν
γὰρ αὐτοὺς μέρος εἶναι δεῖ τῆς πόλεως. τὸ μὲν
10 γὰρ ἐπιβατικὸν ἐλεύθερον καὶ τῶν πεζευόντων
ἐστίν, ὃ κύριόν ἐστι καὶ κρατεῖ τῆς ναυτιλίας·
πλήθους δὲ ὑπάρχοντος περιοίκων καὶ τῶν τὴν
χώραν γεωργούντων, ἀφθονίαν ἀναγκαῖον εἶναι
καὶ ναυτῶν. ὁρῶμεν δὲ καὶ τοῦτο καὶ νῦν ὑπάρχον τισίν, οἷον τῇ πόλει τῶν Ἡρακλεωτῶν·
15 πολλὰς γὰρ ἐκπληροῦσι τριήρεις κεκτημένοι τῷ
μεγέθει πόλιν ἑτέρων ἐμμελεστέραν.

Περὶ μὲν οὖν χώρας καὶ λιμένων τῶν¹ πόλεων
καὶ θαλάττης καὶ περὶ τῆς ναυτικῆς δυνάμεως
ἔστω διωρισμένα τὸν τρόπον τοῦτον.

VI. Περὶ δὲ τοῦ πολιτικοῦ πλήθους, τίνα μὲν
ὅρον ὑπάρχειν χρή πρότερον εἴπομεν, ποίους δέ
20 τινας τὴν φύσιν εἶναι δεῖ νῦν λέγωμεν. σχεδὸν
δὴ κατανοήσειεν ἄν τις τοῦτό γε βλέψας ἐπί τε
τὰς πόλεις τὰς εὐδοκιμούσας τῶν Ἑλλήνων καὶ
πρὸς πᾶσαν τὴν οἰκουμένην ὡς διείληπται τοῖς
ἔθνεσιν. τὰ μὲν γὰρ ἐν τοῖς ψυχροῖς τόποις ἔθνη
καὶ τὰ περὶ τὴν Εὐρώπην θυμοῦ μέν ἐστι πλήρη,
25 διανοίας δὲ ἐνδεέστερα καὶ τέχνης, διόπερ ἐλεύθερα
μὲν διατελεῖ μᾶλλον, ἀπολίτευτα δὲ καὶ τῶν

¹ τῶν ed.: καὶ codd.

but also some of its neighbours, by sea as well as by land) ; but when we come to the question of the number and size of this force, we have to consider the state's manner of life : if it is to live a life of leadership and affairs,[a] it must possess maritime as well as other forces commensurate with its activities. On the other hand it is not necessary for states to include the teeming population that grows up in connexion with the sailor crowd, as there is no need for these to be citizens ; for the marines are free men and are a part of the infantry, and it is they who have command and control the crew; and if there exists a mass of villagers and tillers of the soil, there is bound to be no lack of sailors too. In fact we see this state of thing existing even now in some places, for instance in the city of Heraclea ; the Heracleotes man a large fleet of triremes, although they possess a city of but moderate size as compared with others.

Let such then be our conclusions about the territories and harbours of cities, and the sea, and about naval forces.

VI. About the citizen population, we said before what is its proper limit of numbers. Let us now speak of what ought to be the citizens' natural character. Now this one might almost discern by looking at the famous cities of Greece and by observing how the whole inhabited world is divided up among the nations.[b] The nations inhabiting the cold places and those of Europe are full of spirit but somewhat deficient in intelligence and skill, so that they continue comparatively free, but lacking in political

(4) National character: Hellenic blend of courage and intelligence.

---

[a] *i.e.* active interference with other states—a broader term than hegemony, leadership of an alliance : *cf.* 1265 a 23 n.

[b] c. iv. fin.

1327 b

πλησίον ἄρχειν οὐ δυνάμενα· τὰ δὲ περὶ τὴν
Ἀσίαν διανοητικὰ μὲν καὶ τεχνικὰ τὴν ψυχήν,
ἄθυμα δέ, διόπερ ἀρχόμενα καὶ δουλεύοντα δια-
τελεῖ· τὸ δὲ τῶν Ἑλλήνων γένος ὥσπερ μεσεύει

30 κατὰ τοὺς τόπους, οὕτως ἀμφοῖν μετέχει, καὶ
γὰρ ἔνθυμον καὶ διανοητικόν ἐστιν, διόπερ ἐλεύ-
θερόν τε διατελεῖ καὶ βέλτιστα πολιτευόμενον καὶ
δυνάμενον ἄρχειν πάντων, μιᾶς τυγχάνον πολιτείας. τὴν αὐτὴν δ' ἔχει διαφορὰν καὶ τὰ τῶν
Ἑλλήνων ἔθνη πρὸς[1] ἄλληλα· τὰ μὲν γὰρ ἔχει

35 τὴν φύσιν μονόκωλον, τὰ δὲ εὖ[2] κέκραται πρὸς
ἀμφοτέρας τὰς δυνάμεις ταύτας. φανερὸν τοίνυν
ὅτι δεῖ διανοητικούς τε εἶναι καὶ θυμοειδεῖς τὴν
φύσιν τοὺς μέλλοντας εὐαγώγους ἔσεσθαι τῷ
νομοθέτῃ πρὸς τὴν ἀρετήν. ὅπερ γάρ φασί τινες
δεῖν ὑπάρχειν τοῖς φύλαξι, τὸ φιλητικοὺς μὲν

40 εἶναι τῶν γνωρίμων πρὸς δὲ τοὺς ἀγνῶτας ἀγρίους,
ὁ θυμός ἐστιν ὁ ποιῶν τὸ φιλητικόν· αὕτη γάρ

1328 a ἐστιν ἡ τῆς ψυχῆς δύναμις ᾗ φιλοῦμεν. σημεῖον
δέ· πρὸς γὰρ τοὺς συνήθεις καὶ φίλους ὁ θυμὸς
αἴρεται μᾶλλον ἢ πρὸς τοὺς ἀγνῶτας, ὀλιγωρεῖσθαι
νομίσας. διὸ καὶ Ἀρχίλοχος προσηκόντως τοῖς
φίλοις ἐγκαλῶν διαλέγεται πρὸς τὸν θυμόν·

5   σὺ[3] γὰρ δὴ παρὰ φίλων ἀπάγχεαι.

καὶ τὸ ἄρχον δὲ καὶ τὸ ἐλεύθερον ἀπὸ τῆς δυνάμεως ταύτης ὑπάρχει πᾶσιν· ἀρχικὸν γὰρ καὶ
ἀήττητον ὁ θυμός. οὐ καλῶς δ' ἔχει λέγειν

---

[1] πρὸς ΓΡ[1] : καὶ πρὸς cett.   [2] εὖ ΓΜΡ[1] : εὖ τε cett.
[3] σὺ Schneider : οὐ codd.

---

[a] *i.e.* intelligence and high spirit, capacity for self-govern-
ment and capacity for empire.
[b] The ruling class in Plato's Ideal State, *Republic* 375 c.

organization and capacity to rule their neighbours.
The peoples of Asia on the other hand are intelligent
and skilful in temperament, but lack spirit, so that
they are in continuous subjection and slavery. But
the Greek race participates in both characters, just
as it occupies the middle position geographically, for
it is both spirited and intelligent; hence it continues to be free and to have very good political
institutions, and to be capable of ruling all mankind
2 if it attains constitutional unity. The same diversity
also exists among the Greek races compared with
one another: some have a one-sided nature, others
are happily blended in regard to both these capacities.[a]
It is clear therefore that people that are to be easily
guided to virtue by the lawgiver must be both intellectual and spirited in their nature. For as to what Plato's
is said by certain persons about the character that Guardians
should belong to their Guardians [b]—they should be too fierce.
affectionate to their friends but fierce towards
strangers—it is spirit that causes affectionateness, for
spirit is the capacity of the soul whereby we love.
3 A sign of this is that spirit is more roused against
associates and friends than against strangers, when it
thinks itself slighted. Therefore Archilochus [c] for
instance, when reproaching his friends, appropriately apostrophizes his spirit:

For 'tis thy friends that make thee choke with rage.

Moreover it is from this faculty that power to command and love of freedom are in all cases derived;
for spirit is a commanding and indomitable element.

[c] Archilochus of Paros (one of the earliest lyric poets, *fl.*
600 B.C., the inventor of the iambic metre, which he used for
lampoons), fr. 61 Bergk, 676 Diehl, 67 Edmonds, *Elegy and
Iambus*, ii. 133.

^{1328 a}
χαλεποὺς εἶναι πρὸς τοὺς ἀγνῶτας· πρὸς οὐθένα
10 γὰρ εἶναι χρὴ τοιοῦτον, οὐδ' εἰσὶν οἱ μεγαλόψυχοι
τὴν φύσιν ἄγριοι πλὴν πρὸς τοὺς ἀδικοῦντας, τοῦτο
δὲ μᾶλλον ἔτι πρὸς τοὺς συνήθεις πάσχουσιν, ὅπερ
εἴρηται πρότερον, ἂν ἀδικεῖσθαι νομίσωσιν. καὶ 4
τοῦτο συμβαίνει κατὰ λόγον· παρ' οἷς γὰρ ὀφεί-
λεσθαι τὴν¹ εὐεργεσίαν ὑπολαμβάνουσι, πρὸς τῷ
15 βλάβει καὶ ταύτης ἀποστερεῖσθαι νομίζουσιν· ὅθεν
εἴρηται

χαλεποὶ γὰρ πόλεμοι ἀδελφῶν

καὶ

οἵ τοι πέρα στέρξαντες, οἱ δὲ καὶ πέρα
μισοῦσιν.

Περὶ μὲν οὖν τῶν πολιτευομένων, πόσους τε
ὑπάρχειν δεῖ καὶ ποίους τινὰς τὴν φύσιν, ἔτι δὲ
τὴν χώραν πόσην τέ τινα καὶ ποίαν τινά, διώρισται
20 σχεδόν· οὐ γὰρ τὴν αὐτὴν ἀκρίβειαν δεῖ ζητεῖν
διά² τε τῶν λόγων καὶ τῶν γιγνομένων διὰ τῆς
αἰσθήσεως.

VII. Ἐπεὶ δ', ὥσπερ τῶν ἄλλων τῶν κατὰ φύσιν 1
συνεστώτων οὐ ταῦτά³ ἐστι μόρια τῆς ὅλης συ-
στάσεως ὧν ἄνευ τὸ ὅλον οὐκ ἂν εἴη, δῆλον ὡς
οὐδὲ πόλεως μέρη θετέον ὅσα ταῖς πόλεσιν ἀναγ-
25 καῖον ὑπάρχειν (οὐδ' ἄλλης κοινωνίας οὐδεμιᾶς,
ἐξ ἧς ἕν τι τὸ γένος, ἐν γάρ τι καὶ κοινὸν εἶναι δεῖ
καὶ ταὐτὸ τοῖς κοινωνοῖς, ἄν τε ἴσον ἄν τε ἄνισον

---

¹ τὴν Schneider: δεῖν (vel δεῖ, δὲ) τὴν codd.
² ἐπί Richards.
³ ταὐτά cod. inf.: πάντα Wyse.

---

^a Euripides fr. 965.

But it is a mistake to describe the Guardians as cruel towards strangers; it is not right to be cruel towards anybody, and men of great-souled nature are not fierce except towards wrongdoers, and their anger is still fiercer against their companions if they think that these are wronging them, as has been said before. 4 And this is reasonable, because they think that in addition to the harm done them they are also being defrauded of a benefit by persons whom they believe to owe them one. Hence the sayings

> For brothers' wars are cruel,[a]

and

> They that too deeply loved too deeply hate.[b]

We have now approximately decided what are the proper numbers and the natural qualities of those who exercise the right of citizens, and the proper extent and nature of the territory (for we must not seek to attain the same exactness by means of theoretical discussions as is obtained by means of the facts that come to us through sense-perceptions).

1 VII. But since, just as with all other natural organisms those things that are indispensable for the existence of the whole are not parts[c] of the whole organization, it is also clear that not all the things that are necessary for states to possess are to be counted as parts of a state (any more than this is so with any other association that forms something one in kind, for there must be something that is one and common and the same for the partners, whether the shares that they take be equal or unequal:

B. Internal structure of Ideal State: (1) social and political institutions.

[b] Trag. incert. fr. 78 Nauck.

[c] *i.e.* they are not *all of them* parts: the 'parts' of a thing are among the 'indispensable conditions' of its existence, but there are others also.

1328 a μεταλαμβάνωσιν, οἷον εἴτε τροφὴ τοῦτό ἐστιν εἴτε
χώρας πλῆθος εἴτ' ἄλλο τι τῶν τοιούτων ἐστίν)—
ὅταν δ' ᾖ τὸ μὲν τούτου ἕνεκεν τὸ δ' οὗ ἕνεκεν, 2
30 οὐθὲν ἕν γε τούτοις κοινὸν ἀλλ' ἢ τῷ μὲν ποιῆσαι
τῷ δὲ λαβεῖν[1]· λέγω δ' οἷον ὀργάνῳ τε παντὶ πρὸς
τὸ γιγνόμενον ἔργον καὶ τοῖς δημιουργοῖς· οἰκίᾳ
γὰρ πρὸς οἰκοδόμον οὐθέν ἐστιν ὃ γίνεται κοινόν,
ἀλλ' ἔστι τῆς οἰκίας χάριν ἡ τῶν οἰκοδόμων τέχνη.
διὸ κτήσεως μὲν δεῖ ταῖς πόλεσιν, οὐδὲν δ' ἐστὶν
35 ἡ κτῆσις μέρος τῆς πόλεως. πολλὰ δ' ἔμψυχα
μέρη τῆς κτήσεώς ἐστιν. ἡ δὲ πόλις κοινωνία
τίς ἐστι τῶν ὁμοίων, ἕνεκεν δὲ ζωῆς τῆς ἐνδεχομένης ἀρίστης. ἐπεὶ δ' ἐστὶν εὐδαιμονία τὸ 3
ἄριστον, αὕτη δὲ ἀρετῆς ἐνέργεια καὶ χρῆσίς τις
τέλειος, συμβέβηκε δὲ οὕτως ὥστε τοὺς μὲν
40 ἐνδέχεσθαι μετέχειν αὐτῆς, τοὺς δὲ μικρὸν ἢ μηδέν,
δῆλον ὡς τοῦτ' αἴτιον τοῦ γίγνεσθαι πόλεως εἴδη
καὶ διαφορὰς καὶ πολιτείας πλείους· ἄλλον γὰρ
1328 b τρόπον καὶ δι' ἄλλων ἕκαστοι τοῦτο θηρεύοντες
τούς τε βίους ἑτέρους ποιοῦνται καὶ τὰς πολιτείας.
ἐπισκεπτέον δὲ καὶ πόσα ταυτί ἐστιν ὧν ἄνευ
πόλις οὐκ ἂν εἴη· καὶ γὰρ ἃ λέγομεν εἶναι μέρη
πόλεως, ἐν τούτοις ἂν εἴη, διὸ[2] ἀναγκαῖον ὑπάρχειν.
5 ληπτέον τοίνυν τῶν ἔργων τὸν ἀριθμόν· ἐκ τούτων 4
γὰρ ἔσται δῆλον. πρῶτον μὲν οὖν ὑπάρχειν δεῖ

---

[1] παθεῖν Postgate.
[2] διὸ om. codd. cet.: διὰ τὸ Γ.

---

a The sentence is unfinished.
b Possibly the words from the beginning of § 2 'But
when' to this point should be transferred below to § 3 mid.
after 'different constitutions.'

for example this common property may be food or an area of land or something else of the same sort)—[a] 2 but when of two related things one is a means and the other an end, in their case there is nothing in common except for the one to act and the other to receive the action. I mean for instance the relation between any instrument or artificer and the work that they produce : between a house and a builder there is nothing that is produced in common, but the builder's craft exists for the sake of the house. Hence although states need property, the property is no part of the state. And there are many living things that fall under the head of property.[b] And the state is one form of partnership of similar people, 3 and its object is the best life that is possible. And since the greatest good is happiness, and this is some perfect activity or employment of virtue, and since it has so come about that it is possible for some men to participate in it, but for others only to a small extent or not at all, it is clear that this is the cause for there arising different kinds and varieties of state and several forms of constitution ; for as each set of people pursues participation in happiness in a different manner and by different means they make for themselves different modes of life and different constitutions. And we must also further consider how many there are of these things referred to that are indispensable for the existence of a state ; for among them will be the things which we pronounce to be parts of a state, owing to which their presence is essential. We must therefore consider the list of occupations that a state requires : for from these it will appear what the indispensable classes are. First then a state must have a supply of food ;

Six necessary functions,

571

τροφήν, ἔπειτα τέχνας (πολλῶν γὰρ ὀργάνων δεῖται
τὸ ζῆν), τρίτον δὲ ὅπλα (τοὺς γὰρ κοινωνοῦντας
ἀναγκαῖον καὶ ἐν αὐτοῖς ἔχειν ὅπλα πρός τε τὴν
ἀρχήν, τῶν ἀπειθούντων χάριν, καὶ πρὸς τοὺς
10 ἔξωθεν ἀδικεῖν ἐπιχειροῦντας), ἔτι χρημάτων τινὰ
εὐπορίαν, ὅπως ἔχωσι καὶ πρὸς τὰς καθ' αὑτοὺς
χρείας καὶ πρὸς πολεμικάς, πέμπτον δὲ καὶ πρῶτον
τὴν περὶ τὸ θεῖον ἐπιμέλειαν, ἣν καλοῦσιν ἱερα-
τείαν, ἕκτον δὲ τὸν ἀριθμὸν καὶ πάντων ἀναγκαιό-
τατον κρίσιν περὶ τῶν συμφερόντων καὶ τῶν
15 δικαίων τῶν πρὸς ἀλλήλους. τὰ μὲν οὖν ἔργα
ταῦτ' ἐστὶν ὧν δεῖται πᾶσα πόλις ὡς εἰπεῖν (ἡ γὰρ
πόλις πλῆθός ἐστιν οὐ τὸ τυχόν, ἀλλὰ πρὸς ζωὴν
αὔταρκες, ὡς φαμέν, ἐὰν δέ τι τυγχάνῃ τούτων
ἐκλεῖπον, ἀδύνατον ἁπλῶς αὐτάρκη τὴν κοινωνίαν
εἶναι ταύτην). ἀνάγκη τοίνυν κατὰ τὰς ἐργασίας
20 ταύτας συνεστάναι πόλιν· δεῖ ἄρα γεωργῶν τ'
εἶναι πλῆθος οἳ παρασκευάσουσι τὴν τροφήν, καὶ
τεχνίτας, καὶ τὸ μάχιμον, καὶ τὸ εὔπορον, καὶ
ἱερεῖς, καὶ κριτὰς τῶν ἀναγκαίων[1] καὶ συμφερόντων.

VIII. Διωρισμένων δὲ τούτων λοιπὸν σκέψασθαι
25 πότερον πᾶσι κοινωνητέον πάντων τούτων (ἐνδέχεται γὰρ τοὺς αὐτοὺς ἅπαντας εἶναι καὶ γεωργοὺς
καὶ τεχνίτας καὶ τοὺς βουλευομένους καὶ δικά-
ζοντας), ἢ καθ' ἕκαστον ἔργον τῶν εἰρημένων
ἄλλους ὑποθετέον, ἢ τὰ μὲν ἴδια τὰ δὲ κοινὰ τούτων

---

[1] δικαίων Lambinus.

* *Cf.* ii. i. 7, iii. i. 8, v. ii. 10.

secondly, handicrafts (since life needs many tools) ; third, arms (since the members of the association must necessarily possess arms both to use among themselves and for purposes of government, in cases of insubordination, and to employ against those who try to molest them from without) ; also a certain supply of money, in order that they may have enough both for their internal needs and for requirements of war ; fifth, a primary need, the service of religion, termed a priesthood ; and sixth in number and most necessary of all, a provision for deciding questions of interests and of rights between the citizens. These then are the occupations that *and six correspond-* virtually every state requires (for the state is not *ing classes.* any chance multitude of people but one self-sufficient for the needs of life, as we say,[a] and if any of these industries happens to be wanting, it is impossible for that association to be absolutely self-sufficient). It is necessary therefore for the state to be organized on the lines of these functions ; consequently it must possess a number of farmers who will provide the food, and craftsmen, and the military class, and the wealthy, and priests and judges to decide questions of necessity [b] and of interests.

VIII. These matters having been settled, it re- *Citizenship* mains to consider whether everybody is to take part *and* in all of these functions (for it is possible for the whole *confined to* of the people to be at once farmers and craftsmen *two classes.* and the councillors and judges), or whether we are to assume different classes corresponding to each of the functions mentioned, or whether some of them must necessarily be specialized and others combined.

[b] Perhaps the text should be altered to give ' matters of justice.'

1328 b

ἐξ ἀνάγκης ἐστίν. οὐκ ἐν πάσῃ δὲ ταὐτὸ[1] πολιτείᾳ·
30 καθάπερ γὰρ εἴπομεν, ἐνδέχεται καὶ πάντας κοινωνεῖν πάντων καὶ μὴ πάντας πάντων ἀλλὰ τινὰς
τινῶν. ταῦτα γὰρ καὶ ποιεῖ τὰς πολιτείας ἑτέρας·
ἐν μὲν γὰρ ταῖς δημοκρατίαις μετέχουσι πάντες
πάντων, ἐν δὲ ταῖς ὀλιγαρχίαις τοὐναντίον. ἐπεὶ
δὲ τυγχάνομεν σκοποῦντες περὶ τῆς ἀρίστης πολι-
35 τείας, αὕτη δ' ἐστὶ καθ' ἣν ἡ πόλις ἂν εἴη μάλιστ'
εὐδαίμων, τὴν δ' εὐδαιμονίαν ὅτι χωρὶς ἀρετῆς
ἀδύνατον ὑπάρχειν εἴρηται πρότερον, φανερὸν ἐκ
τούτων ὡς ἐν τῇ κάλλιστα πολιτευομένῃ πόλει, καὶ
τῇ κεκτημένῃ δικαίους ἄνδρας ἁπλῶς ἀλλὰ μὴ
πρὸς τὴν ὑπόθεσιν, οὔτε βάναυσον βίον οὔτ'
40 ἀγοραῖον δεῖ ζῆν τοὺς πολίτας (ἀγεννὴς γὰρ ὁ
τοιοῦτος βίος καὶ πρὸς ἀρετὴν ὑπεναντίος), οὐδὲ
1329 a δὴ γεωργοὺς εἶναι τοὺς μέλλοντας ἔσεσθαι[2] (δεῖ
γὰρ σχολῆς καὶ πρὸς τὴν γένεσιν τῆς ἀρετῆς καὶ
πρὸς τὰς πράξεις τὰς πολιτικάς). ἐπεὶ δὲ καὶ τὸ
πολεμικὸν καὶ τὸ βουλευόμενον περὶ τῶν συμ-
5 φερόντων καὶ κρῖνον περὶ τῶν δικαίων ἐνυπάρχει
καὶ μέρη φαίνεται τῆς πόλεως μάλιστα ὄντα,
πότερον ἕτερα[3] καὶ ταῦτα θετέον ἢ τοῖς αὐτοῖς
ἀποδοτέον ἄμφω; φανερὸν δὲ καὶ τοῦτο, διότι
τρόπον μέν τινα τοῖς αὐτοῖς, τρόπον δέ τινα καὶ
ἑτέροις. ᾗ μὲν γὰρ ἑτέρας ἀκμῆς ἑκάτερον τῶν
ἔργων, καὶ τὸ μὲν δεῖται φρονήσεως τὸ δὲ δυνά-

---

[1] ταὐτὸ Spengel: τοῦτο codd.
[2] [τοὺς] μέλλοντας ἔσεσθαι supra post ζῆν τοὺς 40 Richards.
[3] ἕτερα ⟨ἑτέροις⟩ Coraes.

ᵃ Cf. iv. iv. and xiv.   ᵇ c. i. § 5.

But it will not be the same in every form of constitution; for, as we said,[a] it is possible either for all the people to take part in all the functions or for not all to take part in all but for certain people to have certain functions. In fact these different distributions of functions are the cause of the difference between constitutions: democracies are states in which all the people participate in all the functions, oligarchies where the contrary is the case. But at present we are studying the best constitution, and this is the constitution under which the state would be most happy, and it has been stated before[b] that happiness cannot be forthcoming without virtue; it is therefore clear from these considerations that in the most nobly constituted state, and the one that possesses men that are absolutely just, not merely just relatively to the principle that is the basis of the constitution, the citizens must not live a mechanic or a mercantile life (for such a life is ignoble and inimical to virtue), nor yet must those who are to be citizens in the best state be tillers of the soil (for leisure is needed both for the development of virtue and for active participation in politics). And since the state also contains the military class and the class that deliberates about matters of policy and judges questions of justice, and these are manifestly in a special sense parts of the state, are these classes also to be set down as distinct or are both functions to be assigned to the same persons? But here also the answer is clear, because in a certain sense they should be assigned to the same persons, but in a certain sense to different ones. Inasmuch as each of these two functions belongs to a different prime of life, and one requires wisdom, the other strength,

575

10 μεως, ἑτέροις· ᾗ δὲ τῶν ἀδυνάτων ἐστὶ τοὺς
δυναμένους βιάζεσθαι καὶ κωλύειν, τούτους ὑπομένειν ἀρχομένους ἀεί, ταύτῃ δὲ τοῖς αὐτοῖς· οἱ
γὰρ τῶν ὅπλων κύριοι καὶ μένειν ἢ μὴ μένειν
κύριοι τὴν πολιτείαν. λείπεται τοίνυν τοῖς αὐτοῖς
μὲν ἀμφοτέροις[1] ἀποδιδόναι τὴν πολιτείαν ταύτην,[2]
15 μὴ ἅμα δέ, ἀλλ᾿, ὥσπερ πέφυκεν ἡ μὲν δύναμις ἐν
νεωτέροις ἡ δὲ φρόνησις ἐν πρεσβυτέροις εἶναι,
ἔοικεν οὕτως ἀμφοῖν νενεμῆσθαι συμφέρειν[3] καὶ
δίκαιον εἶναι· ἔχει γὰρ αὕτη ἡ διαίρεσις τὸ κατ᾿
ἀξίαν. ἀλλὰ μὴν καὶ τὰς κτήσεις δεῖ εἶναι περὶ
20 τούτους· ἀναγκαῖον γὰρ εὐπορίαν ὑπάρχειν τοῖς
πολίταις, πολῖται δὲ οὗτοι. τὸ γὰρ βάναυσον οὐ
μετέχει τῆς πόλεως, οὐδ᾿ ἄλλο οὐθὲν γένος ὃ μὴ
τῆς ἀρετῆς δημιουργόν ἐστιν. τοῦτο δὲ δῆλον ἐκ
τῆς ὑποθέσεως· τὸ μὲν γὰρ εὐδαιμονεῖν ἀναγκαῖον
ὑπάρχειν μετὰ τῆς ἀρετῆς, εὐδαίμονα δὲ πόλιν
οὐκ εἰς μέρος τι βλέψαντας δεῖ λέγειν αὐτῆς ἀλλ᾿[b]
25 εἰς πάντας τοὺς πολίτας. φανερὸν δὲ καὶ ὅτι[4] δεῖ
τὰς κτήσεις εἶναι τούτων, εἴπερ[5] ἀναγκαῖον εἶναι
τοὺς γεωργοὺς δούλους ἢ βαρβάρους[6] περιοίκους
λοιπὸν δ᾿ ἐκ τῶν καταριθμηθέντων τὸ τῶν ἱερέων
γένος· φανερὰ δὲ καὶ ἡ τούτων τάξις. οὔτε γὰρ
γεωργὸν οὔτε βάναυσον ἱερέα καταστατέον, ὑπὸ

---

[1] ἀμφότερα ? Susemihl.   [2] ταῦτα ? Susemihl.
[3] εἶναι ἔοικεν . . . συμφέρειν Immisch: ἐστίν· οὔκουν . . .
συμφέρει codd. (sed pro εἶναι *esse* videtur Guil.).
[4] εἴπερ Hayduck.   [5] ὅτι Hayduck.
[6] βαρβάρους Susemihl: βαρβάρους ἢ codd.

---

[a] Or, amending this curious Greek, 'for the constitution
to assign both these functions to the same people.'
[b] A Platonic phrase, *Republic* 500 D.

they are to be assigned to different people ; but inasmuch as it is a thing impossible that when a set of men are able to employ force and to resist control, these should submit always to be ruled, from this point of view both functions must be assigned to the same people ; for those who have the power of arms have the power to decide whether the constitution 4 shall stand or fall. The only course left them is to assign this constitutional function to both sets of men without distinction,[a] yet not simultaneously, but, as in the natural order of things strength is found in the younger men and wisdom in the elder, it seems to be expedient and just for their functions to be allotted to both in this way, for this mode of division 5 possesses conformity with merit. Moreover the ownership of properties also must be centred round these classes, for the citizens must necessarily possess plentiful means, and these are the citizens. For the artisan class has no share in the state, nor has any other class that is not ' an artificer of virtue.' [b] And this is clear from our basic principle ; for in conjunction with virtue happiness is bound to be forthcoming, but we should pronounce a state happy having regard not to a particular section of it but to all its citizens. And it is also manifest that the properties must belong to these classes, inasmuch as [c] it is necessary for the tillers of the soil to be slaves, or serfs of alien race. There remains of the list enumerated the class of priests ; and the position of this class also is manifest. Priests must be appointed The neither from the tillers of the soil nor from the priesthood. artisans, for it is seemly that the gods should be

[c] As this is a new point, perhaps we should transpose ' inasmuch as ' ($εἴπερ$) and ' that ' ($ὅτι$) in the line above.

1329 a

30 γὰρ τῶν πολιτῶν πρέπει τιμᾶσθαι τοὺς θεούς·
ἐπεὶ δὲ διῄρηται τὸ πολιτικὸν εἰς δύο μέρη, τοῦτ᾽
ἐστὶ τό τε ὁπλιτικὸν καὶ τὸ βουλευτικόν, πρέπει
δὲ τήν τε θεραπείαν ἀποδιδόναι τοῖς θεοῖς καὶ τὴν[1]
ἀνάπαυσιν ἔχειν περὶ αὐτοὺς[2] τοὺς διὰ τὸν χρόνον
ἀπειρηκότας, τούτοις ἂν εἴη τὰς ἱερωσύνας ἀποδοτέον.

35 Ὧν μὲν τοίνυν ἄνευ πόλις οὐ συνίσταται καὶ ὅσα
μέρη πόλεως εἴρηται· γεωργοὶ μὲν γὰρ καὶ τεχνῖται καὶ πᾶν τὸ θητικὸν ἀναγκαῖον [ὑπάρχειν][3]
ταῖς πόλεσιν, μέρη δὲ τῆς πόλεως τό τε ὁπλιτικὸν
καὶ βουλευτικόν· καὶ κεχώρισται δὴ τούτων
ἕκαστον, τὸ μὲν ἀεί, τὸ δὲ κατὰ μέρος.

40 IX. Ἔοικε δ᾽ οὐ νῦν οὐδὲ νεωστὶ τοῦτ᾽ εἶναι
γνώριμον τοῖς περὶ πολιτείας φιλοσοφοῦσιν, ὅτι
1329 b δεῖ διῃρῆσθαι χωρὶς κατὰ γένη τὴν πόλιν καὶ τό
τε μάχιμον ἕτερον εἶναι καὶ τὸ γεωργοῦν. ἐν
Αἰγύπτῳ τε γὰρ ἔχει τὸν τρόπον τοῦτον ἔτι καὶ
νῦν τά τε περὶ τὴν Κρήτην, τὰ μὲν οὖν περὶ
5 Αἴγυπτον Σεσώστριος, ὥς φασιν, οὕτω νομοθετή-
σαντος, Μίνω δὲ τὰ περὶ Κρήτην. ἀρχαία δ᾽
ἔοικεν εἶναι καὶ τῶν συσσιτίων ἡ τάξις, τὰ μὲν
περὶ Κρήτην γενόμενα περὶ τὴν Μίνω βασιλείαν,
τὰ δὲ περὶ τὴν Ἰταλίαν πολλῷ παλαιότερα τούτων.
φασὶ γὰρ οἱ λόγιοι τῶν ἐκεῖ κατοικούντων Ἰταλόν
τινα γενέσθαι βασιλέα τῆς Οἰνωτρίας, ἀφ᾽ οὗ τό
10 τε ὄνομα μεταβαλόντας Ἰταλοὺς ἀντ᾽ Οἰνωτρῶν
κληθῆναι καὶ τὴν ἀκτὴν ταύτην τῆς Εὐρώπης

---

[1] v.l. τιν᾽.
[2] περὶ αὐτοὺς post τὰς tr. Richards.   [3] Spengel.

---

[a] *i.e.* the 'appurtenances' are permanently separate from
the army and the deliberative, which are the 'parts,' and

578

worshipped by citizens; and since the citizen body is divided into two parts, the military class and the councillor class, and as it is seemly that those who have relinquished these duties owing to age should render to the gods their due worship and should spend their retirement in their service, it is to these that the priestly offices should be assigned.

We have therefore stated the things indispensable for the constitution of a state, and the things that are parts of a state : tillers of the soil, craftsmen and the labouring class generally are a necessary appurtenance of states, but the military and deliberative classes are parts of the state ; and moreover each of these divisions is separate from the others, either permanently or by turn.[a]

IX. And that it is proper for the state to be divided up into castes and for the military class to be distinct from that of the tillers of the soil does not seem to be a discovery of political philosophers of to-day or one made recently.[b] In Egypt this arrangement still exists even now, as also in Crete ; it is said to have been established in Egypt by the legislation of Sesostris and in Crete by that of Minos. Common meals also seem to be an ancient institution, those in Crete having begun in the reign of Minos, while those in Italy are much older than these. According to the historians one of the settlers there, a certain Italus, became king of Oenotria, and from him they took the name of Italians instead of that of Oenotrians, and the name of Italy was given to all

History of the caste system.

which are separate from each other only 'by turn,' *i.e.* a citizen passes on from one to the other.

[b] Perhaps to be read as denying the originality of Plato's *Republic*.

1329 b

Ἰταλίαν τοὔνομα λαβεῖν ὅση τετύχηκεν ἐντὸς οὖσα
τοῦ κόλπου τοῦ Σκυλλητικοῦ καὶ τοῦ Λαμητικοῦ·
ἀπέχει δὲ ταῦτα ἀπ' ἀλλήλων ὁδὸν ἡμισείας
ἡμέρας. τοῦτον δὴ λέγουσι τὸν Ἰταλὸν νομάδας
15 τοὺς Οἰνωτροὺς ὄντας ποιῆσαι γεωργούς, καὶ
νόμους ἄλλους τε αὐτοῖς θέσθαι καὶ τὰ συσσίτια
καταστῆσαι πρῶτον· διὸ καὶ νῦν ἔτι τῶν ἀπ' ἐκείνου
τινὲς χρῶνται τοῖς συσσιτίοις καὶ τῶν νόμων
ἐνίοις. ᾤκουν δὲ τὸ μὲν πρὸς τὴν Τυρρηνίαν
20 Ὀπικοὶ καὶ πρότερον καὶ νῦν καλούμενοι τὴν
ἐπωνυμίαν Αὔσονες, τὸ δὲ πρὸς τὴν Ἰαπυγίαν καὶ
τὸν Ἰόνιον Χῶνες, τὴν καλουμένην Σύρτιν¹· ἦσαν
δὲ καὶ οἱ Χῶνες Οἰνωτροὶ τὸ γένος. ἡ μὲν οὖν
τῶν συσσιτίων τάξις ἐντεῦθεν γέγονε πρῶτον, ὁ
δὲ χωρισμὸς ὁ κατὰ γένος τοῦ πολιτικοῦ πλήθους
ἐξ Αἰγύπτου· πολὺ γὰρ ὑπερτείνει τοῖς χρόνοις
25 τὴν Μίνω βασιλείαν ἡ Σεσώστριος. σχεδὸν μὲν
οὖν καὶ τὰ ἄλλα δεῖ νομίζειν εὑρῆσθαι πολλάκις
ἐν τῷ πολλῷ χρόνῳ, μᾶλλον δ' ἀπειράκις· τὰ μὲν
γὰρ ἀναγκαῖα τὴν χρείαν διδάσκειν εἰκὸς αὐτήν,
τὰ δ' εἰς εὐσχημοσύνην καὶ περιουσίαν ὑπαρχόντων
30 ἤδη τούτων εὔλογον λαμβάνειν τὴν αὔξησιν· ὥστε
καὶ τὰ περὶ τὰς πολιτείας οἴεσθαι δεῖ τὸν αὐτὸ
ἔχειν τρόπον. ὅτι δὲ πάντα ἀρχαῖα, σημεῖον τὸ
περὶ Αἴγυπτόν ἐστιν· οὗτοι γὰρ ἀρχαιότατοι μὲν
δοκοῦσιν εἶναι, νόμων δὲ τετυχήκασιν ⟨ἀεὶ⟩² κα
τάξεως πολιτικῆς. διὸ δεῖ τοῖς μὲν εὑρημένοις

---

¹ Σιρῖτιν Goettling.　　² Bernays et Susemihl.
³ Lambinus: εἰρημένοις codd.

ᵃ i.e. the south-west peninsula or toe of Italy.
ᵇ i.e. the Gulfs of Squillace and Eufemia.

that promontory *a* of Europe lying between the Gulfs
of Scylletium and of Lametus,*b* which are half a day's
3 journey apart.   It was this Italus then who according to tradition converted the Oenotrians from a
pastoral life to one of agriculture and gave them
various ordinances, being the first to institute their
system of common meals ; hence the common meals
and some of his laws are still observed by certain
of his successors even to-day.   The settlers in the
direction of Tyrrhenia *c* were Opicans, who to-day as
in former times bear the surname of Ausonians ; the
region towards Iapygia *d* and the Ionian Gulf, called
Syrtis, was inhabited by the Chones, who also were
4 Oenotrians by race.   It is from this country that
the system of common meals has its origin, while
the division of the citizen-body by hereditary caste
came from Egypt, for the reign of Sesostris long
antedates that of Minos.   We may almost take it
therefore that all other political devices also have
been discovered repeatedly, or rather an infinite
number of times over, in the lapse of ages ; for the
discoveries of a necessary kind are probably taught
by need itself, and when the necessaries have been
provided it is reasonable that things contributing to
refinement and luxury should find their development ;
so that we must assume that this is the way with
5 political institutions also.   The antiquity of all of
them is indicated by the history of Egypt ; for the
Egyptians are reputed to be the oldest of nations,
but they have always had laws and a political system.
Hence we should use the results of previous dis-

---

c The modern Tuscany, *i.e.* the people of Lucania, Cam-
pania and Latium.

d The south-east promontory or heel of Italy.

1329 b

85 ἱκανῶς χρῆσθαι, τὰ δὲ παραλελειμμένα πειρᾶσθαι
ζητεῖν.

Ὅτι μὲν οὖν δεῖ τὴν χώραν εἶναι τῶν ὅπλα
κεκτημένων καὶ τῶν τῆς πολιτείας μετεχόντων,
εἴρηται πρότερον, καὶ διότι τοὺς γεωργοῦντας
αὐτῶν ἑτέρους εἶναι δεῖ, καὶ πόσην τινὰ χρὴ καὶ
40 ποίαν εἶναι τὴν χώραν· περὶ δὲ τῆς διανομῆς καὶ
τῶν γεωργούντων, τίνας καὶ ποίους εἶναι χρή,
λεκτέον πρῶτον, ἐπειδὴ οὔτε κοινήν φαμεν εἶναι
1330 a δεῖν τὴν κτῆσιν, ὥσπερ τινὲς εἰρήκασιν, ἀλλὰ τῇ
χρήσει φιλικῶς γινομένην κοινήν,[a] οὔτ' ἀπορεῖν
οὐθένα τῶν πολιτῶν τροφῆς. περὶ συσσιτίων τε
συνδοκεῖ πᾶσι χρήσιμον εἶναι ταῖς εὖ κατεσκευ-
5 ασμέναις πόλεσιν ὑπάρχειν· δι' ἣν δ' αἰτίαν συνδοκεῖ
καὶ ἡμῖν, ὕστερον ἐροῦμεν. δεῖ δὲ τούτων κοινωνεῖν πάντας τοὺς πολίτας, οὐ ῥᾴδιον δὲ τοὺς
ἀπόρους ἀπὸ τῶν ἰδίων τε εἰσφέρειν τὸ συντεταγμένον καὶ διοικεῖν τὴν ἄλλην οἰκίαν. ἔτι δὲ τὰ
πρὸς τοὺς θεοὺς δαπανήματα κοινὰ πάσης τῆς
πόλεώς ἐστιν. ἀναγκαῖον τοίνυν εἰς δύο μέρη
10 διῃρῆσθαι τὴν χώραν, καὶ τὴν μὲν εἶναι κοινὴν τὴν
δὲ τῶν ἰδιωτῶν, καὶ τούτων ἑκατέραν διῃρῆσθαι
δίχα πάλιν, τῆς μὲν κοινῆς τὸ μὲν ἕτερον μέρος
εἰς τὰς πρὸς τοὺς θεοὺς λειτουργίας, τὸ δὲ ἕτερον
εἰς τὴν τῶν συσσιτίων δαπάνην, τῆς δὲ τῶν
15 ἰδιωτῶν τὸ ἕτερον μέρος τὸ[1] πρὸς τὰς ἐσχατιάς,
ἕτερον δὲ τὸ[1] πρὸς τὴν πόλιν, ἵνα δύο κλήρων ἑκά-

---

[1] τὸ bis del. Richards.

[a] This vague phrase (based on the proverb κοινὰ τὰ τῶν
φίλων, 'friends' goods are common property') seems to
denote some sort of customary communism in the cultivation
of the land and enjoyment of the produce, combined with
private ownership of the freehold.

covery when adequate, while endeavouring to investigate matters hitherto passed over.

It has been stated before that the land ought to (2) Land be owned by those who possess arms and those who tenure. share the rights of the constitution, and why the cultivators ought to be a different caste from these, and what is the proper extent and conformation of the country. We have now to discuss first the allotment of the land, and the proper class and character of its cultivators; since we advocate not common ownership of land, as some have done, but community in it brought about in a friendly way by the use of it,[a] and we hold that no citizen should be ill supplied with means of subsistence. As to common meals, all agree that this is an institution advantageous for well-organized states to possess; our own reasons for sharing this view we will state later.[b] But the common meals must be shared by all the citizens, and it is not easy for the poor to contribute their assessed share from their private means and also to maintain their household as well. And moreover the expenses connected with religion are the common concern of the whole state. It is necessary therefore for the land to be divided into two parts, of which one must be common and the other the private property of individuals; and each of these two divisions must again be divided in two. Of the common land one portion should be assigned to the services of religion, and the other to defray the cost of the common meals; of the land in private ownership one part should be the district near the frontiers, and another the district near the city, in order that

[b] This promise is not fulfilled.

στῳ νεμηθέντων ἀμφοτέρων τῶν τόπων πάντες μετέχωσιν. τό τε γὰρ ἴσον οὕτως ἔχει καὶ τὸ δίκαιον
καὶ τὸ πρὸς τοὺς ἀστυγείτονας πολέμους ὁμονοη-
τικώτερον. ὅπου γὰρ μὴ τοῦτον ἔχει τὸν τρόπον,
οἱ μὲν ὀλιγωροῦσι τῆς πρὸς τοὺς ὁμόρους ἔχθρας
20 οἱ δὲ λίαν φροντίζουσι καὶ παρὰ τὸ καλόν. διὸ παρ᾿
ἐνίοις νόμος ἐστὶ τοὺς γειτνιῶντας τοῖς ὁμόροις
μὴ συμμετέχειν βουλῆς[1] τῶν πρὸς αὐτοὺς πολέμων,
ὡς διὰ τὸ ἴδιον οὐκ ἂν δυναμένους βουλεύσασθαι
καλῶς. τὴν μὲν οὖν χώραν ἀνάγκη διῃρῆσθαι
25 τὸν τρόπον τοῦτον διὰ τὰς προειρημένας αἰτίας.

Τοὺς δὲ γεωργήσοντας μάλιστα μέν, εἰ δεῖ κατ᾿
εὐχήν, δούλους εἶναι, μήτε ὁμοφύλων πάντων[2] μήτε
θυμοειδῶν (οὕτω γὰρ ἂν πρός τε τὴν ἐργασίαν εἶεν
χρήσιμοι καὶ πρὸς τὸ μηδὲν νεωτερίζειν ἀσφαλεῖς),
30 δεύτερον δὲ βαρβάρους[3] περιοίκους παραπλησίους
τοῖς εἰρημένοις τὴν φύσιν. τούτων δὲ τοὺς μὲν
ἰδίους ἐν τοῖς ἰδίοις εἶναι [ἰδίους][4] τῶν κεκτημένων
τὰς οὐσίας, τοὺς δ᾿ ἐπὶ τῇ κοινῇ γῇ κοινούς. τίνα
δὲ δεῖ τρόπον χρῆσθαι δούλοις, καὶ διότι βέλτιον
πᾶσι τοῖς δούλοις ἆθλον προκεῖσθαι τὴν ἐλευθερίαν,
ὕστερον ἐροῦμεν.

Χ. Τὴν δὲ πόλιν ὅτι μὲν δεῖ κοινὴν εἶναι τῆς
35 ἠπείρου τε καὶ τῆς θαλάσσης καὶ τῆς χώρας ἁπάσης
ὁμοίως ἐκ τῶν ἐνδεχομένων, εἴρηται πρότερον·
αὐτῆς δὲ προσάντη[5] τὴν θέσιν εὔχεσθαι δεῖ κατα-

---

[1] βουλῆς ⟨περὶ⟩ Richards.   [2] πάντων ⟨ὄντων⟩ Richards.
[3] βαρβάρους ⟨ἢ⟩ Schneider (cf. 1329 a 27).
[4] om. cod. deterior.   [5] Immisch: πρὸς αὐτὴν εἶναι codd.

two plots may be assigned to each citizen and all
8 may have a share in both districts. This arrangement satisfies equity and justice, and also conduces
to greater unanimity in facing border warfare.
Where this system is not followed, one set of people
are reckless about quarrelling with the neighbouring
states, and the other set are too cautious and neglect
considerations of honour. Hence some people have
a law that the citizens whose land is near the frontier
are not to take part in deliberation as to wars against
neighbouring states, on the ground that private
interest would prevent them from being able to
take counsel wisely. The land must therefore be
divided up in this manner because of the reasons
aforesaid.

9   Those who are to cultivate the soil should best of Tillage by
all, if the ideal system is to be stated, be slaves, not serfs.
drawn from people all of one tribe nor of a spirited
character (for thus they would be both serviceable
for their work and safe to abstain from insurrection),
but as a second best they should be alien serfs of a
similar nature. Of these labourers those in private
employment must be among the private possessions
of the owners of the estates, and those working on
the common land common property. How slaves
should be employed, and why it is advantageous
that all slaves should have their freedom set before
them as a reward, we will say later.[a]

X. It has been said before that the city should so (3) Plan of
far as circumstances permit be in communication City.
alike with the mainland, the sea and the whole of its aspect.
territory. The site of the city itself we must pray
that fortune may place on sloping ground, having

---

[a] This promise is not fulfilled.

1330 a

τυγχάνειν πρὸς τέτταρα βλέποντας, πρῶτον μέν,
ὡς ἀναγκαῖον, πρὸς ὑγίειαν (αἵ τε γὰρ πρὸς
40 ἕω τὴν ἔγκλισιν ἔχουσαι καὶ πρὸς τὰ πνεύματα τὰ
πνέοντα ἀπὸ τῆς ἀνατολῆς ὑγιεινότεραι, δεύτερον
δὲ κατὰ βορέαν, εὐχείμεροι γὰρ αὗται μᾶλλον),

1330 b

τῶν δὲ λοιπῶν πρός τε τὰς πολιτικὰς πράξεις καὶ 2
πολεμικὰς καλῶς ἔχει.[1] πρὸς μὲν οὖν τὰς πολεμικὰς αὐτοῖς μὲν εὐέξοδον εἶναι χρή, τοῖς δ'
ἐναντίοις δυσπρόσοδον καὶ δυσπερίληπτον, ὑδάτων
τε καὶ ναμάτων μάλιστα μὲν ὑπάρχειν πλῆθος
5 οἰκεῖον, εἰ δὲ μή, τοῦτό γ' εὕρηται διὰ τοῦ κατασκευάζειν ὑποδοχὰς ὀμβρίοις ὕδασιν ἀφθόνους καὶ
μεγάλας, ὥστε μηδέποτε ὑπολείπειν εἰργομένους
τῆς χώρας διὰ πόλεμον. ἐπεὶ δὲ δεῖ περὶ ὑγιείας 3
φροντίζειν τῶν ἐνοικούντων, τοῦτο δ' ἐστὶν ἐν τῷ
10 κεῖσθαι τὸν τόπον ἔν τε τοιούτῳ καὶ πρὸς τοιοῦτον
καλῶς, δεύτερον δὲ ὕδασιν ὑγιεινοῖς χρῆσθαι, καὶ
τούτου τὴν ἐπιμέλειαν ἔχειν μὴ παρέργως. οἷς
γὰρ πλείστοις χρώμεθα πρὸς τὸ σῶμα καὶ πλει-
στάκις, ταῦτα πλεῖστον συμβάλλεται πρὸς τὴν
15 ὑγίειαν· ἡ δὲ τῶν ὑδάτων καὶ τοῦ πνεύματος
δύναμις τοιαύτην ἔχει τὴν φύσιν. διόπερ ἐν ταῖς
εὖ φρονούσαις δεῖ διωρίσθαι πόλεσιν, ἐὰν μὴ πάνθ'
ὅμοια μηδ'[2] ἀφθονία τούτων ᾖ ναμάτων, χωρὶς
τά τε εἰς τροφὴν ὕδατα καὶ τὰ πρὸς τὴν ἄλλην
χρείαν. περὶ δὲ τόπων τῶν ἐρυμνῶν οὐ πάσαις 4
ὁμοίως ἔχει τὸ συμφέρον ταῖς πολιτείαις· οἷον
20 ἀκρόπολις ὀλιγαρχικὸν καὶ μοναρχικόν, δημο-

---

[1] Immisch: ἔχειν codd. [2] Coraes: μήτ' codd.

---

[a] Apparently (1) fresh air, (2) water supply, (3) administration, (4) military requirements.

regard to four considerations [a] : first, as a thing
essential, the consideration of health (for cities
whose site slopes east or towards the breezes that
blow from the sunrise are more healthy, and in the
second degree those that face away from the north
wind,[b] for these are milder in winter) ; and among the
remaining considerations, a sloping site is favourable
both for political and for military purposes. For
military purposes therefore the site should be easy
of exit for the citizens themselves, and difficult for
the adversary to approach and to blockade, and it
must possess if possible a plentiful natural supply of Water-
pools and springs, but failing this, a mode has been supply.
invented of supplying water by means of construct-
ing an abundance of large reservoirs for rain-water,
so that a supply may never fail the citizens when
they are debarred from their territory by war.
And since we have to consider the health of the
inhabitants, and this depends upon the place being
well situated both on healthy ground and with a
healthy aspect, and secondly upon using wholesome
water-supplies, the following matter also must be
attended to as of primary importance. Those things
which we use for the body in the largest quantity, and
most frequently, contribute most to health ; and the
influence of the water-supply and of the air is of this
nature. Hence in wise cities if all the sources of
water are not equally pure and there is not an
abundance of suitable springs, the water-supplies for
drinking must be kept separate from those for
other requirements. As to fortified positions, what Hilly or
is expedient is not the same for all forms of consti- level site.
tution alike ; for example, a citadel-hill is suitable

[b] Literally, ' in the direction in which the north wind blows.'

κρατικὸν δ' ὁμαλότης, ἀριστοκρατικὸν δ' οὐδέτερον
ἀλλὰ μᾶλλον ἰσχυροὶ τόποι πλείους. ἡ δὲ τῶν
ἰδίων οἰκήσεων διάθεσις ἡδίων μὲν νομίζεται καὶ
χρησιμωτέρα πρὸς τὰς ἄλλας πράξεις ἂν εὔτομος
ᾖ καὶ κατὰ τὸν νεώτερον καὶ τὸν Ἱπποδάμειον
25 τρόπον, πρὸς δὲ τὰς πολεμικὰς ἀσφαλείας τοὐναντίον ὡς εἶχον κατὰ τὸν ἀρχαῖον χρόνον· δυσείσοδος
γὰρ ἐκείνη τοῖς ξενικοῖς καὶ δυσεξερεύνητος τοῖς
ἐπιτιθεμένοις. διὸ δεῖ τούτων ἀμφοτέρων μετέχειν
(ἐνδέχεται γὰρ ἄν τις οὕτω κατασκευάζῃ καθάπερ
ἐν τοῖς γεωργοῖς[3] ἃς καλοῦσί τινες τῶν ἀμπέλων
30 συστάδας) καὶ τὴν μὲν ὅλην μὴ ποιεῖν πόλιν εὔ-
τομον, κατὰ μέρη δὲ καὶ τόπους· οὕτω γὰρ καὶ
πρὸς ἀσφάλειαν καὶ κόσμον ἕξει καλῶς.

Περὶ δὲ τειχῶν, οἱ μὴ φάσκοντες δεῖν ἔχειν τὰς
τῆς ἀρετῆς ἀντιποιουμένας πόλεις λίαν ἀρχαίως
ὑπολαμβάνουσιν, καὶ ταῦθ' ὁρῶντες ἐλεγχομένας
35 ἔργῳ τὰς ἐκείνως καλλωπισαμένας. ἔστι δὲ πρὸς
μὲν τοὺς ὁμοίους καὶ μὴ πολὺ τῷ πλήθει διαφέροντας οὐ καλὸν τὸ πειρᾶσθαι σῴζεσθαι διὰ τῆς
τῶν τειχῶν ἐρυμνότητος· ἐπεὶ δὲ καὶ συμβαίνειν ἐνδέχεται[4] πλείω τὴν ὑπεροχὴν γίγνεσθαι
τῶν ἐπιόντων τῆς ἀνθρωπίνης[5] τῆς ἐν τοῖς ὀλίγοις
40 ἀρετῆς, εἰ δεῖ σῴζεσθαι καὶ μὴ πάσχειν κακῶς

---

[1] δυσείσοδος ed. (sic Jackson transpositis δυσείσοδος et δυσεξερεύνητος) : δυσέξοδος codd.
[2] [τοῖς] Immisch, et ἐπιτιθεμένοις supra post ξενικοῖς tr.
Richards.   [3] γεωργίοις Scaliger.
[4] sic ? Richards : δὲ (aut δὲ καὶ) συμβαίνει καὶ ἐνδέχεται codd.
[5] τῆς ἀνθρωπίνης Spengel : καὶ τῆς ἀνθ. καὶ codd.

---

[a] See II. v.
[b] i.e. an enemy's mercenaries ; but the mss. give ' difficult for foreign troops to make sorties from [i.e. presumably

for oligarchy and monarchy, and a level site for democracy ; neither is favourable to an aristocracy, but rather several strong positions. The arrange- ment of the private dwellings is thought to be more agreeable and more convenient for general purposes if they are laid out in straight streets, after the modern fashion, that is, the one introduced by Hippodamus [a] ; but it is more suitable for security in war if it is on the contrary plan, as cities used to be in ancient times ; for that arrangement is difficult for foreign troops [b] to enter and to find their way 5 about in when attacking. Hence it is well to combine the advantages of both plans (for this is possible if the houses are laid out in the way which among the farmers some people call ' on the slant ' [c] in the case of vines), and not to lay out the whole city in straight streets, but only certain parts and districts, for in this way it will combine security with beauty.

As regards walls, those who aver that cities which pretend to valour should not have them hold too old- fashioned a view—and that though they see that the cities that indulge in that form of vanity are refuted 6 by experience. It is true that against an evenly matched foe and one little superior in numbers it is not honourable to try to secure oneself by the strength of one's fortifications ; but as it may possibly happen that the superior numbers of the attackers may be too much for the human valour of a small force, if the city is to survive and not to suffer disaster or

to find their way out when once they have got in, *cf.* Thuc. ii. 4. 2] and for attackers to find their way about in.'

[c] The Roman *quincunx*, each plant of one row being in line with the gap between two plants of the next row, thus : . . . . .

1330 b
μηδὲ ὑβρίζεσθαι, τὴν ἀσφαλεστάτην ἐρυμνότητα
1331 a τῶν τειχῶν οἰητέον εἶναι πολεμικωτάτην, ἄλλως
τε καὶ νῦν εὑρημένων τῶν περὶ τὰ βέλη καὶ
τὰς μηχανὰς εἰς ἀκρίβειαν πρὸς τὰς πολιορκίας.
ὅμοιον γὰρ τὸ τείχη μὴ περιβάλλειν ταῖς πόλεσιν
ἀξιοῦν καὶ τὸ τὴν χώραν εὐέμβολον ζητεῖν[1] καὶ
5 περιαιρεῖν τοὺς ὀρεινοὺς τόπους, ὁμοίως δὲ καὶ
ταῖς οἰκήσεσι ταῖς ἰδίαις μὴ περιβάλλειν τοίχους
ὡς ἀνάνδρων ἐσομένων τῶν κατοικούντων. ἀλλὰ
μὴν οὐδὲ τοῦτό γε δεῖ λανθάνειν, ὅτι τοῖς μὲν
περιβεβλημένοις τείχη περὶ τὴν πόλιν ἔξεστιν
ἀμφοτέρως χρῆσθαι ταῖς πόλεσιν, καὶ ὡς ἐχούσαις
10 τείχη καὶ ὡς μὴ ἐχούσαις, ταῖς δὲ μὴ κεκτημέναις
οὐκ ἔξεστιν. εἰ δὴ τοῦτον ἔχει τὸν τρόπον, οὐχ
ὅτι τείχη μόνον περιβλητέον, ἀλλὰ καὶ τούτων
ἐπιμελητέον ὅπως καὶ πρὸς κόσμον ἔχῃ τῇ πόλει
πρεπόντως καὶ πρὸς τὰς πολεμικὰς χρείας, τάς τε
ἄλλας καὶ τὰς νῦν ἐπεξευρημένας. ὥσπερ γὰρ τοῖς
15 ἐπιτιθεμένοις ἐπιμελές ἐστι δι' ὧν τρόπων πλεονεκ-
τήσουσιν, οὕτω τὰ μὲν εὕρηται τὰ δὲ δεῖ ζητεῖν καὶ
φιλοσοφεῖν καὶ τοὺς φυλαττομένους· ἀρχὴν γὰρ οὐδ'
ἐπιχειροῦσιν ἐπιτίθεσθαι τοῖς εὖ παρεσκευασμένοις.
Ἐπεὶ δὲ δεῖ τὸ μὲν πλῆθος τῶν πολιτῶν ἐν
20 συσσιτίοις κατανενεμῆσθαι, τὰ δὲ τείχη διειλῆφθαι
φυλακτηρίοις καὶ πύργοις κατὰ τόπους ἐπικαίρους,
δῆλον ὡς αὐτὰ προκαλεῖται παρασκευάζειν ἔνια
τῶν συσσιτίων ἐν τούτοις τοῖς φυλακτηρίοις. καὶ
ταῦτα μὲν δὴ τοῦτον ἄν τις διακοσμήσειε τὸν
τρόπον· XI. τὰς δὲ τοῖς θείοις ἀποδεδομένας οἰκή-
25 σεις καὶ τὰ κυριώτατα τῶν ἀρχείων συσσίτια

---

[1] ζητεῖν ⟨ποιεῖν⟩ ? ed.

---

[a] Perhaps a word should be added to the Greek giving

insult, the securest fortification of walls must be deemed to be the most warlike, particularly in view of the inventions that have now been made in the direction of precision with missiles and artillery for sieges. To claim not to encompass cities with walls is like desiring *a* the country to be easy to invade and stripping it of hilly regions, and similarly not surrounding even private dwellings with house-walls on the ground that the inhabitants will be cowardly. Another point moreover that must not be forgotten is that those who have walls round the city can use their cities in both ways, both as walled cities and as open ones, whereas cities not possessing walls cannot be used in both ways. If then this is so, not only must walls be put round a city, but also attention must be paid to them in order that they may be suitable both in regard to the adornment of the city and in respect of military requirements, especially the new devices recently invented. For just as the attackers of a city are concerned to study the means by which they can gain the advantage, so also for the defenders some devices have already been invented and others they must discover and think out ; for people do not even start attempting to attack those who are well prepared.

And since the multitude of citizens must be distributed in separate messes, and the city walls must be divided up by guard-posts and towers in suitable places, it is clear that these facts themselves call for some of the messes to be organized at these guard-posts. These things then might be arranged in this manner. XI. But it is fitting that the dwellings assigned to the gods and the most important of the

‘ desiring to make the country easy to invade, and to strip it—’.

1331 a

ἁρμόττει τόπον ἐπιτήδειόν τε ἔχειν καὶ τὸν αὐτόν
ὅσα μὴ τῶν ἱερῶν ὁ νόμος ἀφορίζει χωρὶς ἤ τ
μαντεῖον ἄλλο πυθόχρηστον. εἴη δ' ἂν τοιοῦτος
τόπος ὅστις ἐπιφάνειάν τε ἔχει πρὸς τὴν τῆ
30 θέσεως ἀρετὴν[1] ἱκανῶς καὶ πρὸς τὰ γειτνιῶντα μέρ
τῆς πόλεως ἐρυμνοτέρως. πρέπει δ' ὑπὸ μὲ
τοῦτον τὸν τόπον τοιαύτης ἀγορᾶς εἶναι κατα
σκευὴν οἵαν καὶ περὶ Θετταλίαν νομίζουσιν[2] ἣ
ἐλευθέραν καλοῦσιν, αὕτη δ' ἐστὶν ἣν δεῖ καθαρὰ
εἶναι τῶν ὠνίων πάντων καὶ μήτε βάναυσον μήτ
35 γεωργὸν μήτ' ἄλλον μηδένα τοιοῦτον παραβάλλει
μὴ καλούμενον ὑπὸ τῶν ἀρχόντων. εἴη δ' ἂ
εὔχαρις ὁ τόπος εἰ καὶ τὰ γυμνάσια τῶν πρεσ
βυτέρων ἔχοι τὴν τάξιν ἐνταῦθα· πρέπει γὰρ
διῃρῆσθαι κατὰ τὰς ἡλικίας καὶ τοῦτον τὸν κόσμον
καὶ παρὰ μὲν τοῖς νεωτέροις ἄρχοντάς τινας δια
40 τρίβειν, τοὺς δὲ πρεσβυτέρους παρὰ τοῖς ἄρχουσιν
ἡ γὰρ ἐν ὀφθαλμοῖς τῶν ἀρχόντων παρουσίο
μάλιστα ἐμποιεῖ τὴν ἀληθινὴν αἰδῶ καὶ τὸν τῶ
1331 b ἐλευθέρων φόβον. τὴν δὲ τῶν ὠνίων ἀγορὰ
ἑτέραν τε δεῖ ταύτης εἶναι καὶ χωρίς, ἔχουσα
τόπον εὐσυνάγωγον τοῖς τε ἀπὸ τῆς θαλάττη
πεμπομένοις καὶ τοῖς ἀπὸ τῆς χώρας πᾶσιν. ἐπε
δὲ τὸ πλῆθος[3] διαιρεῖται τῆς πόλεως εἰς ἱερεῖ
5 καὶ εἰς[4] ἄρχοντας, πρέπει καὶ τῶν ἱερέων συσ
σίτια περὶ τὴν τῶν ἱερῶν οἰκοδομημάτων ἔχειν τὴ
τάξιν. τῶν δ' ἀρχείων ὅσα περὶ τὰ συμβόλαια
ποιεῖται τὴν ἐπιμέλειαν, περί τε γραφὰς δικῶν κα

---

[1] Lambinus : ἀρετῆς θέσιν codd. (ἱερετείας θέσιν Jackson).
[2] Lambinus : ὀνομάζουσι codd.   [3] προεστὸς Newman.
   [4] καὶ εἰς Thomas Aquinas : εἰς codd.

official messes should have a suitable site, and the Temples and public buildings.
same for all, excepting those temples which are
assigned a special place apart by the law or else by
some utterance of the Pythian oracle. And the site
would be suitable if it is one that is sufficiently
conspicuous in regard to the excellence of its position,
and also of superior strength in regard to the adjacent
2 parts of the city. It is convenient that below this
site should be laid out an agora of the kind customary
in Thessaly which they call a free agora, that is, one
which has to be kept clear of all merchandise and
into which no artisan or farmer or any other such
person may intrude unless summoned by the magistrates. It would give amenity to the site if the
gymnasia of the older men were also situated here—
for it is proper to have this institution also divided
according to ages,[a] and for certain magistrates to pass
their time among the youths while the older men
spend theirs with the magistrates ; for the presence
of the magistrates before men's eyes most engenders
true respect and a freeman's awe. The agora for
merchandise must be different from the free agora,
and in another place ; it must have a site convenient
for the collection there of all the goods sent from the
3 seaport and from the country. And as the divisions of
the state's populace include [b] priests and magistrates,
it is suitable that the priests' mess-rooms also should
have their position round that of the sacred buildings.
And all the magistracies that superintend contracts,
and the registration of actions at law, summonses

---

[a] Or 'for in this noble practice different ages should be
separated ' (Jowett).

[b] Perhaps the Greek should be altered to τὸ προεστός, 'as
the governing class is divided into.'

τὰς κλήσεις καὶ τὴν ἄλλην τὴν τοιαύτην διοίκησιν,
ἔτι δὲ περὶ τὴν ἀγορανομίαν καὶ τὴν καλουμένην
10 ἀστυνομίαν, πρὸς ἀγορᾷ μὲν δεῖ καὶ συνόδῳ τινὶ
κοινῇ κατεσκευάσθαι, τοιοῦτος δ' ὁ περὶ τὴν ἀναγκαίαν ἀγορὰν ἐστι τόπος· ἐνσχολάζειν μὲν γὰρ τὴν
ἄνω τίθεμεν, ταύτην δὲ πρὸς τὰς ἀναγκαίας
πράξεις.

Μεμιμῆσθαι[1] δὲ χρὴ τὴν εἰρημένην τάξιν καὶ τὰ
15 περὶ τὴν χώραν· καὶ γὰρ ἐκεῖ τοῖς ἄρχουσιν οὓς
καλοῦσιν οἱ μὲν ὑλωροὺς οἱ δὲ ἀγρονόμους καὶ
φυλακτήρια καὶ συσσίτια πρὸς φυλακὴν ἀναγκαῖον
ὑπάρχειν, ἔτι δὲ ἱερὰ κατὰ τὴν χώραν εἶναι νενε-
μημένα, τὰ μὲν θεοῖς τὰ δὲ ἥρωσιν. ἀλλὰ τὸ
διατρίβειν νῦν ἀκριβολογουμένους καὶ λέγοντας
20 περὶ τῶν τοιούτων ἀργόν ἐστιν. οὐ γὰρ χαλεπόν
ἐστι τὰ τοιαῦτα νοῆσαι, ἀλλὰ ποιῆσαι μᾶλλον· τὸ
μὲν γὰρ λέγειν εὐχῆς ἔργον ἐστί, τὸ δὲ συμβῆναι
τύχης. διὸ περὶ μὲν τῶν τοιούτων τό γε ἐπὶ πλεῖον
ἀφείσθω τὰ νῦν.

XII. Περὶ δὲ τῆς πολιτείας αὐτῆς, ἐκ τίνων καὶ
25 ἐκ ποίων δεῖ συνεστάναι τὴν μέλλουσαν ἔσεσθαι
πόλιν μακαρίαν καὶ πολιτεύσεσθαι[2] καλῶς, λεκτέον.
ἐπεὶ δὲ δύ' ἐστὶν ἐν οἷς γίγνεται τὸ εὖ πᾶσι, τούτοιν
δ' ἐστὶν ἐν μὲν ἐν τῷ τὸν σκοπὸν κεῖσθαι καὶ τὸ
τέλος τῶν πράξεων ὀρθῶς, ἐν δὲ τὰς πρὸς τὸ τέλος
30 φερούσας πράξεις εὑρίσκειν (ἐνδέχεται γὰρ ταῦτα
καὶ διαφωνεῖν ἀλλήλοις καὶ συμφωνεῖν· ἐνίοτε γὰρ
ὁ μὲν σκοπὸς ἔκκειται καλῶς ἐν δὲ τῷ πράττειν
τοῦ τυχεῖν αὐτοῦ διαμαρτάνουσιν, ἐνίοτε δὲ τῶν

---

[1] νενεμῆσθαι ΓΜΡ[1].   [2] Coraes: πολιτεύεσθαι codd.

and other such matters of administration, and also those that deal with the control of the markets and with what is termed policing the city, should have buildings adjacent to an agora or some public place of resort, and such a place is the neighbourhood of the business agora, for we assign the upper agora as the place in which to spend leisure, and this one for necessary business.

The arrangements in the country also should copy the plan described ; there too the magistrates called in some states Wardens of the Woods and in others Land-superintendents must have their guard-posts and mess-rooms for patrol duty, and also temples must be distributed over the country, some dedicated to gods and some to heroes. But to linger at this point over the detailed statement and discussion of questions of this kind is waste of time. The difficulty with such things is not so much in the matter of theory but in that of practice ; to lay down principles is a work of aspiration, but their realization is the task of fortune. Hence we will relinquish for the present the further consideration of matters of this sort. *Country buildings.*

XII. We must now discuss the constitution itself, and ask what and of what character should be the components of the state that is to have felicity and good government. There are two things in which the welfare of all men consists : one of these is the correct establishment of the aim and end of their actions, the other the ascertainment of the actions leading to that end. (For the end proposed and the means adopted may be inconsistent with one another, as also they may be consistent ; sometimes the aim has been correctly proposed, but people fail to achieve it in action, sometimes they achieve all *C. Education of the Citizens. Introduction: happiness virtuous activity.*

1331 b

μὲν πρὸς τὸ τέλος πάντων ἐπιτυγχάνουσιν ἀλλὰ τὸ
τέλος ἔθεντο φαῦλον, ὁτὲ δὲ ἑκατέρου διαμαρ-
85 τάνουσιν, οἷον περὶ ἰατρικήν—οὔτε γὰρ ποῖόν τι
δεῖ τὸ ὑγιαινὸν εἶναι σῶμα κρίνουσιν ἐνίοτε καλῶς
οὔτε πρὸς τὸν ὑποκείμενον αὐτοῖς ὅρον τυγχάνουσι
τῶν ποιητικῶν· δεῖ δ' ἐν ταῖς τέχναις καὶ ἐπιστήμαις ταῦτα ἀμφότερα κρατεῖσθαι, τὸ τέλος καὶ
τὰς εἰς τὸ τέλος πράξεις). ὅτι μὲν οὖν τοῦ τ' εὖ
40 ζῆν καὶ τῆς εὐδαιμονίας ἐφίενται πάντες φανερόν,
ἀλλὰ τούτων τοῖς μὲν ἐξουσία τυγχάνειν, τοῖς δὲ
1332 a οὔ, διά τινα τύχην ἢ φύσιν (δεῖται γὰρ καὶ χορηγίας
τινὸς τὸ ζῆν καλῶς, τούτου[1] δὲ ἐλάττονος μὲν
τοῖς ἄμεινον διακειμένοις πλείονος δὲ τοῖς χεῖρον),
οἱ δ' εὐθὺς οὐκ ὀρθῶς ζητοῦσι τὴν εὐδαιμονίαν
5 ἐξουσίας ὑπαρχούσης. ἐπεὶ δὲ τὸ προκείμενόν ἐστι
τὴν ἀρίστην πολιτείαν ἰδεῖν, αὕτη δ' ἐστὶ καθ' ἣν
ἄριστ' ἂν πολιτεύοιτο πόλις, ἄριστα δ' ἂν πολιτεύοιτο καθ' ἣν εὐδαιμονεῖν μάλιστα ἐνδέχεται τὴν
πόλιν, δῆλον ὅτι τὴν εὐδαιμονίαν δεῖ τί ἐστι μὴ
λανθάνειν. φαμὲν δὲ (καὶ διωρίσμεθα ἐν τοῖς
ἠθικοῖς, εἴ τι τῶν λόγων ἐκείνων ὄφελος) ἐνέργειαν
10 εἶναι καὶ χρῆσιν ἀρετῆς τελείαν, καὶ ταύτην[2] οὐκ
ἐξ ὑποθέσεως ἀλλ' ἁπλῶς. λέγω δ' ἐξ ὑποθέσεως
τἀναγκαῖα, τὸ δ' ἁπλῶς τὸ καλῶς· οἷον τὰ περὶ
τὰς δικαίας πράξεις, αἱ[3] δίκαιαι τιμωρίαι[4] καὶ
κολάσεις ἀπ' ἀρετῆς μέν εἰσιν, ἀναγκαῖαι δέ, καὶ
τὸ καλῶς ἀναγκαίως ἔχουσιν (αἱρετώτερον μὲν[5]

---

[1] ταύτης Schneider.
2 ταύτης ? Stahr. 3 αἱ ⟨γὰρ⟩ Reiz.
a πράξεις διὰ τὰς τιμωρίας Jackson. 5 [μὲν] Coraes.

---

a *i.e.* they misconceive the nature of happiness and select
the wrong thing to aim at.
b *Eth. Nic.* 1098 a 16 and 1176 b 4.

the means successfully but the end that they posited was a bad one, and sometimes they err as to both—for instance, in medicine practitioners are sometimes both wrong in their judgement of what qualities a healthy body ought to possess and unsuccessful in hitting on effective means to produce the distinctive aim that they have set before them ; whereas in the arts and sciences both these things have to be secured, the end and the practical means to the end.)   Now it is clear that all men aim at the good life and at happiness, but though some possess the power to attain these things, some do not, owing to some factor of fortune or of nature (because the good life needs also a certain equipment of means, and although it needs less of this for men of better natural disposition it needs more for those of worse) ; while others, although they have the power, go wrong at the start in their search for happiness.[a]   But the object before us is to discern the best constitution, and this is the one under which a state will be best governed, and a state will be best governed under the constitution under which it has the most opportunity for happiness ; it is therefore clear that we must know what happiness is.   The view that we maintain (and this is the definition that we laid down in *Ethics*,[b] if those discourses are of any value) is that happiness is the complete activity and employment of virtue, and this not conditionally but absolutely.   When I say ' conditionally ' I refer to things necessary, by ' absolutely ' I mean ' nobly ' : for instance, to take the case of just actions, just acts of vengeance and of punishment spring it is true from virtue, but are necessary, and have the quality of nobility only in a limited manner (since it would be preferable that

15 γὰρ μηθενὸς δεῖσθαι τῶν τοιούτων μήτε τὸν ἄνδρα
μήτε τὴν πόλιν), αἱ δ' ἐπὶ τὰς τιμὰς καὶ τὰς
εὐπορίας¹ ἁπλῶς εἰσὶ κάλλισται πράξεις· τὸ μὲν
γὰρ ἕτερον κακοῦ τινος ἀναίρεσίς² ἐστιν, αἱ τοιαῦται
δὲ πράξεις τοὐναντίον, κατασκευαὶ γὰρ ἀγαθῶν
εἰσὶ καὶ γεννήσεις. χρήσαιτο δ' ἂν ὁ σπουδαῖος
20 ἀνὴρ καὶ πενίᾳ καὶ νόσῳ καὶ ταῖς ἄλλαις τύχαις
ταῖς φαύλαις καλῶς, ἀλλὰ τὸ μακάριον ἐν τοῖς
ἐναντίοις ἐστίν (καὶ γὰρ τοῦτο διώρισται κατὰ
τοὺς ἠθικοὺς λόγους, ὅτι τοιοῦτός ἐστιν ὁ σπουδαῖος ᾧ διὰ τὴν ἀρετὴν ἀγαθά³ ἐστι τὰ ἁπλῶς
ἀγαθά, δῆλον δ' ὅτι καὶ τὰς χρήσεις ἀναγκαῖον
25 σπουδαίας καὶ καλὰς εἶναι ταύτας ἁπλῶς)· διὸ
καὶ νομίζουσιν ἄνθρωποι τῆς εὐδαιμονίας αἴτια
τὰ ἐκτὸς εἶναι τῶν ἀγαθῶν, ὥσπερ εἰ τοῦ κιθαρίζειν
λαμπρὸν καὶ καλῶς αἰτιῷντο⁴ τὴν λύραν μᾶλλον
τῆς τέχνης. ἀναγκαῖον τοίνυν ἐκ τῶν εἰρημένων
τὰ μὲν ὑπάρχειν τὰ δὲ παρασκευάσαι τὸν νομοθέτην.
30 διὸ κατατυχεῖν⁵ εὐχόμεθα τὴν τῆς πόλεως σύστασιν ὧν ἡ τύχη κυρία (κυρίαν γὰρ αὐτὴν ὑπάρχειν
τίθεμεν)· τὸ δὲ σπουδαίαν εἶναι τὴν πόλιν οὐκέτι
τύχης ἔργον, ἀλλ' ἐπιστήμης καὶ προαιρέσεως.
ἀλλὰ μὴν σπουδαία πόλις ἐστὶ τῷ τοὺς πολίτας
τοὺς μετέχοντας τῆς πολιτείας εἶναι σπουδαίους·
35 ἡμῖν δὲ πάντες οἱ πολῖται μετέχουσι τῆς πολιτείας.
τοῦτ' ἄρα σκεπτέον, πῶς ἀνὴρ γίνεται σπουδαῖος.
καὶ γὰρ εἰ πάντας ἐνδέχεται σπουδαίους εἶναι μὴ

¹ προεδρίας Jackson.　　² ἀναίρεσίς Schneider : αἵρεσίς codd.
³ Reiz : τὰ ἀγαθά codd.　　⁴ Muret : αἰτιῷτο codd.
⁵ Coraes : κατ' εὐχὴν codd.

ᵃ A conjectural emendation gives ' distinctions.'
ᵇ This is a conjectural emendation ; the mss. give ' the
adoption.'　　　　　ᶜ Eth. Nic. 1113 a 15 ff.

neither individual nor state should have any need of such things), whereas actions aiming at honours and resources [a] are the noblest actions absolutely; for the former class of acts consist in the removal [b] of something evil, but actions of the latter kind are the opposite—they are the foundation and the generation 4 of things good. The virtuous man will use even poverty, disease, and the other forms of bad fortune in a noble manner, but felicity consists in their opposites (for it is a definition established by our ethical discourses [c] that the virtuous man is the man of such a character that because of his virtue things absolutely good are good to him, and it is therefore clear that his employment of these goods must also be virtuous and noble absolutely); and hence men actually suppose that external goods are the cause of happiness, just as if they were to assign the cause of a brilliantly fine performance on the harp to the instrument rather than to the skill of the player. It follows therefore from what has been said that some goods must be forthcoming to start with and 5 others must be provided by the legislator. Hence we pray that the organization of the state may be successful in securing those goods which are in the control of fortune (for that fortune does control external goods we take as axiomatic); but when we come to the state's being virtuous, to secure this is not the function of fortune but of science and policy. But then the virtue of the state is of course caused by the citizens who share in its government being virtuous; and in our state all the citizens share in the government. The point we have to consider therefore is, how does a man become virtuous? For even if it be possible for the citizens to be virtuous

Virtue is the product of nature, habit and reason.

1332 a

καθ᾽ ἕκαστον δὲ τῶν πολιτῶν, οὕτως αἱρετώτερον·
ἀκολουθεῖ γὰρ τῷ καθ᾽ ἕκαστον καὶ τὸ πάντας.
ἀλλὰ μὴν ἀγαθοί γε καὶ σπουδαῖοι γίγνονται διὰ
40 τριῶν· τὰ τρία δὲ ταῦτά ἐστι φύσις ἔθος λόγος.
καὶ γὰρ φῦναι δεῖ πρῶτον οἷον ἄνθρωπον ἀλλὰ μὴ
τῶν ἄλλων τι ζῴων, εἶτα[1] καὶ ποιόν τινα τὸ σῶμα

1332 b καὶ τὴν ψυχήν. ἔνιά τε οὐθὲν ὄφελος φῦναι, τὰ
γὰρ ἔθη μεταβαλεῖν ποιεῖ· ἔνια γάρ ἐστι διὰ τῆς
φύσεως ἐπαμφοτερίζοντα διὰ τῶν ἐθῶν ἐπὶ τὸ
χεῖρον καὶ τὸ βέλτιον. τὰ μὲν οὖν ἄλλα τῶν ζῴων
5 μάλιστα μὲν τῇ φύσει ζῇ, μικρὰ δ᾽ ἔνια καὶ τοῖς
ἔθεσιν, ἄνθρωπος δὲ καὶ λόγῳ, μόνον γὰρ ἔχει
λόγον· ὥστε δεῖ ταῦτα συμφωνεῖν ἀλλήλοις· πολλὰ
γὰρ παρὰ τοὺς ἐθισμοὺς καὶ τὴν φύσιν πράττουσι
διὰ τὸν λόγον, ἐὰν πεισθῶσιν ἄλλως ἔχειν βέλτιον.

Τὴν μὲν τοίνυν φύσιν οἵους εἶναι δεῖ τοὺς μέλλοντας εὐχειρώτους ἔσεσθαι τῷ νομοθέτῃ, διωρίσμεθα
10 πρότερον, τὸ δὲ λοιπὸν ἔργον ἤδη παιδείας· τὰ
μὲν γὰρ ἐθιζόμενοι μανθάνουσι, τὰ δ᾽ ἀκούοντες.

XIII. Ἐπεὶ δὲ πᾶσα πολιτικὴ κοινωνία συνέστηκεν ἐξ ἀρχόντων καὶ ἀρχομένων, τοῦτο δὴ[2]
σκεπτέον, εἰ ἑτέρους εἶναι δεῖ τοὺς ἄρχοντας καὶ
15 τοὺς ἀρχομένους ἢ τοὺς αὐτοὺς διὰ βίου· δῆλον γὰρ
ὡς ἀκολουθεῖν δεήσει καὶ τὴν παιδείαν κατὰ τὴν
διαίρεσιν ταύτην. εἰ μὲν τοίνυν εἴησαν τοσοῦτον

---

[1] mg. cod. inferior: οὕτω cet.
[2] ἤδη ΓΜ.

[a] In c. vi.

collectively without being so individually, the latter is preferable, since for each individual to be virtuous entails as a consequence the collective virtue of all.
6 But there are admittedly three things by which men are made good and virtuous, and these three things are nature, habit and reason. For to start with, one must be born with the nature of a human being and not of some other animal; and secondly, one must be born of a certain quality of body and of soul. But there are some qualities that it is of no use to be born with, for our habits make us alter them: some qualities in fact are made by nature liable to be modified by the habits in either direction, for the 7 worse or for the better. Now the other animals live chiefly by nature, though some in small degrees are guided by habits too; but man lives by reason also, for he alone of animals possesses reason; so that in him these three things must be in harmony with one another; for men often act contrary to their acquired habits and to their nature because of their reason, if they are convinced that some other course of action is preferable.

Now we have already *a* defined the proper natural character of those who are to be amenable to the hand of the legislator; what now remains is the task of education, for men learn some things by practice, others by precept. *Habit and reason need education.*

1 XIII. But since every political community is composed of rulers and subjects, we must therefore consider whether the rulers and the subjects ought to change, or to remain the same through life; for it is clear that their education also will have to be made to correspond with this distribution of functions. If then it were the case that the one class differed from *Unity of education: the same for all young citizens, as no special ruling class.*

1832 b διαφέροντες ἅτεροι τῶν ἄλλων ὅσον τοὺς θεοὺς καὶ
τοὺς ἥρωας ἡγούμεθα τῶν ἀνθρώπων διαφέρειν,
εὐθὺς πρῶτον κατὰ τὸ σῶμα πολλὴν ἔχοντες[1]
20 ὑπερβολήν, εἶτα κατὰ τὴν ψυχήν, ὥστε ἀναμφισ-
βήτητον εἶναι καὶ φανερὰν τὴν ὑπεροχὴν τοῖς
ἀρχομένοις τὴν τῶν ἀρχόντων, δῆλον ὅτι βέλτιον
ἀεὶ τοὺς αὐτοὺς τοὺς μὲν ἄρχειν τοὺς δ' ἄρχεσθαι
καθάπαξ· ἐπεὶ δὲ τοῦτ' οὐ ῥᾴδιον λαβεῖν οὐδ' ἔστιν 2
ὥσπερ ἐν Ἰνδοῖς φησὶ Σκύλαξ εἶναι τοὺς βασιλέας
25 τοσοῦτον διαφέροντας τῶν ἀρχομένων, φανερὸν
ὅτι διὰ πολλὰς αἰτίας ἀναγκαῖον πάντας ὁμοίως
κοινωνεῖν τοῦ κατὰ μέρος ἄρχειν καὶ ἄρχεσθαι.
τό τε γὰρ ἴσον[2] ταὐτὸν τοῖς ὁμοίοις, καὶ
χαλεπὸν μένειν τὴν πολιτείαν τὴν συνεστηκυῖαν
παρὰ τὸ δίκαιον. μετὰ γὰρ τῶν ἀρχομένων
30 ὑπάρχουσι νεωτερίζειν βουλόμενοι πάντες οἱ κατὰ
τὴν χώραν, τοσούτους τε εἶναι τοὺς ἐν τῷ πολιτεύματι τὸ πλῆθος ὥστ' εἶναι κρείττους πάντων τούτων ἕν τι τῶν ἀδυνάτων ἐστίν. ἀλλὰ μὴν ὅτι γε 3
δεῖ τοὺς ἄρχοντας διαφέρειν τῶν ἀρχομένων ἀναμ-
φισβήτητον· πῶς οὖν ταῦτ' ἔσται καὶ πῶς μεθ-
85 έξουσι δεῖ σκέψασθαι τὸν νομοθέτην. εἴρηται δὲ
πρότερον περὶ αὐτοῦ. ἡ γὰρ φύσις δέδωκε τὴν
διαίρεσιν[3] ποιήσασα αὐτῷ τῷ γένει ταὐτὸ τὸ μὲν
νεώτερον τὸ δὲ[4] πρεσβύτερον, ὧν τοῖς μὲν ἄρχεσθαι πρέπει, τοῖς δ' ἄρχειν· ἀγανακτεῖ δὲ οὐδεὶς
καθ' ἡλικίαν ἀρχόμενος, οὐδὲ νομίζει εἶναι κρείτ-
40 των, ἄλλως τε καὶ μέλλων ἀντιλαμβάνειν τοῦτον

---

[1] Richards: ἔχοντας codd.
[2] ἴσον ⟨δίκαιον καὶ⟩ Richards.
[3] Aretinus: αἵρεσιν codd.   [4] τότε μὲν—τότε δὲ MP¹.

---

[a] The emendation suggested by Richards gives 'For

the other as widely as we believe the gods and heroes
to differ from mankind, having first a great superiority
in regard to the body and then in regard to the soul,
so that the pre-eminence of the rulers was indis-
putable and manifest to the subjects, it is clear that
it would be better for the same persons always to be
2 rulers and subjects once for all ; but as this is not
easy to secure, and as we do not find anything corresponding to the great difference that Scylax states to
exist between kings and subjects in India, it is clear
that for many reasons it is necessary for all to share
alike in ruling and being ruled in turn. For equality
means for persons who are alike identity of status,
and also it is difficult ^a for a constitution to endure
that is framed in contravention of justice. For all the
people throughout the country are ranged on the
side of the subject class in wishing for a revolution,
and it is a thing inconceivable that those in the
government should be sufficiently numerous to over-
3 power all of these together. But yet on the other
hand that the rulers ought to be superior to the
subjects cannot be disputed ; therefore the lawgiver
must consider how this is to be secured, and how
they are to participate in the government. And this
has been already ^b discussed. Nature has given the
distinction by making the group that is itself the same
in race partly younger and partly older, of which two
sets it is appropriate to the one to be governed and
for the other to govern ; and no one chafes or thinks
himself better than his rulers when he is governed
on the ground of age, especially as he is going to get
back what he has thus contributed to the common

equality and identity (of status) are just for persons who are
alike, and it is difficult,' etc.   ^b c. viii. § 3, 1329 a 4 ff.

1332 b

τὸν ἔρανον ὅταν τύχῃ τῆς ἱκνουμένης ἡλικίας.
ἔστι μὲν ἄρα ὡς τοὺς αὐτοὺς ἄρχειν καὶ ἄρχεσθαι
1333 a φατέον, ἔστι δὲ ὡς ἑτέρους. ὥστε καὶ τὴν παιδείαν
ἔστιν ὡς τὴν αὐτὴν ἀναγκαῖον, ἔστι δ᾽ ὡς ἑτέραν
εἶναι. τόν τε γὰρ μέλλοντα καλῶς ἄρχειν ἀρ-
χθῆναί φασι δεῖν πρῶτον (ἔστι δ᾽ ἀρχή, καθάπερ ἐν
τοῖς πρώτοις εἴρηται λόγοις, ἡ μὲν τοῦ ἄρχοντος
5 χάριν, ἡ δὲ τοῦ ἀρχομένου· τούτων δὲ τὴν μὲν
δεσποτικὴν εἶναί φαμεν, τὴν δὲ τῶν ἐλευθέρων.
. . .[1] διαφέρει δ᾽ ἔνια τῶν ἐπιταττομένων οὐ τοῖς
ἔργοις ἀλλὰ τῷ τίνος ἔνεκα. διὸ πολλὰ τῶν εἶναι
δοκούντων διακονικῶν ἔργων καὶ τῶν νέων τοῖς
ἐλευθέροις καλὸν διακονεῖν· πρὸς γὰρ τὸ καλὸν καὶ
10 τὸ μὴ καλὸν οὐχ οὕτω διαφέρουσιν αἱ πράξεις καθ᾽
αὑτὰς ὡς ἐν τῷ τέλει καὶ τῷ τίνος ἕνεκεν). ἐπεὶ
δὲ πολίτου[2] καὶ ἄρχοντος τὴν αὐτὴν ἀρετὴν εἶναι
φαμεν καὶ τοῦ ἀρίστου ἀνδρός, τὸν δ᾽ αὐτὸν
ἀρχόμενόν τε δεῖν γίγνεσθαι πρότερον καὶ ἄρχοντα
ὕστερον, τοῦτ᾽ ἂν εἴη τῷ νομοθέτῃ πραγματευτέον,
15 ὅπως ἄνδρες ἀγαθοὶ γίγνωνται καὶ διὰ τίνων
ἐπιτηδευμάτων, καὶ τί τὸ τέλος τῆς ἀρίστης ζωῆς.

Διῄρηται δὲ δύο μέρη τῆς ψυχῆς, ὧν τὸ μὲν ἔχει
λόγον καθ᾽ αὑτό, τὸ δ᾽ οὐκ ἔχει[3] μὲν καθ᾽ αὑτὸ
λόγῳ δ᾽ ὑπακούειν δυνάμενον. ὧν φαμὲν τὰς
ἀρετὰς εἶναι καθ᾽ ἃς ἀνὴρ ἀγαθὸς λέγεταί πως.
20 τούτων δ᾽ ἐν ποτέρῳ μᾶλλον τὸ τέλος, τοῖς μὲν

---

[1] lacunam Conring.
[2] πολίτου ⟨τοῦ ἀρίστου⟩? (cf. 1331 a 13) ed. (ἀρίστου pro τοῦ
ἄρχοντος Spengel). [3] ἔχον? Richards.

---

[a] The sentence here breaks off into a long parenthesis,
after which it is not resumed.
[b] Book III. vi. §§ 6-12, 1278 b 30 ff.

stock when he reaches the proper age. In a sense therefore we must say that the rulers and ruled are the same, and in a sense different. Hence their education also is bound to be in one way the same and in another different. For he who is to be a good ruler must have first been ruled, as the saying is [a] (and government, as has been said in the first discourses,[b] is of two sorts, one carried on for the sake of the ruler and the other for the sake of the subject ; of these the former is what we call the rule of a master, the latter is the government of free men. . . .[c] But some of the commands given differ not in nature of the services commanded but in their object. Hence a number of what are thought to be menial services can be honourably performed even by freemen in youth ; since in regard to honour and dishonour actions do not differ so much in themselves as in their end and object). But since we say that the goodness of a citizen [d] and ruler are the same as that of the best man, and that the same person ought to become a subject first and a ruler afterwards, it will be important for the legislator to study how and by what courses of training good men are to be produced, and what is the end of the best life.

The soul is divided into two parts, of which one is in itself possessed of reason, while the other is not rational in itself but capable of obeying reason. To these parts in our view belong those virtues in accordance with which a man is pronounced to be good in some way. But in which of these two parts the end of man rather resides, those who define the

The aim of education (-c.xv. mid.). Psychology.

---

[c] One sentence or more has been lost here.
[d] Perhaps the Greek should be altered to give ' of the best citizen.'

1333 a

οὕτω διαιρῦσιν ὡς ἡμεῖς φαμεν οὐκ ἄδηλον πῶ
λεκτέον. αἰεὶ γὰρ τὸ χεῖρον τοῦ βελτίονός ἐστι
ἕνεκεν, καὶ τοῦτο φανερὸν ὁμοίως ἔν τε τοῖς κατὰ
τέχνην καὶ τοῖς κατὰ φύσιν· βέλτιον δὲ τὸ λόγον
ἔχον. διῄρηταί τε διχῇ, καθ' ὅνπερ εἰώθαμεν
25 τρόπον διαιρεῖν· ὁ μὲν γὰρ πρακτικός ἐστι λόγος
ὁ δὲ θεωρητικός· ὡσαύτως οὖν ἀνάγκη διῃρῆσθα
καὶ τοῦτο τὸ μέρος δῆλον ὅτι. καὶ τὰς πράξεις
δ' ἀνάλογον ἐροῦμεν ἔχειν, καὶ δεῖ τὰς τοῦ φύσε
βελτίονος αἱρετωτέρας εἶναι τοῖς δυναμένοις τυγχάνειν ἢ πασῶν ἢ τοῖν δυοῖν· αἰεὶ γὰρ ἑκάστῳ
30 τοῦθ' αἱρετώτατον οὗ τυχεῖν ἔστιν ἀκροτάτου.
διῄρηται δὲ καὶ πᾶς ὁ βίος εἰς ἀσχολίαν καὶ εἰς
σχολὴν καὶ πόλεμον καὶ εἰρήνην, καὶ τῶν πρακτῶν
τὰ μὲν εἰς τὰ¹ ἀναγκαῖα καὶ χρήσιμα τὰ δὲ εἰς
τὰ¹ καλά. περὶ ὧν ἀνάγκη τὴν αὐτὴν αἵρεσιν
εἶναι καὶ τοῖς τῆς ψυχῆς μέρεσι καὶ ταῖς πράξε-
35 σιν αὐτῶν, πόλεμον μὲν εἰρήνης χάριν, ἀσχολίαν
δὲ σχολῆς, τὰ δ' ἀναγκαῖα καὶ χρήσιμα τῶν
καλῶν ἕνεκεν. πρὸς πάντα μὲν τοίνυν τῷ πολιτικῷ βλέποντι νομοθετητέον, καὶ κατὰ τὰ μέρη
τῆς ψυχῆς καὶ κατὰ τὰς πράξεις αὐτῶν, μᾶλλον δὲ
40 πρὸς τὰ βελτίω καὶ τὰ τέλη. τὸν αὐτὸν δὲ τρόπον
καὶ περὶ τοὺς βίους καὶ τὰς τῶν πραγμάτων
αἱρέσεις²· δεῖ μὲν γὰρ ἀσχολεῖν δύνασθαι καὶ
1333 b πολεμεῖν, μᾶλλον δ' εἰρήνην ἄγειν καὶ σχολάζειν·

---

¹ [εἰς τὰ] Bonitz.
² Coraes: διαιρέσεις codd.

---

a i.e. the two lower ones, the three being the activities of
the theoretic reason, of the practical reason, and of the
passions that although irrational are amenable to reason.

parts of the soul in accordance with our view will have no doubt as to how they should decide. The worse always exists as a means to the better, and this is manifest alike in the products of art and in those of nature ; but the rational part of the soul is 7 better than the irrational. And the rational part is subdivided into two, according to our usual scheme of division ; for reason is of two kinds, practical and theoretic, so that obviously the rational part of the soul must also be subdivided accordingly. A corresponding classification we shall also pronounce to hold among its activities : the activities of the part of the soul that is by nature superior must be preferable for those persons who are capable of attaining either all the soul's activities or two *a* out of the three ; since that thing is always most desirable for each person which is the highest to which it is possible 8 for him to attain. Also life as a whole is divided into business and leisure, and war and peace, and our actions are aimed some of them at things necessary and useful, others at things noble. In these matters the same principle of preference that applies to the parts of the soul must apply also to the activities of those parts : war must be for the sake of peace, business for the sake of leisure, things necessary and 9 useful for the purpose of things noble. The statesman therefore must legislate with all these considerations in view, both in respect of the parts of the soul and of their activities, and aiming more particularly at the greater goods and the ends. And the same principle applies in regard to modes of life and choices of conduct : a man should be capable of engaging in business and war, but still more capable of living in peace and leisure ; and he should do what is neces-

The chief aim is training for leisure and for peace.

607

1333 b

καὶ τἀναγκαῖα καὶ τὰ χρήσιμα δὲ[1] πράττειν, τὰ
δὲ καλὰ δεῖ μᾶλλον. ὥστε πρὸς τούτους τοὺς
σκοποὺς καὶ παῖδας ἔτι ὄντας παιδευτέον καὶ τὰς
5 ἄλλας ἡλικίας ὅσαι δέονται παιδείας. οἱ δὲ νῦν
ἄριστα δοκοῦντες πολιτεύεσθαι τῶν Ἑλλήνων, καὶ
τῶν νομοθετῶν οἱ ταύτας καταστήσαντες τὰς
πολιτείας, οὔτε πρὸς τὸ βέλτιον τέλος φαίνονται
συντάξαντες τὰ περὶ τὰς πολιτείας οὔτε πρὸς
πάσας τὰς ἀρετὰς τοὺς νόμους καὶ τὴν παιδείαν,
10 ἀλλὰ φορτικῶς ἀπέκλιναν πρὸς τὰς χρησίμους
εἶναι δοκούσας καὶ πλεονεκτικωτέρας. παραπλησίως δὲ τούτοις καὶ τῶν ὕστερόν τινες γραψάντων
ἀπεφήναντο τὴν αὐτὴν δόξαν· ἐπαινοῦντες γὰρ τὴν
Λακεδαιμονίων πολιτείαν ἄγανται τοῦ νομοθέτου
15 τὸν σκοπὸν ὅτι πάντα πρὸς τὸ κρατεῖν καὶ πρὸς
πόλεμον ἐνομοθέτησεν· ἃ καὶ κατὰ τὸν λόγον
ἐστὶν εὐέλεγκτα καὶ τοῖς ἔργοις ἐξελήλεγκται νῦν.
ὥσπερ γὰρ οἱ πλεῖστοι τῶν ἀνθρώπων ζητοῦσι τὸ
πολλῶν δεσπόζειν ὅτι πολλὴ χορηγία γίγνεται τῶν
εὐτυχημάτων, οὕτω καὶ Θίβρων ἀγάμενος φαίνεται
τὸν τῶν Λακώνων νομοθέτην καὶ τῶν ἄλλων
20 ἕκαστος τῶν γραφόντων περὶ τῆς[2] πολιτείας
αὐτῶν ὅτι διὰ τὸ γεγυμνάσθαι πρὸς τοὺς κινδύ-
νους πολλῶν ἦρχον. καίτοι δῆλον ὡς ἐπειδὴ νῦν
γε οὐκέτι ὑπάρχει τοῖς Λάκωσι τὸ ἄρχειν, οὐκ
εὐδαίμονες, οὐδ' ὁ νομοθέτης ἀγαθός. ἔστι[3] δὲ
τοῦτο γελοῖον, εἰ μένοντες ἐν τοῖς νόμοις αὐτοῦ,
25 καὶ μηδενὸς ἐμποδίζοντος πρὸς τὸ χρῆσθαι τοῖς
νόμοις, ἀποβεβλήκασι τὸ ζῆν καλῶς. οὐκ ὀρθῶς

---

[1] om. ΓΜΡ[1]: δεῖ? Stahr.
[2] περὶ τῆς Schneider: περὶ codd.
[3] Congreve: ἔτι codd.

sary and useful, but still more should he do what is
noble. These then are the aims that ought to be
kept in view in the education of the citizens both
while still children and at the later ages that require
education. But the Greek peoples reputed at the
present day to have the best constitutions, and the
lawgivers that established them, manifestly did not
frame their constitutional systems with reference to
the best end, nor construct their laws and their
scheme of education with a view to all the virtues,
but they swerved aside in a vulgar manner towards
those excellences that are supposed to be useful
and more conducive to gain. And following the
same lines as they, some later writers also have pronounced the same opinion : in praising the Spartan
constitution they express admiration for the aim of
its founder on the ground that he framed the whole
of his legislation with a view to conquest and to war.
These views are easy to refute on theoretical grounds
and also have now been refuted by the facts of
history. For just as most of mankind covet being
master of many servants [a] because this produces a
manifold supply of fortune's goods, so Thibron [b] and
all the other writers about the Spartan constitution
show admiration for the lawgiver of the Spartans
because owing to their having been trained to meet
dangers they governed a wide empire. Yet it clearly
follows that since as a matter of fact at the present
day the Spartans no longer possess an empire, they
are not happy, and their lawgiver was not a good one.
And it is ridiculous that although they have kept to
his laws, and although nothing hinders their observing the laws, they have lost the noble life. Also

The Spartan
error that
empire is
the end.

---

[a] Or possibly, ' covet a wide empire.'   [b] Unknown.

1333 b

δ᾽ ὑπολαμβάνουσιν οὐδὲ περὶ τῆς ἀρχῆς ἣν δεῖ
τιμῶντα φαίνεσθαι τὸν νομοθέτην· τοῦ γὰρ δεσποτικῶς ἄρχειν ἡ τῶν ἐλευθέρων ἀρχὴ καλλίων καὶ
μᾶλλον μετ᾽ ἀρετῆς. ἔτι δ᾽ οὐ διὰ τοῦτο δεῖ τὴν
80 πόλιν εὐδαίμονα νομίζειν καὶ τὸν νομοθέτην ἐπαινεῖν, ὅτι κρατεῖν[1] ἤσκησεν ἐπὶ τὸ τῶν πέλας
ἄρχειν· ταῦτα γὰρ μεγάλην ἔχει βλάβην, δῆλον
γὰρ ὅτι καὶ τῶν πολιτῶν τῷ δυναμένῳ τοῦτο πειρατέον διώκειν, ὅπως δύνηται τῆς οἰκείας πόλεως
ἄρχειν· ὅπερ ἐγκαλοῦσιν οἱ Λάκωνες Παυσανίᾳ
85 τῷ βασιλεῖ, καίπερ ἔχοντι τηλικαύτην τιμήν. οὔτε
δὴ πολιτικὸς τῶν τοιούτων λόγων καὶ νόμων
οὐθεὶς οὔτε ὠφέλιμος οὔτε ἀληθής ἐστιν· ταὐτὰ
γὰρ ἄριστα καὶ ἰδίᾳ καὶ κοινῇ, τὸν τε νομοθέτην
ἐμποιεῖν δεῖ ταῦτα ταῖς ψυχαῖς τῶν ἀνθρώπων.
40 τήν τε τῶν πολεμικῶν ἄσκησιν οὐ τούτου χάριν
δεῖ μελετᾶν, ἵνα καταδουλώσωνται τοὺς ἀναξίους,
ἀλλ᾽ ἵνα πρῶτον μὲν αὐτοὶ μὴ δουλεύσωσιν ἑτέροις,
1334 a ἔπειτα ὅπως ζητῶσι τὴν ἡγεμονίαν τῆς ὠφελείας
ἕνεκα τῶν ἀρχομένων, ἀλλὰ μὴ πάντων δεσπο-
τείας· τρίτον δὲ τὸ[2] δεσπόζειν τῶν ἀξίων δουλεύειν.
ὅτι δὲ δεῖ τὸν νομοθέτην μᾶλλον σπουδάζειν ὅπως
5 καὶ τὴν περὶ τὰ πολεμικὰ καὶ τὴν ἄλλην νομοθεσίαν
τοῦ σχολάζειν ἕνεκεν τάξῃ καὶ τῆς εἰρήνης,
μαρτυρεῖ τὰ γιγνόμενα τοῖς λόγοις· αἱ γὰρ πλεῖσται
τῶν τοιούτων πόλεων πολεμοῦσαι μὲν σῴζονται,
κατακτησάμεναι δὲ τὴν ἀρχὴν ἀπόλλυνται· τὴν

---

[1] [κρατεῖν] Reiz.   [2] τὸν ⟨τε⟩ Thurot: τὸν codd.
[3] τῷ Victorius: τοῦ Coraes.

writers have a wrong conception of the power for which the lawgiver should display esteem; to govern freemen is nobler and more conjoined with virtue than to rule despotically. And again it is not a proper ground for deeming a state happy and for praising its lawgiver, that it has practised conquest with a view to ruling[a] over its neighbours. This principle is most disastrous; it follows from it that an individual citizen who has the capacity ought to endeavour to attain the power to hold sway over his own city; but this is just what the Spartans charge as a reproach against their king Pausanias, although he attained such high honour. No principle therefore and no law of this nature is either statesmanlike or profitable, nor is it true; the same ideals are the best both for individuals and for communities, and the lawgiver should endeavour to implant them in the souls of mankind. The proper object of practising military training is not in order that men may enslave those who do not deserve slavery, but in order that first they may themselves avoid becoming enslaved to others; then so that they may seek suzerainty for the benefit of the subject people, but not for the sake of world-wide despotism; and thirdly to hold despotic power over those who deserve to be slaves. Experience supports the testimony of theory, that it is the duty of the lawgiver rather to study how he may frame his legislation both with regard to warfare and in other departments for the object of leisure and of peace. Most military states remain safe while at war but perish when they have won their empire; in peace-time they lose

Proper aim of military training.

---

[a] A probable emendation gives 'that he has trained it with a view to ruling.'

γὰρ βαφὴν ἀφιᾶσιν, ὥσπερ ὁ σίδηρος, εἰρήνην
ἄγοντες. αἴτιος δ᾽ ὁ νομοθέτης οὐ παιδεύσας
10 δύνασθαι σχολάζειν.

Ἐπεὶ δὲ τὸ αὐτὸ τέλος εἶναι φαίνεται καὶ κοινῇ
καὶ ἰδίᾳ τοῖς ἀνθρώποις, καὶ τὸν αὐτὸν ὅρον
ἀναγκαῖον εἶναι τῷ τε ἀρίστῳ ἀνδρὶ καὶ τῇ
ἀρίστῃ πολιτείᾳ, φανερὸν ὅτι δεῖ τὰς εἰς τὴν
15 σχολὴν ἀρετὰς ὑπάρχειν[1]· τέλος γάρ, ὥσπερ εἴρηται
πολλάκις, εἰρήνη μὲν πολέμου, σχολὴ δ᾽ ἀσχολίας.
χρήσιμοι δὲ τῶν ἀρετῶν εἰσι πρὸς τὴν σχολὴν
καὶ διαγωγὴν ὧν τε ἐν τῇ σχολῇ τὸ ἔργον καὶ
ὧν ἐν τῇ ἀσχολίᾳ· δεῖ γὰρ πολλὰ τῶν ἀναγκαίων
20 ὑπάρχειν ὅπως ἐξῇ σχολάζειν. διὸ σώφρονα[2] τὴν
πόλιν εἶναι προσήκει καὶ ἀνδρείαν καὶ καρτερικήν·
κατὰ γὰρ τὴν παροιμίαν, οὐ σχολὴ δούλοις, οἱ
δὲ μὴ δυνάμενοι κινδυνεύειν ἀνδρείως δοῦλοι τῶν
ἐπιόντων εἰσίν. ἀνδρίας μὲν οὖν καὶ καρτερίας
δεῖ πρὸς τὴν ἀσχολίαν, φιλοσοφίας δὲ πρὸς τὴν
σχολήν, σωφροσύνης δὲ καὶ δικαιοσύνης ἐν ἀμ-
25 φοτέροις τοῖς χρόνοις, καὶ μᾶλλον εἰρήνην ἄγουσι
καὶ σχολάζουσιν· ὁ μὲν γὰρ πόλεμος ἀναγκάζει
δικαίους εἶναι καὶ σωφρονεῖν, ἡ δὲ τῆς εὐτυχίας
ἀπόλαυσις καὶ τὸ σχολάζειν μετ᾽ εἰρήνης ὑβριστὰς
ποιεῖ μᾶλλον. πολλῆς οὖν δεῖ δικαιοσύνης καὶ
πολλῆς σωφροσύνης[3] τοὺς ἄριστα δοκοῦντας πράτ-
30 τειν καὶ πάντων τῶν μακαριζομένων ἀπολαύοντας,
οἷον εἴ τινές εἰσιν, ὥσπερ οἱ ποιηταί φασιν, ἐν
μακάρων νήσοις· μάλιστα γὰρ οὗτοι δεήσονται
φιλοσοφίας καὶ σωφροσύνης καὶ δικαιοσύνης, ὅσῳ

---

[1] ὑπερέχειν Susemihl.
[2] [σώφρονα] Susemihl.
[3] σωφροσύνης ⟨μετέχειν⟩ Coraes, ⟨τυγχάνειν⟩ Richards.

their keen temper, like iron.[a] The lawgiver is to blame, because he did not educate them to be able to employ leisure.

16 And since it appears that men have the same end both collectively and individually, and since the same distinctive aim must necessarily belong both to the best man and to the best government, it is clear that the virtues relating to leisure are essential[b]; since, as has been said repeatedly, peace **17** is the end of war, leisure of business. But the virtues useful for leisure and for its employment are not only those that operate during leisure but also those that operate in business; for many of the necessaries must needs be forthcoming to give us opportunity for leisure. Therefore it is proper for the state to be temperate, brave and enduring; since, as the proverb goes, there is no leisure for slaves, but people unable to face danger bravely are the slaves of their assail-**18** ants. Therefore courage and fortitude are needed for business, love of wisdom for leisure, temperance and justice for both seasons, and more especially when men are at peace and have leisure; for war compels men to be just and temperate, whereas the enjoyment of prosperity and peaceful leisure tend **19** to make them insolent. Therefore much justice and much temperance are needed by those who are deemed very prosperous and who enjoy all the things counted as blessings, like the persons, if such there be, as the poets say,[c] that dwell in the Islands of the Blest; these will most need wisdom, temperance and

Psychological inferences.

---

[a] *i.e.* an iron blade when not used loses keenness and has to be re-tempered.
[b] *i.e.* to the state as well as to the individual.
[c] Hesiod, *Works and Days* 170 ff.

1334 a
μᾶλλον σχολάζουσιν ἐν ἀφθονίᾳ τῶν τοιούτων
ἀγαθῶν. διότι μὲν οὖν τὴν μέλλουσαν εὐδαιμονή-
35 σειν καὶ σπουδαίαν ἔσεσθαι πόλιν τούτων δεῖ τῶν
ἀρετῶν μετέχειν, φανερόν· αἰσχροῦ γὰρ ὄντος μὴ[1]
δύνασθαι χρῆσθαι τοῖς ἀγαθοῖς, ἔτι μᾶλλον μὴ
δύνασθαι ἐν τῷ σχολάζειν χρῆσθαι, ἀλλ' ἀσχολοῦν-
τας μὲν καὶ πολεμοῦντας φαίνεσθαι ἀγαθούς,
εἰρήνην δ' ἄγοντας καὶ σχολάζοντας ἀνδραποδώ-
40 δεις. διὸ δεῖ μὴ καθάπερ ἡ Λακεδαιμονίων πόλις
τὴν ἀρετὴν ἀσκεῖν. ἐκεῖνοι μὲν γὰρ οὐ ταύτῃ
1334 b διαφέρουσι τῶν ἄλλων, τῷ μὴ νομίζειν ταὐτὰ
τοῖς ἄλλοις μέγιστα τῶν ἀγαθῶν, ἀλλὰ τῷ γίνεσθαι[2]
ταῦτα μᾶλλον διά τινος ἀρετῆς· ἐπεὶ δὲ μείζω τε
ἀγαθὰ ταῦτα καὶ τὴν ἀπόλαυσιν τὴν τούτων ἢ
τὴν τῶν ἀρετῶν . . .
5 . . .[3] καὶ ὅτι δι' αὐτήν, φανερὸν ἐκ τούτων· πῶς
δὲ καὶ διὰ τίνων ἔσται, τοῦτο δὴ θεωρητέον.
τυγχάνομεν δὴ διῃρημένοι πρότερον ὅτι φύσεως
καὶ ἔθους καὶ λόγου δεῖ· τούτων δὲ ποίους μέν
τινας εἶναι χρὴ τὴν φύσιν, διώρισται πρότερον,
λοιπὸν δὲ θεωρῆσαι πότερον παιδευτέοι τῷ λόγῳ
10 πρότερον ἢ τοῖς ἔθεσιν. ταῦτα γὰρ δεῖ πρὸς
ἄλληλα συμφωνεῖν συμφωνίαν τὴν ἀρίστην· ἐν-
δέχε ται γὰρ διημαρτηκέναι καὶ τὸν λόγον τῆς βελτίστης ὑποθέσεως καὶ διὰ τῶν ἐθῶν ὁμοίως ἦχθαι.
φανερὸν δὴ τοῦτό γε πρῶτον μέν, καθάπερ ἐν τοῖς
ἄλλοις, ὡς ἡ[4] γένεσις ἀπ' ἀρχῆς ἐστι[5] καὶ τὸ τέλος

---

[1] ⟨τοῦ⟩ μὴ Richards.   [2] Schneider : γενέσθαι codd.
[3] lacunam Camerarius.   [4] ἢ ⟨τε⟩ Richards.
[5] ἐστι⟨ν⟩ ante ἄλλου tr. ? Richards.

---

a The end of this sentence and the beginning of the next
appear to have been lost.

justice, the more they are at leisure and have an abundance of such blessings. It is clear therefore why a state that is to be happy and righteous must share in these virtues; for if it is disgraceful to be unable to use our good things, it is still more disgraceful to be unable to use them in time of leisure, and although showing ourselves good men when engaged in business and war, in times of peace and 20 leisure to seem no better than slaves. Therefore we must not cultivate virtue after the manner of the state of Sparta. The superiority of the Spartans over other races does not lie in their holding a different opinion from others as to what things are the greatest goods, but rather in their believing that these are obtained by means of one particular virtue; yet because they both deem these things and their enjoyment to be greater goods than the enjoyment of the virtues . . .[a]

. . . and that it is to be practised for its own sake is manifest from these considerations; but it must now be considered how and by what means this will come about. Now we have indeed previously decided that it requires nature and habit and reason, and among these, what particular quality of nature men ought to possess has been defined previously; but it remains to consider whether men ought to be educated first by means of the reason or by the habits. For between reason and habit the most perfect harmony ought to exist, as it is possible both for the reason to have missed the highest principle and for men to have been as wrongly trained through the habits. This therefore at all events is clear in the first place, in the case of men as of other creatures, that their engendering to start with and the end

Educational system.

Ascent from habit to reason, from bodily training to mental.

^{1834 b}
¹⁵ ἀπό τινος ἀρχῆς¹ ἄλλου τέλους, ὁ δὲ λόγος ἡμῖν
καὶ ὁ νοῦς τῆς φύσεως τέλος, ὥστε πρὸς τούτους
τὴν γένεσιν καὶ τὴν τῶν ἐθῶν δεῖ παρασκευάζειν
μελέτην. ἔπειτα ὥσπερ ψυχὴ καὶ σῶμα δύ᾽ ἐστίν, 23
οὕτω καὶ τῆς ψυχῆς ὁρῶμεν δύο μέρη, τό τε
²⁰ ἄλογον καὶ τὸ λόγον ἔχον, καὶ τὰς ἕξεις τὰς τούτων
δύο τὸν ἀριθμόν, ὧν τὸ μέν ἐστιν ὄρεξις τὸ δὲ νοῦς.
ὥσπερ δὲ τὸ σῶμα πρότερον τῇ γενέσει τῆς
ψυχῆς, οὕτω καὶ τὸ ἄλογον τοῦ λόγον ἔχοντος.
φανερὸν δὲ καὶ τοῦτο· θυμὸς γὰρ καὶ βούλησις, ἔτι
δὲ ἐπιθυμία,² καὶ γενομένοις εὐθὺς ὑπάρχει τοῖς
παιδίοις, ὁ δὲ λογισμὸς καὶ ὁ νοῦς προϊοῦσιν
²⁵ ἐγγίνεσθαι πέφυκε. διὸ πρῶτον μὲν τοῦ σώματος τὴν ἐπιμέλειαν ἀναγκαῖον εἶναι προτέραν ἢ
τὴν τῆς ψυχῆς, ἔπειτα τὴν τῆς ὀρέξεως, ἕνεκα
μέντοι τοῦ νοῦ τὴν τῆς ὀρέξεως, τὴν δὲ τοῦ
σώματος τῆς ψυχῆς.

XIV. Εἴπερ οὖν ἀπ᾽ ἀρχῆς τὸν νομοθέτην ὁρᾶν 1
³⁰ δεῖ ὅπως βέλτιστα τὰ σώματα γένηται τῶν
τρεφομένων, πρῶτον μὲν ἐπιμελητέον περὶ τὴν
σύζευξιν, πότε καὶ ποίους τινὰς ὄντας χρὴ ποιεῖσθαι πρὸς ἀλλήλους τὴν γαμικὴν ὁμιλίαν. δεῖ δ᾽
ἀποβλέποντα νομοθετεῖν ταύτην τὴν κοινωνίαν
πρὸς αὑτούς τε καὶ τὸν τοῦ ζῆν χρόνον, ἵνα
³⁵ συγκαταβαίνωσι ταῖς ἡλικίαις ἐπὶ τὸν αὐτὸν
καιρὸν καὶ μὴ διαφωνῶσιν αἱ δυνάμεις τοῦ μὲν
ἔτι δυναμένου γεννᾶν τῆς δὲ μὴ δυναμένης, ἢ

---

¹ ἀρχῆς ⟨ἀρχὴ⟩ Thurot.
² γὰρ καὶ ἐπιθυμία [ἔτι δὲ βούλησις] ? ed.

---

^a *i.e.* every process and partial end are means to an ultimate
end. A conjecture gives ' the end to which a beginning leads
is itself the beginning of another end.' The active reason is
the completion and purpose of human birth and growth.

616

from any beginning is relative to another end,[a] and that reason and intelligence are for us the end of our natural development, so that it is with a view to these ends that our engendering and the training of our habits must be regulated. And secondly, as soul and body are two, so we observe that the soul also has two parts, the irrational part and the part possessing reason, and that the states which they experience are two in number, the one being desire and the other intelligence ; and as the body is prior in its development to the soul, so the irrational part of the soul is prior to the rational. And this also is obvious, because passion and will, and also appetite,[b] exist in children even as soon as they are born, but it is the nature of reasoning and intelligence to arise in them as they grow older. Therefore in the first place it is necessary for the training of the body to precede that of the mind, and secondly for the training of the appetite to precede that of the intelligence ; but the training of the appetite must be for the sake of the intellect, and that of the body for the sake of the soul.

XIV. Inasmuch therefore as it is the duty of the lawgiver to consider from the start how the children reared are to obtain the best bodily frames, he must first pay attention to the union of the sexes, and settle when and in what condition a couple should practise matrimonial intercourse. In legislating for this partnership he must pay regard partly to the persons themselves and to their span of life, so that they may arrive together at the same period in their ages, and their powers may not be at discord through the man being still capable of parentage and the wife

State regulation of marriage, to produce fit pupils.

[b] These three emotions are subdivisions of ' desire ' above.

1834 b
ταύτης μὲν τοῦ δ' ἀνδρὸς μή (ταῦτα γὰρ ποιεῖ καὶ
στάσεις πρὸς ἀλλήλους καὶ διαφοράς), ἔπειτα καὶ 2
πρὸς τὴν τῶν τέκνων διαδοχήν, δεῖ γὰρ οὔτε λίαν
40 ὑπολείπεσθαι ταῖς ἡλικίαις τὰ τέκνα τῶν πατέρων
(ἀνόνητος γὰρ τοῖς μὲν πρεσβυτέροις ἡ χάρις παρὰ
1335 a τῶν τέκνων, ἡ δὲ παρὰ τῶν πατέρων βοήθεια τοῖς
τέκνοις), οὔτε λίαν πάρεγγυς εἶναι (πολλὴν γὰρ
ἔχει δυσχέρειαν, ἥ τε γὰρ αἰδὼς ἧττον ὑπάρχει
τοῖς τοιούτοις ὥσπερ[1] ἡλικιώταις καὶ περὶ τὴν
οἰκονομίαν ἐγκληματικὸν τὸ πάρεγγυς)· ἔτι δ',
5 ὅθεν ἀρχόμενοι δεῦρο μετέβημεν, ὅπως τὰ σώματα
τῶν γεννωμένων ὑπάρχῃ πρὸς τὴν τοῦ νομοθέτου
βούλησιν. σχεδὸν δὴ πάντα ταῦτα συμβαίνει κατὰ 3
μίαν ἐπιμέλειαν. ἐπεὶ γὰρ ὥρισται τέλος τῆς
γεννήσεως ὡς ἐπὶ τὸ πλεῖστον εἰπεῖν ἀνδράσι μὲν
ὁ τῶν ἑβδομήκοντα ἐτῶν ἀριθμὸς ἔσχατος, πεντή-
10 κοντα δὲ γυναιξίν, δεῖ τὴν ἀρχὴν τῆς συζεύξεως
κατὰ τὴν ἡλικίαν εἰς τοὺς χρόνους καταβαίνειν
τούτους. ἔστι δ' ὁ τῶν νέων συνδυασμὸς φαῦλος 4
πρὸς τεκνοποιίαν· ἐν γὰρ πᾶσι ζῴοις ἀτελῆ τὰ τῶν
νέων ἔγγονα καὶ θηλυτόκα μᾶλλον καὶ μικρὰ τὴν
15 μορφήν, ὥστ' ἀναγκαῖον ταὐτὸ τοῦτο συμβαίνειν
καὶ ἐπὶ τῶν ἀνθρώπων. τεκμήριον δέ· ἐν ὅσαις
γὰρ τῶν πόλεων ἐπιχωριάζεται[2] τὸ νέους συζευγνύναι καὶ νέας, ἀτελεῖς καὶ μικροὶ τὰ σώματά εἰσιν.
ἔτι δὲ ἐν τοῖς τόκοις αἱ νέαι πονοῦσί τε μᾶλλον
20 καὶ διαφθείρονται πλείους· διὸ καὶ τὸν χρησμὸν
γενέσθαι τινές φασι διὰ τοιαύτην αἰτίαν τοῖς

---

[1] ὡς παρ' Ellis.   [2] ἐπιχωριάζει M.

[a] Some editors write θηλύτοκα and interpret 'more likely to
be born females.' (θηλυτόκα, 'likely to bear females,' is applied
to the young parents themselves in *Hist. An.* iv. 766 b 29.)

incapable, or the wife capable and the man not (for this causes differences and actual discord between
2 them), and also he must consider as well the succession of the children, for the children must neither be too far removed in their ages from the fathers (since elderly fathers get no good from their children's return of their favours, nor do the children from the help they get from the fathers), nor must they be too near them (for this involves much unpleasantness, since in such families there is less respect felt between them, as between companions of the same age, and also the nearness of age leads to friction in household affairs) ; and in addition, to return to the point from which we began this digression, measures must be taken to ensure that the children produced may have bodily frames suited to the wish of the lawgiver.
3 These results then are almost all attained by one mode of regulation. For since the period of parentage terminates, speaking generally, with men at the age of seventy at the outside, and with women at fifty, the commencement of their union should cor-
4 respond in respect of age with these times. But the mating of the young is bad for child-bearing ; for in all animal species the offspring of the young are more imperfect and likely to produce female children,[a] and small in figure, so that the same thing must necessarily occur in the human race also. And a proof of this is that in all the states where it is the local custom to mate young men and young women, the people are deformed and small of body. And again young women labour more, and more of them die in childbirth ; indeed according to some accounts such was the reason why the oracle[b] was given to the

[b] Μὴ τέμνε νέαν ἄλοκα (' cut not a new furrow ') schol.

1335 a Τροιζηνίοις, ὡς πολλῶν διαφθειρομένων διὰ τὸ
γαμίσκεσθαι τὰς νεωτέρας, ἀλλ' οὐ πρὸς τὴν τῶν
καρπῶν κομιδήν. ἔτι δὲ καὶ πρὸς σωφροσύνην 5
συμφέρει τὰς ἐκδόσεις ποιεῖσθαι πρεσβυτέραις,
ἀκολαστότεραι γὰρ εἶναι δοκοῦσι νέαι χρησάμεναι
25 ταῖς συνουσίαις. καὶ τὰ τῶν ἀρρένων δὲ σώματα
βλάπτεσθαι δοκεῖ πρὸς τὴν αὔξησιν ἐὰν ἔτι τοῦ
σπέρματος[1] αὐξανομένου ποιῶνται τὴν συνουσίαν·
καὶ γὰρ τούτου τις ὡρισμένος χρόνος, ὃν οὐχ ὑπερ-
βαίνει πληθύον ἔτι. διὸ τὰς μὲν ἁρμόττει περὶ τὴν 6
τῶν ὀκτωκαίδεκα ἐτῶν ἡλικίαν συζευγνύναι, τοὺς
30 δ' ἑπτὰ καὶ τριάκοντα, ἢ μικρὸν πρότερον[2]· ἐν τοσούτῳ γὰρ ἀκμάζουσί τε τοῖς σώμασιν ἢ[3] σύζευξις
ἔσται καὶ πρὸς τὴν παῦλαν τῆς τεκνοποιίας συγκατα-
βήσεται τοῖς χρόνοις εὐκαίρως. ἔτι δὲ ἡ διαδοχὴ
τῶν τέκνων τοῖς μὲν ἀρχομένης ἔσται τῆς ἀκμῆς,
ἐὰν γίγνηται κατὰ λόγον εὐθὺς ἡ γένεσις, τοῖς δὲ
35 ἤδη καταλελυμένης τῆς ἡλικίας πρὸς τὸν τῶν
ἑβδομήκοντα ἐτῶν ἀριθμόν. περὶ μὲν οὖν τοῦ 7
πότε δεῖ ποιεῖσθαι τὴν σύζευξιν, εἴρηται, τοῖς δὲ
περὶ τὴν ὥραν χρόνοις ὡς οἱ πολλοὶ χρῶνται,
καλῶς καὶ νῦν ὁρίσαντες χειμῶνος τὴν συναυλίαν
ποιεῖσθαι ταύτην. δεῖ δὲ καὶ αὐτοὺς ἤδη θεωρεῖν
40 πρὸς τὴν τεκνοποιίαν τά τε παρὰ τῶν ἰατρῶν
λεγόμενα καὶ τὰ παρὰ τῶν φυσικῶν· οἵ τε γὰρ
ἰατροὶ τοὺς καιροὺς τῶν σωμάτων ἱκανῶς λέγουσι,
1335 b καὶ περὶ τῶν πνευμάτων οἱ φυσικοί, τὰ βόρεια τῶν

---

[1] σώματος Γ.
[2] μικρὸν πρότερον Immisch (paulo ante Ramus): μικρὸν
codd., μικρὸν ⟨παραλλάττοντας⟩ Richards (plus minusve
Vittori).   [3] ἢ add. Richards.

people of Troezen, because many were dying owing
to its being their custom for the women to marry
young, and it did not refer to the harvest.   And
again it also contributes to chastity for the bestowal of
women in marriage to be made when they are older,
for it is thought that they are more licentious when
they have had intercourse in youth.   Also the males
are thought to be arrested in bodily growth if they
have intercourse while the seed is still growing ;
for this also has a fixed period after passing which it
is no longer plentiful.   Therefore it is fitting for the
women to be married at about the age of eighteen
and the men at thirty-seven or a little before *—
for that will give long enough for the union to take
place with their bodily vigour at its prime, and for
it to arrive with a convenient coincidence of dates
at the time when procreation ceases.   Moreover the
succession of the children to the estates, if their
birth duly occurs soon after the parents marry, will
take place when they are beginning their prime, and
when the parents' period of vigour has now come
to a close, towards the age of seventy.   The proper
age therefore for union has been discussed ; as to
the proper times in respect of the season we may
accept what is customary with most people, who have
rightly decided even as it is to practise marital co-
habitation in winter.   And people should also study
for themselves, when their time comes, the teachings
of physicians and natural philosophers on the subject
of the procreation of children ; the suitable bodily
seasons are adequately discussed by the physicians,
and the question of weather by the natural philosophers, who say that north winds are more favour-

* The word ' before ' is a conjectural insertion.

1335 b

νοτίων ἐπαινοῦντες μᾶλλον. ποίων δέ τινων τῶν
σωμάτων ὑπαρχόντων μάλιστ᾽ ἂν[1] ὄφελος εἴη τοῖς
γεννωμένοις, ἐπιστήσασι μὲν μᾶλλον λεκτέον ἐν
5 τοῖς περὶ τῆς παιδονομίας, τύπῳ δὲ ἱκανὸν εἰπεῖν
καὶ νῦν. οὔτε γὰρ ἡ τῶν ἀθλητῶν χρήσιμος ἕξις
πρὸς πολιτικὴν εὐεξίαν οὐδὲ πρὸς ὑγίειαν καὶ
τεκνοποιίαν, οὔτε ἡ θεραπευτικὴ καὶ κακοπονη-
τικὴ λίαν, ἀλλ᾽ ἡ μέση τούτων. πεπονημένην μὲν
οὖν ἔχειν δεῖ τὴν ἕξιν, πεπονημένην δὲ **πόνοις**
10 μὴ βιαίοις, μηδὲ πρὸς ἕνα[2] μόνον,[3] ὥσπερ ἡ τῶν
ἀθλητῶν ἕξις, ἀλλὰ πρὸς τὰς τῶν ἐλευθερίων
πράξεις. ὁμοίως δὲ δεῖ ταῦτα ὑπάρχειν ἀνδράσι
καὶ γυναιξίν. χρὴ δὲ καὶ τὰς ἐγκύους ἐπιμελεῖσθαι
τῶν σωμάτων, μὴ ῥαθυμούσας μηδ᾽ ἀραιᾷ τροφῇ
χρωμένας· τοῦτο δὲ ῥᾴδιον τῷ νομοθέτῃ ποιῆσαι
15 προστάξαντι καθ᾽ ἡμέραν τινὰ ποιεῖσθαι πορείαν
πρὸς θεῶν ἀποθεραπείαν τῶν εἰληχότων[4] τὴν περὶ
τῆς γενέσεως τιμήν. τὴν μέντοι διάνοιαν τοὐναντίον τῶν σωμάτων ῥαθυμοτέρως ἁρμόττει δι-
άγειν· ἀπολαύοντα γὰρ φαίνεται τὰ γεννώμενα τῆς
ἐχούσης ὥσπερ καὶ τὰ φυόμενα τῆς γῆς. περὶ
20 δὲ ἀποθέσεως καὶ τροφῆς τῶν γιγνομένων ἔστω
νόμος μηδὲν πεπηρωμένον τρέφειν· διὰ δὲ πλῆθος
τέκνων, ἐὰν ἡ τάξις τῶν ἐθῶν κωλύῃ[5] μηδὲν ἀπο-
τίθεσθαι τῶν γιγνομένων, ὡρίσθαι δεῖ τῆς τεκνοποιίας τὸ πλῆθος, ἐὰν δέ τισι γίγνηται παρὰ ταῦτα
συνδυασθέντων, πρὶν αἴσθησιν ἐγγενέσθαι καὶ ζωὴν

---

[1] M : μάλιστα cet.   [2] ἐν Schneider.
[3] πόνον ? Immisch.   [4] ταῖς εἰληχυίαις Γ.
[5] τέκνων ἡ τάξις—κωλύει P[1] : τέκνων (ἡ γὰρ τάξις—γιγνομένων)
Wallies.

8 able than south. The particular kind of bodily constitution in the parents that will be most beneficial
for the offspring must be dwelt on more in detail
in our discussion of the management of children [a];
it is sufficient to speak of it in outline now. The
athlete's habit of body is not serviceable for bodily
fitness as required by a citizen, nor for health and
parentage, nor yet is a habit that is too valetudin-
arian and unfit for labour, but the condition that lies
between them. The bodily habit therefore should
have been trained by exercise, but not by exercises
that are violent, and not for one form of labour
only, as is the athlete's habit of body, but for the
pursuits of free men. And these arrangements
9 must be provided alike for men and women. And
pregnant women also must take care of their bodies,
not avoiding exercise nor adopting a low diet;
this it is easy for the lawgiver to secure by ordering
them to make a journey daily for the due worship of
the deities whose office is the control of childbirth.
As regards the mind, however, on the contrary it
suits them to pass the time more indolently than as
regards their bodies; for children before birth are
evidently affected by the mother just as growing
plants are by the earth. As to exposing or rearing
the children born, let there be a law that no deformed child shall be reared; but on the ground
of number of children, if the regular customs hinder
any of those born being exposed, there must
be a limit fixed to the procreation of offspring,
and if any people have a child as a result of intercourse in contravention of these regulations, abortion
must be practised on it before it has developed sen-

Exposure of deformed infants.

---

[a] This was never written, or has been lost.

25 ἐμποιεῖσθαι δεῖ τὴν ἄμβλωσιν· τὸ γὰρ ὅσιον καὶ τὸ
μὴ διωρισμένον τῇ αἰσθήσει καὶ τῷ ζῆν ἔσται.
ἐπεὶ δ' ἡ μὲν ἀρχὴ τῆς ἡλικίας ἀνδρὶ καὶ γυναικὶ
διώρισται πότε ἄρχεσθαι χρὴ τῆς συζεύξεως, καὶ
πόσον χρόνον λειτουργεῖν ἁρμόττει πρὸς τεκνο-
30 ποιίαν ὡρίσθω. τὰ γὰρ τῶν πρεσβυτέρων ἔκγονα,
καθάπερ τὰ τῶν νεωτέρων, ἀτελῆ γίνεται καὶ τοῖς
σώμασι καὶ ταῖς διανοίαις, τὰ δὲ τῶν γεγηρακότων
ἀσθενῆ. διὸ κατὰ τὴν τῆς διανοίας ἀκμήν· αὕτη
δ' ἐστὶν ἐν τοῖς πλείστοις ἥνπερ τῶν ποιητῶν τινες
εἰρήκασιν οἱ μετροῦντες ταῖς ἑβδομάσι τὴν ἡλικίαν,
35 περὶ τὸν χρόνον τὸν τῶν πεντήκοντα ἐτῶν. ὥστε
τέτταρσιν ἢ πέντε ἔτεσιν ὑπερβάλλοντα τὴν
ἡλικίαν ταύτην ἀφεῖσθαι δεῖ τῆς εἰς τὸ φανερὸν
γεννήσεως, τὸ δὲ λοιπὸν ὑγιείας χάριν ἤ τινος
ἄλλης τοιαύτης αἰτίας φαίνεσθαι δεῖ ποιουμένους
τὴν ὁμιλίαν. περὶ δὲ τῆς πρὸς ἄλλην ἢ πρὸς
40 ἄλλον, ἔστω μὲν ἁπλῶς μὴ καλὸν ἁπτόμενον
φαίνεσθαι μηδαμῇ μηδαμῶς ὅταν ᾖ[1] καὶ προσ-
αγορευθῇ πόσις, περὶ δὲ τὸν χρόνον τὸν τῆς
1336 a τεκνοποιίας ἐάν τις φαίνηται τοιοῦτόν τι δρῶν,
ἀτιμίᾳ ζημιούσθω πρεπούσῃ πρὸς τὴν ἁμαρτίαν.

XV. Γενομένων δὲ τῶν τέκνων οἴεσθαι δεῖ[2]
μεγάλην εἶναι διαφορὰν πρὸς τὴν τῶν σωμάτων
5 δύναμιν τὴν τροφήν, ὁποία τις ἂν ᾖ. φαίνεται δὲ
διά τε τῶν ἄλλων ζῴων ἐπισκοποῦσι καὶ διὰ τῶν
ἐθνῶν οἷς ἐπιμελές ἐστιν ἄγειν εἰς[3] τὴν πολεμικὴν

---

[1] ὅταν ⟨ἀνὴρ⟩ ᾖ ? Richards.
[2] οἴεσθαι δεῖ Spengel : οἴεσθαι codd.
[3] ἄγειν εἰς Richards : ἄγειν ΓΜΡ¹ : εἰσάγειν cet. : ἀσκεῖν
Coraes.

---

[a] Solon, fragment 27.

ation and life ; for the line between lawful and un-
awful abortion will be marked by the fact of having
ensation and being alive. And since the beginning
of the fit age for a man and for a woman, at which
hey are to begin their union, has been defined, let
t also be decided for how long a time it is suitable
or them to serve the state in the matter of producing
children. For the offspring of too elderly parents,
as those of too young ones, are born imperfect both
n body and mind, and the children of those that have
arrived at old age are weaklings. Therefore the
period must be limited to correspond with the mental
prime ; and this in the case of most men is the age
stated by some of the poets, who measure men's
age by periods of seven years,[a]—it is about the
age of fifty. Therefore persons exceeding this age
by four or five years must be discharged from the
duty of producing children for the community, and
for the rest of their lives if they have intercourse it
must be manifestly for the sake of health or for
some other similar reason. As to intercourse with
another woman or man, in general it must be dishonourable to be known to take any part in it in any
circumstances whatsoever as long as one is a husband
and bears that name, but any who may be discovered
doing anything of the sort during the period of parentage must be punished with a loss of privilege suited
to the offence.

XV. When the children have been born, the par- Regimen
ticular mode of rearing adopted must be deemed an of infants.
important determining influence in regard to their
power of body. It appears from examining the other
animals, and is also shown by the foreign races that
make it their aim to lead to the military habit of

ἕξιν ἡ τοῦ γάλακτος πληθύουσα τροφὴ μάλιστ
οἰκεία τοῖς σώμασιν, ἀοινοτέρα δὲ διὰ τὰ νοσήματα
10 ἔτι δὲ καὶ κινήσεις ὅσας ἐνδέχεται ποιεῖσθα
τηλικούτων συμφέρει. πρὸς δὲ τὸ μὴ διαστρέφε
σθαι τὰ μέλη δι' ἁπαλότητα χρῶνται καὶ νῦν ἔνι
τῶν ἐθνῶν ὀργάνοις τισὶ μηχανικοῖς ἃ τὸ σῶμ
ποιεῖ τῶν τοιούτων ἀστραβές. συμφέρει δ' εὐθὺ
καὶ πρὸς τὰ ψύχη συνεθίζειν ἐκ μικρῶν παίδων
τοῦτο γὰρ καὶ πρὸς ὑγίειαν καὶ πρὸς πολεμικὰ
15 πράξεις εὐχρηστότατον. διὸ παρὰ πολλοῖς ἐστ
τῶν βαρβάρων ἔθος τοῖς μὲν εἰς ποταμὸν ἀπο
βάπτειν τὰ γιγνόμενα ψυχρόν, τοῖς δὲ σκέπασμ
μικρὸν ἀμπίσχειν, οἷον Κελτοῖς. πάντα γὰρ ὅσ
δυνατὸν [ἐθίζειν]¹ εὐθὺς ἀρχομένων βέλτιον ἐθίζει
20 μέν,² ἐκ προσαγωγῆς δ' ἐθίζειν· εὐφυὴς δ' ἡ τῶ
παίδων ἕξις διὰ θερμότητα πρὸς τὴν τῶν ψυχρῶ
ἄσκησιν. περὶ μὲν οὖν τὴν πρώτην συμφέρε
ποιεῖσθαι τὴν ἐπιμέλειαν τοιαύτην τε καὶ τὴ
ταύτῃ παραπλησίαν· τὴν δ' ἐχομένην ταύτης
ἡλικίαν μέχρι πέντε ἐτῶν, ἣν οὔτε πω πρὸ
25 μάθησιν καλῶς ἔχει προσάγειν οὐδεμίαν οὔτε πρὸ
ἀναγκαίους πόνους, ὅπως μὴ τὴν αὔξησιν ἐμ
ποδίζωσιν, δεῖ³ τοσαύτης τυγχάνειν κινήσεως ὥστ
διαφεύγειν τὴν ἀργίαν τῶν σωμάτων· ἣν χρ
παρασκευάζειν καὶ δι' ἄλλων πράξεων καὶ διὰ τῆ
παιδιᾶς. δεῖ δὲ καὶ τὰς παιδιὰς εἶναι μήτ
30 ἀνελευθέρους μήτε ἐπιπόνους μήτε ἀνειμένας
καὶ περὶ λόγων δὲ καὶ μύθων, ποίους τινὰ
ἀκούειν δεῖ τοὺς τηλικούτους, ἐπιμελὲς ἔστω τοῖ
ἄρχουσιν οὓς καλοῦσι παιδονόμους. πάντα γὰρ

---

¹ Richards. ² Richards: μὲν ἐθίζειν codd.
³ δεῖ δὲ codd. cet.

body, that a diet giving an abundance of milk is most suited to the bodies of children, and one that allows rather little wine because of the diseases that it causes. Moreover it is advantageous to subject them to as many movements as are practicable with children of that age. To prevent the limbs from being distorted owing to softness, some races even now employ certain mechanical appliances that keep the bodies of infants from being twisted. And it is also advantageous to accustom them at once from early childhood to cold, for this is most useful both for health and with a view to military service. Hence among many non-Greek races it is customary in the case of some peoples to wash the children at birth by dipping them in a cold river, and with others, for instance the Celts, to give them scanty covering. For it is better to inure them at the very start to everything possible, but to inure them gradually ; and the bodily habit of children is naturally well-fitted by warmth to be trained to bear cold. In the earliest period of life then it is expedient to employ this or a similar method of nursing ; and the next *Discipline of* period to this, up to the age of five, which it is not *childhood.* well to direct as yet to any study nor to compulsory labours, in order that they may not hinder the growth, should nevertheless be allowed enough movement to avoid bodily inactivity ; and this exercise should be obtained by means of various pursuits, particularly play. But even the games must not be unfit for freemen, nor laborious, nor undisciplined. Also the question of the kind of tales and stories that should be told to children of this age must be attended to by the officials called Children's Tutors. For all such

1336 a
δεῖ τὰ τοιαῦτα προοδοποιεῖν πρὸς τὰς ὕστερον
διατριβάς· διὸ τὰς παιδιὰς εἶναι δεῖ τὰς πολλὰς
μιμήσεις τῶν ὕστερον σπουδαζομένων. τὰς δὲ
35 διατάσεις τῶν παίδων καὶ[1] κλαυθμοὺς οὐκ ὀρθῶς
ἀπαγορεύουσιν οἱ κωλύοντες ἐν τοῖς νόμοις·
συμφέρουσι γὰρ πρὸς αὔξησιν· γίνεται γὰρ τρόπον
τινὰ γυμνασία τοῖς σώμασιν, ἡ γὰρ τοῦ πνεύματος
κάθεξις ποιεῖ τὴν ἰσχὺν τοῖς πονοῦσιν, ὃ συμβαίνει
καὶ τοῖς παιδίοις διατεινομένοις. ἐπισκεπτέον δὲ
40 τοῖς παιδονόμοις τὴν τούτων διαγωγὴν τήν τ'
ἄλλην καὶ ὅπως ὅτι ἥκιστα μετὰ δούλων ἔσται.
1336 b ταύτην γὰρ τὴν ἡλικίαν, καὶ μέχρι τῶν ἑπτὰ ἐτῶν,
ἀναγκαῖον οἴκοι τὴν τροφὴν ἔχειν· εὔλογον οὖν
ἀπολαύειν[2] ἀπὸ τῶν ἀκουσμάτων καὶ τῶν ὁραμά-
των ἀνελευθερίαν καὶ τηλικούτους ὄντας. ὅλως
μὲν οὖν αἰσχρολογίαν ἐκ τῆς πόλεως, ὥσπερ[3]
5 ἄλλο τι, δεῖ τὸν νομοθέτην ἐξορίζειν (ἐκ τοῦ γὰρ
εὐχερῶς λέγειν ὁτιοῦν τῶν αἰσχρῶν γίνεται καὶ τὸ
ποιεῖν σύνεγγυς), μάλιστα μὲν οὖν[4] ἐκ τῶν νέων,
ὅπως μήτε λέγωσι μήτε ἀκούωσι μηδὲν τοιοῦτον·
ἐὰν δέ τις φαίνηταί τι λέγων ἢ πράττων τῶν
ἀπηγορευμένων, τὸν ἐλεύθερον μὲν[5] μήπω δὲ κατα-
10 κλίσεως ἠξιωμένον ἐν τοῖς συσσιτίοις ἀτιμίαις[6]
κολάζειν καὶ πληγαῖς, τὸν δὲ πρεσβύτερον τῆς
ἡλικίας ταύτης ἀτιμίαις ἀνελευθέροις ἀνδραπο-
δωδίας χάριν. ἐπεὶ δὲ τὸ λέγειν τι τῶν τοιούτων
ἐξορίζομεν, φανερὸν ὅτι καὶ τὸ θεωρεῖν ἢ γραφὰς
ἢ λόγους ἀσχήμονας. ἐπιμελὲς μὲν οὖν ἔστω τοῖς

---

[1] καὶ τοὺς MP[1] : κατὰ τοὺς Γ.   [2] ἀπελαύνειν codd. cet.
[3] εἴπερ Lambinus.   [4] μέντοι ? Richards.
[5] μὲν hic Richards, ante ἐλεύθερον codd.
[6] [ἀτιμίαις] Buecheler, ὀνείδεσι Richards.

amusements should prepare the way for their later pursuits; hence most children's games should be 6 imitations of the serious occupations of later life. The legislators in the *Laws* [a] forbid allowing children to have paroxysms of crying, but this prohibition is a mistake; violent crying contributes to growth, for it serves in a way as exercise for the body, since holding the breath is the strength-giving factor in hard labour, and this takes place also with children when they stretch themselves in crying. The Tutors must supervise the children's pastimes, and in particular must see that they associate as little as possible with slaves. For children of this age, and up to seven 7 years old, must necessarily be reared at home; so it is reasonable to suppose that even at this age they may acquire a taint of illiberality from what they hear and see. The lawgiver ought therefore to banish indecent talk, as much as anything else, out of the state altogether (for light talk about anything disgraceful soon passes into action)—so most of all from among the young, so that they may not say nor hear anything of the sort; and anybody found saying or doing any of the things prohibited, if he is of free station but not yet promoted to reclining at the public meals, must be punished with marks of dishonour and with beating, and an older offender must be punished with marks of dishonour degrading to a 8 free man, because of his slavish behaviour. And since we banish any talk of this kind, clearly we must also banish the seeing of either pictures or representations that are indecent. The officials must therefore be

---

[a] *Laws* vii. 792 A. Plato merely says that a child's crying shows it to be annoyed, and that it ought to have as little pain as possible or else it will grow up morose.

629

15 ἄρχουσι μηθὲν μήτε ἄγαλμα μήτε γραφὴν εἶναι
τοιούτων πράξεων μίμησιν, εἰ μὴ παρά τισι θεοῖς
τοιούτοις οἷς καὶ τὸν τωθασμὸν ἀποδίδωσιν ὁ
νόμος· πρὸς δὲ τούτους[1] ἀφίησιν ὁ νόμος τοὺς τὴν
ἡλικίαν ἔχοντας ἔτι[2] τὴν ἱκνουμένην καὶ ὑπὲρ
αὐτῶν καὶ τέκνων καὶ γυναικῶν τιμαλφεῖν τοὺς
20 θεούς. τοὺς δὲ νεωτέρους οὔτ᾽ ἰάμβων οὔτε
κωμῳδίας θεατὰς ἐατέον,[3] πρὶν ἢ τὴν ἡλικίαν
λάβωσιν ἐν ᾗ καὶ κατακλίσεως ὑπάρξει κοινωνεῖν
ἤδη καὶ μέθης καὶ τῆς ἀπὸ τῶν τοιούτων γιγνομένης βλάβης ἀπαθεῖς ἡ παιδεία ποιήσει πάντας.
25 νῦν μὲν οὖν ἐν παραδρομῇ τοῦτον πεποιήμεθα
τὸν λόγον· ὕστερον δ᾽ ἐπιστήσαντας δεῖ διορίσαι
μᾶλλον, εἴτε μὴ δεῖ πρῶτον εἴτε δεῖ διαπορήσαντας,
καὶ πῶς δεῖ· κατὰ δὲ τὸν παρόντα καιρὸν ἐμνήσθη-
μεν ὡς[4] ἀναγκαῖον. ἴσως γὰρ οὐ κακῶς ἔλεγε[5] τὸ
τοιοῦτον Θεόδωρος ὁ τῆς τραγῳδίας ὑποκριτής·
30 οὐθενὶ γὰρ πώποτε παρῆκεν ἑαυτοῦ προεισάγειν
οὐδὲ τῶν εὐτελῶν ὑποκριτῶν, ὡς οἰκειουμένων τῶν
θεατῶν ταῖς πρώταις ἀκοαῖς· συμβαίνει δὲ ταὐτὸ
τοῦτο καὶ πρὸς τὰς τῶν ἀνθρώπων ὁμιλίας καὶ
πρὸς τὰς τῶν πραγμάτων· πάντα γὰρ στέργομεν
τὰ πρῶτα μᾶλλον. διὸ δεῖ τοῖς νέοις πάντα
35 ποιεῖν ξένα τὰ φαῦλα, μάλιστα δ᾽ αὐτῶν ὅσα ἔχει
ἢ μοχθηρίαν ἢ δυσμένειαν.

---

[1] τούτους Reiz : τούτοις codd.   [2] [ἔτι] Welldon.
[3] ἐατέον Immisch (εἶναι ἐατέον Jackson): θετέον, θετητέον,
νομοθετητέον codd.
[4] ὅσον Richards.   [5] ἔλυε ? Newman.

---

[a] The ms. text gives ' and in addition to these '; and the
word ' still ' may be an interpolation.

careful that there may be no sculpture or painting that represents indecent actions, except in the temples of a certain class of gods to whom the law allows even scurrility; but in regard to these [a] the law permits men still of suitable age to worship the gods both on their own behalf and on behalf 9 of the children and women. But the younger ones must not be allowed in the audience at lampoons [b] and at comedy, before they reach the age at which they will now have the right to recline at table in company and to drink deeply, and at which their education will render all of them immune to the harmful effects of such things. For the present therefore we have merely mentioned these matters in passing, but later we must stop to settle them more definitely, first discussing fully whether legislation prohibiting the attendance of the young is desirable or not, and how such prohibition should be put in force; but on the present occasion we have touched on the question only in the manner necessary. 10 For perhaps the tragic actor Theodorus [c] used to put the matter not badly: he had never once allowed anybody to produce his part [d] before him, not even one of the poor actors, as he said that audiences are attracted by what they hear first; and this happens alike in regard to our dealings with people and to our dealings with things—all that comes first we like better. On this account we ought to make all base things unfamiliar to the young, and especially those that involve either depravity or malignity.

[b] Iambic verses, often abusive and indecent, recited at festivals of Dionysus.

[c] A great Athenian performer of Sophocles; he took the part of Antigone.

[d] Loosely put for ' to appear on the stage.'

Διελθόντων δὲ τῶν πέντε ἐτῶν τὰ δύο μέχρι τῶν
ἑπτὰ δεῖ θεωροὺς ἤδη γίγνεσθαι τῶν μαθήσεων ἃς
δεήσει μανθάνειν αὐτούς. δύο δ' εἰσὶν ἡλικίαι 11
πρὸς ἃς ἀναγκαῖον διῃρῆσθαι τὴν παιδείαν, μετὰ[1]
τὴν ἀπὸ τῶν ἑπτὰ μέχρι ἥβης καὶ πάλιν μετὰ[1] τὴν
40 ἀφ' ἥβης μέχρι τῶν ἑνὸς καὶ εἴκοσιν ἐτῶν. οἱ γὰρ
ταῖς ἑβδομάσι διαιροῦντες τὰς ἡλικίας ὡς ἐπὶ τὸ
1337 a πολὺ λέγουσιν οὐ κακῶς,[2] δεῖ δὲ τῇ διαιρέσει τῆς
φύσεως ἐπακολουθεῖν· πᾶσα γὰρ τέχνη καὶ παιδεία
τὸ προσλεῖπον βούλεται τῆς φύσεως ἀναπληροῦν.
πρῶτον μὲν οὖν σκεπτέον εἰ ποιητέον τάξιν τινὰ
περὶ τοὺς παῖδας, ἔπειτα πότερον συμφέρει κοινῇ
5 ποιεῖσθαι τὴν ἐπιμέλειαν αὐτῶν ἢ κατ' ἴδιον
τρόπον, ὃ γίνεται καὶ νῦν ἐν ταῖς πλείσταις τῶν
πόλεων, τρίτον δὲ ποίαν τινὰ δεῖ ταύτην.

---

1 μετὰ—μετὰ : κατὰ—κατὰ Richards.
2 Muretus : καλῶς codd.

But when the five years from two to seven have Two passed, the children must now become spectators at the lessons [a] which they will themselves have to learn.
11 And there are two ages corresponding to which education should be divided—there must be a break after the period from seven to puberty, and again after that from puberty to twenty-one. For those who divide the ages by periods of seven years are generally speaking not wrong,[b] and it is proper to follow the division of nature, for all art and education aim at filling up nature's deficiencies. First therefore we must consider whether some regulation in regard to the boys ought to be instituted, next whether it is advantageous for their supervision to be conducted on a public footing or in a private manner as is done at present in most states, and thirdly of what particular nature this supervision ought to be.

Two periods of education.

---

[a] *i.e.* in gymnastics and music.
[b] The MSS. give ' not right.'

Θ

I. Ὅτι μὲν οὖν τῷ νομοθέτῃ μάλιστα πραγμα- 1
τευτέον περὶ τὴν τῶν νέων παιδείαν, οὐδεὶς ἂν
ἀμφισβητήσειεν. καὶ γὰρ ἐν ταῖς πόλεσιν οὐ
γιγνόμενον τοῦτο βλάπτει τὰς πολιτείας· δεῖ γὰρ
15 πρὸς ἑκάστην παιδεύεσθαι,[1] τὸ γὰρ ἦθος τῆς
πολιτείας ἑκάστης τὸ οἰκεῖον καὶ φυλάττειν εἴωθε
τὴν πολιτείαν καὶ καθίστησιν ἐξ ἀρχῆς, οἷον τὸ
μὲν δημοκρατικὸν δημοκρατίαν, τὸ δ' ὀλιγαρχικὸν
ὀλιγαρχίαν· ἀεὶ δὲ τὸ βέλτιον[2] ἦθος βελτίονος
20 αἴτιον πολιτείας. ἔτι δὲ πρὸς πάσας δυνάμεις καὶ 2
τέχνας ἔστιν ἃ δεῖ προπαιδεύεσθαι καὶ προεθίζεσθαι
πρὸς τὰς ἑκάστων ἐργασίας, ὥστε δῆλον ὅτι καὶ
πρὸς τὰς τῆς ἀρετῆς πράξεις. ἐπεὶ δ' ἓν τὸ τέλος
τῇ πόλει πάσῃ, φανερὸν ὅτι καὶ τὴν παιδείαν μίαν
καὶ τὴν αὐτὴν ἀναγκαῖον εἶναι πάντων καὶ ταύτης
τὴν ἐπιμέλειαν εἶναι κοινὴν καὶ μὴ κατ' ἰδίαν, ὃν
25 τρόπον νῦν ἕκαστος ἐπιμελεῖται τῶν αὑτοῦ τέκνων
ἰδίᾳ τε καὶ μάθησιν ἰδίαν ἣν ἂν δόξῃ διδάσκων. δεῖ
δὲ τῶν κοινῶν κοινὴν ποιεῖσθαι καὶ τὴν ἄσκησιν·
ἅμα δὲ οὐδὲ χρὴ νομίζειν αὐτὸν αὑτοῦ τινα εἶναι
τῶν πολιτῶν, ἀλλὰ πάντας τῆς πόλεως, μόριον

---

[1] Susemihl (*disciplinam accommodari* Aretinus): πολιτεύεσθαι codd.   [2] βέλτιον M, βέλτιστον vulg.

BOOK VIII [a]

Book VIII.
THE BEST
CONSTITU-
TION
(continued).
Education
should be
systematic,
universal,
and publicly
organized.

1   I. Now nobody would dispute that the education
of the young requires the special attention of the
lawgiver. Indeed the neglect of this in states is
injurious to their constitutions ; for education ought
to be adapted to the particular form of constitution,
since the particular character belonging to each constitution both guards the constitution generally and
originally establishes it—for instance the democratic
spirit promotes democracy and the oligarchic spirit
oligarchy ; and a better spirit always produces a better
2 constitution.   Moreover in regard to all the faculties
and crafts certain forms of preliminary education and
training in their various operations are necessary, so
that manifestly this is also requisite in regard to the
actions of virtue.   And inasmuch as the end for the
whole state is one, it is manifest that education also
must necessarily be one and the same for all and that
the superintendence of this must be public, and not
on private lines, in the way in which at present each
man superintends the education of his own children,
teaching them privately, and whatever special branch
of knowledge he thinks fit.   But matters of public
interest ought to be under public supervision ; at the
same time also we ought not to think that any of the
citizens belongs to himself, but that all belong to the

---

[a] Book V. in some editions.

30 γὰρ ἕκαστος τῆς πόλεως, ἡ δ' ἐπιμέλεια πέφυκεν
ἑκάστου μορίου βλέπειν πρὸς τὴν τοῦ ὅλου ἐπιμέλειαν. ἐπαινέσειε δ' ἄν τις κατὰ[1] τοῦτο Λακε- 3
δαιμονίους· καὶ γὰρ πλείστην ποιοῦνται σπουδὴν
περὶ τοὺς παῖδας καὶ κοινῇ ταύτην.

Ὅτι μὲν οὖν νομοθετητέον περὶ παιδείας καὶ
ταύτην κοινὴν ποιητέον, φανερόν· τίς δ' ἐστὶν ἡ
35 παιδεία καὶ πῶς χρὴ παιδεύεσθαι, δεῖ μὴ λανθάνειν.
νῦν γὰρ ἀμφισβητεῖται περὶ τῶν ἔργων· οὐ γὰρ
ταὐτὰ πάντες ὑπολαμβάνουσι δεῖν μανθάνειν τοὺς
νέους οὔτε πρὸς ἀρετὴν οὔτε πρὸς τὸν βίον τὸν
ἄριστον, οὐδὲ φανερὸν πότερον πρὸς τὴν διάνοιαν
πρέπει μᾶλλον ἢ πρὸς τὸ τῆς ψυχῆς ἦθος. ἔκ τε 4
40 τῆς ἐμποδὼν παιδείας ταραχώδης ἡ σκέψις, καὶ
δῆλον οὐδὲν πότερον ἀσκεῖν[2] δεῖ τὰ χρήσιμα πρὸς
τὸν βίον ἢ τὰ τείνοντα πρὸς ἀρετὴν ἢ τὰ περιττά·
1337 b πάντα γὰρ εἴληφε ταῦτα κριτάς τινας. περί τε
τῶν πρὸς ἀρετὴν οὐθέν ἐστιν ὁμολογούμενον· καὶ
γὰρ τὴν ἀρετὴν οὐ τὴν αὐτὴν εὐθὺς πάντες τιμῶσιν, ὥστ' εὐλόγως διαφέρονται καὶ πρὸς τὴν
ἄσκησιν αὐτῆς.

II. Ὅτι μὲν οὖν τὰ ἀναγκαῖα δεῖ διδάσκεσθαι
5 τῶν χρησίμων, οὐκ ἄδηλον· ὅτι δὲ οὐ πάντα,
διῃρημένων τῶν τε ἐλευθέρων ἔργων καὶ τῶν
ἀνελευθέρων, φανερόν, καὶ ὅτι[3] τῶν τοιούτων
δεῖ μετέχειν ὅσα τῶν χρησίμων ποιήσει τὸν μετ-

---

[1] Sylburg: καὶ codd.
[2] ⟨διδ⟩άσκειν Busse.   [3] καὶ ὅτι Richards: ὅτι codd.

state, for each is a part of the state, and it is natural
for the superintendence of the several parts to have
3 regard to the superintendence of the whole. And one
might praise the Spartans in respect of this, for they
pay the greatest attention to the training of their
children, and conduct it on a public system.

It is clear then that there should be legislation **Present lack**
about education and that it should be conducted on a **of system.**
public system. But consideration must be given to
the question, what constitutes education and what
is the proper way to be educated. At present there
are differences of opinion as to the proper tasks to be
set ; for all peoples do not agree as to the things that
the young ought to learn, either with a view to virtue
or with a view to the best life, nor is it clear whether
their studies should be regulated more with regard
4 to intellect or with regard to character. And con-
fusing questions arise out of the education that
actually prevails, and it is not at all clear whether
the pupils should practise pursuits that are practically
useful, or morally edifying, or higher accomplishments—for all these views have won the support of
some judges ; and nothing is agreed as regards the
exercise conducive to virtue, for, to start with, all
men do not honour the same virtue, so that they
naturally hold different opinions in regard to training
in virtue.

1 II. It is therefore not difficult to see that the **Curriculum:**
young must be taught those useful arts that are **utility and**
indispensably necessary ; but it is clear that they **edification.**
should not be taught all the useful arts, those pursuits
that are liberal being kept distinct from those that
are illiberal, and that they must participate in such
among the useful arts as will not render the person

1337 b

ἔχοντα μὴ βάναυσον. βάναυσον δ' ἔργον εἶναι δεῖ
τοῦτο νομίζειν καὶ τέχνην ταύτην καὶ μάθησιν
10 ὅσαι πρὸς τὰς χρήσεις καὶ τὰς πράξεις τὰς τῆς
ἀρετῆς ἄχρηστον ἀπεργάζονται τὸ σῶμα τῶν
ἐλευθέρων ἢ τὴν ψυχὴν ἢ τὴν διάνοιαν. διὸ τάς τε
τοιαύτας τέχνας ὅσαι τὸ σῶμα παρασκευάζουσι
χεῖρον διακεῖσθαι βαναύσους καλοῦμεν καὶ τὰς
μισθαρνικὰς ἐργασίας· ἄσχολον γὰρ ποιοῦσι τὴν
15 διάνοιαν καὶ ταπεινήν. ἔστι δὲ καὶ τῶν ἐλευθε- 2
ρίων ἐπιστημῶν μέχρι μέν τινος ἐνίων μετέχειν
οὐκ ἀνελεύθερον, προσεδρεύειν δὲ λίαν πρὸς τὸ
ἐντελὲς ἔνοχον ταῖς εἰρημέναις βλάβαις. ἔχει δὲ
πολλὴν διαφορὰν καὶ τὸ τίνος χάριν πράττει τις ἢ
μανθάνει· αὑτοῦ μὲν γὰρ χάριν ἢ φίλων ἢ δι'
20 ἀρετὴν οὐκ ἀνελεύθερον, ὁ δὲ ταὐτὸ[1] τοῦτο πράττων
δι' ἄλλους πολλάκις θητικὸν καὶ δουλικὸν δόξειεν
ἂν πράττειν.

Αἱ μὲν οὖν καταβεβλημέναι νῦν μαθήσεις,
καθάπερ ἐλέχθη πρότερον, ἐπαμφοτερίζουσιν. ἔστι 3
δὲ τέτταρα σχεδὸν ἃ παιδεύειν εἰώθασι, γράμματα
25 καὶ γυμναστικὴν καὶ μουσικὴν καὶ τέταρτον ἔνιοι
γραφικήν, τὴν μὲν γραμματικὴν καὶ γραφικὴν ὡς
χρησίμους πρὸς τὸν βίον οὔσας καὶ πολυχρήστους,
τὴν δὲ γυμναστικὴν ὡς συντείνουσαν πρὸς ἀνδρίαν·
τὴν δὲ μουσικὴν ἤδη διαπορήσειεν ἄν τις. νῦν μὲν
γὰρ ὡς ἡδονῆς χάριν οἱ πλεῖστοι μετέχουσιν αὐτῆς·
30 οἱ δ' ἐξ ἀρχῆς ἔταξαν ἐν παιδείᾳ διὰ τὸ τὴν φύσιν
αὐτὴν ζητεῖν, ὅπερ πολλάκις εἴρηται, μὴ μόνον
ἀσχολεῖν ὀρθῶς ἀλλὰ καὶ σχολάζειν δύνασθαι
καλῶς· αὕτη γὰρ ἀρχὴ πάντων, ἵνα καὶ πάλιν
εἴπωμεν περὶ αὐτῆς. εἰ γὰρ ἄμφω μὲν δεῖ, μᾶλλον 4

---

[1] Richards: αὐτὸ codd.

who participates in them vulgar. A task and also an art or a science must be deemed vulgar if it renders the body or soul or mind of free men useless for the employments and actions of virtue. Hence we entitle vulgar all such arts as deteriorate the condition of the body, and also the industries that earn wages; for they make the mind preoccupied and degraded. And even with the liberal sciences, although it is not illiberal to take part in some of them up to a point, to devote oneself to them too assiduously and carefully is liable to have the injurious results specified. Also it makes much difference what object one has in view in a pursuit or study; if one follows it for the sake of oneself or one's friends, or on moral grounds, it is not illiberal, but the man who follows the same pursuit because of other people would often appear to be acting in a menial and servile manner.

The branches of study at present established fall into both classes, as was said before.[a] There are perhaps four customary subjects of education, reading and writing, gymnastics, music, and fourth, with some people, drawing; reading and writing and drawing being taught as being useful for the purposes of life and very serviceable, and gymnastics as contributing to manly courage; but as to music, here one might raise a question. For at present most people take part in it for the sake of pleasure; but those who originally included it in education did so because, as has often been said, nature itself seeks to be able not only to engage rightly in business but also to occupy leisure nobly; for—to speak about it yet again[b]—this is the first principle of all things. For if although both business and leisure are

The four normal studies.

Use of leisure.

[a] c. i. § 4.   [b] Cf. VII., 1334 a 2-10.

1337 b

δὲ αἱρετὸν τὸ σχολάζειν τῆς ἀσχολίας καὶ τέλος,
35 ζητητέον τί ποιοῦντας δεῖ σχολάζειν. οὐ γὰρ δὴ
παίζοντας· τέλος γὰρ ἀναγκαῖον εἶναι[1] τοῦ βίου
τὴν παιδιὰν ἡμῖν. εἰ δὲ τοῦτο ἀδύνατον, καὶ
μᾶλλον ἐν ταῖς ἀσχολίαις χρηστέον ταῖς παιδιαῖς
(ὁ γὰρ πονῶν δεῖται τῆς ἀναπαύσεως, ἡ δὲ παιδιὰ
χάριν ἀναπαύσεώς ἐστιν, τὸ δ' ἀσχολεῖν συμβαίνει
40 μετὰ πόνου καὶ συντονίας), διὰ τοῦτο δεῖ παιδιὰς
εἰσάγεσθαι καιροφυλακτοῦντας τὴν χρῆσιν, ὡς
προσάγοντας φαρμακείας χάριν· ἄνεσις γὰρ ἡ
1338 a τοιαύτη κίνησις τῆς ψυχῆς, καὶ διὰ τὴν ἡδονὴν
ἀνάπαυσις. τὸ δὲ σχολάζειν ἔχειν αὐτὸ δοκεῖ τὴν
ἡδονὴν καὶ τὴν εὐδαιμονίαν καὶ τὸ ζῆν μακαρίως.
τοῦτο δ' οὐ τοῖς ἀσχολοῦσιν ὑπάρχει ἀλλὰ τοῖς
σχολάζουσιν· ὁ μὲν γὰρ ἀσχολῶν ἕνεκά τινος
5 ἀσχολεῖ τέλους ὡς οὐχ ὑπάρχοντος, ἡ δ' εὐδαιμονία
τέλος ἐστίν, ἣν οὐ μετὰ λύπης ἀλλὰ μεθ' ἡδονῆς
οἴονται πάντες εἶναι. ταύτην μέντοι τὴν ἡδονὴν
οὐκέτι τὴν αὐτὴν τιθέασιν, ἀλλὰ καθ' ἑαυτοὺς
ἕκαστος καὶ τὴν ἕξιν τὴν αὑτῶν, ὁ δὲ ἄριστος τὴν
ἀρίστην καὶ τὴν ἀπὸ τῶν καλλίστων. ὥστε
10 φανερὸν ὅτι δεῖ καὶ πρὸς τὴν ἐν τῇ διαγωγῇ
[σχολὴν][2] μανθάνειν ἄττα καὶ παιδεύεσθαι, καὶ
ταῦτα μὲν τὰ παιδεύματα καὶ ταύτας τὰς μαθήσεις
ἑαυτῶν εἶναι χάριν, τὰς δὲ πρὸς τὴν ἀσχολίαν ὡς
ἀναγκαίας καὶ χάριν ἄλλων. διὸ καὶ τὴν μουσικὴν
οἱ πρότερον εἰς παιδείαν ἔταξαν οὐχ ὡς ἀναγκαῖον
15 (οὐδὲν γὰρ ἔχει τοιοῦτον) οὐδ' ὡς χρήσιμον (ὥσπερ

---

[1] ⟨ἦν⟩ εἶναι Spengel.   [2] Jackson.

necessary, yet leisure is more desirable and more fully an end than business, we must inquire what is the proper occupation of leisure. For assuredly it should not be employed in play, since it would follow that play is our end in life. But if this is impossible, and sports should rather be employed in our times of business (for a man who is at work needs rest, and rest is the object of play, while business is accompanied by toil and exertion), it follows that in introducing sports we must watch the right opportunity for their employment, since we are applying them to serve as medicine; for the activity of play is a relaxation of the soul, and serves as recreation because of its pleasantness. But leisure seems itself to contain pleasure and happiness and felicity of life. And this is not possessed by the busy but by the leisured; for the busy man busies himself for the sake of some end as not being in his possession, but happiness is an end achieved, which all men think is accompanied by pleasure and not by pain. But all men do not go on to define this pleasure in the same way, but according to their various natures and to their own characters, and the pleasure with which the best man thinks that happiness is conjoined is the best pleasure and the one arising from the noblest sources. So that it is clear that some subjects must be learnt and acquired merely with a view to the pleasure in their pursuit, and that these studies and these branches of learning are ends in themselves, while the forms of learning related to business are studied as necessary and as means to other things. Hence our predecessors included music in education not as a necessity (for there is nothing necessary about it), nor as useful (in the way in which reading

τὰ γράμματα πρὸς χρηματισμὸν καὶ πρὸς οἰκονομίαν καὶ πρὸς μάθησιν καὶ πρὸς πολιτικὰς πράξεις
πολλάς, δοκεῖ δὲ καὶ γραφικὴ χρήσιμος εἶναι πρὸς
τὸ κρίνειν τὰ τῶν τεχνιτῶν ἔργα κάλλιον), οὐδ᾽
20 αὖ καθάπερ ἡ γυμναστικὴ πρὸς ὑγίειαν καὶ ἀλκήν
(οὐδέτερον γὰρ τούτων ὁρῶμεν γιγνόμενον ἐκ τῆς
μουσικῆς)· λείπεται τοίνυν πρὸς τὴν ἐν τῇ σχολῇ
διαγωγήν, εἰς ὅπερ καὶ φαίνονται παράγοντες
αὐτήν, ἣν γὰρ οἴονται διαγωγὴν εἶναι τῶν ἐλευθέρων, ἐν ταύτῃ τάττουσιν. διόπερ Ὅμηρος
οὕτως ἐποίησεν·

25   ἀλλ᾽ οἷον¹ μέν² ἐστι καλεῖν ἐπὶ δαῖτα θαλείην·
καὶ οὕτω προειπὼν ἑτέρους τινὰς
            οἳ καλέουσιν ἀοιδόν
φησιν,
            ὅ κεν τέρπῃσιν ἅπαντας.
καὶ ἐν ἄλλοις δέ φησιν Ὀδυσσεὺς ταύτην ἀρίστην
εἶναι διαγωγήν, ὅταν εὐφραινομένων τῶν ἀνθρώπων
30 δαιτυμόνες δ᾽ ἀνὰ δώματ᾽ ἀκουάζωνται ἀοιδοῦ
ἥμενοι ἑξείης.

III. Ὅτι μὲν τοίνυν ἐστὶ παιδεία τις ἣν οὐχ ὡς
χρησίμην παιδευτέον τοὺς υἱεῖς οὐδ᾽ ὡς ἀναγκαίαν
ἀλλ᾽ ὡς ἐλευθέριον καὶ καλήν, φανερόν ἐστιν·
πότερον δὲ μία τὸν ἀριθμὸν ἢ πλείους, καὶ τίνες
αὗται καὶ πῶς, ὕστερον λεκτέον περὶ αὐτῶν, νῦν δὲ

---

¹ Schneider: οἷον codd.   ² θέμις Ellis.

ᵃ This line is not in our *Odyssey*, but apparently followed
xvii. 383. The passage runs (382 ff.):

τίς γὰρ δὴ ξεῖνον καλεῖ ἄλλοθεν αὐτὸς ἐπελθὼν
ἄλλον γ᾽, εἰ μὴ τῶν οἳ δημιοεργοὶ ἔασι,
μάντιν ἢ ἰητῆρα κακῶν ἢ τέκτονα δούρων,
ἢ καὶ θέσπιν ἀοιδόν, ὃ κεν τέρπῃσιν ἀείδων;

and writing are useful for business and for household management and for acquiring learning and for many pursuits of civil life, while drawing also seems to be useful in making us better judges of the works of artists), nor yet again as we pursue gymnastics, for the sake of health and strength (for we do not see either of these things produced as a result of music); it remains therefore that it is useful as a pastime in leisure, which is evidently the purpose for which people actually introduce it, for they rank it as a form of pastime that they think proper for free men. For this reason Homer wrote thus :

> But him alone
> 'Tis meet to summon to the festal banquet *a*;

and after these words he speaks of certain others

> Who call the bard that he may gladden all.*b*

And also in other verses Odysseus says that this is the best pastime, when, as men are enjoying good cheer,

> The banqueters, seated in order due
> Throughout the hall, may hear a minstrel sing.*c*

1   III. It is clear therefore that there is a form of education in which boys should be trained not because it is useful or necessary but as being liberal and noble ; though whether there is one such subject of education or several, and what these are and how they are to be pursued, must be discussed later,*d* but as it is   *Liberal study.*

---

b The third line quoted corresponds to this, but not exactly.
c *Odyssey*, ix. 5 f.
d This promise is not fulfilled.

85 τοσοῦτον ἡμῖν εἶναι πρὸ ὁδοῦ γέγονεν, ὅτι καὶ παρὰ
τῶν ἀρχαίων ἔχομέν τινα μαρτυρίαν ἐκ τῶν κατα-
βεβλημένων παιδευμάτων· ἡ γὰρ μουσικὴ τοῦτο
ποιεῖ δῆλον. ἔτι δὲ καὶ τῶν χρησίμων ὅτι δεῖ τινὰ
παιδεύεσθαι τοὺς παῖδας οὐ μόνον διὰ τὸ χρήσιμον,
οἷον τὴν τῶν γραμμάτων μάθησιν, ἀλλὰ καὶ διὰ
40 τὸ πολλὰς ἐνδέχεσθαι γίγνεσθαι δι' αὐτῶν μαθήσεις ἑτέρας· ὁμοίως δὲ καὶ τὴν γραφικὴν οὐχ ἵνα 2
ἐν τοῖς ἰδίοις ὠνίοις μὴ διαμαρτάνωσιν ἀλλ' ὦσιν
1388 b ἀνεξαπάτητοι πρὸς τὴν τῶν σκευῶν ὠνήν τε καὶ
πρᾶσιν, ἀλλὰ[1] μᾶλλον ὅτι ποιεῖ θεωρητικὸν τοῦ
περὶ τὰ σώματα κάλλους· τὸ δὲ ζητεῖν πανταχοῦ
τὸ χρήσιμον ἥκιστα ἁρμόττει τοῖς μεγαλοψύχοις
καὶ τοῖς ἐλευθέροις. ἐπεὶ δὲ φανερὸν πρότερον[2]
5 τοῖς ἔθεσιν ἢ τῷ λόγῳ παιδευτέον εἶναι, καὶ περὶ
τὸ σῶμα πρότερον ἢ τὴν διάνοιαν, δῆλον ἐκ τούτων
ὅτι παραδοτέον τοὺς παῖδας γυμναστικῇ καὶ παιδο-
τριβικῇ· τούτων γὰρ ἡ μὲν ποιάν τινα ποιεῖ τὴν
ἕξιν τοῦ σώματος, ἡ δὲ τὰ ἔργα.

Νῦν μὲν οὖν αἱ μάλιστα δοκοῦσαι τῶν πόλεων 3
10 ἐπιμελεῖσθαι τῶν παίδων αἱ μὲν ἀθλητικὴν ἕξιν
ἐμποιοῦσι, λωβώμεναι τά τε εἴδη καὶ τὴν αὔξησιν
τῶν σωμάτων, οἱ δὲ Λάκωνες ταύτην μὲν οὐχ
ἥμαρτον τὴν ἁμαρτίαν, θηριώδεις δ' ἀπεργάζονται
τοῖς πόνοις, ὡς τοῦτο πρὸς ἀνδρίαν μάλιστα
συμφέρον. καίτοι, καθάπερ εἴρηται πολλάκις, οὔτε
15 πρὸς μίαν οὔτε πρὸς μάλιστα ταύτην βλέποντα

---

[1] ἀλλὰ Thurot: ἢ codd. (μᾶλλον ἢ Postgate).
[2] Demetrius: πότερον codd.

---

[a] *i.e.* premature and disproportionate muscular development, directed to some particular competition. *Cf.*
1288 b 12 ff.

we have made this much progress on the way, that
we have some testimony even from the ancients,
derived from the courses of education which they
founded—for the point is proved by music. And it is
also clear that some of the useful subjects as well
ought to be studied by the young not only because
of their utility, like the study of reading and writing,
but also because they may lead on to many other
2 branches of knowledge; and similarly they should
study drawing not in order that they may not go
wrong in their private purchases and may avoid being
cheated in buying and selling furniture, but rather
because this study makes a man observant of bodily
beauty; and to seek for utility everywhere is
entirely unsuited to men that are great-souled and
free. And since it is plain that education by habit   Training of
must come before education by reason, and training   habit.
of the body before training of the mind, it is clear
from these considerations that the boys must be
handed over to the care of the wrestling-master and
the trainer; for the latter imparts a certain quality to
the habit of the body and the former to its actions.
3   Now at the present time some of the states   Gymnastics
reputed to pay the greatest attention to children   and
produce in them an athletic habit ^a to the detriment   athletics.
of their bodily form and growth, while the Spartans
although they have avoided this error yet make
their boys animal in nature by their laborious exercises, in the belief that this is most contributory
to manly courage. Yet, as has often been said, it
is not right to regulate education with a view
to one virtue only, or to this one most of all;
indeed they do not even investigate the question

1338 b

ποιητέον τὴν ἐπιμέλειαν· εἴ τε καὶ πρὸς ταύτην,
οὐδὲ τοῦτο ἐξευρίσκουσιν. οὔτε γὰρ ἐν τοῖς ἄλλοις
ζῴοις οὔτ᾽ ἐπὶ τῶν ἐθνῶν ὁρῶμεν τὴν ἀνδρίαν
ἀκολουθοῦσαν τοῖς ἀγριωτάτοις, ἀλλὰ μᾶλλον τοῖς
20 ἡμερωτέροις καὶ λεοντώδεσιν ἤθεσιν. πολλὰ δ᾽ 4
ἐστὶ τῶν ἐθνῶν ἃ πρὸς τὸ κτείνειν καὶ πρὸς τὴν
ἀνθρωποφαγίαν εὐχερῶς ἔχει, καθάπερ τῶν περὶ
τὸν Πόντον Ἀχαιοί τε καὶ Ἡνίοχοι, καὶ τῶν
ἠπειρωτικῶν ἐθνῶν ἕτερα, τὰ μὲν ὁμοίως τούτοις
τὰ δὲ μᾶλλον, ἃ λῃστικὰ μέν ἐστιν ἀνδρείας δ᾽ οὐ
25 μετειλήφασιν. ἔτι δ᾽ αὐτοὺς τοὺς Λάκωνας ἴσμεν,
ἕως μὲν αὐτοὶ[1] προσήδρευον ταῖς φιλοπονίαις, ὑπερέχοντας τῶν ἄλλων, νῦν δὲ καὶ τοῖς γυμνασίοις
καὶ τοῖς πολεμικοῖς ἀγῶσι λειπομένους ἑτέρων·
οὐ γὰρ τῷ τοὺς νέους γυμνάζειν τὸν τρόπον τοῦτον
διέφερον, ἀλλὰ μόνον τῷ πρὸς μὴ[2] ἀσκοῦντας ἀσκεῖν.
30 ὥστε τὸ καλὸν ἀλλ᾽ οὐ τὸ θηριῶδες δεῖ πρωτ- 5
αγωνιστεῖν· οὐ γὰρ λύκος οὐδὲ τῶν ἄλλων θηρίων
τι ἀγωνίσαιτο ἂν οὐθένα[3] καλὸν κίνδυνον, ἀλλὰ μᾶλλον
ἀνὴρ ἀγαθός. οἱ δὲ λίαν εἰς ταῦτα ἀνέντες τοὺς
παῖδας καὶ τῶν ἀναγκαίων ἀπαιδαγωγήτους ποιήσαντες βαναύσους κατεργάζονται κατά γε τὸ
35 ἀληθές, πρὸς ἕν τε[4] μόνον ἔργον τῇ πολιτικῇ χρησίμους ποιήσαντες καὶ πρὸς τοῦτο χεῖρον, ὡς φησὶν
ὁ λόγος, ἑτέρων. δεῖ δὲ[5] οὐκ ἐκ τῶν προτέρων
ἔργων κρίνειν, ἀλλ᾽ ἐκ τῶν νῦν· ἀνταγωνιστὰς γὰρ
τῆς παιδείας νῦν ἔχουσι, πρότερον δ᾽ οὐκ εἶχον.

IV. Ὅτι μὲν οὖν χρηστέον τῇ γυμναστικῇ, καὶ 1

---

[1] αὐτοὶ ⟨μόνοι⟩ Eucken.
[2] μόνον τῷ ? Reize et πρὸς μὴ ed. : τῷ μόνον μὴ πρὸς codd.
[3] οὐθὲν Goettling.   [4] ἕν τι ? ed.
[5] δεῖ δὲ—εἶχον ante 29 ὥστε transp. Bekker.

whether this virtue is to be had in view at all. For neither in the lower animals nor in the case of foreign races do we see that courage goes with the wildest, but rather with the gentler 4 and lion-like temperaments.[a] And there are many foreign races inclined to murder and cannibalism, for example among the tribes of the Black Sea the Achaeans and Heniochi, and others of the mainland races, some in the same degree as those named and some more, which although piratical have got no share of manly courage. And again we know that even the Spartans, although so long as they persisted by themselves in their laborious exercises they surpassed all other peoples, now fall behind others both in gymnastic and in military contests ; for they used not to excel because they exercised their young men in this fashion but only because they trained and 5 their adversaries did not. Consequently honour and not animal ferocity should play the first part ; for it is not a wolf nor one of the other wild animals that will venture upon any noble hazard, but rather a good man. But those who let boys pursue these hard exercises too much and turn them out untrained in necessary things in real truth render them vulgar, making them available for statesmanship to use for one task only, and even for this task training them worse than others do, as our argument proves. And [b] we must not judge them from their former achievements but from the facts of to-day ; for they have rivals in their education now, but they used to have none before.

1 IV. It is therefore agreed that we should employ Periods of

---

[a] *Hist. An.* 629 b 8 (the lion is gentle except when hungry); Plato, *Soph.* 231 A (the dog the gentlest of animals).
[b] This sentence would come better at the end of § 4.

⁴⁰ πῶς χρηστέον, ὁμολογούμενόν ἐστιν. μέχρι μὲν
γὰρ ἥβης κουφότερα γυμνάσια προσοιστέον, τὴν
βίαιον τροφὴν καὶ τοὺς πρὸς ἀνάγκην πόνους ἀπ-
είργοντας, ἵνα μηθὲν ἐμπόδιον ᾖ πρὸς τὴν αὔξησιν·
1339 a σημεῖον γὰρ οὐ μικρὸν ὅτι δύναται τοῦτο παρασκευάζειν, ἐν γὰρ τοῖς ὀλυμπιονίκαις δύο τις ἂν
ἢ τρεῖς εὕροι τοὺς αὐτοὺς νενικηκότας ἄνδρας τε
καὶ παῖδας διὰ τὸ νέους ἀσκοῦντας ἀφαιρεῖσθαι
τὴν δύναμιν ὑπὸ τῶν ἀναγκαίων γυμνασίων. ὅταν 2
⁵ δ' ἀφ' ἥβης ἔτη τρία πρὸς τοῖς ἄλλοις μαθήμασι
γένωνται, τότε ἁρμόττει καὶ τοῖς πόνοις καὶ ταῖς
ἀναγκοφαγίαις καταλαμβάνειν τὴν ἐχομένην ἡλι-
κίαν· ἅμα γὰρ τῇ τε διανοίᾳ καὶ τῷ σώματι
διαπονεῖν οὐ δεῖ, τοὐναντίον γὰρ ἑκάτερος ἀπεργάζεσθαι πέφυκε τῶν πόνων, ἐμποδίζων ὁ μὲν τοῦ
¹⁰ σώματος πόνος τὴν διάνοιαν ὁ δὲ ταύτης τὸ σῶμα.

Περὶ δὲ μουσικῆς ἔνια μὲν διηπορήσαμεν τῷ 3
λόγῳ καὶ πρότερον, καλῶς δ' ἔχει καὶ νῦν ἀνα-
λαβόντας αὐτὰ προαγαγεῖν, ἵνα ὥσπερ ἐνδόσιμον
γένηται τοῖς λόγοις οὓς ἄν τις εἴπειεν ἀποφαινό-
¹⁵ μενος περὶ αὐτῆς. οὔτε γὰρ τίνα ἔχει δύναμιν
ῥᾴδιον περὶ αὐτῆς διελεῖν, οὔτε τίνος δεῖ χάριν
μετέχειν αὐτῆς, πότερον παιδιᾶς ἕνεκα καὶ ἀναπαύσεως, καθάπερ ὕπνου καὶ μέθης (ταῦτα γὰρ
καθ' αὑτὰ μὲν οὔτε τῶν σπουδαίων, ἀλλ' ἡδέα, καὶ
ἀναπαύει μέριμναν,[1] ὥς φησιν Εὐριπίδης, διὸ καὶ
²⁰ τάττουσιν[2] αὐτὴν καὶ χρῶνται πᾶσι τούτοις ὁμοίως,

---

[1] Goettling: ἅμα παύει μέριμναν aut ἅμα μέριμναν ποιεῖ codd.
[2] πράττουσιν Richards.

---

* *i.e.* compulsion to eat very large rations of prescribed
food—the Greek way of training.

gymnastic training, and how we should employ it. gymnastics and of study.
For until puberty we should apply lighter exercises,
forbidding hard diet and severe exertions, in order
that nothing may hinder the growth; for there is
no small proof that too severe training can produce
this result in the fact that in the list of Olympic
victors one would only find two or three persons who
have won both as men and as boys, because when
people go into training in youth the severe exercises
2 rob them of their strength. But when they have
spent three years after puberty upon their other
studies, then it is suitable to occupy the next period
of life with laborious exercises and strict training
diet[a]; for it is wrong to work hard with the mind
and the body at the same time, for it is the nature
of the two different sorts of exertion to produce
opposite effects, bodily toil impeding the development of the mind and mental toil that of the body.

3 About music on the other hand we have previously Music in education:
raised some questions in the course of our argument,
but it is well to take them up again and carry them
further now, in order that this may give the key so
to speak for the principles which one might advance
in pronouncing about it. For it is not easy to say precisely what potency it possesses, nor yet for the sake
of what object one should participate in it—whether
for amusement and relaxation, as one indulges in
sleep and deep drinking (for these in themselves
are not serious pursuits but merely pleasant, and
'relax our care,' as Euripides says [b]; owing to which
people actually class music with them [c] and employ

[b] *Bacchae* 378 (Bromios) ὃς τάδ᾽ ἔχει, | θιασεύειν τε χόροις
| μετά τ᾽ αὐλῶν γελᾶσαι | ἀναπαῦσαί τε μερίμνας.

[c] Or ' and it is owing to this that people perform music.'

1389 a

ὕπνῳ[1] καὶ μέθῃ καὶ μουσικῇ, τιθέασι δὲ καὶ τὴν
ὄρχησιν ἐν τούτοις)· ἢ μᾶλλον οἰητέον πρὸς ἀρετήν 4
τι τείνειν τὴν μουσικήν (ὡς δυναμένην, καθάπερ
ἡ γυμναστικὴ τὸ σῶμα ποιόν τι παρασκευάζει,
καὶ τὴν μουσικὴν τὸ ἦθος ποιόν τι ποιεῖν, ἐθίζουσαν
25 δύνασθαι χαίρειν ὀρθῶς)· ἢ πρὸς διαγωγήν τι συμβάλλεται καὶ πρὸς φρόνησιν (καὶ γὰρ τοῦτο τρίτον
θετέον τῶν εἰρημένων). ὅτι μὲν οὖν δεῖ τοὺς νέους
μὴ παιδιᾶς ἕνεκα παιδεύειν, οὐκ ἄδηλον· οὐ γὰρ
παίζουσι μανθάνοντες, μετὰ λύπης γὰρ ἡ μάθησις.
30 ἀλλὰ μὴν οὐδὲ διαγωγήν γε παισὶν ἁρμόττει καὶ
ταῖς ἡλικίαις ἀποδιδόναι ταῖς τοιαύταις· οὐθενὶ
γὰρ ἀτελεῖ προσήκει τέλος. ἀλλ' ἴσως ἂν δόξειεν 5
ἡ τῶν παίδων σπουδὴ παιδιᾶς εἶναι χάριν ἀνδράσι
γενομένοις καὶ τελειωθεῖσιν. ἀλλ' εἰ τοῦτ' ἐστὶ
35 τοιοῦτον, τίνος ἂν ἕνεκα δέοι μανθάνειν αὐτούς,
ἀλλὰ μή, καθάπερ οἱ τῶν Περσῶν καὶ Μήδων
βασιλεῖς, ἄλλων αὐτὸ ποιούντων μεταλαμβάνειν
τῆς ἡδονῆς καὶ τῆς μαθήσεως;[2] καὶ γὰρ ἀναγκαῖον βέλτιον ἀπεργάζεσθαι τοὺς αὐτὸ τοῦτο
πεποιημένους ἔργον καὶ τέχνην τῶν τοσοῦτον
χρόνον ἐπιμελουμένων ὅσον πρὸς μάθησιν μόνον.
εἰ δὲ δεῖ τὰ τοιαῦτα διαπονεῖν αὐτούς, καὶ τὰ[3]
40 περὶ τὴν τῶν ὄψων πραγματείαν αὐτοὺς ἂν δέοι
παρασκευάζειν· ἀλλ' ἄτοπον. τὴν δ' αὐτὴν ἀπορίαν 6
ἔχει καὶ εἰ δύναται τὰ ἤθη βελτίω ποιεῖν· ταῦτα

---

[1] ὕπνῳ Aretinus : οἴνῳ codd.
[2] ἀναπαύσεως Richards.
[3] τὰ Argyriades : om. codd.

---

[a] The term διαγωγή, 'pastime,' is idiomatically used of the
pursuits of cultured leisure—serious conversation, music,
the drama.

[b] Or, altering the text, 'relaxation.'

all of these things, sleep, deep drinking and music, in the same way, and they also place dancing in the same class); or whether we ought rather to think that music tends in some degree to virtue (music being capable of producing a certain quality of character just as gymnastics are capable of producing a certain quality of body, music accustoming men to be able to rejoice rightly); or that it contributes something to intellectual entertainment[a] and culture (for this must be set down as a third alternative among those mentioned). Now it is not difficult to see that one must not make amusement the object of the education of the young; for amusement does not go with learning—learning is a painful process. Nor yet moreover is it suitable to assign intellectual entertainment to boys and to the young; for a thing that is an end does not belong to anything that is imperfect. But perhaps it might be thought that the serious pursuits of boys are for the sake of amusement when they have grown up to be men. But if something of this sort is the case, why should the young need to learn this accomplishment themselves, and not, like the Persian and Median kings, participate in the pleasure and the education[b] of music by means of others performing it? for those who have made music a business and profession must necessarily perform better than those who practise only long enough to learn. But if it is proper for them to labour at accomplishments of this sort, then it would also be right for them to prepare the dishes of an elaborate cuisine; but this is absurd. And the same difficulty also arises as to the question whether learning music can improve their characters; for why should they learn to per-

not a mere amusement.

1339 b γὰρ τί δεῖ μανθάνειν αὐτούς, ἀλλ' οὐχ ἑτέρων
ἀκούοντας ὀρθῶς τε χαίρειν καὶ δύνασθαι κρίνειν,
ὥσπερ οἱ Λάκωνες· ἐκεῖνοι γὰρ οὐ μανθάνοντες
ὅμως δύνανται κρίνειν ὀρθῶς, ὥς φασι, τὰ χρηστὰ
καὶ τὰ μὴ χρηστὰ τῶν μελῶν. ὁ δ' αὐτὸς λόγος
5 κἂν εἰ πρὸς εὐημερίαν καὶ διαγωγὴν ἐλευθέριον
χρηστέον αὐτῇ· τί δεῖ μανθάνειν αὐτούς, ἀλλ' οὐχ
ἑτέρων χρωμένων ἀπολαύειν; σκοπεῖν δ' ἔξεστι 7
τὴν ὑπόληψιν ἣν ἔχομεν περὶ τῶν θεῶν· οὐ γὰρ ὁ
Ζεὺς αὐτὸς ᾄδει καὶ κιθαρίζει τοῖς ποιηταῖς. ἀλλὰ
καὶ βαναύσους καλοῦμεν τοὺς τοιούτους καὶ τὸ
10 πράττειν οὐκ ἀνδρὸς μὴ μεθύοντος ἢ παίζοντος.

V. Ἀλλ' ἴσως περὶ μὲν τούτων ὕστερον ἐπι- 1
σκεπτέον· ἡ δὲ πρώτη ζήτησίς ἐστι πότερον οὐ
θετέον εἰς παιδείαν τὴν μουσικὴν ἢ θετέον, καὶ τί
δύναται τῶν διαπορηθέντων τριῶν, πότερον παιδείαν ἢ παιδιὰν ἢ διαγωγήν. εὐλόγως δ' εἰς
15 πάντα τάττεται καὶ φαίνεται μετέχειν. ἥ τε γὰρ
παιδιὰ χάριν ἀναπαύσεώς ἐστι, τὴν δ' ἀνάπαυσιν
ἀναγκαῖον ἡδεῖαν εἶναι (τῆς γὰρ διὰ τῶν πόνων
λύπης ἰατρεία τίς ἐστιν), καὶ τὴν διαγωγὴν ὁμολογουμένως δεῖ μὴ μόνον ἔχειν τὸ καλὸν ἀλλὰ καὶ
τὴν ἡδονήν (τὸ γὰρ εὐδαιμονεῖν ἐξ ἀμφοτέρων
20 τούτων ἐστίν)· τὴν δὲ μουσικὴν πάντες εἶναί φαμεν
τῶν ἡδίστων, καὶ ψιλὴν οὖσαν καὶ μετὰ μελῳδίας
(φησὶ γοῦν καὶ Μουσαῖος εἶναι βροτοῖς ἥδιστον 2
ἀείδειν, διὸ καὶ εἰς τὰς συνουσίας καὶ διαγωγὰς
εὐλόγως παραλαμβάνουσιν αὐτὴν ὡς δυναμένην

ᵃ A semi-legendary bard, to whom a number of oracular
verses that were current were attributed.

form edifying music themselves, instead of learning to enjoy it rightly and be able to judge it when they hear others performing, as the Spartans do? for the Spartans although they do not learn to perform can nevertheless judge good and bad music correctly, so it is said. And the same argument applies also if music is to be employed for refined enjoyment and entertainment; why need people learn to perform themselves instead of enjoying music played by 7 others? And we may consider the conception that we have about the gods: Zeus does not sing and harp to the poets himself. But professional musicians we speak of as vulgar people, and indeed we think it not manly to perform music, except when drunk or for fun.

1 V. But perhaps these points will have to be con- *Moral value* sidered afterwards; our first inquiry is whether *of music.* music ought not or ought to be included in education, and what is its efficacy among the three uses of it that have been discussed—does it serve for education or amusement or entertainment? It is reasonable to reckon it under all of these heads, and it appears to participate in them all. Amusement is for the sake of relaxation, and relaxation must necessarily be pleasant, for it is a way of curing the pain due to laborious work; also entertainment ought admittedly to be not only honourable but also pleasant, for happiness is derived from both honour and pleasure; but we all pronounce music to be one of the pleasantest things, whether instrumental or instrumental and 2 vocal music together (at least Musaeus*a* says, 'Song is man's sweetest joy,' and that is why people with good reason introduce it at parties and entertainments, for its exhilarating effect), so that for this

1339 b

εὐφραίνειν), ὥστε καὶ ἐντεῦθεν ἄν τις ὑπολάβοι
25 παιδεύεσθαι δεῖν αὐτὴν τοὺς νεωτέρους. ὅσα γὰρ
ἀβλαβῆ τῶν ἡδέων, οὐ μόνον ἁρμόττει πρὸς τὸ
τέλος ἀλλὰ καὶ πρὸς τὴν ἀνάπαυσιν· ἐπεὶ δ' ἐν
μὲν τῷ τέλει συμβαίνει τοῖς ἀνθρώποις ὀλιγάκις
γίγνεσθαι, πολλάκις δὲ ἀναπαύονται καὶ χρῶνται
30 ταῖς παιδιαῖς οὐχ ὅσον ἐπὶ πλέον ἀλλὰ καὶ διὰ τὴν
ἡδονήν, χρήσιμον ἂν εἴη διαναπαύειν ἐν ταῖς ἀπὸ
ταύτης ἡδοναῖς. συμβέβηκε δὲ τοῖς ἀνθρώποις 3
ποιεῖσθαι τὰς παιδιὰς τέλος· ἔχει γὰρ ἴσως ἡδονήν
τινα καὶ τὸ τέλος, ἀλλ' οὐ τὴν τυχοῦσαν, ζητοῦντες
δὲ ταύτην λαμβάνουσιν ὡς ταύτην ἐκείνην διὰ
35 τὸ τῷ τέλει τῶν πράξεων ἔχειν ὁμοίωμά τι. τό τε
γὰρ τέλος οὐθενὸς τῶν ἐσομένων χάριν αἱρετόν,
καὶ αἱ τοιαῦται τῶν ἡδονῶν οὐθενός εἰσι τῶν
ἐσομένων ἕνεκεν, ἀλλὰ τῶν γεγονότων, οἷον πόνων
καὶ λύπης. δι' ἣν μὲν οὖν αἰτίαν ζητοῦσι τὴν
εὐδαιμονίαν γίγνεσθαι διὰ τούτων τῶν ἡδονῶν,
40 ταύτην ἄν τις εἰκότως ὑπολάβοι τὴν αἰτίαν· περὶ 4
δὲ τοῦ κοινωνεῖν τῆς μουσικῆς, οὐ διὰ ταύτην
μόνην, ἀλλὰ καὶ διὰ τὸ χρήσιμον εἶναι πρὸς τὰς
ἀναπαύσεις, ὡς ἔοικεν. οὐ μὴν ἀλλὰ ζητητέον μή
1340 a ποτε τοῦτο μὲν συμβέβηκε, τιμιωτέρα δ' αὐτῆς ἡ
φύσις ἐστὶν ἢ κατὰ τὴν εἰρημένην χρείαν, καὶ δεῖ
μὴ μόνον τῆς κοινῆς ἡδονῆς μετέχειν ἀπ' αὐτῆς,
ἧς ἔχουσι πάντες αἴσθησιν (ἔχει γὰρ ἡ μουσικὴ τὴν
5 ἡδονὴν φυσικήν, διὸ πάσαις ἡλικίαις καὶ πᾶσιν
ἤθεσιν ἡ χρῆσις αὐτῆς ἐστι προσφιλής), ἀλλ' ὁρᾶν

reason also one might suppose that the younger men
ought to be educated in music. For all harmless
pleasures are not only suitable for the ultimate object
but also for relaxation ; and as it but rarely happens
for men to reach their ultimate object, whereas they
often relax and pursue amusement not so much
with some ulterior object but because of the
pleasure of it, it would be serviceable to let them relax
at intervals in the pleasures derived from music.
3 But it has come about that men make amusements
an end ; for the end also perhaps contains a certain
pleasure, but not any ordinary pleasure, and seeking
this they take the other as being this because it has
a certain resemblance to the achievement of the end
of their undertakings. For the end is desirable not
for the sake of anything that will result from it, and
also pleasures of the sort under consideration are
not desirable for the sake of some future result, but
because of things that have happened already, for
instance labour and pain. One might then perhaps
assume this to be the reason which causes men to
seek to procure happiness by means of those pleasures;
4 but in the case of taking part in music, this is not
because of this reason only, but also because performing music is useful, as it seems, for relaxation.
But nevertheless we must examine whether it is not
the case that, although this has come about, yet the
nature of music is more honourable than corresponds
with the employment of it mentioned, and it is
proper not only to participate in the common pleasure
that springs from it, which is perceptible to everybody
(for the pleasure contained in music is of a natural
kind, owing to which the use of it is dear to those of
all ages and characters), but to see if its influence

1340 a

εἴ πῃ καὶ πρὸς τὸ ἦθος συντείνει καὶ πρὸς τὴν
ψυχήν. τοῦτο δ᾿ ἂν εἴη δῆλον εἰ ποιοί τινες τὰ
ἤθη γιγνόμεθα δι᾿ αὐτῆς. ἀλλὰ μὴν ὅτι γιγνόμεθα
ποιοί τινες, φανερὸν διὰ πολλῶν μὲν καὶ ἑτέρων,
10 οὐχ ἥκιστα δὲ καὶ διὰ τῶν Ὀλύμπου μελῶν· ταῦτα
γὰρ ὁμολογουμένως ποιεῖ τὰς ψυχὰς ἐνθουσια-
στικάς, ὁ δ᾿ ἐνθουσιασμὸς τοῦ περὶ τὴν ψυχὴν
ἤθους πάθος ἐστίν. ἔτι δὲ ἀκροώμενοι τῶν μιμή-
σεων γίγνονται πάντες συμπαθεῖς, καὶ χωρὶς[1] τῶν
ῥυθμῶν καὶ τῶν μελῶν αὐτῶν. ἐπεὶ δὲ συμβέβηκεν
15 εἶναι τὴν μουσικὴν τῶν ἡδέων, τὴν δ᾿ ἀρετὴν περὶ
τὸ χαίρειν ὀρθῶς καὶ φιλεῖν καὶ μισεῖν, δεῖ δῆλον
ὅτι μανθάνειν καὶ συνεθίζεσθαι μηθὲν οὕτως ὡς
τὸ κρίνειν ὀρθῶς καὶ τὸ χαίρειν τοῖς ἐπιεικέσιν
ἤθεσι καὶ ταῖς καλαῖς πράξεσιν· ἔστι δ᾿ ὁμοιώματα
μάλιστα παρὰ τὰς ἀληθινὰς φύσεις ἐν τοῖς ῥυθμοῖς
20 καὶ τοῖς μέλεσιν ὀργῆς καὶ πραότητος, ἔτι δ᾿
ἀνδρίας καὶ σωφροσύνης καὶ πάντων τῶν ἐναντίων
τούτοις καὶ τῶν ἄλλων ἠθικῶν[2] (δῆλον δὲ ἐκ τῶν
ἔργων, μεταβάλλομεν γὰρ τὴν ψυχὴν ἀκροώμενοι
τοιούτων)· ὁ δ᾿ ἐν τοῖς ὁμοίοις ἐθισμὸς τοῦ λυπεῖ-
σθαι καὶ χαίρειν ἐγγύς ἐστι τῷ πρὸς τὴν ἀλήθειαν
25 τὸν αὐτὸν ἔχειν τρόπον (οἷον εἴ τις χαίρει τὴν
εἰκόνα τινὸς θεώμενος μὴ δι᾿ ἄλλην αἰτίαν ἀλλὰ
διὰ τὴν μορφὴν αὐτήν, ἀναγκαῖον τούτῳ καὶ
αὐτὴν ἐκείνην τὴν θεωρίαν οὗ τὴν εἰκόνα θεωρεῖ
ἡδεῖαν εἶναι)· συμβέβηκε δὲ τῶν αἰσθητῶν ἐν μὲν
τοῖς ἄλλοις μηδὲν ὑπάρχειν ὁμοίωμα τοῖς ἤθεσιν,

---

[1] hic lacunam Γ: ⟨τῶν λόγων διὰ⟩ Susemihl.
[2] ἠθῶν Richards.

---

[a] A Phrygian composer of the seventh century B.C.
[b] Music dramatically expressing various states of emotion.

reaches also in a manner to the character and to the soul. And this would clearly be the case if we are affected in our characters in a certain manner by it. But it is clear that we are affected in a certain manner, both by many other kinds of music and not least by the melodies of Olympus[a]; for these admittedly make our souls enthusiastic, and enthusiasm is an affection of the character of the soul. And moreover everybody when listening to imitations[b] is thrown into a corresponding state of feeling, even apart from the rhythms and tunes themselves.[c] And since it is the case that music is one of the things that give pleasure, and that virtue has to do with feeling delight and love and hatred rightly, there is obviously nothing that it is more needful to learn and become habituated to than to judge correctly and to delight in virtuous characters and noble actions; but rhythms and melodies contain representations of anger and mildness, and also of courage and temperance and all their opposites and the other moral qualities, that most closely correspond to the true natures of these qualities (and this is clear from the facts of what occurs—when we listen to such representations we change in our soul); and habituation in feeling pain and delight at representations of reality is close to feeling them towards actual reality (for example, if a man delights in beholding the statue of somebody for no other reason than because of its actual form, the actual sight of the person whose statue he beholds must also of necessity give him pleasure); and it is the case that whereas the other objects of sensation contain no representation of

Psychology of music and art.

[c] A probable correction of the Greek gives 'by the rhythms and tunes themselves, even apart from the words.'

1340 a
30 οἷον ἐν τοῖς ἁπτοῖς καὶ τοῖς γευστοῖς (ἀλλ' ἐν τοῖς
ὁρατοῖς ἠρέμα, σχήματα γάρ ἐστι τοιαῦτα, ἀλλ'
ἐπὶ μικρόν, κοὐ¹ πάντες τῆς τοιαύτης αἰσθήσεως
κοινωνοῦσιν· ἔτι δὲ οὐκ ἔστι ταῦτα ὁμοιώματα
τῶν ἠθῶν ἀλλὰ σημεῖα μᾶλλον τὰ γιγνόμενα
σχήματα καὶ χρώματα τῶν ἠθῶν, καὶ ταῦτ' ἐστὶν
35 ἐπὶ τοῦ σώματος ἐν τοῖς πάθεσιν· οὐ μὴν ἀλλ' ὅσον
διαφέρει καὶ περὶ τὴν τούτων θεωρίαν, δεῖ μὴ τὰ
Παύσωνος θεωρεῖν τοὺς νέους ἀλλὰ τὰ Πολυγνώτου
κἂν εἴ τις ἄλλος τῶν γραφέων ἢ τῶν ἀγαλματο-
ποιῶν ἐστὶν ἠθικός), ἐν δὲ τοῖς μέλεσιν αὐτοῖς ᵇ
40 ἐστὶ μιμήματα τῶν ἠθῶν· καὶ τοῦτ' ἔστι φανερόν,
εὐθὺς γὰρ ἡ τῶν ἁρμονιῶν διέστηκε φύσις ὥστε
ἀκούοντας ἄλλως διατίθεσθαι καὶ μὴ τὸν αὐτὸν
ἔχειν τρόπον πρὸς ἑκάστην αὐτῶν, ἀλλὰ πρὸς μὲν
1340 b ἐνίας ὀδυρτικωτέρως καὶ συνεστηκότως μᾶλλον,
οἷον πρὸς τὴν μιξολυδιστὶ καλουμένην, πρὸς δὲ
τὰς μαλακωτέρως τὴν διάνοιαν, οἷον πρὸς τὰς
ἀνειμένας, μέσως δὲ καὶ καθεστηκότως μάλιστα
5 πρὸς ἑτέραν, οἷον δοκεῖ ποιεῖν ἡ δωριστὶ μόνη τῶν
ἁρμονιῶν, ἐνθουσιαστικοὺς δ' ἡ φρυγιστί· ταῦτα ᵍ
γὰρ καλῶς λέγουσιν οἱ περὶ τὴν παιδείαν ταύτην
πεφιλοσοφηκότες, λαμβάνουσι γὰρ τὰ μαρτύρια
τῶν λόγων ἐξ αὐτῶν τῶν ἔργων. τὸν αὐτὸν δὲ
τρόπον ἔχει καὶ τὰ περὶ τοὺς ῥυθμούς· οἱ μὲν γὰρ
ἦθος ἔχουσι στασιμώτερον οἱ δὲ κινητικόν, καὶ
10 τούτων οἱ μὲν φορτικωτέρας ἔχουσι τὰς κινήσεις

¹ κοὐ Mueller: καὶ codd.

ᵃ 'Not' is a conjectural insertion.
ᵇ i.e. these visual impressions do vary to some extent in moral effect.
ᶜ Pauson is a painter otherwise little known. Polygnotus decorated the Stoa Poikilē and other famous public buildings

character, for example the objects of touch and taste (though the objects of sight do so slightly, for there are forms that represent character, but only to a small extent, and not^a all men participate in visual perception of such qualities ; also visual works of art are not representations of character but rather the forms and colours produced are mere indications of character, and these indications are only bodily sensations during the emotions ; not but what in so far as there is a difference even in regard to the observation of these indications,^{b} the young must not look at the works of Pauson but those of Polygnotus,^{c} 8 and of any other moral painter or sculptor), pieces of music on the contrary do actually contain in themselves imitations of character ; and this is manifest, for even in the nature of the mere melodies there are differences, so that people when hearing them are affected differently and have not the same feelings in regard to each of them, but listen to some in a more mournful and restrained state, for instance the mode called Mixolydian, and to others in a softer state of mind, but in a midway state and with the greatest composure to another, as the Dorian mode alone of tunes seems to act, while the Phrygian 9 makes men enthusiastic ; for these things are well stated by those who have studied this form of education, as they derive the evidence for their theories from the actual facts of experience. And the same holds good about the rhythms also, for some have a more stable and others a more emotional character, and of the latter some are more vulgar in their

at Athens, in the middle of the 5th century B.C. ‘ Polygnotus represented men as better than they really were, Pauson as worse ’ (*Poetics* 1448 a 5).

1840 b

οἱ δὲ ἐλευθεριωτέρας. ἐκ μὲν οὖν τούτων φανερὸν
ὅτι δύναται ποιόν τι τὸ τῆς ψυχῆς ἦθος ἡ μουσικὴ
παρασκευάζειν, εἰ δὲ τοῦτο δύναται ποιεῖν, δῆλον
ὅτι προσακτέον καὶ παιδευτέον ἐν αὐτῇ τοὺς νέους.
ἔστι δὲ ἁρμόττουσα πρὸς τὴν φύσιν τὴν τηλι- 10
15 καύτην ἡ διδασκαλία τῆς μουσικῆς· οἱ μὲν γὰρ
νέοι διὰ τὴν ἡλικίαν ἀνήδυντον οὐδὲν ὑπομένουσιν
ἑκόντες, ἡ δὲ μουσικὴ φύσει τῶν ἡδυσμένων¹ ἐστίν.
καί τις ἔοικε συγγένεια ταῖς ἁρμονίαις καὶ τοῖς
ῥυθμοῖς εἶναι²· διὸ πολλοί φασι τῶν σοφῶν οἱ μὲν
ἁρμονίαν εἶναι τὴν ψυχήν οἱ δ' ἔχειν ἁρμονίαν.

20 VI. Πότερον δὲ δεῖ μανθάνειν αὐτοὺς ᾄδοντάς τε 1
καὶ χειρουργοῦντας ἢ μή, καθάπερ ἠπορήθη πρότερον, νῦν λεκτέον. οὐκ ἄδηλον δὲ ὅτι πολλὴν
ἔχει διαφορὰν πρὸς τὸ γίγνεσθαι ποιούς τινας, ἐάν
τις αὐτὸς κοινωνῇ τῶν ἔργων· ἐν γάρ τι τῶν
25 ἀδυνάτων ἢ χαλεπῶν ἐστὶ μὴ κοινωνήσαντας τῶν
ἔργων κριτὰς γενέσθαι σπουδαίους. ἅμα δὲ καὶ
δεῖ τοὺς παῖδας ἔχειν τινὰ διατριβήν, καὶ τὴν
Ἀρχύτου πλαταγὴν οἴεσθαι γενέσθαι καλῶς, ἣν
διδόασι τοῖς παιδίοις ὅπως χρώμενοι ταύτῃ μηδὲν
καταγνύωσι τῶν κατὰ τὴν οἰκίαν· οὐ γὰρ δύναται
30 τὸ νέον ἡσυχάζειν. αὕτη μὲν οὖν ἐστὶ τοῖς νηπίοις
ἁρμόττουσα τῶν παιδίων, ἡ δὲ παιδεία πλαταγὴ
τοῖς μείζοσι τῶν νέων. ὅτι μὲν οὖν παιδευτέον
τὴν μουσικὴν οὕτως ὥστε καὶ κοινωνεῖν τῶν

¹ ἡδυσμάτων ? Bywater.
² ⟨ἡμῖν⟩ εἶναι Aretinus : ⟨πρὸς ἡμᾶς⟩ εἶναι Reiz.

ᵃ The former doctrine is Pythagorean, the latter is stated
by Plato, *Phaedo* 93.
ᵇ Archytas a Pythagorean philosopher, mathematician.
660

emotional effects and others more liberal. From
these considerations therefore it is plain that music
has the power of producing a certain effect on the
moral character of the soul, and if it has the power
to do this, it is clear that the young must be directed
10 to music and must be educated in it. Also education
in music is well adapted to the youthful nature ; for
the young owing to their youth cannot endure anything not sweetened by pleasure, and music is by
nature a thing that has a pleasant sweetness. And
we seem to have a certain affinity with tunes and
rhythms ; owing to which many wise men say either
that the soul is a harmony or that it has harmony.[a]

1   VI. We ought now to decide the question raised Lessons in
earlier, whether the young ought to learn music music,
by singing and playing themselves or not. It is
not difficult to see that it makes a great difference
in the process of acquiring a certain quality whether
one takes a part in the actions that impart it oneself ;
for it is a thing that is impossible, or difficult, to
become a good judge of performances if one has
not taken part in them. At the same time also
boys must have some occupation, and one must
think Archytas's rattle[b] a good invention, which
people give to children in order that while occupied
with this they may not break any of the furniture ;
for young things cannot keep still. Whereas then
a rattle is a suitable occupation for infant children,
education serves as a rattle for young people when
older. Such considerations therefore prove that
children should be trained in music so as actually

statesman, and general of Tarentum, contemporary with
Plato. He was interested in mechanics ; but one tradition
ascribes the toy in question to a carpenter of the same name.

1340 b

ἔργων, φανερὸν ἐκ τῶν τοιούτων· τὸ δὲ πρέπον 2
καὶ τὸ μὴ πρέπον ταῖς ἡλικίαις οὐ χαλεπὸν δι-
35 ορίσαι, καὶ λῦσαι πρὸς τοὺς φάσκοντας βάναυσον
εἶναι τὴν ἐπιμέλειαν. πρῶτον μὲν γάρ, ἐπεὶ τοῦ
κρίνειν χάριν μετέχειν δεῖ τῶν ἔργων, διὰ τοῦτο
χρὴ νέους μὲν ὄντας χρῆσθαι τοῖς ἔργοις, πρεσβυτέρους δὲ γινομένους τῶν μὲν ἔργων ἀφεῖσθαι,
δύνασθαι δὲ τὰ καλὰ κρίνειν καὶ χαίρειν ὀρθῶς
40 διὰ τὴν μάθησιν τὴν γενομένην ἐν τῇ νεότητι· περὶ 3
δὲ τῆς ἐπιτιμήσεως ἥν τινες ἐπιτιμῶσιν ὡς ποιούσης
τῆς μουσικῆς βαναύσους, οὐ χαλεπὸν λῦσαι
σκεψαμένους μέχρι τε πόσου τῶν ἔργων κοινωνη-
1341 a τέον τοῖς πρὸς ἀρετὴν παιδευομένοις πολιτικήν,
καὶ ποίων μελῶν καὶ ποίων ῥυθμῶν κοινωνητέον,
ἔτι δὲ ἐν ποίοις ὀργάνοις τὴν μάθησιν ποιητέον,
καὶ γὰρ τοῦτο διαφέρειν εἰκός. ἐν τούτοις γὰρ ἡ
λύσις ἐστὶ τῆς ἐπιτιμήσεως· οὐθὲν γὰρ κωλύει
5 τρόπους τινὰς τῆς μουσικῆς ἀπεργάζεσθαι τὸ
λεχθέν. φανερὸν τοίνυν ὅτι δεῖ τὴν μάθησιν αὐτῆς 4
μήτε ἐμποδίζειν πρὸς τὰς ὕστερον πράξεις, μήτε
τὸ σῶμα ποιεῖν βάναυσον καὶ ἄχρηστον πρὸς τὰς
πολεμικὰς καὶ πολιτικὰς ἀσκήσεις, πρὸς μὲν τὰς
χρήσεις[1] ἤδη πρὸς δὲ τὰς μαθήσεις[1] ὕστερον. συμ-
10 βαίνοι δ᾽ ἂν περὶ τὴν μάθησιν εἰ μήτε τὰ πρὸς
τοὺς ἀγῶνας τοὺς τεχνικοὺς συντείνοντα διαπονοῖεν,
μήτε τὰ θαυμάσια καὶ περιττὰ τῶν ἔργων ἃ νῦν
ἐλήλυθεν εἰς τοὺς ἀγῶνας ἐκ δὲ τῶν ἀγώνων εἰς

---

[1] χρήσεις et μαθήσεις permutanda Boiesen (vel ἤδη et ὕστερον Spengel).

---

[a] It is difficult not to think that either the nouns or the adverbs in the Greek have been erroneously transposed, and that we should translate ' either for learning them now or for practising them later on.'

2 to take part in its performance ; and it is not difficult to distinguish what is suitable and unsuitable for various ages, and to refute those who assert that the practice of music is vulgar. For first, inasmuch as it is necessary to take part in the performances for the sake of judging them, it is therefore proper for the pupils when young actually to engage in the performances, though when they get older they should be released from performing, but be able to judge what is beautiful and enjoy it rightly because of the study in which they engaged in their youth.

3 Then as to the objection raised by some people that music makes people vulgar, it is not difficult to solve it by considering how far pupils who are being educated with a view to civic virtue should take part in the actual performance of music, and in what times and what rhythms they should take part, and also what kinds of instruments should be used in their studies, as this naturally makes a difference. For the solution of the objection depends upon these points, as it is quite possible that some modes of

4 music do produce the result mentioned. It is manifest therefore that the study of music must not place a hindrance in the way of subsequent activities, nor vulgarize the bodily frame and make it useless for the exercises of the soldier and the citizen, either for their practical pursuit now or for their scientific study later on.[a] And this would come about in respect of their study if the pupils did not go on toiling at the exercises that aim at professional competitions, nor the wonderful and elaborate performances which have now entered into the competitions and have passed from the competitions into

1341 a

τὴν παιδείαν, ἀλλὰ καὶ τὰ μὴ[1] τοιαῦτα μέχρι
περ ἂν δύνωνται χαίρειν τοῖς καλοῖς μέλεσι καὶ
15 ῥυθμοῖς, καὶ μὴ μόνον τῷ κοινῷ τῆς μουσικῆς,
ὥσπερ καὶ τῶν ἄλλων ἔνια ζῴων, ἔτι δὲ καὶ πλῆθος
ἀνδραπόδων καὶ παιδίων. δῆλον δὲ ἐκ τούτων 5
καὶ ποίοις ὀργάνοις χρηστέον. οὔτε γὰρ αὐλοὺς
εἰς παιδείαν ἀκτέον οὔτ' ἄλλο τεχνικὸν ὄργανον,
οἷον κιθάραν κἂν εἴ τι τοιοῦτον ἕτερόν ἐστιν, ἀλλ'
20 ὅσα ποιήσει αὐτῶν[2] ἀκροατὰς ἀγαθοὺς ἢ τῆς μουσικῆς παιδείας ἢ τῆς ἄλλης. ἔτι δ' οὐκ ἔστιν
ὁ αὐλὸς ἠθικὸν ἀλλὰ μᾶλλον ὀργιαστικόν, ὥστε
πρὸς τοὺς τοιούτους αὐτῷ καιροὺς χρηστέον ἐν οἷς
ἡ θεωρία κάθαρσιν μᾶλλον δύναται ἢ μάθησιν.
προσθῶμεν δὲ ὅτι συμβέβηκεν αὐτῷ[2] ἐναντίον
25 πρὸς παιδείαν καὶ τὸ κωλύειν τῷ λόγῳ χρῆσθαι
τὴν αὔλησιν. διὸ καλῶς ἀπεδοκίμασαν αὐτοῦ[2] οἱ
πρότερον τὴν χρῆσιν ἐκ τῶν νέων καὶ τῶν ἐλευθέρων, καίπερ χρησάμενοι τὸ πρῶτον αὐτῷ.
σχολαστικώτεροι γὰρ γιγνόμενοι διὰ τὰς εὐπο- 6
ρίας καὶ μεγαλοψυχότεροι πρὸς ἀρετήν, ἔτι τε
30 πρότερον καὶ μετὰ τὰ Μηδικὰ φρονηματισθέντες
ἐκ τῶν ἔργων, πάσης ἥπτοντο μαθήσεως, οὐδὲν
διακρίνοντες ἀλλ' ἐπιζητοῦντες. διὸ καὶ τὴν
αὐλητικὴν ἤγαγον πρὸς τὰς μαθήσεις. καὶ γὰρ ἐν
Λακεδαίμονί τις χορηγὸς αὐτὸς ηὔλησε τῷ χορῷ,
καὶ περὶ 'Αθήνας οὕτως ἐπεχωρίασεν ὥστε σχεδὸν

---

[1] τὰ μὴ Immisch : τὰ codd.
[2] αὐτῶν, αὐτῷ, αὐτοῦ propter hiatum secludenda ? Immisch:
lege ποιήσει τούτων—ἐναντίον αὐτῷ—οἱ πρότερον αὐτοῦ Richards.

---

[a] See 1341 b 33 ff.
[b] A wealthy citizen who undertook the duty of equipping

education, but also only practised exercises not of that sort until they are able to enjoy beautiful tunes and rhythms, and not merely the charm common to all music, which even some lower animals enjoy, 5 as well as a multitude of slaves and children. And it is also clear from these considerations what sort of instruments they should use. Flutes must not be introduced into education, nor any other professional instrument, such as the harp or any other of that sort, but such instruments as will make them attentive pupils either at their musical training or in their other lessons. Moreover the flute is not a moralizing but rather an exciting influence, so that it ought to be used for occasions of the kind at which attendance has the effect of purification rather than instruction.[a] And let us add that the flute happens to possess the additional property telling against its use in education that playing it prevents the employment of speech. Hence former ages rightly rejected its use by the young and the free, although at first they 6 had employed it. For as they came to have more leisure because of their wealth and grew more high-spirited and valorous, both at a still earlier date and because after the Persian Wars they were filled with pride as a result of their achievements, they began to engage in all branches of learning, making no distinction but pursuing research further. Because of this they even included flute-playing among their studies ; for in Sparta a certain chorus-leader played the flute to his chorus himself [b] and at Athens

Musical instruments.

and training a chorus for a religious celebration (especially the production of a drama at Athens) usually had an assistant of lower station to supply the instrumental music. The office of choregus is not elsewhere referred to as existing at Sparta.

1341 a

35 οἱ πολλοὶ τῶν ἐλευθέρων μετεῖχον αὐτῆς· δῆλον
δὲ ἐκ τοῦ πίνακος ὃν ἀνέθηκε Θράσιππος Ἐκ-
φαντίδῃ χορηγήσας. ὕστερον δ' ἀπεδοκιμάσθη διὰ 7
τῆς πείρας αὐτῆς, βέλτιον δυναμένων κρίνειν τὸ
πρὸς ἀρετὴν καὶ τὸ μὴ πρὸς ἀρετὴν συντεῖνον·
ὁμοίως δὲ καὶ πολλὰ τῶν ὀργάνων τῶν ἀρχαίων,
40 οἷον πηκτίδες καὶ βάρβιτοι καὶ τὰ πρὸς ἡδονὴν
συντείνοντα τοῖς ἀκούουσι τῶν χρωμένων,[1] ἑπτά-
1341 b γωνα καὶ τρίγωνα καὶ σαμβῦκαι, καὶ πάντα τὰ
δεόμενα χειρουργικῆς ἐπιστήμης. εὐλόγως δ' ἔχει 8
καὶ τὸ περὶ τῶν αὐλῶν ὑπὸ τῶν ἀρχαίων μεμυθο-
λογημένον· φασὶ γὰρ δὴ τὴν Ἀθηνᾶν εὑροῦσαν
ἀποβαλεῖν τοὺς αὐλούς. οὐ κακῶς μὲν οὖν ἔχει
5 φάναι καὶ διὰ τὴν ἀσχημοσύνην τοῦ προσώπου
τοῦτο ποιῆσαι δυσχεράνασαν τὴν θεόν· οὐ μὴν
ἀλλὰ μᾶλλον εἰκὸς ὅτι πρὸς τὴν διάνοιαν οὐθέν
ἐστιν ἡ παιδεία τῆς αὐλήσεως, τῇ δὲ Ἀθηνᾷ τὴν
ἐπιστήμην περιτίθεμεν καὶ τὴν τέχνην.

VII. Ἐπεὶ δὲ τῶν τε ὀργάνων καὶ[2] τῆς ἐργασίας 1
10 ἀποδοκιμάζομεν τὴν τεχνικὴν παιδείαν (τεχνικὴν
δὲ τίθεμεν τὴν πρὸς τοὺς ἀγῶνας, ἐν ταύτῃ γὰρ ὁ
πράττων οὐ τῆς αὑτοῦ μεταχειρίζεται χάριν ἀρετῆς,
ἀλλὰ τῆς τῶν ἀκουόντων ἡδονῆς, καὶ ταύτης
φορτικῆς, διόπερ οὐ τῶν ἐλευθέρων κρίνομεν εἶναι
τὴν ἐργασίαν, ἀλλὰ θητικωτέραν· καὶ βαναύσους
15 δὴ συμβαίνει γίγνεσθαι, πονηρὸς γὰρ ὁ σκοπὸς

---

[1] χρωμάτων ? Immisch.   [2] ⟨ἔνια⟩ καὶ Immisch.

---

[a] Ecphantides was one of the earliest comic poets ; Thrasippus is not elsewhere recorded. Who the flute-player was
is unknown.

[b] These were old-fashioned forms of the lyre.

[c] A possible emendation of the Greek gives 'those who
listen to their modulations.'

it became so fashionable that almost the majority of
freemen went in for flute-playing, as is shown by
the tablet erected by Thrasippus after having pro-
7 vided the chorus for Ecphantides.*a* But later on it
came to be disapproved of as a result of actual
experience, when men were more capable of judging
what music conduced to virtue and what did not ;
and similarly also many of the old instruments were
disapproved of, like the pêctis and the barbitos *b*
and the instruments designed to give pleasure to
those who hear people playing them,*c* the septangle,
the triangle and the sambyc,*d* and all the instru-
8 ments that require manual skill. And indeed there
is a reasonable foundation for the story that was
told by the ancients about the flute. The tale goes
that Athene found a flute and threw it away. Now
it is not a bad point in the story that the goddess
did this out of annoyance because of the ugly dis-
tortion of her features ; but as a matter of fact it is
more likely that it was because education in flute-
playing has no effect on the intelligence, whereas
we attribute science and art to Athene.

1   VII. And since we reject professional education *Melodies*
in the instruments and in performance *e* (and we *and rhythms.*
count performance in competitions as professional,
for the performer does not take part in it for his
own improvement, but for his hearers' pleasure,
and that a vulgar pleasure, owing to which we do
not consider performing to be proper for free men,
but somewhat menial ; and indeed performers do
become vulgar, since the object at which they aim

   d Three different stringed instruments, the last having
four strings stretched in a triangular frame.
   e The Greek should probably be altered to give ' reject
some instruments and professional education in performance.'

1341 b

πρὸς ὃν ποιοῦνται τὸ τέλος, ὁ γὰρ θεατὴς φορτικὸς
ὢν μεταβάλλειν εἴωθε τὴν μουσικήν, ὥστε καὶ
τοὺς τεχνίτας τοὺς πρὸς αὐτὸν μελετῶντας αὐτούς
τε ποιούς[1] τινας ποιεῖ καὶ τὰ σώματα διὰ τὰς
κινήσεις) σκεπτέον δή τι[2] περί τε τὰς ἁρμονίας 2
20 καὶ τοὺς ῥυθμούς, καὶ πρὸς παιδείαν πότερον πάσαις
χρηστέον ταῖς ἁρμονίαις καὶ πᾶσι τοῖς ῥυθμοῖς ἢ
διαιρετέον, ἔπειτα τοῖς πρὸς παιδείαν διαπονοῦσι
πότερον τὸν αὐτὸν διορισμὸν θήσομεν ἢ τρίτον
δεῖ τινὰ ἕτερον (ἐπειδὴ τὴν μὲν μουσικὴν ὁρῶμεν
25 διὰ μελοποιίας καὶ ῥυθμῶν οὖσαν, τούτων δ’
ἑκάτερον οὐ δεῖ λεληθέναι τίνα ἔχει δύναμιν πρὸς
παιδείαν), καὶ πότεροι προαιρετέον μᾶλλον τὴν
εὐμελῆ μουσικὴν ἢ τὴν εὔρυθμον. νομίσαντες οὖν 3
πολλὰ καλῶς λέγειν περὶ τούτων τῶν τε νῦν μου-
σικῶν ἐνίους καὶ τῶν ἐκ φιλοσοφίας ὅσοι τυγχάνουσιν ἐμπείρως ἔχοντες τῆς περὶ τὴν μουσικὴν
30 παιδείας, τὴν μὲν καθ’ ἕκαστον ἀκριβολογίαν
ἀποδώσομεν ζητεῖν τοῖς βουλομένοις παρ’ ἐκείνων,
νῦν δὲ νομικῶς[3] διέλωμεν, τοὺς τύπους μόνον
εἰπόντες περὶ αὐτῶν. ἐπεὶ δὲ τὴν διαίρεσιν 4
ἀποδεχόμεθα τῶν μελῶν ὡς διαιροῦσί τινες τῶν
ἐν φιλοσοφίᾳ, τὰ μὲν ἠθικὰ τὰ δὲ πρακτικὰ τὰ δ’
35 ἐνθουσιαστικὰ τιθέντες, καὶ τῶν ἁρμονιῶν τὴν
φύσιν πρὸς ἕκαστα τούτων οἰκείαν ἄλλην πρὸς
ἄλλο μέρος[4] τιθέασι, φαμὲν δ’ οὐ μιᾶς ἕνεκεν
ὠφελείας τῇ μουσικῇ χρῆσθαι δεῖν ἀλλὰ καὶ πλειόνων χάριν (καὶ γὰρ παιδείας ἕνεκεν καὶ καθάρσεως—

---

[1] ὁμοίους Busse (*illius modi* Ar.).
[2] δή τι ed.: δέ τι, δ’ ἔτι codd.: δὲ τά, ἔτι τά, δὴ ἔτι edd.
[3] λογικῶς Richards.
[4] μέλος Tyrwhitt.

is a low one, as vulgarity in the audience usually
influences the music, so that it imparts to the artists
who practise it with a view to suit the audience a
special kind of personality, and also of bodily
2 frame because of the movements required)—we
must therefore give some consideration to tunes and
rhythms, and to the question whether for educational
purposes we must employ all the tunes and all the
rhythms or make distinctions; and next, whether
for those who are working at music for education
we shall lay down the same regulation, or ought we
to establish some other third one (inasmuch as we
see that the factors in music are melody and rhythm,
and it is important to notice what influence each of
these has upon education), and whether we are to
prefer music with a good melody or music with a
3 good rhythm. Now we consider that much is well
said on these matters by some of the musicians of
the present day and by some of those engaged in
philosophy who happen to be experienced in musical
education, and we will abandon the precise discussion
as to each of these matters for any who wish it to
seek it from those teachers, while for the present
let us lay down general principles, merely stating
4 the outlines of the subjects. And since we accept Psycho-
the classification of melodies made by some philo- logical
sophers, as ethical melodies, melodies of action, and music.
passionate melodies,[a] distributing the various harmonies among these classes as being in nature akin
to one or the other, and as we say that music
ought to be employed not for the purpose of one
benefit that it confers but on account of several (for
it serves the purpose both of education and of pur-

---

[a] *i.e.* representative of character, of action and of emotion.

1841 b

τί δὲ λέγομεν τὴν κάθαρσιν, νῦν μὲν ἁπλῶς, πάλιν
40 δ' ἐν τοῖς περὶ ποιητικῆς ἐροῦμεν σαφέστερον,—
τρίτον δὲ πρὸς διαγωγήν, πρὸς ἄνεσίν τε καὶ πρὸς
1842 a τὴν τῆς συντονίας ἀνάπαυσιν), φανερὸν ὅτι χρηστέον 5
μὲν πάσαις ταῖς ἁρμονίαις, οὐ τὸν αὐτὸν δὲ τρόπον
πάσαις χρηστέον, ἀλλὰ πρὸς μὲν τὴν παιδείαν ταῖς
ἠθικωτάταις, πρὸς δὲ ἀκρόασιν ἑτέρων χειρουρ-
γούντων καὶ ταῖς πρακτικαῖς καὶ ταῖς ἐνθουσια-
5 στικαῖς (ὃ γὰρ περὶ ἐνίας συμβαίνει πάθος ψυχὰς
ἰσχυρῶς, τοῦτο ἐν πάσαις ὑπάρχει, τῷ δὲ ἧττον
διαφέρει καὶ τῷ μᾶλλον—οἷον ἔλεος καὶ φόβος,
ἔτι δ' ἐνθουσιασμός, καὶ γὰρ ὑπὸ ταύτης τῆς
κινήσεως κατακώχιμοί τινές εἰσιν, ἐκ δὲ τῶν ἱερῶν
μελῶν ὁρῶμεν τούτους ὅταν χρήσωνται τοῖς
10 ἐξοργιάζουσι τὴν ψυχὴν μέλεσι καθισταμένους
ὥσπερ ἰατρείας τυχόντας καὶ καθάρσεως· ταὐτὸ 6
δὴ τοῦτο ἀναγκαῖον πάσχειν καὶ τοὺς ἐλεήμονας
καὶ τοὺς φοβητικοὺς καὶ τοὺς ὅλως παθητικοὺς
τοὺς[1] ἄλλους καθ' ὅσον ἐπιβάλλει τῶν τοιούτων
ἑκάστῳ, καὶ πᾶσι γίγνεσθαί τινα κάθαρσιν καὶ
15 κουφίζεσθαι μεθ' ἡδονῆς· ὁμοίως δὲ καὶ τὰ μέλη
τὰ καθαρτικὰ παρέχει χαρὰν ἀβλαβῆ τοῖς ἀνθρώποις). διὸ ταῖς μὲν τοιαύταις ἁρμονίαις καὶ
τοῖς τοιούτοις μέλεσι θετέον[2] τοὺς τὴν θεατρικὴν
μουσικὴν μεταχειριζομένους ἀγωνιστάς (ἐπεὶ δ' ὁ 7
θεατὴς διττός, ὁ μὲν ἐλεύθερος καὶ πεπαιδευμένος,
20 ὁ δὲ φορτικὸς ἐκ βαναύσων καὶ θητῶν καὶ ἄλλων
τοιούτων συγκείμενος, ἀποδοτέον ἀγῶνας καὶ
θεωρίας καὶ τοῖς τοιούτοις πρὸς ἀνάπαυσιν· εἰσὶ

---

[1] τοὺς Immisch: τοὺς δ' codd.
[2] παιδευτέον Jebb: ἐατέον ⟨χρῆσθαι⟩ Richards.

gation—the term purgation we use for the present without explanation, but we will return to discuss the meaning that we give to it more explicitly in our treatise on poetry [a]—and thirdly it serves for amusement, serving to relax our tension and to give rest 5 from it), it is clear that we should employ all the harmonies, yet not employ them all in the same way, but use the most ethical ones for education, and the active and passionate kinds for listening to when others are performing (for any experience that occurs violently in some souls is found in all, though with different degrees of intensity—for example pity and fear, and also religious excitement ; for some persons are very liable to this form of emotion, and under the influence of sacred music we see these people, when they use tunes that violently arouse the soul, being thrown into a state as if they had received medicinal 6 treatment and taken a purge ; the same experience then must come also to the compassionate and the timid and the other emotional people generally in such degree as befalls each individual of these classes, and all must undergo a purgation and a pleasant feeling of relief ; and similarly also the purgative melodies afford harmless delight to people). Therefore those who go in for theatrical music must be set to compete in harmonies and melodies of this kind 7 (and since the audience is of two classes, one freemen and educated people, and the other the vulgar class composed of mechanics and labourers and other such persons, the latter sort also must be assigned competitions and shows for relaxation ; and just as

[a] In *Poetics* c. vi. tragedy is said to purge the emotion of pity and fear by giving them an outlet; the reference here is probably to the lost Second Book of *Poetics*.

1342 a

δ' ὥσπερ αὐτῶν αἱ ψυχαὶ παρεστραμμέναι τῆς
κατὰ φύσιν ἕξεως, οὕτω καὶ τῶν ἁρμονιῶν παρεκβάσεις εἰσὶ καὶ τῶν μελῶν τὰ σύντονα καὶ
25 παρακεχρωσμένα, ποιεῖ δὲ τὴν ἡδονὴν ἑκάστοις
τὸ κατὰ φύσιν οἰκεῖον, διόπερ ἀποδοτέον ἐξουσίαν
τοῖς ἀγωνιζομένοις πρὸς τὸν θεατὴν τὸν τοιοῦτον τοιούτῳ τινὶ χρῆσθαι τῷ γένει τῆς μουσικῆς)·
πρὸς δὲ παιδείαν, ὥσπερ εἴρηται, τοῖς ἠθικοῖς τῶν ᶜ
μελῶν χρηστέον καὶ ταῖς ἁρμονίαις ταῖς τοιαύταις.
30 τοιαύτη δ' ἡ δωριστί, καθάπερ εἴπομεν πρότερον·
δέχεσθαι δὲ δεῖ κἄν τινα ἄλλην ἡμῖν δοκιμάζωσιν
οἱ κοινωνοὶ τῆς ἐν φιλοσοφίᾳ διατριβῆς καὶ τῆς
περὶ τὴν μουσικὴν παιδείας. ὁ δ' ἐν τῇ Πολιτείᾳ
Σωκράτης οὐ καλῶς τὴν φρυγιστὶ μόνην καταλείπει
1342 b μετὰ τῆς δωριστί, καὶ ταῦτα ἀποδοκιμάσας τῶν
ὀργάνων τὸν αὐλόν. ἔχει γὰρ τὴν αὐτὴν δύναμιν
ἡ φρυγιστὶ τῶν ἁρμονιῶν ἥνπερ αὐλὸς ἐν τοῖς
ὀργάνοις· ἄμφω γὰρ ὀργιαστικὰ καὶ παθητικά.
δηλοῖ δ' ἡ ποίησις· πᾶσα γὰρ βακχεία καὶ πᾶσα ᵉ
5 ἡ τοιαύτη κίνησις μάλιστα τῶν ὀργάνων ἐστὶν ἐν
τοῖς αὐλοῖς, τῶν δ' ἁρμονιῶν ἐν τοῖς φρυγιστὶ
μέλεσι λαμβάνει ταῦτα τὸ πρέπον, οἷον ὁ διθύ-
ραμβος ὁμολογουμένως εἶναι δοκεῖ Φρύγιον, καὶ
τούτου πολλὰ παραδείγματα λέγουσιν οἱ περὶ τὴν
σύνεσιν ταύτην ἄλλα τε, καὶ διότι Φιλόξενος ἐγ-
10 χειρήσας ἐν τῇ δωριστὶ ποιῆσαι διθύραμβον τοὺς
Μύσους[1] οὐχ οἷός τ' ἦν, ἀλλ' ὑπὸ τῆς φύσεως

---

[1] Reiz : μύθους codd.

ᵃ Said to mean divergent from the regular scale in having
smaller intervals.
ᵇ 1342 a 2.   ᶜ 1343 b 3 ff.   ᵈ 399 A.
ᵉ Or perhaps βακχεία and κίνησις denote bodily movement

their souls are warped from the natural state, so those harmonies and melodies that are highly strung and irregular in coloration [a] are deviations, but people of each sort receive pleasure from what is naturally suited to them, owing to which the competitors before an audience of this sort must be allowed to

8 employ some such kind of music as this) ; but for education, as has been said,[b] the ethical class of melodies and of harmonies must be employed. And of that nature is the Dorian mode, as we said before [c] ; but we must also accept any other mode that those who take part in the pursuit of philosophy and in musical education may recommend to us. Socrates in the *Republic* [d] does not do well in allowing only the Phrygian mode along with the Dorian, and that when he has rejected the flute among instruments ; for the Phrygian mode has the same effect among harmonies as the flute among instruments—both are

9 violently exciting and emotional. This is shown by poetry ; for all Bacchiac versification and all movement of that sort [e] belongs particularly to the flute among the instruments, and these metres find their suitable accompaniment in tunes in the Phrygian mode among the harmonies : for example the dithyramb is admittedly held to be a Phrygian metre, and the experts on this subject adduce many instances to prove this, particularly the fact that Philoxenus when he attempted to compose a dithyramb, *The Mysians*, in the Dorian mode was unable to do so,

accompanying the song; or they may denote the emotional frenzy expressed and stimulated by it. The dithyramb was a form of poetry of this class, originally celebrating the birth of Dionysus. Philoxenus, one of the most famous dithyrambic poets, 435–380 B.C., lived at Athens, and later at the court of Dionysius of Syracuse.

1342 b

αὐτῆς ἐξέπεσεν εἰς τὴν φρυγιστὶ τὴν προσήκουσαν
ἁρμονίαν πάλιν. περὶ δὲ τῆς δωριστὶ πάντες 10
ὁμολογοῦσιν ὡς στασιμωτάτης οὔσης καὶ μάλιστ᾽
ἦθος ἐχούσης ἀνδρεῖον. ἔτι δὲ ἐπεὶ τὸ μέσον μὲν
15 τῶν ὑπερβολῶν ἐπαινοῦμεν καὶ χρῆναι διώκειν
φαμέν, ἡ δὲ δωριστὶ ταύτην ἔχει τὴν φύσιν πρὸς
τὰς ἄλλας ἁρμονίας, φανερὸν ὅτι τὰ Δώρια μέλη
πρέπει παιδεύεσθαι μᾶλλον τοῖς νεωτέροις. εἰσὶ
δὲ δύο σκοποί, τό τε δυνατὸν καὶ τὸ πρέπον· καὶ
γὰρ τὰ δυνατὰ δεῖ μεταχειρίζεσθαι μᾶλλον καὶ τὰ
20 πρέποντα ἑκάστοις· ἔστι δὲ καὶ ταῦτα ὡρισμένα
ταῖς ἡλικίαις, οἷον τοῖς ἀπειρηκόσι διὰ χρόνον οὐ
ῥάδιον ᾄδειν τὰς συντόνους ἁρμονίας, ἀλλὰ τὰς
ἀνειμένας ἡ φύσις ὑποβάλλει τοῖς τηλικούτοις.
διὸ καλῶς ἐπιτιμῶσι καὶ τοῦτο Σωκράτει τῶν περὶ 11
τὴν μουσικήν τινες, ὅτι τὰς ἀνειμένας ἁρμονίας
25 ἀποδοκιμάσειεν εἰς τὴν παιδίαν,[1] ὡς μεθυστικὰς
λαμβάνων αὐτάς, οὐ κατὰ τὴν τῆς μέθης δύναμιν,
βακχευτικὸν γὰρ ἤ γε μέθη ποιεῖ μᾶλλον, ἀλλ᾽
ἀπειρηκυίας. ὥστε καὶ πρὸς τὴν ἐσομένην ἡλικίαν,
τὴν τῶν πρεσβυτέρων, δεῖ καὶ τῶν τοιούτων
ἁρμονιῶν ἅπτεσθαι καὶ τῶν μελῶν τῶν τοιούτων.
30 ἔτι δ᾽ εἴ τίς ἐστι τοιαύτη τῶν ἁρμονιῶν ἣ πρέπει
τῇ τῶν παίδων ἡλικίᾳ διὰ τὸ δύνασθαι κόσμον
τ᾽ ἔχειν ἅμα καὶ παιδείαν, οἷον ἡ λυδιστὶ φαίνεται πεπονθέναι μάλιστα τῶν ἁρμονιῶν. δῆλον οὖν[2]
ὅτι τούτους ὅρους τρεῖς ποιητέον εἰς τὴν παιδείαν,
τό τε μέσον καὶ τὸ δυνατὸν καὶ τὸ πρέπον.[3]

---

[1] Immisch olim : παιδείαν codd.
[2] δῆλον οὖν Schneider : δῆλον codd., ᾗ δῆλον Goettling.
[3] *Reliqua huius operis in Graeco nondum inueni* Guil.

but merely by the force of nature fell back again into
10 the suitable harmony, the Phrygian. And all agree
that the Dorian mode is more sedate and of a specially
manly character. Moreover since we praise and say
that we ought to pursue the mean between extremes,
and the Dorian mode has this nature in relation to
the other harmonies, it is clear that it suits the
younger pupils to be educated rather in the Dorian
melodies. But there are two objects to aim at, the
possible as well as the suitable ; for we are bound
rather to attempt the things that are possible and
those that are suitable for the particular class of
people concerned ; and in these matters also there
are dividing lines drawn by the ages—for instance,
those whose powers have waned through lapse of
time cannot easily sing the highly strung harmonies,
but to persons of that age nature suggests the re-
11 laxed harmonies. Therefore some musical experts
also rightly criticize Socrates [a] because he disapproved
of the relaxed harmonies for amusement, taking them
to have the character of intoxication, not in the sense
of the effect of strong drink, for that clearly has more
the result of making men frenzied revellers, but
as failing in power. Hence even with a view to the
period of life that is to follow, that of the comparatively old, it is proper to engage in the harmonies and
melodies of this kind too, and also any kind of harmony that is suited to the age of boyhood because it
is capable of being at once decorous and educative,
which seems to be the nature of the Lydian mode
most of all the harmonies. It is clear therefore that
we should lay down these three canons to guide
education, moderation, possibility and suitability.

[a] *Republic* 338 e.

INDEX I.—SUBJECTS

INDEX I. SUBJECTS

678

INDEX I. SUBJECTS

679

INDEX I. SUBJECTS

INDEX II.—PERSONS AND PLACES

References as noted on p. 677.

Short foot-notes on some of these names will be found in the text.

INDEX II. PERSONS AND PLACES

INDEX II. PERSONS AND PLACES

Printed in Great Britain by R. & R. CLARK, LIMITED, *Edinburgh*

THE LOEB CLASSICAL LIBRARY

VOLUMES ALREADY PUBLISHED

LATIN AUTHORS

1

THE LOEB CLASSICAL LIBRARY

OVID : THE ART OF LOVE AND OTHER POEMS. J. H. Mozley.
OVID : FASTI. Sir James G. Frazer.
OVID : HEROIDES AND AMORES. Grant Showerman.
OVID : METAMORPHOSES. F. J. Miller. 2 Vols.
OVID : TRISTIA AND EX PONTO. A. L. Wheeler.
PETRONIUS. M. Heseltine ; SENECA : APOCOLOCYNTOSIS.
    W. H. D. Rouse.
PHAEDRUS AND BABRIUS (Greek). B. E. Perry.
PLAUTUS. Paul Nixon. 5 Vols.
PLINY : LETTERS, PANEGYRICUS. B. Radice. 2 Vols.
PLINY : NATURAL HISTORY. 10 Vols. Vols. I-V. H. Rack-
    ham. Vols. VI-VIII. W. H. S. Jones. Vol. IX. H. Rack-
    ham. Vol. X. D. E. Eichholz.
PROPERTIUS. H. E. Butler.
PRUDENTIUS. H. J. Thomson. 2 Vols.
QUINTILIAN. H. E. Butler. 4 Vols.
REMAINS OF OLD LATIN. E. H. Warmington. 4 Vols.
    Vol. I (Ennius and Caecilius). Vol. II (Livius, Naevius,
    Pacuvius, Accius). Vol. III (Lucilius, Laws of the XII
    Tables). Vol. IV (Archaic Inscriptions).
SALLUST. J. C. Rolfe.
SCRIPTORES HISTORIAE AUGUSTAE. D. Magie. 3 Vols.
SENECA : APOCOLOCYNTOSIS. *Cf.* PETRONIUS.
SENECA : EPISTULAE MORALES. R. M. Gummere. 3 Vols.
SENECA : MORAL ESSAYS. J. W. Basore. 3 Vols.
SENECA : NATURALES QUAESTIONES. T. H. Corcoran. 2 Vols.
SENECA : TRAGEDIES. F. J. Miller. 2 Vols.
SENECA THE ELDER : CONTROVERSIAE SUASORIAE. M.
    Winterbottom. 2 Vols.
SIDONIUS : POEMS AND LETTERS. W. B. Anderson. 2 Vols.
SILIUS ITALICUS. J. D. Duff. 2 Vols.
STATIUS. J. H. Mozley. 2 Vols.
SUETONIUS. J. C. Rolfe. 2 Vols.
TACITUS : AGRICOLA AND GERMANIA. M. Hutton ; DIALOGUS.
    Sir Wm. Peterson. Revised by R. M. Ogilvie, E. H.
    Warmington, M. Winterbottom.
TACITUS : HISTORIES AND ANNALS. C. H. Moore and J.
    Jackson. 4 Vols.
TERENCE. John Sargeaunt. 2 Vols.
TERTULLIAN : APOLOGIA AND DE SPECTACULIS. T. R. Glover ;
    MINUCIUS FELIX. G. H. Rendall.
VALERIUS FLACCUS. J. H. Mozley.
VARRO : DE LINGUA LATINA. R. G. Kent. 2 Vols.
VELLEIUS PATERCULUS AND RES GESTAE DIVI AUGUSTI.
    F. W. Shipley.

THE LOEB CLASSICAL LIBRARY

VIRGIL. H. R. Fairclough. 2 Vols.
VITRUVIUS : DE ARCHITECTURA. F. Granger. 2 Vols.

GREEK AUTHORS

ACHILLES TATIUS. S. Gaselee.
AELIAN : ON THE NATURE OF ANIMALS. A. F. Scholfield.
3 Vols.
AENEAS TACTICUS, ASCLEPIODOTUS AND ONASANDER. The
Illinois Greek Club
AESCHINES. C. D. Adams.
AESCHYLUS. H. Weir Smyth. 2 Vols.
ALICIPHRON, AELIAN AND PHILOSTRATUS : LETTERS. A. R.
Benner and F. H. Fobes.
APOLLODORUS. Sir James G. Frazer. 2 Vols.
APOLLONIUS RHODIUS. R. C. Seaton.
THE APOSTOLIC FATHERS. Kirsopp Lake. 2 Vols.
APPIAN'S ROMAN HISTORY. Horace White. 4 Vols.
ARATUS. Cf. CALLIMACHUS : HYMNS AND EPIGRAMS.
ARISTIDES. C. A. Behr. 4 Vols. Vol. I.
ARISTOPHANES. Benjamin Bickley Rogers. 3 Vols. Verse
trans.
ARISTOTLE : ART OF RHETORIC. J. H. Freese.
ARISTOTLE : ATHENIAN CONSTITUTION, EUDEMIAN ETHICS,
VIRTUES AND VICES. H. Rackham.
ARISTOTLE : THE CATEGORIES. ON INTERPRETATION. H. P.
Cooke ; PRIOR ANALYTICS. H. Tredennick.
ARISTOTLE : GENERATION OF ANIMALS. A. L. Peck.
ARISTOTLE : HISTORIA ANIMALIUM. A. L. Peck. 3 Vols.
Vols. I and II.
ARISTOTLE : METAPHYSICS. H. Tredennick. 2 Vols.
ARISTOTLE : METEOROLOGICA. H. D. P. Lee.
ARISTOTLE : MINOR WORKS. W. S. Hett. "On Colours,"
" On Things Heard," " Physiognomics," " On Plants,"
" On Marvellous Things Heard," " Mechanical Prob-
lems," " On Invisible Lines," " Situations and Names of
Winds," " On Melissus, Xenophanes, and Gorgias."
ARISTOTLE : NICOMACHEAN ETHICS. H. Rackham.
ARISTOTLE : OECONOMICA AND MAGNA MORALIA. G. C.
Armstrong. (With METAPHYSICS, Vol. II.)
ARISTOTLE : ON THE HEAVENS. W. K. C. Guthrie.
ARISTOTLE : ON THE SOUL, PARVA NATURALIA, ON BREATH.
W. S. Hett.

THE LOEB CLASSICAL LIBRARY

ARISTOTLE: PARTS OF ANIMALS. A. L. Peck; MOVEMENT AND PROGRESSION OF ANIMALS. E. S. Forster.

ARISTOTLE: PHYSICS. Rev. P. Wicksteed and F. M. Cornford. 2 Vols.

ARISTOTLE: POETICS; LONGINUS ON THE SUBLIME. W. Hamilton Fyfe; DEMETRIUS ON STYLE. W. Rhys Roberts.

ARISTOTLE: POLITICS. H. Rackham.

ARISTOTLE: POSTERIOR ANALYTICS. H. Tredennick; TOPICS. E. S. Forster.

ARISTOTLE: PROBLEMS. W. S. Hett. 2 Vols.

ARISTOTLE: RHETORICA AD ALEXANDRUM. H. Rackham. (With PROBLEMS, Vol. II.)

ARISTOTLE: SOPHISTICAL REFUTATIONS. COMING-TO-BE AND PASSING-AWAY. E. S. Forster; ON THE COSMOS. D. J. Furley.

ARRIAN: HISTORY OF ALEXANDER AND INDICA. 2 Vols. Vol. I. P. Brunt. Vol. II. Rev. E. Iliffe Robson.

ATHENAEUS: DEIPNOSOPHISTAE. C. B. Gulick. 7 Vols.

BABRIUS AND PHAEDRUS (Latin). B. E. Perry.

ST. BASIL: LETTERS. R. J. Deferrari. 4 Vols.

CALLIMACHUS: FRAGMENTS. C. A. Trypanis; MUSAEUS: HERO AND LEANDER. T. Gelzer and C. Whitman.

CALLIMACHUS: HYMNS AND EPIGRAMS, AND LYCOPHRON. A. W. Mair; ARATUS. G. R. Mair.

CLEMENT OF ALEXANDRIA. Rev. G. W. Butterworth.

COLLUTHUS. Cf. OPPIAN.

DAPHNIS AND CHLOE. Cf. LONGUS.

DEMOSTHENES I: OLYNTHIACS, PHILIPPICS AND MINOR ORATIONS: I-XVII AND XX. J. H. Vince.

DEMOSTHENES II: DE CORONA AND DE FALSA LEGATIONE. C. A. Vince and J. H. Vince.

DEMOSTHENES III: MEIDIAS, ANDROTION, ARISTOCRATES, TIMOCRATES, ARISTOGEITON. J. H. Vince.

DEMOSTHENES IV-VI: PRIVATE ORATIONS AND IN NEAERAM. A. T. Murray.

DEMOSTHENES VII: FUNERAL SPEECH, EROTIC ESSAY, EXORDIA AND LETTERS. N. W. and N. J. DeWitt.

DIO CASSIUS: ROMAN HISTORY. E. Cary. 9 Vols.

DIO CHRYSOSTOM. 5 Vols. Vols. I and II. J. W. Cohoon. Vol. III. J. W. Cohoon and H. Lamar Crosby. Vols. IV and V. H. Lamar Crosby.

DIODORUS SICULUS. 12 Vols. Vols. I-VI. C. H. Oldfather. Vol. VII. C. L. Sherman. Vol. VIII. C. B. Welles. Vols. IX and X. Russel M. Geer. Vols. XI and XII. F. R. Walton. General Index. Russel M. Geer.

DIOGENES LAERTIUS. R. D. Hicks. 2 Vols. New Introduction by H. S. Long.

DIONYSIUS OF HALICARNASSUS : CRITICAL ESSAYS. S. Usher. 2 Vols.

DIONYSIUS OF HALICARNASSUS : ROMAN ANTIQUITIES. Spelman's translation revised by E. Cary. 7 Vols.

EPICTETUS. W. A. Oldfather. 2 Vols.

EURIPIDES. A. S. Way. 4 Vols. Verse trans.

EUSEBIUS : ECCLESIASTICAL HISTORY. Kirsopp Lake and J. E. L. Oulton. 2 Vols.

GALEN : ON THE NATURAL FACULTIES. A. J. Brock.

THE GREEK ANTHOLOGY. W. R. Paton. 5 Vols.

THE GREEK BUCOLIC POETS (THEOCRITUS, BION, MOSCHUS). J. M. Edmonds.

GREEK ELEGY AND IAMBUS WITH THE ANACREONTEA. J. M. Edmonds. 2 Vols.

GREEK MATHEMATICAL WORKS. Ivor Thomas. 2 Vols.

HERODES. Cf. THEOPHRASTUS : CHARACTERS.

HERODIAN. C. R. Whittaker. 2 Vols.

HERODOTUS. A. D. Godley. 4 Vols.

HESIOD AND THE HOMERIC HYMNS. H. G. Evelyn White.

HIPPOCRATES AND THE FRAGMENTS OF HERACLEITUS. W. H. S. Jones and E. T. Withington. 4 Vols.

HOMER : ILIAD. A. T. Murray. 2 Vols.

HOMER : ODYSSEY. A. T. Murray. 2 Vols.

ISAEUS. E. S. Forster.

ISOCRATES. George Norlin and LaRue Van Hook. 3 Vols.

[ST. JOHN DAMASCENE] : BARLAAM AND IOASAPH. Rev. G. R. Woodward, Harold Mattingly and D. M. Lang.

JOSEPHUS. 9 Vols. Vols. I–IV. H. St. J. Thackeray. Vol. V. H. St. J. Thackeray and Ralph Marcus. Vols. VI and VII. Ralph Marcus. Vol. VIII. Ralph Marcus and Allen Wikgren. Vol. IX. L. H. Feldman.

JULIAN. Wilmer Cave Wright. 3 Vols.

LIBANIUS : SELECTED WORKS. A. F. Norman. 3 Vols. Vols. I and II.

LONGUS : DAPHNIS AND CHLOE. Thornley's translation revised by J. M. Edmonds ; and PARTHENIUS. S. Gaselee.

LUCIAN. 8 Vols. Vols. I–V. A. M. Harmon. Vol. VI. K. Kilburn. Vols. VII and VIII. M. D. Macleod.

LYCOPHRON. Cf. CALLIMACHUS : HYMNS AND EPIGRAMS.

LYRA GRAECA. J. M. Edmonds. 3 Vols.

LYSIAS. W. R. M. Lamb.

MANETHO. W. G. Waddell ; PTOLEMY : TETRABIBLOS. F. E. Robbins.

THE LOEB CLASSICAL LIBRARY

MARCUS AURELIUS. C. R. Haines.

MENANDER. F. G. Allinson.

MINOR ATTIC ORATORS. 2 Vols. K. J. Maidment and J. O. Burtt.

MUSAEUS: HERO AND LEANDER. *Cf.* CALLIMACHUS: FRAGMENTS.

NONNOS: DIONYSIACA. W. H. D. Rouse. 3 Vols.

OPPIAN, COLLUTHUS, TRYPHIODORUS. A. W. Mair.

PAPYRI. NON-LITERARY SELECTIONS. A. S. Hunt and C. C. Edgar. 2 Vols. LITERARY SELECTIONS (Poetry). D. L. Page.

PARTHENIUS. *Cf.* LONGUS.

PAUSANIAS: DESCRIPTION OF GREECE. W. H. S. Jones. 4 Vols. and Companion Vol. arranged by R. E. Wycherley.

PHILO. 10 Vols. Vols. I-V. F. H. Colson and Rev. G. H. Whitaker. Vols. VI-X. F. H. Colson. General Index. Rev. J. W. Earp.
Two Supplementary Vols. Translation only from an Armenian Text. Ralph Marcus.

PHILOSTRATUS: THE LIFE OF APOLLONIUS OF TYANA. F. C. Conybeare. 2 Vols.

PHILOSTRATUS: IMAGINES; CALLISTRATUS: DESCRIPTIONS. A. Fairbanks.

PHILOSTRATUS AND EUNAPIUS: LIVES OF THE SOPHISTS. Wilmer Cave Wright.

PINDAR. Sir J. E. Sandys.

PLATO: CHARMIDES, ALCIBIADES, HIPPARCHUS, THE LOVERS, THEAGES, MINOS AND EPINOMIS. W. R. M. Lamb.

PLATO: CRATYLUS, PARMENIDES, GREATER HIPPIAS, LESSER HIPPIAS. H. N. Fowler.

PLATO: EUTHYPHRO, APOLOGY, CRITO, PHAEDO, PHAEDRUS. H. N. Fowler.

PLATO: LACHES, PROTAGORAS, MENO, EUTHYDEMUS. W. R. M. Lamb.

PLATO: LAWS. Rev. R. G. Bury. 2 Vols.

PLATO: LYSIS, SYMPOSIUM, GORGIAS. W. R. M. Lamb.

PLATO: REPUBLIC. Paul Shorey. 2 Vols.

PLATO: STATESMAN, PHILEBUS. H. N. Fowler; ION. W. R. M. Lamb.

PLATO: THEAETETUS AND SOPHIST. H. N. Fowler.

PLATO: TIMAEUS, CRITIAS, CLITOPHO, MENEXENUS, EPISTULAE. Rev. R. G. Bury.

PLOTINUS. A. H. Armstrong. 6 Vols. Vols. I-III.

PLUTARCH: MORALIA. 17 Vols. Vols. I-V. F. C. Babbitt. Vol. VI. W. C. Helmbold. Vol. VII. P. H. De Lacy and

THE LOEB CLASSICAL LIBRARY

B. Einarson. Vol. VIII. P. A. Clement, H. B. Hoffleit.
Vol. IX. E. L. Minar, Jr., F. H. Sandbach, W. C.
Helmbold. Vol. X. H. N. Fowler. Vol. XI. L. Pearson,
F. H. Sandbach. Vol. XII. H. Cherniss, W. C. Helmbold.
Vol. XIII, Parts 1 and 2. H. Cherniss. Vol. XIV. P. H.
De Lacy and B. Einarson. Vol. XV. F. H. Sandbach.

PLUTARCH : THE PARALLEL LIVES. B. Perrin. 11 Vols.

POLYBIUS. W. R. Paton. 6 Vols.

PROCOPIUS : HISTORY OF THE WARS. H. B. Dewing. 7 Vols.

PTOLEMY : TETRABIBLOS. *Cf.* MANETHO.

QUINTUS SMYRNAEUS. A. S. Way. Verse trans.

SEXTUS EMPIRICUS. Rev. R. G. Bury. 4 Vols.

SOPHOCLES. F. Storr. 2 Vols. Verse trans.

STRABO : GEOGRAPHY. Horace L. Jones. 8 Vols.

THEOPHRASTUS : CHARACTERS. J. M. Edmonds ; HERODES,
etc. A. D. Knox.

THEOPHRASTUS : DE CAUSIS PLANTARUM. G. K. K. Link and
B. Einarson. 3 Vols. Vol. I.

THEOPHRASTUS : ENQUIRY INTO PLANTS. Sir Arthur Hort.
2 Vols.

THUCYDIDES. C. F. Smith. 4 Vols.

TRYPHIODORUS. *Cf.* OPPIAN.

XENOPHON : ANABASIS. C. L. Brownson.

XENOPHON : CYROPAEDIA. Walter Miller. 2 Vols.

XENOPHON : HELLENICA. C. L. Brownson.

XENOPHON : MEMORABILIA AND OECONOMICUS. E. C. Marchant ; SYMPOSIUM AND APOLOGY. O. J. Todd.

XENOPHON : SCRIPTA MINORA. E. C. Marchant and G. W
Bowersock.

VOLUMES IN PREPARATION

LATIN AUTHORS

MANILIUS. G. P. Goold.

DESCRIPTIVE PROSPECTUS ON APPLICATION

Short Loan Collection

CAMBRIDGE, MASS.　　　　　　LONDON
HARVARD UNIV. PRESS　　　WILLIAM HEINEMANN LTD